ST IVES (1860-1930)

THE ARTISTS AND THE COMMUNITY

A SOCIAL HISTORY

DAVID TOVEY

ABOUT THE AUTHOR

David Tovey was born in 1953 and was educated at his father's preparatory school, Tockington Manor, near Bristol, and at Clifton College, before reading Jurisprudence at Pembroke College, Oxford. After twenty years as a solicitor, he returned to University in 1996 to read History of Art and is now an independent art historian, specialising in Cornish Art. His particular interest in St Ives art derives from the fact that his great-grandfather, William Titcomb, was one of the early settlers in the colony. Since 2000, he has curated several exhibitions and written numerous books on Cornish art. In particular, he published in 2003 a history of the first 25 years of the St Ives Society of Artists (1927-1952), entitled *Creating A Splash*, and curated the resultant exhibition, which toured six venues during 2003-4. Then, in 2008, he was lead Curator of *Dawn of a Colony*, a joint exhibition staged by Tate St Ives and Penlee House Gallery & Museum, Penzance, which reviewed art in St Ives from 1811 to 1914, and published two extensive histories to accompany these shows. He lectures widely on Cornish representational art, particularly to members of the National Association for Design and Fine Arts Societies. His previous books include:-

George Fagan Bradshaw - Submariner and Marine Artist - and the St Ives Society of Artists
(Wilson Books, 2000 ISBN 0 9538363 0 4)

W.H.Y.Titcomb : A Newlyner from St Ives, dealing with the years 1858-1908
(Wilson Books, 2003 ISBN 0 9538363-2-0)

W.H.Y.Titcomb : Bristol, Venice and the Continental Tours, covering the years 1909-1930
(Wilson Books, 2003 ISBN 0 9538363-1-2)

Creating A Splash - The St Ives Society of Artists - The First Twenty-Five Years (1927-1952)
(Wilson Books, 2003 & 2004 ISBN 0-9538363-4-7)

St Ives Art pre-1890 - The Dawn of the Colony
(Wilson Books, 2008 ISBN 9780953836352)

Pioneers of St Ives Art at Home and Abroad (1889-1914)
(Wilson Books, 2008 ISBN 9780953836369)

First published in 2009 by
WILSON BOOKS
11-13 Mill Bank, Tewkesbury, Gloucestershire, GL20 5SD
(01684 850898) Email : dwt4@talktalk.net

A catalogue record for this book is available from the British Library.

ISBN for this paperback edition
9780953836376

Printed and bound in England by
R.Booth Print, The Praze, Commercial Road, Penryn, Cornwall TR10 8AA

ST IVES (1860-1930)

THE ARTISTS AND THE COMMUNITY - A SOCIAL HISTORY

CONTENTS

ILLUSTRATIONS

Front Cover	Edward King	*Sale of Herrings, St Ives*	(photo: St Ives Town Council)
Back Cover	Frederick Sargent	*Catch of Pilchards off St Ives*	(photo: St Ives Town Council)
Part Dividers	Edmund Fuller	From *In and About St Ives*	(Priscilla Fursdon)

Colour Plates

MAP OF ST IVES

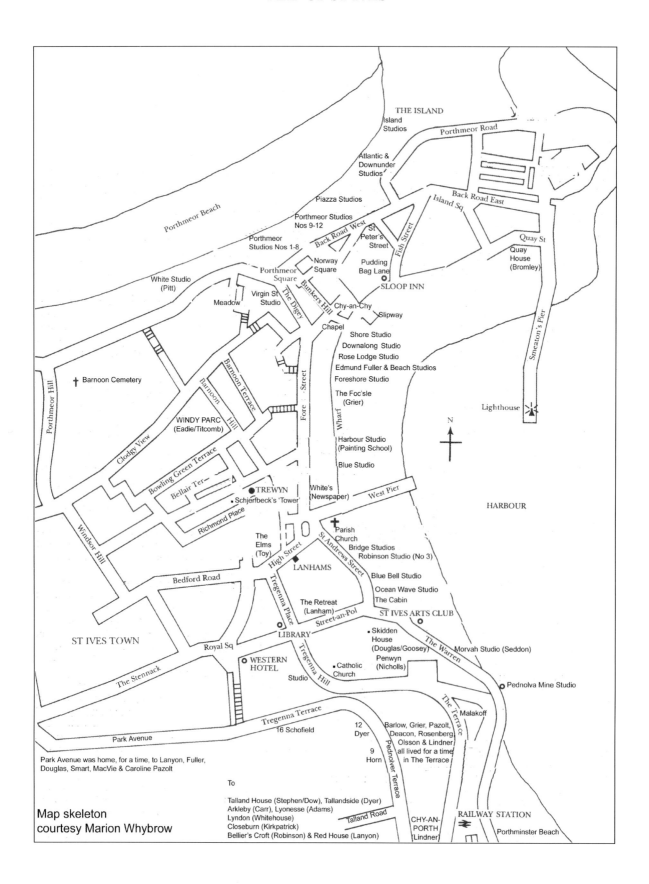

Map skeleton
courtesy Marion Whybrow

AUTHOR'S NOTE

When, following the success of *Creating A Splash : The St Ives Society of Artists (1927-1952)*, I decided to turn my attention, in the autumn of 2003, to the earlier history of the St Ives art colony, I envisaged that I would be able to produce a single volume history in a couple of years. I had not realised, however, the quite astonishing number of artists, who had found inspiration in St Ives, in the early years of the colony, or the wealth of material that had remained undiscovered. Now, six years later, this is the third volume in a four part series, the last part of which, provisionally entitled *Sea-Change : Art in St Ives 1914-1930*, will be published in September 2010 to coincide with an exhibition on the subject that I will be curating for Penlee House Gallery & Museum, Penzance. This third volume in the series, whilst covering the same period as the other three parts combined, is very different to those other parts, as it is a social history, not an art history. It is also a subject that would not be easy to research and write about from scratch, and I have drawn upon all sorts of material that I have unearthed during the many decades that St Ives art has enthralled me. What results is a fascinating blend of art, architecture, literature, theatre, music, religion, temperance, local politics, fishing, mining etc, and I have uncovered a wide range of interesting characters from all stratas of St Ives society, plus the occasional healthy whiff of scandal. It will appeal, therefore, to a far wider range of reader than the other parts of the series, albeit it will not be able to be promoted by an exhibition. I hope that much of the pleasure that I have derived from delving into these new and fascinating topics is evident from what I have written, and that the illustrations, which include many evocative images of people and long-lost spaces, are equally interesting. Finally, once again, I must stress that as a one-man researcher, writer, editor, designer, publisher and publicist, I need YOUR help. If you do enjoy the book, please spread the word.

INTRODUCTION

My previous books, covering this period of St Ives art, have concentrated, principally, on the paintings produced by the leading artists working in the town. This book, for the very first time, looks at the way of life enjoyed by the artists, and at the impact that they had on the town and the townspeople. It raises, and seeks to answer, a number of novel questions about the artists and the manner in which they lived, worked and socialised, and considers the wide variety of ways that they had an effect on the town, not only from a commercial perspective, but also from social, cultural and physical standpoints.

In Part One - The Arrival of the Artists - I look at the fragile state of the town before the artists began to visit it and at how the colony developed. How long did the artists tend to stay, at first, and at what juncture did they change from being regular visitors to settlers? When, as far as the locals were concerned, did they become conspicuous? What time of year did artists tend to visit and what differences in character were there between the summer and winter seasons? How did the colony evolve over the years?

Part Two - The Artists at Home, at Work and at Play - concentrates on the artist community itself. I start by investigating, for the first time, the backgrounds of the artists, and this analysis reveals that the only thing that they had in common was their interest in art. Far from being a homogenous group of sophisticated and privileged persons, with a tidy private income, one finds that they are drawn from widely diverse backgrounds that range from the aristocracy, through the Church and the military, to humble craftsmen or labourers. However, surprisingly few come from artistic families, and the battle to pursue their chosen calling will have been, in many instances, one of the few shared experiences.

In selecting accomodation, visiting artists had a variety of choices. Did they stay in a hotel, take lodgings or rent a house? Did they select a property near the harbour for the views, or did they find a place in Up-along away from the noise and smells of the fishing quarter? Or did they stay in the much quieter surroundings in one of the outlying villages and use the train to get into town? Having enjoyed their initial experiences, at what stage did they commit themselves to the colony by taking a long lease? Was buying or, even, building their own home an option? Separate chapters look at the range of answers that individual artists, and their literary friends, devised to these questions, both in and out of town, and the mark that these homes made on the locality.

As regards studios, the verdict of nearly all artists was that they wanted a workspace, with a view, in the centre of town. Studios, therefore, appeared all over the fishing quarter in a range of dilapidated and incommodious buildings, bringing the artists in daily contact with the fisherfolk. The vistas on offer were widely divergent - the harbour from any number of angles, the view across St Ives Bay to Godrevy or Atlantic breakers pounding on to the sands of Porthmeor, flanked by the Island. This raises the

Fig. 0.1 Herbert Lanyon
John Douglas
(courtesy Andrew Lanyon)

Fig. 0.2 Herbert Lanyon
Self Portrait
(courtesy Andrew Lanyon)

intriguing question, to what extent did studio vistas affect artists' subjects? When disused buildings ran out, enterprising locals erected purpose-built studios and, taking heed of the artists' preference for northern light, these were often built on Porthmeor. By the First World War, the Porthmeor area, which had been the industrial section of town, had become almost exclusively an artists' enclave. It is a fascinating story, untold before, and I make no excuse for dealing with it at length.

All colonies contain numerous artists, who are not well-known through their exhibited works, but these lesser artists can still contribute significantly to the community spirit. Indeed, as they may not have been so committed to their art, they are often the people who organise social activities or have talents in other directions - as musicians, as actors, as sportsmen or as wits. This book, therefore, gives me the opportunity of recording the characters and careers of some of these artists, who have not been given much attention previously, but who rented homes and studios in the colony for extended periods. However, for those artists, whose works I have discussed in detail in my other books, I merely give the briefest of biographical information.

The colony also boasted a significant number of artist-photographers, such as Herbert Lanyon, John Douglas and Sydney Carr, whose camera work, often of considerable merit in its own right, has provided essential records of people and places, particularly artists' studios. Finally, in the pre-War period, there were a number of resident writers, such as Leslie Stephen, Charles Lewis Hind, Charles Marriott, Cyril Ranger-Gull and Havelock and Edith Ellis, who mixed with the artists. Some have left memoirs of great interest and importance, but, in other cases, I have quoted extracts from their works of fiction, as these often capture the spirit of the colony and the manner in which it inter-reacted with the local community.

There is no doubt that the St Ives Arts Club was the centre of the social life of the colony and that the entertainments put on by the artists, both there and in venues around the town, were important for promoting the spirit of unity in the colony. I also reconstruct the parties that the artists threw in their homes and in their studios, their Carnival Masquerades and other frolics. Unsurprisingly, given the magnificent scenery in all directions, walking was a popular pastime, with artists being some of the first to write walking guides, whilst golf, for both male and female artists, also proved a popular communal activity. Cricket matches with or against the Newlyn artists, or for or against the local club, and sometimes even between the sexes, were less regular, but, when arranged, were eagerly anticipated events. The caricatures of H.G.Fitzherbert also show that the artists joined in with the local hunt and shoot and that, during the winter evenings, amidst the constant haze of pipe smoke, billiards and cards were popular.

I devote a separate chapter to student life in the town, as the Schools of Painting were of such importance in attracting fresh blood to the colony, and the student body formed a distinct element in the community. A range of different sources make it possible to recreate the hopes and aspirations, the doubts and despair and the fun and frolic of the classes of 1901-2 to an extraordinary degree.

Comic art may not feature on the walls of Burlington House, but there were a number of artists with a comic eye in the colony, such as Edmund Fuller, Herbert Fitzherbert, Sydney Carr and Frank Ver Beck, who became well-known in other spheres. These are featured, not only because they will have kept their peers amused, but because they have provided us with a wide range of caricatures, not only of their fellow artists, but also of others in the community with whom the artists fraternised. Indeed, these caricatures are of crucial importance in demonstrating the way in which the artists melded into the community.

In Part Three, I look specifically at the inter-reaction between the artists and the locals, albeit this is a constant theme that runs throughout the book. What exposure did the artists get in the local press, and was this favourable? How long was it before the artists were accepted by the middle classes in the town, and to what extent did they socialise together? What impact did the artists have on local businesses? Which sections of the local community and what types of business profited from the artists' presence, and did raised prices benefit all or did they cause resentment in some quarters? Were there particular entrepeneurs, who took advantage of the artists' special requirements? Did artists become involved in serving the community, for example, by becoming Councillors or Borough Magistrates? What romances occurred between the artists and the locals?

Whilst friendships between the artists and middle class businessmen and clergy might be anticipated, how did the artists get on with the fisherfolk, given that anyone from outside the Duchy was considered a "foreigner"? To what extent did the lives of the artists impinge on the fisherfolk at all? Could they simply be ignored? What percentage of the fisherfolk were prepared to act as models, and did the sex of the artists affect their willingness? What was the reaction of the fisherfolk to the numerous foreign artists working in the town? Were there any instances of xenophobia? Were

Fig. 0.3 Cordier   *View of St Ives*   (from *Picturesque World* 1880)
This unpicturesque scene shows the extent of mining operations close to town.

Fig. 0.4 *St Ives* - engraving after photograph by Edward Ashton (detail)   (from *Pictorial World* 1877)

the artists generally considered as wealthy sophisticates and categorised as "natural foes", like all the monied classes who lived Up-along, or did the fishermen react differently to individual approaches? How did the artists cope with certain aspects of their lives being affected by the superstitions, fervent beliefs and outdated moral code of the fishermen? What tensions did exist, and how often did disagreements occur? Were disputes the result of distinctions in class, wealth, education or religion, or were other issues, such as temperance or local politics, at play? Was it only newcomers, be they painters, preachers or politicians, who caused problems?

At one Mayoral Banquet, the comment was passed that one of the most significant contributions of the artists had been their enlargement of "the mental vision of the townspeople". A heightened appreciation of art was clearly one aspect of this, but to what extent did the locals show any interest in the artists' paintings and what opportunities were they given to view them? Did any local collections get formed? How else did the artists contribute to the improvement of the cultural activities of the town and the mindset of the populace? To what extent did artists get involved in local musical or dramatic societies, or influence the type of entertainments that were put on in the town? What part did the artists play in encouraging new sports, such as golf and cricket, and how involved were they in local clubs? What charitable activities did the artists support or encourage? What impact did the way of life led by female artists have on local attitudes towards women, and what role did such females play in furthering women's rights? What types of behaviour did the artists persuade the locals were cruel or inappropriate?

In Part Four - War and Aftermath - , I look at the manner in which the outbreak of War impacted on St Ives society and the ways in which the artists, who were unable to fight, combined with the locals in a whole range of fund-raising activities for various relief causes, not least of which was the plight of numerous Belgian refugees that were taken in by the town on the initiative of some of the artists. The post-War period saw many changes in the town, in the colony and in society as a whole. It was not an easy period, with the fishing industry decimated and the heyday of the rural art colony long past. The artists not only widened their range of artistic endeavours, with the decorative arts receiving unprecedented attention, but they were joined in the colony by numerous retired writers, playrights, actors and musicians, as well as some highly decorated military figures. The Arts Club was transformed, with non-artist members putting on a wide range of entertainments on a regular basis, and the formation of Literary and Dramatic Societies, coupled with literary buff, Greville Matheson, assuming an editorial role at the *St Ives Times*, rendered painting no longer the dominant member of the Fine Arts in St Ives society. As the local Council sought to modernise St Ives, not only to appeal to a wider range of tourists, but also for the benefit of the health of the working classes, relations between the artists and local dignitaries deteriorated, as quaint parts of the town were swept away.

Finally, in Part Five, I summarise the impact of the artists on the town. I review one of the principal themes running through the entire book - the effect of the artists on the town's development as a tourist centre. How did the artists change the nature of the town's burgeoning tourist industry, and what part did they play in its subsequent significant growth? Did the artists become a tourist spectacle themselves? Was a superior type of tourist attracted to St Ives by virtue of the artists, and what impact did this have on the manner in which the town was developed? To what extent did the artists and the Arts Club draw writers, actors, musicians and other professionals to the town? Whilst one local Mayor passed the comment "A locality can have no better friend than an art colony", was this a widely prevailing view?

Pulling together other themes from the book, I also look at how the artists impacted on commercial interests in the town and make a final assessment of how the artists affected the physical aspect of the town, not only by their homes and studios, but also by their efforts to combat "the spirit of Mr Gradgrind".[1]

The result of this study of the artists' social life and their interreaction with the townsfolk provides a totally new, and exceptionally important, perspective on the town and the colony, and demonstrates that the artists played a far more important role in shaping St Ives than they are normally given credit for. However, it also reveals the foresight of many of the local dignitaries and entrepreneurs, who quickly realised the importance of the artists to the local economy and worked with them so as to ensure that the town offered everything that an artist community required.

---

1 This expression was used by Louis Grier, when he was elected on to the local Town Council. Mr Gradgrind was the philistine teacher in Charles Dickens' *Hard Times*.

A NOTE ON SOURCES

St Ives is extraordinarily lucky in the wealth of sources that have survived. Well-known are the records of the St Ives Arts Club and the extraordinarily detailed coverage in the contemporary local press. However, for this book, I have been able to draw upon two under-utilised sources, first drawn to my attention by Brian Stevens of the St Ives Museum, namely the Rate Books held by the Museum and the Mornington Estate papers, held at the County Records Office in Truro, which relate to the properties rented out in St Ives by the town's major landowner of the period, Lord Cowley.

The Rate Books list the owner and ratepayer for every single property in St Ives, including studios, and so are a vital record of where artists are likely to have been working or living in any particular year. However, a little caution is required, as it soon becomes quite clear that the named ratepayer can sometimes have little correlation to the actual occupier. The Rate Books are, nevertheless, invaluable, but, unfortunately, there is not a full run. Indeed, before 1898, there are only extant relevant Rate Books for the years 1886, 1888, 1893 and 1894, with those of 1886 and 1888 being of little assistance. This means that I often have to speculate as to the position in the years 1889-1892 and 1895-1897. Whilst there is then a full run of Rate Books from 1898-1917, the only extant Rate Book for subsequent years is for 1925.

Henry Arthur Mornington Wellesley (1866-1919), the third Earl Cowley, who inherited the title in 1895, was an absentee landlord and, upon his demise, the local paper merely commented, "His death removes from Society one of its most romantic figures, who had in many ways a varied career. He first came before the public in a breach of promise case in 1889 and, again, in 1905, in the famous Hortopp divorce suit"![2] As many artists either rented homes or studios from Lord Cowley, the Mornington Estate papers contain valuable correspondence from artists, albeit normally complaining about some problem or other. On the death of the third Earl in 1919, the title was inherited by his son, Christian Arthur Wellesley (1890-1962), who had previously pursued a career as a music-hall artist and scenery painter, and who had been brought before the Official Receiver in 1916.[3] Accordingly, one of his first acts, as the new Earl, was to organise a mass sale of some one hundred and sixty of his St Ives properties. A large number of artist's studios were included in such sale, albeit that they did prove some of the hardest properties to shift. The total realised was over £31,000.[4] Therefore, the threat of sale, followed by redevelopment, hung thereafter over any remaining properties owned by the Cowley Estate.

Whilst St Ives is lucky that the colony was visited by numerous foreign artists, whose accounts of their stay have been preserved in archives in their own countries, there is a sad lack of material relating to the principal British artists working in the colony. Artists such as Adrian Stokes, Arnesby Brown, Julius Olsson and William Titcomb have left no correspondence or comments from their time in the colony. In assessing the inter-reaction with the locals, one is frequently working off scraps. It is perhaps not surprising that there are few accounts by the locals of the period, but those that do exist make hardly any mention of the artists. The most surprising omission is in the Reminiscences of William Paynter. Here was one of the men who showed great initiative by building the Piazza Studios for the artists and who enjoyed a good income from them for over thirty years, and yet he does not mention the art colony at all! One can only assume that he felt that it was inappropriate to pass comment on his social superiors, or that he was only likely to make himself look ridiculous by discussing an aspect of life that he knew little about.

ABBREVIATIONS

BAPFA	Bristol Academy for the Promotion of the Fine Arts
GER	Gross Estimated Rental, as recorded in the St Ives Rate Books
RCPS	Royal Cornwall Polytechnic Society, Falmouth
RHA	Royal Hibernian Academy
SBA (RBA)	Society of British Artists (later Royal Society of British Artists)
SWA	Society of Women Artists
WCAU	West Cornwall Art Union, Penzance

---

2 *St Ives Times*, 17/1/1919.

3 See *St Ives Times*, 17/1/1919 and *New York Times*, 28/5/1911.

4 For details of properties sold, see *St Ives Times*, 12/9/1919 and 3/10/1919..

PART ONE

OLD HOUSES BEACH ST. IVES.

Edmund G. Fuller

THE ARRIVAL OF THE ARTISTS

1.1   St Ives before the artists

At the beginning of the nineteenth century, St Ives was a prosperous town, dominated by fishing, shipbuilding, rope-making and mining industries. Fishing, however, was the activity with which the majority of the town's residents were involved, and there were distinct fishing seasons - the principal ones being the pilchard season, which ran from August to November, and the herring season, which ran from October to December, whilst the less important mackerel season ran from February to June. During the relatively barren summer months, a number of boats went to fish for herring in the North Sea. John Hobson Matthews, in his history of the district, published in 1892, commented, "St Ives was at the height of its prosperity during the first quarter of the present century, when its mines were all working, its fisheries remunerative and its agriculture in full swing. At that happy time, St Ives was the metropolis of West Cornwall and its inhabitants were noted for the polished gaiety of their mode of life; balls, concerts and dinner parties in the winter season, and picnics and boating excursions in the summer made up the annual round of fashionable pleasure at St Ives."[5]

The industries in St Ives continued to prosper until the 1860s. Record numbers of pilchards were still being caught - for instance, 18,000 hogsheads were landed between 1st and 24th October 1851, whilst the record catch for a season was the 28,000 hogsheads landed in 1871.[6] One old salt, recalling that extraordinary year, commented, "All this bay was a great lump of solid pilchard".[7] The 1861 Census shows the population of the town at 7027, an increase of 500 from 1851, and the highest figure of the century. This was largely due to the mid-century mining boom. In the 1850s, the St Ives Consols Mine, at the top of The Stennack, was considered to be one of the largest tin concerns in the County, whilst Wheal Providence in Carbis Bay was another large operation that employed hundreds of workers.[8] In 1860, a mine was even opened in the middle of town, on Pednolver Point, and there were numerous other mining operations all around the town.[9] Accordingly, it might appear that, in 1860, the beginning of the period covered by this book, St Ives was at the height of its prosperity. However, despite all this commercial activity, John Sampson Courtney reveals that, even as early as 1845, everything was not harmonious in the town.

> "Not a century has passed away since St Ives was the chief town in the west, and the resort of all the fashionable people of the neighbourhood. But the blight of a parliamentary character has rested upon it and its inhabitants have been divided into opposing parties, jealous and envious of each other; and consequently while other towns around it have been flourishing and improving, it has not only failed to keep pace with them, but has actually fallen back into that state of relative inferiority from which they have happily emerged."[10]

Inadequate infrastructure was one of the issues that failed to be addressed during this period, as St Ives suffered from a defective water supply and poor drainage. This, when coupled with the effluvia from the pilchard cellars, which ran through open channels in the streets, meant that the town stank. For those unused to them, the odours in the town were intolerable, and the early guide books to Cornwall recommended visitors to view St Ives from a distance, but not to venture any closer.[11] In addition, Trewren's Bus, the main means of getting to the town, only ran three days a week and, as a result, visitors were so rare that "if a stranger walked down Tregenna Hill, the women occupiers would look out of their windows or doorways and enquire who he was and what he wanted."[12] Unsurprisingly, therefore, the American artist, William Trost Richards, as late as 1878, reported to his patron that St Ives was "one of the least frequented towns of this district, partly because of a bad reputation as a dirty fishing town, and partly because it has been a little out of the main line of travel".[13]

The ability of the town to prosper, without visitors, was severely hampered in the third quarter of the century, by the collapse of its main industries. Matthews recorded that "the invention of steam navigation dealt a death blow to her numerous fleet of sailing vessels and to shipbuilding in the town", whilst the importation of cheap tin from the colonies killed off the mines. Furthermore, the fisheries had become far less dependable.[14] Accordingly, in the 1870s, St Ives was in serious trouble, and the Town Council

---

5 J.H.Matthews, *A History of the Parishes of Saint Ives, Lelant, Towednack and Zennor in the County of Cornwall*, London, 1892 at p.358.

6 *St Ives Times* 12/9/1913.

7 *St Ives Weekly Summary* 1/1/1905. This report puts the haul in 1871 at 35,000 hogsheads.

8 Murray's Handbook for Devon and Cornwall, 1859 (1971 reprint at p.181). Stennack means 'place of tin'.

9 See Plan of Saint Ives, Uny Lelant and Towednack Mining Districts, reproduced in C. Noall, *The Book of St Ives*, Buckingham, 1977 at p.97.

10 J.S.Courtney, *A Guide to Penzance and its Neighbourhood*, Penzance, 1845 at p.172.

11 See, for instance, Murray's *Handbook for Devon and Cornwall*, 1859 (1971 reprint at p.180).

12 W.J.Jacobs, *Memories of Eighty Years 1880-1960*, privately published, 1960 (copy at St Ives Archive Centre) at p.3-4.

13 Letter from W.T.Richards to G.Whitney dated 29/9/1878 - Archives of American Art, W.T.Richards Papers, Reel 2296.

14 J.H.Matthews, *A History of the Parishes of Saint Ives, Lelant, Towednack and Zennor in the County of Cornwall*, London, 1892 at p.358.

decided that the town needed to re-invent itself as a health resort. This concept was not universally welcomed. William Jacobs, the founder and editor for fifty years of *The Western Echo*, recalled in his memoirs that, in his youth, "St Ives was divided into two parties, up-along and down-along. The down-along party was opposed to any public expenditure to attract visitors, but the up-along party realised that the fisheries were declining, and a violent clash of local interests ensued".[15]

For the health resort plan to succeed, access to the town had to be made far easier. This was finally achieved in 1877, when a branch line was completed from St Erth.[16] Far from being welcomed, however, old St Ives folk from the Down-along district would stand on The Malakoff, making derisive comments at the railway contractors. "What a lot of fools to bring a railway to St Ives. Trewren's bus will bring in all the people we want."[17] Also required were some drastic improvements to the water supply and the drainage. Even the latter proved difficult to achieve, and it was left to a young, newly arrived doctor, John Michael Nicholls, to urge action, as he was shocked at local mortality rates, particularly amongst children. Jacobs recalled, "At first they refused to listen to him. The local rate was only 1s 8d in the £ and that seemed to be all the local people cared about. Eventually, Dr Nicholls had to threaten the Council that unless they did something to remedy the state of affairs, he would report the matter to London, when the Government would carry out a scheme at probably three times the cost."[18]

The railway could not save the industries, upon which St Ives had relied on the past, and Edward Hain, one of the most enlightened figures in the town, whose decision, in 1878, to start building up a fleet of steamships, was to prove an inspired move, later recalled that, in the railway's early years, "the main purpose for which it seemed to be employed then was to take people out of the place, because they could not get a proper and adequate living in it".[19] This view is confirmed by the Census figures, which saw the population drop from 6965 in 1871, to 6445 in 1881, and, yet further, to 6094 in 1891.[20]

Fig. 1.1 The laying of the foundation of the extension to Smeaton's Pier 1888

In addition to organising infrastructure improvements, the Town Council, led by Edward Hain, also authorised a number of works to improve the harbour, including an extension to Smeaton's Pier in 1888-90 and the erection of the West Pier in 1894. (St Ives Museum/St Ives Trust)

15 W.J.Jacobs, *Memories of Eighty Years 1880-1960*, privately published, 1960 at p.83 (copy at St Ives Archive Centre).

16 Previous efforts in 1844, 1846, 1853 and 1862 had all foundered - See Cyril Noall, *Yesterday's Town*, Buckingham, 1979 at p.60.

17 W.J.Jacobs, *Memories of Eighty Years 1880-1960*, privately published, 1960 at p.3 (copy at St Ives Archive Centre).

18 W.J.Jacobs, *Memories of Eighty Years 1880-1960*, privately published, 1960 at p.13 (copy at St Ives Archive Centre).

19 Speech at the 1911 Mayoral Banquet, *St Ives Weekly Summary* 10/11/1911.

20 See Janet Axten Dissertation *Migration into and out of St Ives, Cornwall 1871-1901* dated June 2003 - copy held at St Ives Archive Centre.

Fig. 1.2 Edward Cooke   *Carrick Gladden Cove, St Ives Bay* (11th October 1848)   (Private Collection)

However, the railway did bring, for the first time, non artist visitors to the town, and the transformation by the Great Western Railway Company in 1878 of Tregenna Castle into a high class hotel ensured that there was quality accomodation available for wealthy tourists. This was an immediate draw, for William Trost Richards records in 1878 that "the Duke of Newcastle and other swells" had been lodging there.[21] However, the tourist season extended only over August and September and, accordingly, when the artists first settled in the town, in the mid-1880s, St Ives was in an extraordinarily fragile position.

1.2   The pattern of settlement

1885 is taken as the year when the St Ives art colony was established, as it was that year that three artists - the Englishman Henry Harewood Robinson (known as Harry), his Irish wife Maria Dorothea Webb Robinson (known as Dorothy) and the Scot William Eadie - decided to overwinter in the town. In retrospect, the date of the formation of an art colony is given great weight, but to what extent did the local inhabitants notice any difference in the artistic presence in the town from previous years?

Ever since the completion of the rail link to Penzance in 1859, artists had become much more regular visitors to Cornwall, and St Ives soon attracted the distinguished new Academician, James Clarke Hook, who stayed in the town from 3rd July to 16th September 1860, and the Bristol watercolourist, George Wolfe, who returned on a number of occasions throughout the 1860s. At this juncture, artists tended to go off on sketching trips in late summer/early autumn, avoiding the heat and haze of mid-summer. Whilst, on occasion, these tours might last for a couple of months, the artists tended to move around regularly, as they explored as many new areas as possible. So, for example, the week that Edward Cooke spent in St Ives in October 1848 was the longest period that he spent in any one place during his two-month tour of Devon and Cornwall that autumn. Even a regular long-term visitor to Cornwall, such as the marine painter, John Brett, who set out intending to work in particular locations, rarely stayed anywhere for more than a few weeks, and so the period of a month that he spent in St Ives in September 1872 was probably quite unusually long for a visitor to the town, whilst Hook's length of stay in 1860 had been extraordinary. Artists, therefore, would only have been seen around the town at certain times of year and their numbers will have been small. However, given the rarity of visitors to the town and their sketching habits, they would have been conspicuous.

The launch of St Ives as a health resort in the late 1870s coincided with a change of outlook on the part of a number of artists, for there was a surge of interest, from artists returning from France, in replicating the art colony existence that they had experienced there. Accordingly, artists started to consider relocating,

---

21 Letter from W.T.Richards to G.Whitney dated 29/9/1878 - Archives of American Art, W.T.Richards Papers, Reel 2296.

for significant periods, to similar out of the way, unspoilt places on the coast of Britain. As a result, lengths of visits extended. With Newlyn having attracted artists to settle there in 1882, it was not surprising to find other artists exploring nearby towns. Accordingly, John Hobson Matthews in the Guide to St Ives, that he produced in 1884, commented that the quaintness of the town had already "given weeks of work to a considerable number of eminent artists". Indeed, the Guide is directed, in large part, at the artist visitor. One of the artists who does seem to have spent some considerable time in the town in the early 1880s is the Nottingham-born artist, Edwin Ellis, as he exhibited a series of paintings featuring the fishing industry in St Ives at the winter exhibition of SBA in 1882. Given that a number of works featured the seine fishery, he too is likely to have been an autumn visitor. However, there are few sources from which to work out quite how many artists were working in the town in the early 1880s, what time of year they visited and how long they stayed. Accounts of Whistler's visit in January 1884, however, make it clear that his party, which also comprised his pupils Mortimer Menpes and Walter Sickert, were not the only artists in residence at that time, and so the season was extending.

Given the nomadic nature of most early artist visitors, they tended either to work in watercolour, which was far more convenient than oils, or to do small panels. If, like Edward Cooke or John Brett, they did decide to use these sketches for a major work, then this was done back in their studios at home. However, figure painters, such as James Clarke Hook or Edith Hume, would have had to have done detailed portrait studies of their fishermen models in St Ives, even if their major works, utilising these sketches, were executed in their home studios. However, in the early 1880s, when the cult of Bastien-Lepage was at its height, the inquisitive amongst the fisherfolk would have witnessed a new phenomenon - the sight of artists attempting to paint exhibition-sized canvases *en plein air*. Walter Sickert recounted his amusement, in 1883, at seeing a *plein airist* at work on the beach in St Ives in a full gale, with bemused fishermen being employed to hold his easel and the four corners of the canvas steady with ropes. However, such an approach was probably now common-place, for Mortimer Menpes indicated that the other artists in St Ives at the time found Whistler "a continual source of wonder". " "The man must be idling." they said. "How can one work in earnest sitting on a borrowed chair and with nothing but a small pochade box and a grey-tinted panel? Real hard work necessitates a great canvas and easel, large brushes, and at least a sketching umbrella." "[22] Artists, therefore, were not only more numerous, but more visible - or most probably, in the eyes of the fisherfolk, more risible.

Fig. 1.3 An elderly artist, possibly Émile-Louis Vernier, attracting interest, as he paints on the harbour beach

22 Mortimer Menpes, *Whistler as I Knew Him*, London, 1904, p.138-9.

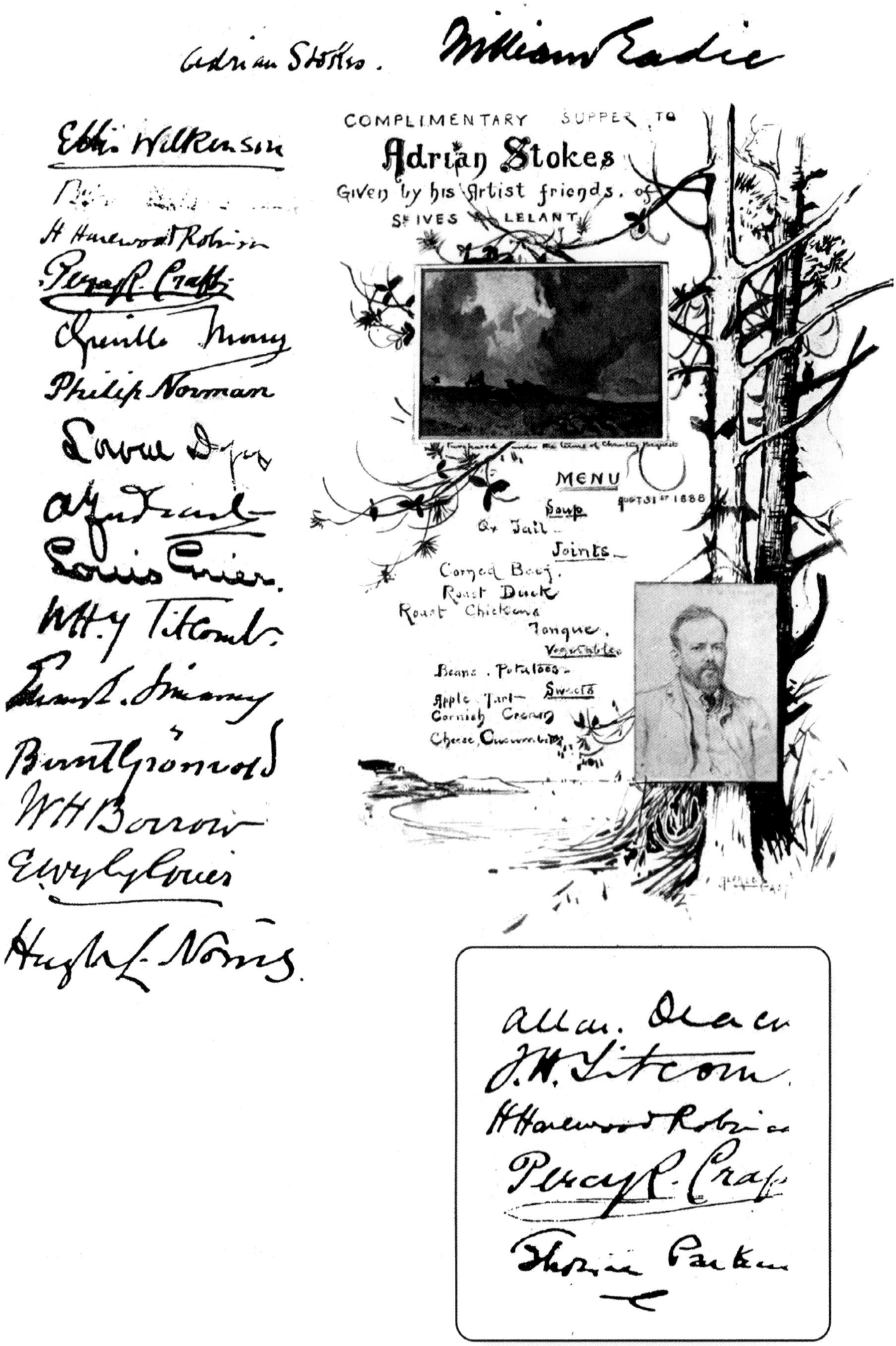

Fig. 1.4 The menu, designed by Alfred East, for Adrian Stokes' Chantrey Supper on 31st August 1888
Note the faces in the trees.

Some indication that artists were beginning at this time to consider longer sojourns in the town is revealed by Harry Robinson's confirmation that the Hon Duff Tollemache had created, in 1884, a studio out of a disused and ruinous building on Carn Crowse. There are no previous references to studios in the town, and clearly the expense of obtaining a suitable building, and fitting it out, would not have been merited for artists intending only to visit for a few weeks. Therefore, Tollemache's decision to renovate a ruin suggests an intention to make an extended stay. The following year, the Robinsons and Eadie also decided to create studios, but they then determined to stay on in St Ives "as winter residents". Furthermore, they did not merely over-winter in the town, but rented houses on a long-term basis, used St Ives as their exhibiting address and, in effect, made St Ives their permanent base.

The decisions taken by the Robinsons and Eadie to settle in the town in 1885 mark the formation of the St Ives art colony, but their early commitment to the town was quite unusual, and it was some years before other artists changed from being regular visitors to permanent residents. What does occur, though, is that visiting artists stayed for longer than previously. In part, this may be due to the large number of foreign artists, who decided to work in St Ives in the next couple of years - artists who had known the Robinsons from their time in the ateliers of Paris and the art colonies of Brittany. These foreigners did not have any other home or studio in England, to which they could return from time to time, and, accordingly, they based themselves in St Ives for periods of months, rather than weeks, for they decided during their stays, not only to complete series of sketches, but also to finish or, in any event, make major progress with their large exhibition-destined works. Accordingly, for example, the visits of the American, Howard Russell Butler, in 1886 and 1887, which extended between July and October each year, might have exceeded that of Hook in 1860, but were in fact shorter than any of his principal companions - the Simmonses and the Chadwicks, whose stays were nearer to nine months. These new long-term visitors clearly needed good studio space in the town, which they found exclusively in the fishing quarter, and so artists and fishermen were thrown together in a way that had not necessarily occurred before. From 1886, a variety of sources begin to provide an indication of the number of artists in the town at any one time. Accordingly, one can gauge from the extant letters of Howard Russell Butler and Stanhope Forbes that, in the summer of 1886, there were at least eleven artists present, although there are likely to have been a number of other short-term visitors as well. Both Stanhope Forbes and Butler confirm that, in 1887, the colony became much busier. In June that year, Forbes predicted, "St Ives will be crowded this year with people from all parts of the world. Plenty of new Americans.....There will be many more people there than there were last year."[23] This was confirmed by Butler, who returned in early July, in a letter to his sister, Harriet, "The colony at St Ives has doubled. There are to be twenty artists here this summer." In fact, taking into account the artists who exhibited St Ives scenes at the exhibitions held in Penzance and St Ives that year, the number rose to at least thirty. In 1888, the sources are not so numerous, but twenty artists attended the supper held on 31st August to celebrate Adrian Stokes' sale to the Chantrey Trustees. As this was at the height of the tourist season, the number of attendees probably reflects almost the maximum number of artists that would have been in the colony at any one time, although there would have been plenty of other visitors at other times of the year.

With the colony having been established in 1885 and with this level of artist visitors subsequently, one might imagine that, by 1888, more would have settled in the town. However, the 1888 Rate Book lists only Eadie and the Robinsons as ratepayers for houses, and only Robinson, Louis and Wyly Grier as ratepayers for a studio. All the other artists, however long they stayed, had yet to commit themselves, even to a studio.

It was in the winter of 1888 that Louis Grier started the Saturday evening social get-togethers in his studio, 'The Foc'sle', fronting the harbour, that ultimately led to the formation of the St Ives Arts Club in 1890. In his account of these, he contends that as many as sixty people took part. In the past, it has been assumed that these were all artists (plus the odd writer, such as Leslie Stephen), and their spouses, indicating a winter community of at least thirty painters. Yet 1889 sees the first review of the Private Views held by the artists in March, prior to the submission of their works to the London exhibitions - the event that became known as Show Day -, and only ten artists were involved - Adrian and Marianne Stokes, William Eadie, Harry and Dorothy Robinson, Louis and Wyly Grier, Edward Simmons, Julius Olsson and William Titcomb. It seems clear, therefore, that quite a few of the participants in these social evenings were local friends of the artists, revealing the extent to which the artists were already intermingling with the community.

The list of ten artists who held Private Views in 1889 is, however, most informative, for, without exception, all these artists were to play a significant role in the development of the colony. Whereas the artists known to be in the colony in previous years, normally during the summer months, included many, who were short-term visitors and who had little to do with the colony subsequently, these ten artists had

---

23 Letter to his mother dated 5/6/1887 - Tate Gallery Archives 9015-2-1-430.

21

worked hard together in the colony over the winter months on their Royal Academy submissions and now showed off to their colleagues, and the local friends with whom they had socialised, the fruits of their labour. Not only was a core group developing, but also a pattern of life. For the fisherfolk, the artists were no longer an occasional curiosity; they were now a permanent feature.

1.3   The pattern of the seasons

An article on St Ives artists in 1905 passed the comment, "St Ives is mostly a winter colony, most of the artists flying before the tourist and the holiday-maker...'Anything for a quiet life' is the general motto".[24] This marks a distinct change from the position in the pre-colony period, and in the very early years of the colony, when artists had tended to descend on the town in the summer and autumn. The development of St Ives as a winter base for artists was largely due to the enthusiasm of the period for *plein air* painting, as it became recognised, in artistic circles, that the equable climate of West Penwith meant that it was one of the few areas in Britain where open air painting could be practised all the year round. Accordingly, most of the regular members of the colony were to be found in residence during the winter months, and there were a fair number of winter visitors as well. As most artists did not have homes or studios with electricity, their working days were curtailed by the diminishing hours of daylight. As a result, greater attention was given during these months to evening entertainments at the Arts Club and other venues around the town. The President of the Arts Club was elected each November, when most of the artists had settled down for the winter, and the fact that a part-year resident, such as Arnesby Brown, could be elected President, suggests that the artists accepted that the months from November to April were the key period in the Arts Club calendar. In addition to the regular Saturday nights at the Club, there seem to have been some key dates set aside for entertainments - Boxing Night for a local charitable cause, New Year at the Club and a Fancy Dress Ball in February, the final release of tension before the highlight of the colony's artistic calendar - Show Day - an event in which all committed residents of the colony tried to participate.

Soon after Show Day, the colony began to dissipate, as artists left to attend Varnishing Day at the Academy or went to view the exhibitions in London, and often Paris as well. A contributor to *The Artist*, visiting the town in June, commented, "Now that the bustle and excitement of Academy time are well over, St Ives appears almost deserted by its artist population. The jolly little fraternity which met nearly every evening at the cosy Arts Club, to discuss the day's doings and each other's pictures, has nearly entirely disappeared."[25] After the stress of the weeks leading up to Show Day, many artists were quite glad not to think of painting for a while and took breaks with their long-suffering wives and children. Others, always keen to find new sources of inspiration, began to plot that summer's sketching sorties, perhaps having spotted a subject that interested them in one of the exhibitions. Escaping the tourist masses, who began to flock to St Ives in ever greater numbers, was, in many instances, also a key objective.

The extent to which the regulars in the colony could dissipate completely by the end of May is graphically demonstrated by the replies received by Nottingham Castle Museum to its invitations to exhibit at the Cornish Artists Exhibition, which were sent out at the end of May 1894, for hardly any came from St Ives. Several artists had gone to France - Adrian and Marianne Stokes were in Longpré-les-corps-saints on the Somme, Sydney and Alexandrina Laurence were on the banks of the Seine at Vétheuil and Harry and Dorothy Robinson were staying at a hotel in Marlotte, Seine et Marne and painting in the Forest of Fontainebleau. Lowell Dyer was staying at the Hotel du Luxembourg in Laroche in Belgium. Jessie Davidson, having returned from the Continent, went up to Lennoxtown in Scotland. Julius Olsson was experiencing life in another of Britain's coastal art colonies in Walberswick, whereas Louis Grier was in Wells-by-the-Sea in Norfolk, hoping that some students would respond to his advertisement in *The Studio*. William Titcomb was at his recently inherited property in Wickersley in South Yorkshire, where he was painting the local steel works, Arthur Meade was in Dorchester, with his wife's family, and Emily Latham Greenfield was in the depths of Wales. Fred Milner had gone back to Cheltenham and Eardley Blomefield had returned to his native Mansfield. Greville Morris was initially in Bushey, possibly for further study, before joining Charles Bartlett at The Manor in Steventon, Berkshire, whilst Noble Barlow was in Broadway, Worcestershire and Trythall Rowe was painting in Tewkesbury. The Canadian, Mary Bell, was staying with her friend Edith Fuller in Croydon Only Algernon Talmage, William Eadie and Edmund Fuller replied from St Ives. This snapshot of a typical summer's scattering of artists is most illuminating.

The departure of the resident artists from St Ives during May did not mean that the town was empty of artists, as the first published Visitors' Lists of the year in the local paper, normally in late May/early

24 J.M.Gibbon, *St Ives and its Artists*, *Black and White*, 30/12/1905.
25 Reproduced in *St Ives Weekly Summary*, 16/6/1894.

June, reveal that other artists had already arrived. Their lengths of stay varied, not unnaturally, but often such visitors would stay for several months. These early Visitors' Lists each year, as well as those in September and October, reveal just how important artists were to the tourist trade of the town, as artists consistently make up a significant percentage of the visitors staying in these off-peak months.

It is difficult to say how much such summer artist visitors fraternised with the artist residents. Their presence in the town, if not discovered through their sketching habits, would have been publicized by the Visitors' Lists and, in the case of distinguished or well-known figures, might have elicited some invitations to tea. However, an invitation to the Arts Club was less likely, as its activities were drastically curtailed during the summer months. Acquaintance could have also been made through the sub-letting of neighbouring studios, as there appears to have been both a formal, and informal, system of matching visitors with temporarily available studio space. After the opening of the first Schools of Painting in 1895, there was a noticeable increase in summer artist visitors, as many students would use their vacation periods from their principal places of study to experience the unique methods of the St Ives schools. In addition to the numerous short-term visitors, there was, of course, a continual stream of artists joining and leaving the colony, but, certainly in the years prior to the War, there was a distinct change in the character of the colony between the winter and summer periods.

1.4   The pattern of the day

Charles Lewis Hind, during his time as a student under Julius Olsson and Louis Grier in 1896, indicated that everyday life within the artistic community in St Ives followed a familiar pattern.

> "One day at St Ives passes much like another. About the hour of ten, you may see the painters who live on the road that climbs on to Carbis Bay, clad in knickerbockers and Norfolk jackets, sauntering down towards their studios. Arrived there, they may sit for for half-an-hour smoking the meditative morning pipe, studying the work upon the easel, and considering the attack of a new day's task. Painting follows, and about lunchtime, you may again see them sauntering homewards up the hill road. An hour later, the return to the studios begins, where, if it is winter-time, they remain until sunset, when those who play billiards foregather at the hostelry. On summer evenings, the train may carry a load of men and canvases to Lelant, to make sketches in the open, or some will play a round of golf, or take part in a four at tennis. Subsequently, there is a constant interchange of festivities and, on Saturdays, everybody makes a point of being at the Club. So the winter months pass by, and if, as sending-in day approaches, the members of the colony become a little serious, a trifle moody, or a thought more detached than usual, it is understood that as soon as the pictures are despatched, this mantle of aloofness will be thrown off, and the old hospitable life resumed."[26]

Fig. 1.5 Charles Lewis Hind   (Andrew Lanyon)

---

26 C.Lewis Hind, *In Painters' Land, The Ludgate*, October 1896.

Fig. 1.6 Sydney Carr   *Cyril Ranger-Gull*
(David Wilkinson, Book Gallery, St Ives)

Whilst making passing reference to some summer activities, this description is primarily of the pattern of life during the winter months, a period of serious endeavour for ambitious artists during which they were based largely in their studios. This book, however, is not confined to successful members of the colony, and Cyril Ranger-Gull's descriptions of the typical lifestyle of the artists in his satirical novel, *Portalone* (1904), might be closer to the truth for some of the less committed artists, for whom a small private income "forbade strenuousness". A *bon viveur* himself, Ranger-Gull nevertheless mercilessly cast his satirical eye over certain sections of the artistic community, particularly those who "played at being celebrities long before they could establish any claim to distinction". Like the author, these artists could frequently be found in the pub.

In Ranger-Gull's colony, "a hole of idleness and folly", populated by "golfers and loafers", the artist, again clad in knickerbockers and a Norfolk jacket, but perhaps sporting a loud waistcoat and gaudy stockings, also made certain that he was at his studio in the morning, but he probably arrived a little later, and with a thumping headache, being "a whisky drinking backslider". Although attempting to work, he did not achieve very much, and was delighted when a colleague from a neighbouring studio popped in. This enabled him to sound off on the hot art topics of the moment, or to give voice to his lofty ambitions and objectives, even if both he and his colleague knew that he had neither the talent nor the application to achieve them. With a bit of luck, whilst puffing away on their ever-lit pipes, there was also a tasty exchange of "sally-lun scandal". Both were delighted when the hour struck eleven, and they could saunter along to meet some further colleagues at 'The Brigantine', a very thinly disguised reference to 'The Sloop Inn'. This pub had been taken over by the artists "as a theatre where they saw themselves playing congenial parts", and they had hung it with paintings of sea and moor, despite the initial protestations of the landlord, in an effort to reproduce the Bohemian ambience of hostelries that they had experienced in France. "Most of those who came carried a paint-box, a folding tripod easel and some a sheaf of brushes. This was a more or less invariable habit. Each man had, in the course of time, come to believe that he had just dropped in for a minute or two and would shortly be back at work". By 2 p.m., however, they could always find an excuse for not pursuing their sketching that afternoon, even if no-one suggested a round of golf. "On brilliant days of clement weather, the colour of the sea and sky was far too "hot" and "glaring" to paint. When it rained, "mere studio work never did a man any good yet; made a man paint everything in too low a key. *Plein air* was the only thing."."[27] Even if they did return to their studio, they only succeeded in scrubbing out what they had painted that morning and, when the light failed, they probably frequented a further hostelry, where billiards could be played, before climbing, rather unsteadily, the hill back to their homes. Ranger-Gull summarised the artists in the colony as "Genial, kindly, idle, and pretentious, with "art" in their mouths, their tongues in their cheeks, and the ever-lasting flagon at their lips. Here were men of middle age aping the *Quartier Latin* with bleary eyes".[28] A number of characters in Ranger-Gull's novel were recognised as based on local artists and, unsurprisingly, the book did not go down too well!

1.5   The patterns of change

The American artist, Edward Simmons, who witnessed the development of the art colonies at Concarneau, between 1880 and 1885, and St Ives, from 1886 to 1892, commented in his autobiography, "Seeing this colony form in St Ives made me study out how such things happen. The artist finds a place that is beautiful, undiscovered, and suits his pocket-book. He goes there for two years. The third year other artists follow him; the fourth year come the retired British admirals and 'vamps'; the fifth year the artist leaves; the sixth come the wealthy people who spend a lot of money on it, making it as ugly and dear as possible, but soon tire and go away. Then the artist comes back again and begins all over, picking the bones of what the Money Bags had killed."[29] It is difficult to pinpoint the precise trends in the development of St Ives, which gave rise to this somewhat cynical viewpoint, but there is no doubt that the atmosphere in the town will have changed, as its attractions became more well-known, and the expanding group of artists was accompanied by ever increasing hordes of tourists, and businessmen keen to take advantage of the new opportunities.

There would have been changes too in the spirit within the artistic community, as it grew in size. Whilst the vast majority of artists in the early years of the colony were young, enthusiastic and ambitious, with much in common, following their French experiences, a generation gap appeared as the decades rolled by and, whilst equally earnest young painters arrived and settled, there were bound to be attracted to the colony the less committed type of artist, lampooned by Ranger-Gull, who merely wanted to mix in artistic circles. Indeed, Folliott-Stokes also complained about the arrival of a type of female artist, who "belonged to a sort of neuterdom, which at that time, to the amazement of every one, was making a fungus-like appearance in the circles where people talked about Art."[30]

Fig. 1.7 Hubert Vos   *Edward Simmons*
(sketched at the Stokeses' New Year's Day
party 1890)

---

27 C Ranger-Gull, *Portalone*, London, 1904 at p.12-3.

28 C Ranger-Gull, *Portalone*, London, 1904, p.74.

29 E E Simmons, *From Seven to Seventy*, New York and London, 1922 at p.165.

30 A.G.Folliott-Stokes, *A Moorland Princess*, London, 1904 at p.91-2.

Fig. 1.8   Herbert Lanyon *Louis Grier*   (St Ives Arts Club)

Musing on how things had changed, an artist, most probably based on Louis Grier, commented in Folliott-Stokes' novel *A Moorland Princess*, published in 1904, "[St Ives] as an art centre has ceased to exist; it's as dead as a door nail, swamped by dilettantism and shekels. You should have known it in the early days, my boy. A few of us came straight from Paris, and led a life of primitive simplicity and bohemianism. We were all equally poor, and used to meet together in each other's lodgings every evening, and discuss art and our work, over a glass of whisky and a pipe. A common enthusiasm bound us together, irrespective of sex and social rank. Now all is changed. The bourgeois prejudices and customs of middle-class English society have stolen into the community, inflated numerically beyond all knowledge. Champagne and cigars have supplemented beer and pipes; while art and work, as subjects of conversation, have given way to tennis and gossip. Besides all this, some of the older ones amongst us have discovered that the fame dreams of youth will never be realised, and are content to admire where we formerly worshipped. We still give the mornings to the mistress of our youth; but we devote the afternoon to tennis, tea parties and scandal."[31]

The First World War changed British society completely and the colony at St Ives took on a very different character in the 1920s. Its appeal as a centre for both the practice and teaching of landscape and marine painting had passed, and its resident artists ceased to be at the forefront of developments in British art. Fashion, economics and the demographic effects of the War led to a surge in interest in the decorative arts, whilst the colony now attracted retired writers, playrights, actors and musicians, so that as much interest was shown in literature, drama and music, as in art. Accordingly, the colony was constantly evolving and its relationship with the local community was never static either. The following account provides a series of snapshots, capturing relationships between various segments of 'art and town' at different times.

---

31 A.G.Folliott-Stokes, *A Moorland Princess*, London, 1904 at p.131.

PART TWO

THE WHARF ST. IVES

Edmund G. Fuller

THE ARTISTS AT HOME, AT WORK

AND AT PLAY

ARTISTS' BACKGROUNDS

It is too easy to portray the artists as wealthy sophisticates who, unsurprisingly, faced difficulties inter-reacting with the locals - dour, cash-strapped, abstemious Methodists. Such categorisations, however, are far too simplistic and an analysis of the backgrounds of the artists reveals a surprising diversity, not only in social standing and wealth, but also in origin. It also needs to be remembered that, in an era of large families and primogeniture, younger children, of even the wealthiest families, may not have received an over-generous allowance or inheritance. There was also an accepted moral duty placed upon sons to provide for unmarried sisters, who appear, during this period, to be numerous.

2.1.1 Place of origin

One of the strange features of the first fifty years of the St Ives art colony is the lack of Cornish-born artists who decided to settle in the town. Whereas some of the earliest exhibited depictions of the area were by Cornish-based artists, such as Thomas Hart and Richard Harry Carter, or by Cornish-born artists, such as Edith Hume and Melicent Grose, executed during return visits to relatives, the only artists with Cornish parentage resident in St Ives for an extended period were Gertrude Talmage and the photographer, Herbert Lanyon, both of whom were born in Redruth. There was also, surprisingly, no weighting towards West Country families. Ease of access to Cornwall, therefore, played no part in the make-up of the colony. Artists were drawn to the town from all over the country and included Irish, such as Dorothy Robinson and Monica MacIvor, Scots, such as William Eadie and Thomas Millie Dow, and Welsh, such as Mia Brown. The attraction of the quaint hideaway, far from the regions decimated by the industrial revolution, may have resulted in there being a particularly strong contingent from the Liverpool-Birkenhead-Manchester region, and there were also a number of artists, who came from big towns such as London, Birmingham and Bristol. However, there were also plenty of artists, who had grown up in more rural surroundings.

2.1.2 Artistic families

Surprisingly few of the resident artists came from artistic families. John Bromley's pedigree was the most distinguished in this respect. His great-grandfather, William Bromley ARA, had engraved the Elgin Marbles for the Government, his grandfather, John Bromley, was an engraver, and his father, William, was an RBA, whilst his brother, Val, was also a distinguished painter. Not unnaturally, he had commenced his studies under his father. Will Ashton's father, James, had also had a distinguished career as an artist and art tutor on emigrating to Australia, where his pupils included not only his son but Richard Hayley Lever. Louis Sargent's father, Louis Phillippe Sargent, had had a successful career in France as an engraver, whilst Gertrude Rosenberg came from a Bath family of artists. However, her father, George Frederick Rosenberg, a watercolour artist, died when she was just two. These, though, are isolated examples, and most St Ives artists will have had to go through the difficult process of persuading sceptical parents that a career in art was not only appropriate, but viable.

2.1.3 Landed Gentry, Church and military families

The Victorian era remained one where landed estates tended to pass to the eldest son, leaving younger sons to find careers in the armed forces or in the Church. These were occupations, therefore, which tended to be the province of 'old money'. Claude Francis Barry was the only artist who was the heir to a title. However, this was a relatively newly created one - his grandfather, Sir Francis Tress Barry, who had amassed a fortune by washing the residue from exhausted Portugese copper mines, being granted the title Baron de Barry of Portugal in 1876. Due to the machinations of his stepmother, though, he was effectively disinherited.

Without doubt, the most common occupation for artists' fathers was as a clergyman. Sydney Carr and the Titcomb brothers, William and John (always known as Jack), were the sons of Bishops. However, Carr's father, who was Bishop of Oxford, died when he was young, and he owed his means to his uncles, who were newspaper proprietors in Bristol. The Titcombs' father, Jonathan Holt Titcomb (1820-1887), was an evangelical Anglican, who was appointed the first Bishop of Rangoon and later the first Bishop of North and Central Europe. Moulton Foweraker's father was the Head of Exeter Cathedral School and numerous other artists, such as Alfred Hartley, Algernon Talmage, Folliott Stokes, Gwilt Jolley, Eardley Blomefield, Mia Brown and Annie Falkner, were also from Church families.

Fig. 2.1 Sydney Carr's father when Bishop of Oxford
(the late Derek Wintle/Andrew Eggleston)

A number of artists also came from military backgrounds. Edmund Fuller's father was an Army General and he himself was educated at Sandhurst. Charles Simpson's father was an Army Major General and Colonel of the Lincolnshire Regiment, and Charles might well have followed his father into an Army career, had it not been for a fall off the family pony, which affected his hearing. William Parkyn's father was also an Army man, where he rose to the rank of Lieutenant-Colonel.

2.1.4 Backgrounds in the professions

Unsurprisingly, a number of artists had fathers, who had had successful careers in one of the professions. Those of Millie Dow, Frank Emanuel, John Chadwick Lomax, Alfred Conquest and Gordon Killmister were all lawyers, whilst those of Wyly and Louis Grier, the Sealy sisters, Nell Cuneo and Percy and Marjorie Ballance were in the medical profession. Edward King's father was a banker, Leslie Hervey's an accountant, whilst the Jackson sisters' family wealth derived from stockbroking. Teachers did not amass fortunes, but Ellis Wilkinson's father was the Headmaster of Harrow Board School and Adrian Stokes' father was an Inspector of Schools. More unusually, the father of the Kirkpatrick sisters was the Governor of Newgate Prison, whilst Guy Kortright's father was appointed the Colonial Governor of Canada.

2.1.5 'Trade' backgrounds

In a sign of the changing times, some of the wealthiest artists came from families that had recently made their money from 'trade' and, in an era where the upper classes looked down on 'new money' so acquired, this is likely to have caused some tensions, particularly, as in the case of Henry Detmold and Moffat Lindner, their fathers were of German origin. Lindner was the wealthiest artist in St Ives, despite being one of nine children. His father, Maximilian, described himself as a "foreign merchant" and wanted Moffat to follow his two elder brothers into the family business. This he did, until it became quite clear to his father that he was desperately unhappy, and he was finally allowed to pursue his artistic bent. This was an experience shared by a number of other artists, such as Elmer Schofield, whose family were in the cotton trade, but not all fathers were so accomodating. Terrick Williams, who was born in Liverpool but brought up, from the age of seven, in Lewisham, was forced to work in the family soap and perfume business for eight years, until at the age of 25, he suffered a physical and mental breakdown.

Fig. 2.2   Julius Olsson   (Lewis & Fry)
His father was a Swedish timber merchant

Due to his father's early demise, Charles Muirhead was still working in the family fishmonger business in Liverpool at the age of 27, and he probably did not escape to pursue his love of art until his early thirties.   The one artist to make some sort of success out of a family business was Alfred East, who spent twenty years in the footwear manufacturing business established by his elder brother, Charles, becoming a partner, before deciding in 1879 to sell out his stake to fund his art education.

There were all sorts of other trading activities that had helped to build up wealth in the families of artists.   The father of the Whitehouse sisters supervised a nail manufacturing business, whilst Allan Deacon's father ran an alkali factory, Mary McCrossan's an iron foundry and Helen Knapping's a brickworks. Various families were specialist merchants, often with an interest in foreign trade, of such commodities as sugar (Romilly Fedden), cotton (Sydney Lee), wool (Harry Robinson), lace (Lewis Hind) or timber (Julius Olsson), whilst the fathers of Arnesby Brown, William Fortescue and Hilda and Ann Fearon were all Wine Merchants. In addition to those who came from wealthy families, who had enjoyed considerable success in their trading ventures, there were a surprisingly large number of artists whose fathers appear to have been quite ordinary tradesmen.   Noble Barlow's father was an upholsterer, Arthur Meade's a poulterer and fishmonger, Percy Craft's a cheesemonger, Beale Adams' a baker, John Park's a decorator and William Cave Day's a cabinet maker.

2.1.6   False starts and second careers

A number of artists encountered strong resistance to their preferred career as an artist and were encouraged by their families to enter into other occupations. Few lasted long. Julius Olsson, Fred Milner and Louis Grier worked initially as bank clerks, William Fortescue had a spell as an engineering draftsman, Adrian Stokes as a cotton broker, Jack Titcomb as a Lloyds underwriter, Harry Robinson as a barrister, Folliott Stokes as a land agent and Allan Deacon in the medical profession. None appear to have been particularly successful. Perhaps unsurprisingly, a number of architects, such as Charles Mottram, Hurst Balmford, Gordon Killmister and George Turland Goosey, decided to turn their energies to painting later in life. Of those who had pursued military careers initially, George Bradshaw and Francis Roskruge were well decorated, albeit Bradshaw's career as a submarine commander ended in a messy court martial.

2.1.7   Deceased parents

The wealth and status that families had enjoyed could soon be decimated by the death of the head, and a number of artists appear to have experienced the difficulties that this caused. For daughters, in particular, the loss of prospects, following the early demise of their father, could spell a life-long spinsterhood. Artists like Gwendoline Hopton and the Horn sisters, therefore, appear to spend their formative years constantly moving between relations, spreading the burden that they were no doubt perceived to be. Others so afflicted, like Mia Edwards and Leonora Locking, did manage to find husbands - Arnesby Brown and Alfred Hartley respectively - whilst the beauty of Augusta Baird-Smith, having lost her father, before she was four, and her mother, before she was fourteen, caught the attention of Moffat Lindner.

Another problem could be caused by a wide disparity of ages between parents. William Whitehouse, the father of the four Whitehouse sisters, was twenty-two years older than their mother and, by the time that their mother died after nearly twenty years of widowhood, their inheritance had reduced significantly.

2.1.8   Artists' income - painting sales or private means?

The existing source material does not permit a detailed analysis of the level of income artists received from painting sales, but I would be extremely surprised if more than a handful of artists could have survived at all, let alone in relative comfort, solely from the proceeds of painting sales. Arnesby Brown post-1895 and Julius Olsson post-1900 might have been able to do so but, however much critical acclaim artists received, sales still proved difficult. William Titcomb, at the height of his reputation, appears not to have sold any of his major Royal Academy exhibits in the period 1895-1905, something which may have been a factor in his decision to leave St Ives. The American, William Wendt, also indicated that John Noble Barlow, at the very time that he was winning his greatest critical acclaim in France and America, was constantly strapped for cash, whilst a lesser artist, such as Lizzie Whitehouse, bemoaned that she could not sell anything at all.

The vast majority of artists, therefore, relied to a significant degree on some private means. As can be gauged from their diverse backgrounds, the level of such means varied extensively. Very few could live extravagantly. Most just about got by, sometimes with the aid of handouts from other members of the family. For instance, Middleton Jameson's art career was almost entirely funded by his brother, the renowned Dr Lanner Jameson, who had invested in South African gold mines alongside Cecil Rhodes. Fred Milner seems to have been largely reliant on his wife's brother, who was in the cork trade in Portugal, but, more than once, he tells his regular correspondent, Mrs Brumfit, the popular New Zealand singer, also known as Ethel Goode, that he will not be visiting the Royal Academy exhibition, because he cannot afford the fare to London.

Fig. 2.3 Arnesby Brown   (Russell & Son)
His father was a wine merchant.

TABLE A   BACKGROUNDS OF SOME PRE-WAR RESIDENT ARTISTS

ARTIST	OCCUPATION OF FATHER	PLACE OF BIRTH / CHILDHOOD	ARTIST	OCCUPATION OF FATHER	PLACE OF BIRTH / CHILDHOOD
Beale Adams	Baker	Bath	G. Hopton	Army - Deceased	Pennal, N. Wales
W. Ashton	Artist	York - Adelaide	Horn sisters	Deceased	Pulloxhill, Beds
A Bailey	Railway Engineer	Brighton	R.L. Hutton	Broker	India - Scotland
Bainsmith/Douglas	Bookseller	Stroud, Glos	Jackson sisters	Stockbroker	Liverpool
J. N. Barlow	Upholsterer	Manchester	M.A.Jameson	Newspaper Editor	Edinburgh
C. F. Barry	Titled / M.P.	Windsor	G Walter Jevons	Merchant	Birkenhead
Evelyn L. Beckles	Flour Mill M.D.	London - Devon	M.Gwilt Jolley	Clergyman	Croydon
E. W. Blomefield	Clergyman	India - Leeds	C G Killmister	Solicitor	Macclesfield
J.M. Bromley	Artist	London	Edward King	Bank Clerk	Enfield
J.A.A Brown	Wine Merchant	Nottingham	Kirkpatrick sisters	Prison Governor	Holborn
Mia Brown	Clergyman	Monmouthshire	Helen Knapping	Brickmaker	S.Shoebury, Essex
S Carr	Bishop	Lincoln - Bristol	R.G. Kortright	Colonial Governor	Clifton - Canada
A. Conquest	Solicitor	Woodford, Essex	W.H. Lanyon	Gas Works	Redruth
P.R. Craft	Cheesemonger	London	Sydney Lee	Cotton Merchant	Manchester
Nell Cuneo	Naval Doctor	London	Augusta Lindner	Army Captain	Cheshire
W. Cave Day	Cabinet Maker	Dewsbury, Yorks	Moffat Lindner	Foreign Merchant	Birmingham
A. Deacon	Alkali Factory	Widnes, Cheshire	E.T. Lingwood	Miller	Needham, Suffolk
H.E. Detmold	Colonial Merchant	Kingston, Surrey	W.E.Linton	Warehouseman	Bristol
T.M. Dow	Scottish Lawyer	Fife	J.C. Lomax	Barrister	K'sington- Suffolk
W. Eadie	Silk Dyer	Paisley	M. McCrossan	Ironfounder	Liverpool
A East	Shoemaker	Kettering	Arthur Meade	Poultry / Fish	Near Taunton
C.H.Eastlake	Managing Clerk	Wandsworth	C. Greville Morris	Cotton Spinning	Salford
F.L.Emanuel	Solicitor	Kensington	Charles Mottram	Clergyman	Rotherham-L'don
A. Falkner	Clergyman	Dorchester	Julius Olsson	Timber Merchant	Islington - Purley
H. & A. Fearon	Wine Merchant	Banstead, Surrey	John Park	Painter/Decorator	Preston
A. R. Fedden	Sugar Merchant	Bristol	William Parkyn	Army Colonel	Lee, Kent
P.Feeney	News Reporter	Birmingham	Harry Robinson	Wool Merchant	Almondbury, Yorks
S.A. Forbes	Railway Manager	Dublin - London	G. M. Rosenberg	Artist	Bath
W. Fortescue	Wine Merchant	Birmingham	L. Sargent	Artist	London
A. Foweraker	Clergyman- Head	Exeter	W E Schofield	Cotton	Pennsylvania
E. Fuller	Army General	Brompton	Sealy sisters	G.P.	Weybridge
L. & W. Grier	Doctor	Australia-Canada	Adrian Stokes	School Inspector	Southport-L'pool
Alfred Hartley	Clergyman	Stocking Pelham	Folliott Stokes	Clergyman	Goring, Oxon
Nora Hartley	Doctor - Dec'd	London	A. Talmage	Clergyman	Fifield, Oxon
J.H. Hay	Architect	Liverpool	G. Talmage	Chemist	Redruth
Edith Hayes	Naval Captain	Portsea, Hants	W. & J. Titcomb	Bishop	Cambridge-L'don
H P Heard	Baltic Trader	Bideford, Devon	Whitehouse sisters	Nail Merchant	Leamington
L. Hervey	Accountant	Lightcliff, Yorks	Ellis Wilkinson	Headmaster	Harrow
C Lewis Hind	Lace	Nottingham	T Williams	Soap Maker	L'pool-Lewisham

Others, though, were quietly comfortable and had little incentive to produce anything to sell. Accordingly, there are a number of artists, such as Lowell Dyer, Jack Titcomb and James Elgar Russell, who rented studios for decades, without seemingly producing much work at all, or certainly much that warranted exhibiting. Nevertheless, this does not mean that they were not important members of the community. Dyer, for instance, was the resident wit and was President of the Arts Club on a number of occasions. Jack Titcomb, or 'Titters', as he seems to have been known, who was clearly an organiser, was also President on three occasions and was a well-liked colleague on the golf course or at the billiards table, whilst Elgar Russell organised musical activities. They may not, even with application, have made great artists, but they enjoyed the company of artists and contributed to the spirit of the community, without which the colony would have been short-lived.

ACCOMODATION FOR ARTISTS AND THEIR LITERARY FRIENDS IN TOWN

2.2.1   Lodgings and landladies

Lodgings were ideal for artists. Hotels, such as Tregenna Castle, which had been acquired by the Great Western Railway in 1878, and the Porthminster Hotel, which opened in 1894, were too expensive for long stays, and were used sparingly by artists.[32] Lodgings were much cheaper and, unlike rented accomodation, artists did not need to commit themselves to any time-frame, and so were free to move on at a moment's notice, as and when new pastures called. Landladies soon learnt, however, that projected stays of a couple of weeks would most probably extend to several months, as the charms of the town worked their magic.

Whistler and his pupils, Menpes and Sickert, during their stay in January 1884, lodged with an old lady at 14 Barnoon Terrace.[33] Menpes recalled, "Very small and very humble rooms they were, no doubt; but many and charming are the memories that cling to them. Lodging house or palace, it was all the same. The presence of the Master acted as a charm; and to us enthusiastic admirers it mattered not that the chairs were of horsehair and the ornaments aggressive, while the accomodation was very scant."

On his first visit to St Ives in 1886, the American, Howard Butler, took lodgings in Up-along, in an establishment which enabled him to keep an eye open for weather effects - probably on The Terrace. Although delighted at the easy availability of farm produce, which made "a most agreeable change after the artificiality of Parisian dinners", he was non-plussed by the accounting system utilised. "Although I am surrounded by friends, I am obliged to eat alone as it is impossible to alter the English system and keep the accounts straight. Here you pay for every potato, chop, egg or pot of cream that you consume". But such annoyances were worthwhile for "they know how to cook and such baked apples and cream as I get here were never equalled, even by the Queen of Sheba herself."[34]

On his return the following year, he rented a little house owned by Mrs Dumble, the widow of a fisherman, possibly in Bowling Green Terrace.[35] "She gives me the whole house and does my cooking and all the house service for twelve shillings a week", he reported to his family. To begin with, he assumed responsibility for shopping, but Mrs Dumble soon took the view that he was extravagant and did it herself, getting much better deals than Butler could have dreamed of. However, Butler had to put up with her standing behind his chair, as he ate his meals. When he had finished, she invariably said, "Yer don eat mor'n a sparrow", but when he indulged his fondness for clotted cream, she would sigh disapprovingly, "Thre'penny worth of cream"! Nevertheless, her eye for a bargain served him well. He records, "Time meant nothing to Mrs Dumble. She would go down to the end of the pier and stand where she could be seen by the fishermen in the bay and hold up her hands with all the fingers extended. This meant that she was willing to give one penny for ten whiting. If no fisherman responded, she would put down one finger and then another until her offer were accepted. She would get six or eight but sometimes if the run was exceptionally good, she would get ten and then Mrs Dumble was happy."[36]

The early Visitors' Lists show properties in The Terrace, Bowling Green Terrace and Bellair Terrace as being particularly popular. Mrs Pearson at 6, The Terrace, who was an amateur painter herself, had a number of artists staying with her on a long-term basis, including Louis and Wyly Grier, Eardley Blomefield, William Titcomb, David Davies and Allan Deacon. Titcomb, however, was not particularly impressed, for he commented at the opening of the 1894 Nottingham Castle Museum exhibition; "We have to be fearfully moral and fearfully uncomfortable. We live in miserable lodgings and are at the

---

32 Unfortunately, there are no records for the Tregenna Castle Hotel, but the guests at the Porthminster Hotel are often recorded on the Visitors' Lists. Harry Browne, a London-based artist, who was a very regular visitor over a period of some twenty-five years, seems to have been the only artist who, without fail, stayed here - often for months at a time.

33 The two lodging houses in Barnoon Terrace listed in Kelly's Directory in 1883 are in the names of Sampson Noall and Thomas Williams.

34 Letter from H.R.Butler to Mary Butler dated 8/8/1886, Archives of American Art, Smithsonian Institution, Washington DC, Howard Russell Butler papers, Reel 1189.

35 *St Ives Weekly Summary* 10/2/1906 notes the death of Mrs Catherine Dumble, of Bowling Green Terrace, aged 77.

36 H.R.Butler, Unpublished Autobiography, p.174, Archives of American Art, Smithsonian Institution, Washington DC, Howard Russell Butler papers, Reel 93.

TABLE B   ARTISTS RECORDED ON VISITORS' LISTS DURING 1889
(commencing 24th May - terminating 9th November)

ARTIST (in order of arrival)	LODGINGS	PERIOD OF STAY
Eardley Blomefield	6, The Terrace (Mrs Pearson)	1st June - [9th November]
Robert Rouse	6, Bellair Terrace (Mrs Wm Noall)	1st June - 29th June
Wyly Grier	6, The Terrace (Mrs Pearson)	8th June - 19th October
Louis Grier	6, The Terrace (Mrs Pearson)	8th June - 19th October
Sydney and Alexandrina Laurence	Ayr House (Mrs Richards)	8th June - [9th November]
Mrs Llewellyn and family	The Warren (Miss Couch)	29th June - 21st September
Lowell Dyer and wife	24, The Terrace (Miss Harry) then 2 Bowling Green from 24/8 (Mrs D) and 21/9 (Lowell D)	6th July - [9th November]
Henry Detmold	7, Bellair Terrace (Mrs Wm Williams)	6th July - [9th November]
A G Folliott-Stokes and wife	9, Bowling Green (Mrs Noall) then from 20/7 5 Bowling Green Terrace (Miss Bellman), then from 7/9 30 Bowling Green Terrace, then from 26/10 3 Draycot Cottages	6th July - [9th November]
Lucius O'Brien and family	Albany House (Mrs Williams)	20th July - 2nd November
Allan Deacon	6, Bellair Terrace (Mrs Wm Noall)	20th July - 5th October
Maria Wiik & Helene Schjerfbeck	8, Bellair Terrace (Mrs Hy Williams)	20th July - [9th November]
Percy Northcote and wife	26, Bowling Green Terr	27th July - [9th November]
Ernest Taylor	16 Bowling Green Terrace	27th July - 31st August
Leslie Giffen Cauldwell	4, Richmond Place (Robinsons)	27th July - 21st September
May Houghton and her mother	St Andrews Street (Mrs Behenna)	5th August - [9th November]
William Cave Day	Mount Zion (Mrs S Williams)	10th August - 31st August
Misses Ellen and Rose Welby	18 Bowling Green Terrace	August
F Rede Fowke	Carbis Bay (Mrs Arthur)	August
John Chadwick Lomax	Tregenna Castle	August
Edward and Vesta Simmons	4 Bellair Terrace (Mrs Rd Uren)	24th August - 7th September
Charles Mottram and family	30 Bowling Green Terrace	31st August - 14th September
Fred Reilly	4, Richmond Place (Robinsons)	31st August - [9th November]
George Hillyard Swinstead & family	The Warren (Mrs Murgatroyd)	7th September - 21st September
Ayerst Ingram	12, The Terrace	7th September - 21st September
Edward Lingwood	27, Bowling Green	21st September
Alfred Haigh	Carbis Bay (Mrs Arthur)	21st September - 5th October
Mary Bell	St Andrews Street (Mrs Behenna)	28th September - [9th November]
Arnesby Brown	1, Academy Place (Mrs Noall)	28th September - 2nd November
Middleton Jameson (probably)	4, Bellair Terrace	26th October - [9th November]
Margaret Waterfield	25, The Terrace	26th October - [9th November]

This Table shows the lodging houses selected by artists, and their lengths of stay, as recorded in the Visitors' Lists during the first year that they were published. Many of the artists listed went on to become regulars or settlors, but others were one-off visitors.

mercy of Wesleyan landladies, whose forté is certainly not cooking".[37] In later years, properties in Albany Terrace, Tregenna Terrace, Richmond Terrace and Carrack Dhu Road also proved popular, as the number of properties taking guests proliferated significantly. Some artists returned to the same landlady every visit. For instance, the Cheshire contingent - the Baird-Smith, Kennedy and Jackson sisters - always stayed at 7 Bowling Green Terrace. The arrangements demanded by, or agreed with, landladies probably differed from house to house, but it is interesting that, by the time of the 1893 Kelly's Directory, a change in nomenclature had come into play; the term 'lodging house' was no longer used and, instead, owners advertised 'apartments'. This clearly suggests that visitors did not want to share common rooms with other guests, but required their own living/dining room. It is unlikely, though, that they would have had, or wanted, their own kitchen. The arrangement recorded by the American, Walter Norris, in 1904 is likely to have been fairly typical. Lodging at 5 The Terrace, he told his friend, John Sloan, "We have a bed-chamber on the second floor and a parlor (which is also our dinng room) on the first. Mrs Norris purchases at the markets what she desires and it is cooked and served by the landlady and her maid."[38]

There must have been many letters written home by artists telling of the eccentricities of their landladies, but few seem to have survived. The Canadian art student, Emily Carr, who lodged in the winter of 1901-2 with the Curnow family, next to the churchyard in St Andrew's Street, recorded that her request for hot water once a week was considered most odd - the family themselves washing, if at all, in the sea. Accordingly, a secret ritual had to be arranged after supper each Saturday night, when Ma Curnow would come into her room and say, "The cauldron, Miss, it is heated to wash your feet" - the concept of Carr having an all-over wash, being too terrible even to contemplate![39]

St Andrews Street, where both Carr and fellow student, Will Ashton, stayed, was not the most salubrious place at that time. A visitor, who took lodgings there in 1908, commented, "In twilight, the place looked more like a London slum than anything else, but passing through a narrow passage, and up a stair leading directly out of the kitchen, you are at once in a big room with windows looking straight down into the sea and on to the rocks which form the foundation of the houses. Above this room is a big

Fig. 2.4 Emily Carr at St Ives
(image courtesy of Royal BC Museum, BC Archives, B-877)

37 *Nottingham Express*, 29/9/1894.
38 Letter from W. Norris to J.Sloan dated 23/8/1904, Sloan papers, Delaware Art Museum, Wilmington.
39 Emily Carr, *Growing Pains*, Toronto, paperback edition 1966, p.170.

Fig. 2.5   Herbert Lanyon Waves hitting the houses in St Andrew's Street in a gale
(courtesy Andrew Lanyon)

bedroom, which shakes in the wind and trembles when the waves roar, so that it is more easy to imagine oneself in a cabin than in a bedroom." Indeed, whilst such lodgings afforded fine views of the harbour, they could provide guests with rather too close an acquaintance with the sea, as artists, such as Franz Muller-Gossen and Frank Emanuel, experienced.[40] "In St Ives today, you may lie in your bed and feel it shake under you as the wind comes up from the sea and shakes the houses in its grip, as a terrier strikes a rat. Nay more, there are days and nights when the sea comes up in mighty waves, and lifting herself on high actually pours over the roofs and down the chimneys of the daring householders, putting out their fires, swamping their floors, "and they go on as if nothing was happening", said a St Ives man to me." If, like the locals, one could put up with a bit of seawater coming down the chimney from time to time in big storms, the attraction of such a location was not only the view, but the price. "Quarters such as these cost in winter about 9s a week, a price which includes fires, lights, attendance and boot-cleaning. Your food, if you will for the time renounce meat and put quantities of Cornish cream into your menu instead, may come to 7s per week."[41]

The constant stream of artist visitors ensured that letting rooms were much in demand and artists were very popular, for they often stayed for months at a time and were just as likely to arrive in the winter, when the holidaymakers had long gone. One enterprising landlady, a Mrs Hodge, even advertised for 'Lady Artists and Students' in *The Studio*.[42]

2.2.2   Artists' Homes - An overview

Whilst there was always a keen demand for lodgings or apartments from short-term visitors, those artists, who had decided to settle in the town, tended, particularly if they were married, to look for houses to rent. Very few actually bought properties. When the artists first arrived, suitable housing stock in the town was limited. Those able to find, and afford, large houses, were lucky. William Eadie, the only early artist to have a large family already, managed to find suitable accomodation at 'Windy Parc', off Ayr Lane, for eight years, but, when served notice, found that he had to move to Halsetown. After the

40 F L Emanuel, *The Charm of the Country Town - St Ives, Cornwall, Architectural Review*, July 1920 and see M Whybrow, *St Ives 1883-1993 - Portrait of an Art Colony*, Woodbridge, 1994 at p. 26.
41 *St Ives Cornwall - As Others See Us*, St Ives Weekly Summary, 29/2/1908.
42 *The Studio*, 9/1899, Vol 78, No 17.

property had been renovated in 1895-6, William Titcomb then took possession and, at much the same time, Thomas Millie Dow took over 'Talland House' from the renowned man of letters, Leslie Stephen, who had been using it as a summer residence for his extended family since 1881. However, other large properties were in short supply. Accordingly, in the early 1890s, artists tended to rent terraced houses in various parts of the town, with one of the new terraces, Richmond Place, proving particularly popular. This was built by Robert Toy and he seems to have been the builder most in tune with the artists' requirements, for, repeatedly, artists are some of the first to move into his new developments. Toy also tried to buy some land on Porthmeor Beach to build studios for them and was used to build the extension to the West Cornwall Golf Club at Lelant that had been designed by the artist, William Brooke.

At the time of his marriage, at the age of thirty, in 1876, Toy was described as a joiner. His father was a baker and his wife, Caroline (née Fry), who was nine years his junior, was the daughter of a master mariner. Toy was then living in Bellair Terrace, one of the first terraces, for which he was responsible. Richmond Place, which he built next and to which he moved himself, ran parallel to it. Another group of houses built by Toy, that proved perennially popular with artists, was the small terrace of three properties just before the coastguard cottages on Porthminster Hill. Toy was also responsible for a number of other developments in the town, which found favour with the artists, such as Pednolver Terrace.[43] With a rapidly expanding family, which in the end totalled thirteen children, he himself moved quite regularly. However, at the turn of the century, he built for himself 'The Elms' (Fig. 2.8), now on the edge of Trewyn Gardens, close to Richmond Place. This is very different in style to his normal homes, having an Arts and Crafts influence, possibly resulting from his erection of 'St Eia' for Julius Olsson at much the same time. In 1916, however, inspired by the view of a sunset over the ocean, he moved to 1 Clodgy View, part of a new terrace that he had constructed, where he remained until his death in 1928.[44] In his obituary, he was called "the leader in building modern St Ives".[45]

Fig. 2.6 St Ives from the harbour beach

This photograph is pre-1888, as the pier has not been extended and the Mine Engine House on Pednolver Point has not been reduced in height. What is most interesting is the lack of development on Porthminster Hill To the very left is a new built property (c.1881), William John Paynter's 'Shun Lee'; in the middle the coastguard cottages, then half of Draycott's Terrace. This would all soon change, with Edward Hain's 'Treloyhan Manor', Capt Harry's 'Morwenstow' (later 'Chy-an'Dour'), John Eccles Brown's 'Scot's Craig', the Porthminster Hotel, Robert Toy's terrace, comprising 'Godrevy', Zareba' and 'Porthia' and the completion of Draycott Terrace.

43 His obituary also records that he built Porthminster Terrace and Sea View Terrace and Barclays Bank. *St Ives Times*, 28/9/1928.
44 Some of his descendants lived here until 1972.
45 *St Ives Times*, 28/9/1928.

Fig. 2.8 'The Elms', by Trewyn Gardens, in 2009
Built by Toy for his own family, this property later
became the home of Martin Cock, the founder
of the *St Ives Times* and the owner, from 1919,
of James Lanham Ltd

Fig. 2.7 Robert Toy and his first child, Katie,
whose portrait was painted by W. Eadie in 1892.
(Pamela Robinson)

Fig. 2.9 Robert Toy and his family outside 'The Elms' in 1900.   (Pamela Robinson)

The available housing stock in town, however, was not all new and pristine, and Murielle Schofield's problems at 16 Tregenna Terrace, in 1903, reveal that conditions could still be horrendous. Tregenna Terrace was a popular street for lodging houses and rented property, but it was built into the side of a hill. No 16 was very dark at the back and very damp. It was also infested with fleas. She then found herself over-run by rats. One evening, the rat man had a three and a half hour battle, until 1.45 a.m., with a cat-sized rat, which ran up his trouser leg and leapt at his throat three times. When cats, traps and poison had no effect, he resorted to flushing out the other rats with his ferret.[46] Unsurprisingly, Murielle started to look for another house to rent, but found that there was very little suitable accomodation on the market. The few properties available were too dark, overlooked or the wrong side of town. With the success of the colony, accomodation had become scant.

As children came along, and the concept of having a separate studio integrated into the home grew in popularity, the requirements of the artists altered, and their desire for larger than standard housing, away from the noise and smells of the fishing quarter, led them to review the new developments that were taking place in the higher part of town and, in certain cases, to search out potential building sites for themselves.

In the late 1890s, a number of factors combined to make the artists much more confident of their prospects. Queen Victoria's Jubilee in 1897 had been a rousing celebration of the glory of the Empire. Cornwall was experiencing a tourist boom, with visitor numbers in St Ives in 1897 and 1898 being higher than ever before. The artists too were making a name for themselves in London circles and sales of paintings were buoyant, whilst the finances of several members of the colony were also boosted by inheritances. All this led to decisions by a significant number of artists to commit themselves more firmly to the colony by moving to larger houses in the Up-along district of town and signing long-term leases. There was probably an element of 'keeping up with the Joneses' to the trend as well, as good friends from the local community, such as Edward Hain, Captain Thomas Row Harry, Robert Read and William Trewhella, had, during the mid-1890s, moved into sumptuous large, often newly built, residences.[47] Accordingly, in the years around the turn of the century, Moffat Lindner, and his new wife, Augusta Baird-Smith, Louis Grier, Allan and Kate Deacon, newly arrived from France, and the American-born marine painter, Alfred Pazolt, and his sister, Caroline, all took substantial villas on The Terrace, the American, Lowell Dyer, took the end-terrace house in the new Pednolver Terrace, which gave him fine views of the harbour, and Sydney Carr, the Kirkpatrick sisters and the Whitehouse sisters took significant properties in Talland Road.

Some artists even bought plots of land a little further out of town and had houses built for them, to their own specifications. These were often influenced by the Arts and Crafts movement and so introduced into St Ives novel designs. 'St Eia', on Porthminster Hill, built by Robert Toy in 1898 for occupation by Julius Olsson, was one of the first properties to reflect this movement, and was soon joined by the Robinsons' new home, 'Belliers Croft', built for them in 1899 on a field off The Belliers. Toy may well have been responsible for its erection as well, as he had been a neighbour of the Robinsons when they lived in Richmond Place. At the same time, Edmund Fuller designed a number of significant homes for William Fortescue, Albert Lang and himself in the Carbis Bay area. The only artists to turn their attention to a site in Down-along were John and Selina Bromley, who bought some dilapidated cottages at the end of Smeaton's Pier and turned them into 'Quay House'. The change was noted by the locals, and William Faull, at the Mayoral Banquet in 1901, commented that he was "glad that the artists were settling down and building villas".[48] Ranger-Gull, in *Portalone*, highlights this phenomenon as well, referring to some half-dozen big modern houses with roofs of red tiles, built by artists wealthier than the rest, thrusting themselves into the little remaining available space in the town.[49]

The enthusiasm of the late 1890s boom was soon dissipated by the Boer War, which not only raised doubts as to the true merits of the Empire, but also gave rise to a significant financial burden, which led to increased taxes. Tourists were not as plentiful, and the art market slowed. Julius Olsson, despite burgeoning critical success, and Edmund Fuller did not stay too long in their new dream homes, and Beale Adams downsized significantly. Fuller, though, moved into one of Toy's new properties in Clodgy View. Toy also seems to have been responsible for the first six houses in Park Avenue, which were far superior to the rest of the terrace, completed in a new style a few years later by J.R.Sandry.[50] These

46 Smithsonian Institution, Archives of American Art, Schofield Papers, Letter from Murielle to Elmer Schofield dated 25/12/1903.

47 Trewhella bought 'Trewyn' in 1891, which he extended significantly, Hain built Treloyhan Manor in 1892 to the design of Silvanus Trevail, whilst Trevail also designed Captain Harry's new home on Porthminster Hill, 'Morwenstow' (later called 'Chy-an-Dour'), which had three reception rooms and eight bedrooms. Read moved into 'Beaumont', Talland Road.

48 *St Ives Weekly Summary*, 9/11/1901.

49 C.Ranger-Gull, *Portalone*, London, 1904 at p.128-9.

50 Sandry also built the new Catholic Church but was killed in the War in France in November 1917 - see *St Ives Times*, 16/11/1917.

Fig. 2.10 Nos. 1-4 Park Avenue in 2009.
Herbert Lanyon lived for a while in No. 4

afforded pleasant views across the Stennack Valley and over the harbour to The Island, framed on one side by the tower of the Parish Church and, on the other, by the steeple of the newly erected Catholic Church. Herbert Lanyon and, later, Edmund Fuller took one of the big houses, but the smaller ones proved attractive to a series of artists, such as John and Mabel Douglas, Borlase Smart, Dr Adam MacVie and Caroline Pazolt. Only the wealthiest artist of them all, Moffat Lindner, created a major new home in the decade prior to the War, when he bought 'Chy-an-Porth', on the junction of The Terrace and Albert Road, in 1910 and added a vast extension to it, whilst Herbert Lanyon, at the time of his late marriage in 1916, moved into 'The Red House', a significant property in The Belliers, dating from the turn of the century.

Some of the artists' homes were substantial properties, which became significant landmarks in the area. A number were later converted into hotels. Sadly, few now survive intact, and this aspect of the artists' contribution to the town has been totally neglected. The recent destruction by arson of 'Belliers Croft', the purpose-built home of two of the colony's initial settlers, Harry and Dorothy Robinson, was greeted with barely a whisper of outrage, as few were aware of its significance in the history of St Ives.

2.2.3 Domestic help

Another benefit from the arrival of the artists was an increased demand for domestic servants. Most artists employed at least one female domestic to help with the cleaning and heating of their homes. Several others employed a cook as well. However, other live-in staff, such as Governesses or seamstresses, normally came from outside the area. Whereas some servants became family retainers for many years, other relationships went awry. For instance, Moulton Foweraker, who ran a boarding house with his wife at 'Headlands', Carbis Bay, experienced difficulties, in 1905, with his cook, who was completely unreliable and who refused to open the door to guests when their housemaid was out. Matters came to a head one Sunday afternoon, when the Fowerakers had gone out without their key and could not get her to open the door. Foweraker dismissed her on the spot, with a month's wages, but she would not leave. The constable that he summoned refused to act, and so Foweraker "carried her into the garden", where her boxes had been put. She sued for unfair dismissal, but the case was thrown out.

Fig. 2.11 St Ives from Parc-an-Roper before the completion of Park Avenue. On the right is No. 4..

Mary Lovett Cameron had a worse experience, when she was brutally assaulted at her home, 'Borallan', which was a mile or so outside St Ives, by a former employee, Thomas Trevorrow, but it was felt that this was due to the man having become "odd since he returned from sea".[51] Her friend, Jessie Titcomb, who had discovered her, indicated that her dress was not torn, so that there was no suggestion of a sexual motive.

Young lads could also find employment, for various tasks. Howard Butler hired the services of a boy, Daniel Lander, to carry his things, run errands, wash his brushes and generally keep his studio in order. Daniel, whom Butler praised for his industry, was on call from nine in the morning until nine at night, and received just five pence a day. The boy, though, was probably totally bemused by Butler's insistence on calling him 'Deronda'. The Titcombs employed Humphrey Hart as their donkey boy, as they used a donkey, called 'Buller', to ferry their shopping up Barnoon Hill to their home 'Windy Parc'. Humphrey's father was an invalid and, therefore, his family was always in need and grateful for every additional penny that their children could bring in. Photos of Humphrey (see Fig. 2.12) show him with trousers much too short and boots way too big for him, as his family could not afford to buy the correct sizes. The Titcombs even had panniers made so that their children could be taken for rides on the donkey. Murielle Schofield was quite taken with this idea and arranged to borrow 'Buller' off them, but soon reneged on the deal, for she was told by the policeman that the donkey was being "dreadfully abused" by a group of at least half a dozen local boys on the sand, and she herself had witnessed one of the boys kicking it unmercifully as he rode it.[52] Several other artists advertised for trustworthy boys to run errands for them and, in the pre-telephone age, they must have been extremely useful.[53] However, again, the artists' actions had an impact on prices that was not welcomed by all. For instance, Eliza Smedley, who was looking for a housekeeper, complained to her granddaughter, Edith, "The town is swarmed with artists giving high wages."[54]

Fig. 2.12   Frank and Loveday Titcomb on their donkey, 'Buller', with Humphrey Hart, their donkey boy.

---

51 *St Ives Weekly Summary*, 11/6/1898.

52 Letters to Elmer Schofield dated 28/12/1903 and 4/1/1904 - Smithsonian Institution, Archives of American Art, Schofield Papers (Reel 5043).

53 For instance, Helen Ludby advertised for a boy 'for mornings' in *St Ives Weekly Summary*, 30/8/1902, whilst Mrs Fortescue advertised for a 'good, general servant, small family' in same paper.

54 Letter from Eliza Smedley to Edith Ramsdell dated 7/2/1897.

TABLE C - HOMES OF SOME PERMANENT RESIDENTS

ARTIST FAMILY	DATES	PROPERTY	OWNER	GER
Adams	1898 - 1905 1905 - c.1914 by 1925 - C.1939	Porthia, The Terrace Primrose Cottage, The Warren Lyonesse, 4 Talland Road	M Davis S Couch	£25 £13 £50
Barlow	1894 - before 1898 by 1898 - 1899 1901 - 1908	9, Barnoon Terrace Carrack Dhu 25, The Terrace	Mary Rosewarne J C Boase Ed Stevens	£12 £20 £19-10
Bromley	1899 - 1905 1907 - 1939	St Peter's Street Quay House, Quay St	Berriman Self	£6 £27
Carr	by 1898 - 1901 1902 - 1912	8, Albany Terrace Arkleby, Talland Road	Ed Hain Leddra	£30 £35
Deacon	1900 - 1910	The Terrace	G J A Staff	£40/£45
Douglas	by 1898 - [1899] [1900] - 1901 1902 - 1915 1916 1917- 1938	Atlantic Terrace Talland Skidden House, Skidden Hill Terrace 10, Park Avenue	Geo Jenkyn G Noall Lord Cowley J T Short J R Sandry	£12 £28 £12 £22 £25
Dow	1895 - 1919 by 1898 from 1899	Talland House with orchard, studio and land with stable and coach house	Self	£56 £83 £88
Dyer	by 1891 - 1899 1900 - 1923 1923 - 1939	Richmond Place 12, Pednolver Terrace Tallandside, Talland Road	Geo Jenkyn G Noall F Dow	£17 £35 £30
Eadie	1886-1894 by 1898 - 1902	Windy Parc, Ayr Lane Halsetown	Thos Rosewall T Jenkyns reps	£22 £8
Fortescue	by 1898 - 1898 1899 - 1924	Richmond Terrace Trelyon Cottage, Trelyon Downs	H H John Self	£18 £38
Fuller	by 1893 -1900 1900 - 1911 1911 - 1925	1 Barnoon Terrace 'Dunvegan', Trelyon 6 Clodgy View	Kate Thomas Self R Toy	£24 £20
Horn	1901 -09	9, Pednolver Terrace	S & M Hodge then J Hearne	£28
Kirkpatrick	by 1893 - 1906	Closeburn, Talland	W H Care / Dow	£35 / £38
Lindner	1899 - 1910 1910 - 1949	The Warren House, The Terrace Chy-an-Porth, The Terrace	Daniell & Lang Self	£60 £150
Meade	1895 - beyond 1930	Godrevy, Porthminster Hill	M Davis	£25
Milner	by 1898 - 1900 1901 - 1939	Draycott Terrace Zareba, Porthminster Hill	Thos Banfield M Davis	£10 £19
Olsson	by 1893 - 1898 1899 - 1909 from 1902 1909 -1911	Porthia, Porthminster Hill St Eia, Porthminster Hill with studio 26, The Terrace	R Toy R Toy/ M Davis M Davis Dr Jenkyn	£25 £40 £65 £18
Pazolt	1903 - 1910	Algonquin, The Terrace	M Davis	£55
Robinson	by 1888 - c.1898 by 1898 - 1899 1900 - 1917	4, Richmond Terrace Carrack Dhu Belliers Croft, Bellyars	Toy / Rosewarne J C Boase Self	£14 £20 £55
Rosenberg	1907 - 1912	The Terrace	Self	£30
Russell	1901 - 1916 1917-1927	The Warren St John's, Primrose Valley	S Noall	£7 £42
Talmage	by 1893 - c.1898 by 1898 - 1906 1906	9, Richmond Terrace 14, Draycott Terrace The Warren x 2	M W Ninnis Sampson Rowe B Hichens x 2	£14 £27-10 £8 & £3
Titcomb	by 1893 -1896 1896 - 1904	Richmond Terrace Windy Parc, Ayr Lane	 Cleveland	£15 £30
Whitehouse	1899 - c1921	Lyndon, Talland	T Jenkyn	£38

2.2.4 The Stephen family at 'Talland House'

When the artists first settled in St Ives, the figure described by Walter Sickert as "the most impressive personage in the area" was the distinguished man of letters, Leslie Stephen, who, since 1881, had rented 'Talland House' (GER £56) as a summer residence for his extended family.[55] Stephen's second wife, Julia, had modelled for Holman Hunt, George Frederick Watts and Burne-Jones, and their large family included Leslie's daughter, Laura, from his first marriage, Julia's three children from her first marriage to Herbert Duckworth, and their own four children, Vanessa (later Bell), Virginia (later Woolf), Thoby and Adrian.

The property was part of the Tregenna Castle estate, that had been bought by the Great Western Railway in the late 1870s, and Leslie Stephen had discovered it on a walking holiday in the area. Although newly restored after a fire in 1873, it had few illusions of grandeur at that juncture. Stephen called it, in his memoir, "a small but roomy house, with a garden of an acre or two all up and down hill, with quaint little terraces divided by hedges of escallonia, a grape-house and kitchen-garden and a so-called 'orchard' beyond", whilst Virginia described it as "a square house, like a child's drawing of a house, remarkable only for its flat roof, and the criss-crossed railing that ran around the roof".[56] It was then reasonably secluded from the rest of town and afforded magnificent views of the ever-changing colours of the waters of the Bay, particularly from the large French windows on the first floor, which opened out on to small, attractive, wrought-iron encompassed balconies. The furnishings in the house, however, were nothing fancy - normally cast offs from their London home - and, as the years went by - and the hordes of children traipsed more and more sand into the carpets - , they became distinctly shabby. The house itself, shut up for much of the year, was also, not surprisingly, very damp.

The Stephen family spent the summer months in St Ives, and the house and garden were always awash with children and distinguished visitors. One of the terraces was converted into a cricket pitch, which kept the children amused for hours, and they even painted the ball with luminous paint, so that it could be seen in the dark. Another sheltered area was called 'Love Corner', the scene of the betrothment, in 1890, of the journalist, Leo Maxse, later editor of the right-wing *National Review*, and Kitty Lushington, the daughter of a great friend of Julia, who had exercised her renowned match-making skills. There were also other areas labelled by the family 'The Coffee Garden' and 'The Lookout Place'.

Fig. 2.13 Talland House in the 1880s
(Leslie Stephen album, Mortimer Rare Book Room, Smith College)

---

55 Frances Spalding, *Vanessa Bell*, London, 1996, at p.11.
56 Virginia Woolf, *A Sketch of the Past*, in Ed. Jeanne Schulkind, *Virginia Woolf - Moments of Being*, New York, 1985 at p.127-8.

Fig. 2.14 Julia Stephen and her children outside the dining room of 'Talland House' in 1894.
Virginia is bending down to pet the family dog.
(Leslie Stephen album, Mortimer Rare Book Room, Smith College)

Leslie Stephen, who had been editor of the *Cornhill* magazine for eleven years, and who had published important works not only on philosophical history and theory, but also on mountaineering, was clearly a very welcome and highly regarded visitor in St Ives, whilst his wife, Julia, also made herself very popular with the locals with her concern for the poor and needy and for her other good works. After her death, the St Ives Nursing Association was set up in her memory.[57] By the time the artists began to settle in the town, Stephen was working on the first *Dictionary of National Biography*, and it is unsurprising, therefore, that they courted him and were welcomed at 'Talland House'. Stephen, after telling his American friend, Charles Norton, in September 1889 that St Ives attracted him more than ever, commented, "We have even made a pleasant acquaintance with some of the school of artists which has strangely sprung up here within the last three or four years....One of them is a Yankee named Simmons, who once attended your lectures & is married to a lovely Californian. Another is Adrian Stokes, who sells pictures now for good prices & has an Austrian wife."[58] Despite, in Virginia's view, her father having "no feeling for pictures, no ear for music and no sense of the sound of words", his friendship with the artists led him to

---

57 In the Journal that she maintained during a return visit to St Ives in 1905, Virginia records how her mother was still recalled with great affection.

58 Ed. J W Bicknell, *Selected Letters of Leslie Stephen*, London, 1996 Vol 2 at p.369. Stephen may have liked Vesta Simmons but Virginia recorded that Vanessa was not impressed when she came to lunch on Vanessa's birthday in 1892 and gave her a tie as a present. Marion Dell and Marion Whybrow, *Virginia Woolf & Vanessa Bell, Remembering St Ives*, Padstow, 2003, at p.57.

become involved with the St Ives Arts Club in its early days, albeit his visits in the summer coincided with the quiet period of the Club's year. Nevertheless, most probably at the suggestion of Adrian Stokes, he was elected its second President in 1891, but ill health meant that he could not take up the position.[59]

In 1894, the construction of the Porthminster Hotel interrupted the view from the property, much to the family's annoyance. However, by this juncture, for financial and other reasons, Leslie had been planning to give the property up, and his wife's death in 1895 hastened the decision. Virginia commented, "When they took Talland House, father and mother gave us - me at any rate - what has been perennial, invaluable". Their childhood experiences in St Ives proved the inspiration for Virginia's *To the Lighthouse* and other novels, and gave Vanessa an insight into an artistic coterie.[60] Both girls also developed, during their time in St Ives, an interest in photography, which was to play an important role in their lives.

Fig. 2.15   Leslie and Julia Stephen reading in the Drawing Room, Talland House',
with Virginia in the background.
(Leslie Stephen album, Mortimer Rare Book Room, Smith College)

After Julia's death, Stephen noted beside this photograph, "When I look at certain little photographs—at one in which I am reading by her side at St. Ives with Virginia in the background... I see as with my bodily eyes the love, the holy and tender love which breathes through those exquisite lips, and I know that the later years were a deep strong current of calm inward happiness, and the trials, so to speak, merely floating accidents on the surface." (Leslie Stephen's Mausoleum Book at p.58)

---

59 Virginia Woolf, Typed script of *A Sketch of the Past*, at p.8.
60 ibid.

Fig. 2.16   Detail from Willis' 1844 engraving of St Ives showing the extensive parkland surrounding
'Barnoon House' or 'Windy Parc' (to left)

2.2.5   The Eadie family at 'Windy Parc', Ayr Lane

The first artist to be recorded as a ratepayer for a property was William Eadie (1846-1926), who is shown in the 1886 Rate Book as the tenant of 'Barnoon House', known locally as 'Windy Parc' (GER £22), in Ayr Lane, a property then owned by Thomas Rosewall, but, reputedly, first built by a nobleman for his mistress. Eadie, who was the son of a Scottish silk dyer and who had been born and brought up in Paisley, was one of the first three artists to settle in St Ives over the winter of 1885-6. However, his artistic background was very different to all the other early settlers in the colony, for he did not arrive in St Ives after a spell spent training in France, but came direct from London, where he had been based since at least 1871. He was also rather older than his colleagues and had been married to his wife, Annie, a fellow Scot, who was five years younger than him, since 1880. They had already produced four children - shortly to be joined by a fifth.[61] Quite why a portrait and figure painter of modest ability, with an extensive young family, should decide to settle in such a remote spot, far away from his native Scotland, is unknown, but his decision to relocate to St Ives was certainly a brave one. He also committed himself to the town, far earlier than most of his colleagues, by immediately taking a long lease of the property, an imposing residence with extensive grounds off Barnoon Hill, which was sufficiently sizeable to accomodate his large family.[62] He converted one of the outhouses into a studio.

With his family responsibilities, Eadie does not seem to have socialised with the other artists over much, but he was a regular churchgoer, becoming good friends with the Vicar, Canon John Balmer Jones, and his curate, the Reverend Edward Griffin. The American, Howard Russell Butler, who was also a regular at the Parish Church, commented, in a letter to his sister in 1887, "I have just been in to Mr Eadie's where there are five little things that all seemed to be about four years old. Eadie is a Scotch artist, who lives here permanently. Last year I went in nearly every Sunday afternoon to see the children."

Eadie enjoyed some initial success as a portrait painter, and his genre paintings depicting the interiors of the homes of the fisherfolk, such as Figs 2.17 and 2.18, are of social historical interest. However, in November 1893, Eadie wrote to the property agent, Reginald Glanville, enquiring as to the availability of 2, The Terrace, as he was being forced to leave 'Windy Parc', as it had fallen in hand to the Duchess of Cleveland, who wanted to make alterations and repairs to it.[63] He commented, "I don't want to leave St Ives but find it difficult to get a suitable house for my family at the present time."[64] Unfortunately, his search proved fruitless, and he was eventually forced to settle in Halsetown.[65] As a result, he ceased to take part in Show Days and became rather a peripheral figure until his departure back to London in 1902.

61 Their fifth child was born in St Ives in 1886.
62 In a letter to R Glanville dated 16/11/1893, Eadie confirms that he has been living at 'Windy Parc' for eight years. - Mornington Estate Papers, County Records Office, Truro, GHW/12/3/6/1/61/10.
63 It was re-let to William Titcomb after the alterations.
64 Letter from W Eadie to R Glanville dated 16/11/1893 - Mornington Estate Papers, County Records Office, Truro, GHW/12/3/6/1/61/10.
65 Eadie felt obliged in March 1896 to insert an advert in the local paper indicating when his work would be available for view at his studio in Halsetown. This was a different day to Show Day. In 1894, he is recorded as the ratepayer for a small house (GER £4) in Back Road West but this will have been too small for his large family and was probably used by him as a studio.

Figs. 2.17 & 2.18 William Eadie   *A cottage interior*   *A Cornish Fisherman's Sunday*

2.2.6   The Robinsons and the initial attractions of Richmond Place

Harry and Dorothy Robinson, the other two initial settlers in the town, were also, by the time of the 1888 Rate Book, recorded as ratepayers for a tenanted property - 4, Richmond Place. This was part of a new terrace constructed by the developer, Robert Toy. Following the completion of Bellair Terrace and Mountpleasant Terrace, Toy turned his attention in the mid-1880s to a new parallel terrace, running uphill away from the harbour, in the grounds of the large property, 'Brunswick House' (later 'Trewyn'). Therefore, the new properties afforded pleasant views, down to the harbour and across to Tregenna Terrace and its adjoining parkland, known as Parc-an-Roper, on the other side of the Stennack Valley.

The terrace seems to have been constructed in various phases, one part initially being called Richmond Place and the other Richmond Terrace. This was most probably due to the existence of an old music pavilion, which presumably had originally been built by the owners of 'Brunswick House', and it was the presence of this in their garden plot that clearly made No 4 attractive to the Robinsons, who let it out as a studio to the Finn, Helene Schjerfbeck, during her visit in 1887-8 (see Chapter 2.4.2).

By 1893, a number of other artists had taken up residence in the terrace, including the Americans Sydney Laurence (No 1) and Lowell Dyer (No 2), Algernon Talmage and his mother (No 9) and William Titcomb. The houses were relatively modest in size, having GERs of no more than £17. They had two small reception rooms on the ground floor, plus a kitchen and utility area, with two bedrooms on the first floor. However, what may have made them particularly attractive to artists was a large attic, reached by a set of stairs, into the roof of which, at the rear of the property, could be inserted a north-west facing skylight or dormer window, thus making it an ideal space for a studio. Indeed, a number of artists continue to live in these properties, using the attics for this very purpose.

By 1898, Toy seems to have overcome any reluctance on the part of the local council to the demolition of the music pavilion and the terrace had been completed. By this juncture, however, artists were beginning to get grander ideas as to the type of properties that they wished to live in and, although artists rented properties in the terrace from time to time, it was never again the artistic enclave that it was at the beginning of the 1890s.[66]

Fig. 2.19 Richmond Place in 2009

---

66 Of the initial group, all had left by 1898, except Dyer who stayed until 1899. William Fortescue (1898) and Charles Mottram (1900-4), lived there briefly. However, art student, Ida Praetorius and her mother, Helen, lived in No 6 from 1905 until at least 1919 and Frederick Beaumont took No 9 between 1916 and 1919.

2.2.7   An artist enclave on Porthminster Hill

In the early 1890s, Robert Toy completed a small terrace of just three houses on land adjoining the coastguard cottages on Porthminster Hill. For many years, these properties, which are first listed in the Rate Book of 1893 (and in Kelly's Directory that year), were to be the home of artists, and they still retain their original names. The two end of terrace properties, 'Porthia' and 'Godrevy' (both GER £25) were rented off Toy initially by the artists, Julius Olsson and William Dickson, whilst the middle section, 'Zareba', was rented by Louis Grier's father, Charles.

Olsson, a self-taught artist, who was the son of a Swedish timber merchant and his English wife, had been involved with the colony from the time of his marriage in 1888 to Katherine Mary Butt, the daughter of a merchant, then aged 27. However, it is not clear where they had stayed before, as they do not appear on the Visitors' Lists. They were based at 'Porthia' until 1898, when they moved to the grander, detached house, 'St Eia', built on the adjoining plot. 'Porthia' was then rented by one of Olsson's former students, Charles George Beale Adams, the son of a Bath baker, who enjoyed some success as a marine painter, particularly at the RBA, and was a stalwart of the Arts Club. He and his London-born wife, Kate, an accomplished musician, stayed at 'Porthia' until 1905, when they moved to 'Primrose Cottage' in Primrose Valley. However, Kate died, after a lingering illness, in 1909.[67]

William Dickson and his wife are first recorded in the town in July 1891, when they were staying at 'Barnoon Villa', but appear to have settled in the colony shortly afterwards, as they took part in the Carnival Masquerade in March 1892. However, although he was represented in the Cornish Artists' Exhibition at Nottingham Castle in 1894, there is no further reference to him locally after that year. It is likely, therefore, that former Bushey student, Arthur Meade, who is recorded as the ratepayer for 'Godrevy' in 1898, took over from the Dicksons in 1894-5, when he decided to settle in the town with his wife, Mabel, and newly-born daughter, Celia. Mabel came from Dorchester in Dorset and, as they disliked the tourist crowds in St Ives, they frequently spent the summer months in Dorset, letting out 'Godrevy' to holidaymakers. Their domestic servant, Emma Lane, also came from Dorset and, at the time of her death in 1922, had been a faithful friend of the family for fifty years. The Meades remained at 'Godrevy' until the mid-1930s, but after his wife's death, Meade moved, for his final few years, to a bungalow at Lelant, 'Penhale', adjoining his beloved golf course.

Fig. 2.20 Porthminster Hill c.1895   (postcard detail, courtesy St Ives Trust Archive Study Centre)
A comparison with Fig. 2.6 reveals not only the erection of Robert Toy's terrace (top, as in 2009) but the completion of Draycott Terrace in a more grandiose style (1894), whilst, on the left, William John Paynter's 'Shun Lee' has been joined by Capt Harry's 'Morwenstow' and John Eccles Brown's 'Scot's Craig'.

---

67 In the 1920s, Beale Adams moved to 'Lyonesse' in Talland Road and lived there until his death in 1939. He and Kate are buried at St Uny, Lelant.

Fig. 2.21 Wyly Grier *Portrait of a Physician* (Ruth Grier)
This is a portrait of the artist's father, Charles.

Charles Grier was a retired doctor, originally from Ireland, who had married an Australian and who had practised in Australia, Canada and England. His two youngest children, Wyly and Louis Grier, were both artists, who were prominent members of the colony in its early years, and he had a further son, a doctor, who lived at Mevagissey. After his death in 1898, 'Zareba' was let out for a year to the American artist, Sydney Laurence, before, in 1901, becoming the home of the Yorkshire-born landscape painter, Fred Milner, who lived there, with his wife, Sophia, until his death in 1939. Milner, then living in Cheltenham, is first recorded in St Ives in 1890, and spent a decade making regular visits to the town before deciding to settle there. He always contended that the three houses commanded one of the finest views in St Ives, and he and Meade were next-door neighbours for over thirty years. Milner's wife died in 1947 and both are buried at St Uny, Lelant.

2.2.8 The Titcomb family at 'Windy Parc', Ayr Lane

After its refurbishment by the Duchess of Cleveland, resulting in an increase in GER to £30, 'Windy Parc' was let out to William Titcomb in 1896. Titcomb had first visited St Ives in 1887 and had become one of the leading figure painters in the colony. He was also a stalwart of the Arts Club, serving on the first committee and being President in 1900. Following his marriage in St Ives in April 1892 to Jessie Morison, a fellow artist, who was the daughter of a shipowner of Scottish extraction, they had rented property in Richmond Terrace, but now, perhaps with a family in mind, decided to live in a more significant property.

One of the attractions of the property was its large garden, which afforded fine views over the harbour and across the Bay. William painted a number of works set in the garden, such as his mythological subjects *Circe and the Pigs* and *Orpheus*, as well as his fine painting of three old St Ives characters, *The End of the Day* (Fig. 2.24). He also painted there his depiction of Christ walking on the water (*Ego Sum Nolite Timere* - Fig. 3.24), having arranged with some of the local fishermen to haul up to the garden one of the old seine boats from Porthminster Beach. Given the steepness of Barnoon Hill, this must have elicited some curses, and the boat eventually had to be cut in half.

Fig. 2.22 'Windy Parc' in 2009
now hemmed in by development

Fig. 2.23 William and Jessie Titcomb and their son, Frank,
at 'Windy Parc' in 1900

Fig. 2.24 W H Y Titcomb   *The End of the Day*
This features Old Bull, One-Eyed Barber and Prussian Bill sitting in the garden of 'Windy Parc'

Fig. 2.25 Jessie Titcomb *A Hymn to Pan*
The Titcombs' donkey boy, Humphrey Hart, modelled for the boy holding
the goat and his sister, Miriam, for the girl playing the pipe.

Jessie, too, found the privacy of the garden welcome, as she was fond of painting children in the nude in outdoor settings, a practice that many locals would have frowned upon. Her work, *A Hymn to Pan*, accordingly, was painted in the garden, as was, possibly, *Springtide*. For models, she used their donkey boy, Humphrey Hart, and his sister, Miriam. However, Jessie soon found that motherhood impinged upon her painting, after their son, Frank, was born in 1898 and their daughter, Loveday, in 1900.

At the time of the 1901 Census, the Titcombs had a number of servants to assist them. These included Mary Wright, a domestic cook, aged 22, from Mousehole, and Margaret Perkins, a domestic servant, aged 16, from St Ives. However, the person who ran the household was an old family retainer, Phoebe Rice, then aged 66, whom they trusted so much that, at the time of the Census, the Titcombs were actually away, leaving Phoebe in charge of their two small children, one only a few months old! A nanny, Ethel Dickinson, joined the family soon afterwards in February 1902.

In June 1904, however, the freehold of the property was one of a number of properties in the town sold by the Bolton Estate. Along with seven cottages in Ayr Lane, it was sold for £1510 to William Trewhella and this may well have hastened the Titcombs' decision to leave St Ives for Dusseldorf in 1905.[68]

2.2.9 The Millie Dow family at 'Talland House'

When Leslie Stephen decided to give up 'Talland House' in 1895, the lease was acquired by the Scottish artist, Thomas Millie Dow, the son of the Town Clerk of Dysart in Fifeshire. Dow had first visited St Ives in 1889 and, upon his marriage in 1891 to Florence Pilcher (née Cox), an old flame now widowed with two children, the family had settled initially in Hillhead, Glasgow. However, in 1894, following his father's death, they based themselves in St Ives for a year, to see whether the town's climate improved the health of Florence's son, Luke Pilcher. Finding that it did, they decided to settle in the town. Marion Whybrow records a story, recalled in the Dow family, of how Stephen, when initially showing Millie Dow around the property, suddenly put his finger to his lips, saying 'shush' before lifting a floorboard and whistling. Several rats emerged from below the floor, which he fed with cheese. He then suddenly clapped his hands, a signal for the rats to disappear from sight.[69] Having taken over the lease, Dow bought the freehold of the property from the Great Western Railway Company and, in order to protect it from development, he also acquired the orchard in front (GER £12). The Dows soon settled in and, in February 1896, Dow told his great American friend, Abbott Thayer, "We are all very happy here and have no regrets at the change we have made. It is such a pleasure to wake and find every one healthy and well."[70]

---

68 *St Ives Weekly Summary*, 18/6/1904.

69 Marion Whybrow, *St Ives - Portrait of an Art Colony 1883-1993*, Woodbridge, 1994 at p. 44.

70 Letter from Millie Dow to Abbott Thayer dated 7/2/1896 - Archives of American Art, Smithsonian Institution, Thayer papers, Dow correspondence, 1.27.

Fig. 2.26 The Millie Dow family outside 'Talland House'   (Dow family archive)

Fig. 2.27 Pietro, Millie Dow's Italian servant, outside 'Talland House'   (Dow family archive)

The Millie Dow family, one of the wealthiest in the colony, made great changes to the property over the years. They renovated the house completely and inserted far more elaborate glazing into the distinctive bay windows. They also added an extension to one side and built, in 1898, a coach house and stables (GER £5). Thomas decided that he needed a separate studio, and built this (GER £15) on land acquired on the other side of Talland Road, near the junction with The Bellyars. The 1899 Rate Book also shows him as the owner of a further property (GER £38) on Talland Road, 'Closeburn' (now known as 'The Cottage'), which was let out to the Kirkpatrick sisters.

The 1901 Census revealed that the Dows had more live-in staff than any other artist family, for in addition to a cook and a 'table maid', they had a 'sewing maid' from Switzerland and a Governess, who had been born in India. They are later known to have brought servants back from their regular trips to Italy. Thomas described the garden at the house, which he also remodelled extensively, as "an unfailing source of delight to us" and spent many happy hours working in it, being renowned for his cultivation of flowers, particularly roses and chrysanthemums.[71] He often used these in his paintings and Elizabeth Forbes commented, "Mr Dow is one of those rare artists who can reach the souls of flowers, and give you back, from the painted surface, the sense of their pathetic frailness and faint perfume."[72]

The precise extent of Dow's involvement with St Ives society is hard to gauge, as he appears to have been quite a private man. His paintings reveal a poetic mysticism. As he did not submit work to the Royal Academy, preferring to exhibit in Scotland, and as his studio was away from the centre of town, he did not participate in Show Days. However, he was elected President of the Arts Club in 1898, and signed in distinguished visitors on a number of occasions. In later years, though, the family tended to spend their winters in Italy. Nevertheless, Norman Garstin, a friend of Dow's from time spent together in a French atelier, recorded, on Dow's death in 1919, how the house and garden had been very much the centre of Dow's life, a base for work and play and a continuing centre for friendship and enjoyable hospitality.[73]

The memory of childhood days spent at 'Talland House' remained dear to Virginia Woolf and she could never resist the urge to view it on her return visits to St Ives. In 1905, her sister, Vanessa, and herself found themselves peering at the house through a chink in the escallonia hedge. "There", Virginia recorded in her diary, "was the house, with its two lighted windows; there on the terrace were the stone urns, against the bank of tall flowers; all, so far as we could see, was as though we had but left it in the morning; but yet, as we knew well, we could go no further; if we advanced the spell was broken."[74] However, in 1914, when her husband, Leonard Woolf, brought her down to Cornwall in the hope that it would help her recover from her first breakdown, she mentioned that they had "crept into Talland House itself yesterday, and found it wonderfully done up and spick and span, and all the garden brimming with flowers and rock gardens - very unlike what it was in our day."[75]

Florence Dow continued to live in 'Talland House' until her death in 1952 aged 95. She was a keen supporter of the St John Ambulance Brigade and the Edward Hain Memorial Hospital and retained many friends amongst the older fisherfolk, with whom she loved to mix. An old friend described her as "sweet and wise and humorous and infinitely kind".[76]

2.2.10 The homes of Lowell Dyer

Lowell Dyer (1856-1939) was an American artist, who came over to St Ives for a summer holiday in 1888 and stayed for the rest of his long life, a period of over fifty years. Renowned as the wit of the colony, a regular remark passed between Arts Club members was "Have you heard Dyer's latest?". However, he remains a rather elusive, enigmatic character.

Dyer was the son of Oliver Dyer, credited as one of the pioneers of stenography in America, for he established the first American periodical devoted to shorthand - the *American Phonographic Journal* - and started the first experimental high school classes in the subject.[77] However, in mid-life, he turned

---

71 ibid.

72 Elizabeth Forbes, *Two Painters of St Ives - Julius Olsson - T. M. Dow*, The Paperchase, Newlyn, Summer No 1909 at p.39.

73 Norman Garstin, *The late T Millie Dow - An Appreciation*, St Ives Times 1/8/1919.

74 Leonard Woolf, *Virginia Woolf at St Ives*, St Ives Times 4/1964.

75 Letter from Virginia Woolf to Violet Dickinson, dated April 1914 - Ed. Nigel Nicolson and Joanne Trautmann, *Virginia Woolf - The Collected Letters*, New York, 1979-80, Vol II No 704.

76 *St Ives Times*, 22/2/1952.

77 Eugene Garfield, *The History and Evolution of Stenographic Languages*, 7/1/1985. In his obituary, he was also hailed as the first shorthand reporter in the United States Senate and he wrote several books, including one of his recollections of the great senators of 1848-9 - see *The New York Times* 14/1/1907. Other books included a life of General Andrew Jackson.

Fig.2.29 'Tallandside', Talland Road in 2008.
Originally, the purpose-built studio of Millie Dow,
it was converted into a home by Lowell Dyer.
Louis Sargent also lived there.

Fig. 2.28 Nos 10-12 Pednolver Terrace in 2009

to religion, becoming at first a clergyman of the Episcopal Church, but he "tended later in life to adopt a mystical or Swedenborgian interpretation of religious truth".[78] Accordingly, he became a Swedenborgian minister in Mount Vernon, New York, before retiring to Boston, where he died in 1907. As a result, presumably, of sharing his father's mystical views, Lowell Dyer himself was known to fellow artists as 'the Boston Swedenborgian'.[79]

Dyer was born in Brooklyn and studied art in Paris for a time under Gérome at the Beaux Arts and at Julian's Academy with Collin. He also studied in Venice, where he developed a passionate admiration for the Italian Old Masters, particularly Botticelli, which was to influence his own art. He is first recorded in St Ives when he was present at the Complimentary Supper thrown to celebrate Adrian Stokes sale to the Chantrey Trustees on 31st August 1888. He went back to New York for three months in the spring of 1889, but then returned to the colony with his wife, Anna. Although not a founder member of the Arts Club in 1890, he joined soon afterwards and became a stalwart, being President in 1893/4 and again in 1918, and Treasurer in 1898-1900 and 1915-1917. When it came to electing a punchmaster for parties, Dyer was always the man.

By 1891, the Dyers were part of the artistic enclave in Richmond Place, living in No 2 (GER £17), then owned by George Jenkyn. As Dyer is not recorded as being the ratepayer for a separate studio during his occupation of this house, he may have used its attic as his workplace. He was primarily a figure painter, with a predeliction for paintings of young women or children as angels, often imbued with a heavy symbolism. His work echoes that of the Pre-Raphaelites, but examples are rare, for he was not a regular exhibitor. The first mention of a painting of an angel, simply entitled *An Angel* and showing the divine figure clutching a bunch of Annunciation lilies, was on Show Day in 1899 (see Fig. 2.31). It was said that the praise given to this work persuaded Dyer to specialise in this subject.

In 1900, like many of their colleagues at that time, the Dyers decided to move to a bigger house further away from the centre of the town. They did not buy, however, but took a lease from G.Noall of 12 Pednolver Terrace (GER £30).[80] This was the end house in a fine new terrace built by Robert Toy on Albert Road, from which there were magnificent views of the harbour and out over the Bay. It was a special location, which the Dyers enjoyed

Fig. 2.30 Dyer in his studio (1909)
(photo : W G Batchelor,
courtesy Marion Whybrow)

78 *St Ives Times*, 7/7/1939.

79 Charles Marriott, *Memories of Cornwall's Art Colonies*, *The Cornish Review*, Spring 1949, No 1 at p.68.

80 In the Rate Books, the house is listed as part of Talland Road in 1901, of Pednolver Place in 1902, of Pednolver Road from 1903 to 1914 and then of Pednolver Terrace, the name by which it is known today.

Fig. 2.31 Lowell Dyer
Angel of the Annunciation

for twenty-three years. Long-term neighbours included Edward Hain, the son of Sir Edward Hain, next door in No 11, and fellow artist, Frances Horn and her family in No 9, whilst, at the time of the 1901 Census, there were also living nearby John and Mabel Douglas and early settlers, the American Frank Chadwick and his Swedish wife, Emma, who were back in town for one of their most extended visits.

Encouraged by the response to his art, Dyer also took in 1902 one of the Porthmeor Studios. However, his output seems to have ground almost immediately to a standstill. Dyer is quite clearly identifiable as the basis for the character Harrison in Ranger-Gull's novel *Portalone*, an artist "who painted angels without models, which no-one ever bought". Clearly no fan, Ranger-Gull continued, "Like most of the others, he had a small private income which forbade strenuousness" and "Like Lucas, he was a whiskey-drinking backslider who was attempting to drown his sorrows."[81] Clearly, these comments about a fictional character should not necessarily be accepted as an accurate reflection of Dyer's own personality, but, from what we do know - for instance, after 1903, Dyer did not exhibit again on Show Day until 1919 - , it would not be surprising if they had some resonance of truth.

Dyer seems to have found a kindred spirit, with a similar mystical approach, in Thomas Millie Dow, and they became good friends. Indeed, the pair may have met originally in Paris, when studying under Gérome. 'Talland House' was no distance away from Pednolver Terrace and the pair of families socialised with each other often. Following Dow's death in 1919, the Dyers appear to have acquired off Dow's widow, Florence, his old studio and its surrounding land, which was on Talland Road, close to the junction with The Bellyars. They incorporated this into a new property, which they called 'Tallandside' (GER £30) and moved into it in 1923.[82] The property was of an unusual design for St Ives, the exterior of the first floor being covered with grey slate tiles (see Fig. 2.29). It did not boast views of the quality of those from their previous home in Pednolver Terrace, but there were less stairs and it was more easily maintained - two attributes that would have been welcomed by a couple in their late sixties. Furthermore, the incorporation of a sizeable workspace in the property meant that Dyer no longer needed to make the trek to and from his Porthmeor Studio. The house also had a pleasant garden, and it was to be their home for the rest of their lives. The American artist, Wilson Henry Irvine, on visiting the Dyers in their new home, in 1923, noted in his Journal, "Bully place, fine studio".[83] Perhaps due to the more convenient studio, Dyer began to exhibit some of his paintings of angels again during the 1920s. Many felt that these were reminiscent of the style of Burne Jones and would not look out of place in Florentine churches, but they were a world away from modern trends.

Irvine, who described Dyer as "a small, nervous little man", who told funny stories and complained of bad eyes, recorded Dyer's description of an encounter with Augustus John in the Café Royal. Dyer had gone up to John's table, where he was "surrounded by a group of young artists indeterminate in sex", and said to him, "I know many of your friends through the Chelsea Club, but have never been presented to you". John, who was "drunk more or less", responded, "Go to hell you poor stiff - etc etc". Dyer retreated, mortified, to the door, but then returned to John's table, "What I wanted to say to you was that your poor, weak, futile attempts to imitate Michelangelo are done for, played out". John, for once, was lost for words.[84]

Dyer's eyesight became increasingly worse, until he was almost totally blind by the date of his death in 1939. His obituary stated that his loss would be greatly felt by many old friends "who relished his quaint humour and admired his independence and his high ideals."[85] The use of the word "quaint" might suggest that his line in witticisms had not stood the test of time. However, writing in 1949 with his

81 C Ranger-Gull, *Portalone*, London, 1904, at p.15-6.
82 Dyer is still noted as at Pednolver Terrace in the Water Rate Book for 1922. However, it is likely that the house that drew admiration from W H Irvine in April 1923 was 'Tallandside'.
83 Journal of Wilson Henry Irvine, 5/4/1923, Archives of American Art, Smithsonian Institution, Irvine papers, Reel 3564.
84 Journal of Wilson Henry Irvine, 29/4/1923, Archives of American Art, Smithsonian Institution, Irvine papers, Reel 3564.
85 *St Ives Times*, 7/7/1939.

reminiscences of the colony in the early years of the century, Charles Marriott recalled Dyer as "the wit of the community" and was moved to include a couple of examples of Dyer's humour - the only ones that have come down to us.

"On a famous liar, who lied for the fun of the thing, he wrote this epitaph: "Here lies Blank Dash. As Usual".

Dyer played croquet. One afternoon he said to the then Vicar, a rather solemn person, "Why, Vicar, you're a regular dab." "Dab, dab," said the Vicar, crossly. "What's a dab?" "Quite common place", retorted Dyer, turning away impatiently.

Of a painter known as Wicked Willie, on account of his extreme mildness, Dyer was heard to observe reflectively : "Here comes Wicked Willie, looking like a fresh-water mermaid in a cow pasture." [86]

Despite his modest output and reputation as an artist during his lifetime, Dyer's work is represented in a number of public collections. *Spring* at Kirkcaldy Art Gallery and *Reverence* at the Victoria Art Gallery, Bath are typical examples of his style, the former having been donated, when the Gallery first opened in 1925, by Allan Maclean, Millie Dow's brother-in-law. *Woman in a Florentine cloister* (Plate 12) sold well recently in America. 'Tallandside' was later the home of Louis Sargent, who died there in 1965.

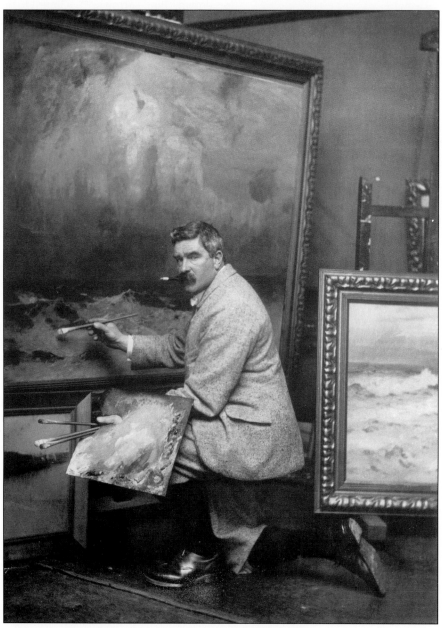

Fig. 2.32 Julius Olsson in his studio at 'St Eia', March 1909
(Walter G Batchelor)   (courtesy A.Wormleighton)

86 Charles Marriott, *Memories of Cornwall's Art Colonies, The Cornish Review*, Spring 1949, No 1 at p.68-9.

Fig. 2.33 'St Eia' and its studio (on the left) during the Lloyds' ownership
(Lloyd family archive)

2.2.11 The Olsson and Lloyd families at 'St Eia', Porthminster Hill

In 1899, following his father's death, which presumably resulted in an inheritance, Julius Olsson moved from 'Porthia' into 'St Eia' (GER £40), a newly-built property on the neighbouring triangular plot. Again, Robert Toy is listed as the initial owner, although, by 1900, he had sold the freehold, and that of 'Porthia', 'Zareba' and 'Godrevy', to Mrs Davis. The style of 'St Eia', with its protruding first floor windows, owes much to the Arts and Crafts movement, and is so unlike any other St Ives property of the period that one suspects that Olsson played a significant part in selecting its design. Indeed, it would have fitted much better into Surrey suburbia, where Olsson grew up and where his brothers still lived, than it did in St Ives. Shortly afterwards, Olsson arranged for an impressive studio (GER £25) to be added, which boasted fine views over St Ives Bay and from which he could study the effects of the moon upon the waters of the Bay - a subject which was to win him great acclaim. It is rather strange, therefore, to discover that Olsson never owned the freehold. For Toy to have built a significant property of unusual design merely to rent it out might not have been too speculative, given its enviable position, but to construct in its grounds as well a huge studio, far beyond the means of most artists, seems a little foolhardy, and one wonders whether Toy was let down by Olsson. In any event, Olsson enjoyed showing off his fine new home - his students record being invited to dinner with some regularity, whilst Murielle Schofield tells her husband about a number of tea parties thrown by Olsson and his wife.

In the past, it has always been assumed that Olsson, whose career took off in the first decade of the century, stayed at 'St Eia', until he moved to London to pursue Academy election, following his sale to the Chantrey Trustees in 1911. Yet, the Rate Book for 1909 records him as the ratepayer for a much smaller property, 26 The Terrace (GER £18), whilst the musician, Will Lloyd, has taken over 'St Eia'. It appears that the supreme confidence engendered by the tourist boom in the late 1890s quickly dissipated and a number of artists were forced to retrench. Olsson, who did have a reputation in his family for extravagance, had probably overstretched himself, despite his success.

Will Lloyd had enjoyed a most unconventional childhood. His mother, Frances or Fanny Lloyd (1855-1921), was the daughter of the prominent American portrait and history painter, William Henry Powell, and was not only an artist herself, but also an opera singer. Whilst studying under M.Drouet in Paris in 1883, she had fallen for a fellow student, Walter Lloyd, but he was not a standard student, for he was a retired English naval officer, of some distinction, who was twenty-seven years her senior.[87] They married in 1883 and it is believed that they first came to St Ives in 1884, before the art colony was formed. After the death of their first child in infancy in Paris, they moved to Rome, where Will was born in 1885. In 1889, however, Walter Lloyd died from cholera, and Fanny, unenthused by New York society, decided to bring her son up as an Englishman, utilising her Navy Widow's pension of £90 per annum.

87 Captain Walter Lloyd had joined the navy aged 14 and had seen service in the Chinese opium wars, the Crimean War and the Baltic, where he was decorated for bravery. He had then become a Queen's Messenger, carrying military intelligence through the Middle East, where he kept extensive journals and made watercolour paintings of any scene which interested him.

She appears to have moved about with some regularity, and stayed for periods with her late husband's many siblings, some of whom lived in Yorkshire and some in Wadebridge in Cornwall. Indeed, she based herself at 'Rose Cottage', Wadebridge for a number of years, Will attending Cottrell's School. She first went to Zennor in 1893 and, charmed by its spectacular scenery and unspoilt ambience, was, thereafter, a regular visitor with her paints. Each Christmas, Fanny and Will joined other members of the Lloyd family at Cowesby Hall, a large estate in the North Yorkshire Moors, with an impressive house, built, in 1832, to the design of Anthony Salvin, for Will's grandfather, George Lloyd, and now owned by one of her late husband's brothers, Thomas.[88] Will clearly made a good impression on these visits, as, on Thomas' death, childless, he left the estate to Will, then still at school at Charterhouse.

Will had wanted to be an engineer, but poor health forced him to give up his university course, and, with fond memories of visits to Zennor, he decided, in 1903, to try painting in the healthy environs of St Ives. He appears to have attended the classes of both Talmage and Louis Grier (see Fig. 2.236) and both his mother and himself exhibited on Show Day in 1904. Back at Cowesby Hall, he fulfilled his duties as local squire conscientiously and, in 1907, married Constance Primrose Rawson, from Sowerby in Yorkshire. They shared a joint passion for music - Will playing the flute or piccolo, and Primrose the piano and several string instruments, including the violin and viola. In addition to a love of chamber music, which they performed together, Will was, due to his mother, also an opera *aficionado*. His son, George, who won early acclaim for his Cornish opera, *Iernin*, recalled his father's influence, "He knew an immense amount about opera, in particular all the early Italian writers.....all Italian opera was grist to his mill."[89]

Although, after 1904, Will did not pursue his artistic aspirations any further, he enjoyed his brief spell in the colony at St Ives so much that, shortly after his marriage, he decided to acquire a property in the town, which they could use for part of the year. Accordingly, he took over 'St Eia' from Olsson, whose studio now became a music room. Recalling his childhood, their son, George, commented that the studio was so enormous that "you could get, quite literally, a small orchestra" into it. "Every weekend, people gathered together - there were trios and quartets.... I grew up with chamber music and used to creep in and hear all this."[90]

Fig. 2.34 Fanny Lloyd *Self-Portrait*
(Lloyd family archive)

88 The Lloyd family had been successful wool merchants and entrepreneurs in the Manchester and Leeds area from the mid-1600s. Colonel Thomas Lloyd, commandant of the Leeds Volunteers in the Napoleonic Wars, was an industrialist, who built Armley Mills, the largest factory in the world in its day. I am deeply indebted to Bill Lloyd for all information about the Lloyd family.
89 From conversation between George Lloyd and Chris de Sousa on *Iernin* CD 1986
90 From conversation between George Lloyd and Chris de Sousa on *Iernin* CD 1986

Fig. 2.35 Will Lloyd   (Lloyd family archive)

Fig. 2.36 Primrose Lloyd   Fig. 2.37 Primrose and Will Lloyd
          (Lloyd family archive)   (Lloyd family archive)

Despite regular visits to the Yorkshire estate, Will Lloyd still played a significant role in the colony, being Secretary of the Arts Club in 1911-2 and President in 1919. He wrote a memoir of Vincenzo Bellini, which was published in 1908, and followed this, in 1911, with a book of poems, *The Return from the Masque and other poems*. The American painter, Paul Dougherty, who will have known his maternal grandfather, became a firm friend and, in 1913, the pair went on a walking holiday to Switzerland, where they climbed the Matterhorn, amongst other peaks. Will may also have introduced Dougherty to the cliffs at Zennor, which became a favourite subject for him.

After Will's marriage, his mother returned to America for five years and then took a flat in St John's Wood, but, on discovering that she was not looking after herself properly, Will invited her down to live with them in St Ives in 1914. When this did not work out, Fanny rented 'Bridge Cottage' in Zennor (see Fig. 2.98). In the meantime, Will had volunteered for active service and fought in France, winning the Military Cross, but the horrifying scenes that he witnessed at Passendale and elsewhere changed his outlook completely, making him unhappy with the role of English gentleman.

During the War, Fanny took art lessons from the Belgian refugee artist, Louis Reckelbus, and made great strides with her painting, finding that the medium of tempera suited her (see Plates 2 & 3). The series of works that she exhibited at Lanham's in 1919 and on Show Day in 1920, which included *Light and Sound* and *The Planetary Spirit*, won high praise, not only for their technique, but also for their very different allegorical subject-matter. Such subjects suggest also the influence of Reckelbus' Belgian colleague, Emile Fabry, the renowned symbolist painter, who was also in St Ives during the War years. However, sadly, Fanny died in February 1921, and a small retrospective was held in 'St Eia' on Show Day in 1921.

By now, however, the Lloyds were finding the increasing tourist hordes in St Ives a trial, and they gave up 'St Eia' in 1922, thereafter using 'Bridge Cottage' at Zennor as their Cornish base. Here, Will was able to write more poetry and, in 1929 and 1931, he published further books of poems, which were well received. Some were lyrical (*Ode in Spring*), some dealt with the War (*A Grave on the Vimy Ridge*), some had a philosophical tenour, but most were written in sonnet-form and possessed qualities of naturalness and simplicity.[91] Will also acquired a property in London, as he liked to attend operas at Covent Garden, and, each year, he invited his good friend, Walter Barnes, of the Penzance Orchestra, to join them. On one occasion, in 1933, during a conversation bewailing the lack of an opera tradition in England, Barnes, who had just performed George Lloyd's first Symphony, written when he was just nineteen, had promised to put on in Penzance any opera that they might write. Within four days, Will had produced the *libretto* and, over the course of the next twelve months, George, finding inspiration from the moorland scenery around Zennor, had written the opera *Iernin*, based on the Cornish legend of the Nine Maidens, who were turned to stone for dancing on a Sunday. This was first performed in Penzance in November 1934. Reviewed very favourably by the critic of *The Times*, who happened to be on holiday in the area, the work then enjoyed the second longest run in London for an opera in English and attracted all the big names in music. Will, having now divested himself of Cowesby Hall, was largely responsible for funding the opera company and considered the work's success one of the highlights of his life.

Fig. 2.38 Cowesby Hall, from the courtyard   (Lloyd family archive)

---

91 See review by Herbert Laurie in *St Ives Times*, 4/1/1929. The third volume was called *Azrael*.

Fig. 2.39 The Terrace, with , on immediate left, Chy-an-Drea Hotel and then No 27 (Dr Nicholls),
No 26 (Olsson), No 25 (Grier and Barlow) etc
(L.E.Comley - St Ives Museum/St Ives Trust Archive Study Centre)

2.2.12 Artists in The Terrace

The run of villas on The Terrace, which had been built by Sir Christopher Somerton in the 1820s, were still desirable properties, despite the main road into town now passing by them, as they were spacious and elegant and afforded fine views across the Bay. Accordingly, they too started to become extremely popular with the artists at the turn of the century. In 1899, following their marriage, Moffat and Gussie Lindner moved into one of the most impressive properties, 'The Warren House' (GER £60). This had three reception rooms, eight bedrooms and a pretty garden, and they stayed there for a decade. Other artists to take properties in this section of The Terrace, on a long-term basis, were Allan Deacon and his wife, Kate, both former Bushey students, in 1900 (GER £40), the landscape painter, John Noble Barlow and his American wife, Elizabeth, in 1901 (No 25 - GER £19) and the American-born marine painter, Alfred Pazolt, in 1903 ('Algonquin' - GER £55). Later in the decade, in 1907, Gertrude Rosenberg moved into No 18 and, in 1909, Louis Grier replaced Noble Barlow in No 25 and Julius Olsson moved into No. 26.

2.2.13 Harry and Dorothy Robinson at 'Belliers Croft'

In John Hobson Mathews' history of the district, published in 1892, he mentions that The Belliers was an attractive, wooded lane running along the boundary of the Tregenna Estate and that, adjoining it, was a field, Belliers Croft. It was this field that Harry and Dorothy Robinson bought in the late 1890s and they arranged for the erection upon it of a significant dwelling house for themselves, with a number of features reflecting the Arts and Crafts movement (Fig. 2.40). In addition to spacious reception rooms, this property (GER £55) had eight bedrooms and an attractive two-storey wooden veranda at the gable end that afforded vistas of the Bay. There was a separate studio measuring over 31' x 20'.[92] Despite the property's size, they retained the name 'Belliers Croft'. The Robinsons had no children and so this huge house was occupied merely by themselves and one servant. They still retained their studio in St Andrew's Street, and it is possible that the studio in the home was used more for musical activities as, by this juncture, Harry Robinson was devoting more of his energies to music (and civic duties), rather than to art. As his contributions to the *West Country Arts Review* demonstrate, he also wrote poetry. If the Cassilises in *Portalone* are indeed based on the Robinsons, then they liked to show off their splendid new house by throwing regular parties, and they gained a reputation for having food and drink readily available at all hours. However, the couple were only able to enjoy their

---

92 See particulars of sale dated 3/1/1921 reproduced in the *St Ives Times* during January 1921.

Fig. 2.40 Bellier's Croft as a hotel.
The old studio can be seen to the right.

new home together for a few years, as Harry died from heart failure in 1904. This was a severe blow to the colony, for not only was Robinson the first of the early settlers to pass away, but he had been one of the lynchpins of the Arts Club, having been President on two occasions and Secretary for nine years. Pallbearers at his funeral were Louis Grier, Allan Deacon, Arthur Meade, Lowell Dyer, William Titcomb, Folliott Stokes, Julius Olsson and Walter Jevons, whilst, among the numerous artists present at his funeral, was Stanhope Forbes, with whom he had become great friends during Forbes' time in St Ives in 1886-7.

Despite now being on her own, Dorothy continued to live in the property until 1917, albeit she stopped painting almost entirely and, apart from one appearance on the Ladies Committee of the Arts Club in 1909, vanished off the social scene.[93] The involvement of the Lunacy Commissioners in her affairs in 1917 suggest that the last few years of her life - she died in York in 1920 - were beset by mental problems. The contents of 'Belliers Croft', including their collection of oil paintings, were sold in December 1917.

The next occupants of 'Belliers Croft' were also artists - Claude Francis Barry and his wife, Doris. Despite objections from his family, Barry had married, in 1908, Doris Hume-Spry, who was descended from the Dukes of Rutland, whom he had met at art school in Bournemouth, and they had lived in St Ives for much of the pre-War period, whilst Barry pursued his studies under Alfred East, Frank Brangwyn, Stanhope Forbes, Julius Olsson and others. On their return in 1918 - Barry having been a conscientious objector - , they took a three year lease of the Robinsons' property. He held several exhibitions of his work at 'St Leonard's Studio' and she also exhibited her needlework pictures, to considerable acclaim. However, shortly after the end of the lease, he deserted his wife and family and moved to the Continent.

After being used as a hostel in the Second World War, for which wall hangings were provided by Phyllis Pulling, the property eventually became a hotel for many years but, in 2007, was razed to the ground in a fire, having been empty for a while after the refusal of planning permission for redevelopment. Now, of course, that redevelopment is occurring and St Ives has lost another crucial part of its artistic heritage.

2.2.14 The Kirkpatrick sisters at 'Closeburn', Talland Road

'Closeburn' is the property situated on the corner of Talland Road, opposite the back entrance to 'Talland House', which is now known as 'The Cottage'. It was first recorded as owned by Thomas Millie Dow, and occupied by the Kirkpatrick sisters, in 1899.[94] There were three sisters - Ida (1866-1950), Ethel (1869-1966) and Lily (c.1862-1902) - , all of whom were exhibiting artists. However, Lily, a figure painter, with a love of music, who was always of delicate health, is the best known, because of her lesbian love affair with Edith Ellis (see Chapter 2.3.2.3). Edith's husband, Havelock, commented, "Lily was a St Ives artist, who lived with an elder sister, by whom she was jealously tended and guarded, in a little home of refined culture. She had studied in Paris without, however, being touched by the Bohemian life of the Latin Quarter, and as the sisters had private means, she was not dependent on her art for a living."[95]

---

93 She signed into the Arts Club a Miss Webb from Belfast, presumably a sister or a niece, on various occasions between 12/1907 & 3/1908.

94 Despite being ratepayers for this property until 1906, they do make occasional appearances on the Visitors' List, presumably on their return from their travels having let out 'Closeburn'.

95 Havelock Ellis, *My Life*, Heinemann, 1940.

The sisters' father was Captain Thomas Sutton Kirkpatrick of Dublin, who, after retiring from the 3rd Dragoon Guards, had become Governor at Newgate Prison. Ida and Ethel first exhibited in 1890, when both showed marine paintings, the results of a trip to Polperro. Other Cornish scenes were included in their exhibits over the next couple of years. In 1893, the family moved to Harrow-on-the-Hill, and the three sisters are recorded as visitors in St Ives in both July 1893 and July 1894. Lily may well have decided to move permanently to St Ives at this juncture, and she exhibited her work for the first time ever on Show Day in 1895. Her painting, *An Old Score*, was, however, well-received. "Beautiful in colour and composition, this painting depicts a girl poring over a piece of music which lies on a small table in front of her. The effect of the draperies and golden hair of the girl against the dark background is very good."[96]

The sisters used Rock Studio (GER £6), the converted Mine Engine House on The Warren, and, although only Lily participated in Show Days, Ethel exhibited a St Ives subject at the SWA in 1895 and Ida in 1899. Lily too exhibited paintings of the harbour and Hayle Bar at the RHA, where she showed from 1897, but her major works were oils which combined her joint loves of music and art, and depicted girls playing musical instruments. A typical example is *The Duet* (Fig. 2.41), which was illustrated as a Picture of the Year in 1899.[97]

After Lily's death in 1902, Ethel Kirkpatrick retained both 'Closeburn' and the studio until 1906, exhibiting a further St Ives subject at the SWA in 1905, but then both she and Ida transferred their attentions to the art colony at Walberswick, which they had visited from 1897 and with which they were to be closely associated until 1920.[98]

The name 'Closeburn' seems to have been changed to 'The Cottage', immediately after the Kirkpatricks' departure, and it was occupied, from 1915, by Sir Herbert Thirkell White, who was known to Florence Dow, as he had served with her first husband in the Civil Service in Burma, and who became a close friend of a number of artists.

Fig. 2.41 Lily Kirkpatrick   *The Duet*   (1899)
The identity of the models is not known, but presumably they were her sisters or other members of the artistic community. The instrument is Louis Grier's guitar lyre from the band of Charles II.

96 *St Ives Weekly Summary*, 4/4/1895.

97 She also exhibited a painting called *The Concert* on Show Day in 1899 and *Girl with Violin* was one of her exhibits in the Whitechapel show in 1902.

98 *St Ives Weekly Summary* 2/6/1906 records the death from a weak heart of a Miss Kirkpatrick, an Irish lady, at The Belliers, but it is not clear what relationship this woman had with the sisters.

2.2.15 The Whitehouse sisters at 'Lyndon', Talland Road

The art of the four Whitehouse sisters - Sarah Elizabeth (Lizzie) (1854-1933), Mary Jane (Jeannie) (1855-1933), Louise Caroline (Louie) (1856-1932) and Frances Charlotte (Daisy) (1863-1950) - was showcased at Penlee House Gallery & Museum, Penzance in September/October 2004. Only Lizzie enjoyed any success on the national stage, and this was relatively moderate, whilst Daisy exhibited locally for a number of years, and yet the exhibition was of considerable interest, for it demonstrated the depth of unheralded talent that was in the colony. Whatever their accomplishments as painters, the four sisters clearly played a significant part in both the artistic and local communities for some thirty years. They all remained unmarried - albeit it was discovered, at one juncture, that two of them had got engaged simultaneously to the same man! - and we know rather more about them, than many other artists in the colony, because of surviving correspondence in the Whitehouse Family Archive at the Gloucester Records Office.[99] Letters from British artists in the colony have rarely survived and so this correspondence is valuable, particularly, as, unlike, for instance, the Stanhope Forbes letters, it is not about the problems of art, but the problems of survival. Brought up without regard to the necessity of a career, but left as spinsters with a small income from which to eke out an existence, they organised their lives so as to reduce their living costs to a minimum, whilst still hoping to squeeze in some summer travel for sketching or educational purposes. Their plight will have been similar to a number of other impoverished painters, particularly spinsters without prospects, who tried to pursue artistic careers in the town and, accordingly, their accounts of their day to day trials are invaluable for throwing light on a whole section of the art colony.

William Whitehouse, the father of the four sisters and their three brothers, managed a nail-manufacturing business in the West Midlands, and was sufficiently successful at one juncture to rent 'Packwood House', the impressive manor house in Lapworth, Warwickshire, dating from Tudor times, that is now a National Trust property. However, he died in 1882. Both he and his wife, Sarah, were descended from the Hately family, one that was well-known in the Midlands. Louie later wrote, "The Hately branch...has brought... all our artistic inheritance...the colour sense, facility in drawing, music...voice...and my best gift, a love of literature etc."[100] Mrs Whitehouse and her daughters, who were then living in Leamington, are first recorded as visiting St Ives in July 1890, when they stayed with Miss Couch in The Warren until the end of September. They returned in July 1891 for a similar length of time, this time lodging with Mrs Grenfell in 4, Draycot Cottages. Indeed, Lizzie, who was the eldest and most accomplished of the sisters, and who had first exhibited her work in 1882, gave St Ives as her exhibiting address in 1891. She also joined the Arts Club that year and, the following year, seems to have been an active member of the sketching group, for she made a suggestion that a book be kept at the Club with a list of models, a description of their appearance and their address (see Fig. 2.42). It was also in 1892 that she completed a group portrait of her three sisters (Fig. 2.44). She then went to study in Paris, winning a bronze medal at the Academie Delecluse in 1893, and her two successes at the Royal Academy were in 1893 and 1894. During her absence in France, Mrs Whitehouse and two of her daughters took part in the Carnival Masquerade at the Arts Club in February 1893.

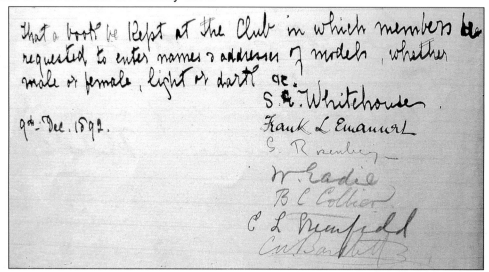

Fig. 2.42 Suggestion made by Lizzie Whitehouse in Arts Club Suggestions Book, co-signed by Frank Emanuel, Gertrude Rosenberg, William Eadie, B.C.Collier, Emily Latham Greenfield and Charles Bartlett

99 The archive consists principally of the papers of Arnold A G Whitehouse (Arnold), the eldest surviving son of the Whitehouse sisters' brother, Arthur Edward Whitehouse (Arthur). Its reference is Churchdown District - D6035.
100 Letter dated 1/4/1922 to Arnold Whitehouse, quoted in catalogue to 2004 Exhibition prepared by Roger Whitehouse.

Fig. 2.43 Sarah Elizabeth Whitehouse   *The Cabbage Sellers, St Ives*
(exhibited Show Day 1909)
(Anne Whitehouse/Penlee House Gallery & Museum)

The family are again recorded on the Visitors' List in April and May 1894 and it seems that, at this juncture, they decided to base themselves more permanently in the colony. Certainly, Lizzie participated for the first time on Show Day in 1895, when her exhibits included a portrait of her mother, which was described as "a lifelike and dignified portrait with the draperies exquisitely painted".[101]   By 1898, the sisters had taken various small studios around the town - Lizzie one on St Andrew's Street (GER £7), Daisy one on the harbour beach (GER £2) and Louie one in Palace Yard (GER £2). Lizzie's work began to gain good reviews and, in 1897, she was awarded by the Royal Academician Solomon Solomon first prize in the Mellins Art Competition for her work, *Interior and Figure*. Her greatest success, however, came in 1900, when her painting, *In Praise of Love*, was illustrated as a Picture of the Year. A representation of it was published on autotype by Hyde Park Fine Art Gallery, run by her brother, and a copy was purchased by H.M.Queen Alexandra.[102]

In their initial years in the colony, the family seem to have taken rooms.[103] Lizzie later commented, "The great advantage of rooms lies in not being tied - you can move when you like, whereas with a house you are tied down."[104] However, in 1899, they took over, from the Laurences, 'Lyndon', a large property (GER £38) on Talland Road, committing themselves to a seven year lease. However, their mother was only able to enjoy the ambience of the property for a short while, as she died on 16th November 1900 and was buried in Barnoon Cemetery. Perhaps perturbed by their continued unmarried status, the sisters clearly agreed, following their mother's death, to have a wholesale revision of their ages and so, in the 1901 Census, Lizzie became 33, not 46, Jeannie 32, not 45, Louie 30, not 44, and Daisy 27, not 37! One finds, particularly with women, that ages given in Census returns have been massaged somewhat, but audacity on this scale was rarely contemplated!

In 1902, Lizzie discovered that her brother, Arthur, despite being frame-maker to the Princess of Wales and having a client list that included many members of the aristocracy, was in serious financial difficulties.

---

101 *St Ives Weekly Summary*, 6/4/1895. In 1895, she was elected a member of the 91 Art Club. The Whitehouse Family Archive reveals that she spent several weeks that summer with a group of art students in Bosham, Chichester - see letter dated 11/8/1895 from Lizzie to Arnold from Bosham (Bundle 1/8).

102 Originally called *The Power of Love*, it showed a fair and gracious woman with children clustered around her - at her feet, by her chair, in her arms - whilst doves hovered reverently around this personification of Divine Love.

103 For instance, letters dated in February and March 1896 are from 20, The Terrace, whilst one in May 1896 is from 12, The Terrace.

104 In 1917, Lizzie was again asked for financial advice by her brother's widow. In the course of a lengthy exposition in a letter dated 12/1/1917 (Bundle 2/4), she commented, "We once had to meet something of the same difficulty you are faced with. Mother had not income enough to keep on our home and we, on the advice of a friend who had tried it, went in to rooms and they always had to be cheap ones and mother did not dislike it and was not unhappy till at last, besides living, she had saved enough money to move and settle again. The great advantage of rooms lies in not being tied - you can move when you like, whereas with a house you are tied down."

Fig. 2.44 Lizzie (S.E.) Whitehouse   *The Whitehouse sisters* (1892)
(Michael Whitehouse/Penlee House Gallery & Museum, Penzance)

Figs. 2.45 & 2.46 'Lyndon', Talland Road (top) and
Sarah, the mother of the Whitehouse sisters, in 'Lyndon' (1900)
(Roger Whitehouse/Penlee House Gallery & Museum, Penzance)

She bailed him out with a loan of £300, but, in so doing, set out her own financial philosophy.[105] "I am quite positive that only by knowing to a nicety what you can spend a year and then resolutely living within that sum, can anyone ever have peace of mind about money affairs, or keep free of some debt - to pay ready money and to go without what one can't afford and to put something by, however small, against the inevitable rainy day is the only way to keep straight."[106] When told of Arthur's anticipated expenditure, she commented, "Gas at £10 a year seems a big sum - we spend about £3 burning oil lamps and candles as we can't afford gas with our income - but here some who wish to be economical have 1/- in the slot gas and use some lamps and candles in bedrooms."[107]

Letters in the Family Archive also demonstrate that holidays could not be contemplated, unless their own house was let first, and part of the house was let out anyway, whenever possible. The New Zealander, Margaret Stoddart, was one of their tenants, and she may have become a good friend as well, as she exhibited in Lizzie's studio on Show Days in 1902-4 and 1906. Certainly, she shared the sisters' frugal outlook, for she told Frances Hodgkins, in 1902, that she managed to live on £1 a week.[108]

In a letter to her nephew, Arnold, in December 1903, Jeannie Whitehouse mentioned that the sisters were attracted by a property opposite the Porthminster Hotel. "It is small and compact, easy to run with one servant, has a small garden and would let well - a consideration to us with small means. It has four bedrooms and a dressing room and three letting rooms - unfortunately so many people feel like us that I am afraid we shall stand no chance of either buying or renting it...and unfortunately we have this house on our hands for three and a half years longer, and there, at present, does not seem so great a demand for large houses as a few years ago."[109] As predicted, they did not get the house and, when the lease of 'Lyndon' came up for renewal in 1906, the sisters decided to stay on.

Lizzie continued to be a regular participant in Show Days and recorded in December 1903 how she had had a particularly hard-working week, as she had hired a professional model.[110] In 1906, she moved from her St Andrew's Street studio to one on St Peter's Street, and this remained as her work-base until 1915. However, although the 2004 exhibition revealed that she continued to produce some attractive work (see, for example, Plate 9), she had no success in London and found it difficult to effect sales. At the time of his father's financial crisis in 1902, she commented to her nephew, Arnold, "I had always hoped that by the time you boys and Stella [Arthur's children] were grown up, I might have got into some steady selling of pictures and I always planned the money for just these emergencies, but pictures won't sell and I can't make money unfortunately or I wouldn't mind how hard I worked and you should be welcome to it all."[111]

Daisy also started to exhibit her paintings, mainly floral subjects, at the RCPS in 1902, but did not participate in Show Days until 1907. Mainly working in watercolours, she was a keen advocate of cream, rather than gold, mounts, which were then the fashion. Although she exhibited in such shows until 1919, her work elicited little comment. A painting of Venice is owned by St Ives Arts Club. Jeannie and Louie, who admitted to a "nervous self-conscious temperament", do not appear to have exhibited at all, although Louie did enjoy sketching, sowing and craft work.[112] However, she was not as permanently based in St Ives as the others.

Paintings by Lizzie reveal relatively modest holidays to Northumberland (1907), the Cotswolds (1908) and Picardy (1909).[113] However, in June 1909, all the sisters resigned from the Arts Club, as they intended to be away for a year, and they did not, in fact, exhibit on Show Day again until 1912. Their destination was Italy, and works mentioned on their return indicate that Rome, Florence and Sicily were

105 As the value of her securities were low at that time, she bravely borrowed the money off the bank herself. Interestingly, it was always Lizzie that Arthur's family approached when in need of funds, rather than the other sisters, and under the original terms of the loan, Lizzie agreed that, should she die first, the loan would be forgiven, implying that she felt no commitment financially towards her sisters.

106 Letter dated 19/1/1902 to Arnold Whitehouse (Arthur's son) (Bundle 2/4).

107 Letter dated 28/1/1902 to Arnold Whitehouse (Bundle 2/4).

108 Letter from Frances Hodgkins to Isabel Field dated 7/3/1902 - Ed L Gill, *The Letters of Frances Hodgkins*, Auckland, 1993 at p.123.

109 Letter dated 6/12/1903 from Jeannie to Arnold Whitehouse (Bundle 2/4).

110 Letter dated 6/12/1903 to Arnold Whitehouse (Bundle 2/4).

111 Letter dated 2/2/1902 to Arnold Whitehouse (Bundle 2/4).

112 In a letter to Arnold dated 20/5/1896, Louie comments, ""I myself know with my nervous self-conscious temperament that had I had the advantages of mixing in good society as a girl, what a boon it would have been. What a lot of gaucherie it would have saved. How much pleasant even it makes one for others to live with if one can also have gracious manners and ways - this is the outcome of a charming afternoon spent with Baroness Farina. I would that I had her ease of manner and readiness of expression." Later, in 1926, when confined to her room in Venice with severely impacted vision and heart weakness, she told Arnold, "So life is ended for me as far any enjoyment goes - never to read, sketch, sow or craft work ever again." Letter dated 18/4/1926 from Domus Civica, San Rocco in Venice (Bundle 2/10).

113 These dates are the years the works depicting these places were exhibited on Show Day and so the trips themselves are likely to have been during the previous summer. The painting in the 2004 show entitled *A Cotswold Evening* is a view of Burford likely to have been executed in 1907.

amongst the places visited. Indeed, Lizzie sold a watercolour of almond blossom in Rome from a small exhibition that she had in St Ives in March 1913 with Mrs Lucy Bodilly and former Talmage student, Ida Praetorius.[114] Louie, however, stayed on in Rome and entertained there, in 1913, the Fortescue family and, later, Mabel Douglas, clearly a good friend of the sisters, and Kitty Hain, the daughter of Edward Hain. The deteriorating situation in Europe meant that, when the lease of 'Lyndon' came up for renewal in 1913, the sisters again opted to stay on, but their enjoyable Italian trip had planted the seed of an idea.

With the outbreak of War, the sisters devoted themselves to a range of charitable activities in the town, which are discussed elsewhere (Chapter 4.1). They had less time for art, but Lizzie and Daisy were involved in Show Days until 1919. However, in 1920, when their lease ran out, they decided, on this occasion, to give up 'Lyndon', store their furniture in Allan Deacon's Virgin Street Studio and live in Italy for a few years. It was a severe blow, then, when Deacon's studio was destroyed by fire in 1921, for their furniture was uninsured. Louie settled in Venice, but Lizzie and Daisy, accompanied by Jeannie, continued touring and sketching, for both were asked in 1926 to contribute to an International Exhibition in Assissi and to mount an exhibition of their sketches at a new hotel in Bordighera. From letters and postcards within the Whitehouse archive, places visited included Rome, Assissi, Florence, Venice, Spoleto and Bordighera. In fact, Lizzie died and was buried in Bordighera in Italy in 1933. Louie and Jeannie also died in 1932-3, but Daisy lived on for a further 27 years, dying in England at the age of 97. Nevertheless, she insisted on being buried alongside Lizzie in Bordighera.

The property agent, George Toman, labelled Lizzie Whitehouse a "whimsical old maid". The expression "old maid" was probably used quite frequently to describe the Whitehouse sisters, but "whimsical" seems a little harsh for Lizzie, in any event. She comes across in her letters as very practical. In their straightened circumstances, the sisters seem to have been able, by living a frugal existence, to create a genteel home where art, literature, music and travel were fully appreciated. For thirty years, they were an integral part of the art colony.

Fig. 2.47 Sarah Elizabeth Whitehouse *Daisy Whitehouse*
(Michael Whitehouse/Penlee House Gallery & Museum)

114 During this Exhibition, she sold some jewellery designed and made by her niece, Stella, for whom high hopes were held in this connection for a while.

Fig. 2.48 Sydney Carr
(the late Derek Wintle/Andrew Eggleston)

2.2.16 The Carr family at 'Arkleby', Talland Road

Sydney Herbert Carr (1864-1917), quite understandably, is never mentioned in histories of St Ives art, as, despite exhibiting locally with some regularity between 1889 and 1902, he was an artist of limited ability.[115] However, he was an important member of the artistic community, for he also gained some success as a photographer, produced some amusing caricatures of his fellow artists, and played his part at the Arts Club and in the town. A friendship with *bon viveur*, Cyril Ranger-Gull, whose portrait photograph by Carr (Fig. 1.6) is a good example of his skill with the camera, suggests a similar maverick outlook and, indeed, in 1903, Ranger-Gull dedicated his book, *The Adventures of Mr Topham, Comedian*, to "Sydney H Carr, my friend, in whom I discern something of the essential Topham spirit".[116] Carr's own bookplate (Fig. 2.49) certainly confirms that he was an unconventional character.

Carr was born in Lincoln and his father subsequently became Bishop of Oxford. However, he was orphaned at an early age, and his brother, Dudley, who was blind, and himself, were bought up by two uncles, the Somertons, who had newspaper interests in Bristol. He is believed to have studied at Oxford and to have undertaken some art training in London. He exhibited for the first time at the RWA in 1887, when his address was 27 Kilburn Priory in London, and the title of his 1888 exhibit, *A Batchelor's Dessert - A Study*, casts some light on his character and sense of humour! He was offered the chance to design art nouveau crafts for Liberty's, but, having been left some money by one of his uncles, he married his girlfriend, Mary, from Spilsby, Lincolnshire, and settled initially in Penzance. He contributed to the 1889 WCAU Exhibition, but is referred to as a newcomer on Show Day in Newlyn in 1891. However, he then began to pay visits to St Ives, staying at the Tregenna Castle Hotel in March 1891 and with Mrs Ashton at Hawke's Point in August 1892. He was still living in Penzance when he was first signed in to the Arts Club by Olsson in October 1894, but he may have moved to St Ives at this time, as he exhibited on Show Day in the town for the first time in 1895, when his paintings of Land's End and Sennen coastal scenery were considered "delicately painted and happy in restful effect of silver haze on sea and sky and rock".[117] Certainly, by 1898, he was living in 8, Albany Terrace in St Ives, a not insubstantial property (GER £30), owned by Edward Hain.

---

115 He was involved in Show Day in 1895, [1896], 1897, 1898, 1901 and 1903. and exhibited work at WCAU 1889, WCAU 1891, RCPS (62) 1894, RCPS (64) 1896, RCPS (66) 1898, RCPS (67) 1900, Whitechapel 1902 and RCPS (68) 1902.

116 I am indebted to David Wilkinson of The Book Gallery, St Ives for this information.

117 *St Ives Weekly Summary*, 6/4/1895. He also contributed to the first exhibition at the Passmore Edwards Gallery in Newlyn in 1895.

Fig. 2.49 Sydney Carr   Bookplate   (Carr family archive)

Fig. 2.50 Sydney Carr   *A Dry Game*   (from '*The Black Monks*')
The presence of fine silver candlesticks and a bishop's chair might indicate that he had used his own living room at 'Arkleby' for this set.

Carr was particularly fond of painting coastal scenes, with sandy bays, and St Ives street scenes and, in September 1897, he held an exhibition of his works in his Porthmeor studio, which James Lanham publicised. Carr, therefore, may well have been one of the initial tenants of the new block of studios constructed at Porthmeor in 1895. However, in 1899, he took the cheaper 'Blue Bell Studio' in St Andrew's Street.

In 1902, the Carr family moved to 'Arkleby', a large property in Talland Road. Carr now appears to have turned his attention more towards photography, his camera capturing many fascinating scenes in and around the harbour beach. A number of these are illustrated throughout this book. However, his excellent photographs of St Ives scenes, despite winning several prizes, are not widely known.

Always keen to try different things, Carr also executed silhouettes and a number of bookplates, full of fantastical figures reminiscent of Hieronymous Bosch, and put together a somewhat bizarre album, entitled *The Black Monks*, which features photographs of models of German monks placed in interior and exterior set pieces. They drink, they take snuff, they play skittles and cards and sidle up to dancing girls. Accordingly, they generally behave in a very un-monkish manner, master minded by a slightly zany brain.

Carr was a popular figure in the Arts Club and played a full part in dramatic productions. His caricatures of fellow Arts Club members playing cards and billiards will be roughly contemporaneous with those by Fitzherbert, but are unknown, as they were not published (see further Chapter 2.7.3). He also is frequently mentioned as the donor of prizes at sporting functions and played his part in the local community. However, in September 1911, he gave up 'Blue Bell Studio', saying he was going abroad in March 1912, and, in 1913, he moved to Teignmouth, where he died in 1917.[118]

2.2.17 The homes of the Rowe and Talmage families

Recalling his time in St Ives in the early years of the century, Charles Marriott later commented, "One of the most talented and certainly the most popular of the St Ives painters was Algernon Talmage. He was, indeed, a most attractive personality: modest, slightly reserved but always ready to do a kind action for a friend."[119] Algernon Talmage (1871-1939) was the second son of the second wife of the Rector of Fifield, Oxfordshire. His mother, Susan, was twenty-seven years younger than his father, John, the latter dying when he was just twelve. Both his mother and his father's mother came from old Cornish families.

---

118 Letter from S H Carr to Glanville and Hamilton dated 28/9/1911 - Mornington Estate Papers, County Records Office, Truro, GHW/12/3/6/1/152/31.

119 Charles Marriott, *Memories of Cornwall's Art Colonies*, *The Cornish Review*, Spring 1949, No.1.

Having studied at West London School of Art and Bushey, Talmage first came down to St Ives in 1893, and lived initially with his mother in Richmond Place. In 1896, he married Gertrude Rowe, who, unusually, was an art student from the locality.[120] She was one of the five talented children of Sampson Taylor Rowe, who had run a chemist and druggist business in Redruth for forty-four years, as well as being a registered dentist. He was also a member of the Pharmaceutical Society and the Society of Public Analysts. Gertrude's elder sister, Lily, attained wide celebrity as a contralto of great power, before marrying an Army officer, Major Julian, whilst her younger sister, Louise, known as Bessie, took leading parts in the D'Oyley Carte opera company, before marrying, in 1893, William Geoffrey Bouchard de Montmorency, 6th Viscount Mountmorres (1872-1936), who became a clergyman and who occasionally assisted at services at the Parish Church.[121]

In 1897, shortly after Gertrude's marriage, her father retired from business, and he and her mother, Fanny, moved to St Ives, buying 14 Draycott Terrace (GER £27-10), one of the run of fine properties, with attractive ironwork, just underneath the Porthminster Hotel, which had been built in 1894 to the design of Silvanus Trevail for the Rouncefield family (see Fig. 2.20). In the 1899 Rate Book, Talmage is shown as the joint occupier of the property with Sampson Rowe, and, therefore, seems to have opted to live with his in-laws. In fact, at the time of the 1901 Census, Gertrude and he were not only sharing the house with her parents, but also her two sisters and her two nieces, the daughters of Lily Julian, whose husband was fighting in the Boer War and who had endured the siege of Ladysmith.[122] There cannot have been much privacy.

Sampson Rowe himself was interested in art and wrote a number of articles and short stories for the local paper on art related topics.[123] He also acquired for Talmage a property in Carnglaze Street (GER £7) to use as a studio. However, he died in 1903, aged 78, from a cancerous growth in his throat and tongue.[124]

Although, by 1902, Talmage is shown as the owner of a separate property in Draycott Terrace, this seems to have been an investment, as it is always occupied by others, and he remained living with his mother-in-law. He did, though, change studios, giving up the Carnglaze Street studio and taking No 5 Porthmeor Studios, newly created out of Olsson's vast studio. It was also at this time that he started to become the leading figure in the Cornish School of Landscape and Sea Painting, taking over responsibility for the Harbour Studio from Olsson. Gertrude seems to have helped at the School, as a number of the students are signed into the Arts Club by her.

Talmage, who was well-liked by his students, also played a significant role in the artists' entertainments, gaining a good reputation as a comic actor. Lily Julian also performed in a number of concerts, whilst Viscount Mountmorres and his wife were frequent guests at the Arts Club. Talmage, however, left St Ives and his wife in 1907 and moved to London. Gertrude did not pursue her art, after his departure, with any great vigour, although she did participate in Show Day in 1915 and 1916. After her mother's death in 1915, she continued to live in 14, Draycott Terrace and, although she is still recorded there in Kelly's Directory of 1930, she held an auction of the property's contents in 1928.

2.2.18 The homes of the Bucknall - Bainbridge - Douglas families

Sarah Bucknall and her two artistically inclined daughters, Sarah Georgina (1858-1937) and Mabel Maud (1861-1956), arrived in St Ives in the mid-1890s to make a fresh start. Sarah's husband, Samuel, had been a Stroud bookseller, but the onset of locomotor ataxy left him a severe invalid, and the family moved to Weston-super-Mare, where they lived opposite London University Professor Francis Newman, who had become a good friend.[125] Samuel passed away in 1881, but it was the unexpected death, in 1893, of Henry Bainbridge, the talented sculptor that Georgina had married, that prompted the move,

120 In August 1889, the Misses Rowe from Camborne stayed at Hendra's in Carbis Bay and Gertrude first exhibited at the RCPS show in 1893.

121 He became Vicar of Swinton in 1917, having travelled in the Congo and served as Hon.A.D.C. to the Governor of Jamaica. See *St Ives Times*, 26/10/1917.

122 See *St Ives Weekly Summary*, 1/8/1903.

123 One story entitled *A St Ives Artist*, published in June 1900, concerned a London artist, called George Lawrence, who had come down to St Ives in the 1840s to try to regain his health. He was inspired to produce a final masterpiece by the daughter of his landlady, Isabel Adams, who tidied his studio and accompanied him on his sketching trips to Knill's Monument and, on his death bed, he gave her the cheque for £200 that he had secured from its sale. However, in grief at his parting, she drowned herself in the lily ponds of Tregenna Castle.

124 See *St Ives Weekly Summary*, 1/8/1903. His estate totalled £3726.

125 She won a medal at Taunton in 1885. See Georgina Bainsmith, *Francis Newman in Private Life*, in Giberne Sieveking, *Memoir and Letters of Francis W. Newman*, London, 1909.

Fig. 2.51 Georgina Bucknall, aged 22, in 1881
(courtesy Marion Whybrow)

Fig. 2.52 Mabel Bucknall, aged 19, in 1881
(courtesy Marion Whybrow)

for Georgina was left with a young son, Bruce, to raise. The family shortly settled in 'Fairholme' on Barnoon Terrace and also rented 'Simcock's Garden', a 550 square yard piece of land with a frontage on to Barnoon Hill.[126]

Georgina was herself a sculptor and had trained initially in Taunton before attending art school in London.[127] She was later described as "the pupil and friend of eminent artists". Between 1895 and 1908, she regularly exhibited her work on Show Days, achieving a not insignificant reputation, which led her, in 1909, to be elected a Fellow of the North British Academy of Arts, Newcastle-upon-Tyne.[128] Her portrait busts included a representation of Capt Thomas Row Harry, when mayor of St Ives, in embossed bronze, a marble bust of Canon Alfred Ainger (1837-1904), Canon of Bristol Cathedral and Master of the Temple, London and a bronze bust of Francis Newman, which she had modelled in her early student days and which she gave to University College, London in 1907.[129]

Possibly inspired by her brother-in-law, Georgina began to show an interest in photography around the turn of the century and took premises for a few years on the High Street that she used as a studio. Reviewing her photographic exhibits at the 1902 RCPS exhibition, the *Cornish Post* commented, "The artistic carbon portraits from the studio of Mrs Bainsmith, St Ives, are on the plane of London photographic artists, though the posing, arrangement of draperies and lighting are on quite original lines". Her portraits of children and adults were felt to "resemble the soft-toned natural effects of copies of fine paintings" and to be "notable for the texture, the grouping and the lighting". In 1905, she showed some of her photographs at the Royal Photographic Society in Regent Street. Unfortunately, although reference is made to her artistic photos throughout her life, none have been identified. After 1908, however, Georgina seems to have given up her artistic endeavours and concentrated on championing women's rights and various local causes. She tried on a number of occasions to get elected on to the local Council, but found it difficult to break down the prejudice against females. However, from various references to her in the newspapers, it appears that she was not particularly well-liked and, in Arts Club minutes dealing with resolutions or demands from her, one can detect the raising of a quizzical eyebrow to its furthest extent!

It is not known whether Mabel studied elsewhere before coming to St Ives but, like her sister, the first mention of her work is on Show Day in 1895, when she exhibited a portrait *Grief*, and she was a

126 Simcock's Garden was offered for sale in July 1913 for building land.

127 See Georgina Bainsmith, *Francis Newman in Private Life*, in Giberne Sieveking, *Memoir and Letters of Francis W. Newman*, London, 1909.

128 *St Ives Weekly Summary*, 6/9/1902 & 15/5/1909.

129 This is illustrated in my book *Pioneers of St Ives Art at Home and Abroad*, Tewkesbury, 2008 at p.261. Bainsmith wrote, for Giberne Sieveking's book, "The bust has always been one of my greatest treasures; and after the lapse of years that have gone by since it was first modelled, I still revere and reverence his memory and his truly beautiful life. Whatever he wrote, this is what his actual life and deeds expressed strongly - "he lived to do good." This is what impressed me most as a young girl, and my life has been richer and nobler for the honour and privilege of knowing Francis Newman."

member of the Arts Club by the following year. Work executed prior to her marriage to the photographer and artist, John Christian Douglas, in February 1897 is rare, but a portrait of her sister was sold at the Penzance Auction House in 1991.[130] However, she did not begin to exhibit regularly until 1904, by which time she was specialising in portrait miniatures.

John Christian William Douglas (1860-1938) was born in Mundesley, Norfolk and was educated in Blandford Forum.[131] He came to St Ives in the mid-1890s and was a member of the Arts Club by January 1894, when he signed in a relative, Howard Douglas. A Mr Douglas from London is also listed as a Visitor staying at Albany Terrace with Mrs Pearce in July and August 1894. After their marriage, the Douglases lived initially in Atlantic Terrace (GER £12), then at 5 Talland Road (GER £28) before taking, in late 1901, 'Skidden House' on Skidden Hill (GER £12), which had formerly been occupied by the cabinet maker, John Daniel. It needed quite a bit of work on it, as it had dry rot on two floors. However, in April 1902, Douglas wrote enthusiastically to the property agents, "You will hardly know John Daniel's house now - my wife and myself have done wonders in improving the property generally and it is now very habitable."[132] He put the total cost at £40, of which half was set against the rent. They also took a lease of the adjoining cottage, which was let to Ann Stevens, as they hoped to combine the two in due course, but this never happened as Ann Stevens did not die until 1926, aged 87.[133] There was a yard behind the property, upon which extensions have subsequently been built, and it is now the Skidden House Hotel.

Douglas was a long-term occupant of a Porthmeor Studio. He is certainly recorded as a ratepayer for one in 1898 and, given the date of his arrival, he may well have been one of the first occupants of the group erected in 1895. Although he did do some painting, particularly coastal studies, and exhibited at the RCPS exhibition in 1896, he is best known for his photography, where his skills were wide-ranging. In particular, he had a good sense of design and was prepared to move his camera closer to his subject than some of his contemporaries in St Ives, such as Edward Ashton and L.E.Comley. In addition to portrait photographs of artists and their families, Douglas is responsible for many of the iconic images of artists in their studios. He was also used by the artists to take photographs of their paintings, for record purposes or for use in publications such as Royal Academy Pictures. In addition, Douglas was a fine landscape and marine photographer, capturing the ever-changing scene in the harbour, as well as the splendours of the Cornish coast, and was awarded various medals at the RCPS exhibitions - a silver in 1900 for *The Sunken Rock* and a bronze in 1902 for *Breakers*. He also had a particular fascination with the hordes of gulls that hovered over the harbour, waiting for easy pickings, and took numerous images of the play of light through and over the dense mass of birds (see Fig. 3.53).

Douglas' photographs were used by Folliott Stokes to illustrate his three books on the Cornish coastline and moors, published between 1908 and 1912, and were bought by the visiting American artist, Wilson Henry Irvine, to assist him with completing his Cornish marine paintings once back home. Indeed, it is from Irvine's Journal that we learn most about Douglas, as he was one of the few St Ives artists to make an effort to befriend the American, and found that Irvine shared an interest in photography. Irvine was most impressed with Douglas' work, commenting. "He is a really corking photographer. Never saw as fine ones of the sea."[134] Irvine also liked one of gulls in the harbour and was not surprised to learn that Douglas had sent his series of the sea to Paul Dougherty, "who certainly would find them useful in marine painting".[135] Irvine was amused to be told by Douglas that photography was a sideline for him, and then to be told by Lowell Dyer that, for Douglas, painting was the sideline. On a photography expedition to Hor Point, Douglas admitted as much, confirming that his camera had been "his un-doing artistically" and regretting that "he hadn't quite hit if off" as an artist.[136] Unfortunately, after his death, a number of his plates became mixed up with those of Herbert Lanyon and so it is not possible, in all instances, to be certain of authorship. However, other sources reveal more and more the extent and quality of Douglas' work.

---

130 Sale dated 20/6/1991, Lot 79. Although catalogued as 'An Edwardian lady', Marion Whybrow confirmed it was of Georgina - M Whybrow, *St Ives 1883-1993 - Portrait of an Art Colony*, Woodbridge, 1994 at p.82.

131 At the time of his marriage in 1897, he was described as the son of the late John Douglas EICS.

132 Letter from J.C.Douglas to Glanville and Hamilton dated 22/4/1902 - Mornington Estate Papers, County Records Office, Truro, GHW/12/3/6/1/111.

133 *St Ives Times*, 19/2/1926.

134 Journal of Wilson Henry Irvine, 2/4/1923, Archives of American Art, Smithsonian Institution, Wilson Henry Irvine papers, Reel 3564.

135 Journal of Wilson Henry Irvine, 7/4/1923, Archives of American Art, Smithsonian Institution, Wilson Henry Irvine papers, Reel 3564. It is most interesting, therefore, to find in the Paul Dougherty Papers at the Archives of American Art, Reel 950, a series of "reference photos" of the Cornish coast. These are likely to have been taken by Douglas and be the photos Irvine is referring to.

136 Journal of Wilson Henry Irvine, 21/4/1923, Archives of American Art, Smithsonian Institution, Wilson Henry Irvine papers, Reel 3564. Recording the walk back from Hore Point, Irvine made one of the most unusual descriptions of St Ives. "In looking down from the moors on the town, that portion between the Island and the main, it looked exactly like a pile of shark guts under the table of the skinners, delicate pinks, grays and violet"!

Fig. 2.53 John Douglas   *Self-Portrait - Double-Exposure*
(courtesy Andrew Lanyon)

Fig. 2.54 Herbert Lanyon *John Douglas*
(probably in his conservatory at Park Avenue)
(St Ives Arts Club)

In 1915, the Douglases decided to move to somewhere bigger and gave up their home on Skidden Hill. They had taken a twenty-one year lease in December 1901, but there was a fourteen year break clause, which they took advantage of by getting their solicitor to serve notice in June 1915. At that time, it was envisaged that Frances Hodgkins would take over the tenancy, but the more oppressive restrictions on outdoor sketching introduced that autumn, which put paid to her painting classes, clearly scotched this plan. One reason why Douglas was in a blind fury when he met George Toman in Porthmeor Square in July (see Chapter 2.4.1) might have related to the landlord's charge for dilapidations. Despite the work that the Douglases had done in 1901, potential tenants of the property in late 1915 did suggest that it was in a poor condition and that it did not have a bathroom. The Douglases moved initially to 2 The Terrace but, by 1917, had settled in 13, Park Avenue (GER £25) and they were based in that road for the rest of John's life. 'Skidden House', after the War, became the home of the architect/artist, George Turland Goosey, who made extensive renovations to the interior.

Sarah Bucknall seems to have enjoyed a wide circle of friends amongst both the artistic and local communities, and her funeral in April 1923 was well attended. Irvine records in his Journal on 1st May that year, "Met Douglas who tells me of the tyranny of his departed mother-in-law and her Will not mentioning his wife, who had cared for her and sacrificed. Sore at the sister".[137] The fact that Douglas was peddling this story perhaps explains why Georgina Bainsmith, several years later, took the most unusual step of having her mother's will published, in its entirety, in the local papers, for this quite clearly shows that she had left her residuary estate as to two thirds to Georgina and one third to Mabel. This was a perfectly reasonable decison, given that Georgina had lived with and looked after her mother, whilst her son, Bruce, had been badly wounded in the First World War.[138] As with his outburst at George Toman, the story does not reflect well on Douglas. Georgina, for her part, not needing so much room, had moved, by 1925, to 5, Albert Place. Both sisters spent the rest of their lives in St Ives, Georgina dying in 1937 and Mabel not until 1956, having lost her husband in 1938. However, neither of the sisters were accorded an obituary notice.

2.2.19 John and Selina Bromley at 'Quay House', Quay Street

As already mentioned, John Bromley came from an artistic family. Although he did not give a St Ives exhibiting address until 1897, a watercolour, *Porthminster Sands*, exhibited at the RBA in 1895 demonstrates that he had visited before.[139] Shortly after his arrival, he fell in love with an art student, Selina Wing (b.c.1857), who was the second daughter of Thomas Wing of Brackendene, Upper Tooting. She had been a regular visitor to the colony since 1891 and probably settled more permanently in the town in 1895.[140] They married in Penzance on 6th April 1899 and took, initially, a small house (GER £6) in St Peter's Street, St Ives. However, in 1905, they acquired from John Tregerthen Short, a local ship and property owner, certain dilapidated cottages in Quay Street, at the end of Smeaton's Pier, which had previously been owned by Canon John Balmer Jones, between 1891 and his death in 1901. Although some of the old thick cottage walls were retained, the outward appearance was completely transformed into a two-storeyed property, with bigger rooms and windows, which they named 'Quay House'. A significant feature was a central large, curved window on the ground floor, whilst the good-sized entrance hall had an ornate staircase, with Breton carvings. A conservatory type studio appears to have been added on the Smeaton's Pier side at the front and this afforded fine views down the pier and across the harbour.[141]

This is one of the only examples of an artist buying property in Down-along, but the fantastic position, that the site enjoyed, outweighed the noise and smells that would have affected them, being so close to the pier. They clearly enjoyed their home, as they stayed there for the rest of their lives, and it afforded John an ideal position from which to paint pictures of the harbour and the bay. However, they were disinclined to open their home on Show Days. Bromley, who always classified himself principally as a Gentleman, was reputedly one of the first St Ives residents to get a car and a telephone.

Bromley acted as Treasurer of the Arts Club in the years 1906-1911 and was often involved in the organisation of the artists' entertainments. He eventually died in May 1939 and Selina in November 1940. The property then passed to John's nephew, Cecil Magnus, who had been much involved with the Arts Club since the mid-1920s, but he sold it in 1941. It has since been the subject of several further substantial renovations, so that it is now unrecognisable from the property designed by the Bromleys. The area of beach by Smeaton's Pier in front of the property is still called Bromley's Foresand.

---

137 Journal of Wilson Henry Irvine, Archives of American Art, Smithsonian Institution, Wilson Henry Irvine papers, Reel 3564.

138 See *St Ives Times* 24/1/1926 re Will. In 1960, Bruce Bainsmith was living at 'Little Wheal Speed' and wrote an article, under the pseudonym, Er-An-Mor, for *Old Cornwall* on the Fuggan Pit there - *Old Cornwall* Vol 5 at p.463-4.

139 His 1894 exhibits at the Winter Exhibition of the RBA - *The Old Lighthouse* and *Over Moor and Sea* could well be Cornish, with the former being of the light on Smeaton's Pier.

140 She is recorded in the Visitors' Lists fromJuly to October 1891 (with Miss A Hall), and in September and October 1894 & 1895. She exhibited at the opening exhibition of the Passmore Edwards Gallery in. Newlyn in 1895 and in Falmouth in 1896 & 1898.

141 I am indebted to Michael Bailey, the current owner of 'Quay House', for much information about the property.

Fig. 2.55 The dilapidated houses in Quay Street which Bromley converted into Quay House   (postcard)

Fig. 2.56 'Quay House' (with conservatory to right) from Smeaton's Pier in the 1950s
(Michael Bailey)

Fig. 2.57 'Chy-an-Porth', The Terrace   (H.J.Healey, Tregenna Studio)   (courtesy Nik Halliday)
This shows the main elevation of the new section added by the Lindners.

2.2.20 Moffat and Gussie Lindner at 'Chy-an-Porth'

The most impressive home created by an artist was Moffat Lindner's 'Chy-an-Porth', situated on the junction of The Terrace and Albert Road, just down the hill and across the road from the Porthminster Hotel. The property had been the home of Dr George Staff, who was well known and liked by the artists, and was bought by the Lindners at auction in 1909, following Staff's death in August 1908. The particulars stated, "The House is built of Granite, is in good repair, of attractive elevation, and commands uninterrupted views of St Ives Bay, Porthminster Beach and Hill", with grounds comprising "nice Flower and Kitchen Gardens and Lawn". This, though, was insufficient for the Lindners, who extended it significantly, adding an impressive full height extension, and completely altering the principal focus of the house. The new elevation, facing the garden, now became the main frontage, with an attractive double arched Loggia leading into a sizeable new main entrance hall, in which the arch shape was repeated. Huge triple windows on each floor are an attractive and unusual feature of this elevation, which is topped off by twin gables and a tall chimney made with alternative layers of brick and stone. The house already had a sitting room (16'4" x 14'4") and a dining room (15' x 22'), both with views across the Bay, but now the Lindners added a further massive Drawing Room (27' x 28'). A rear entrance hall leading on to Talland Road was also created, over which they placed a stone inscribed 'L (Lindner) / M & G (Moffat & Gussie) / 1910' (Fig. 2.58). They also wanted an Italianate style garden and brought over craftsmen from Italy for this purpose. The alterations resulted in the Rate Books recording a GER of £150, more than double that of 'Talland House'.

The purchase and redevelopment of 'Chy-an-Porth' sealed the Lindners' connections with St Ives, as it became their principal home until Moffat's death in 1949. Lindner, therefore, began to exhibit on Show Days for the first time and he became President of the Arts Club for six out of the next seven years, leading the artists through the dark days of the War. However, Lindner also used his wealth to support good causes in the town and to help some of the less well-off artists, such as the New Zealander, Frances Hodgkins, to whom he gave commissions. He was one of the principal organisers of the exhibition by St Ives artists in Cheltenham in 1925, in an effort to get further exposure for the colony, and he gave

Fig. 2.58 'Chy-an-Porth'
Design over rear entrance
L - M & G - 1910

Fig. 2.59 'Chy-an-Porth' - the new main Entrance Hall
(Daphne Pearson)   (courtesy Nik Halliday)

his support to the formation of the St Ives Society of Artists, of which he was President from its formation in 1927 to 1945, when he was well into his nineties. As will be seen, he was also the crucial figure in saving the Porthmeor Studios from development. Gussie Lindner also played a significant role in the community, and 'Chy-an-Porth' became the centre for debates on women's suffrage and other political issues and the location for fund-raising activities for a range of local charitable causes. Sadly, the significance of the property, which was converted into apartments many years ago, has not been appreciated, and it is now in a sorry state, awaiting yet further development in the garden.

Fig. 2.60 The Drawing Room of 'Chy-an-Porth', with Wilson Steer's
portrait of Gussie Lindner to the left of the fireplace
(Daphne Pearson)   (courtesy Nik Halliday)

Fig. 2.61 'Tolvean', the family home of Herbert Lanyon in Redruth   (Schofield family archive)

2.2.21 The homes of Herbert Lanyon

William Herbert Lanyon (1863-1936) was one of the very few locals to be an integral part of the artist community in St Ives, albeit he was primarily a musician and a photographer. Born in Redruth, Lanyon was one of eleven children. His father owned the local gasworks and had made money investing in Malaysian tin mines. Herbert was the only member of the family to have artistic sensibilities and, as a result, at home, he felt like a fish out of water, whilst his relatives thought him odd. Lanyon was clearly a very intense young man and he prepared, for delivery to his father, a thirty page document, which he entitled *Address by the Defendant in Reputation of Charges preferred by the Prosecution*. He later told a woman that he had met in America, in typically convoluted style, "We have been strangers all our lives - my father, my mother, brothers and, alas, all my sisters, and myself, and we are strangers yet, to remain so, until some power, more than human, remove the obscuring veils from eyes that are blind, and let in more spiritual light, revealing more of eternal truth, to give those who judge, knowledge wherewith to do so with justice."[142]

Lanyon attended The Leys, Cambridge, a Wesleyan school, before studying the piano at the Royal College of Music. In 1887, he was appointed Professor of Music at the College, Harrogate.[143] He is first recorded as visiting St Ives in August 1890, when he stayed with Mrs Mitchell in Royal Square throughout the autumn. He became an early member of the Arts Club, where his musical ability will have been much appreciated. In fact, one of the first suggestions, to which he put his name, was that one of the ladies' nights should, in future, be open to all members and be devoted to music. He was also happy for one of the men's evenings to be devoted to drawing. In November that year, Wyly Grier and himself provided the entertainment for the St Ives Parish Church Club in the National School, with Grier singing songs and Lanyon playing a piano solo. In 1891, he was back staying with Mrs Mitchell between July and late October, and offered music tuition. In 1892, he gave an innovative lecture in the Wesley Hall, advocating that musical societies should be open to all comers, with no restrictions as to social standing or monetary qualifications, and that Churches should put on musical entertainments for the public at large.[144] However valid and interesting his arguments, he is likely to have lost his audience, as the talk lasted one hour forty-five minutes!

---

142 Letter dated 8/12/1899 from 'Tolvean', Redruth to Mrs W.R.Bond of Kankakee - Lanyon family archive.

143 See *Cornish Telegraph* 1/12/1887. He was also appointed Organist at the Trinity Wesleyan Chapel in Harrogate.

144 *St Ives Weekly Summary*, 30/1/1892.

A watercolour, dated 1886, demonstrates that Lanyon had an early interest in art and, in 1891, he had an oil, *Summer Evening on Porthmeor Beach*, hung at the RCPS exhibition in Falmouth. However, although, as late as 1909, he was still attending art classes - those run by the American, Frank Shill - , he does not appear to have exhibited a painting again.[145]

In the mid-1890s, Lanyon decided to try to pursue his musical career in America. He based himself in Kankakee, near Chicago, during 1895-6, and not only performed concerts and taught the piano, but also gave lectures. He was hampered, however, by lack of funds, for he could not afford a studio in the centre of town. In a bitter mood, for in his "inmost heart", he held his father "solely responsible" for his failures, he told his mother, "My lectures set people talking, but the lecturer was lost to sight; my music elicited the applause of my audiences, but the musician was buried in oblivion. To find, W.H.Lanyon, in a city of nearly two million inhabitants, was more hopeless than to search for a hair in a haystack".[146] However, according to Charles Marriott, his professional career in America was cut short, when he was involved in a railway accident and injured his hand.[147] Indeed, it seems that he was so seriously hurt that he read his own obituary in the paper! He returned to Kankakee again in 1898-9, when he gave music lessons, but left in April 1899 "to obey duty's bidding".

Fig. 2.62 Edmund Fuller Bookplate for Herbert Lanyon
(Lanyon family archive)

---

145 Martyn Rowe, Redruth - auction dated 30/1/2009 Lot 19.
146 Letter to his mother dated16/2/1896 from Chicago - Lanyon family archive.
147 Charles Marriott, *Memories of Cornwall's Art Colonies, Cornish Review*, Spring 1949, No 1, at p.70.

Fig.2.63 Herbert Lanyon   *Sydney Schofield*
(the second son of Elmer and Murielle Schofield)
(Schofield family archive)

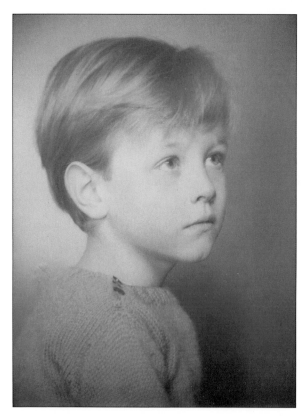

Figs. 2.64 & 2.65 Herbert Lanyon
(left)   *Peter Lanyon*
(right)   *Peter and Mary Lanyon on north cliffs*
(Schofield/Lanyon family archive)

Fig. 2.66   Herbert Lanyon   *The Wave* (or *The Cornish Giant*)   (RCPS award 1906)
(courtesy Andrew Lanyon)

In St Ives, the layman could detect no impairment to his musical prowess, and he again played an important role in the musical activities of the town, organising musical evenings at various venues, which often featured his own compositions. In 1903, he advertised lessons in "pianoforte playing, voice culture and singing to a strictly limited number of pupils" at 4 Sea View Terrace on Wednesday and Saturday afternoons. However, it was the 'At Home' musical parties that he hosted on Sunday evenings that proved particularly popular.

Lanyon is now best remembered as a photographer, and we are indebted to him for many of the portrait photos of his contemporaries, such as those of Fred Milner, Herbert Fitzherbert, John Douglas and Elmer Schofield. He seems to have started by doing portrait photographs of women. Murielle Schofield, however, was not impressed by him initially, passing scathing comment on his appearance in a letter to her husband; "What a dreadfully untidy, dissipated young man he looks - long hair, long trousers and Norfolk jacket with belt dangling and his face crying out to be shaved."[148] However, she later went down to have a look at some of his work in his studio and, despite thinking that a number of the women photographed looked a little "frowsy", decided that her two sons and herself should be taken. She was very pleased with the results (see Fig. 2.63) and thought the charge of 15/- per photo was very reasonable. Lanyon went on to win awards at the RCPS, in 1906, for a photographic portrait and, in 1908, for 'Portrait of a Lady'. By this juncture, he had taken a tenancy of one of the loft studios in the building next to the churchyard in St Andrew's Street, which he named 'The Attic Studio' and this was to be his work base for the next decade.

Lanyon also did landscape and marine photography and, on Show Day in 1914, the comment was passed that "his artist-comrades have often found his studies of sea and coast scenes of help and inspiration for their works in oil and watercolour".[149] A photo called *The Wave* or *The Cornish Giant* (Fig. 2.66) also won an award at Falmouth in 1906 and was widely reproduced. Lanyon said that the wave itself knocked him off the rock upon which he had been standing to take the shot and so he was lucky that the photograph was not damaged. In order to advertise his work, Lanyon arranged for a fine mahogany case containing "several artistic and well-executed specimens of the photographers art" to be erected at the railway station.

Lanyon did eventually marry in 1916, his wife being a Camborne girl, Lilian Vivian, the daughter of the draper, John Vivian, who had served as a member of Cornwall County Council from its inception.[150] She had been married before, but had been left widowed with a young child, Gerald.[151] They shared

---

148 Letter from Murielle Schofield to Elmer Schofield dated 26/11/1903 (Schofield Archive).

149 *St Ives Weekly Summary*, 27/3/1914

150 This probably prompted Lanyon to stand in the County Council elections in 1919.

151 Her first husband, Gerald Gordon-Smith, whom she married on 1/2/1907 was a talented sportsman, playing rugby for England, but he died on the boat returning from South Africa, where the Vivians had mining interests, in 1911. Her son, Gerald, died from TB in South Africa aged only 23 in 1931.

Fig. 2.67 'The Red House' in 1962 (since demolished).
Lanyon and his neighbours allowed their grounds to be used
once a year for the Scouts' 'Jolliday'.
(St Ives Trust Archive Study Centre)

a great interest in music, Lilian being a capable violinist, and, indeed, before her first marriage, they had performed together in a number of concerts. On their marriage, they moved into 'The Red House', a significant property in The Bellyars, which had been built at the turn of the century and comprised drawing, dining and breakfast rooms, a servants' hall, kitchen, scullery and butler's pantry and eleven bedrooms.[152] Herbert created a studio in his new home, which he also called 'The Attic Studio', and in addition to himself, this was to be used during the First World War by the Belgian refugee artist, Louis Reckelbus. The American illustrator, Frank Ver Beck, was another foreign artist, who became a good friend during the War years.

After the War, Lanyon became more involved with the running of the Arts Club, serving as Treasurer between 1920 and 1922, before being elected President in 1922 and 1923. He continued his photography and now had two very attractive new models - his two children, Mary and Peter, who were born in 1917 and 1918 respectively. A picture of his son, Peter, (Fig. 2.64), who was to become the best known of the Cornish-born artists, also won an award. It was about this time that Herbert cut off his little finger, whilst using his printing press. Although he stuck it back on, it never bent properly again, and this impeded his piano playing yet further.[153] During the 1920s, though, Lanyon devoted himself increasingly to a wide range of local causes and, upon his death in 1936, his contribution to the community, which is discussed further below, was much lauded.

Fig. 2.68 Lilian and Herbert Lanyon in later life

152 See advert in *St Ives Weekly Summary*, 2/9/1910, which indicates that it was subject to a lease for 999 years from 1901.
153 This story was told to me by the family and therefore seems to be a different accident to that mentioned by Marriott.

ACCOMODATION FOR ARTISTS AND THEIR LITERARY FRIENDS OUT OF TOWN

2.3.1   Introduction

St Ives, for all its attractions, often stank of fish. Catches were gutted on the beach and the remains left for the gulls. The open stone channels, along which pilchard juices used to run, can still be seen in parts of the town, and these not only smelt but were an attraction for rats, which were a common problem. As the fishing fleet returned in the middle of the night, there was also much activity in the early hours and a good deal of noise as pony-led carts were drawn over the cobbles. Sleep, on occasion, must have been difficult for those living anywhere near the harbour. Unsurprisingly, therefore, some artists, right from the outset, decided that it was far more congenial to stay in one of the neighbouring villages, even if they had taken a studio in St Ives. The trip to and from town each day was easily done by train, using the branch line stations at Carbis Bay or Lelant.

2.3.2   Carbis Bay - General

Carbis Bay has been so completely and utterly spoilt by over-development of the worst kind that it is hard to imagine that, when the art colony at St Ives was first established, there were hardly any buildings in the area at all. Indeed, the name Carbis Bay had only recently been coined by the railway company for their station in the Carbis Valley. Previously, as when Edward William Cooke had been sketching, in October 1848, the storage huts on the beach, with roofs made from upturned seine boats (Fig. 1.2), it had been known as Carrick Gladden Cove. The railway, however, did more than merely change the name of the area, and its presence led to a burgeoning tourist industry, as the remains of the tin and copper mining activity, that had dominated the landscape in mid-century, were tidied up, and a series of pleasure gardens, which catered for tourists and school parties, were laid out. Payne's Tea Gardens, Hawke's Bay Picnic Grounds and the Carbis Valley Picnic Grounds were some of the areas, where the public could enjoy the scenery and visit a grotto and wishing well, whilst children could find things to do and places to play.[154] Even as early as July 1881, some fifteen hundred schoolchildren and their teachers were entertained there.

2.3.2.1 Hotels and lodgings in Carbis Bay

Soon a demand arose for accomodation and this was met initially by Maria Hendra (née Jenkin), a Scorrier-born girl, who had been working as a confectioner and pastry cook with her husband, Charles, in Camborne (Fig. 2.69). As her husband's health had suffered during his time as a miner in South America, she felt that the bracing air at Carbis Bay might be beneficial and so, in 1887, she built a small property, 'Maria Villa', on the cliff edge in Carbis Bay, and took in lodgers. As her reputation grew, so did the size of the property. In 1889, it was considerably extended and, by 1892, it was known as 'Hendra's Hotel'. Guests came from all walks of life - "Cabinet ministers, Colonial governors, famous painters, soldiers and sailors, engineers, diplomats, North Country manufacturers, newspaper editors, schoolmasters, ministers of religion of all denominations, University professors, men and women from every quarter of the compass".[155] However, Maria Hendra was known for her "singular gift of making all classes at ease with each other" and, despite her refusal to obtain a licence, the hotel became well-known nationally for its excellent food and friendly welcome. On her death in 1931, it was taken over by her nephew, Thomas Scott Brown, who had been assisting her since her husband died in 1908, and the hotel was run by this one family for ninety-eight years. Sadly, not even this provenance has prevented it from being demolished recently.

---

154 The first of these was Payne's Tea Gardens set up by William and Jane Payne on land belonging to Little Gonwin Farm but they abandoned this in 1868 for what was then an unpromising stretch of neglected mining land nearer the beach, where they planted trees and shrubs and created winding paths down to the beach. In 1897, their son, John, opened a new picnic ground north of the railway and various amusements were installed. A grotto, wishing well, boating lake and a room with a fine floor for dancing followed over the years. In 1883, Edward Ashton, a pharmacist and photographer from St Ives, and his wife, who was also a pharmacist, took over Hawke's Point Picnic Grounds, which they ran well into the 1920s. The Carbis Valley Picnic Grounds were set up by a Mr Williams in the 1890s and were run by him into the 1930s, whilst there are also references to Annie's Picnic Grounds in Carbis Valley. See Wendy Smaridge's research paper *Carbis Bay After the Mines Closed - Tea Gardens and Picnic Gardens*, St Ives Archive Centre.

155 *The Cornishman and Cornish Telegraph*, 8/4/1931.

Fig. 2.69 Charles and Maria Hendra   (Little Hendra)

Fig. 2.70 The original 'Maria Villa', Carbis Bay
(Little Hendra)

Fig. 2.71 'Hendra's Hotel', after several extensions   (Little Hendra)

The first artists to lodge with Maria Hendra, in August 1889, were Evelyn and Ethel Stocker, two St Austell-born sisters, who both worked as art teachers and who returned to study in St Ives on a number of occasions. The most important group of artists, though, who stayed with Mrs Hendra in the days when the property was still known as 'Maria Villa', congregated there in the autumn of 1890. Laurence Scott, a landscape painter from Cheltenham, in fact, arrived with his wife in May and stayed for some five months. They were joined in early August by another Cheltenham-based landscape painter, Fred Milner and his wife, to whom they had no doubt recommended the establishment. Then, at the end of August, Alfred East and his wife arrived and stayed for five weeks. It was most probably during their time together at Hendra's in September 1890 that Milner developed his great admiration for the work of East, and a lifetime's friendship, which was to have a major impact on his career, was forged.

Possibly after hearing from East of the great "kindness and attention" that he had received from Mrs Hendra, Edward and Vesta Simmons, and their two children, booked in to 'Maria Villa' on 1st December 1890 and stayed four months. Despite being based in St Ives for some six years, they never seemed to have a settled abode, but moved between London, St Ives and the Continent with some regularity. The marine painter, Alfred Warne-Browne and his family, who had been living in Charlestown, Carbis Bay at the time of the Census earlier that year, moved to 'Maria Villa' by April 1891 and stayed for several months, whilst Laurence Scott and his wife, having clearly enjoyed their long stay the previous summer, returned in July 1891. Other artists to stay with Mrs Hendra that year included Percy Northcote, one of the Bushey trained men, and Gertrude Rosenberg.

The artist, who formed the closest connection with Hendra's Hotel, however, was John Ward Girdlestone, a civil engineer, who took up painting in his retirement and was a regular student of Julius Olsson. Writing in the hotel's Visitors' Book in December 1908, he commented that his wife, Ellen, and himself had "since the autumn of 1891, with the exception of but a few months, made Hendra's Hotel their home and headquarters". It seems clear from the 1901 Census, which lists them in "part of" Hendra's Hotel, with Girdlestone being named as head of the household, that they took an apartment in the hotel, albeit most probably taking meals with regularity with the other guests. Certainly, in January 1904, they met the young art student, Brian Hatton, and his family friends the Lancasters, who were staying in the hotel, and it was through Girdlestone that Hatton managed to meet a number of the leading artists in the colony (see Chapter 2.6.4).   On his departure, Hatton did in the Visitors' Book a quick sketch of his dog, 'Gyrth', who seems to have enjoyed terrorising the local cats. When the Girdlestones did eventually leave after seventeen years, they did not go far, but moved into 'The Nest' (now known as 'Cliff Cottage'), a nearby property that had been built in 1889 by Captain Josiah Thomas. A reserved man, Girdlestone did not socialise with the other artists very much and, when he died in 1911, no artist attended his funeral. However, the presence of their grand-daughter, Miss Lola Lee, who had become "a famous and refined dancer", caused a stir in 1914, as she performed as a captive in a Siberian prison to great acclaim in the Public Hall during her stay.[156] Ellen Girdlestone died in 1919.

Another painter, who stayed on a regular basis for extended periods of time at Hendra's Hotel, was the Edinburgh-born artist, Stuart William Tatton Hobkirk (1868-1940). This was principally because the hotel was the favoured residence of his mother, who styled herself Baroness Farina Firras, although the 1891 Census, when she was living in Cheltenham, records her name as simply Marella Firras. She is first recorded in the Visitors' Book in July 1897, when both Stuart Hobkirk and her much younger son, Raffael Firras, were with her, and was a regular there until 1904, when she acquired property first in St Ives and then in Lelant. Like the Girdlestones, she may have taken a separate apartment in the hotel, as she too is described as 'Head' of the household in the 1901 Census, although she and Stuart are listed under Hendra's Hotel. She was a red-headed woman, who clearly made quite an impression on the young Brian Hatton, and was welcomed in artistic circles. Louie Whitehouse, after "a charming afternoon spent with Baroness Farina", commented, "I would that I had her ease of manner and readiness of expression."[157]

Another artist, whose experiences at Hendra's Hotel led him to decide to settle in Carbis Bay, was Albert Moulton Foweraker. Foweraker was the son of the Headmaster of Exeter Cathedral School and his family first stayed at Hendra's in July 1898. They settled in the village in 1901 and he and his wife ran 'Headlands', a new lodging house built by the Freeman family a few years before. Foweraker made a big impression in the colony with his acting and musical talents, and ran frequent painting trips to Spain. When the Fowerakers left shortly after the War, 'Headlands' became a school and is now a Care Home.[158]

---

156 *St Ives Times*, 1/5/1914.

157 Letter from Louie to Arnold Whitehouse dated 20/5/1896, Whitehouse Family Archive, Gloucester Records Office, Churchdown District, D6035, (Bundle 2/2).

158 Rocklands School from Hastings was at 'Headlands' during the Second World War.

Fig. 2.72 W E Freeman   *Sketch from Visitors' Book, Hendra's Hotel*   (Little Hendra)

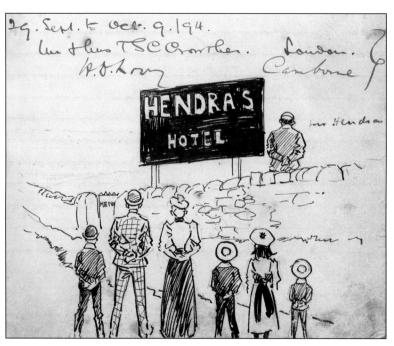

Fig. 2.73 A.D.Lowry   *Sketch from Visitors' Book, Hendra's Hotel*
(Little Hendra)

Guests at the Hotel occasionally did sketches in the Visitors' Book and the most impressive (Fig. 2.72) is by Wilfred Freeman, who stayed in October 1904. Eating, playing golf and sleeping seem to be the principal pastimes that he indulged in, but he fitted in some painting as well, for he exhibited several of his watercolour sketches of St Ives and Hayle at the RCPS exhibition in Falmouth in 1906.

Another place to stay in Carbis Bay was in the cottage owned by the Ashtons at Hawke's Point. Edward Ashton and his wife were both pharmacists and had a shop in a large corner house opposite the Market House in St Ives. She acquired a reputation as "the lady with the magic hands", due to her ability to save lives and limbs through her massages and magnetic touch.[159] She was also a water diviner, which led some to view her as a witch. She was certainly a teller of tall stories and claimed that she was descended from Robert Bruce. Artist visitors would also have been told about her two family portraits by Henry Raeburn, which she had loaned to South Kensington Museum. Edward Ashton was one of the earliest photographers in St Ives and, in addition to the pharmacy, he had a further shop for his photographic activities at the top of Skidden Hill, where the Catholic Church now stands. In addition to these professional activities, the Ashtons ran the Hawke's Point Picnic Grounds and let rooms. They also had a large studio, with exquisite views, that could be rented. Emma Loam, who was one of the Ashtons' first lodgers in 1885, described this studio, which she and her husband hired, in addition to the three rooms in the cottage, as the sitting room was small. "The view from this studio was exquisite, and we never tired of it whether in fine or wet weather. The golden sands below always made it appear sunny even if it did rain, and then the magnificent bay, in its ever changing colours, sometimes blue as an Italian picture, purple, green, grey and, in a storm, almost black" [160] The existence of this studio in 1885 clearly makes it one of the very first in the district. It had originally been a mining shed at the head of a shaft and was presumably converted into a studio by Ashton for his photographic work shortly after he took over the property in 1883.[161]

It was this combination of rooms and a fine studio that attracted a number of artists. Sydney Carr stayed there for most of August 1892 on one of his first trips over from Penzance before deciding to move across to St Ives permanently. However, it was the London society painter, George Frederick Sargent,

Fig. 2.74 The Hawkes Point Studio
The upturned half boat in which Havelock Ellis worked can be seen on the right

159 See *Woman's Magic Hands - Saving Lives and Limbs, St Ives Times*, 11/7/1924.
160 Emma Loam, *Carbis Bay - Past and Present*, St Ives Archive Centre. This is a most interesting account, written in 1929, of life at Mrs Ashtons in the 1880s.
161 See Havelock Ellis, *My Life*, London, 1940 at p.273.

Fig. 2.75 Edmund Fuller   *The Rocket* (RA 1899)
This was a reconstruction of the wreck of the *Rosedale* during the *Cintra* gale.

who perhaps stayed there most frequently, on his visits to St Ives in the last few years of his life. Although he did stay at Hendra's Hotel in August 1898, he tended to prefer to lodge with Mrs Ashton. However, his first visit in late 1893, when he was accompanied by his niece, Agnes Richardson, who was also an artist, involved high drama, for they were there the day of what is now referred to as the *Cintra* gale - the terrible occasion when three steamers were wrecked at Carbis Bay and seven members of the crew of the *Cintra* lost their lives. The local paper recorded, "The scenes from the cliffs at Carbis Bay and St Ives on Saturday will be remembered as among the grandest, most terrible and exciting that have ever been witnessed on our Cornish coast."[162] There were many tales of exceptional bravery, and some fifty of the shipwrecked sailors were put up by Mrs Hendra and Mrs Ashton.

A guest at Hendra's Hotel commented, in the Visitors' Book, that, despite having dozens of ship-wrecked sailors to look after, Mrs Hendra ensured that her other guests were hospitably entertained, whilst the local paper recorded, "The kindness of Mr F.Sargent, his niece, Miss Richardson, Mrs Ashton of the picnic grounds and Mr Ashton of St Ives was unlimited. Garments, stimulants, food, medicine, money - everything, in short, was freely given by Mrs Ashton and her lodger, Mr Sargent, so that every want of Cromwell and Edward Jones, [two of the *Cintra* survivors] who had escaped death, were fully met, regardless of the cost and personal inconveniences. This kindness and hospitality was also extended to those who had assisted in any way in rescue work."[163]

It was during this first visit that Sargent painted his most famous Cornish work, *Catch of Pilchards off St Ives* (Back Cover), now hanging on the stairs of the St Ives Guildhall. His niece, Agnes Richardson, who appears to have modelled, but not in the nude, for both John William Waterhouse and Herbert Draper, was clearly his pupil, and she had five small works included in the RCPS exhibition in Falmouth in 1894.[164] Her greatest success, though, was a Dartmoor landscape, which was hung at the Royal Academy in 1896 and rated by the art critic of *St James' Gazette* as "the strongest landscape by a woman that he had ever seen".[165] The pair returned to Carbis Bay and St Ives a number of times before Sargent's death in 1899. Without his encouragement, Agnes ceased exhibiting in 1902 and she was living at Clarence House, Penzance when she later joined the West Cornwall Golf Club.

---

162 Unidentified paper in St Ives Archive Centre.

163 Unidentified paper in St Ives Archive Centre.

164 See Simon Toll, *Herbert Draper 1863-1920 - A Life Study*, Woodbridge, 2003 at p.59 and p.171. Draper, to whom Agnes was introduced by Waterhouse, apparently felt that Agnes' sister, Edith, was a better model. Sargent's niece is not the postcard designer, Agnes Richardson, who was born in 1884.

165 *St Ives Weekly Summary* 6/3/1897 but page heading dated 6/2/1897. A note in *St Ives Weekly Summary* 1/2/1896 makes mention of her work *For men must work and women must weep*, which was engraved, and *The Engagement Ring*, featuring a sailor and his sweetheart.

The studio at Hawke's Point subsequently became the writing base of Havelock Ellis for ten years. He described it as "a rough little building", "convenient and yet solitary and isolated" and recalled how his friend, the gay socialist poet and philosopher, Edward Carpenter, had declared that "my hermitage had one of the finest outlooks on the whole English coast".[166] Outside, half a boat had been set on end against the hillside, and Ellis, who preferred working out of doors, found that, in this little ivy-covered shelter, he was often able to read or write, even during the winter months. Ellis fondly remembered his time in the studio - "I was able to work in complete freedom and under conditions that suited me perfectly". His tenure only came to an end when Mrs Ashton decided that she wanted "to put the place to other uses", and so it presumably ceased thereafter to be a studio.[167]

The most impressive and expensive hotel in Carbis Bay, known simply as the Carbis Bay Hotel, was erected in 1894 to the design of the leading Cornish architect of the nineteenth century, Silvanus Trevail. It opened within a week of the Porthminster Hotel in St Ives and was aimed at much the same market. However although a number of artists, or their relatives, are recorded as staying the odd night in the hotel, cost considerations, as much as anything, dictated that it was not a regular haunt for anyone, other than the Exeter-born art student, John Littlejohns, whose father seems to have been an investor in the hotel company.

Fig. 2.76 Havelock Ellis in the studio at Hawke's Point in 1897

---

166 Havelock Ellis, *My Life*, London, 1940 at p.273.
167 ibid at p.274.

2.3.2.2 Rented property in Carbis Bay

The St Ives Rate Books do not cover the Carbis Bay area and no residents listed in Kelly's Directory for that area during the 1890s are artists. However, it is known that the American, Frederick Waugh, rented Fern Cottage during his stay in the area in 1895-6 and, indeed, his son, Coulton, was born there. However, the 1901 Census reveals that Arnesby and Mia Brown, Max and Helen Ludby, Herbert Turner and the Australian, David Davies, and his wife, Janet, had taken properties on the Longstone Downs behind Carbis Bay.

It is likely that Arnesby Brown, following his marriage in 1896, required more genteel surroundings than Tregethas Farm, near St Erth, where he appears to have lodged in the preceding years, but there is no mention of his name in the St Ives Rate Books until 1906, when he took a property in Pednolver Terrace for a couple of years. On the few occasions that he is signed into the Arts Club, an address of 'Carbis Bay' is given and it is likely, therefore, that he was based here during the winter months in the decade spanning the turn of the century.

The Davieses returned to St Ives for their second visit in 1898 and stayed in the area until 1904. They lived initially in the town, but, in 1899, they decided to move out and their son, Hanbury, was born in Carbis Bay. Davies took students during this period and a number may have stayed with him or in the locality. The Ludbys too, at the time of the Census, had had a child within the last year, called Jessie. They are first recorded in St Ives shortly after their marriage in September 1894 and were regular visitors. Both were artists, Max at that time working principally in watercolour. He was also a stalwart of drama productions in the town. It seems that a stay at Hendra's Hotel, when they visited in 1897, led them to decide to base themselves in Carbis Bay during their further visits in the first decade of the new century. In 1904, Ludby used an exhibiting address of 'The Croft', Carbis Bay - this is the property in Porthrepta Road, now known as 'The Old Vicarage'. They returned for an extended visit in 1907-8, during which time Ludby's work caused some discussion for its daring use of primary colours only, but they resigned from the Arts Club in August 1908 to paint in Paris. Although there is no further reference to them in artistic circles, they are still recorded at 'The Croft' in Kelly's Directory of 1910. At the end of the War, 'The Croft' was rented by David and Frances Horne, who sponsored the foundation of the Leach Pottery, and, in the 1920s, it was occupied by two promising young artists, Percy and Marjorie Ballance, and their parents.[168]

Herbert William John Turner, an artist from Bristol, was a long-term resident of Carbis Bay, living initially in 'Endsleigh', a detached double-fronted villa with ten rooms, before moving in 1920 to 'Briardene', where he was still living in 1930. His wife, Louisa, was from Zennor and they had, at the time of the 1901 Census, a daughter aged one, who had been born in Morvah.[169] However, little is known about his work - he only exhibited between 1898 and 1908 - and, although he became a member of the Arts Club in December 1904, he does not appear to have socialised with the other artists overmuch. However, his daughters, Dorothy and Irene, were regular performers at the Carbis Bay Institute in the 1920s and became great friends of the Horne's daughter, Margery, leading them to be actively involved in the St Ives Handicraft Guild, which Frances Horne set up.

2.3.2.3 The Carbis Bay homes of Havelock and Edith Ellis

It is difficult to believe that Havelock and Edith Ellis were ever fully embraced by St Ives society, despite Havelock's extraordinary erudition on a wide range of subjects, which encompassed drama, literary criticism, poetry, science, psychology, travel, translation, editing and, of course, the study of sex, for which he is now best known. Their unconventional marriage, which, within its first year, saw both having relationships with other women, and, during which they frequently lived apart, would have raised eyebrows, particularly as a frustrated suitor of Havelock's mistress, Mneme Barker Smith, highlighted the affair in public. Whilst the quick-tempered Edith became friends with a number of artists, her lesbian relationships were bound to have initiated gossip and, at that time, would have been considered improper. If social contact was a little strained beforehand, then the furore surrounding the publication in 1897 of Havelock's book on homosexuality, *Sexual Inversion*, will have made matters much worse. This was just two years after Oscar Wilde had been jailed for sodomy and the book led to the criminal trial of a bookseller, George Bedborough, for obscenity in 1898.[170]

168 Their mother, Isabel, died on 9/11/1931 aged 67. Both her and her husband, John des Carriere Ballance, who died aged 57, are buried at St Uny, Lelant.

169 The death of Mrs Turner is recorded in *St Ives Times*, 30/12/1927.

170 The position would not have been helped by the further publicity surrounding the publication in 1899 of the second volume in the series - *Studies in the Psychology of Sex* - , for this, contrary to Ellis' express directions, had been printed in England also and, when the police eventually tracked down the publisher in 1902, he committed suicide and the whole edition was destroyed. See Havelock Ellis, *My Life*, London, 1967 (original 1940) at p. 313.

However, it was not only Havelock's writings that caused outrage, for, in 1898, Edith published a novel *Seaweed - A Cornish Idyll*, which also scandalised certain sections of society, not only because of its subject, but also because of the occasional unconventional freedom of its language. In the novel, a Cornish seaman, rendered impotent by an accident, not only forgives, but encourages, adultery by his wife, whilst she eventually comes to the conclusion that there is a greater, spiritual love than mere physical passion. The story, as Havelock admits, was inspired by their own relationship, for they did love each other deeply, despite the lack of physical relations between them, and he accepted, if not actively encouraged, her lesbian affairs.[171]

The very unusual love affair between Havelock and Edith did, in fact, blossom in Cornwall. They had met initially in London in 1887, at a time when Edith (née Lees) had been Secretary of the socialist Society, *Fellowship of the New Life*, but had been unimpressed with each other. Then, by chance, in 1890, they found themselves staying at the same cottage in Lamorna - she in the midst of a walking tour, he, whilst serving as a medical locum. A few days later, they bumped into each other again in St Ives and realised that they were overjoyed to see each other. They had vastly contrasting personalities - he was reserved, diffident and sensitive - always a dreamer -, whilst she had an ever fresh and eager vivacity that was quite childlike. She used to tell her friends, "I am his champagne, and he is my opium."[172]

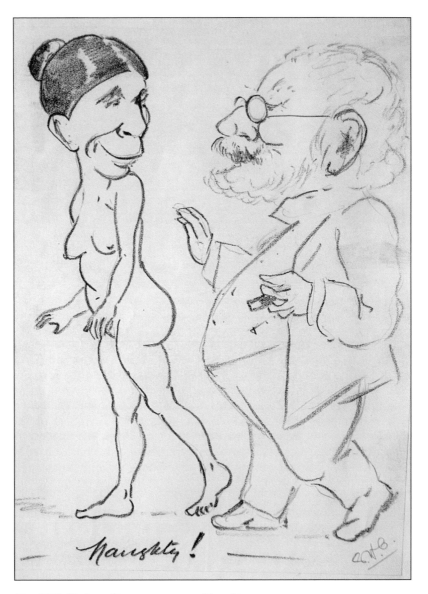

Fig. 2.77 Sydney Carr   *Naughty*
(the late Derek Wintle/Andrew Eggleston)

---

171 The book was an unfortunate casualty of the collapse of Havelock's publisher, but a longer version was subsequently published in 1907 under the name *Kit's Woman : A Cornish Idyll*.
172 Havelock Ellis, *My Life*, London, 1967 (original 1940) at p. 216.

Fig. 2.78 Edith and Havelock Ellis in 'The Count House' in 1896.
This was Ellis' favourite photo of the diminutive Edith.

After their marriage in December 1891, Havelock tended to join Edith during the winter months in Carbis Bay, where she had taken a cottage, which she called 'The Cot', "from a woman artist friend" - unfortunately not identified - but, during the summer months, when Edith was busily engaged in her various business ventures, Havelock would base himself in London and they would only meet up occasionally. Edith fraternised with the artists, as she had been an art student herself, and she seems initially to have taken one of the new Porthmeor Studios. Indeed, she knew some members of the colony from time spent in Brittany. The American, Edward Simmons, recorded in his autobiography, "There came to Concarneau a young girl, wide-eyed, eager and temperamental, thirsting for a knowledge of life, but knowing about as much of it as the bird just out of the egg. She was alone and studying Art. She asked of the women folk the meaning of marriage and....not so long after her enlightenment, she announced her wedding, and with none other than the now well-known writer - Havelock Ellis." On linking up with her again in St Ives, Simmons found "the one-time timid and childish wife had developed into a charming woman, and, strange to say, a full-fledged raiser of blooded stock."[173] This is a reference to the little farm that Edith established, involving cows, pigs, donkeys, fowls and ducks, which Havelock felt benefitted her fragile health and gratified her native instincts for practical activity and close contact with Nature and Earth.[174] As the farm expanded, she employed a number of locals to assist her.

173 E.E.Simmons, *From Seven to Seventy*, London and New York, 1922 at p.149. Somewhat surprisingly, I have had scholars of Edith Eliis doubting Simmons' account, on the basis that Havelock Ellis states at p.251 of *My Life* that, prior to their honeymoon in Paris, she had only been abroad once and then to Switzerland.

174 Havelock Ellis, *My Life*, London, 1940 at p.279. Simmons commented further on her farming venture, "She it was who tended the wants of the baby bulls and colts, was in at the birth and deaths of the animals; while Havelock sat by the warmth of his very delightful fire-place, smoking his pipe and probably mulling over the psychological effect of all this on the feminine mind. Anyway, I had a delightful time and, upon his refusal to help her, I held the head of a baby calf while she slipped a dose of oil down its throat, oblivious to the fact that I was ruining a beautiful new pair of white flannel trousers." E.E.Simmons, *From Seven to Seventy*, London and New York, 1922 at p.149-50.

Deciding after a while that 'The Cot' was too small, Edith, probably in 1894, rented on a long-lease 'The Count House', built some forty years previously as the headquarters of the nearby mine.[175] Havelock, who was not consulted in this decision, commented, "With windows blocked up all the winter by boards, and never built for a home, it had looked to me a peculiarly dreary, dilapidated, God-forsaken building. But Edith always had an eye for the possibilities of a place; the artist in her delighted to develop these possibilities. Her artistic instincts in the domestic sphere were always right, although her calculation as to the cost of her creative activities were apt to be wrong."[176] Writing in 1906, Edith agreed that it would have been much better financially "to build than to patch and remake a house undermined by dry rot, rats, and leakages", needing a new roof, and with every room "dyed with a flaming terra cotta distemper which took two years to extinguish".[177] Cornish workmen, who made procrastination a profession, drove her witless, and she commented, "As I built up, with the aid of dreamy dwellers in the neighbourhood, some portion of the place one week, I was saved from monotony by another part falling down the next."[178] Indeed, Havelock and herself were lucky to escape serious injury when defective work by their mason led to the bay window in their bedroom collapsing as they slept. In all, the refurbishment took five long years to complete. Whilst the house had a beautiful outlook over sea and moor, Charles Marriott, visiting in the winter of 1903-4, recalled that it was "surrounded by the waste heaps of its activity and furzy crofts, so that the approach was all in the Wuthering Heights atmosphere of my expectations".[179] However, he enjoyed his first meal there, remembering that "the appointment of the house, and the meal, struck me as vaguely and pleasantly foreign - simple furniture, unsecluded books, small dishes, and aromatic things to drink."[180]

Having moved to 'The Count House', Edith then embarked on her other major business venture - holiday lets, as she did not give up 'The Cot', but let it out and, over time, took three other cottages in the neighbourhood, which she did up artistically and let to visitors.[181] These included 'Rose Cottage', on the main road, and the two isolated Moor Cottages.[182] Marriott's first summons to join the Ellises for dinner had been to meet the artist, Frederick Cayley Robinson, who had taken one of these cottages.

Fig. 2.79 Edith Ellis and a friend outside 'The Count House'

175 Havelock Ellis states that they left 'The Count House' in 1906, having been there 12 years.

176 Havelock Ellis, *My Life*, London, 1940 at p.278.

177 Mrs Havelock Ellis, *A Cornish Experiment in Cottages*, The World's Work and Play, September 1906 at p. 361-2.

178 ibid.

179 Charles Marriott in the Preface to Mrs Havelock Ellis, *The Mine of Dreams*, London, 1925 at p.iii.

180 ibid at p.iv.

181 Marriott records that she put in Liberty curtains - C.Marriott, *Memories of Cornwall's Art Colonies*, Cornish Review, Spring 1949, No 1, at p.69.

182 In her article, *A Cornish Experiment in Cottages*, The World's Work and Play, September 1906 at p. 361-3, Edith indicates that she was motivated to put into practice Kant's dictum that every human being should be an end in himself or herself, and not a mere means to an end of another, which had been one of the ideals of the 'Fellowship of the New Life', a socialist Society of which she had been Secretary before her marriage.

Fig. 2.80 Edith Ellis c.1914

He commented that "Mrs Ellis delighted to bring people together; and her hobby of letting cottages... made plenty of opportunities". In addition to Cayley Robinson, he met, in this way, Mr and Mrs Alfred Sidgwick, for whom he found a permanent home at 'Trewoofe', in the Lamorna valley, the writer, Winifred James, and the prominent British Christian Socialist, Conrad Noel, amongst many others. Havelock also recalled how the cottages drew a wide range of visitors. "The most extraordinarily varied people drifted into them. Amid the sprinkling of stodgy suburbans, there were exquisite artists, noted men of letters, soldiers and diplomats, eccentric foreign scholars, runaway wedded couples, people with obscure Continental titles, victims of alcohol and of morphia, on two occasions mysterious and clever adventurers, who of course escaped, even when their true character had been discovered, without paying rent".[183] In particular, Havelock mentioned the future Royal Academician, Henry Bishop, the novelist, Somerset Maugham, the eminent Platonist scholar, Wincenty Lutoslawski, the author, Edward Verrall Lucas, and the South African editor, Edward Garratt.

Edith was a small, round, bustling woman, with a low, musical voice, and extraordinarily bewitching eyes, with the lightest of irises.[184] She had a highly-strung, emotional nature and, therefore, was prone to dramatic mood swings, particularly when ill. She had a reputation in St Ives as "a rough-tongued but warm-hearted woman". Henry Bishop, who became a good friend due to his regular use of her cottages, summed up her character with the words, "Much of the angel and something of Billingsgate"![185] She also liked to cultivate an aura of eccentricity, riding everywhere on a 'jingle' - a donkey and cart - and ostentatiously feeding her donkey on cigarettes![186] She did not attempt to hide her sexual proclivities, openly saying in respect of any good looking female companion, "Isn't she the most beautiful thing you ever saw? Don't you just love her?", a trait that Charles Marriott, for one, found a trifle embarassing.[187] Gussie Lindner, who shared a passion for women's rights, was one of her closest friends amongst the artist community, but it was the delicate Lily Kirkpatrick, with whom she fell in love. Havelock, who seems to have viewed his wife's lesbian affairs as good, first-hand case material, wrote at some length on their relationship.

183 Havelock Ellis, *My Life*, London, 1940 at p.280-1.
184 Charles Marriott in the Preface to Mrs Havelock Ellis, *The Mine of Dreams*, London, 1925 at p.iii.
185 Havelock Ellis, *My Life*, London, 1940 at p.520.
186 ibid at p.vi.
187 ibid at p.vi.

"Edith and Lily only came to know each other slowly. Circumstances - especially the circumstance of the elder sister who ever watched over Lily like a mother - seldom permitted more than occasional and difficult private meetings. Sometimes these were stolen and took place in a quiet wood between St Ives and Carbis. But they often met more openly in Lily's studio at Porthminster [the Pednolva Mine Studio]. On one occasion I gave up my studio at Hawkes Point for the day, to enable them to picnic quietly there. It was but rarely indeed that they could spend the night together and that Lily would hurry to Carbis with her little nightdress at a late hour when she had almost been given up.... [Edith] was indefatigable in her devotion and endlessly inventive in a lover's attentions. At such times she had all the air and spirit of an eager boy, even the deliberate poses and gestures of a boy, never of a man, and on one side of her, deeply woman-hearted as she was, it was more than a pose, with her restless activity and her mischievousness and her merry ringing laugh...To Lily this boyish ardour was certainly delightful, as delightful as was Lily's ethereal fragility to Edith.....Lily's purity, with its brightness and reserve - a reserve that seemed to both of them deeper than the more superficial reserve of the English - and its flashes of audacity, together with her charming wit, and the touch of the instinctive artist in all her actions, suited Edith perfectly. Throughout her life she had numerous intimate relationships with women, but no woman, before or after, ever appealed to her so deeply, or satisfied her so utterly, as Lily."[188]

When Lily became terminally ill in 1902 with Bright's disease, a kidney disorder, her sister made it difficult for Edith to see her, and, when she did, she was scarcely ever alone with her. After her death that June, Edith "dedicated to her a kind of worship which increased rather than lessened as the years went by".[189] She bought the adjoining burial plot at Lelant and visited her grave in times of trial, finding rest and consolation there.[190] "Every little present that Lily had given her was cherished, constantly used indeed, but guarded with anxious care", particularly Lily's brooch which she wore at all times, and she spent the next ten years putting together an anthology of love poems, *The Lover's Calendar*, which was inspired by Lily and their relationship and which she called "the epitome of a love-history".

Fig. 2.81 Lily Kirkpatrick, shortly before her death in 1902

---

188 Havelock Ellis, *My Life*, London, 1940 at p.325-6.
189 Havelock Ellis, *My Life*, London, 1940 at p.327.
190 She eventually gave the plot up when she decided in favour of cremation.

Fig. 2.82 Moor Cottages, Carbis Bay
The hut on the left was constructed for Havelock to write in.

After Lily's death, Edith started to write humorous short stories based on her experiences in Cornwall and these were published together, to considerable acclaim, as *My Cornish Neighbours*, in 1906. I utilise extracts from them on a number of occasions, as they provide a most valuable insight into the foibles of the locals and their reactions to the artists and other 'foreigners' living in their midst.

The Ellises stayed at 'The Count House' for twelve years, before being approached in 1906 by a Company that wanted to re-open the mine.[191] They offered Edith £10 to clear out, but she managed to negotiate a fee of £200. The timing was ideal, as she had grown tired of the farm, hating, in particular, the slaughter of the animals. 'The Count House' later became the home of Bernard Leach, who divided it into two, and the base of a prehistoric hut dwelling was found in the garden.

The Ellises simply moved to the two Moor Cottages, occupying one each. Havelock explained, "The two Moor cottages in a single building stood inland at an isolated and awkwardly situated spot behind the mine and off the road, only approached by rough paths. It was a beautifully peaceful place, with no houses in sight, facing the south, the grounds running down to a little streamlet near to a well... They were small plain ordinary labourers' cottages containing altogether four small and four very small rooms. The two upper front rooms were the best and with the pleasantest outlook. That in the right hand cottage became Edith's study and bedroom and that on the left mine."[192] Edith also set up two summer houses in the garden for them each to use as further studios, as she too now concentrated on her writing, producing novels and short stories, and preparing lectures on a variety of socialist, philosophical and scientific topics.[193] She also arranged for *The Subjection of Kezia*, one of the stories in *My Cornish Neighbours*, to be transformed into a play and it received good notices at various leading London theatres and in the provinces. However, during their time in Moor Cottages, Edith was frequently ill, with a heart condition and a bout of broncho-pneumonia.

As her writing and lecturing activities took her more and more to London, and as she had received advice that the climate of Cornwall was not good for her health, Edith decided in 1910 to give up the Moor Cottages and, henceforth, to use 'Rose Cottage', as their Cornish base, whenever they were in the area. Havelock commented that, once before, they had lived in it for a few weeks, but had not found it "home-like". "Gradually, however, with her usual ingenuity, Edith had introduced a number of improvements; it had become as pleasant and comfortable as one can expect an old Cornish cottage to be." [194]

191 In *St Ives Weekly Summary* 18/5/1907, there is a note from Mrs H.Ellis of 'The Count House' concerning an anonymous letter writer who had libelled her and so they appear not to have moved out until 1907 at the earliest.
192 Havelock Ellis, *My Life*, London, 1940 at p.351.
193 In March 1906, she gave three lectures in Penzance - (i) *Edward Carpenter - A Forerunner*, (ii) *Nietzche and Morals*, and (iii) *James Hinton - A Mythical Scientist*.
194 Havelock Ellis, *My Life*, London, 1940 at p.357.

Edith enjoyed immersing herself in the London social scene, becoming an active member of the Lyceum Club, but a further health shock came when she learnt that she had diabetes, for which treatment by insulin had not then been devised. Through an American woman artist, who had been a fellow former lover of Lily Kirkpatrick, Edith was invited in 1914 to make a lecturing tour of America and the success of that led to an invitation for a further longer tour in 1915, which left her physically exhausted. Her various physical ailments exacerbated her tendency to manic depression and, in the last year of her life, she suffered severe mental problems, even demanding a separation from Havelock. When back in Carbis Bay, St Ives friends, such as Gussie Lindner and her sister, Isabel, (known to Edith as 'Blue'), tried to help, but it was a very difficult time, with the local doctor advising them that she could be a danger to their children.[195] She had a spell in the Convent Nursing Home in Hayle, during which she tried to commit suicide, but she eventually died in London in 1916, having caught a chill watching a Zeppelin raid. Seemingly, prescient of her impending death, she had put the lease of 'Rose Cottage' into joint names, thinking it would be a good source of profit to Havelock, but he let one of her artist friends have it for a trifling sum and vowed not to besmirch his vision of Carbis Bay as "Paradise" by visiting it again.[196] In the 1920s, 'Rose Cottage' became the home for many decades of the artist, Shearer Armstrong, and her husband.

3.2.4   The architectural designs of Edmund Fuller in the Carbis Bay locality

At the close of the century, at the same time as some artists were seeking plots in Up-along for new properties, other artists began to look for unspoilt locations outside St Ives upon which to build. William Fortescue, who decided to move from Newlyn to St Ives in 1897, wrote in April that year to the Cowley Estate, saying, "I am looking about the neighbourhood of St Ives for a piece of ground with the idea of building a small cottage residence." He indicated that a plot between St Ives and Carbis Bay on the outskirts of the village of Trelyon, then consisting of the 'Cornish Arms' and a few cottages, had taken his fancy.[197] Having acquired a two acre piece of ground, he asked his artist colleague, Edmund Fuller (1858-1940), to design a new house for him.

This was Fuller's first architectural commission. He had settled in St Ives wth his wife, Emma, in 1892 and, by this juncture, was making a name for himself as a marine painter. It is not known what prompted him to begin to take an interest in the study of architecture, or what persuaded Fortescue to entrust what, for him, was such an important commission, to an untried hand. Perhaps, Fuller had already been considering designs for a home of his own. In any event, as Fuller produced fine plywood models of his designs to aid him in his perspective elevations, Fortescue is likely to have seen a model of his proposed home before confirming the commission. The property, which Fortescue called 'Trelyon Cottage', despite being of some considerable size, was built of granite and had a tiled roof. It faced north, as this enabled the principal rooms to enjoy the view out towards Godrevy. From an unusually spacious hall, a stairway, with a fine balustrade, led up to five bedrooms on the first floor. A large room on the second floor, which afforded not only the best views of Godrevy, but also a view of Knill's Steeple to the rear was Fortescue's home studio. As Fortescue lived in the house, for the rest of his life, the design was clearly satisfactory.

Fig. 2.83 Edmund Fuller *Self-Portrait*

---

195 Havelock indicates that Edith called Gussie's sister, 'Blue'. This is her sister, Isabel, who visited regularly, rather than her half sister, Ethel Kennedy, who married MacIvor Bassett and lived in Lelant.

196 Havelock Ellis, *My Life*, London, 1940 at p.358.

197 Letter dated 15/4/1897 from W. Fortescue to R Glanville - Mornington Estate papers, County Records Office, Truro GHW/12/3/6/1/82/27.

Edward Fuller Maitland (b.1860), another former Bushey student, also wrote to the Cowley Estate in January 1899, stating "My wife and I wish to build a house in the neighbourhood of St Ives". He was particularly interested in a plot between the footpath going to Carbis Bay and the sea, but was put off by the fact that a development of seventy villas was planned by the Estate nearby. He blustered, "I have to say I do not see what class of person are likely to inhabit such houses. They would be quite unsuitable as lodging houses, being away from the sea-shore, and no artist would wish to possess one; and to the retired tradesmen, of whom there are very few in St Ives, the price would be prohibitive."[198] This proposal for a huge housing estate on the land between the main road at Trelyon and the sea caused considerable consternation to others, not least Edward Hain, whose property 'Treloyhan Manor' flanked the proposed development and whose view would have been severely impaired. As a result, in 1899, he paid the enormous sum of £10,000 to buy the whole section of land himself. Unfortunately, as Hain's only son was killed in the War, this land became available for development after Hain's own death in 1917.

Hain's purchase will have been a great relief to Arts Club member, Thomas Albert Lang, as he had acquired from Thomas Bedford Bolitho, in 1897, a plot on the cliff top at Carbis Bay, which would also have been adjacent to the proposed development. Albert Lang had an interest in the quarry and building contracting business, run principally by his father, Thomas, and his elder brother, John, and he had first come to St Ives in 1892 to supervise the construction of the West Pier. The family had then built in 1894 'Treloyhan Manor', to the design of Silvanus Trevail, for Edward Hain and the Porthminster Hotel, in which both Hain and Thomas Lang senior had significant stakes. Quite what credentials Albert possessed in artistic, literary, musical or dramatic matters is unknown, but his wealth, his golfing prowess and his general club-ability meant that no objection was raised to his election as an Arts Club member. Indeed, he went on to serve as President in 1906-7.

Despite his family's connections, Lang decided to use Edmund Fuller as the architect of the substantial new residence for his family that he built on this plot and called 'Tremorna', whilst Fuller designed a residence, 'Dunvegan', for his own occupation on the adjoining plot, albeit that this may have been owned by Lang as well. Both houses were constructed at much the same time in 1900-1, with Lang, presumably, obtaining the requisite building materials and labour at a discounted rate.[199] A photograph taken from Hawke's Point in 1901 demonstrates how these two houses and 'Treloyhan Manor' are the only houses on the cliff top on this side of the Bay. They enjoyed commanding vistas down the pine clad steep slopes and across the Bay towards Godrevy. On the later sale of 'Tremorna', the view was described as one "not to be excelled even in North Cornwall".[200]

The design of both houses have similarities, although 'Tremorna' was significantly bigger than 'Dunvegan'. One of the most surprising features of the houses, given that Lang will have had access to good quality stone, is that they are both rendered, and seem to have been so from the outset. Such a finish will have been novel at this time and, perhaps, it was one that Lang's firm was promoting. Unfortunately, a rendered finish is not highly regarded now and, as various sections have been re-rendered in a different colour, it does the houses no favours at all. Fuller's design for the facades is based on a vertical impulse being provided by a tower-like feature on the right-hand side, balanced by horizontal impulses from attractive wooden verandas, backed by large windows to the left. In the case of 'Dunvegan', there is just one veranda at first floor level, which winds around along a portion of the side of the property from which equally fine views are obtainable, whereas at 'Tremorna', there are verandas on both ground and first floors, with that on the ground floor linked into a veranda in front of a separate one-storey section - possibly a later addition - on the side. Fuller's papers contain various designs for fireplaces in yellow pine, and some abstract Art Nouveau patterns, but it is unclear to what extent he also designed the interior of the properties.

'Dunvegan', a modest sized property, (see Fig. 2.88) remains relatively unchanged. Whilst there is a two-storey extension clearly added to the right-hand side of the property, this appears to have been done by Fuller, so as to provide himself with a studio at home. This was on the top floor of the extension, and, as it faced almost due north, the whole of the front pitch of the roof was originally glass. The view from the studio remains superb and one suddenly becomes aware that it is the subject of an important painting. However, it is not one by Fuller. It is no less than the vista captured by Julius Olsson in his 1911 Chantrey painting, *Moonlit Shore* - a fascinating indication of a close friendship between the two leading seascape artists in the colony.

198 Letter from E Fuller Maitland to Glanville and Hamilton dated 12/1/1899 - Mornington Estate Papers, County Records Office, Truro, GHW/12/3/6/1/99/40. Fuller Maitland was the son of a barrister and had been born in Wargrave, Berkshire. He had attended Oxford University before studying at Bushey. Although as a result of this exchange, the Fuller Maitlands aborted their plans to move to the locality, settling instead in Rye, they returned to visit on many occasions and remained members of the local Golf Club until 1937.

199 The 1901 Census records merely House on Cliff Nos 1 and 2 but both the Fullers and the Langs are in occupation.

200 1923 Sales Particulars (St Ives Museum)

Figs. 2.84 - 2.87
'Tremorna', Carbis Bay
(all courtesy John Cross)

Clockwise

Main house and croquet lawn, in
the1930s, although the scene is very
similar to a 1923 photograph. To the
left is 'Little Parc Owles', created from
Garage and Cottage initially erected
by the Hornes

Distinctive verandas from original
Fuller design

View of house from Carbis Bay beach

View from house, which featured often
in Olsson paintings

Fig. 2.88 'Dunvegan' (far left) and 'Tremorna' (far right), with 'Little Parc Owles'
behind, in 2007, upon the 120th anniversary of the opening of the branch line
(*St Ives Times & Echo*)

In 1911, Fuller decided to leave 'Dunvegan', and he moved back into St Ives, taking one of the properties
in Clodgy View that had just been erected by Robert Toy. His reasons for moving from his own designed
home are not known, but he was certainly not downsizing, as 6 Clodgy View contained eight bedrooms,
two reception rooms, kitchen, scullery, larder, cool house, bathroom and water-closet. Perhaps, with
advancing years, he wanted to be closer to the town's amenities. He gave up the Clodgy View property
in 1920, and spent his last five years in town at 6 Park Avenue, one of the original group of quality
houses in this street. In 1920, 'Dunvegan' was acquired by Norman Cooke, who was a stalwart of the
Arts Club until 1940 and whose daughters, Dorothy and Iris, were both artists.[201] The studio, therefore,
remained in use for its original purpose for many years.

Albert Lang was an integral figure in the artistic community for over twenty years, socialising with his
friends from the Arts Club and the Golf Club. These clearly included the American maverick, Sydney
Laurence, several of whose paintings he acquired, and Julius Olsson, given the number of times he
depicted the view from the garden of 'Tremorna' under the light of the moon. In the 1901 Census,
Lang described himself as 'retired railway contractor', despite only being aged 41, and he and his wife,
Bessie, who was four years younger and who had been born in Plymouth, appear to have devoted
themselves over the next decade to the development of the grounds of the property. The presence of
one-storey blocks on either side of the main house would also suggest that additions were made over
time, with Fuller, presumably, being asked to advise. Lang's final year as Treasurer of the Arts Club was
in 1914, and there is a brief note, in the Arts Club Minutes, of a dinner in his honour in 1915, suggesting
his departure from the area, possibly on war duties. However, it was not until September 1919 that
'Tremorna' was acquired by David Horne, a rice merchant, and his wife, Frances, from Richmond, who
had fallen in love with the locality, during the War years, and who, as mentioned above, had been renting
'The Croft'.

In the four years that the Hornes owned the property, before David Horne's early death, at the age of
only 48, they clearly did a considerable amount of work to the property, and, therefore, it is uncertain
what features mentioned in the sale particulars, produced when the property was sold in 1923, were
original, what were added by the Langs during their ownership or what were innovations of the Hornes.[202]
However, the house, at that juncture, was described as having two significant reception rooms overlooking
the Bay, with windows to the covered balcony. The Drawing Room was 29' x 15', and the Dining Room
was 24' x 18'. Each had a glazed brick fireplace, the former with a mahogany chimneypiece, the latter
with an oak one. The single storey building on the left of the main frontage - probably an addition during
Lang's occupancy - housed a billiard room, measuring 33' x 19', completely panelled in selected teak.
It also had a polished block floor, suitable for dancing, fitted bookcases and cupboards and, unusually,
a steel fireplace. The principal bedroom on the first floor was 21' x 16', and had French windows to the
the covered balcony on two sides. There were eight bed and dressing rooms in all.

---

201 The 1923 Sales particulars for 'Tremorna' indicate that Cooke bought 'Dunvegan' from David Horne, who appears. therefore,
to have owned both properties for a while. See Special Condition 11 (St Ives Museum).
202 A copy of the Sale Particulars is held at St Ives Museum. I am grateful to Lady Carol Holland for a copy of these.

"The Pleasure Grounds" of the property, comprising some two and a half acres, included, in addition to the tennis or croquet lawn and a large kitchen garden, many delightful Terrace Walks, bordered by flower beds and shrubberies, a Terrace Rock Garden, a Rose Garden on the cliffside and a Veronica path. The gardens included a quantity of very rare plants, including flowering shrubs from Australia and New Zealand Myrtles. Winding paths led down to the cliff path that provided access to the beach.

One of the major innovations made by the Hornes was the installation of new Electric Plant. This was contained in a separate Engine House. Their funding of the Leach Pottery resulted also in the insertion of a new fireplace, showing early examples of Leach tiles. They also built, to the rear, a substantial garage and servants' cottage, which was later converted into the property, 'Little Parc Owles', famous for its associations during the Second World War with the art critic Adrian Stokes, his wife, Margaret Mellis, and their guests, Ben Nicholson, Barbara Hepworth and Naum Gabo. It was also, later, the home of Peter Lanyon.

Following its sale in 1923, 'Tremorna' remained largely unspoilt until the Second World War but, sadly, subsequently, has had numerous unsympathetic extensions added over the years. Furthermore, it has now been converted into eight apartments and so, internally, has been largely destroyed as well. It remains, though, Fuller's finest accomplishment as an architect, and the lifestyle enjoyed at the property by the Langs, and their artist friends, with private facilities for billiards, tennis and croquet and extensive manicured grounds, was far more sophisticated than any that the artists could have aspired to in their first decade in the town. Fuller's other known architectural commissions are the Trevessa Hotel in Primrose Valley, St Ives (Fig. 2.90) and the library at 'Boskerris Vean', Carbis Bay (see Figs. 4.13-4).

Fig. 2.89 Albert Lang (right) and the Secretary, W.C.Perry, at
the West Cornwall Golf Club (Golf Club)

Fig.2.90 Edmund Fuller   Design of frontage of the Trevessa Hotel
Fuller is also known to have been the architect for the Trevessa Hotel in Primrose Valley, St Ives, which was run by a Miss Newton. The property was burnt down in an insurance scam in the 1970s. The properties subsequently erected in Primrose Valley clearly owe a debt to this design.

2.3.3   Lelant

Lelant, which was the next stop after Carbis Bay on the branch line from St Ives, was also, in the early days of the colony, a quiet, unspoilt place. Nearby were the sand dunes, known as the Lelant Towans, covered in grey-green grass, which overlooked the entrance to the Hayle Estuary and the quaint old ferry house. Here was a spot where one could "commune with Nature with very little prospect of being disturbed".[203]

Adrian Stokes was the first artist to select Lelant for his home, and his major works of 1888-9 are all Lelant scenes. As a local resident, he was also involved in the discussions leading up to the establishment of the West Cornwall Golf Club on the Lelant Towans in December 1889, and he served on the founding committee. It has proved difficult, however, to establish quite where the Stokeses lived initially.[204] After their spell in Italy in 1891-3, they seem to have settled back in Lelant, as their names do not appear in the 1894 St Ives Rate Book and Lewis Hind, recounting his time as a student in St Ives in 1895-6, recalled "the blue pools and dunes of Lelant, in those days the painting ground of Adrian Stokes, now R.A.".[205] Certainly, Kelly's Directory records them as living in Church Lane (now Church Road), Lelant not only in 1897 but also, somewhat surprisingly, in 1902, as they had little connection with the colony after 1898.

Alfred East was another artist, who enjoyed painting in the Lelant area, although, on his visits to the locality, he appears to have stayed principally with his sister, Mrs G.F.Monson, in Hayle or in St Ives. However, he used an old apple loft in Lelant as a studio and this was taken over by the Australian, David Davies, when he moved to Carbis Bay in 1899. Davies remained based there until 1904 and, in March 1901, signed into the Arts Club a New Zealand artist, Samuel Hales, who is recorded as lodging in Lelant at the time of the 1901 Census and so presumably was studying under Davies. Avery Lewis, an artist from Hastings, was also lodging in the village at that time.[206]

203 W.H.Bartlett, *Summer Time in St Ives*, Cornwall, *Art Journal*, 25/9/1897.

204 They also may have moved into St Ives in late 1889, for Helene Schjerfbeck tells her brother, Magnus, that she went almost every day to the Stokeses at that time, something that would have been unlikely if they were still out in Lelant. She also adds, "Marianne sends her love; she is delighted with her maid and with her home, but she is usually in raptures about something or other." Letter dated 1889, the 26th, Saturday evening, translated by Erkki Toivanen.

205 C Lewis Hind, *Napthali*, London, 1926 at p.162.

206 I am indebted to John Sell of St Ives Trust Archive Study Centre for his perusal of the 1901 Census for Lelant.

In 1906, the American artist, Percy Simpson FRGS MSA, moved out from St Ives to Lelant, living in 'Riverside Studio' and stayed there until 1910. Simpson had first been involved in the colony between 1900 and 1902, during which time he took part in Show Days and the exhibitions in Falmouth. He was back again in 1904 before settling in Lelant.[207] Following the death of his wife in 1913, he appears to have returned to America.[208] In the 1920s, 'Riverside' became the home of Moffat Lindner's mother.

The West Cornwall Golf Club at Lelant proved a considerable attraction. William Brooke, who was asked to design the new Pavilion at the Golf Club in 1900, decided to move to 'Littlewood', Lelant in 1902, when he was made Club Captain, and thereafter directed his energies more towards golf than art. Other golfers, who decided to take property in Lelant, included Stuart Hobkirk's mother, Baroness Farina, who lived until 1910 in 'Chy-an-Chy', and Hilda and Maud Sealy from Weybridge, who first came down to St Ives to study under Julius Olsson. They lived in Lelant for many years, initially at 'Elm Cottage', then 'Tyringham Row' and finally 'Tremar'.[209] Maud was recalled by Dorothy Meade as one of the characters of the village. "Perhaps one of the most colourful was Miss Sealy with her large raffia hats, heavily decorated with incredible gardens of brightly coloured raffia flowers. She was always to be seen, and heard, striding through the village followed by two or three poodles and a minute but noisy Yorkshire terrier, panting in their efforts to keep up with her. She lived in the early years in Elm Cottage at the turn of Abbey Hill. The cottage faced up the hill and had red roses all over it and also had a well-kept gay garden. Her very chatty green parrot used to stand on a perch by the gate and greet the passers-by with a shrill, "Good morning, nice day," in the exact tone of his mistress."[210]

Katherine Horn (d.1949), one of the Horn sisters from East Moseley, who, like the Sealy sisters, had come down to St Ives to study art, also ended up by settling in Lelant, at 'Chygwidden Cottage', making more regular appearances on the golf course than at Lanham's. Gussie Lindner's half sister, Ethel Kennedy, another former student, also settled in Lelant, having married Frederick MacIvor Bassett, and they ran a preparatory school at 'Chygwidden' for a number of years, before moving to 'Treglaze Vean'. The 1920s saw the well-known illustrator, John de Walton RWA, living at Abbey Cottage, and the painter, Mary Grylls, and her husband, Reginald, a Councillor, in the large property, 'Ar-Lyn', now a care home, where they were resident until the 1950s.[211] Other artists, such as Edmund Fuller, Fred Milner, Jack Titcomb, and Mary McCrossan, whilst based in St Ives, clearly had an affinity for St Uny, the beautifully positioned church at Lelant, for they chose to be buried there.[212]

Fig. 2.91 Donald Shaw MacLaughlan   *Lelant*   (1919)

207 An uninspiring painting of St Ives harbour merely signed 'Simpson' in the St Ives Museum is presumed to be by him.

208 *St Ives Times* 12/9/1913 records the death of Mrs Simpson, then living at 'St Cyres', Stratton, near Bude, from heart failure at Sans Souci Hotel, Clarens, Montreux, Switzerland.

209 Miss H M Sealy died in 1936. A Miss Sealy is still recorded in Kelly's at Tremar in 1939.

210 From Dorothy Meade, *Reminiscences of Lelant*, Lelant website.

211 Mary Grylls died on 25/10/1956 and Reginald on 28/11/1955 and both are buried at St Uny, Lelant.

212 Artists buried there include Edmund Fuller and his wife, although he moved away in c.1925 and died in Portishead in 1940, Mary McCrossan, Gertrude Rosenberg, Fred Milner and his wife, Ida and Dotte Praetorius, William Spittle, Jack Titcomb, Nina Weir Lewis, Mabel Shone, Mary Grylls, Henry Rutherfoord and Lady Blumberg (formerly Eliza Tudor Lane).

2.3.4   Zennor

Zennor, on the coast to the north of St Ives, did not have a rail connection to the town and was too remote to be selected as the permanent home for any artist in the pre-War period, but the spectacular cliff scenery in the locality and the mystery of the moors of the Cornish Hinterland attracted many artists to visit this ancient village. It was, accordingly, a popular destination for a walk, or for Sunday tea parties. However, those, like Arnesby Brown, who tried to walk there and back, with their painting equipment, did not do so a second time! Therefore, artists wanting to paint in the area needed somewhere to stay. Such stays were normally for no more than a week However, some became fascinated with the wildness of the area and stayed much longer, whilst others made repeated return visits.

Adrian and Marianne Stokes were again some of the first artists to base themselves in the village for a significant period, as, at the time of the 1891 census, they were lodging at 'Tregerthen Cottage' at Zennor, whilst Adrian was working on his major painting of the year, *The Setting Sun*. They were joined there by one of their patrons, John Westlake QC DCL (1828-1913), a barrister, Liberal M.P. and Professor of International Law at Cambridge University. He had been born in Lostwithiel and he and his wife, Alice, regularly stayed in Zennor, later using, as their summer residence, 'Eagle's Nest', the spectacularly sited property, just outside the village (see Fig. 2.99), that has subsequently been home to a succession of artists. Alice Westlake was herself an artist and her portrait of her husband, dating from 1896-7, is owned by the National Portrait Gallery, as is one by Marianne Stokes, dating from 1902 (Fig. 2.92).

Zennor, however, became synonymous with one establishment - the lodging house run by Mrs Griggs, which was situated opposite the old Church. Arnesby Brown claimed to be her first visitor in 1897 and was a regular until 1909. Allen Gardner Folliott Stokes (1855-1939) also recorded spending "many and many a happy month in Mrs Griggs' comfortable home".[213] Folliott Stokes, more than any other artist, brought the attractions of the area to the attention of the public, both locally and nationally, describing the moors as "a vast expanse of primeval country as yet unconquered by man".[214]

Fig. 2.92 Marianne Stokes *Portrait of John Westlake*
(National Portrait Gallery)

213 Mrs Griggs' Visitors' Book
214 A.G.Folliott-Stokes, *The Cornish Coast and Moors*, London, 1931 edition at p.151.

Figs. 2.93-4 H.G.Fitzherbert   Caricatures of Folliott Stokes, as *A Moorland Prince* in
Caricatures of the Cornish Riviera (left), and in *Everyone's Doing It* (right)

Folliott Stokes was born in Goring, Oxfordshire, and was the eldest son of William Stokes, the Vicar, and his wife, Emily, who was sixteen years his junior. At the time of the 1881 Census, he was working as a land agent in Bridgnorth, but, by 1884, he had married Charlotte Vansittart Frere, the daughter of a barrister, and had a daughter, Muriel, who had been born in Kingston-upon-Thames. The family are first recorded as visitors to St Ives in July 1889 and settled in the town soon after. However, at the time of the 1901 Census, Folliott Stokes seems to have separated from his wife, who was living with their daughter in Penzance. In the next few years, he spent more and more of his time on his own, exploring the moors and coast around Zennor, an area populated by dwellers "who live a different life to the rest of Cornwall".[215] He was intoxicated by the wild and terrible beauty of the region, by its loneliness and by the romance of the prehistoric remains that were scattered over the area. "These tor crowned hills that face the sea, these secluded valleys, hung with the gold of the whinbush and the purple of the heath, these laughing streams which hurry to the great water, guarded by rocks, veined and patterned more cunningly than human brain e're dreamed of..., stir the finest instincts of the soul and kindle that spirit of poetry which, though inarticulate, lies latent in almost every heart".[216] One spring, he even took a broken down cottage just under the crest of Zennor Hill, which had been unoccupied for so long that "the upland wildings no longer shunned it". As a result, he witnessed at close quarters rarely seen animal behaviour. Stokes' unbridled enthusiasm for the Hinterland led him to be dubbed by the artists of St Ives and Newlyn as "The Man of the Moor".[217]

Not all his fellow artists could be persuaded of the merits of this often bleak, storm-lashed moorland, but he introduced its delights to the writer, Cyril Ranger-Gull, who also stayed at Mrs Griggs', whilst finishing his controversial novel, *When It Was Dark*. Accordingly, in *Portalone*, his subsequent novel, 'the Hinterland' around Zennor, which he described as utterly unspoilt "as the artists are too lazy and the tourists don't know", featured extensively. Indeed, Ranger-Gull dedicated the book to Folliott Stokes, and confirmed that one of the main characters, Gerald Ffoulkes, was based substantially upon him. Ffoulkes had broken away from the other artists in the colony and sought an ideal and simple life, communing with Nature. "To him every natural object seemed to possess more or less of a moral or spiritual life, to be capable of a companionship with man".[218] The company of Ranger-Gull inspired Folliott Stokes to write a novel himself, and *A Moorland Princess*, published at the same time, also features Zennor extensively, and he went on to write a number of guide books to the Cornish Coast and Moors, published later in the decade.

---

215 C.Ranger-Gull, *Portalone*, London, 1904 at p.76-7 and 80.

216 *Our Hinterland*, an article by Folliott Stokes published in *The Cornishman* and reproduced in *St Ives Weekly Summary* 15/4/1905.

217 *St Ives Weekly Summary*, 28/3/1907.

218 C.Ranger-Gull, *Portalone*, London, 1904 at p.144.

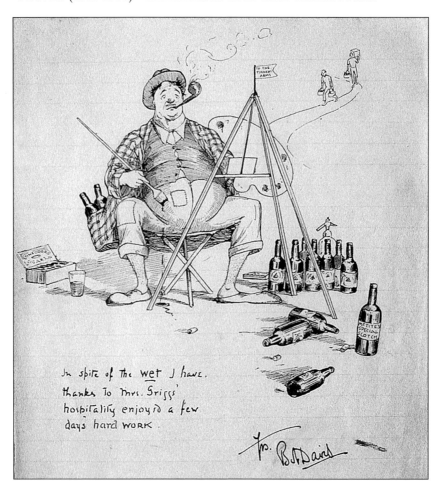

Figs. 2.95-2.97
Sketches in Mrs Griggs' Visitors' Book
        Bob Davis (top)
        Alfred Munnings (bottom left)
        and William Parkyn (bottom right)
(Alison Symons)

Many visitors to Mrs Griggs rated their Zennor stay as the best of their lives. The artists, Emily Allnutt and Alice Nicholson, who first became involved with the colony in 1911, were not unusual when they commented, "We have travelled in many foreign places but have never enjoyed ourselves more".[219] William Parkyn and Alfred Munnings were two of the many artists who filled a page of her Visitors' Book with a sketch (see Figs. 2.95-97), Parkyn praising her teas after a stiff walk, whilst Munnings shows himself lounging comfortably in a chair after an ample repast.[220] Munnings stayed there for five weeks in 1913, taking over her front parlour for himself, whilst his groom and model, Ned, had a bedroom and fed in the kitchen with the landlady. Munnings was enchanted by the area, seeing scores of potential subjects, but forced himself to concentrate on his depictions of Ned on his horse, Grey Tick, on Zennor Hill. It was a productive time, resulting in a number of paintings that were hung at the Royal Academy and sold well. The most well-known of these is *Going to the Meet of the Western Foxhounds*, which was acquired by the Laing Art Gallery in Newcastle-upon-Tyne. The Griggs family enjoyed the artists staying with them and Mrs Griggs' son, Maurice, married Florence Dow's daughter, Elizabeth Pilcher, in 1920.

Another visitor to Mrs Griggs' was Count Larisch, who had married into the Bavarian Royal Family, and who had been feted by the artists at the Arts Club during his visits to the colony since 1910. However, his interest in the coastline might have been rather more sinister, for it was contended after his hurried departure, in February 1915, that he was a spy and, thereafter, artist visitors to Zennor found their sketches being destroyed by over eager coast watchers. This phobia explains the expulsion from the area by the local authorities of D.H.Lawrence and his German wife, Freida. The Lawrences had taken, in 1916, 'Upper Tregerthen', a cottage overlooking the coast less than a mile from Zennor, where they painted the walls pale pink and the cupboards bright blue. They persuaded Katherine Mansfield and John Middleton Murry to take the cottage next door, but Katherine hated it there and they left after only a few weeks. It was here that Lawrence wrote *Women in Love*. Lawrence, in his green corduroy suit, and Freida, in her long-flowing purple dresses, attracted attention whenever they visited St Ives, and the discovery that Freida was not only the subscriber to a German newspaper, but the cousin of the German air ace, the 'Red Baron', led to a number of unfounded rumours circulating that she was a spy. After several raids on their home, they were expelled from the County in October 1917.[221]

As already mentioned, Fanny Lloyd and her son, Will, were regular visitors to Zennor from 1893 onwards and, in addition to enjoying Mrs Griggs' hospitality frequently, they also rented 'Bridge Cottage' in the village. It was here that Fanny settled during the War years and produced some colourful tempera works of buildings in the locality, including a depiction of the interior of the living room in the cottage (see Plates 2 & 3). After her death, Will and Primrose Lloyd, having given up 'St Eia' in 1922, used the cottage, which Will purchased, as their principal Cornish base. They took a great interest in the history of the locality and the ancient methods of farming employed and Primrose, in conjunction with Colonel Hirst and the West Cornwall Field Club, set up and ran the Wayside Museum, which now boasts a fascinating collection. Will died in Zennor in July 1951, but Primrose lived until January 1985.

Fig. 2.98 'Bridge Cottage', Zennor   (Lloyd family archive)

---

219 Mrs Griggs' Visitors' Book.

220 Other sketches are by Bob Davis (possibly an American), F R Fitzgerald, Iris Leveson Gower, Mrs Laurence Davies, Frank Russell Butler, the Thompson family from St Albans and the novelist, C.Ranger-Gull.

221 Freida Lawrence, *Not I, But The Wind*, London, 1935.

Fig. 2.99 'Eagle's Nest, near Zennor
(Roger Slack/St Ives Trust Archive Study Centre)

Despite the Lloyd's decision to be based on a more permanent basis in Zennor, it was still very basic, as the American artist, Wilson Henry Irvine, and his wife, found out in 1923, when they decided to rent a cottage in the village, near to the Inn, for a fortnight in mid-May. "We have to pick up gorse brush to kindle our fire, meat man once a week, baker twice, coal man seldom. Water at the town pump by the roadside. Privy up three of the dampest stone steps one ever negotiated. Stone floors."[222] The cottage creaked at night and was very cold. The meat man did not stop, a chicken promised by a local did not materialise and they were left to eat bacon and eggs for several days. The scenery, however, was inspiring. Irvine had never seen such fine heads before.

Another couple, who decided to base themselves out at Zennor permanently after the War, were William and Katherine Arnold-Forster, who rented, and then subsequently bought, 'Eagle's Nest', off Alice Westlake. The son of an M.P., Will had studied at the Slade between 1905 and 1908 and exhibited his work at various venues until the mid-1930s, showing some 120 paintings at the Goupil Gallery. He was a guest of John Douglas at the Arts Club in 1909, whilst his wife, Katherine, (née Cox, and always known as 'Ka'), was a guest in 1913. After serving in the Navy during the War, Will decided, in an effort to recover from its horrors, to install his young family at 'Eagle's Nest', which Ka's friend, Virginia Woolf, described, after a visit in 1921, as "a windswept, bleak house high above the cliff, with few trees, neighbours or modern conveniences.....Ka and Will sit among the rocks in Mrs Westlake's stone mansion, rather windblown, but sublime, observing hail storms miles out to sea, and the descent of the sun".[223] Although it was very basic when they first moved in, Will created a studio there and they worked hard over many years to transform the garden. Will eventually published in 1948 the classic gardening book, *Shrubs for the Milder Counties*. However, Will was seduced from his art by politics. He was actively involved with the League of Nations and joined the Labour Party, standing in St Ives at the 1928 election - the first time that St Ives had had a Labour candidate. He eventually served as Secretary to Lords Cecil and Parmoor in the second Labour Government. In the meantime, Ka got involved in a number of local causes and was the town's first female magistrate. The garden at 'Eagle's Nest', which was subsequently to provide inspiration to Patrick Heron, was the setting for a number of fund-raising functions, for such causes as the League of Nations Union, the Women's Peace Pilgrimage and the Labour Party. Ka died in May 1938, aged only 51, and Will, who also designed the Memorial Gardens in St Ives, died in October 1951.

---

222 Journal of Wilson Henry Irvine, 10/5/1923, Archives of American Art, Smithsonian Institution, Irvine papers, Reel 3564.
223 *The Question of Things Happening Vol 2, The Letters of Virginia Woolf, 1912-1922*, The Hogarth Press.

ARTISTS IN THEIR STUDIOS

Whene'er I wander to and fro
To right, to left, above, below,
In corners odd, or in a row,
I'm bound to see a studio![224]

2.4.1 Introduction

2.4.1.1 Overview

The availability of good, cheap studio space is of prime importance to the health of any art colony, and the collapse of the mining and shipbuilding industries, and the reduction in the level of fishing catches, led to a number of industrial buildings being available in St Ives. These were often very basic, having not been designed for human habitation, but when situated on one of the town's beaches or overlooking the sea, they became much sought-after workspaces, particularly if a northern facing skylight could be inserted into their roofs. In his account of the fledgling colony, Harry Robinson commented that, soon, "large skylights appeared everywhere among the grey roofs of the old town", and this new feature was the first physical change to the appearance of the town wrought by the artists.[225] Initially, a vast array of different types of building were pressed into service. William Eadie seems to have converted an outhouse in the grounds of his home, 'Windy Parc', whilst Harry Robinson used, initially, a carpenter's shop, probably in Back Street.[226] In the garden of his home in Richmond Place, however, there was also an old, dilapidated Music Pavilion, with an attractive upper room, decorated with plaster reliefs, which was also kitted out as a studio, having been used for the previous forty years purely as a store.

Howard Butler was the first to see the conversion potential of the town's net and rope lofts and created the first studio on Porthmeor Beach out of a loft previously used for storing ropes from the pilchard fishery.[227] In addition to the fabulous views afforded by the studio, it also faced north, and other artists, who seem to have created their early studios from net lofts in this popular area of town, were William Titcomb, who took one in Porthmeor Road, and Julius Olsson, who rented one in Back Road East. Louis Grier was one of the first artists to have a studio on the harbour beach. This was a position from which all the activity of the fishing fleet could be studied, and, by the early 1890s, Edmund Fuller and others had taken nearby properties for use as studios. The American, Edward Simmons, during his stay between 1886 and 1892, had a studio in a large net loft in St Andrew's Street, next to the Churchyard, and Percy Craft and Harry Robinson also used cottages on the seaward side of that rather dilapidated street as studios. These properties again had fine views of the harbour, but took the full brunt of gales and, accordingly, suffered severe water damage at times. Further along, in The Warren, another unusual studio was created from the old Mine Engine House on Pednolver Point. These early studios show that a location with a good view over the Bay was the major prerequisite and that, whilst the smells of Down-along might make it a disagreeable area in which to live, the artists enjoyed working in the midst of their models, witnessing at close quarters the ebb and flow of the fishing seasons. The artists' requirements for studio space also saved many of these buildings from redevelopment.

By the mid-1890s, however, the constant stream of artists visiting the town meant that available studio space with sea vistas had become scarce, with the result that artists started to create studios in areas, such as Norway and Virgin Street, which may not have had good views but had the advantage of being cheaper. Harry Robinson confirmed that it was the locals, who responded to this need, for, in 1896, he commented that, "by the enterprise of the townspeople, new studios were built, some of imposing size".[228] Robinson here is referring, in particular, to the creation of the Porthmeor Studios complex by George Williams, in the years 1889-1895, and the new Piazza Studios, initially five in number, erected by William Paynter in 1896.

---

224 From poem *Art in St Ives* (Anon, but probably Greville Matheson), *St Ives Times*, 14/12/1923.

225 Harry Robinson, *St Ives as an Art Colony*, in *Babcock's Historical Sketch of St Ives and District*, 1896.

226 See *St Ives as an Art Colony* in *Badcock's Historical Sketch of St Ives and District*, 1896.

227 Letter from H.R.Butler to Mary Butler dated 8/8/1886, Howard Russell Butler papers as aforesaid, Reel 1189.

228 Harry Robinson, *St Ives as an Art Colony*, in *Babcock's Historical Sketch of St Ives and District*, 1896.

George Williams, who was born in St Ives in 1818, lived in Salubrious Place.[229]   He turned his hand to a range of activities, describing himself as a fish salesman, basket maker and cooper. He was clearly highly regarded in the town, for he became a Justice of the Peace and was Mayor in 1872-3 and 1878-9. In 1889-90, he converted some of the buildings that he owned in Back Road West into three studios and, then buoyed by the success of these, created a further six more nearby in 1895, including a vast studio purpose-built for Julius Olsson's new Painting School.   Clearly, Williams had been persuaded by the continuing influx of artists that here was a long-term investment opportunity, and, furthermore, he was prepared to take a risk that Olsson's proposed new venture would take off. It was a considerable act of faith, particularly by someone in their seventies, and must have involved some detailed discussions with the artists as to their particular requirements. Williams' nine studios in this block gave him an annual income of £105 and, upon his death in 1902, all were bought at auction by the local bank, Bolitho and Co. A speculative venture had become in just over a decade an appropriate investment for a bank, a tribute not only to the foresight and enterprise of George Williams, but also to the strength of the art colony.

Whilst Williams was the freehold owner of the Porthmeor Studios site and so had an asset of value, even should the art craze dissipate, William Paynter, who lived at 9 The Terrace, was merely a lessee of some adjoining land, and his decision to erect a purpose-built block of studios demonstrated considerable faith not only in the art colony, but also in his own longevity. In 1896, Paynter was approaching sixty years of age and his lease of the property from Lord Cowley came to an end on the death of the survivor of his slightly younger brother, James, and himself. The period during which the family might expect a return from their investment was, accordingly, very uncertain, and yet they decided to proceed. Unsurprisingly, therefore, the studios were built completely of wood, but they provided a total yearly income of £60. Although described in Kelly's Directory in 1883 as a shipright, Paynter had prospects, as his father's second wife, Elizabeth, came from a monied family.[230]   He was described as "a man of amazing health and strength", with broad views and a generous nature, and proved a popular landlord. In the end, his studio venture proved an inspired investment, as he did not die until 1930.[231]

One of the fascinating aspects of these two new developments was that provision was made for fishermen to share sections of the premises with the artists, so that artists and fishermen have worked side by side in these properties ever since. The Porthmeor Studios were built over new or modified fish cellars, now equipped with new concrete tanks, whereas, in the Piazza Studios, there were also four storage areas for use by fishermen. This may well have been due to the fishermen having occupied the sites previously, with the provision of space for them being part of the deal which enabled the developments to occur.

A   Site of Butler's first Porthmeor Studio
B   Area developed by George Williams in 1889–1890
C   Area developed by George Williams in 1895
D   Original building for Porthmeor Studio No. 8
E   Area developed by William Paynter in 1896
F   Site of Island Studios

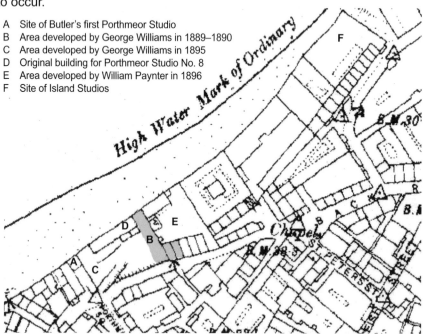

Fig. 2.100 Extract from 1877 Ordnance Survey map showing Porthmeor Beach
properties prior to the development of the Porthmeor and Piazza Studios

229 At the time of the 1891 Census, he shared his home not only with his wife Jane (then 78), but also his son, George, (then 53), who may have been handicapped, as he was called a 'Gardner's Boy', his daughter, Silistra, (then 34) and her husband, Isaac Pearce, a local butcher and farmer.
230 Her father Tonkin Young was a magistrate, shipowner and chemist and, shortly after her marriage to William John Paynter (father of William) in late 1881, they had built 'Shun Lee', the first of the new houses on Porthminster Hill (see Fig. 2.6).
231 See obituary notice - St Ives Times, 28/2/1930.

Plate 1　Frances Hodgkins　　*The Edwardians*
　　　　(Auckland Art Gallery Toi o Tamaki)
　　　　This depicts Edgar and Edith Skinner, and their maid, Elsa,
　　　　in their home, 'Salubrious House', Salubrious Place, St Ives

Plates 2 & 3　Fanny Lloyd
　　　　　　The Living Room, Bridge Cottage &
　　　　　　Duckpond and David's House, Zennor

Plate 4   Hurst Balmford   *The Piazza and Porthmeor Studios from the Island*
          (Private Collection)

Plate 5   Sara Maclean   *The Island Studios from the Island*
          (Private Collection)

Plate 6   Borlase Smart   *The Pilot's Boathouse*
(Leamington Spa Art Gallery & Museum, Warwick District Council)
Note that a poster advertises an exhibition of pictures in the blue painted studio
above the boathouse.

Plate 7   Adrian Stokes   *Ship in difficulties off Porthmeor*
(ex-Griffin collection, courtesy Newlyn School Gallery)

Plate 8   Edward Simmons   *The Carpenter's Son*
(painted in his St Andrew's Street studio)

Plate 10   K.M.Handyside
Girl with sticks
(W.H.Lane & Son)

Plate 11 Harry Robinson
Music
(Lanhydrock House)

Plate 9   Sarah Elizabeth Whitehouse
St Martin's - Summer at St Ives
(Jane Cooper/Penlee House Gallery & Museum)

Plate 12 Lowell Dyer
Woman in a cloister
(Kelley Gallery, Pasadena/
Bridgeman Art Library)

Whilst these were clearly the two principal studio developments in the town in the mid-1890s, it appears that quite a number of other properties fronting Porthmeor Beach had also been adapted into studios, for Howard Russell Butler expressed his astonishment, on his return to the town in 1895, that "all this row of lofts, some twenty-four, had been converted into studios". It is not easy from the Rate Books, or any other source, to verify this statement, particularly as several developments of studios fronting the beach are known to have occurred later. However, these major new initiatives at the Porthmeor and Piazza Studios in 1895-6 kick-started the process whereby almost the whole of this industrial segment of St Ives was converted into an art enclave. Surprisingly, there are few photos of the run of buildings fronting Porthmeor Beach in the pre-War period, but two paintings from the 1920s by Hurst Balmford (Plate 4) and Sara Maclean (Plate 5), when taken together, show an uninterrupted block of properties built on the sea-wall, with numerous skylights and enlarged windows revealing the haunts of artists. More than any other part of the town, here was an area totally transformed by the artistic fraternity.

Porthmeor Beach, however, was not the only location for new studios and these continued to appear all over the town, as new arrivals hunted out other appropriate spaces. However, not all outlasted the departure of their initial creators. After the War, the number of studios in the town grew significantly - in 1921, it was estimated that there were over 200 - and there seems to have been a move towards smaller, cosier quarters, where the studio doubled as living and reception area, reflecting not only the state of the art market and the economy in general, but the change in demographics resulting from the War's huge death toll. Accordingly, the odd inserted rooflight might be the only sign that an artist worked there.

By the time of the Second World War, a number of studio complexes, such as the Island Studios, created in 1910 by the American artist, Henry Keasbey, had ceased to exist, and the total number of studios was put at around 100. In the years immediately after the War, there was an alarming drop in numbers, as landlords converted them into more profitable uses, and, at the time of the campaign to save the Porthmeor Studios in the late 1940s, only 38 survived. Now, the Porthmeor Studios alone from these early studio complexes remain and yet, at the time of writing, it is still proving difficult to persuade funding bodies of their unique status. However, one major achievement of the present campaign has been to secure Grade II listing as a building of historic interest.

2.4.1.2 The influence of location and size

Of all the studios in St Ives, only the Porthmeor Studios have previously been written about, and then only recently, in Ben Tufnell's book, published in 2007 by Tate St Ives, *On the very edge of the Ocean - the Porthmeor Studios and Painting in St Ives*. Unfortunately, Tufnell, then a Curator at Tate Britain, clearly had no interest in pre-Modernist painting in St Ives or in doing any detailed research into the pre-1949 history of the studios, and so his account of the earlier period is a work of pure fiction. Mistakenly believing that Olsson and his School of Painting operated exclusively from the Porthmeor Studios, he argues that the studios, with their unique position at the edge of the ocean, played a key role in the 'place-myth' of St Ives as a centre for marine painting. He, therefore, failed to appreciate that Olsson did not produce his famous moonlit pictures at Porthmeor - the studios face north-west and, therefore, are the place to see the setting sun, not the rising moon - but, instead, executed there the paintings of sirens and mermaids that represent the nadir of his career. He also failed to appreciate that the School of Painting was run from 1898 from the Harbour Studio on the harbour beach. If he had cared to do an analysis of artists who did occupy the Porthmeor Studios in the early years, he would have found that, despite the studios offering an artist the ability to "sit in his easy chair and study the wave forms as if they were simply an attraction of his back garden", very few occupants were actually marine painters, and even those that were did not feel compelled, that often, if at all, to paint pictures of Porthmeor Beach and the Island.[232] So, for instance, whereas Sydney Laurence's *Setting Sun on the Cornish Coast* (Southampton Art Gallery) and Moffat Lindner's *The Flowing Tide - Afterglow* (Ferens Art Gallery, Hull) were clearly inspired by Porthmeor sunsets witnessed from the studios, they are rare treatments of the subject in either artist's oeuvre, particularly as Lindner had an association with the studios for over fifty years. Furthermore, Arthur Meade, a leading landscape and marine artist who worked for over forty years in a Porthmeor Studio, did not, to my knowledge, produce a single major painting of Porthmeor Beach or the Island. This lack of influence of location might seem rather odd, as Tufnell argues more convincingly that the size, location and ambience of the studios had a marked impact on the work of modernist artists, such as Ben Nicholson and Patrick Heron. However, whilst the earlier period did see St Ives gain a reputation internationally, as a centre for marine and landscape painting, the artists at that time were fervent advocates of *plein air* sketching and, therefore, tended to use their studios for working up into major exhibition pieces sketches done elsewhere, not as places of inspiration in themselves.

---

232 C.Lewis Hind, *In Painters' Land, The Ludgate*, October 1896.

Fig. 2.101 The various complexes of Porthmeor studios seen from the Island
(St Ives Trust Archive Study Centre)

In making his claims for the uniqueness of the Porthmeor Studios at all times, Tufnell ignores the other groups of studios fronting Porthmeor Beach, but similar analyses of the artists working in the Piazza Studios or the Island Studios results in the same conclusion - that there was no special marine element drawn to them. Indeed, an analysis of the studios occupied by the leading marine artists in the colony demonstrates that they were dotted about all over the town, with Adrian Stokes not even having a sea view!

Nevertheless, there were clearly occasions when artists sought out studios in specific locations, as they wanted to concentrate on a particular type of work. For instance, Millie Dow, who had a studio in Talland Road, was keen, at one juncture, to rent the studio on Pednolver Point, as he wanted to do some marine studies, and artists on the harbour beach were constantly inspired by the scene unfolding before them, leading Charles Simpson, for instance, to do a series of paintings capturing the various aspects of the herring season that he witnessed from 'Shore Studio'. However, the influence of the location of a studio on subject matter should not be overplayed. The artists created any 'place myth', not the studios.

One feature of St Ives studios, that often resulted in comment, was their sheer size. Previously, it has been thought that this resulted primarily from the size of the original spaces converted into studios, often lofts that had had to house lengthy seine nets. However, the recent discovery that a significant proportion of the extra-large studios in the Porthmeor and Piazza studio complexes were purpose-built gives this aspect a new dynamic. Indeed, it was the fact that London could not boast a single studio as big as that built initially for the School of Painting that led Herbert Draper to come down to St Ives for his ceiling commission. St Ives became known, therefore, not just for its superb location and thriving colony, but also for its big studios. Large workspaces had a certain aura. As Borlase Smart said in relation to Fred Milner's vast studio in the Piazza block, "It conveyed the impression that big things had been created there."[233] Nine foot canvases, which were not uncommon before the War, could not be painted in a little hovel - space was needed for their execution and appreciation.

233 From Borlase Smart's Appreciation, *St Ives Times* 10/1939.

2.4.1.3 The principal landlord's local agent

A large number of the studios in the town were owned by the Cowley Estate, whose property agent was Reginald Glanville, a man whom the artists liked enormously and who built up a collection of paintings by them. However, Glanville was based in Truro, and so, for urgent matters, the artists had to deal, after 1901, with Glanville's local representative, George Toman, who lived at Meadow. This invariably led to disputes, as Toman was a bull-nosed, self-righteous individual, who seemed to enjoy wielding what power he had, particularly as, being a devout member of the Methodist New Connexion Society, he was a critic of the artists' Bohemian ways.[234] As a result, the archives of Glanville's firm, which are part of the Mornington Estate Papers, contain a fascinating series of letters from both the artists and Toman, complaining about each other and often giving their respective accounts of the same incident. Given that extant letters from St Ives artists are so rare, these reveal previously unknown character traits of individual artists, whilst highlighting that there was still a good deal of ill-feeling between the artists and certain sections of the community.

The attitude adopted towards the artists by Toman is perfectly encapsulated in a single sentence in one of his letters to his office in Truro - "These paint-wasters seem to think they can do as they please."[235] Often one can have some sympathy with Toman, as the artists are frequently in the wrong, but his manner clearly riled every artist with whom he came into contact. Lizzie Whitehouse complained of him being "insulting and rude", Sydney Carr objected to his aggressive manner, Dr A.G.Richardson indicated he had been "impertinent", whilst Herbert Lanyon accused him "of quite intolerable insolence" and of being "utterly blind to all reason with passion". Most told Reginald Glanville that they never wanted anything to do with Toman again, but circumstances meant that they had little choice.

One of the biggest bones of contention was the prohibition against sub-letting without consent contained in every studio lease. Most artists spent some time - often months - away from St Ives each year and were keen, for financial reasons, during that period, to let out their studios to any artist who happened to be visiting the town at the time. Keys were left with friends, and, accordingly, various artists would utilise the studio during the lessee's absence. It was quite impracticable to get consent, which involved the sub-lessee submitting references, on each occasion, and the artists rarely bothered. However, the incident which caused Toman's outburst makes his reaction a little more understandable. Lizzie Whitehouse had sublet her studio in St Andrew's Street, without consent, to the family of the artist, Betty Thompson, who, in attempting to unblock the chimney in the front room, had dislodged some bricks, with the result that smoke from their fires went straight into the adjoining property, asphyxiating its occupants, who were already incapacitated with influenza!

If the artists made clear their opinion of Toman to Reginald Glanville, then Toman was not to be outdone. He called A.G.Richardson, a retired doctor of medicine, who had turned to painting, "a complete drunken nuisance with neither money nor manners". Lizzie Whitehouse he considered was "an old maid and very whimsical". After a spat with Herbert Lanyon, he commented, "However, it is Lanyon all round it seem, in speaking or writing, moderation is out of the question, especially when the Moon is growing." Sydney Carr, an artist to whom he had a particular antipathy, he labelled a double-dyed villain, one of his favourite expressions. After having had a blazing row wirh Toman, Carr apologised to Glanville for losing his temper, but added, "These psalm-singing oily gentlemen go against my grain", whilst Toman, in recounting the incident to Glanville, commented, "I think that is the first time during my life that I have been Hell'd on." However, the artist whom Toman seems to have goaded more than any other was John Douglas. The incident which brought matters to a head in 1915 seems relatively innocuous - Reginald Glanville's partner, Hamilton, had turned up at Douglas' house on Skidden Hill without an appointment. As Douglas had just served notice to quit after fourteen years, Hamilton may have come to prepare a schedule of dilapidations. Anyway, Douglas was in a towering rage when he chanced upon Toman in Porthmeor Square. Toman's account of the incident, whilst showing Douglas' behaviour to be completely unacceptable, gives an insight into his own character. "He said you brought him [Hamilton] there at my place, you dirty burglar going about - at least twice repeated - , you blood sucker, you dirty sponger, going about poking your nose everywhere looking at people's property, you son of a whore, thrice repeated, you scoundrel, many times repeated. He called me many other things but I don't seem to remember them all. They were just such as could come from a double-dyed Villain. It was only when I threatened to summon him that he left me. His hands were clenched all the time and he himself in an attitude to strike..... I shall see what you have to say before I take action against him. Of course, there is defamation of character here. I have maintained that, unsullied from infancy to the present - that must be vindicated at all costs." Hamilton, though, seems to have persuaded him not to pursue the matter.

---

234 It is perhaps telling that, even in his obituary, Toman was only described as an "acceptable" local preacher - St Ives Times, 4/7/1924. It also seems unsurprising that Toman became, during the war, that other figure of authority that so annoyed the artists, a coast-watcher, who ensured that restrictions on outdoor sketching were rigidly enforced.

235 Letter from G Toman to Glanville and Hamilton dated 15/10/1918 re St Andrew's Street Studio let to Miss S E Whitehouse - Mornington Estate Papers, County Records Office, Truro, GHW/12/3/6/1/200/55.

Fig. 2.102 'Bridge Studios', St Andrew's Street. The skylights are those of Herbert Lanyon's 'Attic Studio', which suffered severe problems with rats and water damage. (St Ives Trust Archive Study Centre)

2.4.1.4 Common complaints

The correspondence with Glanville's firm also reveals that the artists experienced a number of problems with neighbours, who were locals, which will not have aided good relations between the two communities. For instance, Herbert Lanyon's studio in St Andrew's Street was infested by rats, as a Mr Pearce kept slaughter-house offal in the basement beneath it, whilst Hurst Balmford, in his studio in the Island Studios block, had to cope with the damage caused by tar and creosote dripping through the ceiling, as a fisherman, called Thomas, insisted on tarring his nets in the loft above. In a blatant case of misogyny, Mary Williams, in Norway Square, suffered a brutal campaign of harassment from her neighbour, James Carbines, which ended with him building a wall blocking completely the entrance to her home and studio. These may be isolated incidents, but demonstrate that, beneath the surface, there were always tensions.

The artists endured a whole range of other problems with their studios - and, as a consequence, their landlords, who were never over-eager to spend money on them. As many studios had originally been built as cellars or lofts or other spaces not intended for human habitation, it is not surprising that they often proved not the most commodious accomodation. Few of the properties were watertight and roofs, which were the responsibility of the landlords, leaked incessantly. As now, gales and blizzards constantly blew off tiles and caused considerable damage, which even the local practice of covering the roofs with what Herbert Lanyon referred to as "a form of cement slurry", failed to counteract. Rotting timbers of roofs and windows were a constant headache and the artists' desire for skylights to provide better lighting conditions in the studio often proved a curse, as they invariably leaked, causing damage to the interior. Split lead gutters were another regular cause of problems and, as these were often sizeable, constant, and normally ineffectual, patching resulted. As a result of all these problems, plasterwork in the studios was invariably old and damp, and the dust falling from this was a constant annoyance and, as William Cock put it, "unfortunate for wet canvases". Studios were, accordingly, cold and damp spaces, in which a stove was an essential, but often ineffectual, fitting. In winter, when the artists were often working in their studios the most, conditions must regularly have been dire but, at other times, these vast rooms, with fantastic views, were treasured as the unique spaces that they truly were, the envy of many a visiting artist.

2.4.1.5 Sources

One might have anticipated that reviews of Show Day each year would have been helpful in determining the identity and location of the studio in which each artist was exhibiting but, in fact, the reviews hardly ever mention studio names, and it was only in the 1920s that a programme, listing the names of the open studios and their occupants, was produced, to which a much-needed map was added later in the decade. For the early years of the colony, accordingly, reliance has to be placed, in the main, on the extant St Ives Rate Books (see A Note on Sources), in which artists are often listed as ratepayers not only for premises labelled studios, but also for lofts, cellars and other small premises clearly used by them as workplaces. However, it soon becomes quite clear that the named ratepayer might have little correlation to the actual occupier. For instance, Wyly Grier is recorded as a ratepayer for a Porthmeor Studio for some six years after he emigrated to Canada, whilst Stuart Hobkirk is listed as the ratepayer for a Piazza Studio as late as 1917, when there is no other record of him in St Ives after 1904. It is also clear that there were frequent sub-lettings during periods of absence or illness, so that the Rate Books, for all their immense value, do not even begin the tell the full story of which artists found inspiration in particular spaces.

Comments made from time to time over the years as to the number of studios in the town also suggest that there were many other premises utilised as studios, which are not revealed by the Rate Books. For instance, Walter Norris tells his American colleague, John Sloan, in 1904 that there are sixty-five studios occupied in the town, whilst the Rate Book that year records just forty-eight, several of which are noted as vacant. Accordingly, there were clearly other properties owned or rented by locals that were made available as studios, perhaps, principally, on short-term lets. Furthermore, as artists began to be able to afford to rent or buy bigger properties, they created studio spaces in their homes as well, so that, particularly during times of inclement weather, they could choose between the warmth, comfort and convenience afforded by a studio at home, and the vista, ambience and privacy from a young family offered by a studio in the fishing quarter.

Fig. 2.103 Waves crashing over the rooftops of St Andrew's Street properties in October 1922   (postcard)

Figs. 2.104-5   Helene Schjerbeck   Sketches of the interior and exterior of her 'Tower' studio
from her letter to Maria Wiik   (courtesy : Carl Appelberg)

2.4.2   Helene Schjerfbeck's 'Tower' Studio, Richmond Place

One of the earliest, most interesting but, sadly, shortest-lived, studios was a tower, which is variously described as a Summer House or a Music Pavilion, which was in the grounds of the Robinsons' house at 4 Richmond Place, and which is likely to have been built originally by the owners of 'Brunswick House' (later renamed 'Trewyn'). It can be clearly seen, in its original garden setting, in the engraving of Edward Ashton's photograph of the town included in *The Pictorial World* in 1877 (Fig. 0.4). This was occupied by the Finnish artist, Helene Schjerfbeck, during her initial visit to the colony in 1887-8. Writing from Barnoon Villa, where she was staying, she exclaimed excitedly to her Finnish friend, Maria Wiik,

"I cannot but describe to you my tower once again because I love it more every day that passes. Through the arch on the ground floor one can walk straight into the Robinsons' garden; on one side, there is my green door with a big padlock hanging on it. On the first floor, there is a very small room with a single window. That's where I keep coals &c and, if need be, also sketch still lives. A flight of steep stairs leads up through the ceiling to a kind of chicken coop from which you emerge into the middle of my atelier. The brazier in the fireplace is black, but all the rest is white. From the centre of the ceiling the friendly face of the sun beams down on me, surrounded by Aries and Taurus among the 12 signs of the Zodiac and, in the four corners, lightly clad figures represent the four seasons. At the top of each wall, there is a large round plaster frame with the figure of a goddess at its centre. All these are made of plaster. The view is over the town, to the harbour and to the sea, and everything is in such a state of decay that I could not ask for better. For 40 years, they used the tower as a store room. Now it has been cleaned up and I have furnished the rooms with some items in the appropriate style."[236]

The final sentence suggests that the Robinsons themselves had not been using the building previously as a studio, and there is no other record of an artist occupying this intriguing space. As already mentioned, the Tower, clearly already somewhat dilapidated, was demolished in the mid-1890s to enable the completion of the terrace.

2.4.3   St Andrew's Street Studios

The properties facing the harbour in St Andrew's Street proved popular as studios from the outset, for, at that juncture, they rose up direct from the beach and afforded fantastic vistas, which even the completion of the West Pier in 1894 did not impact upon materially. The area was also cheap as, even in 1901, the street was described as full of "forsaken, battered, woebegone, tumbledown, dismantled and unsightly remains of houses".[237] One of the reasons for this was that the properties took the full force of gale-driven high seas, and there are several photographs of waves going over their roofs (see Fig. 2.103). Therefore, the fine vistas were accompanied, on occasion, by severe drawbacks, for seawater gushing through one's studio took realism a little too far!

---

236 Letter to Maria Wiik, undated, 1887, translated by Erkki Toivanen.
237 *St Ives Weekly Summary,* 2/3/1901

2.4.3.1 'Bridge Studios', St Andrew's Street

Net lofts built over fish cellars in the substantial property next to the churchyard (now the site of Chy-an-Eglos apartments), owned by the Cowley Estate, were converted into studios at an early juncture and were referred to, in the Estate's papers, as 'Bridge Studios' (see Fig. 2.102) .[238] Edward Simmons was one of the first artists to have his studio in this building, and it will have been of some considerable size, as one of the first meetings of the newly formed St Ives Arts Club was held in it, as well as the Annual General Meetings of the Tennis Club. The interior of the studio is probably featured in Simmons' paintings *The Carpenter's Son* (Plate 8) and *The Mother*, his controversial depictions of casually dressed members of his family as the Holy Family. Referring to the graveyard next door, Simmons commented, "Here the staunch Cornishmen were buried four or five layers deep, and occasionally the tide would wash a hole in the wall, scattering the bones and rolling skulls up and down the beach."[239] Proximity to the churchyard also gave rise to perennial problems with rats.

Artists using studios in this property included the American Edith Cockcroft (1906), John Park (1906-11) and the photographer, Herbert Lanyon (1906-1916).[240] Lanyon, who called his studio 'Attic Studio', experienced a particularly bad year in 1909. His first problem was caused by defective skylights. Writing to the landlord's agents in September, he bewailed, "During the last heavy rains, literally gallons of water were caught in pails, trays, dishes etc in the higher studio... No amount of patching can remedy the mischief; the old and rotten rafters on which the glass rests must be replaced."[241] However, he was soon faced with a far more distressing problem, caused by the activities of another tenant of his building - an invasion by "legions of rats". "For three weeks past, I have had a man trapping and poisoning these repulsive creatures, over 60 of them having been caught in cages and judging from the amount of *Rough on Rats* and *Rodine* consumed, not to mention *Rat Virus*, hundreds have probably succumbed by poison. Still they come, however, and I am persuaded that the task of ridding my premises of the pest will be a hopeless one so long as Mr Pearce occupies the cellar and is permitted to utilize it as a dumping place for slaughter-house offal."[242] A couple of weeks later, he wrote, "I have had all the old woodwork forming a rude dado in the lower studio pulled down to discover scores of rat holes and numerous nests".[243] Having filled the holes and replastered the walls, he match-boarded the whole interior at his own cost to make sure there was no possible means of ingress.

In such crises, Lanyon tended to act hastily and organise the remedial work himself, without waiting for the landlord's approval, and this often resulted in him bearing unnecessary expense. However, just a week later, heavy seas did considerable damage to one of the studio roofs and "tons of water flooded the interior".[244] Seemingly unperturbed by the need for constant repairs, he took out a new seven year lease in 1911, which took in all four of the original net lofts in the building and he converted these into three studios. However, on his marriage in 1916, he moved his studio to his new home, 'The Red House', albeit still calling it 'Attic Studio'.

Arthur White, whose watercolours of the streets and harbour of St Ives are well-known, took over the 'Attic Studio' in St Andrew's Street, and allowed his friend, Robert Langley Hutton, to have an exhibition of his work there in August 1919, shortly before his death, aged only 36, that October. The whole block, which comprised four studios, a cellar and two workshops, was sold by the Cowley estate in 1919 to G.Warren for £755, but White continued to work in 'Attic Studio' until 1927, when he moved to 'Tregenna Hill Studio', which was a large, commodious studio opposite the Catholic Church, measuring 27' x 14', with its own toilet, which had previously been occupied by Claude Francis Barry and then Francis Raymond Spenlove. There is no further mention of 'Attic Studio' thereafter.

2.4.3.2 The studio at No 3 St Andrew's Street

The Robinsons always seemed to have several studios available to them, both in the town and in their home. Clearly, as they were both artists, they needed separate working spaces. By 1890, Harry Robinson had moved from his original studio in Back Street to another of Lord Cowley's

---

238 I am indebted to Pam Badman for this information, resulting from her extensive research into the Mornington Estate papers, where this property is listed as lot 47.

239 E.E.Simmons, *From Seven to Seventy*, London and New York, 1922 at p.163.

240 Frustratingly, this property is noted in the Rate Books each year in the name of Lord Cowley and so these are no help in determining the occupants of the studios. However, some correspondence in the Mornington Estate papers does relate to it.

241 Letter from W.H.Lanyon to Glanville and Hamilton dated 9/9/1909 - Mornington Estate papers GHW/12/3/6/1/142/25.

242 Letter from W.H.Lanyon to Glanville and Hamilton dated 11/10/1909 - Mornington Estate papers GHW/12/3/6/1/142/26.

243 Letter from W.H.Lanyon to Glanville and Hamilton dated 23/10/1909 - Mornington Estate papers GHW/12/3/6/1/142/27.

244 Letter from W.H.Lanyon to Glanville and Hamilton dated 28/10/1909 - Mornington Estate papers GHW/12/3/6/1/142/28.

Fig. 2.106 The seaward side of the houses on St Andrew's Street, Westcott's Quay and part of The Warren. The St Ives Arts Club is the half-timbered building. The large window in the property below the Church tower will be that of Harry Robinson's studio at 3, St Andrew's Street, whilst ,to the left of it, is Blue Bell Yard. (detail from postcard)

Fig. 2.107 The Warren and Westcott's Quay seen from the harbour
(St Ives Trust Archive Study Centre)

properties at 3 St Andrew's Street and this became his principal studio in town.[245] Photographs (see Fig. 2.106) show that he was permitted to insert a large picture window, facing the sea. However, the studio was fairly basic. Writing in 1903, Robinson commented, "I write to call your attention to the state in which the cottage occupied by me in St Andrew's Street as a studio now is. For years, it has been more or less tumbling about my ears but it has reached such a condition as to be absolutely unfit for occupation... The ceiling became thoroughly saturated with salt water at the time of the blizzard some years ago and the plaster both of it and the walls is constantly falling down." He ends with a plea for something to be done soon "as my work is suffering".[246] The landlord did respond promptly, but Robinson had little time to enjoy the improved surroundings, as he died the following year. One might have imagined that Dorothy Robinson would have given up the tenancy after her husband's death, as she effectively gave up painting herself and, in any event, had a fine studio in her home, 'Belliers Croft'. However, she continued to rent it until 1917, when it was taken over by Lizzie Whitehouse. When Whitehouse was subsequently pulled up for sub-letting, she commented that it had been frequently sublet previously by Mrs Robinson, without objection, but the identity of the occupants from 1904 are not known.[247]

Toman was not too enthusiatic about Whitehouse's application for the tenancy, branding her "an old maid and very whimsical" and recalling the trouble that she had given him in relation to another tenancy (St Peter's Street Studio).[248] They soon fell out again, when Toman was "so insulting and rude to my sister in the street" over some misunderstanding, that Lizzie decided to have nothing more to do with him.[249] However, she found, during the winter months, that the property was unusable, as it leaked like a sieve, with water coming through the roof and through the windows, running down the walls and flowing over the floor. In the autumn of 1918, she decided to sublet it to the Thompson family, whose daughter was an art student, and their attempts to dry the place out, by lighting a fire, resulted in the asphyxiation of the neighbours - the saga that led to Toman's exasperated comment, "These paint-wasters seem to think they can do as they please."[250] The young art student was Mary Elizabeth Thompson, known as Betty, who was a dwarf with severe curvature of the spine. During her time in St Ives, she studied under both Alfred Hartley and Émile Fabry and went on to become well-known for her depictions of the Welsh slate and granite quarries.[251] With the property in a poor state, Lord Cowley had little hesitation in including it in the 1919 estate sale, where it was bought by James Lanham Limited for a client for £110. It appears to have reverted to residential use for a while, but, in the late 1930s, it was taken on as a studio again by Pauline Hewitt and used by her until she left St Ives in 1954.

2.4.3.3 'Blue Bell Studio', St Andrew's Street

In August 1888, Percy Craft, the Newlyn artist then working on his St Ives subject *Hevva! Hevva!*, took a three year lease of a loft studio in St Andrew's Street and was permitted access to Blue Bell Yard that fronted on to the harbour. However, he had to give this yard up in November 1889, when William James Hebblethwaite (d.1899) took a lease of 'Blue Bell Studio' and its yard. This was the former Blue Bell Inn that had been a noted resort for smugglers and had been the headquarters of the old freebooter Hans Breton - described as "a Dutchman in every particular - breeches like a balloon up to his armpits, thick jersey, leather braces and dirty red cap".[252]

Hebblethwaite was the son of a Leeds wine merchant and had himself been a woollen manufacturer, but he got into serious financial difficulties due to a partnership venture in Austria. Having been bailed out by his father and given an annuity of £120, he decided, in 1889, to try his hand at art in St Ives. He also had an interest in photography.[253] The studio was clearly in a pretty poor state when Hebblethwaite took it over, as it had been unlet for some while, and a storm in 1891 "nearly polished the whole place off".[254] He also had battles with his neighbours, the Curnows and the Plummers, concerning Blue Bell Yard, telling Glanville, "The yard is of very little use as it is - the neighbours amuse themselves watching my movements and as I told you frequently trespass and I do not care to be sworn at for telling Chas Curnow

245 In a letter from H H Robinson to R Glanville dated 21/6/1891, he asks permission to remove the wooden and glass building that he used as a studio in the garden of a property in Back Street - Mornington Estate Papers, County Records Office, Truro, GHW/12/3/6/1/52/30. Permission may well have been refused, as the Back Street Studio appears to have been occupied by Edith Hayes at the time of the 1891 Census and then by a Miss Little before being sold to William Trewhella in December 1893.

246 Letter from Harewood Robinson to R Glanville dated 11/10/1903 - Mornington Estate Papers, GHW/12/3/6/1/116/22-3

247 Letter from S.E.Whitehouse to R Glanville dated 18/10/1918 - Mornington Estate Papers, GHW/12/3/6/1/63/1.

248 Letter from G Toman to R Glanville dated 10/9/1917 - Mornington Estate Papers, GHW/12/3/6/1/196/84.

249 Letter from S.E.Whitehouse to R Glanville dated 28/12/1917 - Mornington Estate Papers, GHW/12/3/6/1/196/94.

250 Letter from G Toman to R Glanville dated 15/10/1917 - Mornington Estate Papers, GHW/12/3/6/1/200/55.

251 See David Tovey, *Creating A Splash - The St Ives Society of Artists 1927-1952*, Tewkesbury, 2003-4 at p.269-70.

252 *St Ives Weekly Summary* 2/3/1901.

253 Mornington Estate Papers, County Records Office, Truro, GHW/12/2/2/1 - various.

254 Letter from W J Hebblethwaite to R Glanville dated 4/5/1891 - Mornington Estate Papers, GHW/12/3/6/1/43/4.

to keep out and threatened by the next door people to be thrown into the sea".[255] Here, clearly, artist and fishermen did not see eye to eye - the pedantic Hebblethwaite sticking to the strict legalities, whilst the fishermen had probably beforehand enjoyed unfettered access over the whole yard. Eventually, Hebblethwaite got a partition erected in the yard, but they could not even agree what colour to paint it![256] However, despite these problems and repeated complaints to the landlord, he seems to have enjoyed the spot, creating a small bedroom and arranging to extend his lease for a further three years in 1896. However, Hebblethwaite was an amateur artist and, although he was elected as a member of the Arts Club, his work is never mentioned on Show Days and was not included in any exhibitions.[257] In poor health, he seems to have divided his time between a property Millhook, Poundstock, Stratton, Cornwall and St Ives, and, when he was ill in 1896 and 1898, Frederick Sargent sublet the studio for a while.[258] On his death in 1899, his brother, the Reverend E.P.Hebblethwaite, a Vicar in Ashby de la Zouch, dealt with his affairs.

The next tenant of 'Blue Bell Studio' was Sydney Carr, who had previously worked in one of the new Porthmeor Studios. He took possession in February 1900 and used it until March 1912. By this juncture, he had largely given up painting and had decided to concentrate on photography. He may, therefore, not have needed any longer the vast space offered at Porthmeor or he may have appreciated the lower rent - £6, as opposed to £10. He was clearly very taken with his new workplace, as he arranged to have his own headed notepaper, featuring a blue bell. He also took delight in showing visitors all the exits and entrances and the stowing away holes and corners used by the smugglers, and in pointing out the cavernous sound under the basement flooring, as the cellars were believed to be as deep as a well.[259] His bust-up with Toman, in 1909, concerned a leaking skylight, which Toman did not consider was the landlord's responsibility. Carr told Glanville after the incident, "The man's manner was so aggressive that I confess I lost my temper and had to tell him that if he came here again, I would kick him out." [260]

From the windows of his studio, Carr will have been able to keep an eye on the unfolding scene before him and the bulk of his surviving photographs are of the harbour, capturing boats and fisherfolk at interesting moments. Low tide was a particularly fruitful time for him, with vessels keeled over at different angles and fisherfolk spread over the beach, unloading catches, working on their boats or simply chatting, whilst light played off the pools of water collected on the sand. The view, from the harbour beach near Smeaton's Pier across to the Salvation Army building, the West Pier, the Church and Bridge Studios, was a popular one, and perhaps his best photo (Fig. 5.2) shows a young girl and boy, hand in hand, by the water's edge in the foreground of such a scene, as they watch another youngster, who has gone into the water to help a gig land. His photographs gained some recognition, for, in the West of England Industrial Exhibition at Plymouth in November 1907, he was awarded a Diploma (Silver Shield) in the Photographic Section and, in the Western Counties Exhibition in 1908, he was awarded a Diploma of Merit in the Architecture Photography Section.

After Carr's departure to Teignmouth in 1912, 'Blue Bell Studio' was rented by Mabel Douglas, who occupied it until 1919. By this juncture, she was concentrating on miniature portraits in watercolour (see Plate 36), and a reviewer commented, "Her delicacy of treatment and rich colouring impart a jewel-like quality to her work".[261] She also painted still life scenes in oil and watercolour. It is not certain where she had worked previously, but she might have used part of the vast space in her husband's Porthmeor Studio or, given her speciality, she could easily have worked from home. In any event, she now felt that she needed her own space.

Mabel was successful at the Royal Academy on a regular basis between 1904 and 1937 and many of her portraits were of fellow artists or other well-known figures in the town. These included Hilda Fearon (Show Day 1906 - possibly also RA 1911), her friend, Kitty Hain, daughter of Edward Hain (Show Day 1908 and 1909), Miss Chadwick (RA 1909), Mrs Herbert Lanyon (RA 1916), Doris Barry, the needlework expert who was the wife of Claude Francis Barry, (RA 1917) and Katherine Sargent, wife of Louis Sargent, (Show Day 1920). A number of her miniatures were done on ivory.

'Blue Bell Studio' was one of the properties sold by the Cowley Estate in 1919 and Mabel Douglas reverted to exhibiting on Show Days in other people's studios, often with Fred Milner in his large Piazza Studio. In 1920, planning consent was given to the purchaser, Edward Charles Paynter, to convert the

255 Letter from W J Hebblethwaite to R Glanville dated 2/5/1896 - Mornington Estate Papers, GHW/12/3/6/1/43/4.

256 Letter from W J Hebblethwaite to R Glanville dated 17/7/1896 - Mornington Estate Papers, GHW/12/3/6/1/43/4.

257 Mornington Estate Papers, County Records Office, Truro, GHW/12/2/2/1 - various.

258 See Mornington Estate Papers, County Records Office, Truro, GHW/12/2/2/1 - various.

259 *St Ives Weekly Summary* 2/3/1901.

260 Letter from S.Carr to R Glanville dated 852/1909 - Mornington Estate Papers, GHW/12/3/6/1/122/14.

261 *St Ives Times*, March 1922.

Figs. 2.108-110   St Ives harbour - Views by Sydney Carr
(courtesy Derek Wintle/copy photo Andrew Eggleston)

Figs. 2.111 - 113   St Ives harbour - Views by Sydney Carr
(courtesy Derek Wintle/copy photo Andrew Eggleston)

property into a fried fish shop! In doing this, he rendered over the attractive old stone walls, a common practice abhorred by the newly formed St Ives Old Cornwall Society.[262] A local was moved to write a poem on the loss.

In a street I loved and knew well
Stood a house they called the 'Blue Bell'.
Its sign and doors and windows too
Blazed alike in azure hue,
A joy to all the busy throng
Passing up and down-along.
But now no more that joyful wall
The senses charm, the eyes enthrall.
Now, instead of colour gay,
A dull expanse of stucco grey -
But yet not wholly lost those hues,
They have passed on to me - the blues.

Paynter's fish venture seems to have been short-lived, as a Miss A.H.Holt exhibited in 'Blue Bell Studio' on Show Day in 1924.[263] There are few references to it thereafter, although, in 1945, the artist, Medora Heather Bent, gave her address as 'Blue Bell Studio', when applying for a tenancy of one of the Piazza Studios, whilst Hilda Jillard exhibited there on Show Day in 1949. The property is still called 'Bluebell'.

2.4.3.4 'Beach Studio' and 'Ocean Wave Studio', St Andrew's Street

Other artists to rent studios in St Andrews Street were the successful amateur painter, William Cock, whose work is included in a number of Cornish Public Collections, and his son, Garstin Cox (1892-1933), one of the few locally-born artists to make a name for himself prior to the Second World War. William was a director of Holman's Engineering and lived at 'Roskear Villa', Camborne, and father and son are recorded as working together in St Ives from as early as February 1907, when they are signed in to the Arts Club. Although he had created a studio in his own property in Camborne, William wrote to the agents for the Estate of Lord Cowley in October 1910, asking if he could take a small room at the back of their St Ives office in St Andrew's Street as a studio for his son and himself. "The studio is rough as you say, but it will serve our purpose admirably. I have often - with my son when working at St Ives - had to leave all our gear (canvases, easels etc) in a friend's studio or at a lodging house. The greatest gain about this room is that one can easily pull a sketch together on the spot before bringing it to Camborne, which sometimes is a great advantage."[264] He mentioned that his son was presently on tour with Noble Barlow, but would be delighted to get this room. They called it 'Beach Studio'.

The following year, though, they decided they needed more space and took, in addition, a lease of the adjoining 'Ocean Wave Studio' at 6 St Andrew's Street. This had most recently been in the occupation of Dr Richardson, a doctor forced to retire through deafness, who had taken up painting. However, he had been another to feel the lash of Toman's tongue, perhaps understandably, as he appears to have been in occupation without authority and with little inclination to pay much rent.[265] This extra commitment by the Coxes may not have been a success as the studio was in a poor state. In December 1912, William wrote, "The inside studio has given me no end of trouble. I am unable to use it from October to March. The chimney absolutely refuses to draw and the walls and roof are crumbling on my work in fine shale. I have spent about £6 on same; nevertheless, it is a horror."[266]

The onset of War made matters difficult for the family. Even as early as 1911, William struggled to pay the full rent (£6) on time and, in December 1915, he was finally forced to accept defeat. "I can hardly point out that the present crisis has dealt a death blow to our work at St Ives, so that both my son and myself have for the last eight months been working on munitions at Camborne. In fact, it is fifteen months since we have been at the studios in St Ives. This working from 6-30 to 9 in the evenings practically ends all art work and we are trying to settle a few accounts as best we can."[267] It was agreed that the tenancy would come to an end in March 1916 and Cock finally settled his debt that September.

---

262 See *St Ives Times*, 16/4/1920.

263 *St Ives Times*, 12/2/1926 notes the death of E.C.Paynter's daughter-in-law, aged only 23, at 'Bluebell', St Andrew's Street.

264 Letter from W Cock to Glanville and Hamilton dated 26/10/1910 - Mornington Estate Papers, GHW/12/3/6/1/147/144/18.

265 See Mornington Estate Papers, County Records Office, Truro, GHW/12/3/6/1/144/43-5.

266 Letter from W Cock to Glanville and Hamilton dated 3/12/1912 - Mornington Estate Papers, GHW/12/3/6/1/147/152/24-6.

267 Letter from W Cock to Glanville and Hamilton dated 4/12/1915 - Mornington Estate Papers, GHW/12/3/6/1/147/182/27.

Fig. 2.114 The interior of a Borlase Smart studio, probably 'Ocean Wave Studio'
(Smart family archive/St Ives Trust Archive Study Centre)

The purchaser of the studios and the adjoining Cowley Estate Office, at a price of £350, at the time of the Estate Sale in 1919 is noted in the local paper as James Lanham Limited, but 'Ocean Wave Studio' was conveyed to Bertha Cockerham and Florence Canning, two artist friends from Devon.[268] As noted below, Cockerham had been working for some years from a studio in the Norway area of town, but there is no record of her exhibiting at her new studio prior to her death in 1922-3.[269] Florence Canning, who had exhibited at Harris and Sons in Plymouth and who had helped Cockerham run a painting class in Yelverton, came to stay with her in 1911 and joined the Arts Club in 1912, but she no longer painted, due to eye problems.[270] She is still recorded as the ratepayer for the studio (GER £15) in 1925 and she appears to have converted the various parts of the property into a much more commodious home, for when it came up for auction in April 1928, it was said to contain a large studio living room, 28' x 24', with two top lights, a bedroom, 7'6" x 19', coal house, scullery, indoor sanitation, with a large cellar storehouse beneath, 28' x 45', and a balcony frontage of 30', giving a fine uninterrupted sea view. Following the auction, the property was used by Borlase Smart, until the late 1930s.

2.4.4   Studios in The Warren and Westcott's Quay

Similar vistas to those enjoyed from the St Andrew's Street studios were also enjoyed from properties on the adjoining Westcott's Quay, where the Arts Club was located, and the seaward side of The Warren, the road that led from Westcott's Quay past Pednolver Point to Porthminster Beach (see Fig. 2.107). Here again, though, the properties took the full force of gale-driven high seas.

2.4.4.1 The Mine Engine House studio on Pednolver Point

Another unusual type of disused building that was converted into a studio early on was the North Providence Mine Engine House on Pednolver Point - now the site of the Pedn Olva Hotel in The Warren. This mine had been started in 1860 and was to have been worked below the sea, but little was ever done to it. However, the tower of the engine house made an attractive feature opposite the entrance to the harbour. Indeed, it appears that its owner, Lord Cowley, may have incorporated crenellations into its top, after the roof had fallen in, to give it the appearance of a castle. It was often included by artists in early depictions of the town, albeit they tended to depict it as taller and narrower than it was (see , for example, Fig. 2.116).

---

268 I am indebted to Pam Badman for this information, resulting from her extensive research into the Mornington Estate papers, where this property is listed as part lot 35.

269 She was a member of West Cornwall Golf Club and its list of members records her death in the 1922-3 season.

270 See Arts Club Minutes March 1912. The studio was used on Show Day in 1927 by Ellen Fradgley.

Fig. 2.115 View of the Mine Engine House on Pednolver Point and the wooden pier c.1880
(St Ives Trust Archive Study Centre)

Fig. 2.116 James Clarkson Uren   *St Ives*   (Private Collection)
This watercolour, dating from c.1887, shows an artist sketching by the Mine Engine House studio.

Fig. 2.117 This postcard of Pednolver Rocks shows the ivy-clad, truncated Mine studio with sloping roof

Louis Grier, who worked in St Ives in both 1884 and 1886, before settling in the town on a more permanent basis in 1887, may well have been the first artist to use it as a studio, as, in 1888, he gave his exhibiting address, for both his Royal Academy and BAPFA exhibits, as 'Ivy Tower', St Ives. This would not appear to be Schjerfbeck's Tower, as not only was she herself occupying it in early 1888, but her drawing of it shows no hint of ivy. On the other hand, works dated 1888 by Louis Grier depict not only the mine engine house itself, but also the exact view that he would have seen from the Pednolva Studio.[271] Grier certainly indicated to the landlord subsequently that he had formerly been in occupation of the cottage adjoining the studio and it seems likely that this was his first painting base in the town.[272] Grier, in selecting the name 'Ivy Tower', no doubt realised the likelihood of an association with 'Ivory Tower'. However, later in 1888, Grier decided to move to a studio on the harbour beach. His decision may have been prompted by concerns about the stability of the structure, as, in April 1889, the upper-most part of the engine house was taken down and the far less picturesque remnant of the building re-roofed. Whilst detracting from the ambience of the harbour scene, this work, of course, did not affect the fine vista from the property itself and, in June 1889, a three year lease of it, at a yearly rent of £6, was taken by Eardley Wilmot Blomefield, who was then lodging with Grier at 6, The Terrace.

Blomefield, who was born in Calcutta, but who had been living in Mansfield prior to his arrival in St Ives, exhibited at the Paris Salon in 1885 and, therefore, may have known some of the early settlers from his Paris student days. Not unnaturally, given the studio's location, Blomefield seems to have concentrated on marine work whilst in St Ives, and his painting *Landing Fish, St Ives*, which he exhibited in his studio on Show Day in 1891, was described as "a work eloquent in its tranquility and truth...full of sunlight and restful with the repose of a summer sea."[273] He had success at the Royal Academy with *A Cornish Beach* in 1890 and *In the Sun* in 1891. However, he also did some portrait work (see Plate 37). Blomefield was a keen sailor, having a pleasure boat, *Chloe*, and he made headlines in the local paper in June 1891, when he rescued from drowning the son of Matthew Stevens, whom he had seen fall off Pednolver Rocks and get into difficulties.

Blomefield, who was the initial Treasurer of the Arts Club, rented the studio until his departure from the town in 1894, when it was taken over by the Kirkpatrick sisters until 1906. Lily Kirkpatrick, the most talented of the trio, is likely to have used it the most and was the only one to participate in Show Days, but Ethel exhibited a St Ives subject at the SWA in 1895 and Ida in 1899. However, it is unlikely that Ethel and Ida used it that much after Lily's death in 1902. Millie Dow, from whom the Kirkpatricks rented their home, felt that he had been promised first refusal on their departure, for he wanted to use the studio for some marine work, and, accordingly, he was rather annoyed to find out, in early 1907, that it had been rented out on a permanent basis to Moulton Foweraker, who had sublet it off the Kirkpatricks

---

271 See my book *Pioneers of St Ives Art* at p.111.

272 See Letter dated 23/7/1908 - Mornington Estate Papers, County Records Office, Truro, GHW/12/6/3/8/2.

273 *St Ives Weekly Summary*, 11/4/1891.

from May 1906. By now, it had become known as 'Rock Studio' and Foweraker soon wanted to extend his lease as "the studio suits me very well for exhibition purposes".[274] He stayed there until 1909, when, during a brief period of renewed hope for the Cornish mining industry, St Ives Consols showed an interest in re-opening the mine.[275] However, mining activity never resumed and the studio was taken over by the American, J.S.Bristol, until 1911 and then by the marine painter, Charles Tracy, until 1913. Millie Dow was eventually able to rent it in 1914 and his painting of the entrance to the harbour owned by Kelvingrove Art Gallery, Glasgow clearly depicts the view from the studio. The studio was eventually sold off in 1919 and demolished to enable the construction of the property now known as the Pednolva Hotel.

2.4.4.2 'The Cabin Studio', Westcott's Quay

'The Cabin', Westcott's Quay, a property still known by that name that is right on the edge of the sea, opposite the Arts Club, was used between 1899 and 1901 as an accomodation address by girl art students from the Slade, who were studying at the Olsson/Talmage School, and it seems that, in 1906, Algernon Talmage took the opportunity of buying the property. The Rate Books indicate that it comprised two small properties, one a house and studio (GER £8) and one merely a house (GER £3). It is likely that Talmage intended this to be an independent home for Gertrude and himself, something that they had not enjoyed since their marriage in 1896, and he gave 'The Cabin' as his address when he was first elected to Chelsea Arts Club. However, the new arrangement proved short-lived, as he deserted his wife in 1907.

Fig. 2.118 Borlase Smart standing in the doorway of 'The Cabin', Wescott's Quay.
Note the additional boarding on the lower section of the Arts Club at this time.
The property on the left has been demolished.
(Smart family archive/St Ives Trust Archive Study Centre)

274 Mornington Estate Papers, County Records Office, Truro, GHW/12/3/6/1/131/28.

275 There does appear to be a Conveyance dated 28/4/1910 to St Ives Consols which includes the studio and a Licence to Mine of the same date. See Mornington Estate.Papers, GHW/12/2/12/9/1 but see also 12/3/204/15.

Gertrude is still recorded as the ratepayer of the property in 1925, and she appears to have used it as a home and studio at least until the death of her mother in April 1915, aged 87, who, at that juncture, was living with her there. In the 1920s, though, when Gertrude had moved back to the family home at 14, Draycott Terrace, 'The Cabin' was sublet, and the Californian artist, Euphemia Charlton Fortune, indicated that she worked from there during her time in the colony in 1922-3. Writing to her friend, Ethel Grubb, shortly after she and her mother had arrived in the town, Effie Charlton Fortune enthused, "We are quite mad about the studio. At high tide, as it is at the moment, the spray dashes past the windows up to the roof and there are enormous crowds of gulls flying about."[276] However, she may not have been quite so enthusiastic after St Ives was buffeted by an enormous storm in October 1922, during which a well-known photograph (Fig. 2.103) was taken showing waves breaking over the roof of the studio. When it was published in the *Daily Graphic*, the caption read, "The biggest wave is breaking over the Cabin Studios, in which were two Californian women artists, busy with buckets." However, this frightening experience did not dampen her enthusiasm, and she produced some of the best work of her career in the town, including *Summer Morning, St Ives*, which won a silver medal at the Paris Salon in 1923. She told Grubb, "This place would make a sick cat paint. You never saw such ripping stuff in your life to do."[277]

In 1929, Borlase Smart, when writing to protest about proposals for a new road from West Pier to Westcott's Quay, indicated that he had lived in 'The Cabin' for three years and could, accordingly, "claim to speak with authority as to the terrific backwash between the West Pier and Westcott's Quay, running into the harbour mouth during heavy weather", which he felt would be greatly exacerbated by the proposed new road.[278] Fig. 2.118 shows him standing in the doorway.

2.4.4.3 Other studios in The Warren

No other studios appear to have been created in this area of the town in the nineteenth century, but a few others are recorded early in the new century. James Elgar Russell, who was the eldest son of John Russell of St John's, Sutton at Hone, Kent, created a studio in his home (GER £7) next to the Arts Club, into which he moved in 1901. He had first come to study art in St Ives in 1896 and quickly displayed not only his musical and theatrical talents, but also his genial nature and capacity for organisation, for he was elected Secretary of the Arts Club in 1897.[279] For New Year's Eve celebrations in 1902, a covered walkway was erected between his home and the Arts Club, so that both premises could be used for the festivities. In October 1905, Russell seems to have contemplated moving, for he offered the Club first refusal on his cottage. However, instead, he ended up by taking, that year, one of the Porthmeor Studios as his principal workplace and continued to live in the cottage until 1917, when he moved to a much more substantial property in Primrose Valley (GER £42), which he named 'St John's' after his family home.

The watercolourist and flower painter, Helen Seddon, however, was the artist who occupied a studio in The Warren for the longest period. Although the daughter of a New Zealand sheep farmer, she was born in Shropshire and studied art in Edinburgh and Paris, before coming to St Ives in the early 1920s. She exhibited initially at 'Crab Rock Studio', before creating, prior to 1926, 'Morvah Studio' at No 17, where she remained until her death in the early 1970s.

2.4.5   The first studios in the Porthmeor Area

Let us move now to the other side of St Ives, to the area backing on to Porthmeor Beach, which had, for most of the nineteenth century, been the industrial section of town. Initially undevelopable due to wind-blown sand from Porthmeor Beach, the area had only been able to be built upon following the completion of John Smeaton's sea-wall along the back of the beach in the late eighteenth century. As this coincided with the zenith of the fishing industry, huge industrial-scale fish cellars and nets lofts had been constructed, many built directly on to the sea-wall itself. With the fishing industry in ever-deepening decline, more and more of these huge spaces became available, which not only combined fantastic vistas over Porthmeor Beach and the Island, but, of great import to the artists, faced north. Local entrepeneurs also picked up on the particular attractions of this area for artists and erected purpose-built studios wherever there was some spare ground. By the War, this area had been completely transformed, with paintings, not pilchards, the leading commodity.

---

276 Letter dated 29/1/1922 - Fortune papers, Monterey Peninsula Museum.

277 ibid.

278 See Smart's letter *Municipal Bye-Election - A Serious Outlook*, St Ives Times 22/11/1929.

279 See his Obituary in *St Ives Times* 8/4/1927.

Fig. 2.119 Detail from a photo of Porthmeor Wall from the late 1880s, showing, arrowed, on the right,
a small loft believed to be the first Porthmeor Studio created by Butler, and, on the left,
what became Porthmeor Studio No 8. The latter, and probably also the former, have skylights
already inserted.   (Brian Stevens)

Fig. 2.120 Aerial view of St Ives taken in 1936, showing the old industrial fish stores fronting Porthmeor
Beach now converted into studios. The black-roofed building is the Piazza Studios.
(Aero-Films/St Ives Trust Archive Study Centre)

Fig. 2.121 Adrian Stokes
(St Ives Trust Archive Study Centre)

2.4.5.1 Howard Russell Butler and "the first studio on Porthmeor"

In his unpublished autobiography, the American Howard Russell Butler claimed that he created the first studio on Porthmeor Beach during his initial visit to the town in 1886. A letter to his sister that year also records how he located the studio, and the following paragraph is an amalgam of these two accounts.

> "There were no big studios to be had but after a two day search among the lofts in the old fishing part of town, I secured one of the smaller ones, having an exposure toward the north, which had formerly been used for storing the ropes used in the pilcher fishing. It forms the top of a building which at high tide rises almost out of the sea. I had to sign a year's lease but the rental was only four pounds for the year and I had the right to put in a studio window in the roof, which I did at trifling expense. It was a two-day job to cut a hole in the roof and have a window put in and another day was devoted to whitewashing or rather grey-washing the interior and putting the place in thorough order. This was the first studio on Porthmeor... There was no staircase and the loft was reached by a ladder which entered through a trap-door in the floor. By pulling up the ladder, I was indeed isolated. I found this very servicable when Simmons, who was an inveterate talker, would come around determined to finish some argument began the night before and I did not want to be disturbed."[280]

Butler, having rented the studio for a year, presumably used the same space, when he returned in 1887. However, in this area of town, there is no mention of a studio in either the 1886 or 1888 Rate Books. On the other hand, there are only two lofts recorded that have.a GER of about £4, the rent paid by Butler - one owned by William Hambly and let to William Bastian for £3 and one owned by John Williams and let to Richard Lander for £3-10. The latter suddenly looks the most likely possibility when one finds that, in the 1893 Rate Book, it is listed as a studio. Not unnaturally, Lander, therefore, added 10/- to the rent when he sublet it to Butler. Looking at the Ordnance Survey Map of 1877 (Fig. 2.100), the rope loft appears to have been situated right next to the site that was developed into Porthmeor Studios Nos 1-5 (i.e. it is now part of the property known as 'The Doll's House'). I have marked the building on Fig. 2.119, a long-range, and very grimy, photograph showing the Porthmeor wall, taken before the principal studio developments of the 1890s. I believe that it is possible to detect a skylight in the roof of this, although there are clearly two skylights in the other building marked, to its left, which became Porthmeor Studio No 8. This clearly raises the possibilty of this latter building having housed Butler's studio, but I do not

---

280 H.R.Butler, Unpublished Autobiography, p.167, Archives of American Art, Smithsonian Institution, Washington DC, Howard Russell Butler papers, Reel 93 and Letter from H R Butler to Mary Butler dated 8/8/1886 - Archives of American Art, Smithsonian Institution, Howard Russell Butler papers.

believe that it did, for it is listed in the Rate Books as a cooperage, rather than a loft, at a GER of £7-10, and is not noted as a studio until 1898. John Williams' loft/studio was certainly outside the Porthmeor and Piazza studio complexes, for it is recorded in the Rate Books as a separate entity, after those developments were completed.[281]

In the Rate Book for 1893, the name of the ratepayer for this Loft Studio is initially shown as Adrian Stokes, implying that he had been the ratepayer previously. However, he is also shown that year as the ratepayer for a large studio in Virgin Street, which was to be his base for the rest of his time in St Ives. As Stokes had only just come back to St Ives, having left in late 1891, not intending to return, there is the possibility that this studio had been his initial painting base. Indeed, if this was Butler's studio, then Stokes, having arrived in the town in the summer of 1887, might even have taken it over from Butler after his departure that October. This is all total speculation, of course, but two of Stokes' 1890 Show Day exhibits were Porthmeor scenes (see also Plate 7).

Stokes' name in the 1893 Rate Book is replaced by that of the American, Sydney Laurence, who may well have taken occupation initially on Stokes' departure in 1891. As Laurence was the ratepayer in 1894 as well, then this studio will have been the location where Laurence completed his amazing nine-foot masterpiece, *Setting Sun on the Cornish Coast*, depicting waves on Porthmeor Beach lit up by the rays of a beautiful sunset. It is likely that Laurence retained this studio until he decided, in 1898, to try his hand as a roving reporter and, certainly, in 1898, the ratepayer is shown as Selina Wing, an art student, who was shortly to marry John Bromley. Bromley already had a studio on the harbour beach (GER £3) and, in 1901, took the St Peter's Street Studio, after which there seems no further mention of this historical studio.

2.4.5.2 Julius Olsson's Back Road East Studio

The Rate Books for both 1893 and 1894 have Julius Olsson as the ratepayer for two adjoining studios (GER £5 each) in Back Road East, which he was renting off the personal representatives of J.Quick. These, therefore, could have been his initial working base in the town, following his arrival in 1888, and two photographs in the Olsson family archive, which show a young Olsson flanked by canvases in a fairly rough-looking attic, are probably a record of this studio. After Olsson's move to his Porthmeor Studio in 1895, the studio seems to have had few takers, although, in 1901, James Lanham became the ratepayer for it for a few years. However, whether he let it out or used it for storage is not known.

Fig. 2.122 Julius Olsson most probably in his Back Road East studio   (Olsson family archive)

---

281 See the Rate Books of 1898 and 1899.

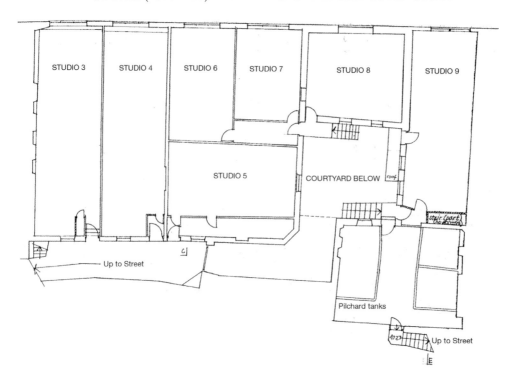

Fig. 2.123 Current floor plan of Porthmeor Studios complex (Long & Kentish, architects, London)

2.4.6   The Porthmeor Studios complex - General

Of all the studio complexes in St Ives, the Porthmeor Studios, with their vast windows which give unequalled views over Porthmeor Beach, have proved the most enduring and, accordingly, are the most well-known, having inspired both traditional and modern painters alike with their location and size. Previously thought to have been converted from sail and net lofts, new research carried out on behalf of the Borlase Smart Trust, which has owned the complex since 1949, suggests that a large number of the studios were, in fact, purpose-built, thus giving a completely new dimension to their historical importance. Although the structures may lack refinement, the studios have always proved impressive workspaces, as a visitor to one of them in the 1920s recorded.

> "We are struck by a rude, bare shed. The masonry is rough and unfinished, sheets of brown paper obscure the light, giving the studio the dim glow of some old cathedral. Stacks of canvases in various stages of completion lie against the walls. The furniture consists of an old wicker arm chair, two or three delightful Chippendales worm-eaten and decayed, and that without which no studio is complete, an old fashioned mirror in which from time to time the artist glances as he works. Here too there is a stove, a tin of milk, an old battered kettle, and other scatterings of a hasty tea party. [The artist] leads us on, and then, with the air of a magician, draws us behind the screen. The studio windows fly open and we stand amazed. In front of us, the Atlantic rolls in on golden sands. A glimpse is caught of distant rocks, and, to the right, the edge of the Island cliffs. There is not a soul to be seen - only the sea sporting for the artist's sake. Here he may catch her in all her moods, and paint the tones of her many dresses. Noon and night the sea will "sit" for him, bringing a new charm every time he looks out from that studio window. Here, too, the copper sails will come out and all unconsciously glitter in the sun."[282]

In times of crisis, the unique qualities of this group of studios have been appreciated and they have been saved from development, thus ensuring that they have continued to inspire the muses of countless artists. Their future now, though, is uncertain, as they need a huge amount of costly remedial work to survive and be habitable. This will, in any event, affect their ambience, as many will need to be subdivided, if there is any hope of them paying their way in the future.

It has not proved easy to link the listings in the Rate Books with the actual studio spaces - see Table D. Be warned, therefore, that the following analysis might prove incorrect in some details.

---

282 D.I.Sedding, *St Ives and its Studios, St Ives Times*, 1/1921.

TABLE D PORTHMEOR STUDIOS PUZZLE

I have spent many, many hours, poring over the available sources, trying to work out which artists occupied which studios in the Porthmeor complex, but I have not found any analysis that fits with all sources. Accordingly, this Table sets out the relevant source material and notes some of the difficulties thrown up. I can only assume that, at some juncture, there was a complete or partial re-numbering.

Ratebook Order (GER)	Current No (best guess)	Ratepayers 1898-1917	Ratepayers 1925
A (£10)	11?	1898 Grier (also 1893-4), 1899-1917 A Meade (in occupation from at least 1895)	A Meade
B (£10)	10	1898 Bosch Reitz (also 1893-4) then Thomas Simmonds (until 1906), 1907-1914 void, 1915-6 Evans Linton, 1917 F Beaumont	R B Smart
C (£10)	1 or 2	1898-1917 J C Douglas	JC Douglas
D (£10)	4?	1898 void, 1899-1907 M Lindner, 1908-1913 A Hartley, 1914 void, 1915-1917 F Hodgkins	M Lindner
E (£10)	1 or 2	1898 S Carr (by 1897) then F W Brooke (until 1901), 1902-1917 L Dyer	L Dyer
F (£10)	3	1898 Ellis then C G B Adams until 1917	B Adams
G (£10)	8	1898-1901 W Jevons, 1902-5 S Bosch Reitz, 1906-7 void, 1908-1917 M Lindner	Emily Hartley?
H (10)	9?	1898 W Osborn, 1899-1901 void, 1902-1911 J Titcomb, 1912-1917 N Hartley	A Hartley
I (£25)	5 - big	1898-1900 J Olsson, 1901 E P Fox, 1902 H Draper, 1903 converted into J, K and L	N/A
J (£11)	5	1903-1913 A Talmage, 1914 A Hartley, 1915-6 void, 1917 C F Barry	A Hayward
K (£10)	6 or 7	1903-4, J Thurston, 1905-1916 J N Barlow, 1917 M Smith	M Smith
L (£10)	6 or 7	1903-4 C Mottram, 1905-1916 J E Russell, 1917 F Ewan	F Ewan

The above Table has been compiled purely from the Rate Books and lists the studios in the order that they appear in the Rate Books from 1898 to 1925 - Studios A-L are, therefore, my designations. There is good reason to believe that this order was not altered at any time as, for instance, in the 1925 Rate Book, Meade is first, Douglas is third and Adams is sixth, an order that had not changed since 1899. In relation to Studios A and B, the named ratepayer in 1898 is the same as for 1893-4 and so these are clearly two of the original 'Back Road Studios' created in 1889-90. One might anticipate, therefore, that the third studio listed, Studio C, would be the other 'Back Road Studio', occupied in 1893-4 by Amy Llewellyn, but this does not appear to be the case.

On the sale of the studios in 1902, the auction particulars refer to five newly erected studios in the occupation of Messrs Fox, Adams, Brooke, Douglas and Lindner. These, therefore, are, respectively, Studios I, F, E, C and D. Studio I is clearly identifiable as the large studio, built for Olsson, which was sub-divided into three in 1903 - Studios J-L. There is also a reference in the sale particulars to a studio, measuring 27.5' x 24', in the occupation of Bosch Reitz. As these measurements conform with those of Studio 8, it seems that Studio G on the list is Studio 8. The three 'Back Road Studios' are said at the time of the sale to be in the occupation of Meade (Studio A) and Gardner Symons, clearly a sub-lessee, with one void. This does not really help to identify the third 'Back Road Studio', but, by a process of elimination, this appears to be Studio H. This all makes the order in which the studios are listed in the Rate Books very strange, albeit seemingly consistent on a year by year basis.

As and when Beale Adams does exhibit on Show Day in the 1920s, he is recorded at Studio No 3, which suggests that Studio F is No 3. However, other artists exhibit there as well. Lindner in the 1920s is said to occupy Studio No 4 and so Studio D is probably No 4. This leaves Dyer (Studio E) and Douglas (Studio C) as long-term occupants of Studio Nos 1 & 2, but I have found no indication of who was in which.

An account of Elgar Russell's exhibition at his studio in 1916 confirms that he occupied either Studio No 6 or 7.

The letters of Frances Hodgkins show her address as 7 Porthmeor Studios. This does not tally with the Table at all. She also calls her studio "a huge barn", which does not really fit Studio No 7, but would fit Studio No 4, which the Table suggests that she will have occupied.

Arthur Hayward's adverts for his painting school in the mid-1920s refer to him operating from Studio No 4. On Show Days in the 1920s, Borlase Smart is recorded as exhibiting at Studio No 1, Frances Ewan at No 2, Marcella Smith at No 3 and Alfred Hartley at No 7. In 1920, Marcella Smith also ran a painting class from No 3. Although all are shown as ratepayers in 1925, none of these numbers tally with the Table, suggesting a re-numbering. On the other hand, the St Ives Society of Artists are said to take, in 1928, Studio No 5 for their Gallery, expanding into No 4 in 1932, and such numbering does match the current one employed. Qué?!!!!!!.

Fig.2.124 The exterior in 2009 of Porthmeor Studios Nos 9-12,
formerly known as 'Back Road Studios',
the home of the St Ives School of Painting since 1938.

2.4.6.1 The Porthmeor Studios complex - Studios now numbered 9 to 12

The first mention in a Rate Book of studios on Back Road West is in 1893 - there being no extant Rate Books for the years 1889-1892. This lists a group of three separate studios, each having a GER of £10, occupied by the Dutch artist, Sigisbert Bosch Reitz, an artist called Grier, whom, given Louis Grier's lease of 'The Foc'sle', will be his brother, Wyly, and a relatively unknown artist, Amy Llewellyn (or Lluellyn). However, it now seems likely that these three studios were created in 1889-90. They were originally called the 'Back Road Studios', and it was only in the 1930s that the current numbering came into being.[283] The owner of the studios was George Williams, who, as mentioned above, was a former Mayor of the town, whose trades included barrel-making. The Rate Book for 1888 records him as owning, in this area, two small houses, with a combined GER of just £7-20, a cooperage (GER £4) and a stable (GER £4-10). It appears to be the cooperage, the stable and one house that he converted into the three studios, which, as they had a combined GER of £30, indicates that a considerable amount of new development took place. This has been confirmed by the recent survey carried out on behalf of the Borlase Smart Trust - see also Fig. 2.100. Therefore, these would appear to be the first purpose-built studios in St Ives - a venture that reflected great faith in the future of the fledgling colony.

Fig. 2.125 The beach-side exterior in 2009 of (from the left) Studio No 9, with No 10 above
(new build 1889-90), No 8 (original) and Nos 6 and 7 (formerly part of No 5)
(new build 1895).

---

283 See, for example, the Show Day report in 1907 (*St Ives Weekly Summary*, 30/3/1907), which refers to Meade exhibiting at the Back Road Studios and also Show Day listings during the 1920s.

Fig. 2.126 The interior of Sigisbert Bosch Reitz's Back Road Studio c.1891
(Six Art Promotion Ltd, Amsterdam)

It seems likely that Bosch Reitz, who came to St Ives with a group of student friends from Paris in mid-1890, took his studio shortly after his arrival, and a photograph of the interior of this (Fig. 2.126) is the earliest known image of a Porthmeor Studio. This photo is likely to date from 1891-2, as it shows, on the easel, his painting of a fish market in St Ives, which he exhibited on Show Day in 1892, whilst a number of portrait sketches, used for it, hang behind. A big, old sail is used to divide up the space, something done by a number of artists in order to try to isolate an area free of the cold draughts that swept through the studios during the winter months. Nets can also be seen hanging from the ceiling. Analysis of the roof timbers shown in this photo suggest that Bosch Reitz was in occupation of what is now known as Studio No 10. Therefore, the group of three studios, listed in the Rate Book of 1893, will represent the three studios in this part of the complex, now known as Nos 9, 10 and 11.

Bosch Reitz is listed as the ratepayer for his studio until 1898, but his presence in the town is rarely mentioned in the years 1893-7 and it is likely that he sublet it repeatedly. However, he will have used it to paint his masterpiece, *Harbour at St Ives* (Stedelijk Museum, Amsterdam), which won a medal at the Paris World Exposition in 1900 and was the first work that he sold to a public gallery. Between 1899 and 1906, however, the ratepayer for the studio was Thomas Charles Simmonds (b.1842), a Cheltenham-born landscape artist, who taught at Nottingham and Derby Schools of Art. Indeed, he was Head of the latter. No St Ives work by him is known, though. After that, for some reason, the studio has no recorded ratepayer for a number of years, although the animal painter, Evelyn Beckles, recently married to William Evans Linton, and the figure painter, Frederick Beaumont, used it for a while during the War. The studio, however, has recently been known as the workplace of Hyman Segal, who occupied it, until his recent death, for more than fifty years.

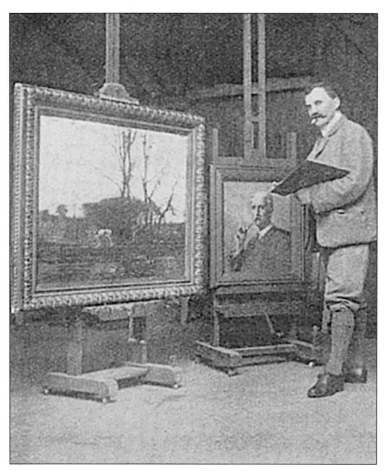

Fig. 2.127 Arthur Meade in his Back Road Studio in 1905
(*Black and White*)

Fig. 2.128 The St Ives School of Painting, with Leonasrd Fuller, second from right
(St Ives Trust Archive Study Centre)

I suspect that Amy Llewellyn occupied Studio No 9. Her name is also spelt locally as Lluellyn and an artist of that name, from Kensington, is recorded in the *Dictionary of British Artists 1880-1940*. She lived at Ayr Cottage and took part in the Carnival Masquerades in 1892-3, but there is no reference to her after 1894. As indicated in Table D, it is not easy to work out who used this studio subsequently, but it is likely that it was taken over by the Australian artist, Will Osborn, who was particularly involved with the colony between 1892 and 1897. After a void break, Jack Titcomb appears to have used it between 1902 and 1911, and then Nora Hartley, until she moved into the St Peter's Street Studio in 1916.

Wyly Grier, who was a figure painter, was the initial occupier of Studio No 11 and he is shown as the ratepayer for this studio until 1898. However, as he emigrated to Canada in 1892, where he became that country's leading portrait painter, the studio was clearly sublet. Arthur Meade, shown as the ratepayer for 1899, was certainly in occupation by 1895, as he suffered a serious fire in the studio that December. The cause of the fire was not known, as the stove had not been lit for several days, but a number of Meade's partially completed canvases were either blistered with the heat or damaged by the water used to put out the fire. Meade occupied this studio for more than forty years, during which time he had over sixty works hung at the Royal Academy. On his reluctant decision to give up the studio after his move to Lelant in the late 1930s, it has been used, ever since, by the St Ives School of Painting, originally established by Leonard Fuller and Marjorie Mostyn in 1938 and still thriving. An additional studio - No 12 - was in operation by Show Day in 1949. This was converted from 17 Back Road West, the other house that George Williams had owned, and was, for many years, until his recent death, used by Bryan Pearce. Such long periods of occupancy demonstrate how artists fully appreciated their exceptional fortune, having once gained access to such magnificent spaces.

2.4.6.2 The Porthmeor Studios complex - Studios now numbered 1 to 7

The Rate Book in 1894 still only lists three studios in this run but, in the mid-1890s, major development clearly occurred, for the next extant Rate Book in 1898 lists nine studios here. When the freehold of these studios was sold in 1902, five of them were described as "newly-erected" and "recently built", but it transpires that such development occurred in 1895.[284] The fact that concrete, a novel building material for this period, was used in their construction confirms that they were purpose built. The development consisted of a block of four studios, each with a GER of £10, of which the ground floor ones (now Nos 3-4) measured 18' x 59' and the first floor ones (now Nos 1-2) 18' x 49'. The fifth studio (GER £25), which was adjoining, was a vast barn of a place, measuring 36' x 57'. Its floor, underneath which was constructed a new concrete tank for storing salted fish, was supported by ship's timbers used as very long floor beams and carried on cast-iron water pipes, probably formerly used as rising mains from mine shafts.[285] This studio was subsequently sub-divided into three to form Studios Nos 5-7. Immediately, the uniqueness of these magnificent workspaces was appreciated. Writing about them in 1896, Lewis Hind commented, "The most spacious studios are those on the Porthmeor Beach. Long, low and light, they border on the yellow sands, and when the high windows are thrown open, the painter can sit in his easy chair and study the wave forms as if they were simply an attraction of his back garden."[286]

It is not certain who were the initial occupants of studios Nos 1-4. An artist called Ellis is noted initially in the 1898 Rate Book. This may well be Edith Ellis, as Havelock indicates that, in their early years in Carbis Bay, he would walk into St Ives at lunchtime from his studio at Hawke's Point "to join Edith for lunch at the little restaurant kept by Miss Kevern as a resort for artists".[287] This suggests that she was pursuing her art at this juncture. However, this studio was taken over during 1898 by Beale Adams, a painter of "fresh", "breezy" and "vigorous" seascapes, whilst Sydney Carr was certainly using one in September 1897, when he had an exhibition of his work in it. However, this was taken over the following year by Frederick William Brooke, most probably an architect who had taken to landscape painting, who, after an initial visit in 1891, appears to have settled in the town in 1894, first exhibiting on Show Day in 1895.[288] He lived initially in Ayr Cottage - presumably taking over from Amy Llewellyn - and, despite having this workplace at Porthmeor, seems to have converted the stable in the grounds of the cottage into a further studio.[289]

---

284 See sale advert in *St Ives Weekly Summary*, 9/8/1902 & 6/9/1902.

285 I am indebted to Eric Berry and Nick Cahill for their survey of the construction process prepared on behalf of the Borlase Smart Trust.

286 C.Lewis Hind, *In Painters' Land*, The Ludgate, October 1896.

287 See Havelock Ellis, *My Life*, London, 1940 at p.274. This was in Tregenna Place.

288 Brooke first exhibited at the RBA in 1886 and had been living at Saxmundham in Suffolk. He was first signed in as a guest at the Arts Club in 1891 by fellow Suffolk resident John Chadwick Lomax. He had certainly become a member of the Arts Club by November 1894.

289 Lilian Faull records that, during the renovation work initiated after her father had bought Ayr Cottage in 1904, her family had lived in this studio. "For over a year, we lived in what had been a Studio, walking over wood and builders' effects as if they didn't exist. That studio had been built from a stable and had wood panelling about four feet high and above that brown hessian walls, and a glass roof in eaves high up." After Brooke's departure, the house had been let to Bernard Walke and his brother, William, who seems to have taken part in art classes in the town, and their mother. Lilian Faull remembered that the Walkes had curtains in the bedroom that had glistening metallic circles on them. Lilian Faull, *The Faulls of St Ives*, Penzance, 1972 at p.98.

Fig. 2.129 The beachside exterior of original Porthmeor Studios Nos 1-5 in the 1960s. The two windows to the left have now become the windows of Studios Nos 6 and 7, with No 5 no longer having a beach prospect. The windows on the very right are in the property thought to be Butler's first Porthmeor Studio, which appears, from the skylight, to be still in use as a studio.   (Roy Ray)

Fig. 2.130 The entrance ramp to Porthmeor Studios Nos 1-8 in the 1960s   (Roy Ray)

His exhibits over the next few years, often of marshes and cornfields, such as *Spring Melody* and *Thistledown*, were considered quietly harmonious in colour, and he was successful at the Royal Academy in 1895, 1897 and 1899. Prior to moving to Lelant in 1902, where he became a stalwart member of the Golf Club, he took an active part in the community, becoming Secretary of the Arts Club in 1898-9.[290]

By 1899, these four studios were occupied by John Douglas, William Brooke, Beale Adams, and Moffat Lindner and, although Lowell Dyer took over from William Brooke in 1902, and Alfred Hartley took over from Moffat Lindner in 1907, when he moved across to Studio No 8, there were no other changes in ratepayers for many years. This does not mean that there were no changes of occupants, for Wilson Henry Irvine recorded his impressions of a visit to Douglas' studio in 1923. Whilst admiring many of his fine photographs, Irvine could not help noticing that the studio had "an accumulation of over thirty years. Other painters leave their things with him and never come back. At least ten paint boxes. He melts up the old tin paint tubes and has 75lbs of pure tin worth several £s."[291]

The very large studio, whose GER was £25, was taken initially by Julius Olsson, and the fact that it was purpose-built suggests that it was specifically designed for his new School of Painting - a demonstration of supreme confidence in the success of the undertaking not only from Olsson but also from George Williams. Indeed, the *Pall Mall Gazette* of 27th July 1895, when reporting on the establishment of the new School, comments, "A spacious studio - and studios without the adjective are large in St Ives - will also be provided for the use of students". This is the first reference that I have found to one of the new studios, and the basis for my conclusion that they were completed earlier that year.

The vastness of Olsson's studio always provoked comment. "Mr Olsson's studio is as long and as high as many a Methodist chapel. From ceiling to floor, great fishing smack sails hang across in folds, stained by a thousand winds to the colour of brown velvet. On one side a bowl of water hissed upon a big stove, on the other a deal bench was strewn with tubes of pigment squeezed into decrepit shapes, and bore a china jar from which a score of good square brushes sprouted. On the wall was stretched a length of canvas ploughed and ridged with palette scrapings and behind, against the sail curtains, stood a mirror. Such was the painting room."[292] Photographs of the studio (Figs. 2.131-3), taken by John Douglas, also enable us to appreciate what a truly impressive space it comprised before its sub-division. Two huge windows gave magnificent views out over the beach, whilst that on the right also had a large skylight inserted in the roof above it. However, the photographs show that Olsson's principal working area was at the back of the studio - the section that is now in Studio No.5. Here, Olsson had blocked up the two small windows facing the courtyard and arranged for a further skylight to be inserted (see Fig. 2.132). A huge sail, acting as a curtain, enables the light or draughts from the front section of the studio to be cut out, and this section is presented as a vast uncluttered space. There is little evidence from these photographs, taken in 1896, of the activities in this studio of the School of Painting and, indeed, by 1898, at the latest, this was operating from the Harbour Studio on The Wharf.

The size of Olsson's studio enabled other activities to take place therein and, in December 1895, the artists performed in it the comedy, *Our Boys*, for the benefit of the Fire Brigade, after Arthur Meade's studio fire.[293] Edmund Fuller also appears to have hired it, during the summer of 1897, to hold a major exhibition, comprising some 120 of his works.

Although, inter alia, due to Douglas' photographs, Olsson is so strongly associated with the Porthmeor Studios, he does not appear to have worked there for more than six years. Indeed, an intriguing comment passed by Murielle Schofield in a letter to her husband, after a tea party at the Olssons, in late 1903, suggests that Olsson may not have had exclusive use of his Porthmeor studio at any juncture. She tells Elmer, "Mr Olsson also asked me again about Mr Woodbury [the Bostonian seascape painter, Charles Herbert Woodbury] and said that he had taken the only really good studio which he (Olsson) had had every winter until now and, as far as he could hear, Mr Woodbury intended to keep it."[294] Assuming that the reference is to the Porthmeor studio - and it is difficult to think of another relevant one - this comment would seem to suggest that Olsson had merely rented it during the winter months, as he did spend much of the rest of the year away from St Ives.

In any event, according to the Rate Books, Olsson's large studio was taken over in 1901/2 by the Australian, Emanuel Phillips Fox, who returned to St Ives in order to paint his Captain Cook commission.

290 A portrait of his wife by Arthur Meade was exhibited at the RBA in 1897.
291 Journal of Wilson Henry Irvine, 7/4/1923, Archives of American Art, Smithsonian Institution, Irvine papers, Reel 3564.
292 *In Painter's Land*, *Black and White*, 12/9/1896 at p.331.
293 See *St Ives Weekly Summary* 27/7/1895 re a studio for the School of Painting and 12/12/1895 & 28/12/1895 re the fire.
294 Letter dated 14/12/1903 from Murielle to Elmer Schofield, Archives of American Art, Smithsonian Institution, Schofield papers.

Fig. 2.131 Julius Olsson in the front section of the original Studio No 5. As a result of the subdivision in 1902-3, this area is now Studios Nos 6 and 7.   (John Douglas, courtesy Andrew Lanyon)

Fig. 2.132 Julius Olsson in the back section of the original Studio No 5. After the sub-division in 1902-3, this area remained part of Studio No 5.   (John Douglas, courtesy Olsson family archive)

Fig. 2.133 Julius Olsson in the original Studio No 5   (John Douglas, courtesy Andrew Lanyon)

Then, in 1902/3, it was used by Herbert Draper, who was working on an enormous 20' x 30' canvas for the ceiling of the great Livery Hall of the Draper's Company. Certainly, in Draper's case, his sole reason for coming down to St Ives was the size of this studio. Even still, the panel was so large that four feet of canvas, either at the top or at the bottom, had to be rolled up at any one time, and the problems that this caused made Draper vow, in his notebook, that he would never again paint a picture that he could not see in its entirety. In fact, Draper sent his daughter, Yvonne, a charming caricature of himself, precariously balancing at the top of a ladder, trying to flatten out the painting across the ceiling with a broom.[295] This ladder and various other sets of steps, together with many of his preliminary drawings, can be seen in a fascinating photograph of Draper at work in his Porthmeor studio (Fig. 2.134).

George Williams' death in 1902 led to the sale of the freehold of the studios, and, from the sale particulars, one can work out that Adams, Brooke, Douglas and Lindner were in occupation of Studios Nos 1-4, Phillips Fox of the big Studio No 5, Bosch Reitz of Studio No 8 and Meade of Studio No 11, whilst the American, George Gardner Symons, was a sub-lessee of either Studio No 9 or 10, the other being unoccupied. The freehold was bought by the private bank, Bolitho and Co, and it soon arranged for the large studio to be divided into three. The front section overlooking the beach was easily divided into two, with each section (now Studios Nos 6 and 7) having a large window. The back section (which retained the name Studio No 5) was now only top lit by the skylight and no attempt was made to open up the windows on to the courtyard. Despite being considerably smaller than Studios 1-4, the new studios at the front were let out at the same rental (£10), whereas the larger back section, despite not having any view, was let out at £11. This meant that the subdivision increased the rental income by £6 per year.

Algernon Talmage (No 5), the watercolourist, Charles Mottram, and the student, John Thurston, were the three initial occupiers of the newly formed studios. Talmage remained as the ratepayer for No 5 until 1913, despite moving to London in 1907, and so may well have sublet it for a number of years.

---

295 S Toll, *Herbert Draper (1863-1920) - A Life Study*, Woodbridge, 2003 at p.116.

Fig. 2.134 Herbert Draper in his Porthmeor Studio working on *Prospero Summoning Nymphs and Deities*

On Thurston's departure in 1904, his studio was taken over by Noble Barlow, until his death in 1917, whilst on Mottram's departure at much the same time, Elgar Russell moved in. He rented it until 1916, having one success at the Paris Salon in 1905 (*The Haunt of the Heron*) and one at the Royal Academy in 1907 (*Sea Breezes*). In August 1916, probably shortly before giving the studio up, he had an exhibition of thirty-five of his paintings there and invited his friends to *Tea and Pictures*. It appears that, even then, the approach to these studios, was not inviting, as a guest reported. "Down a narrow slope confined between high walls, under a washing line still containing remnants of garments which had received attention none too soon, playing 'hide and seek' amongst the packing cases and other litter, the explorer found himself in a small square evidently originally designed for a rat-pit. Exploring further, he mounted an outside stone stair, with the easy gradient of a fire escape" before discovering the studio. This was packed, for Russell was "known to everybody in St Ives, from the celebrated R.A. to the small boy with the cacchinnatory jodel", and he was "persuaded to part with about a dozen of his jewels".[296]

2.4.6.3 The Porthmeor Studios complex - Studio now numbered 8

As previously mentioned, the Rate Book for 1898 lists nine studios owned by George Williams in this complex - the three created in 1889-90, the five newly erected in 1895 and one other. The dimensions given when this studio was sold on Williams' death in 1902 - 27.5' x 24' - make it certain that this additional studio was what is now Studio 8. The fabric of the studio (see Figs 2.125 and 2.136), which backs on to the same courtyard as Olsson's big studio, clearly demonstrates that it was not newly erected in the 1890s, but was an existing building that was converted into a studio. Albeit it is not mentioned as a studio in the 1893 and 1894 Rate Books - George Williams in this section only owning an unoccupied cooperage (GER £7-10) - , it seems clear from Fig. 2.119 that rooflights had been inserted well before the 1895 redevelopment, so that it had been in use as a studio previously. However, it was no doubt refurbished in 1895, for, despite being considerably smaller in size than the newly created studios, its GER was still £10, which probably meant that the occupant also had the use of the cellar below it.

The ratepayer in 1898 was George Walter Jevons (b.c.1855), a Liverpudlian, who was one of the student friends of Bosch Reitz, who accompanied him to St Ives in 1890. As he was quite involved with the colony throughout the 1890s, although moving to live in Roswick Cottage, St Martin in 1894, he is likely to have been the initial occupant. Bosch Reitz took over the studio from him in 1902, but does not appear to have used it much. Moffat Lindner, though, moved into it in 1908 and occupied it until at least 1917 and again for much of the 1930s and 1940s.

---

296 *St Ives Times*, 4/8/1916.

Fig. 2.135 The exterior, today, of the original large Studio No 5, as seen from the courtyard or 'rat-pit'. The two windows on to the courtyard, blocked up by Olsson, are visible. On the right, can be seen the doorway, created at the time of the sub-division, to give access to the new studios 6 and 7, created out of the front section of the original large studio. The current parlous state of the studios is clear.

Fig. 2.136 The exterior, today, of Studio 8, from the courtyard. The steps "with the easy gradient of a fire escape" also lead to the doorway to Studios 6 and 7.

2.4.6.4 Frances Hodgkins and the Porthmeor Studios complex in wartime

During the War years, activity in the studios was probably quite limited, as a combination of war related work and financial pressures made it difficult for artists to find either the time or the enthusiasm for art. The ratepayers remained largely unchanged, but a dynamic new occupant of the studios was the New Zealander, Frances Hodgkins. She described her new abode to her mother in 1914, "It is [a] huge barn that will do nicely for a Class, not pretty but useful. It gives on a yellow sandy beach & at high tide the waves beat against the walls & sometimes the window; for this commodious loft - studio - pigsty - barn, I pay £10 sterling a year - & no supplements as in Paris where you first tip the concierge, postman, policeman and dustman before installing *yourself*."[297] She had some initial problems with the studio - the cowl blew off the chimney out to sea, causing the stove to smoke - and she was warned that her window *often* blew in during Easterly gales, but she soon appreciated its uniqueness. "I will go a long way before I find another Studio like the one I have now."[298] However, as her pupils dropped off, due to the imposition of sketching restrictions, she was forced to give up her lodgings and use the studio as her living quarters as well.

Hodgkins' letters quite clearly indicate that she occupied No 7 Porthmeor Studios, but, as noted in Table D, I am by no means certain that this equates with Studio 7 today, particularly as this studio is not "a huge barn" and would not seem particularly apposite either for a painting class or as a bedsit. On the basis of the Rate Books, I place her in Studio No 4, but there must remain doubt.

In November 1915, Hodgkins was sleeping in the studio when the worst storm for forty years hit the town. "The Studio rocked like a baby's cradle & at dawn looked like a drunkard's home. The sky light blew in & of course floods of rain. About 4 o'c, a fisherman came round & begged me to shelter in their house but I stuck it out.....Tiles rained down in the courtyard & windows and chimneys crashed and banged. One man's Studio close by was blown clean down & half out to sea."[299] Not put off, she stayed there another two years, but the cold and the constant noise of the sea eventually got to her. "It's like a noisy cab rank below my windows - the shingles being hurled about by the high tides", she complained

---

297 Letter dated 19/11/1914 - Ed L Gill, *The Letters of Frances Hodgkins*, Auckland, 1993 at p.299.

298 Letter dated 17/2/1915 - Ed. L Gill, ibid, at p.303.

299 Letter dated 16/11/1915 - Ed. L Gill, ibid, at p.312.

to her mother in February 1916.[300] Having finally decided to move to an unidentified Wharf Studio in October 1917, she confided to a friend, "I moved in here last week & am so much more comfy & warm in this smaller Studio, facing the East & out of the bleak winds from the sea. It is such a rest not to have the waves nagging at one night and day. I can breakfast with the sun on me & have all the mysteries of the harbour unfolded to me, & keep an eye on the British navy at the same time."[301]

2.4.6.5 The Porthmeor Studios complex in the 1920s

Because there is only one extant Rate Book after 1917, it is extremely difficult to be certain which artists occupied which studios during the 1920s, particularly as artists, such as Alfred and Nora Hartley and Lindner, seemed to move between studios, and others did not necessarily exhibit on Show Days in the studios that they occupied. However, the 1925 Rate Book lists eleven ratepayers for studios in this run - Meade, Borlase Smart, Douglas, Emily Hartley (an unknown unless a mistaken reference to Nora), Dyer, Adams, Lindner, Alfred Hartley and, in what I am fairly certain are Studios 5-7, Arthur Hayward, Marcella Smith and Frances Ewan. Douglas, Dyer and Adams are in the same position in the Rate Book listings as always and, therefore, do not appear to have moved from Studios 1-3. However, if one looks at the numbering used in the extant official lists of exhibitors on Show Day during the 1920s, Borlase Smart exhibits in No 1, Frances Ewan, on the one occasion she exhibits, is in No 2, Beale Adams and Marcella Smith exhibit in different years in No 3, Moffat Lindner shows in No 4 and Alfred and Nora Hartley are in No 7! Further confusion is caused by Marcella Smith advertising in 1920 that pupils should contact her at No 3 and Arthur Hayward advertising in 1924-6 that he is running the St Ives School of Portrait Painting from No 4!

What is clear, however, is that the Porthmeor Studios were not being used that much at this juncture and very few of them were open on Show Days. The American artist, Wilson Henry Irvine, visited Dyer's Porthmeor Studio in 1923 and, despite thinking a few of Dyer's religious paintings had "real tone and interest", was amazed at the state of his workplace. "His enormous studio is filled with old drawings in charcoal and black and white oil, with which he starts on his canvases of birds, gulls, eagles and sparrow wings, from which he makes his angels' wings, frames and palettes thrown about, canvases on and off stretchers, old frames, broken rags for draperies, <u>dust</u>, old lanterns - piles of junk thrown down for thirty years and never picked up or dusted."[302] Douglas' studio was similarly filled with old junk and Adams rarely exhibited now. Marcella Smith, who had been one of the most promising artists during the War years, had gone to live with Dorothea Sharp in London, whilst Frances Ewan, who was making a name for herself as an illustrator in London and who retained a Porthmeor studio until her death in the 1960s, was only occasionally in residence at this juncture. Arthur Hayward, fresh from Newlyn, soon moved to the Harbour Studio. Whilst Lindner, Hartley and, to a lesser extent, Meade, continued to exhibit, they were all in their seventies, and the young, enthusiastic Borlase Smart was really the only artist with vitality. However, even he left the colony for a while, selling up the contents of his Porthmeor Studio in September 1926.[303]

Fig. 2.137 Notepaper heading of St Ives Society of Artists from the 1930s, showing an exhibition in Studio No 5 and the new entrance into Studio No 4

---

300 Letter dated 10/2/1916 - Ed. L Gill, ibid, at p.313.

301 Letter to Isabel Field dated 23/10/1917 - Ed. L Gill, ibid, at p.328.

302 Journal of Wilson Henry Irvine, 5/4/1923, Archives of American Art, Smithsonian Institution, Irvine papers, Reel 3564.

303 On offer was a Lay Figure in papier mâché (£10), oak studio easels (£10 and £7), two further easels (5/- and 3/-), a portfolio and stand (£1), two movable large dividing wooden screens (£3-10s each) and a Model's Throne (£2). *St Ives Times*, 24/9/26.

Fig. 2.138 Dame Laura Knight's *Myself and Model* hanging in Studio No 5 and being admired by the 1937 Committee of the St Ives Society of Artists, comprising from the left Borlase Smart, John Millar Watt, Moffat Lindner, Shearer Armstrong, Bernard Ninnes and, adjusting the frame, George Bradshaw.

2.4.6.6 The Porthmeor Galleries of the St Ives Society of Artists

When, in 1928, the newly formed St Ives Society of Artists started to look for a new exhibition venue, independent of Lanham's, Moffat Lindner suggested that they use No 5 Porthmeor Studios. Lindner managed to get the rent down to £8 and the artists set about the studio's redecoration and refurbishment with great enthusiasm. Gas needed to be installed for both lighting and heating and the total cost came to £21. Olsson, who had worked in the area now comprising Studio 5, when he had occupied the vast studio, came down to open the inaugural exhibition. For the first time, a Porthmeor Studio was open to the public on a daily basis and, as the Society's reputation grew, thousands of visitors enjoyed the works of an increasingly distinguished and lauded group of artists.

In 1929, though, the future of the Porthmeor Studios was rendered most uncertain, when the freeholder, Barclays Bank, who had taken over Bolitho and Co in 1915, indicated that it wanted to sell. The timing will have resulted from the Wall Street Crash, but, luckily, even in such dreadful economic conditions, the colony had a saviour - Moffat Lindner, who bought the whole group, thus preventing, in the words of Borlase Smart, "what might have been a serious crisis in the history of St Ives art".[304] Even before Lindner's acquisition of the Studios, he seems to have had the ear of the landlord, as seen in some choices of occupants - e.g. Frances Hodgkins in 1914 and the Society in 1928. Accordingly, he had always appreciated their significance and he now used his position as freeholder for what he perceived was the benefit of the colony as a whole. Whilst loathe to force out long-standing tenants, he was also keen to ensure that these magnificent studios were made available to some of the most energetic and deserving of the younger artists in the colony, such as George Bradshaw, who took No 3, Shearer Armstrong, who took No 9, Hugh Gresty and the celebrated painter-etcher, Job Nixon, who ran a painting class from his studio two nights a week for some time.

The success of the Society in the early 1930s meant that additional exhibition space was required and so, in 1932, Lindner made available, at a cheap rate, the adjoining studio, No 4, which he had been using himself. A doorway was created between the two, and watercolours and etchings tended to be

---

304 Vote of thanks given to Lindner at the AGM of the Society in January 1930.

hung separately in the new area. These two studios were the home of the Society until 1945, during which they displayed work by some thirteen Royal Academicians, who joined the Society during this period, and were visited by ever increasing numbers of art lovers. At no time, before or since, has the public been able to appreciate the ambience of these wonderful spaces to such a degree, and it is a shame that the re-development proposals continue to ignore this period of the Studios' history.

With Moffat Lindner in his nineties in the mid-1940s, the future of the Studios was again uncertain. This was of concern not only to Lindner himself, but also to Borlase Smart, who had been so involved in the Society's success and who had himself been an occupant of several of the studios. Smart set up, in his will, a charitable trust with the objective of trying to ensure the Studios' preservation and, upon his death in 1947, members of the Society, led by Smart's successor as Secretary, David Cox, campaigned to raise funds for this purpose. With the aid of a significant Arts Council grant, the Borlase Smart Trust was able to purchase the studios for £6000 from Moffat Lindner shortly before his death in 1949. Since then the role of Smart, in the preservation of the Studios, has been championed, and Lindner has almost been portrayed as 'the bad guy'. In fact, without Lindner, the Porthmeor Studios would not exist today and his contribution to their preservation deserves far greater appreciation.

Fig. 2.139 David Cox painting in Studio No 5. Cox not only took over the Secretaryship of the Society from Smart but also this studio, which Smart had been using since the Society moved to the Mariners' Chapel in 1945. Smart even persuaded the Walker Art Gallery in 1945 to put on in his studio an exhibition *Great Masters of British Art*, which included works by Reynolds, Gainsborough and Turner and many others!

Fig. 2.140 Artists involved in the campaign to save the Porthmeor Studios in 1948-9 in Studio No 1. From the left, Olive Dexter (occupant of No 4), Sven Berlin, Denise Williams, Leonard Richmond (No 4), Misome Peile, David Cox (No 5) and Wilhelmina Barns-Graham (No 1).

2.4.7 The Piazza Studios, Porthmeor - General

The size, location and ambience of the Porthmeor Studios has always given them immense significance in the history of the colony, now amplified by virtue of them being the sole survivors. However, for over sixty-five years, the adjoining Piazza Studios, also fronting Porthmeor Beach, seem to have been the venue of choice for many of the colony's leading artists. This purpose-built block of studios was erected by William Paynter in 1896 on what was largely a piece of open ground, albeit a small smithy, in the corner of the site, will have been demolished (see Fig. 2.100). Because Paynter only had a lease of the property which expired on the death of the survivor of his brother and himself, the new studios were built completely of wood. The roof, which was also of wood, was simply covered with felt and then tarred. Outside steps and gangplanks led to the various studios. To begin with, there were five studios of varying sizes, but one of the two particularly large ones was later divided into two. No floor plan has survived and so the exact location of the various studios in the block is unknown. There were also four stores used by fishermen, although one of these began in the 1920s to be taken, on occasion, by artists for pupils. The studios proved immensely popular, with Paynter being described as an excellent landlord. However, the block was never intended to be a permanent feature and the fact that the studios were in demand for so long is testament to their continuing appeal to artists, despite their deteriorating condition.

TABLE E   RATEPAYERS AT THE PIAZZA STUDIOS

Ratebook Order (GER)	Ratepayers 1898-1917	Ratepayers & No 1925
A (£15)	1898-1905 W Titcomb, 1906-1917 F Milner	F Milner (No 2)
B (£15)	1898 Wynne, 1899-1902 J N Barlow, 1903 converted into B1 and B2	N/A
B1 (£7-10)	1903 W Wendt, 1904 void, 1905 R Brundrit, 1906-1913 F Freyburg, 1914-1916 M Dougherty, 1917 L Sargent	A Falkner (No 3)
B2 (£7-10)	1903-7 E Schofield, 1908 void, 1909 Janson, 1910-1913 MacIvor, 1914 void, 1915-1917 W Evans Linton	W H Truman (No 4)
C (£9-10)	1898-1909 A Brown, 1910 M McCrossan, 1911 void, 1912-7 L Sargent or N Faberge	J A Park (No 5)
D (£11)	1898-1905 F Milner, 1906-7 void, 1908 G Symons, 1909-1913 C F Barry, 1914-1916 W M Spittle, 1917 void	R Davenport (No 6)
E (£9-10)	1898-1917 S Hobkirk	N Faberge (No 1)

Fig. 2.141 Hurst Balmford Detail of Plate 4, showing front of Piazza and Porthmeor Studios

Figs. 2.142-3 Views of the courtyard at the rear of the Piazza Studios, showing stairs and gangways giving access to the studios (St Ives Trust Archive Study Centre)

2.4.7.1 The Piazza Studios with William Paynter as landlord

There is no mention of the Piazza Studios until the Rate Book of 1898, when the ratepayers are listed as William Titcomb (GER £15), Kendrick Wynne (GER £15), Arnesby Brown (GER £9-10), Fred Milner (GER £11) and Stuart Hobkirk (GER £9-10). However, Titcomb, who appears to be one of the initial occupants, mentions in a letter to his previous landlord that his new studio should be ready for him by Christmas 1896.[305] Accordingly, the block appears to have been constructed during 1896. Titcomb's studio was one of the two large studios created initially, and he rented it until he left the town in 1905. However, he also had a small studio on the harbour beach and worked in a studio at his home, 'Windy Parc', into which he also moved in 1896. Upon Titcomb's departure, Fred Milner, who had worked initially in one of the other studios, moved in to this huge studio and stayed there for the rest of his life. However, he was happy to share it with good friends, such as Alfred East and Gardner Symons. Borlase Smart, on Milner's death in 1939, commented that he was always impressed by "the personality and dignity of his vast studio.... It conveyed the impression that big things had been created there."[306]

The other large studio (also GER £15), after the departure of Kendrick Wynne, was used by the landscape painter, Noble Barlow, himself a painter of vast canvases, between 1899 and 1902, but this was then divided into two. The sub-division, on this occasion, did not result in an increased rental and, accordingly, appears to have been motivated by a slackening of demand for large, expensive studios. The American artists, William Wendt and Elmer Schofield, were the initial occupants of the newly divided studio - the light being far better in Wendt's than it was in Schofield's.[307] It was probably at this stage that the studios were re-numbered - Hobkirk No 1 (GER £9-10), Titcomb No 2 (GER £15), Wendt No 3 (GER £7-50), Schofield No 4 (GER £7-50), Brown No 5 (GER £9-10) and Milner No 6 (GER £11). Although Schofield is listed as the ratepayer for No 4 in the years 1903-7, it is clear, from his correspondence with his wife, that a succession of artists used it during his regular stays in America in the winter months. For instance, on 22nd February 1904, Murielle told Elmer, "[George Gardner Symons] has taken on your studio until you return. It will only mean 5/-, and 15/- from the women who had it before, but it will buy you some paints." She also mentioned, on another occasion, that she had been down to sweep it out, but that "Mr Milner had said it would be quite a pity as the dead matches looked homelike and natural"![308] Symons, during his extended visit in 1908, took Milner's old studio, No 6, whilst Alfred East's protégé, Claude Francis Barry, took over this studio in the years 1909-1913.[309]

Fig. 2.144 Fred Milner in his Piazza Studio in1905
(*Black and White*)

---

305 Mornington Estate Papers, County Records Office, Truro, GHW/12/3/6/1/75/36-7.

306 From Borlase Smart's Appreciation, *St Ives Times* 10/1939.

307 Letter from Murielle to Elmer Schofield dated 10/12/1903. Alfred East, who considered sub-letting Schofield's studio, turned it down because of the light - Letter dated 18/1/1904.

308 Letter to Elmer Schofield dated 9/11/1905.

309 The Rate Books indicate that No 6 was void for a few years after Milner's move to No 2 in 1905, but Max Ludby was exhibiting in a Piazza Studio on Show Day in 1907 and may have used it.

Figs. 2.145-6 Arnesby Brown   *Boats off Smeaton's Pier*
                                  Pony and Cart on St Ives beach
                                  (both pencil sketches, courtesy Gay Jarman)

In the early part of his time in St Ives, Arnesby Brown used a studio owned by Robert Toy in Market Strand (GER £8), the small street running between, and parallel to, Fore Street and The Wharf.[310] However, for much of the period that he spent in the colony, his base was Piazza Studio No 5, although no doubt he sub-let it during the summer months when he was working in Norfolk. It is intensely frustrating that there should be no descriptions or images of the St Ives workplace of this fine painter, but he preferred his own company. A visitor's account of his Norfolk studio, however, throws some light on what one might have expected to see. "Stacks of small panels caught my attention. They were all rapid sketches made by the artist for his larger pictures. I sought a reason that they had not passed into the hands of art dealers and collectors. Then it dawned on me that Mr Arnesby Brown is the severest critic of his own work and would probably object to any but the very pick of these spontaneously executed impressions leaving his possession. I fancy, however, a deeper reason is that he retains a personal attachment to many of them, for do they not contain his immediate reactions to the subjects dealt with in his larger pictures? I recalled his remark of a few minutes before: "Always try to keep the first impression as fresh as possible" ".[311]

---

310 See *A Picture I have seen in St Ives St Ives Weekly Summary* 19/3/1892 and Rate Book 1893.

311 H. L., *Arnesby Brown RA - The Artist at Home*, Undated article from unknown paper in the Brown archive at Norwich Museum and Art Gallery.

The landscape painter, Frank Freyburg, took No. 3 Piazza Studios in 1906 and was noted as its occupier for the next seven years. On his arrival, Freyburg was already married, but it appears that, in 1908, his marriage broke down, as his wife, Mary, an avid reader from the Art Club's library, is not referred to again after March. The previous year, Freyburg had been painting in Ireland, and he paid repeated return visits to Ireland over the course of the next few years and, in 1909, he was joined in St Ives by an Irish girl, Monica MacIvor (1881-1939), who became his pupil. Although her parents were Irish, MacIvor was born in Bushire, Iran and had trained in Paris, exhibiting for the first time at the Paris Salon in 1908. By 1910, she had taken her own Piazza Studio, No.4, and, that year, she won a silver medal at Versailles with *A Visit to the Basket-Makers*.[312] Her speciality was portraits and her sitters included her tutor Frank Freyburg, his relative, Margaret Proschwitzy, and her own sister, posing with a guitar, in a work called *The Lost Chord*, which was classed as of "refined taste and treatment" (Plate 35). She also painted a fellow pupil, the New Zealander, Mrs K M Handyside, who had come over to England in 1904 and who had initially studied at Newlyn under Stanhope Forbes. In a letter to to his mother, Forbes commented, "We have such a charming elderly lady...who hails from New Zealand but originally from Ireland. She is such a nice woman and is going to stay some time...She has come to England determined to learn to paint, and is making capital progress. She is a fine handsome woman and as active as any of the young ones in spite of her years."[313] Having spent several years with Forbes, she joined the Arts Club in St Ives in November 1907 and exhibited in the studio of Frank Freyburg on Show Day in 1908 (see Plate 10). She may have studied under Freyburg for a while as he signed her in to the Arts Club in January 1910 and she clearly sat for Monica MacIvor at that time as well.[314] Hayley Lever, who was not a great fan of Freyburg, told Elmer Schofield in February 1912, "Freyburg is putting on tubes of paint - he has found out <u>another</u> way to <u>do</u> it? He is going to marry a Miss MacIvor, a student of his, I understand."[315] It appears that, following their marriage, they decided to settle in Kensington.[316]

Fig. 2.147 Piazza Studio trio   (Andrew Lanyon)
My best guess is that this shows Frank Freyburg and his pupils Monica MacIvor (left) and the New Zealander, Mrs K.M.Handyside (right) in Piazza Studio No 3 c.1910.

312 *St Ives Weekly Summary*, 24/3/1911. She did a smaller version for her 1911 Show Day exhibit and a work of this title was hung at the Paris Salon in 1912.

313 Letter to his mother dated 7/7/1904.

314 Two Miss Handysides from New Zealand, presumably her daughters, are also signed in as guests in January 1910. There are no further references to her but seven works by her of good quality appeared out of the blue in the W.H.Lane & Son auction of 28th October 1999. The majority were portraits or figure studies, which clearly showed the influence of Forbes. *Young Girl carrying a bundle of sticks* (Plate 10) and *The Daisy Chain*, showing two girls in a rolling landscape setting, were of particular merit. One work, *Corn Stooks*, was dated 1911.

315 Letter from Hayley Lever to W E Schofield dated 12/2/1912 - Schofield Archives, Godolphin House.

316 A 1916 RA exhibit *You and I* could be a portrait of his wife and himself.

Fig. 2.148 Elmer Schofield in No 4 Piazza Studios   (Andrew Lanyon)

Stuart Hobkirk's first exhibit was a painting of St Ives at the RCPS show in 1896 and, accordingly, he may well have been the first occupier of Studio No 1. He is certainly recorded as the ratepayer of this studio each year between 1898 and 1917, but there is no mention of him in a St Ives context after 1904 and, from his concentration on Paris flower market scenes in the years 1899-1904, he may well have been away for significant periods during these years as well. Therefore, he will clearly have sublet it, but I have found no information about other occupants during this extended period.[317] He will have returned from time to time, as his family continued living in the area for many years, and he himself was back in St Ives at the time of his death in 1940, when he was buried at St Uny, Lelant.

During the War years, the ratepayers for the Piazza Studios chop and change with some regularity, only Fred Milner in No 2 continuing in permanent occupation. In the years 1914-6, Matilda Dougherty is recorded as the ratepayer for No 3. This is presumably a reference to Marthe, the second wife of the American marine painter, Paul Dougherty, as they had both been regular visitors to St Ives since 1908. However, Paul Dougherty is not recorded in St Ives after 1914 and it was at this juncture that he and his wife, a musician, split up. Therefore, to what degree either of them used the studio is unclear. The animal painter, William Evans Linton, took over No 4 on 1st January 1915 and is recorded as the ratepayer until 1917, but again there is no other record of his presence in St Ives at this time. No 6, however, was used by the Birmingham figure painter, Walter Maxwell Spittle RBA, RBSA (1858-1917). Inspired by its position, Spittle, who had settled in St Ives in 1913, started to paint colourful rock pools and other marine scenes. Unfortunately, though, he died in 1917 and is buried at St Uny, Lelant.

The position in relation to No 5 is rather more intriguing, as, for a number of years, the noted ratepayer alternated between Louis Sargent, who was making a name for himself for his brightly coloured marine pieces, and Nicholas Leopold Fabergé (1884-1939). A connection between this well-known, and highly regarded, family of craftsmen and St Ives has never been made before, and the only evidence of it is in the Ratebook entries for the Piazza Studios, for, in 1914 and 1917, Nicholas Fabergé is recorded as the ratepayer for No 5 and, in 1925, for No 1.

In 1903, Carl Fabergé decided to open up a shop in London and, in 1909, his youngest son, Nicholas, joined his London agent, Henry Charles Bainbridge, in running the venture.[318] The shop, which was

---

317 When after a long gap, he exhibited again at the RA in 1920, his exhibiting address was in Tonbridge.

318 It is not known whether this Henry Bainbridge was related to Georgina Bainsmith's husband, Henry, who died in 1893.

the only one set up by Fabergé outside Russia, was highly successful, attracting not only the King and Queen but other leading members of the aristocracy. Nicholas developed an interest in art and photography, and it was clearly this that led him to be drawn down to St Ives just before the War. In 1915, however, the shop received orders to close, as foreign capital had to be repatriated to Russia to finance the War effort, but it was not until 1917 that trading ceased and Nicholas decided to return to St Ives. How long he spent in the colony, and when he switched studios, is not known. After his father's death in 1920, Nicholas did not link up with his brothers in 1924 in their attempt to revive the Fabergé brand in Paris, but concentrated on his photographic work. In 1922, he had a liaison with one of his photographic models, Dorise Cladish, resulting in the birth of a son, Theo, who was brought up by Dorise's sister and was unaware that he was a Fabergé until his fifties.[319] Although Nicholas is still recorded as the ratepayer for No 1 studio in 1925, this had been used by others on Show Day since 1920 and, on Theo's birth certificate, Nicholas, still describing himself as 'Artist and Photographer', gives his address as 11 Avenue Studios, Fulham.[320] There are scant records of his photographic work, and nothing relating to St Ives.

This coming and going of artists in the Piazza Studios during the War years did mean that, in stark contrast to the Porthmeor Studios, where long-term occupants clung on to rarely used workspaces, there were studios available in the Piazza block, as a new flush of artists joined the colony in the early 1920s. Fabergé's studio - No 1 - was used in the years 1920-5 by the siblings, Marjorie and Percy Ballance, the children of a Birmingham surgeon, who had been born in.1898 and 1899 respectively. Percy was considered, at that juncture, to be an up-and-coming marine painter of much talent, who painted boldly and expansively. Apparently, on Show Day one year, a cat walked into his Piazza studio, took one look at a large painting of an ocean swell and promptly threw up, much to the merriment of Ballance's colleagues. The artist enquired, "Am I to understand that my seas are emotional? Bit of a risk for the RA Jury - what?!"[321] Marjorie, who had studied previously at the Slade and in Paris, also enjoyed success at the Royal Academy and the Paris Salon in this period, with her brilliantly coloured and highly decorative paintings depicting textiles of the past. Alixe Shearer Armstrong (1894-1983), who was to become one of the leading female painters in the colony, took over the studio in 1925 and used it for a decade.

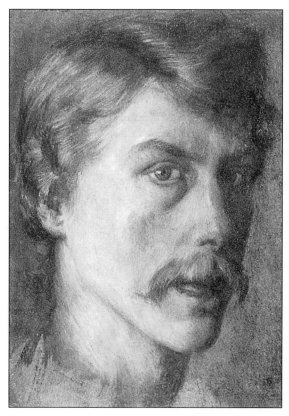

Fig. 2.149 Louis Sargent *Self-Portrait*

---

319 On hearing that he was a Fabergé, Theo, who had been a successful engineer, became a highly acclaimed craftsman himself - see obituary in *The Independent* 6/10/2007.

320 Nicholas married Marion Tattershall but their relationship was childless and he died in London in 1939.

321 *St Ives Times*, 15/3/1940.

With Studio No 2 continuing to be occupied by Milner, No 3 was used by Annie Falkner and her companion, Leslie Hervey, who first became involved with the colony in 1907. Annie, who was born in Dorchester in 1862 and Leslie, who had been born into a large family in Lightcliff, Yorkshire in 1857, had lived together since at least 1893. They appear to have taken over the studio during the War, as, writing in 1930, Annie commented, "We have held the Studio, 3 Piazza, for 15 or 20 years now and have had an excellent landlord in Mr Paynter. We should be very reluctant to give it up at any time."[322] Nevertheless, it is not certain to what extent they used the studio. After participating in Show Day in 1909 and 1910, a year when Annie was successful at the Royal Academy with *The Breeze, St Ives*, they only took part in one further Show Day - that in 1916. Leslie, after a last success at the Royal Academy in 1920, did not exhibit again, whilst Annie, who specialised in decorative pictures, often featuring farm animals (such as *The Lunch Hour* - Southampton Art Gallery), seems to have spent a considerable amount of time in France in the 1920s, where her work was hung at the Salon d'Automne in Paris between 1921 and 1928. Indeed, she was a Societaire of this Salon and was invited to serve on the Hanging Committee in the year of her death. Accordingly, they probably sublet the studio with regularity.[323]

Studios 4 and 5 were the home of the Simpson School of Painting between 1918 and 1924. The animal and bird painter, Charles Simpson, had studied in St Ives under Arnesby Brown and Noble Barlow after coming down from Bushey in 1905, but had based himself for much of the previous decade in Newlyn and Lamorna. However, in 1916, he and his wife, Ruth, a figure painter, whom he had met whilst she was studying at the Forbes School in Newlyn, decided to move across to St Ives. After the War, they set up a School of Painting and took two studios in the Piazza block - No 4 for the School and, directly below it, No 5 for Ruth. No 5 had a large picture window, jutting out over the sand, enabling students to paint marine subjects indoors, when the weather was bad (see Fig. 2.155).

The size of the studios made them useful for other functions as well and a much-reproduced photograph shows the Simpsons holding a lunch party in Studio No 5 in c.1922. Ruth's portrait of the American artist, Charles Rollo Peters, is on the easel behind her. Guests include the artist Robert Hughes from St Buryan (bearded to right) and his New Zealand born wife, Eleanor, (on his right), whom he had met at the Stanhope Forbes School in Newlyn, whilst, to his left, is the artist and jeweller, Ella Naper, who posed nude for Laura Knight in Fig. 2.138. On the far left are Professor Alfred Sidgwick and his wife, the author, Cecily Sidgwick from Lamorna, whilst, to the left of the easel, is one of the Simpson's current students, Kathleen Slatter who married George Bradshaw, whom she had met at the Simpson School.

Fig. 2.150 The Simpsons entertaining in No 5 Piazza Studios (c.1922]

---

322 Letter from A L Falkner to Glanville and Hamilton dated 29/7/1930 - Mornington Estate Papers, GHW/12/3/6/1/51/81.

323 This is confirmed by the correspondence with the Cowley estate in the years 1930-3.

When the Simpson School closed in 1924, Studio No 4 was taken by Herbert Truman, a Dawlish born artist, who had just spent thirteen years as chief inspector of the art and trade schools in Egypt, and Studio No 5 by John Park.

Studio No 6 was occupied from 1917 by Ruth Davenport, who had trained at South Kensington and who described herself as "formerly of Oxford Street, London".[324] However, unlike the other artists, she actually resided in her studio. Her speciality was art needlework pictures, and she held an exhibition of her work at Lanham's Galleries in February 1919. However, she also exhibited on Show Days some oil and watercolour sketches, principally of flowers, some hand-beaten pewter and copper work and some jewellery. She advertised for students from time to time and, in letters to the property agents, mentions a keen and wealthy student from Canada, Miss Northwood, who stayed with her for some time. In 1927, she held an exhibition in her studio with Helen Knapping, who appears to have been her one close friend, and, in 1936, works by both herself and her students were included in a further exhibition in her studio, held jointly with R.J.Enraght-Moony, a painter of Cornish fancies. Generally, however, she comes across as a difficult lady, who antagonised most of her fellow artists.

According to Ruth Davenport, Studio 7 in the Piazza block had been created prior to her arrival in 1917, by converting the loft under No 6.[325] As the studio's GER was £13, substantially more than for any loft previously, it appears that the loft was extended,   However, the first reference that I have found to it is in 1920, when it was used by Noble Barlow's widow to stage an exhibition of his pictures during May that year. Thereafter, it is occasionally used by students of Simpson or Park, but does not appear to have been in great demand.

2.4.7.2 The Piazza Studios under the Cowley Estate

On William Paynter's death in 1930, the block reverted to the Cowley Estate, albeit that it had tried to sell the freehold of it in the 1919 sale. Given that the Estate had leased to the Paynter family a bare stretch of land in 1842 and received back a block of studios and lofts with an annual income of £80, Paynter's widow was not too impressed to be served with a dilapidations notice, requiring remedial work of several hundred pounds, as the block was not in good condition. Martin Cock of James Lanham Limited, who had been managing the studios on behalf of the Paynter family, wrote to the Estate, fearing that the site might be redeveloped. "The dearth of studios at St Ives at present is very great and it will be a calamity from the point of view of the Art Colony if this valuable block of studios got into the hands of one who did not consider their interests."[326] The Estate took the advice of their normal property agents, Glanville and Hamilton, who felt that it would be difficult, in the conditions of the time, "to sell to advantage", the structure "being mostly built of wood and not of a durable nature".[327] Accordingly, the studios were re-let at increased rates to the existing tenants. - Shearer Armstrong (No 1 at £16), Fred Milner (No 2 at £16), Annie Falkner (No 3 at £12-12), Herbert Truman (No 4 at £14), John Park (No 5 at £14), Ruth Davenport (No 6 at £12) and John Park for his students (No 7 at £13).   The total annual income from the block, taking into account the other stores, was now in excess of £100.

Whatever remedial work was carried out under the dilapidations notice, the studios were still in poor condition and the Cowley Estate received persistent complaints from the artists. Annie Falkner told them in 1930, "The stairs and gangways have been in the most *disgraceful state* for a long while.... The wood is all *rotten* through and through. It is certainly not safe for the artists and their friends - let alone Show Day. The gangway to No 3 has never had more than one plank safe to walk on."[328] She then recounted how, when it rained, water from Ruth Davenport's defective gutter poured down on unsuspecting visitors on the stairs.

More alarming problems of a structural nature were reported by Herbert Truman in 1932, when the crowds visiting the studios on Show Day caused the floor in his and the adjoining studio "to sag to such an extent that the floor left the partition walls, causing a gap of an inch or two between them."[329] He had been forced to close his studio on several occasions, and there were clearly serious safety issues to be addressed. Truman was also frustrated that the local police and the St Ives Society of Artists, who organised Show Days, quickly denied responsibility for crowd control. However, problems of leaking roofs, sagging floors and dangerous access paled into insignificance in comparison with the difficulties

---

324 Advert in *St Ives Times* 28/3/1919.

325 In a letter to Glanville and Hamilton dated 29/6/1930, Ruth Davenport comments that this space "has been a studio ever since I came here - thirteen years ago". Mornington Estate Papers, GHW/12/3/6/1/74/12.

326 Letter dated 3/3/1930 - Mornington Estate Papers, County Records Office, Truro, GHW/12/3/6/1/74/2.

327 Letter dated 1/7/1930 - Mornington Estate Papers, GHW/12/3/6/1/74/15/1-2.

328 Letter from A L Falkner to Glanville and Hamilton dated 18/10/1932 - Mornington Estate Papers, GHW/12/3/6/1/229/27.

329 Letter from H.Truman to Glanville and Hamilton dated 1/10/1932 - Mornington Estate Papers, GHW/12/3/6/1/229/63.

that the artists experienced with one of their fellow tenants, Ruth Davenport. Her anti-social behaviour almost beggars belief, and it eventually forced John Park to write to the landlord's agent.

"I am writing to make a complaint against my neighbour at No 6 Piazza Studios - Miss Davenport. For years I have been subjected to petty annoyances from her in the shape of false statements regarding clients coming to my door and tiresome notes being dropped through my letterbox. These I have dismissed as more or less trivial and ignored them but latterly the methods she is employing to annoy are past a joke. She has not used the decent lavatory in the yard for years but deposits parcels of dung in front of my door or scatters it in newspaper in the yard or burns it on her fire thereby smelling us out for hours. She also puts orange peel in dangerous positions (deliberately placed) on the steps, so that anyone visiting the studios after dark could easily fall and break their necks. Her notes too have become scurrilous...and she has brazenly opened important private letters of mine....Clients naturally jib at climbing stairs that are strewn with cabbage leaves and dustbin refuse and I have no time or inclination to be constantly removing dung from my threshold and other conspicuous places."[330]

Herbert Truman, in No.4, also complained along substantially similar lines, calling her "highly strung and abnormal" and blaming "the conditions under which she is allowed to exist".[331] He concluded "her mental condition is such that she is impossible to deal with". Annie Falkner and Leslie Hervey also attempted to have the environmental health officers take action against her. W.Couch reported to the landlord's agents that she was using the sink in the yard as a toilet and that "the gully at the corner is in a very bad state - enough to breed a plague".[332]

Park felt that any reluctance to turn her out was not warranted, as she had taken a further studio in Fish Street, but the landlord's solicitors advised that they felt that the letters of the other tenants were motivated simply by a desire to take over her studio! In the end, Davenport stayed and Park left, leaving his successor, Leonard Richmond, to fight similar battles. However, it was not only artists who found her ways distressing. One of the fishermen, Humphrey Geen, who used the lofts at the Piazza Studios for storage, was driven a couple of years later to do a most uncommon thing - write a letter. "I have a Complaint to Loge Against Mis Demport   She have floded my Loft With Water Last Sunday and Monday night   She Do have her Winders open And the Rain Do Bate in   Every thing was Runen in Water   I have Got Lots of Gear Wet thru here   She is A Verry Bad Woman the Last 6 Months   She have Bean Wicked A Ganst Me   Yo Cant Go in the Loft And Come out With She is up hover throwen down Something Maken a nois   I had the Plyce for Last Sumer And it Dident Make Eney Diference   She thinks She Can Do just Wat She Likes   I ham Asken for Peace And Quite ness."[333]

Fig. 2.151 Herbert Truman in No 4 Piazza Studios in 1934

330 Letter dated 8/10/1931 - Mornington Estate Papers, GHW/12/3/6/1/226/55.
331 Letter dated 31/10/1931 - Mornington Estate Papers, GHW/12/3/6/1/226/74.
332 Letter from W Couch to Glanville and Hamilton dated 21/6/1933 - Mornington Estate Papers, GHW/12/3/6/1/230/8.
333 Letter dated 6/12/1934 -- Mornington Estate Papers, GHW/12/3/6/1/232/36.

Fig. 2.152 Francis Barry in No 2 Piazza Studios in 1945   (David Capps)

Fig. 2.153 Leonard Richmond, with two students, in No 5 Piazza Studios in the 1930s
(Gilbert Adams)

Other changes in personnel during the 1930s included Phyllis Pulling, who took over No 3 from Annie Falkner. Realising that she did not have long to live, Falkner arranged for Lanham's to sell her studio effects in June 1933. Being one of the only known inventories of a St Ives studio, it may be interesting to list the items for sale - three studio tables, chairs, sketching easels, four-fold screen, several canvases, frames, sketching boxes, drawing boards, china, books, mirror, paints, brushes, still life drapery, oil stove, lamps, two deck chairs and the artist's own framed watercolour drawings.[334] Pulling, who had studied at various London art schools, was a decorative artist and was later joined in the studio by her brother, Edward, also an artist, for the rest of the 1930s. In 1935, Shearer Armstrong moved to 9, Porthmeor Studios, as she "felt that a change of lighting etc would be a good thing", and Bernard Ninnes used No 1 for a couple of years before it was taken over, in 1937, for a decade, by Agnes Drey and Eleanor Rice.[335]

The outbreak of War in 1939 saw many changes in occupation. Phyllis Pulling gave up No 3 and moved to London, whilst Herbert Truman ceased to occupy No 4 and Ruth Davenport was finally evicted from both No 6 and No 7. The German, Franz Muller-Gossen, who had taken over No 5 from Leonard Richmond in 1937, remembered his horrific internment on the Isle of Wight, during the First World War, and so moved to Switzerland. Fred Milner also died in 1939 and his large studio (No 2) was taken over in 1942 by Francis Barry, who returned to the colony, having been forced to leave Bordighera in Italy on the outbreak of War. Barry, though, found the view and the light distracting, and had all the windows blacked out. Misomé Peile, who befriended him at this juncture, said that his studio was like another world. It was here that he created his vibrantly coloured Moscow firework paintings which "seemed to blast the studio asunder". Peile herself used it for a while after his departure at the end of the War.

Fig. 2.154 Bill Redgrave working by the fabulous picture window in No 5 Piazza Studios in the 1950s
(St Ives Trust Archive Study Centre)

---

334 Whether the sale proceeded is unclear, as she died on 24th June and the sale was fixed for 26th June. Leslie Hervey was reported to be seriously ill at the same time - see St Ives Times 7/7/1933.
335 Letter to Glanville and Hamilton dated 21/6/1933 - Mornington Estate Papers, GHW/12/3/6/1/233/3.

Fig. 2.155 The Piazza Studios shortly before their demolition
(St Ives Trust Archive Study Centre)

In 1942, Harry Rountree, the New Zealand born illustrator, settled in the colony, and he took over Studio No 5 from the etcher and watercolourist, Robert Herdman Smith, who had used it in the early years of the War. Rountree soon became a Councillor, championing the preservation of the town's architectural antiquities. At much the same time as the campaign was launched to save the Porthmeor Studios, Rountree, in February 1948, with much less fuss, bought the freehold of the Piazza Studios from the Cowley Estate for £2000. This philanthropic action of Rountree, being the *bete noire* of the modernists, has, of course, never been mentioned before and, although, unfortunately, he died unexpectedly in 1950, the ever shorter reviews of Show Day still mention artists in the Piazza Studios as late as 1958.[336] In 1963, however, it appears that the block had become such a liability that there was little alternative to a sale for redevelopment. The studios had only been intended to be temporary structures and yet they provided inspiration for artists for over sixty years - far longer than originally envisaged.

2.4.8   The Porthmeor Road Studios

Porthmeor Road runs off Back Road West down to The Island end of Porthmeor Beach and the properties on the road that backed on to the beach were originally huge fish stores, many of which were owned by the Cowley Estate. Gradually, more and more segments of these vast spaces were converted into studios. A watercolour by Sara Maclean (Plate 5) captures the view of the beach side of these studios, as seen from The Island.

2.4.8.1 The first Porthmeor Road Studio, later 'Downunder Studio'

The first studio in Porthmeor Road was created in the early days of the colony, for the Rate Book of 1893 lists a net loft owned by Lord Cowley in the occupation of William Titcomb. With a GER of £10, it was clearly quite sizeable and it appears to have been situated in what is now known as The Old Pressing Yard, with access to it down a ramp underneath one of the Porthmeor Road cottages. A photograph of Titcomb and Jessie Morison, around the time of their marriage in April 1892, in a studio setting (Fig. 2.156), is likely to depict this studio, and this may have been Titcomb's initial working environment. He continued to use the studio until Christmas 1896, when he moved into one of the new Piazza Studios, after which it was rented by Margaret Helen Knapping (1848-1935).

Helen Knapping was the daughter of Dale Knapping (1823-1878), who had made his fortune from the development of brickworks in South Shoebury, Essex, which had served the rapid growth of Southend. One of three unmarried sisters, she was, in fact, entitled to call herself Lady of the Manor of South Shoebury. A landscape and flower painter in oils and watercolour, she studied under Edmund Aubrey

---

336 Show Day reports in the 1950s record the following artists exhibiting in the Piazza Studios - Bernard Ninnes, Misomé Peile, Thomas Heath Robinson, Isobel Heath, Violet Digby, Edith Lovell Andrews, Eileen Izard, Hilda Jillard, Gai Layor, Maurice Hill, Una Shaw Lang, Miss L Staniland Roberts and Mary Phillips.

Hunt (1855-1922) in England, France and Belgium and began exhibiting at the RBA in 1876. She subsequently became a member of the Women's International Art Club. She is first recorded in St Ives in January 1896 and became a reasonably regular visitor, albeit basing herself in London and retaining substantial property in Essex.[337] However, she only took part in Show Day on one occasion - 1912 - before the War. She was more regularly seen on the golf course. In 1908, she experienced some problems with her studio when her neighbour, the carpenter, Mr Lander, proposed putting a gas engine and sawing machine in her yard, the noise and vibration from which would have severely hampered her ability to work.[338] This was prevented, but the correspondence revealed that she had recently had to spend money on the studio "to prevent the old dust of the plaster from falling down and destroying her pictures."[339]

At the time of the 1919 sale by the Cowley Estate, the studio was offered together with the adjoining 'Atlantic Studio', but, when no offers were forthcoming, Knapping bought the freehold to her own studio, with the cellar underneath, which she had used for some years. She exhibited on each of the Show Days between 1921-5 and continued to use the studio intermittently until her death in 1935. Under her Will, she left it to the RBA, with the request that it be used for the benefit of art students or other deserving artists, preferably with St Ives connections.

Fig. 2.156 William & Jessie Titcomb in his Porthmeor Road Studio in 1892.
The painting on the easel is *A Mariner's Sunday School.*

337 For instance, she is listed as a Visitor in August 1898, 1901 and 1902 and in September 1906 and 1908. In March 1908, she was also in St Ives staying at 14 Carrack Dhu - Mornington Estate Papers, GHW/12/3/6/1/136/26.

338 Letters from Helen Knapping and George Toman to Glanville and Hamilton dated 4/3/1908 - Mornington Estate Papers, GHW/12/3/6/1/136/26.

339 Letter from G Toman to Glanville and Hamilton dated 4/3/1908 - Mornington Estate Papers, GHW/12/3/6/1/136.

Fishermans Cottages, St Ives.

Fig.2.157 *Fishermen's Cottages, Porthmeor Road, St Ives*
This drawing by an unknown hand, which was made into a postcard, shows, in the foreground on the left, the entrance ramp under the cottages to Down-under and Atlantic Studios. At the back can be seen the chimney of the Cryséde factory, which was adjacent to Island Studios.

There are few references to the studio thereafter, possibly because the RBA students used it for short periods, which did not coincide with Show Day, but Hugh Ridge (d.1976), who was to have a long and fruitful career in St Ives, appears to have been given the opportunity of using it when he first came down to the colony, as the review of his first Show Day in 1949 mentions that he was working in the "RBA studio", then known as 'Down-under Studio', Porthmeor Road. He worked here until 1953, putting up a sign for his studio over the access ramp, after which there is no further mention of the studio. Having established a Knapping Prize in 1948, to be awarded to a meritorious art student, the RBA may well have disposed of the property, and applied the proceeds towards the funding of this prize, but the St Ives connection was lost.[340]

2.4.8.2 'Atlantic Studio', Porthmeor Road

In 1910, the late P.Lander's boathouse and the late William Berriman's workshop in Porthmeor Road, which adjoined Helen Knapping's studio, were converted into 'Atlantic Studio' by Alfred Charles Bailey. It was a slightly convoluted property, as the entrance to the studio was under Nos 1 and 2 Porthmeor Road, whilst No 3 Porthmeor Road projected about two foot into the studio.

Bailey was born in Brighton in 1883, and his father, Wilfred, was an engineer, who had worked for the Great Northern Railway and, in Canada, for the Grand Trunk Railway. Alfred studied art initially in Brighton, and then came down to St Ives to study further under Louis Grier. His work is first mentioned on Show Day in 1908 and he joined the Arts Club in 1909. In addition to the conversion costs, Bailey committed himself to a seven year lease, and needed Grier to provide him with a reference and his father to act as guarantor. In 1917, having had a trouble free initial term, he extended the lease for another fifteen years, but, no sooner had he renewed, than he started to experience problems. He was disturbed from the cottage above him by new tenants with screaming children, and from the cellar below by fishermen hanging heavy nets and fishing gear on his floor rendering it unsafe.[341] By 1920, he was also having severe problems with the roof and leaking gutters. "There are very few dry places on the floor at the studio on a wet day and consequently we get a lot of our canvases spoilt by the wet."[342] This was a problem that was never truly solved, as one of the causes was a leaking lead gutter that was seventy feet long and two foot six inches wide, which had been patched, and patched again, for the cost of replacing it was prohibitive.

340 She also bequeathed £59,253 to the National Gallery for the purchase of work by artists living within twenty-five years of the date of purchase. I am most grateful to Norma Neal for providing me with much new information on Knapping.
341 Mornington Estate Papers, GHW/12/3/6/1/ 205/4 & 210/2. His solicitors were Baileys, Shaw and Gillett, two of whose partners were E Horsmann Bailey and Norman C Bailey, most probably relations.
342 Letter from A C Bailey to Glanville and Hamilton, 2/2/19320 - Mornington Estate Papers, GHW/12/3/6/1/ 205/3.

Fig. 2.158 H.G. Fitzherbert *Caricature of Alfred Bailey*
(from *Caricatures of the Cornish Riviera*)

Bailey, who was a tall man, worked in the studio for twenty-two years and, for much of that time, was joined by James Stephen Yabsley, a moderate painter of landscape, marine and still life subjects, who lived at 'Sunrise', Penbeagle and exhibited for the first time on Show Day in 1913. In about 1915, Bailey gave up painting in oils and developed his own individual style of watercolour painting. This was well-regarded at the time, resulting in a number of one-man London shows. The fishermen, however, thought that he was colour blind! The last occasion on which he exhibited in his studio on Show Day was in 1925 and, thereafter, he seems to have spent more of his time in Chelsea. By the date of the expiry of his lease in 1932, the studio, which had failed to attract interest in the 1919 auction, was in such a poor condition that new applicants, such as Leonard Richmond, were put off. Accordingly, the Cowley Estate sold it in 1933. Nevertheless, Borlase Smart is recorded as exhibiting there on Show Day in 1935.

2.4.8.3 The Island Studios, Porthmeor Road

1910 seems to have seen a surge of interest in studios, and the third major block of studios fronting Porthmeor Beach was developed that year. However, this was not an entrepreneurial venture by one of the locals, but by the American artist, Henry Turner Keasbey (1882-1953), and was a unique instance of a visiting foreign artist making a large financial commitment to the colony.

Keasbey was from Philadelphia and first visited St Ives in 1904, no doubt on the recommendation of Elmer Schofield, who had a group of friends from Philadelphia join him that summer. One of four children, his father, Henry Griffiths Keasbey, was a very wealthy businessman.[343] Whether or not this affected his application, he was not an accomplished artist. Although he seems have gone on the 1906 Picardy sketching trip organised by Talmage and exhibited occasionally on Show Day and at the RCPS, his landscape paintings made little impression, and there is no record of him exhibiting after 1910. Keasbey, however, immersed himself in the life of the colony. He appears, from Fitz's caricature of him (see Fig. 2.270), to have shared an enjoyment of country pursuits and to have been exceptionally tall and thin, his huge feet making him more than a little clumsy.

---

343 He worked with his college friend Dr Mattison to perfect quinine compounds for the treatment of malaria and then perfected a process for using asbestos for insulating pipes. The firm of Keasbey-Mattison became huge.

Having concluded that art was not for him, Keasbey decided, in August 1910, to make a property speculation and took a twenty-one year lease of the cellar and lofts in Porthmeor Road, previously occupied by William Warren, converting them into five studios, which he named the Island Studios. The rent was £20 p.a. and, interestingly, one of the conditions of the lease was that all presses, barking vats and other fixtures had to be retained. In addition to putting into the lofts larger windows fronting the beach and skylights, he also made a larger entrance, as he was concerned to ensure that big pictures, and even bulkier packing cases, could be taken in and out. The existing large entrance on to the beach, not surprisingly, was considered inconvenient.[344] Although he could not see the cellar being of much use, he decided to take it as well "to ensure no trade or business is carried on there which would be objectionable to myself or anyone else above. It would also be extremely useful for storing packing cases, studio effects etc and would ensure a certain amount of privacy and quietness."[345] As has been seen from the experiences of Herbert Lanyon and others, this was a wise precaution. Access to Studios 1-4 was gained through the yard at the south end of the block, but Studio 5 was quite independent of the other studios, being sited at the north end, adjoining what became the Cryséde works.

Keasbey used Lanham's to arrange sublettings and some of the first tenants were Nora Hartley, the marine painter and scientist Charles Tracy, Miss Norman and Miss Quick. Leaking roofs - the landlord's responsibility - proved a problem in the early years, and the property also suffered constantly from damp and damaged plasterwork as, when it had first been built, sea-water had been used for the mortar in the walls, as fresh water had, at the time, been in short supply. Salt from the mortar, therefore, kept on being drawn into the plaster - a problem for which there was no solution. However, a bigger problem was lack of demand, for numbers in the colony fell significantly after 1910, and the War merely exacerbated the situation. Keasbey's timing could hardly have been worse.

In 1917, the landlord's agents were rather alarmed to discover that Keasbey had returned to the States. Lanham's sought to appease them, writing, "Mr Keasbey is a most straightforward and honourable man. He left for America soon after his country entered into the War to join up for military service - that, so far as we are aware, is the only and entire reason for his going."[346] Keasbey, however, never returned, and the uncertainty clearly put off bidders when the block was included by the Cowley Estate in the 1919 sale. Thereafter, Lanham's had a real struggle to manage the studios until the lease expired in 1931, using whatever monies they could obtain from subletting to pay the rent due to the landlord.[347]

Fig. 2.159 Sara Maclean *The Island Studios* (detail of Plate 5)

---

344 Letter from H T Keasbey to Glanville and Hamilton dated 18/6/1910 - Mornington Estate Papers, GHW/12/3/6/1/147/11/2.

345 Letter from H T Keasbey to Glanville and Hamilton dated 9/5/1910 - Mornington Estate Papers, GHW/12/3/6/1/147/11.

346 Letter from James Lanham Ltd to Glanville and Hamilton dated 12/12/1917 - Mornington Estate Papers, GHW/12/3/6/1/196/51.

347 Keasbey died, unmarried, in Chester County, Pennsylvania in 1953. In 1960, his sister set up the Keasbey Memorial Fund in memory of their parents and this gives scholarships to Americans wanting to study at Oxford and Cambridge.

Artists using the studios for significant periods included William Cave Day, and his wife, Kathleen, (No.1), John Park and his students (No.4) and Hurst Balmford (No.5).[348] In 1922, however, a collapsed chimney rendered utter devastation to two of the studios - fortunately, at a time when they were unoccupied. In 1925, two of the main props under Kathleen Day's studio were found to be rotten, rendering the building unsafe, whilst, in 1929, storm damage caused much of the already rotten roof of the two centre studios to collapse, sending slates crashing through the toplights of the adjoining studios. This rendered the two centre studios untenantable and the others little better. By 1931, only two were let - No 2 to Miss Maud Gunn of Leicester and No 5 to Hurst Balmford (b.1871), a Huddersfield born painter, who had been Head of Morecambe School of Art. Balmford, though, had experienced problems of his own. Firstly, boys kept on throwing stones at and breaking his side window - a nuisance the police had not been able to stop - and secondly, the tenant of the loft above, Mr Thomas, had taken to tarring his nets there. Not only was this a great fire hazard but he was prone to spill tar and creosote, which leaked through the ceiling damaging Balmford's wall hangings and paintings.[349]

Upon the expiry of Keasbey's lease, the Cowley Estate did little to remedy the situation. Marjorie Ballance, after viewing the studios in 1935, wrote in disgust to the landlord's agents, "One cannot be got into at all, one has no glass in the skylight and another has floorboards warped and unsafe with damp. With the shortage of studios in St Ives and the consequent enormous demand for them, it really is hard to understand how the owners can allow these, which have been some of the best in the town in the past, to fall into this appalling state."[350] However, apart from Major Alan St John Youall, who advertised portraits of pets and hand-painted Cornish and Devon ware, who took over No 5 for two years from March 1934, there is no further record of their use, albeit the Estate retained ownership until 1946.

Fig. 2.160 Hurst Balmford *Self-Portrait*

---

348 There is a reference in a letter from Lanhams dated 11/12/1915 to a tenant, who is "a gentleman of some distinction", possibly Emile Fabry. Other artists who used the studios include A. Mackenzie Grieve and D. Allen (No. 4 - SD 1921), Dr A MacVie (No 3 - SD 1922), G.F.Bradshaw (No.1 - SD 1928) & J.M.Bromley (No.2 - SD 1928).

349 Mornington Estate Papers, GHW/12/3/6/1/ 51/87 & 226/6.

350 Letter from Marjorie Ballance to Glanville and Hamilton dated 19/2/1935 - Mornington Estate Papers, GHW/12/3/6/1/233/4/4.

Fig. 2.161 'White Studio'
(Marion Whybrow)

Fig. 2.162 Headstone of Lynn Pitt in Barnoon Cemetery

2.4.9 'White Studio', Porthmeor Cliff

'The White Studio' was the workplace of James Lynn Pitt (c.1860-1922) and was a wooden structure above Porthmeor Beach - located where the house 'Sunset' now stands. Described on his death as the son of the late James Pitt of Cobham, Lynn Pitt was related to the two distinguished Prime Ministers, William Pitt. Born and brought up in Bristol, he was confined to a wheelchair and had a manservant to look after him. He also had two devoted sisters, who lived in Clifton, one of whom was an artist herself. Pitt was one of Olsson's initial students in 1895 and he later indicated that he erected the studio the following year.[351] A reviewer commented, "The studio overlooks Porthmeor Beach and the North Channel and Mr Pitt's favourite subject is, naturally, "the mighty ocean" which he paints in its varied moods."[352] He did not, however, exhibit any work until 1901 and did not feature on Show Day in St Ives until 1908. By this juncture, he had become an Associate of the Bristol Academy, possibly reflecting his donation in 1906 to the Academy of his work *The Squall - Fishing Boats running for St Ives Harbour*.[353] However, his paintings rarely received comment in St Ives and examples seen recently in the salerooms indicate a fondness for depictions of waves crashing on the foreshore, executed in a competent but uninspired manner. In October 1907, he placed an advert in the St Ives paper, inviting visitors to view the permanent exhibition of his work in his studio. He was the only artist to do this regularly and, in August 1909, he amended it to record that, on Tuesday, Thursday and Saturday afternoons, pupils would be in attendance at his studio, indicating that he had commenced giving art classes.

In 1910, Pitt applied for permission to replace the wooden structure, with one built in brick or stone, but this merely alerted the authorities to the fact that he had not obtained permission to erect the structure in the first place, and he suffered a series of run-ins with the Council, who wanted the site of his studio for road widening. Frances Hodgkins' comment, after the severe gale in November 1915, that "One man's Studio close by was blown clean down & half out to sea" is likely to apply to Pitt's studio.[354] He also suffered problems with break-ins - in 1920, a local boy, Arthur George Wright, climbed up from the beach, tore off a shutter and squirted paint all round the studio, particularly in the fireplace. He also used a number of brushes and daubed several of his paintings, including one of his Royal Academy submissions, with strong yellow paint. Arthur White, in giving evidence at the boy's trial, commented that "it was a delicate matter to judge the value of another artist's work, but Mr Pitt himself estimated the damage at £60"![355] Known to the locals as 'Owld' Pitt, his obituary recorded, "In spite of being physically afflicted, he was very brave and cheerful and many of his old friends will recall pleasant hours spent in his company".[356] An artist's palette decorates his headstone in Barnoon Cemetery. His studio did not long survive him, for it was demolished in a gale, scattering paints and brushes far and wide.

---

351 A Mr Pitt from Bristol stayed at 4 St Andrew's Street in September 1895. This is almost certainly him as his three unmarried sisters lived in Clifton, Bristol and the venue at which he exhibited principally was BAPFA. At the time of his dispute with the Council in 1910, he said that his studio had been up for 14 years without complaint.

352 *St Ives Times*, 27/3/1909.

353 This work no longer appears to be in the RWA collection. His sister, Miss E K Pitt, a miniaturist, was also an ARWA.

354 Letter dated 16/11/1915 - Ed. L Gill, *The Letters of Frances Hodgkins*, Auckland, 1993, at p.312.

355 *St Ives Times*, 6/8/1920. The boy was sent to an industrial school.

356 *St Ives Times*, 17/11/1922. Arthur White was one of the chief mourners at his funeral and Borlase Smart and Alfred Hartley were also in attendance. Herbert Babbage had also been a close friend.

2.4.10 St Peter's Street Studio

One surviving studio in this area of town is the St Peter's Street Studio, now called simply 'The Studio'. It is in St Luke's Court, off St Peter's Street, close to its junction with Back Road West. This was another property owned by the Cowley Estate, and had originally been a loft connected to a blacksmith's shop. It is first recorded in the Rate Books as a studio in 1901 (GER £5), when it was occupied by John and Selina Bromley, and it tended to be referred to in the Estate's correspondence as 'Loft Studio', Back Road West.[357] However, when the Bromleys completed their renovation of 'Quay House', they gave up the studio, and it was taken over by Lizzie Whitehouse in March 1906. She exhibited there on Show Days from 1906-1909 and from 1912-1916, but probably sublet it during her trip to Italy with her sisters in 1909-1911. When requesting a new stove in November 1915, she commented, "I am a quiet, good tenant (in some studios, I know the rent is not always forthcoming to date and again some are empty half the year)."[358] Her request seems to have been motivated, not by her own comfort requirements, but by a desire to sub-let the studio to Nora Hartley, who had complained that she could not work in it without a stove. Keen to rid herself of the commitment, as financial pressures mounted during wartime, Whitehouse was frustrated by Toman's contention that, for the rental she paid (£5), she could not expect a stove, and by Hartley's refusal to take over the lease without the studio being put into proper repair.[359] However, Hartley did assume responsibility for the rates from 1st July 1916. The studio was vacant, though, when it was sold by the Cowley Estate in 1919, as Hartley, by then, had moved to one of the Porthmeor Studios.

The freehold of the property was acquired by Beatrice Pauline Hewitt (1873-1956) in May 1921 and she used it as her home and studio (GER £8) for the rest of the 1920s. She called it 'St Peter's Street Studio'. Pauline Hewitt had not been able to persuade her family to allow her to study art, but a small legacy, when she was twenty-one, enabled her to be independent, and she spent six years at the Slade School, where her contemporaries included Augustus John and William Orpen. A scholarship then enabled her to study further in Germany and Paris. Marriage, though, curtailed her painting career, and it was only when her son was twelve that she started to paint again. However, she then found that she could paint much better than before, and she became one of the leading female artists in the colony until her departure in 1954. She was a great friend of Nell Cuneo, with whom she performed in dramatic productions, and Terence Cuneo, in his autobiography, labelled her "a first rate painter". She remained at 'St Peter's Street Studio' until December 1930. For the next few years, she exhibited in various different studios on Show Day but, by the late 1930s, had settled in 3, St Andrews Street, the cottage that had been the studio of the Robinsons, where she will have had a far better view.

Later artistic owners of the studio include the etcher, Raymond Ray Jones, who used it from October 1940 until his tragic suicide in 1942, and the illustrator, Michael Foreman, who lived there in the 1970s.[360]

Fig. 2.164 'St Peter's Street Studio' in 2009

Fig. 2.163 Pauline Hewitt in the St Peter's Street Studio in 1928

357 I am indebted to Pam Badman for this information, resulting from her extensive research into the Mornington Estate papers, where this property is listed as part lot 116.

358 Letter from S E Whitehouse to R Glanville dated 3/11/1915 - Mornington Estate Papers, GHW/12/3/6/1/182/100.

359 Mornington Estate Papers, County Records Office, Truro, GHW/12/3/6/1/191/1-3

360 I am grateful to Lady Carol Holland for a list of owners of the property.

2.4.11 Studios on the Harbour Beach

Unsurprisingly, artists found the constant and varied activity taking place in the harbour endlessly fascinating and, accordingly, studios fronting the harbour beach proved perennially popular, despite the noise and smells that will have accompanied the vistas. However, the regularity with which small studios were created and then disappeared, when coupled with possible changes of name, makes it difficult to give a full picture.

Figs.2.165-6   The principal run of artists' studios fronting the harbour beach
(top, from right, 'The Foc'sle', Paynter's Boatyard, Customs House, 'Harbour Studio',
'Blue Studio', Lifeboat Inn, Salvation Army building)
(bottom, from left, 'The Foc'sle, ?further Grier studio, 'Foreshore Studio' (hidden in nook),
Edmund Fuller studio)   (St Ives Trust Archive Study Centre)

Fig. 2.167 'The Foc'sle', with shutters open, and other artists' studios on the harbour beach.
Paynter's Boat-building shop and slipway is to the left.
(Marion Whybrow)

2.4.11.1   Louis Grier's 'The Foc'sle'

Grier's studio on the harbour beach, 'The Foc'sle' (GER £8), into which he moved in late 1888, was situated next to Paynter's boat-building shop - approximately where the Amusement Arcade now stands. It was owned by the local Lloyds agent, John Tregethren Short of The Terrace, whose St Ives born nephew, Captain Richard Short (1841-1916), enjoyed success as a coastal painter based in Cardiff.[361] 'The Foc'sle' became one of the best known studios in St Ives, largely because of the social habits of its occupant. It had double doors, painted yellow, and access was via a set of steps "as steep as a foc'sle ladder", no doubt the reason for Grier's choice of name.[362] Lewis Hind commented, "The rafters are stained by multi-coloured palette scrapings into the likeness of a thousand remembered sunsets, and when the doors are open how haunting the opalescent waters of the Bay, the boats that skim round the point like great brown birds, and the sands that curve all the way to white Godrevy."[363] Viewing it during the 1889 Private Views, when Grier was sharing it with his brother, Wyly, the local correspondent commented, "Surely it is an ideal studio for a marine painter. He need never move from the open door to find a subject. A whole lifetime might be spent in depicting the ever varying light and life of the old harbour of St Ives. Here are the forest-like masts of the fishing fleet, all ready for the opening of the spring mackerel season, the sides of the older boats gleaming in the sunshine with all the hues that go to make the auiline dyes. Here are quaintly clad men, women and children; here the clean, trim fishing- and pilot-gigs; there lies groups of fish on the foresand awaiting the auctioneer's hammer. There is Smeaton's Pier and, beyond it, lie four miles of shining water, backed by green slopes and yellow sand-hills, which are, again, backed by the blue, hazy heights of Carn Brea."[364] The studio was big enough to hold gatherings of sixty people in the days before the formation of the Arts Club, and will have been the venue for the 'studio tea parties', for which Grier became well-known. These were recognised as *the* event at which to meet other artists in the colony.

The earliest surviving photograph of the interior of the studio, taken by William Trevorrow and used by Grier in his article on the Arts Club in 1895 (Fig. 2.168), depicts a cluttered workroom. His palette lies on a table, canvases are stacked here and there and the beams are covered in paint scrapings. However, amongst the muddle, a number of curios can be seen and a few musical instruments are propped up against the far wall. Just a year later, a photograph taken by John Douglas and used by Lewis Hind in his article on the School of Painting set up by Grier and Olsson (Fig. 2.169), reveals a totally different ambience of elegance and sophistication. It is now furnished more in the manner of a living room than a studio, with antique chairs, a grandfather clock, a glazed corner cupboard and many curios. Grier's prized possession, the guitar lyre from the band of Charles II, has been given pride of place. This transformation may be partly due to the art of the photographer, but it does appear that Grier actually made his home at 'The Foc'sle' for a number of years, as, in 1899, it is referred to, for the first time, in the Rate Book, as 'Studio and House', with an increased GER of £10. Certainly, he stayed there overnight on many occasions, when he was working on his moonlight paintings.

---

361 Captain Richard Short RCA was self-taught but his successes at the RA in 1887-8 were enthusiastically reported in the local papers (*Cornish Telegraph* 5/5/1887 and 10/5/1888) and he went on to exhibit 14 times at the RA and also regularly at Birmingham and Liverpool. His St Ives connection, however, has now been totally forgotten, and yet he must be one of the very first St Ives born artists to achieve national success.

362 See *In Painter's Land, Black and White,* 12/9/1896 at p.331.

363 See *In Painter's Land, Black and White,* 12/9/1896 at p.331.

364 *The Cornishman,* 11/4/1889.

Fig. 2.168 The interior of 'The Foc'sle' (1895)   (William Trevorrow)

Fig. 2.169 The interior of 'The Foc'sle' (1896). Grier is sitting on the right.   (John Douglas)

Fig. 2.170 Louis Grier in his studio in front of a naval work   (courtesy Denys Wilcox)

Fig. 2.171 Louis Grier in his studio (1905)   (*Black and White*)

Fig. 2.172 The interior of 'The Foc'sle' from the window end (1896)
(John Douglas, courtesy Denys Wilcox)

J.M.Gibbon, who did an article on St Ives artists for the magazine, *Black and White* in 1905, commented that, whereas most studios in St Ives were little more than workshops, 'The Foc'sle' seemed "rather an inner sanctum of the House of Beauty". Curios that he mentioned in particular included Korean hats and "spoils from the Imperial Palace at Pekin".[365]

In *Portalone*, Ranger-Gull describes, at some length, the studio occupied by Lucas, the character based on Grier, which he considered was "more pretentious" than most of the others in the colony, "where people troubled little about accessories of the picturesque. The few men who worked did not need toys; the idle majority did not care one way or the other". Lucas, though, "secretly hankered after the sort of glories he saw photographed in the popular magazines when an academician receives an interviewer." Ranger-Gull also recounted Lucas' curtain ceremony, which he performed for newcomers, having read of the device in a biography of Leonardo. He would habitually keep, behind a purple curtain, the painting upon which he was working at the time, and, then, when a student or newcomer came to the colony, he "used to get him to the studio, lock the door with an air, and, in the manner of a bishop making a confidence to a curate, withdraw the curtain".[366] The presence of a curtain behind an unusual naval work by Grier (Fig. 2.170) might well confirm that he was, indeed, the inspiration for this conceit.

When Grier decided to split with Olsson and run his own painting school, he took extra studio space nearby on the harbour beach - initially, one with a GER of £6 and, then, in 1901, he rented from Dr Rouncefield a much larger studio with a GER of £13. Both Figs 2.166 and 2.167 show a property with a large picture window to the right of 'The Foc'sle' and this is likely to have been one of the additional studios taken by Grier, which were presumably used for his classes. However, he continued as the ratepayer for all three studios until at least 1917, despite ceasing to take many students after 1908 and completing very little new work himself in the new century.

2.4.11.2   Edmund Fuller's Beach Studio

Shortly after his arrival in St Ives in 1892, Edmund Fuller took a loft studio (GER £6) in an unusual building, a few doors down from 'The Foc'sle', which was to be his workplace throughout his time in St Ives - a period in excess of thirty years.[367] The loft area was bigger than that of the cellar underneath and so was supported on the edges by additional wooden struts. It was a large space, with a width of some 77', which enabled him to have his easels, paints and canvases at one end, and a fine lathe and carpenter's bench at the other end, where he did his metal working. Access was up a set of outside wooden steps and there were three windows overlooking the harbour.

---

365 J.M.Gibbon, *Pictures and Painters - St Ives and its Artists*, *Black and White*, December 1905 at p.886.

366 See C.Ranger-Gull, *Portalone*, London, 1904 at pp.113-4.

367 The landlords were the Executors of W Bazeley.

Fig. 2.173 Wharf Road in the 1920s, featuring, in the centre, Edmund Fuller's studio, with 'Rose Lodge' to its right and 'Foreshore Studio' and 'The Foc'sle' to its left.
(St Ives Trust Archive Study Centre)

Fuller made his reputation principally as a marine painter and enjoyed considerable success at the Royal Academy, not only with his paintings of dramatic incidents at sea, but also with pure seascapes, featuring just rocks and sea. Works, such as *Clear Shining after Rain* (RBA 1895), showing white gigs being launched from the harbour beach, will reflect scenes witnessed from his studio. However, as 'Dunvegan', the home that he designed for himself at Carbis Bay, had a fine studio incorporated into the house, with magnificent views over St Ives Bay, he may well have done much of his marine painting there in the decade that he lived there - 1901-1911.

Fuller's beaten copper designs, which were characterised by a fine sense of lettering and beautiful spacing, were in much demand in the town, and it became fashionable for artists to commission copper nameplates from him for their studios. He also made the copper plaque in the Arts Club, noting the four members who had lost their lives in the War, although his design for this was rejected in favour of one by Borlase Smart.

Fuller was a multi-talented individual, and he also did a lot of work in black and white, obtaining "a good effect with a strong line and a broad massing of his light and shade".[368] His pencil, and pen and ink, drawings of old houses about the town are fascinating records of long-lost buildings, and he published a series of these, in 1905, in a booklet, *In and Around St Ives*. He also produced a calendar featuring them in 1912. In addition, he did a number of woodcuts of scenes in the harbour.

Fuller had a fine sense of design, and his black and white work was in demand for a wide range of other purposes as well. Accordingly, in addition to producing many of the leaflets and posters to accompany the artists' entertainments (see Fig. 3.49), he designed letterheads and advertisements for local businesses, such as for the printer and stationer, James Uren White, (see Fig. 3.9) and even the certificate for the St Ives Schools Swimming Association (see Fig.4.21), into which he introduced a touch of humour. He also took advantage of the fashion of the period for bookplates, which illustrated the personal hobbies and pastimes of the owner, and produced a series of bookplates for fellow artists, such as Walter Jevons and Folliott Stokes, and for other Arts Club members, such as the photographer, Herbert Lanyon, and the writer, Greville Matheson. His various designs for his own letterhead and bookplate invariably featured a medieval ship on the high seas, which was a favourite motif (Fig. 2.179).

368 Bleistift, *Art and Artists, St Ives Times*, 7/11/1913.

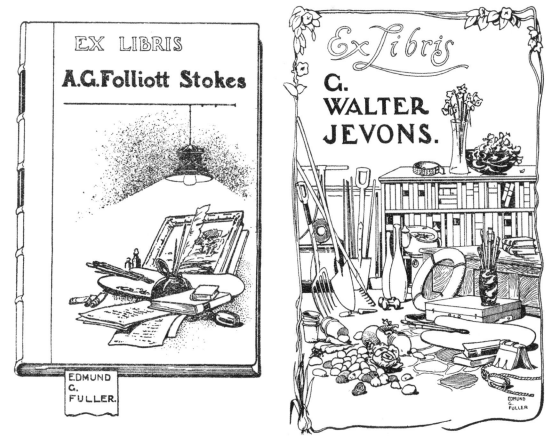

Figs. 2.174-5 Edmund Fuller   Bookplates for fellow artists, Folliott Stokes and Walter Jevons

Fig. 2.176 E.G.Fuller *View from the artist's studio*
(from 1912 Calendar)

However, his interest in Art Nouveau styles led him to win more significant commissions for advertisements and posters, such as for Jacques croquet mallets, and Pirle skirts. A very interesting series of drawings of girls in a style not dissimilar to Alphonse Mucha (see Fig. 2.177) all have the same reference number on them, and these appear to relate to a play, *Blue Moon*.[369] However, perhaps his finest achievement were his designs for the Union Castle Line (see Figs. 2.179-81), a commission most probably won due to a friendship with Greville Matheson, of the publicity department of the firm, who was a regular St Ives visitor. Knowledge of these aspects of Fuller's work comes almost entirely from a suitcase filled with items from his studio, mostly dating from 1910-1913, which suddenly appeared at auction in Clevedon in 2008. Accordingly, he may have done other work in these spheres at different times during his career, which remains completely unknown.

In 1925, the freehold of Fuller's studio and the fish cellar underneath, along with Frank Moore's Beach Studio next door, was put up for sale by auction. The purchaser, who wanted to convert the properties, was keen to obtain vacant possession, and Fuller's studio effects were auctioned by William Benney on 22nd March 1926. Having lost his wife, Emma, in March 1923 and his sister, Clara, who lived with him, in February 1925, Fuller decided to move to Portishead, where he lived until his death in 1940.

Figs. 2.177-181   Various designs by Edmund Fuller, including three for Union Castle Line

369 A musical comedy, *The Blue Moon*, ran at the Lyric Theatre in London in 1905-6.

Fig. 2.182 The staircase entrance to Alfred Pazolt's 'Foreshore Studio,
with nameplate, fashioned by Edmund Fuller.   (postcard)

2.4.11.3   Alfred Pazolt's 'Foreshore Studio'

One of the artists to sport a copper plaque, designed by Edmund Fuller, at the entrance to his studio, was Alfred Joseph Pazolt (1872-1956), who rented, between 1900 and 1910, a loft studio between that of Grier and Fuller, which he named 'The Foreshore Studio'. Access to this was up a wooden staircase to the side of the property, in a little nook. Pazolt was a wealthy Boston-born seascape painter and keen sailor. His forebears, originally called Patzold, were from Austria, but the family had made their money as Boston furriers.[370] On taking early retirement from the business, probably in the mid-1880s, Alfred's father, Henry, decided to return to Europe with his family and to live in Bonn.[371] Alfred began to show an interest in art and studied under P.Jansen at Dusseldorf.[372] It was probably this interest that led Henry and Alfred to relocate, first to Bayswater in London in c.1897, and then to St Ives in 1900. By June that year, the family were staying at 'Seaforth', Park Avenue and Alfred and his sister, Caroline, took lessons from Louis Grier.[373] Both exhibited two works at the 1900 RCPS exhibition, but, whereas Alfred was thereafter a regular contributor to Show Days, Caroline does not seem to have exhibited again.

Although occasionally depicting craft on the high seas, Pazolt concentrated on realistic depictions of the vastness of the ocean and particularly favoured those dramatic moments before, during and after storms, with threatening clouds and waves whipped up into a frenzy (see Plate 24). He had an early success at the Royal Academy in 1901 with *The Rain Squall* and, in 1903, his three canvases on Show Day, *Sunbright Seas*, *Trackless Deep* and *The Passing Squall* were considered noteworthy "for their clever rendering of wave movement, sea atmosphere, and for the truth of their sea colour".[374] The critic was particularly

---

370 Pazolt's grandfather, Thomas, moved to the United States and his father, Henry, was born in New York in 1838. By 1845, Thomas had established himself as a furrier in Boston and Henry also later worked in the family business. Alfred was, accordingly, born in Boston, in 1872. I am completely indebted to Dr Heiner Gillmeister of the Department of English, American and Celtic Studies at the University of Bonn for all of the information about Pazolt's family and much else in this section.

371 Dr Heiner Gillmeister has discovered from the Boston Directory that Henry's brother, Louis, seems to have taken over Henry's share of the family business by at least 1885.

372 Dr Gillmeister indicates that on the foreigners' list of 1895 in the Municipal Archive of Bonn, Pazolt styles himself as an artist - 'Maler'. However, in 1896, he enrolled as a philosophy student at the University of Bonn, only to leave in his third term.

373 Alfred was first signed in to the Arts Club as a guest of Louis Grier in November 1900.

374 *St Ives Weekly Summary*, 28/3/1903.

taken with *The Passing Squall*, which, although small, he considered an important work. "Through the driving storm mist the run of the sea is admirably shown, as the waves with streaming crests fly before the ever increasing fury of the gale. In fact, a feeling of old ocean, its mystic power and majestic movement pervades the entire picture, and will, we believe, achieve for it notable success."[375] In 1904, Pazolt was elected on to the Committee of the Arts Club and, that year, had a painting *Sunlit Seas* hung at the St Louis World Fair.

In October 1907, Pazolt witnessed the wreck of the *Susan Elizabeth* on Porthminster Beach and depicted the scene in a painting called *Her Last Voyage* (donated by the artist to Salcombe Yacht Club). The vessel had been caught in a hurricane on its way back to St Ives from Newport, loaded with coal. When she eventually arrived in St Ives Bay at 5 a.m., she had lost the majority of her sails. Pazolt later commented, "My attempt to portray the scene was as I first saw her, soon after dawn. The men were clinging to the rigging as tremendous seas washed over the ship. After several attempts, the lifeboat was launched from the beach into a roaring smother of sea, spray and foam.[376] A gallant fight with wind and sea, and the wreck was reached. The exhausted crew were taken with difficulty from the gyrating rigging. Barely was the lifeboat clear when the *Susan Elizabeth* started going to pieces. It looked as though a box of matches had suddenly burst, when her planks and spars were tossed about by the mighty sea".[377] The painting originally showed the lifeboat ploughing its way through mountainous winter seas on its errand of mercy but, at a later date, the lifeboat has been removed. Pazolt also witnessed, a few months later, the gale which drove the schooners *Lizzie R. Wilce* and *Mary Barrow* on to Porthminster Beach in January 1908, and he bought the figurehead of the former from the salvage sale.

Although Pazolt continued to have success occasionally at the Royal Academy, his first love seems to have been sailing, and, in addition to 'The Foreshore Studio', he also rented some cellars nearby, where he probably kept his sailing gear. In 1901, he advertised for sale a yacht called *Spinaway*, after which he acquired a most impressive vessel, *Stella Maris*, which was moored in the harbour and was featured in one of the classic early postcards of St Ives (Fig.2.183). He was a keen and highly respected sailor and, in 1902, he presented the prizes at the St Ives Bay Regatta - an event that attracted several thousand spectators - and organised an impromptu gig rowing race between the crew of the local boat, *Grace Veal*, and one selected from three French crabbers anchored in the Bay.[378] However, to what extent Olsson and he sailed together is not known, and students who crewed with Olsson, such as Will Ashton and Arthur Burgess, make no mention of Pazolt. His move to the Isle of Wight in 1910 was clearly influenced by sailing, rather than artistic, considerations.

Fig. 2.183 St Ives Harbour full of mackerel boats.
Pazolt's yacht, *Stella Maris*, is the central boat.   (postcard)

---

375 ibid.

376 Aware of the ship's difficulties, the lifeboat had been launched in readiness to assist some seven hours previously but was itself immediately driven on to Porthminster beach when it first went to help. Hundreds of people waded into the tumultuous surf and, despite ropes snapping and people being constantly swept off their feet, the lifeboat was eventually refloated.

377 *The Seagoer*, Vol 16 No 2 Winter 1951 pp.70-1.

378 *St Ives Weekly Summary* 28/8/1902.

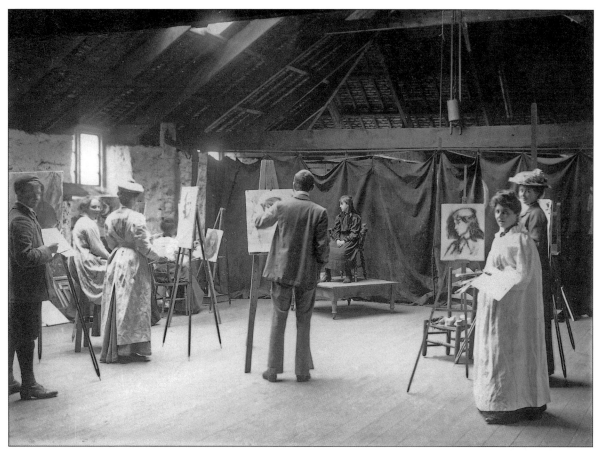

Fig. 2.184 Students at the 'Cornish School of Landscape and Sea Painting' at work in the Harbour Studio c.1901. This well-known image features, on the left, Will Ashton, Hilda Fearon and Emily Carr. See Chapter 2.6 *Student Life in the Colony* for other members of this class.

2.4.11.4 The Harbour Studio

By 1898, Julius Olsson had decided that his original plan of sharing his large Porthmeor Studio with his students was not working, presumably because he faced constant interruptions. However, instead of looking for a separate studio for himself, he was so taken with the ambience of the Porthmeor Studio, despite it being far bigger than he needed, that he rented from William Paynter for his students further large premises fronting the harbour beach (GER £17). These he converted into the Harbour Studio and this studio became the base for his Painting School for the rest of its existence. It appears to have been situated between the Lifeboat Inn and the Customs House (see Figs.2.186 & 2.165).[379] Olsson's decision gave him a rental commitment of £42 per year, when most artists' studios cost them between £6 and £10 - perhaps an indication of the extravagance to which Olsson was deemed to be prone. Unsurprisingly, therefore, when, by 1902, Algernon Talmage began to take a leading role in the School, Olsson ensured that Talmage replaced him as the ratepayer for the studio.

Apart from students in the very early years of the Painting School (1895-7), who probably alternated between Olsson's Porthmeor Studio and Louis Grier's 'The Foc'sle', most students, who came down to St Ives to study under Olsson and/or Talmage, will have worked in the Harbour Studio. A number used it as their exhibiting address, when they were successful at the Royal Academy, and Will Ashton, in 1904, held his farewell exhibition, of over fifty works, in the studio. Talmage continued to be noted as the ratepayer for the studio until 1907, when his departure from St Ives and his wife Gertrude, seems to have resulted in some adjustments, as, for the years 1908-1916, Talmage is shown as both the owner and the ratepayer of a studio on the harbour beach with a GER of just £10. This is a little puzzling, given that Talmage is rarely referred to in St Ives during this period. However, one year, Gertrude Talmage is recorded as the ratepayer and it is possible that she continued to give lessons. Certainly, the Australian student, Penleigh Boyd, in 1912, used the Harbour Studio as his exhibiting address. It is also listed occasionally on Show Day notices in the 1920s - Arthur Hayward showed there in 1928-9 - , but no artist seems to have made it their base for any appreciable length of time. There is no reference to it after 1930, and so it may have been sold off following William Paynter's death that year.

379 The only indication of its position that I have found is on Roskruge's 1929 Map of the Studios, when it was occupied by Arthur Hayward - see Fig. 3.38.

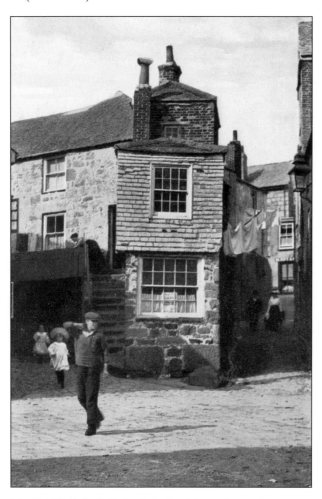

Fig. 2.185 Folliott Stokes' studio at the entrance to
Capel Court/Pudding Bag Lane

2.4.11.5   The Capel Court Studio of Folliott Stokes

Capel Court, the name which, "by order of the Council", the quaint street, Pudding Bag Lane, was to be called after 1890, was, until its demolition in 1936, a small, curving cul de sac, whose entrance was on the right-hand side of 'The Sloop Inn'.[380] It was here that Folliott Stokes had a studio (GER £4) for over twenty-five years.[381] As most of the cottages in the street were small and dark, with few facilities, I assume, but cannot prove, that his studio was the narrow property right at its entrance, for this had large windows and fine views over the harbour.

Stokes, who settled in the colony in 1889, may have had limited art training. He did not exhibit on Show Day until 1892, but he was also hung at the RBA for the first time that year. His paintings were principally of the wild moorland scenes that he so loved, and he was very fond of capturing the effects of the moon. He had a work, *Evensong*, illustrated as a Picture of the Year in 1895, and had two late evening effects hung at the Royal Academy in both 1897 and 1898 and another in 1902. His work, however, was not selected for any of the principal exhibitions held by the Cornish artists.

In the new century, following the apparent break-up of his marriage, Folliott Stokes devoted less time to his art and more to writing. His output was very varied. His initial foray into this field seems to have been his contributions to the *West Country Arts Review* in 1896, which comprised an impassioned article, *Landscape Painters and their Critics*, and a poem. His friendship with the novelist, Cyril Ranger-Gull, persuaded him to try his hand at story-telling and he initially published some short stories in the local paper in 1902-3, before producing in 1904 a novel, *A Moorland Princess*, set in St Ives and Zennor, which is referred to regularly throughout this book because of the insight that it provides into the discussions that the artists had on Art.[382] Folliott Stokes clearly played a central role in such discussions

---

380 The site of the demolished street now forms the car park behind 'The Sloop Inn'.

381 He is first recorded as the ratepayer in the Rate Book of 1893, but probably had been there since his arrival or at least from 1892. He is still recorded there in 1917, but not 1925.

382 See *St Ives Weekly Summary - A Cornish Cameo* on 13/12/1902 and *A Western Tragedy* on 24/1/1903. The former clearly draws on the rescues made during the *Cintra* gale.

and he produced a series of articles on the work of some of his fellow artists, such as Julius Olsson, Algernon Talmage, Alfred Hartley and Louis Sargent, for *The Studio*. However, Stokes is best known for his guide books on the Cornish coast and moors, in which he demonstrates an erudite mind, well-versed in literature, history, mythology, geology and botany. His unbounded enthusiasm for Nature marked him out as a distinctive character, whose intelligence and learning was much appreciated.[383] Following a serious illness, which necessitated an operation in London in 1910, he seems to have re-directed his attention back towards art, and took part in Show Days from 1913 with regularity. However, he did not enjoy any further significant successes.

2.4.11.5 'Chy-an-Chy Studio'

Long-term student, Gertrude Rosenberg (c.1869-1912), created, in the late 1890s, a small studio (GER £4) overlooking the harbour in Chy-an-Chy, the area where Fore Street meets The Wharf, and stayed there until 1910. It was right on the junction of Chy-an-Chy and The Wharf and proved a popular studio for many years. Occupants included Mary Nicholson (1911-2), Agnes Bousfield (1913 to at least 1917), Mabel Shone, whose husband Captain Richard Shone was President of the Arts Club in 1935, (1919-32), Fred Bottomley (1933-7) and Amy Watt (1938-1945).[384] The latter, although primarily a still life painter, was inspired by the studio and her five Royal Academy exhibits in 1938-9 were all St Ives harbour scenes.

2.4.11.6 Other studios on the Harbour Beach prior to the War

Several of the intermittent studios fronting the harbour were quite small, with GERs of less than £3. Other artists to rent studio space here in the early years of the colony were William Titcomb, the Newlyner, Percy Craft, and the Essex artist, Alfred Conquest, who had first visited the colony in 1884. Others, who took studio space in this area for more significant periods, were John Bromley, who was the ratepayer during the years 1899-1909 of a studio with a GER of £3 owned by Simon Noall, Louie Whitehouse, who rented from Lord Cowley, in the years 1898-1904, a studio with a GER of £2, the American, Percy Simpson, who rented, again off Lord Cowley, in the years 1900-1904, a separate studio with a GER of £3, and the Australian, Hayley Lever, who rented various studios in the area in the years 1902-1911. There were also various other premises in the area that acted as small studios from time to time.

2.4.12 Other studios on Wharf Road

A few new studio names do appear along the harbour beach in the 1920s, although it is not always clear whether these are new creations. However, the character and ambience of all these studios was changed significantly by the completion of the construction of Wharf Road, along the back of the beach, in the early 1920s. Instead of having direct access on to the sands, there was now a sizeable road passing in front of the properties that attracted traffic and pedestrians. Whilst there were few objections, as the need for better access will have been evident for many years, the road eventually led to the complete transformation of this section of town. Landlords, instead of owning rather dilapidated cellars and lofts no longer required for the fishing industry, now found themselves with properties of potential in a position that attracted tourists in droves. The relatively meagre rents paid by artists for the use of the properties as studios soon became less attractive. By the 1930s, cafés had started to proliferate, as Greville Matheson recorded in one of his pieces of comic verse.

I'd like to find a studio with windows on the quay,
Where I might sit sometimes at ease and see the passing show,
Where I might paint some pictures of the harbour and the sea,
And watch the flannelled visitors stroll slowly to and fro.
Where I might watch the sea-gulls as they hover up on high,
And the silver on the water when the moon comes up o'nights,
And paint the great cloud galleons as they sail across the sky,
And see the fishing fleet go out ashine with glow-worm lights.

But I find it is no-go,
I can't find a studio,
For there's come a funny change upon the scene,
There might be a chance for me
of a studio on the quay,
If it wasn't for the cafés in between![385]

---

383 It was recorded in March 1906 that he had just returned from an extensive tour of Russia, Turkey, Italy and other countries.

384 Mabel Shone, who died in 1940 aged 72, and her husband, who died in 1944 aged 77, are buried at St Uny, Lelant.

385 Greville Matheson, *Painters, Poets and others in St Ives*, St Ives, 1936 at p.5.

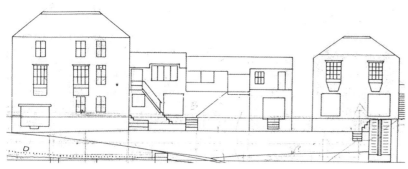

Fig. 2.186
1921 elevation drawing of The Wharf, showing from the left, the Lifeboat Inn, 'Blue Studio', 'Harbour Studio' & the Customs House (St Ives Trust Archive Study Centre)

2.4.12.1 'Blue Studio', Wharf Road

'Blue Studio' (GER £10) is first mentioned by this name on Show Day in 1919 and it was situated next to the Lifeboat Inn (see Figs. 2.186 & 2.165). The name of the studio, which had a large picture window, was clearly given to it, as its woodwork was painted blue. It was taken over in 1922 by Mary Grylls (fl.1921-1956) of 'Ar-Lyn', Lelant, who occupied it for many years. She was the wife of Thomas Reginald Grylls, a local Councillor, and was primarily a still life painter in watercolour. She was a founder member of the St Ives Society of Artists and had one success at the Royal Academy in 1934. It was later used in the 1940s and 1950s by the retired architect, George Pennington (1872-1961), who settled in Carbis Bay in 1939. He held a number of exhibitions in the studio of watercolours from his travels and his black and white sketches of the town were used for Leonard Spray's book, *If You Are "Going to St Ives"*.

2.4.12.2 'Downalong Studio', Wharf Road

'Downalong Studio' was the creation of the figure painter, Nell Cuneo, the London-born widow of the American illustrator, Cyrus Cuneo. After her husband's tragic death from blood-poisoning in 1916, she moved to Dartmoor and then to Cornwall, living initially in Halsetown. She first exhibited on Show Day in 1922, but then bought 'Downalong House' (GER £32), a large but dilapidated property which was next door to the Pilot's Boathouse. In her restoration of the property, she not only created living accomodation for herself and her sons, Desmond and Terence, but also created 'The Copper Kettle' café, which became a popular haunt, and a studio for herself on the top floor. However, Nell Cuneo's visits to St Ives became sporadic after 1930, and she may well have sublet the studio regularly.

Fig.2.187 Herbert Truman's popular postcard of The Wharf, showing 'Downalong House', with the roof-lights of 'Downalong Studio'. On its right is 'The Pilot's Boathouse', with a studio above.

Fig. 2.187A   Charles Simpson sketching outside 'Shore Studio' in 1923

2.4.12.3   'Shore Studio', Wharf Road

The first reference that I have found to the name 'Shore Studio' was in 1913.[386]   By 1919, it had become the personal workspace of Charles Simpson, and a photograph of him in 1923, said to be taken outside his studio, shows him on the nearby slipway.[387] At this juncture, Simpson was a keen bird painter and Vera Hemmens recorded how he would stand at the studio window, studying the flights of birds over the Bay through powerful field glasses. She also commented, "In one corner of the studio is a kind of bird mortuary, where hang all kinds of stuffed birds. These are used to learn the formation and colouring of their feathers."[388]   Simpson was also inspired by the location of his studio to do a series of paintings, in 1923-4, featuring all aspects of the herring fishing season, of which the principal work was *The Herring Fishing Season - From My Studio Window* (Laing Art Gallery).

After Simpson's departure from St Ives in 1924, there is no further reference to 'Shore Studio' until 1930, when it was used on Show Day by Arthur Hayward. In 1933, having sold all three of his Royal Academy exhibits, Hayward decided to build a studio in his garden and to convert 'Shore Studio' into an Art Gallery. Hayward, who had fallen out with Borlase Smart and the St Ives Society of Artists, linked up with Dod and Ernest Procter, Hugh Gresty, Harold and Gertrude Harvey, Midge Bruford and Alison Rose, and they exhibited together for a few years in the studio as the 'Cornwall Group'.

Fig. 2.188 Arthur Hayward and Dod Procter in 'Shore Studio'
during an exhibition of the 'Cornwall Group'

---

386 A postcard in 1913 from Hanna Rion, the second wife of the American illustrator, Frank Ver Beck, is addressed to her daughter from her first marriage, Theresa Abell, at 'Shore Studio'. Theresa was then an art student.

387 See Roskruge's 1929 Map (Fig. 3.38), when it was occupied by Hampden Minton.

388 Vera Hemmens, *A Cornish Chelsea*, *The Daily Graphic*, reproduced in *St Ives Times* 8/1923.

2.4.12.4   'Rose Lodge Studio', Wharf Road

'Rose Lodge Studio' was created from one of the fishing lodges built in the early years of the century that are unique to St Ives. Due to the tidal nature of the harbour, there was a lot of hanging around as the fishermen waited for confirmation that weather and tide permitted departure, and the five lodges became social centres for the fisherfolk. With the decline in the fishing industry, however, they began to become otiose and, as early as in 1913, 'Rose Lodge', which was at the back of the Harbour Beach, close to Edmund Fuller's studio (see Fig. 2.173), was used on Show Day by two long-term friends, Emily Allnutt (c.1867-1944) and Alice Hogarth Nicholson (b.1865). From an artistic family, Emily Allnutt was born in Windsor, and studied at the Slade, in Paris and also at Bushey, where she enrolled in 1894. She first started to show her work in 1899 and moved to St Ives in 1912. She was successful at the Royal Academy in 1915 with a St Ives scene, *Mending the Nets*, and later became an Associate of SWA.

Born in Withington, on the outskirts of Manchester, Alice Nicholson was the second daughter of a College Registrar at Victoria University, but was fifteen years younger than her elder sister. She studied at the Manchester School of Art, at South Kensington, where she won a medal, and at Colarossi's in Paris. Primarily a figure painter in oils and pastels, she first showed her work in 1899, when she was living with her family in Wilmslow, Cheshire. In St Ives, she is first mentioned on Show Day in 1911, when she was exhibiting in the studio of Fred Milner, which may indicate that she was his pupil. By 1913, she was sharing a studio with Emily Allnutt, and her painting, *Mending the Sardine Net*, was accepted by the Royal Academy in 1914. She too became an Associate of SWA, where she was a regular exhibitor.[389]

Fig. 2.189 W.H.Lanyon   Helen Stuart Weir in 'Rose Lodge Studio'
(Lanyon family archive)

389 Her painting, *Idleness*, was presented to the Municipal Art Gallery, West Hartlepool.

Fig. 2.190 Herbert Lanyon   Helen Stuart Weir and Nina Weir-Lewis in 'Rose Lodge Studio'
(Lanyon family archive)

In December 1913, the local art critic recorded that a group of women artists were meeting regularly at 'Rose Lodge Studio' in the evenings "with the object of making studies of lamplight effects". Allnutt's painting of a girl, with a Japanese lantern in her lap, done at such a session, was considered particularly clever and charming.[390] However, in 1915, both women moved to Gerrards Cross, where they lived together for nine years, but they might have retained the studio, for a number of Allnutt's exhibits with SWA between 1917 and 1923 were St Ives scenes. On Show Day in 1916, however, it was used by Pauline Hewitt and Sara Maclean. In 1924, Allnutt decided to settle back in St Ives, living at 15, Sea View Terrace.[391] However, by that time, 'Rose Lodge Studio' had been taken over by the American-born still life painter, Helen Stuart Weir (d.1969), and her mother, Nina Weir-Lewis (d.1937).[392] Having previously studied in America and Germany, Stuart Weir arrived in St Ives with her mother in 1913 and both exhibited that September at Lanham's. Stuart Weir became friendly with another American student, Marcella Smith, and they both took lessons from Fred Milner, whilst her mother studied under Frances Hodgkins. Indeed, when the sketching restrictions were at their most stringent, Hodgkins was thankful for the use of Nina Weir Lewis' garden. Stuart Weir produced some sculpture to begin with, exhibiting a work called *The Caress* at the Royal Academy in 1919 and winning a medal for sculpture in Bucharest. However, she became best known as a still life painter in oils and was acting President of the Society of Women Artists in the years 1933-6. She divided her time between London and St Ives, but this studio was to be her painting base in the colony for the rest of her long life, although she clearly allowed other friends, such as Eleanor Charlesworth, to use it for Show Day on occasion. The studio provided good views of the fish auctions on the beach, and John Park found the steps outside the studio a great vantage point when sketching the harbour, as he did repeatedly.

2.4.12.5   'Beach Studio', Wharf Road

'Beach Studio', at No 93, Wharf Road, adjoined Edmund Fuller's studio, and is first mentioned by that name in November 1914, when it was taken by the etcher Frank Moore (b.1876). Born in Watford, Captain Frank Moore was educated at Highgate School and University College, London. Although he joined the Arts Club in January 1911, he still used Winkleigh in Devon as his exhibiting address for the RWA in 1913, and he does not appear to have settled in St Ives until 1914, when his etchings, drypoints and aquatints were highly regarded on Show Day. His masterly technique, and the great variety in his work, were consistently praised, and he had his own printing press in the studio so that he could personally supervise the important printing process. He remained in 'Beach Studio' until it was sold, along with Fuller's studio, in 1925. After the property's conversion into a studio flat, with large sitting room, two bedrooms, kitchen and bathroom, it was still called 'Beach Studio' and was occupied, for a number of years in the late 1920s, by Hurst Balmford.

---

390 Bleistift, *Art and Artists*, *St Ives Times*, 19/12/1913.

391 Nicholson, who moved to Hindhead in Surrey, came to visit her with some regularity and her portrait by Nora Hartley was exhibited on Show Day in 1925. Allnutt moved, in 1931, to Chalfont Cottage, Carbis Bay and the pair stayed with Mrs Griggs at Zennor in 1933.

392 They exhibited there on Show Day in 1923.

Fig. 2.191 Wharf Road, shortly after its construction in the early 1920s.
'Balcony Studios' are in the foreground   (postcard)

2.4.12.6   Other new studios on Wharf Road

Other studios on Wharf Road mentioned periodically on Show Days during the 1920s were 'Green Studio', occupied by Francis Algernon Spenlove-Spenlove, then calling himself Francis Raymond, and 'West Pier Studio' and the two 'Balcony Studios', which all had a succession of occupants. The 'Balcony Studios' were built on part of the site that had been the home of the Salvation Army prior to its destruction by fire in 1915. An advert in 1927 indicated that 'Upper Balcony Studio' had three rooms, kitchen and bathroom, and boasted not only a balcony with a fine view of the harbour, but also a piano. For this, the extremely high rental of five guineas a week was being asked.[393]

2.4.13 The Malakoff Studios

The Malakoff studios were unique. Seemingly made of just timber and glass, they were basic structures built on the rocky outcrop by the entrance to the station, known, since the days of the Crimean War, as The Malakoff. However, they boasted one of the finest views in St Ives, down over the harbour and out across the Bay towards Godrevy. The two initial studios (each with a GER £6) appear to have been built in 1899 and, although the Rate Books show artists as owner-occupiers, it is very unlikely that they actually acquired any freehold rights.

The longest occupant of a Malakoff Studio was William Fortescue, who worked in one from 1899 until his death in 1924. Fortescue produced, in the main, typical genre scenes of the streets and houses of St Ives, and his studio tended to be the first port of call for visitors to Show Day, who had come by train. However, a particularly fine large work, *Loading Fish at Low Tide, St Ives* (Plate 34), has recently come up for auction in New York. His widow retained the studio and it was used in August 1925 for an exhibition of needlework by Lucy Bodilly, the wife of Arthur Bodilly of 'Rosemorran', and her daughter, Vera, which was highly regarded by Borlase Smart, who wrote a lengthy review praising the quality of the workmanship and the originality of the designs.

The initial occupier of the other studio was noted as 'Jamieson', probably Middleton Jameson, who did exhibit with the St Ives artists at the Whitechapel exhibition in 1902, but, in 1901, the studio was taken over by Moffat Lindner. Possibly, it was used by his wife, Gussie. It was rarely mentioned on Show Day, but Henry Keasbey used it in 1907. In 1911, it was taken over by former Mayor and shipowner, Robert Sawle Read, a good friend of the artists, perhaps for one of his family. On her return to the town in 1924, it was then used by Emily Allnutt, who appears to have called it 'Poncyn Studio'. It is shown on Roskruge's 1929 Map of the studios (Fig. 3.38).

In 1909, Fortescue seems to have created a further studio, which he let out to William Parkyn, who called it 'Trevose Studio'. The son of an Army Lieutenant-Colonel, Parkyn was born in Lee, Kent, and was educated privately, before studying art at Blackheath and Rochester. After a spell in Newquay in 1896-7, he first came to St Ives in 1900 to study under Louis Grier.[394] After a further visit in 1903, he settled

---

393 *St Ives Times*, 22/7/1927.
394 He exhibited Newquay scenes at RCPS in 1896-7. See brief Curriculum Vitae in Tate Gallery Archives 724.252 re Grier.

in the colony in 1907, initially in 'Reculvers House', Hawke's Point, where he had a studio.[395] However, in 1913, after his marriage to Margaret Day, the daughter of the Rector of Sandwich, he moved into a property on Ventnor Terrace, which he called 'Richboro' '.[396] Principally a marine painter, he initially depicted a range of boats at sea but, during the First World War, concentrated on naval vessels. Works from this era that were reproduced as prints include *The Lone Patrol* and *Hun Hunters* and his picture of a hospital ship, in the Royal Collection, is hung at Sandringham. During the War, he was employed as a deputy coast watching officer, and shortly afterwards, he left St Ives to live on The Lizard.

By the end of the 1920s, it was recognised that there was need for a place for char-a-bancs to turn and/or park and, amidst some furore, the Malakoff was chosen as the appropriate site, resulting in the removal of the studios.

2.4.14 The Norway Studios

Nearly all the studios considered to date have been studios with a view and it has been easy to see why the position of such studios would have appealed to artists. Norway is the name given to the area of the town around Norway and Porthmeor Squares, with easy access both to the harbour and Porthmeor Beach. It did not boast any views, but it had one great alternative attraction - it was cheap.

Two studios had been created in the Norway area as early as 1893 and, with a GER of just £2-10 each, they were the cheapest on offer. Yet again, the landlord was George Williams, the creator of the Porthmeor Studios complex. Ratepayers in 1893-4 were Mrs Emily Latham Greenfield and an artist recorded as 'Mead', probably the newly arrived Arthur Meade, rather than C.W.Mead, who was in the colony at the turn of the century.

Born in Westminster in c.1845, Emily Greenfield was first recorded in St Ives in June 1891 and was principally a landscape painter, but she also exhibited some figure paintings, such as *The Fisherman's Wife*, which was the most significant work that she showed at Falmouth (1893 - £95). She stayed in the colony for over a decade, living at 5 Bellair Terrace, with her elder sister, Rose Cooper (born Brighton c.1841), who also was a painter and who took part in entertainments put on by the artists (see Figs. 2.208 & 3.50). Emily enjoyed one success at the Royal Academy and one in Paris, and rented this studio until 1899, before moving to one in St Andrew's Street. By 1901, her Norway studio had been taken over by Marion Frances Horn, a student at the Olsson/Talmage School and she used it until 1906.

Fig. 2.192 A property in Norway Square that may well have been used as a studio.
Was this 'The Hutch'? The buildings on the right were demolished when
the Mariners' Church was built   (St Ives Trust Archive Centre)

---

395 See RWA catalogue 1908. He joined the Arts Club in December 1907 and he first exhibited on Show Day in 1908.

396 However, by 1919, he had moved to 14 Barnoon Terrace. See St Ives Rate Books, Kelly's Directory for 1914 & 1919 and RWA 1915 catalogue.

By 1898, the other small studio was occupied by the visiting American, Richard Levick, and then by further Olsson students, Frank Dobbs (1899), the future Royal Academician, Leonard Campbell Taylor (1901-2), and the Liverpudlian Charles Baxter (1903-5).[397]   After 1906, both properties, although still referred to as studios, are either marked 'void' or shown as occupied by Henry Williams, a relation of George Williams, who had died in 1902. It was only in 1911 that artists again occupied them. Jack Titcomb, downsizing dramatically from a Porthmeor Studio, took one, and was still noted as the ratepayer there in 1925. However, he spent the war years with his brother, William, in Bristol, and will have sublet it for a number of years.

The other small studio, which she now named 'The Hutch Studio', was taken in 1911 by Bertha Cockerham, who lived in nearby 'Brick House' (GER £4). Bertha was another art student, who had been a regular visitor from at least 1901, before settling in the colony in 1909.[398] She first exhibited on Show Day in 1911 and, by 1913, her art had progressed sufficiently for the reviewer of Show Day to comment, "The variety of subjects treated by Miss Cockerham spoke of versatility, whilst their execution was a revelation of exquisite taste and craft. Extravagancy of colour Miss Cockerham evidently avoids, and it is in the poetry of things, even of the commonplace, that she finds her true expression in art."[399] In 1914, she exhibited three works at the London Salon, but this was the only year that she exhibited outside St Ives. Cockerham probably moved from the studio in 1919, when she bought, in conjunction with her friend, Florence Canning, 'Ocean Wave Studio' in St Andrew's Street off the Cowley Estate (see above).

Fig. 2.193 The Canadian art student, Helen McNicoll,
in an unidentified St Ives studio in 1905.

397 Dobbs was involved with the colony between 1895-9 and exhibited a portrait of Gertrude Talmage on Show Day in 1898. This is the only known reference to Taylor in St Ives, but his later portrait of Guy Kortright (RA 1932) might result from a friendship forged as fellow pupils at this time. Baxter was involved with the colony between 1901-5, exhibiting on Show Days in 1901 and 1904 and living in The Terrace at the time of the 1901 Census.

398 Not surprisingly, Bertha's surname is often mis-spelt and so it is difficult to be certain when she first visited St Ives. However, a Mr and Mrs Cochram from Bristol, with their daughter, stayed at 9 Bowling Green Terrace in July 1893. Bertha herself, who was by this juncture living in Plymouth, definitely stayed at 'The Headland', Carbis Bay, Foweraker's guest house, throughout September and October 1901 and may well have returned during 1902, as her parents are listed as Visitors in August that year. A Miss Cockerham from Tavistock also stayed at 2, Springfield Villas in September and October 1903.

399 *St Ives Times*, 28/3/1913.

Fig. 2.194 Porthmeor Square, with the rooflight visible in Norway House Studio   (postcard)

With cheapness a priority for students, it is not surprising that this area attracted artists studying at the Painting Schools in town and the most enduring studio in Norway, which still exists, is Norway House Studio, which was created by the Australian art student, Arthur Burgess, in 1901. In October that year, he described it in detail to his girlfriend, fellow art student, Muriel Coldwell. "It is one of those majestic buildings situated in Porthmeor Square at the top of Bunker's Hill. It is not a bad little crib - 34ft long but only 10ft 6 wide in the widest place. The owner put a top light in to suit myself. I have been very busy fixing it up. J.O. [Olsson] has provided me with two curtains, two chairs and a table, which I had to patch up and cover with a piece of sail cloth....I have also a cosy corner. The framework I made out of old pieces of timber rescued from J.O.'s old studio. Over that I spread my wallaby rug. At the back I have tacked up a strip of chiffon or cretonne which hangs in small folds from shelves....I spend all my spare time in the studio now, evenings as well. I have fallen to sleep reading three nights now on my seat"[400] He includes sketches of both the outside of the studio and the seating arrangement in his 'cosy corner'. Having his own place to work boosted his output and he was soon telling Muriel that he was doing two panels a day and had a frieze of panels along two sides of his studio.

After Burgess' departure in 1902, there is strangely no record of this studio until Show Day in 1919, when it was used by the visiting American artist, Vernon Ellis. However, later that year, the property was bought by Mary Frances Agnes Williams (b.1870), but her ownership led to one of the most unfortunate disputes between an artist and a local. The daughter of a clergyman, Mary Williams seems to have taken to art quite late and to have done most of her art training in Paris, where she won silver medals at the Atelier Colarossi in the annual 'concours' for drawing and painting from the nude. She is first recorded in St Ives as a guest of Lizzie Whitehouse at the Arts Club in November 1917. At the time that she acquired the property, it had no water or water closet and the only access from the ground floor to the studio above was via a trap door. She sought to overcome this problem, by adding a porch and enclosing some outside steps, and, having made a number of enquiries, obtained the consent to this work of the Council, who were reputed to own the land, for it looked as if it formed part of a passage to the Digey. However, James Carbines, who subsequently leased from the Cowley Estate a neighbouring property, found out that the land upon which the porch had been built fell within the curtilage of his property, and he persecuted her unmercilessly. In a plea for help to Lord Cowley's agents, who had failed to appreciate that the land was owned by the Estate when she first enquired of them, she recounted the hassle that she had suffered. Initially, "he obstructed my door with wood and watched my goings in and out with other men round my door - but I just managed then to squeeze past it". Eventually, however, Carbines built a solid wall out from his property, which prevented her from gaining any access to the door of the porch and, accordingly, to her home. "I am a woman and an artist and he intends to bully me", she told the agents, implying that her sex and occupation were a significant factor in Carbine's actions.[401] The porch is still there, and so Carbines was told to desist. However, he

---

400 Letter from Arthur Burgess to Muriel Coldwell dated 9/10/1901 (Stephen Bartley).
401 Mornington Estate Papers, County Records Office, Truro, GHW/12/3/6/1/206/94.

then applied in 1920 to erect two water closets in the passage, right by her front door.[402] His application was rejected, but his intolerable attitude led her in 1923 to move to a property in Victoria Place, which had a self-contained studio, which she called 'Enys Studio'.

Two other studios, although listed in the Rate Book as in Back Road West, seem to have had Porthmeor Square addresses. These were initially occupied by the two New Zealand friends, George Sherriff (1846-1930) and Herbert Babbage. Sherriff had been born in Brighton, but had emigrated with his family to Wanganui in 1862. He returned to England in 1904 for further study at the Slade and the West London School of Art, but based himself for the winter and early spring each year in St Ives. His studio, which he rented initially in 1905, was above a blacksmith's shop and had a view of the sea.[403] This appears to have become known as 'Den Studio' (GER £5). Babbage may well have shared this for a while, as he used a Porthmeor Square address long before taking his own studio (GER £6-10) in 1912. His friends put on an exhibition of his work there, during one of his breaks on leave from the Home Guard, shortly before his untimely death in 1916. It is just possible that this is the studio known as 'St Leonard's Studio', used by Claude Francis Barry and his wife, Doris, for a couple of exhibitions of their work in the years 1919-1921. By 1925, it was occupied by the writer, Rolf Bennett. On Sherriff's final departure back to New Zealand in 1913, 'Den Studio' was taken over by the American illustrator, Frank Ver Beck, who held a small exhibition there, in August 1919, shortly before he returned to America, of the original watercolour drawings for his children's books. It was then used in the early 1920s by Annie Bliss Smith, originally from Hampstead, who specialised in coloured woodcuts.[404] In 1925, the ratepayer was another printmaker, Dossie Cooke, later Dorothy Bayley.

The Rate Book of 1925 records two further studios in the Norway area, albeit these were generally known as the Loft Studios, Back Road West. I believe, although I have no firm proof, that these were in the building that now houses the Penwith Gallery. The first mention of them is in the listing for Show Day in 1923, when they were occupied by Elizabeth Cork, a local amateur, and George Turland Goosey, the Northampton-born architect, who had made a considerable reputation in America, but who had decided to retire from practice and devote himself to furthering his painting skills. Lilas Trewhella, Bernard Ninnes, Fred Bottomley, Mary Williams, the Tiel Jordans and Phyllis Pulling all exhibited there subsequently for one Show Day, but the studios do not appear to have attracted a long-term resident. If my understanding of the location of these studios is correct, then the building was later the home of Peter Lanyon's 'St Peter's Loft' studio.

Fig. 2.195 Herbert Babbage
in his St Ives studio
(Marion Whybrow)

---

402 See *St Ives Times*, 26/3/1920.

403 *A Wanganui Artist in England*, *Wanganui Chronicle*, 16/1/1908. Sherriff was represented at the Colonial and Indian Exhibition in London in 1886 and at the Centennial Exhibition in Melbourne in 1888-9. He was a founder member of the Wanganui Arts and Crafts Society and was elected on to its first committee in July 1901.

404 See Show Day notices 1922-3 and the 1925 Rate Book. On Show Day in 1921, Smith is listed as exhibiting in Back Road West, which may be the same studio.

Fig. 2.196 H.G. Fitzherbert *Caricature of Allan Deacon*
(from *Caricatures of the Cornish Riviera*)

2.4.15   The Virgin Street Studio

The most tragic event involving a St Ives studio was the Virgin Street fire in 1921, in which not only was Allan Deacon's studio destroyed, but Fireman William Paynter Uren killed. Virgin Street was an unusual place for a studio, for it comprised, principally, a row of small cottages, with no sea views. The studio, however, was in a big wooden property that was in multiple occupation, and was clearly of some size, as its GER was £12. At the time of the fire, the lower portion was used by fishermen to store nets, the next floor contained Deacon's studio, a room used by the Plymouth Brethren and a store for the lessee of Porthmeor Beach for tents, chairs and bathing machines, and the top floor was used by a cabinet maker.

The first artist to use space in the building as a studio was Adrian Stokes, who appears to have moved there in 1893. It was again owned by George Williams. Unfortunately, there are no photos or descriptions of it to indicate why a studio on the first floor of a building in multiple occupancy in such a location, some distance from the harbour, was attractive. Stokes remained on record as the occupier there until 1900, when Deacon's name is inserted in his place, but, in practice, Deacon is likely to have taken it over in early 1899, when he decided to settle in the town, as Stokes had already left. Deacon is then recorded as the occupier of the studio until its destruction, despite apparently leaving St Ives in 1912-3. However, he returned in 1920, exhibiting a selection of old and new work in his studio on Show Day that year, including a work called *Prodigal* (most probably *The Peacemakers* - Fig. 2.197), which depicts a corner of the studio.[405] In addition to a number of valuable paintings, he was also said to have lost some antique furniture in the blaze. The Whitehouse sisters, who had stored much of their furniture in the studio, as they had gone on an extended trip to Italy, were also severely inconvenienced financially by the fire. These losses, however, paled into insignificance on learning of the loss of life of Fireman Uren in the fierce blaze, which started in the store, took hold quickly and demolished the whole building.[406]

---

405 *St Ives Times*, 5/3/1920.
406 *St Ives Times*, 15/4/1921.

Fig. 2.197 Allan Deacon *The Peacemakers*   (David Wilkinson, Book Gallery, St Ives)
This was said to depict the interior of Deacon's Virgin Street Studio

2.4.16 The trend towards small studios in the 1920s

After the War, the number of studios in the town grew significantly - in 1921, it was estimated that there were over 200 - and there seems to have been a move away from the huge, barn-like spaces of the past, with their attendant problems of cold and damp, to more personal, cosy quarters. This will, in part, be due to the falling demand for vast canvases, but will also reflect the precarious financial position of artists at this time. Many of the new arrivals were also spinsters of various ages, whose marriage prospects had been severely curtailed by the War's huge death toll.

Many of the wealthier artists, by now, had more than one studio, for they had a room in their homes set aside for painting, in addition to their principal workplace in Down-along. There were also studios of the salon type, fitted out with beautiful objects, where the easel may have been more for display than serious work. However, there were a number of other artists, particularly women, who lived a more bohemian existence, in which their modest studio also acted as their sole reception and living area, and names, such as 'The Den', 'The Hutch' and 'The Cuddy', indicate intimate working spaces. Many of these smaller studios had relatively short lives or were re-named by new occupants and, accordingly, there are few descriptions or records of them.[407] However, 'Ship Studio', created by George and Kathleen Bradshaw, is probably a good example. Newly-wed and financially strapped, they created a small home and studio for themselves out of an old pilchard cellar, with loft above, in the Norway area of town, opposite what is now 'Norway Stores', and occupied it for nearly forty years. A photograph of the living area (Fig. 2.198) shows a tastefully designed, well-lit space, but the rest of the property was very dark and damp, and it is now merely used as a store.

2.4.17 The Artist's Lament

It is noticeable how many more photographs exist of the artists' working environment than of their homes. Whether their studios comprised bare barns or had some tasteful acoutrements, this was the space that defined them. Despite all the inconveniences and the crippling cold, artists often became emotionally attached to the place where some of their greatest dreams had been realised. This is best encapsulated in a poem, entitled *The Artist's Lament*, written by Louis Grier when a change of landlord in 1916 threatened him with eviction from 'The Foc'sle'.

---

407 Other examples, some of which have been mentioned already, are 'Balcony Studio' (Cuneo & others 1922, then Fradgley 1925), 'Little Studio', Market Strand (Hurst - 1919, Ellis - 1923, Dale - 1928-30), 'Loft Studio Nos 1 & 2' (Goosey and Cork 1923-4, Pulling 1933), 'Fire Station Studio' (Mackenzie Grieve - 1924), 'Carrack Dhu Studio' (Bradshaw - 1924), 'Meadow Studio' (Burne - 1924-5, Angier 1930, A F G Henderson 1936), 'Skiber War Vor Studio' (Webb - 1924), 'West Pier Studio' (Tysoe Smith - 1924), 'Alison Studio' (Turvey - 1925, Larking/Ballance - 1938), Mount Zion Studio (Nicoll 1930-3).

Fig.2.198 The Bradshaw and Slatter families in 'Ship Studio'   (Bradshaw family archive)

Fig. 2.199 Marcella Smith in an unidentified St Ives studio   (Smith family archive)

What have I done that I should lose,
The eerie where I woo the muse,
The place of all, which I should choose,
My studio?

The home of all my pots and pans,
The place I lay my deepest plans,
Where I think out my can'ts and cans,
My studio.

The place of warming pans galore,
Which I had bought before the war,
They're not for sale, they're only for
My studio

For thirty years I've labored there,
And planned and thought and torn my hair,
It is my only private lair
My studio.

The landlord so the bills have said,
Has sold the place above my head,
He might as well have sold my bed,
O! studio

How hard it is you can't believe,
I wish I could get a reprieve,
It really breaks my heart to leave,
My studio

Now I must gird my loins and find
Another place in which to bind
The fleeting sketches in my mind,
A Studio[408]

The poem's publication in the *St Ives Times* won him the reprieve desired and he enjoyed the studio until his death.[409] What lament there would be, if we now lost the Porthmeor Studios, which are not only themselves such an integral part of the history of the colony, but also the surviving example of a much wider imprint that the artists made on the heritage of St Ives.

---

408 *St Ives Times*, 2/6/1916.

409 The last reference that I have found to the studio was on Show Day in 1928, when various artists exhibited in it.

SOCIAL LIFE PRIOR TO THE WAR

2.5.1 'More genial, kindly, hospitable society does not exist'

Speaking at the opening of the Cornish Artists' exhibition at Nottingham Castle Museum in 1894, William Titcomb commented, "Living in Cornwall, we painters miss the cultured life of London. We have no music, no drama, no pleasant wickednesses. We have to be fearfully moral and fearfully uncomfortable. We live in miserable lodgings and are at the mercy of Wesleyan landladies, whose forté is certainly not cooking. The compensation, however, comes in painting side by side with many congenial spirits."[410] Clearly over-stating the position to gain a laugh, Titcomb nevertheless highlights an important question, namely, how did a group of well-educated British artists, used to the cultural refinements of life in a metropolis, meld with artists of various different nationalities, who were not always fluent in English, and amuse themselves in a small, remote town, dominated by Methodists, who frowned upon any form of light entertainment?

The answer, at first sight, might seem obvious - namely, that they socialised with each other, talked about what they had in common, principally painting, entertained each other with such gifts as they had as musicians, actors and comedians, and took part together in whatever recreational activities were available. However, it soon becomes apparent that the artists were very aware of the danger of being perceived, locally, as an exclusive, privileged enclave, and that they sought, individually, and as a group, to widen their social circle and to make a difference to the entertainments and pastimes that were available to the townsfolk generally. Several artists became involved in promoting various musical societies, whilst others took part in, or organised, a range of theatrical entertainments. Sports-minded artists were intimately involved with the formation of new golf and cricket clubs or played important roles in the tennis club. In this way, the artists made a significant and welcome contribution to the social and cultural life of the whole town. In this chapter, though, I concentrate principally on the social activities that they pursued with each other.

Life in lodgings, under a Weslyan landlady, may not have been too stimulating, but, once the artists had set up their own homes, and developed a range of entertaining pastimes, their lifestyle proved really quite attractive. Indeed, a correspondent to the *Westminster Gazette*, after a visit in 1896 - just two years after Titcomb's speech -, was moved to comment, "I can say without hesitation that more genial, kindly, hospitable society does not exist in England than in the artist colony, who dwell in the villas and terraces on the heights above St Ives. Simplicity of life, refinement and cultivated taste, love of outdoor nature, and freedom from convention, combine to form a moral atmosphere which is like a tonic, an antiseptic, after the sickly 'decadence' of much of the artistic society of London".[411] It is hardly surprising that this combination of qualities proved so alluring.

2.5.2 'The Early Days'

"You should have known it in the early days, my boy. A few of us came straight from Paris, and led a life of primitive simplicity and bohemianism. We were all equally poor, and used to meet together in each other's lodgings every evening, and discuss art and our work, over a glass of whisky and a pipe. A common enthusiasm bound us together, irrespective of sex and social rank."[412] So reminisces a character in Folliott Stokes' novel, *A Moorland Princess*, and this is likely to be an accurate summary of the early social life of the colony. Both Emma Zorn and Howard Butler record evenings spent at the lodgings of fellow artists. Edward Simmons, a frequent visitor to the Zorns, was described by Emma as "clever at conversation and cards", whilst Butler enjoyed playing logomachy - a word game - when he went round to the Simmonses, as he felt that it was one of the only ways of keeping Simmons quiet!

Butler also socialised with some of the middle class members of the community and came to like, in particular, the elderly banker, James Read, the Reverend John Balmer Jones and his curate, C.F.Jones, who became Butler's tennis partner. It took him some time, however, to get used to the

---

410 *Nottingham Express*, 29/9/1894.

411 Reproduced in *St Ives Weekly Summary*, 19/9/1896.

412 A.G.Folliott-Stokes, *A Moorland Princess*, London, 1904 at p.131.

Fig. 2.200 Henry James on the steps of 'Talland House',
with Julia and Adrian Stephen
(Leslie Stephen album,
Mortimer Rare Book Room, Smith College)

town's social etiquette. "They have a curious custom of inviting you to supper at eight. They begin with music and social talk and nothing is served to eat until ten o'clock. I found this exceedingly trying until I caught on and had my own supper before I left."[413]

Edward Simmons recorded that he spent many occasions with the family of Leslie Stephen at 'Talland House', which he described as "a gathering place for all sorts of interesting persons".[414] Robert Louis Stevenson, Edmund Gosse, the art and literary critic (and brother-in-law of Alma Tadema) and the American poet, James Russell Lowell, were amongst those that he met there. As for Stephen himself, Simmons commented, "One day Stephen remarked that music, like eating, should be done in the bathroom. It always sounded to him like an infernal din. He was the ultra-literary type, who wished to be rid of all things physical; he even envied Harriet Martineau, who had no sense of taste."[415] Adrian and Marianne Stokes were other regular guests at 'Talland House', and Stephen also became friendly with the Dutch artist, Sigisbert Bosch Reitz, whose portrait of him was highly regarded by the *Spectator*, when it was exhibited at the New Gallery in 1892. Julius Olsson also recalled, many years later, the pleasure of dining with the Stephen family at 'Talland House', and Will and Jessie Titcomb and the Griers are amongst others recorded as socialising there.[416] Other guests that they are likely to have met were Henry James, who was a regular visitor, and Joseph Wolstenholme, who, in Stephen's words, "consoled himself with mathematics and opium" and whose personality was used by Virginia Woolf for the character of Augustus Carmichael in *To the Lighthouse*.

2.5.3   Fraternising with the Newlyners

In the early years of the colony, the St Ives artists socialised quite a bit with their brother brushes from Newlyn. This was largely due to a number of Newlyners working for extended periods in St Ives in the late 1880s. Stanhope Forbes, his new fiancée, Elizabeth Armstrong, and their respective mothers, lodged

---

413 H R Butler, Unpublished Autobiography, p.175, Archives of American Art, Smithsonian Institution, Washington DC, Howard Russell Butler papers, Reel 93.

414 Edward Simmons, *From Seven to Seventy*, New York and London, 1922 at p.165.

415 ibid, p.166.

416 *St Ives Times*, Christmas Number, 1925.

with Mrs Rodd at 6 Barnoon Terrace during July and August 1886 and, during the summer, were visited by quite a number of Forbes' Newlyn colleagues. He mentions by name Fred Hall, Frank Bramley, Henry Detmold, William Fortescue, Fred Millard, Norman Garstin and Arthur and Jack Bateman. As Forbes selected a St Ives subject, *Their Ever-Shifting Home*, for his principal Royal Academy submission for the following year, he was back and forth between St Ives and Newlyn over the whole of the winter period, storing his canvas in Harry Robinson's studio and dining with the Robinsons, Howard Butler, William Eadie and some of his London friends, who were working in the town that autumn, J.Langton Barnard, his wife Kate, and her sister, Leonora Locking (who was to marry Alfred Hartley). In return, Forbes invited them over to Sunday lunch in Newlyn, on a couple of occasions, and took them on a tour of the Newlyn studios. As a result, when there was a Ball held in the Public Hall in Fore Street in St Ives in February 1887, Forbes was invited, and was asked "to bring as many dancing men" as he could. In the end, the party from Newlyn comprised Forbes, Lizzie Armstrong, Chevallier Tayler, Fred Millard and Jack Bateman. The St Ives artists present included the Robinsons, the Simmonses and the Chadwicks, with Frank Chadwick causing a twitter amongst the damsels of St Ives, with his white waistcoat, black page-coat and gibus - a folding opera hat. They all had what Tayler called a "punching time", with Lizzie Armstrong impressing on the dancefloor.[417]

Clearly, on Forbes' recommendation, Percy Craft lodged with Mrs Rodd, at 6 Barnoon Terrace, the following summer, whilst Elizabeth Armstrong and her mother took rooms in The Manor House, Green Court, St Ives from July 1887 to March 1888. Forbes came over to stay most weekends, and Norman Garstin and his wife and young child lodged in the town in September. This led that month to the first cricket match between the colonies, which is discussed in greater detail below. In October 1887, Forbes was in St Ives for a "grand silhouette evening", during which the artists did profiles of each other, whilst the St Ives artists came across to Newlyn, on a foul night in February 1888, to watch two plays - *Turn Him Out* and *Checkmate* - put on by the Newlyn Artists' Dramatic Society.[418]

At this juncture, Arthur and Jack Bateman may have moved across to St Ives on a permanent basis for a while, as Arthur used 6 The Terrace as his exhibiting address throughout 1888. Percy Craft and his wife again took rooms in the town that summer, but, on this occasion, Craft took a studio as well, as his major work of the year, *Hevva! Hevva!*, was a St Ives scene. Accordingly, he was in St Ives at the time of the supper held on 31st August to celebrate Adrian Stokes' sale to the Chantrey Trustees. Craft continued to come across to St Ives with some regularity, as he retained a studio in the town for his use until the mid-1890s.

In 1889, Henry Detmold also worked in St Ives for an extended period, lodging at 7 Bellair Terrace from early July until at least November. In 1890, he was back in the colony for a similar length of time, lodging at the Restaurant run by Miss Kevern in Tregenna Place, whose sign featured an artist's palette. He was joined, in August, by Thomas and Caroline Gotch, who lodged at 9 Bellair Terrace, and Edward Docker, who stayed with Mrs Hosking at 'Trenwith House'. As a result, all four were founder members of the St Ives Arts Club in August 1890. However, although, that December, a number of Newlyn artists were members of 'Louis Grier's Company', when he produced *Trial by Jury* in Penzance, the Arts Club soon became the centre of the artists' social life in St Ives and, as the colony grew and became more self-sufficient, fraternisation with the Newlyners diminished. Norman Garstin, who was a good friend of Millie Dow, came over, with some regularity, in the mid-1890s, and included St Ives artists in his 'Notes' for *The Studio*, but the presence of Newlyn artists as guests at the Arts Club is surprisingly rare.

2.5.4   The St Ives Arts Club

When comparing the art colonies at St Ives and Newlyn, Lewis Hind felt that the existence of the Arts Club in St Ives was one of its major advantages. "For beauty of environment, Newlyn cannot be compared to St Ives, and if Newlyn is the possessor of an art gallery, with periodical exhibitions, St Ives has its Club, and a Bohemian camaraderie that the sister colony lacks. Gala night is Saturday, when the painters, men and women, foregather to talk art and life, to skim papers and magazines, to sing glees, and to show their skill in acting. Saturdays everybody makes a point of being present at the Club."[419] The Club, therefore, became the focal point of the colony and played a significant role in ensuring that the resident artists developed a good camaraderie, particularly as it was quite unusual for such a club to be open to both sexes. The artists became quite proud of the reputation that the Club gained and were keen to bring visiting practitioners of the fine arts as guests, whilst visitors to the town soon learnt that securing an invitation was an important objective of their stay.

---

417 Letter from Stanhope Forbes to his mother dated 8/2/1887 - Tate Gallery Archives 9015-2-1-398.

418 Letter from Stanhope Forbes to his mother dated 2/10/1887 - Tate Gallery Archives 9015-2-1-443.

419 C.Lewis Hind, *Newlyn v. St Ives*, The Studio, 1895.

2.5.4.1 Formation

The manner in which the Arts Club came into being was recounted by Louis Grier in an article in *The Studio* and it seems a shame to paraphrase a piece written in his typically droll fashion.

"In the autumn of 1888 a few good men and true met together in my studio (commonly known as 'The Foc'sle') to discuss the advisability of forming an Arts club in our little fishing town, and over the pipe of peace and a little of the dew of Bonnie Scotland, we decided to start an institution to be called The St Ives Arts Club. We arranged to meet on Saturday nights only, and the rendezvous chosen as the most suitable was 'The Foc'sle'.

After a few meetings some judged it rather slow, for many of the attractions usually appertaining to a club were of necessity impossible in a room which was devoted to the worship of a goddess of Art during six days of the week. At the third or fourth 'club night', one member bolder than the rest, and possibly possessing more of the spirit of the gambler, dropped a bolt from the blue by proposing the introduction of lady members; and so persuasive was his manner, that we were speedily won over, and his motion was carried almost without opposition.

The following Saturday we mustered over sixty members of both sexes, and it was conceded by all that we had started a going and pleasant concern. This time we had a piano on the spot, and as we boasted some members possessing considerable vocal and instrumental talent, things began to 'hum' a little more. The light charade was indulged in too (much to the detriment of 'The Foc'sle' draperies) and it was amusing to see a heavy weight in the shape of one of England's hopes in Landscape Art [Adrian Stokes], chirping about on settles and things as little Tom Tit guised in simple drapery with a seven foot mahlstick under it by way of a tail; whilst a six-foot genius from Boston [Edward Simmons] stalked him with a mighty gun.

On fine nights, the large doors at the end of the studio would be opened, and then we had a series of nocturnes that would have merited the artistic appreciation of Mr Whistler. The lights of the incoming herring boats, the rippling waves dancing the lantern's reflections, and right in the foreground the wet scintillating sand, and the groups of hurrying fisherfolk, made a scene of great beauty."[420]

Fig. 2.201 Louis Grier *The Night Watch*   (David Wilkinson, Book Gallery, St Ives)

---

420 Louis Grier, *A Painters' Club*, The Studio, Vol 5, 1895, pp.101-2.

In the spring of 1889, the artists went their separate ways but, when they re-assembled in the autumn, Grier refused to allow 'The Foc'sle' to be used as a club room again, as he "was preparing a masterpiece, and was afraid of interruption". This was his famous work, *The Night Watch* (Fig. 2.201). The club nights, therefore, fell into abeyance that winter. In 1890, though, it was decided to take steps to form an official Arts Club and, at a meeting of artists, chaired by William Eadie, at the Western Hotel on 1st August 1890, a Committee was elected. This comprised three officers - Adrian Stokes as President, Harry Robinson as Secretary and Eardley Blomefield as Treasurer - and four other members - William Eadie, Charles Greville Morris, William Titcomb and Edward Simmons, all of whom had been in St Ives for some years and had most probably taken part in 'The Foc'sle' evenings. The name of the Club was agreed and some draft rules prepared. Membership was to be restricted to "Professional Painters, Engravers, Sculptors, Architects, Authors and Musicians, resident or visiting St Ives and their wives, husbands and relations".

On 4th August, Robinson sent out a letter of invitation to those people in the town that the Committee felt were eligible for membership. This indicated that "A large and convenient Club Room, overlooking the Bay, will, it is expected, be ready to receive the Club in a few weeks". Thirty-two people attended the general meeting held at Edward Simmons' studio in St Andrew's Street on 8th August, becoming founder members, and three others, Leslie and Julia Stephen and Marianne Stokes also pledged membership, although they could not be there in person. Those present were Arthur George Bell, Frederick Bertram, Henry Bishop, Eardley Blomefield, Sigisbert Bosch Reitz, Mary Cameron, Charles Davis, Henry Detmold, Edward Docker, William and Annie Eadie, Miss Harriet Ford, Emanuel Phillips Fox, Thomas and Caroline Gotch, Charles and Mina Grier, Wyly Grier, Miss Edith Hayes, Walter Jevons, John Chadwick Lomax, Charles Greville Morris, Mrs Pansy Rainey, Harry and Dorothy Robinson, Mrs M J Rogers, George Roller, Edward Simmons, Adrian Stokes, Folliott-Stokes and his wife, and William Titcomb. One notable absentee was Louis Grier, who must have been away at the time. However, his brother, Wyly, his mother, Mina, his father, Charles, and his sister, Pansy Rainey, were in attendance.

Given that these meetings had been held at the height of the visitor season in August, it is not surprising that some of the founder members had little future involvement with the Club. In fact, Thomas and Caroline Gotch, George Roller, Arthur Bell and Mrs M J Rogers do not make any other appearance in the Club's records, and Charles Davis, Frederick Bertram and the Newlyners, Henry Detmold and Edward Docker, had left the town by the end of the year. There were also a number of foreign visitors amongst those present - the American Edward Simmons, the Australian, Emanuel Phillips Fox, the Canadian, Harriet Ford (with her friend, Edith Hayes) and the Dutchman, Sigisbert Bosch Reitz - and their involvement with the Club was naturally limited, although both Fox and Bosch Reitz made return visits. In fact, other than the members of the Committee (and, in the case of Eadie, Robinson and Adrian Stokes, their wives), only Folliott-Stokes and his wife proved to be long-term members of the Club. By September, however, the membership included, not only Louis Grier, but also Julius Olsson, Terrick Williams, Herbert Lanyon, Gwilt Jolley, Percy Northcote and Harry Browne, the majority of whom were to have extended St Ives connections.

2.5.4.2 The Club-room

Without doubt, Harry Robinson seems to have been one of the key figures in the Club and it was he who located a suitable Club-room. The premises were on the first floor of an unique building on Westcott's Quay, approximately forty foot square, which had just been acquired by the carpenter, John Jenkyn. The property (see Figs 2.106-7) had been built by the recently deceased Charles Eathorne, as a warehouse for his water grist-mill nearby, probably in the late 1850s, and the upper storey, leased by the Club, which had previously been used for the storage of corn, was constructed solely of wood - tarred weather boarding outside, and wood-lining inside.[421] The ground floor, which had several wide openings in it, as the neighbouring fish cellar had rights of way through it, was used by Jenkyn for his carpenter's shop. Louis Grier called it "a very marine spot indeed....under our feet comes the roar of the ground sea as it struggles with the rocks at the base and rushes madly up the granite walls of our foundations".[422] In September, the Club agreed with Jenkyn that they could put in a large window overlooking the Bay and that a large skylight measuring 11' x 6' should be inserted on the east side of the building between the dormer windows. The result was "a room with curious windows turning up in the most unexpected places, all on different levels, and with a quaint Dutch-like roof, with here and there a skylight, and here and there a swinging window."[423]

---

421 For further details, including a discussion of its unusual construction, see the website of the St Ives Arts Club.

422 Louis Grier, *A Painters' Club*, The Studio, Vol 5, 1895, pp.101.

423 ibid

Although this building has been the home of the Arts Club ever since, it came perilously close to being destroyed within a few months of the Club being formed. In March 1891, West Cornwall experienced the heaviest fall of snow then known, coupled with a furious north-easterly gale, and the building took a fearful battering from wind and sea. Grier recalled the storm in his usual inimitable fashion, by commenting that, one morning, "I announced the interesting fact to my landlady at breakfast that, while dressing, I had seen a considerable portion of the Arts Club washing round the Island head on an excursion up the English Channel. My eyesight had not failed me on that occasion, and a little later on, we had a string of painters, clad in sea-boots, sou'westers and oilskins, handing the club furniture through the town to a neighbouring studio for greater safety, as we found the sea had removed a corner of the roof and carried away a quarter of the foundation, so there was every chance of the whole structure coming down by the run. Carting about odds and ends of furniture is good enough in decent weather, but dodging green seas, as they come sweeping up the alley ways, with rows of hanging lamps and other gimcracks swung on poles across one's shoulders, is no joke."[424] Whilst the artists managed to salvage their furniture, most of the timber in Jenkyn's shop beneath the Club-room was washed away and was soon smashed by the sea into matchwood.

Access to the Club-room was by a very steep set of stairs and the ladies, in danger of their lives in their long clothes, soon demanded a rope as a stair rail (see Fig. 2.202). The conditions of the room appear to have been rather primitive, with plaster falling off from the ceiling into the artists' beer and candles being the only form of light. The Suggestions Book contains a typically dry comment from Louis Grier; "That a thing to hold a candle should be placed on the writing table - the Beer Bottle is, of course, useful but not decorative". Buckets of sand were felt to be a useful fire safety device if lamps were knocked over. Ventilation was another problem at the Club, sometimes members complaining of the arctic conditions, and other times of it being so hot that the ink gave off a bluish steam and the quill pens began curling up! Eventually, it was resolved in 1901 "to match-board the roof of the Club-room as the only effectual method of preventing the constant falling of particles of lime which made it impossible to keep the chairs, tables and floor clean and free from dust"[425]. John Jenkyn did the work for £10-10.

The Club adopted a firm policy of not accepting sketches by members for the decoration of the walls. This is an interesting stance, as it was quite common to find sketches by visiting artists adorning the walls of many of the establishments that the artists will have experienced during their sojourns in France. Instead, the Club permitted photographs of Old Masters or of exhibited pictures by members (see Fig. 2.203). Grier commented, "Photographs are at least harmless in the matter of colour, which is more than can be said of the majority of sketches."[426]

2.5.4.3 Membership and guests

Initially, the Club Rules designated that Tuesday and Thursday evenings should be reserved for female members and Monday, Wednesday and Friday for males, but there were soon suggestions that one of the female nights should be devoted to musical activities and that one of the male nights be given over to a drawing class. By 1895, a fairly set timetable had been agreed of Tuesday for the ladies, Wednesday and Friday for the men and Monday and Thursday for the Drawing Class. Saturday night was open to all and entertainments were often put on by the members themselves.

In recognition of the number of short-term visiting artists, monthly membership was permitted from the outset and members could sign in visitors. Once students became an integral part of the colony, a reduced monthly fee was agreed for them. The rules relating to visitors were changed from time to time, as there were always concerns that people, who did qualify for membership, should not avoid joining, by repeatedly being invited as guests, and that residents in St Ives, who did not qualify, should not be guests too regularly. Visitors needed to be signed in, and the resultant Visitor Books are a vital source, revealing an astonishing range of both British and foreign artists and writers who enjoyed the unique atmosphere of the Club. In fact, the list of introducing members is also of great importance, as the high turnover of members means that the Minute Books of the Club fail to give anything like a full account of changes in the membership. Nevertheless, there were probably many evenings, particularly entertainment evenings, when no-one bothered with the Visitors' Book formalities.

Edward Simmons' comment in his autobiography that, by the time he left St Ives in 1892, membership of the Arts Club had reached one hundred is frequently repeated, but it needs to be remembered that this was written over thirty years later and the figure is clearly over-exaggerated. An attempt to list members during the 1892-3 season has just over 50 names and Grier, writing in 1895, puts membership at about 70. Nevertheless, numbers were constantly changing due to the monthly membership arrangement.

---

424 ibid
425 Arts Club Minutes 4/10/1901.
426 Louis Grier, *A Painters' Club*, The Studio, Vol 5, 1895, pp.102.

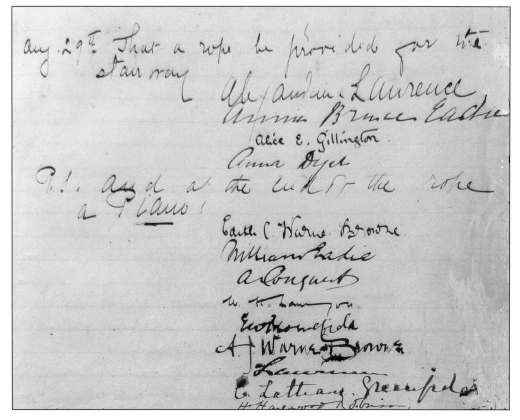

Fig. 2.202 Extract from Arts Club Suggestions Book - "That a rope be provided for the stairway
And at the end of the rope a piano"

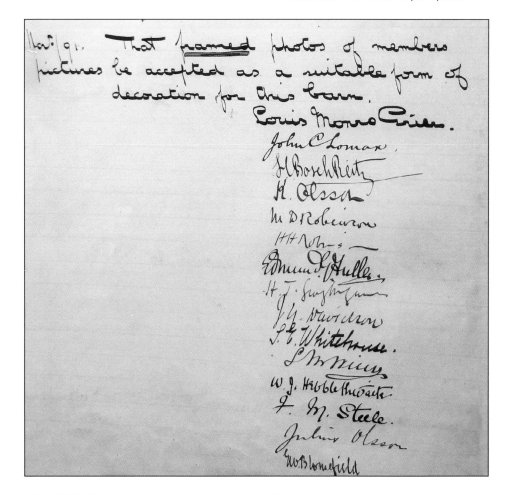

Fig. 2.203 Extract from Arts Club Suggestions Book re photos of members' work

Fig. 2.204 John Douglas   The Club-room of the St Ives Arts Club   (courtesy Andrew Lanyon)
Among the photographs on the wall of members' work is Edward Simmons' *The Mother*.

2.5.4.4 Officers

Appendix A, which lists the officers of the Club, demonstrates quite clearly who were the key figures in the pre-War years. Harry Robinson was the prime organiser and, between the Club's formation in 1890 and his death in 1904, he was Secretary for nine years and President twice. Adrian Stokes, who was regarded as the leading artist in the colony in its early years, was President for three years, as was Olsson, whose School of Painting did so much to encourage students to the town. Most of the principal artists in the early years of the colony, such as Arnesby Brown, William Titcomb, Fred Milner, Arthur Meade, Moffat Lindner and Millie Dow also took a turn as President, whilst the wit of the Club, the American, Lowell Dyer, not only had successive years as President in 1893-4, but also acted as Treasurer between 1898 and 1900. Allan Deacon, who was President in 1903, then had the unenviable task of taking over as Secretary from Robinson between 1904-6, whilst Jack Titcomb had two years as Secretary in 1908-9 before being elected President in 1910. Others to have lengthy stints as Treasurer included Eardley Blomefield, Albert Lang and John Bromley. Despite being always acknowledged as the 'founder' of the Club, Louis Grier's absence from the list of Presidents and his limited contribution as an officer of the Club is telling. Without doubt, he was considered a wag, but clearly he was not felt to be suitable officer material.

2.5.4.5 The Ladies Committee

The first reference to a "Ladies Committee" is in 1892, when a group of female members took it upon themselves to organise a Carnival Masquerade Ball. However, it was not until 1904 that the Minutes of the Club record the formal appointment of a Ladies Sub-Committee, although it seems clear that female members will have organised, right from the start, the food, and much else besides, for the entertainments put on at the Club. The Minutes of the Ladies Committee reveal that, in addition to organising the sustenance, including drink, at functions, it assumed responsibility for the caretaker and the decor. Bridge teas on a Tuesday were started, during the winter months, and these proved very popular. Most of the female members took their turn on these committees (see Appendix A) and they clearly played a vital role. Hayley Lever, in fact, complained to Elmer Schofield in 1912 that the women were now taking over control of the Club completely. "At the Club, the place has been coveted by the women I'm sure. If they all came in full force, they could place whoever they liked on any Committee."[427]

---

427 Letter dated 12/2/1912, Schofield family archive.

Fig. 2.205 John Douglas   A Saturday 'smoker' at the Arts Club in 1895, featuring, from the left,
F.W.Brooke (legs), Alexander, Louis Grier, Middleton Jameson (standing at back), Will Osborn,
Jack Titcomb, Greville Morris, John Bromley (standing), William Titcomb, Walter Jevons (legs)

Fig. 2.206 John Douglas   A Saturday 'smoker' at the Arts Club in 1895, with work by the sketching
class on view. On the left, Louis Grier, with Alexander, John Bromley and Harry Robinson standing
at rear. On the right, at foreground table, Lowell Dyer and Helen Ludby; at next table, Dorothy
Robinson and, possibly, Max Ludby and at the rear, Lily Kirkpatrick and Daisy and Lizzie Whitehouse.

Both photos courtesy St Ives Arts Club.

2.5.4.6 Drawing classes

Drawing classes were an important feature of the Club's existence in its early years. Writing in 1895, Louis Grier commented, "Our club is not all frivol, for we have a model twice a week, and it is no cheery place for idlers then, as there is little to disturb the monotony of silence save the grating of charcoal and the occasional 'flick' of a rag."[428] However, these model nights did not always go smoothly. Olsson, writing in the Suggestions Book one evening, urged the Committee "to look to the arrangements for drawing nights and appoint responsible 'massiers'. Tonight, no massier, no model, no anything!" and, in December 1892, Lizzie Whitehouse suggested "that a book be kept at the Club in which members be requested to enter names and addresses of models, whether male or female, light or dark etc." (see Fig. 2.42). On another occasion, the class came to a premature end, when the young male model fled on hearing the lifeboat rocket, as he was a member of the crew. However, once formal Schools of Painting became established in the colony, which provided sketching opportunities all day, the classes at the Arts Club, not surprisingly, seem to have lapsed. Interestingly, they were reintroduced in 1907, on Monday evenings, at the suggestion of Mabel Douglas, probably in response to Talmage's departure from the town, which really brought to an end any formal system of teaching. A small platform was obtained for the model and a light placed over the centre of it so that the model could be better illuminated.[429]

2.5.4.7 Entertainments

In the pre-War period, there are few Club records of particular entertainments staged, and such records as there are tend to relate to New Year's Eve or President's Night (see below). It is unclear, therefore, to what extent organised entertainments were put on during the winter season. Indeed, in November 1907, a proposal that Special Entertainments should take place once a month was soon abandoned, and the first time that an Entertainments Sub-Committee was elected was in December 1911. The American, Walter Norris, when telling his friend, John Sloan, of the activities of the Arts Club in 1905, does not mention entertainments at all, and merely refers to buffets and "evening smokers".[430] John Douglas' well-known photographs of a Saturday night at the Club in 1895 (see Figs. 2.205-6) would appear to capture one such evening, with the atmosphere distinctly fuzzy, as artists puff away, whilst chatting over a drink. Nevertheless, music clearly played a role in the Saturday night get-togethers, as a piano was hired for each winter season. Furthermore, the Club-room had a small stage, which was draped in fishing nets and old barked sails, giving an effect that was "pleasantly mellow in low-toned browns".[431] Although this was removed in 1901, when space became at a premium, it was re-introduced later. It is likely, therefore, that the majority of the entertainments put on were informal affairs, and that periods of high activity in the public domain (see Chapter 3.4.3), reflecting an influx of talented entertainers, will have led to the transformation of Saturday nights at the Arts Club as well.

In the pre-War period, there were a number of artists who were accomplished musicians, and performances of instrumental selections, from a wide range of styles of music, are likely to have featured on many evenings. Harry Robinson was, again, a key figure initially, as he played the piano well, and also wrote and performed his own compositions. However, Herbert Lanyon, who enjoyed a brief career as a professional performer, was recognised as the outstanding pianist in the colony, and, in the early 1890s, and after his return in the new century from America, his performances of his own and others' compositions were always popular. Beale Adams' wife, Kate, and Lily Kirkpatrick were also talented pianists, as was the former architect, turned art student, Gordon Killmister, who again wrote and performed his own compositions. The cello playing of William Fortescue, after his arrival from Newlyn in 1897, is also likely to have featured with regularity, and there were a number of local and visiting violinists that completed trios from time to time. Another student, Hugh Blackden, captivated local audiences with his mandolin playing, during his time in the colony in the late 1890s.

Singing would have been another popular part of Arts Club entertainments, and here again the range of styles covered will have been wide. Harry Robinson was an expert on early English songs and several members performed for the local Choral Society. However, Robinson also encouraged a group of artists to band together and sing glees and other popular songs. Wyly Grier had a particularly good tenor voice and was in great demand as a soloist, whilst his brother, Louis, and Arthur Meade, also sang well. In the new century, Moulton Foweraker, reflecting his training at Exeter Cathedral School, was also a highly regarded singer.

---

428 Louis Grier, *A Painters' Club*, *The Studio*, Vol 5, 1895, pp.101-2.

429 See Minutes of Ladies Committee 1907.

430 Undated letter, Spring 1905, Sloan Papers, Delaware Art Museum, Wilmington.

431 Louis Grier, *A Painters' Club*, *The Studio*, Vol 5, 1895, pp.102.

Fig. 2.207 John Douglas   Entertainment featuring from the right Harry Robinson, Edmund Fuller,
Miss Harry and (to rear) Georgina Bainsmith. Inscribed *"I swear it by dis leetle hand"*

Fig. 2.208 John Douglas   Entertainment featuring, from the right, Harry Robinson, Mrs Hackman and Rose
Cooper. Inscribed - *What fun it'll be to see Missus a down the cistern and Masta a blacking the boots. Ha Ha.*
Both photos are marked, interestingly, J.C.Douglas, Munchen.

 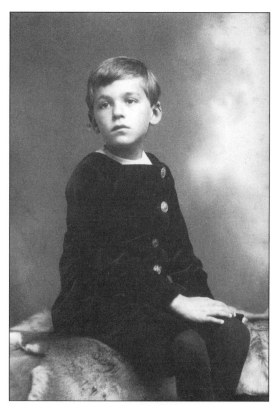

Figs. 2.209-10   John Douglas   *Frank and Loveday Titcomb*
Such child portraits are likely to have been a useful source of income for Douglas.

Fig. 2.211 Edmund Fuller Bookplate for Walter Jevons
This second, and very different, bookplate for Jevons (compare Fig. 2.175) was done after his move to the thatched 'Roswick Cottage', St Martin, in 1894, where he kept a menagerie and devoted himself to his garden. Thomas Carlyle was clearly a favourite author. Jevons still kept in close contact with his St Ives friends and was a pall-bearer at Harry Robinson's funeral.

Humorous recitations are also likely to have played a regular role in Saturday night entertainments, with John Douglas and Lowell Dyer being popular performers. In the early years of the colony, there is also mention of an artist conjuror, possibly founder member Frederick Bertram.[432]   Charades were popular, as well, and the artists occasionally presented various *tableaux vivants* on a chosen theme, such as nursery rhymes. In 1908, members even staged a comic bull fight.

New Year's Eve was always considered to be one of the principal Club nights of the year, and so was well attended. Fancy Dress was a regular feature, but other formal entertainments were staged from time to time. For instance, on 31st December 1912, *The Hypochondriac*, a farce in four scenes, by the New Zealand artist, George Sherriff, was performed. Dancing was usually the concluding activity of the evening's entertainment.

There is little doubt that these evenings were great fun and were thoroughly enjoyed by all. They were a fantastic way of promoting a communal spirit, and the ability of the two sexes to enjoy themselves together will have been rare in Victorian and Edwardian England. One can easily imagine, though, as staunch and sober Methodists wandered up The Warren on a Saturday evening, that the Arts Club seemed the very den of iniquity, as frivolous music, boisterous singing and the sounds of female gaiety filtered out on to the street. "What a bohemian and degenerate crowd!" - and there certainly would have been harsh words spoken, if the entertainment had continued beyond midnight into the blessed Sabbath.

2.5.4.8 Children's parties

The Titcombs ruffled a few feathers in 1905, when they asked if they could hold a children's party in the Club-room one afternoon in February. William explained that "it was intended to ask almost twenty small children the parents of three or four of whom were not members of the Club, but residents of St Ives".[433] After considerable debate, the request was eventually granted, on payment of a charge of 5/-, but it was emphasized that this should not set a precedent and that any future similar request would be judged "entirely on its merits and the circumstances of the moment".[434] However, as more artists had children, it became a regular feature to hold a children's party, often with a fancy dress theme, in the week after Christmas. By the War, such children had become young adults and were often taking roles in entertainments both at the Club and in the town.

2.5.4.9 Lectures and the Library

Surprisingly, records of lectures or debates are rare, but a few were organised during William Titcomb's Presidency in 1901. One evening that year, papers were delivered on the subject *Is Science Inimical to Art?* by the Newlyn artist, Norman Garstin, as well as by the artists Peregrine Feeney and Folliott Stokes. On another occasion, Harry Robinson gave two lectures on English songs of the sixteenth and seventeenth centuries, with musical illustrations by members of the Club, whilst, later in the decade, Alfred East talked about his visit to Japan. On a few occasions, Arts Club members also gave lectures in the town. Again, William Titcomb seems to have initiated this trend and, in 1903, gave a lecture, with lantern slides, to a Young Persons' Guild on *Some Great Italian Painters of the Middle Ages*, which was apparently well attended. Another Club member, whose unusual speciality led to him giving fascinating lectures, was Rupert Vallentin FLS (1859-1934). Vallentin, whose portrait by Alfred Hartley was exhibited on Show Day in 1908, was a distinguished naturalist, who had made an extended study of flora and fauna on the Falkland Islands. He rented Algernon Talmage's house in Draycott Terrace from 1903-8, with his wife, Elinor (1873-1924), who was from the Falklands, but who had studied botanical illustration at Kew. Vallentin not only gave a lecture on *A Naturalist of the Falkland Islands*, illustrated with his own photos, in 1905, but also gave one on *The Oyster* in February 1906.[435] Elinor suffered from poor health, but Rupert eventually arranged for sixty-four of her sketches of flowering plants and ferns from the Falklands to be published in 1921 and this book now fetches over £1,000.[436]

From the outset, the Club subscribed to a number of papers and magazines, and one of the most frequent topics, referred to in the Suggestions Book, is the range of periodicals that should be taken. *The Studio* and *Punch* were two favourites. In 1899, however, a special attempt was made to build up a decent library, and Frederick Sargent and Peregrine Feeney were amongst those who contributed works. In 1904, the post of Librarian was created on the Committee. Louis Grier was initially appointed but, after

---

432 No indication is given of his identity, but Charles Bertram became a well-known conjuror.
433 Arts Club Minutes 21/1/1905.
434 ibid.
435 *St Ives Weekly Summary*, 17/2/1906.
436 E.F.Vallentin, *Illustrations of the flowering plants and ferns of the Falkland Islands*, London, 1921.

just a year, was replaced by Beale Adams. In 1907, John Douglas took on the role and retained it for the next decade. In 1912, it was decided that out of date periodicals should be taken to the Seamen's Mission and the lighthouse on Smeaton's Pier, so that they could be read by the fishermen. Magazines such as *The Studio*, *The Artist*, *Colour*, *The Art Journal*, *Magazine of Art* and *Punch* were retained and, bolstered by repeated gifts, a valuable collection was formed over the years, which, by 1950, comprised over 750 volumes. The book recording Library loans is again a fascinating source and shows that the Library was well utilised. Some visiting foreign artists, such as the Canadian, Harry Britton, clearly found it of immense assistance. Sadly, though, despite being considered to be one of the finest collections in the South-West, in 1979, in an effort to raise funds for repairs, the entire contents of the library were sold at auction, for a pitiful return.

2.5.4.10 Literary members and visitors

Membership of the Club was open to authors, as much as artists, albeit that the number of long-term residents that were writers were few. However, there was nothing to preclude non-artist members becoming officers and, indeed, the second President elected, Leslie Stephen, was a man of letters, albeit ill-health prevented him from performing the role. One of the most regular winter visitors, who was a writer, was Havelock Ellis, but he was a shy, diffident man, who did not enjoy company or the sort of entertainment laid on at the Club. He recalled, however, that his wife, Edith, would nearly always make a point of attending the New Year's Eve celebrations at the Club. She is occasionally signed in by Lily Kirkpatrick at other times, but was not a regular. Whilst the Ellises writing activities resulted in front-page news, it was not the type of publicity that would have been welcomed in Club circles.

More popular was the exposure that Charles Lewis Hind (1862-1927) gave to the colony. The son of a Nottingham lace manufacturer, Hind had a spell at the *Art Journal*, before becoming editor of *The Pall Mall Budget* in 1893. When this folded in 1895, he decided to learn how to paint, as he felt that this would improve his art criticism. During his time in St Ives in 1895-6, and later in 1903-4, he divided his time between art and journalism, and he published a number of articles, in a variety of London magazines, on the work of individual artists, and on such matters as Show Day, the art schools in St Ives and landscape painting in the colony. He also incorporated his experiences in St Ives into a number of his subsequent books.

In November 1895, a new rule was introduced, permitting "persons of eminence in Literature, the Arts and Sciences or the learned professions" to be made Honourable Members on the recommendation of the Committee. This was prompted by the desire to make the prominent lawyer, John Westlake, who, as mentioned above, had a summer residence at Zennor, an Honourable Member, for he was a good patron of Adrian and Marianne Stokes. However, Westlake (see Fig. 2.92) does not appear to have made much use of his membership.

Writers appear more regularly amongst the guest list, during the period that Charles Marriott (1869-1957), then a fledgling novelist, was a member of the Club (1902-9), for he became a stalwart, being elected Secretary in 1907 and President in 1908. Marriott was the son of a Bristol brewer and, having worked for twelve years as a photographer and dispenser at Rainhill Asylum in Lancashire, he won huge acclaim in 1901 for his first novel, *The Column*, which was set in Cornwall. This prompted him to move to the Duchy, where he lived initially in Flagstaff Cottage, Lamorna, the house that was to become John Lamorna Birch's home, before settling in St Ives in 1902. In 1903, he published his second novel, *The House on the Sands*, again set in Cornwall, and, in 1904, *Genevra*, which featured a Welsh artist working in the Lamorna area. Others with Cornish settings included *The Remnant* and *Women in the West* (1906). He also produced the occasional short story and a piece called *The Wreck - An Impression from a Cornish Seaport*, about the wreck of a ketch at St Ives on the night of 28th January 1908.[437] He then branched out into travel books - that on Spain (1908), documenting a trip, taken, most probably, with Bernard Walke, being illustrated by Moulton Foweraker, and that on the Rhine (1911), being illustrated by William Titcomb. Marriott knew Ranger-Gull from his time at Rainhill, but Marston, the character in *Portalone* clearly based on Marriott, was not spared Ranger-Gull's cutting tongue.[438] Marriott's "quick-moving figure, hatless, and clad always in the roughest of corduroys, often attracted attention" and, although he recorded his best friends in St Ives as two non-artists - Herbert Lanyon and

---

437 Reproduced in *St Ives Weekly Summary*, 9/5/1908.

438 "Marston was one of those peripatetic writers who spend a year or two in a place for strictly business purposes. He regarded a locality simply as fallow land from which he should raise his crop of words". As a result, everyone was slightly on edge in his presence, for he always appeared to be taking notes. In a clear reference to *The Column*, Ranger-Gull continued, "His first novel freed him at once from his menial drawing board. The style was an odd torturing of words into harsh, though sometimes, vivid phrase. He wrote of a class above his own and without experience of it, but the angular intellectuality of the thing struck a new note. His work was icy cold. His analysis of character was detached and scientific, brilliant as far as it went, but without blood or humanity". C.Ranger-Gull, *Portalone*, London, 1904, at p.59.

Fig. 2.212 Herbert Lanyon   *Charles Marriott*
(courtesy Andrew Lanyon)

Bernard Walke -, he seems to have got on well enough with members of the colony.[439] Indeed, he was given a Special Dinner by the artists when he left in 1909, and the knowledge of art that he acquired from his companionship with them led him, in the future, to turn to art criticism, as his principal livelihood.

In his reminiscences, Marriott mentioned some of the other writers that he had met during his time in the colony. These included the prolific author, Fergus Hume (1859-1932), who was signed into the Arts Club by John Douglas in November 1905, whom Marriott recalled had "some dodge for warming his feet and legs by suggestion". Hume, who was born in Worcestershire but who had emigrated with his parents to New Zealand in 1863, trained initially as a lawyer, but decided, during his time as a solicitors' clerk in Melbourne, Australia, to turn his hand to novel writing. His first book, *The Mystery of a Hansom Cab*, published in 1886, has been described as "the most successful detective story of all time".[440] Hume, accordingly, was quite a celebrity, and he spent several months in the colony, during which time he sat for a portrait bust, modelled in clay, by Georgina Bainsmith.[441] He also wrote a three-part farce, *Aunty in Africa*, which was performed in the Drill Hall to "a large and fashionable audience" in January 1906. The story concerned one Dick Grenville, who received an inheritance from his uncle, on condition that his aunt came to no harm. Grenville then married the daughter of an African Consul, but, despite every effort to keep his aunt quietly at home, she rampaged through Africa attempting to annex all and sundry to the Empire.[442] The play would now be considered totally politically incorrect. Moulton Foweraker played the role of Grenville, and other leading parts were taken by John Bromley, Louis Grier's niece, Hazel Rainey, and Horace Taylor, a caricaturist friend of Marriott, who had been involved with the colony from time to time since 1901. Bromley and Edmund Fuller designed and painted the scenery, and a full orchestra entertained the audience before the show and during the intervals. It was clearly felt to be a major event that St Ives should premier such a play.[443]

---

439 Leonard Spray, *A Novelists' Hunting Ground*, in *The Star*, reproduced in *St Ives Weekly Summary* 6/1/1912. In addition to Marriott's work, Spray also discusses books by Folliott Stokes, Lewis Hind, Edith Ellis, Harold Begbie and the Rev R.J.Campbell. The latter wrote his *New Theology* in Carbis Bay, in which a vivid description of a storm was inspired by the sight of the Bay lashed into fury by a rough nor'easter.

440 Everyman's Dictionary of Literary Biography 1960.

441 *St Ives Weekly Summary*, 19/5/1906 records that a photograph of this was illustrated in *The Sphere*.

442 A full description is given in *St Ives Weekly Summary* 6/1/1906.

443 It was noted in *St Ives Weekly Summary* that Hume's book *A Son of Perdition*, published in 1912, was set in Cornwall and featured an artist as a wooer, but it does not appear to be based to any great degree on his St Ives experiences.

Another literary visitor at this time mentioned by Marriott was the naturalist, W.H.Hudson, who was an old friend of Alfred Hartley, who had painted his portrait in 1889 (exhibited RBA 1891).[444] Hudson first visited in December 1905, and returned again in April 1907, and was delighted to meet a "native naturalist" - Tom Whatty, the ferryman at Lelant.[445] However, in his book *The Land's End - A Naturalist's Impressions in West Cornwall*, published, with illustrations by A.L.Collins, in 1908, he criticised most severely the St Ives practice of setting baited hooks in gorse bushes to catch birds and recounted the ferryman's sad story of how the pet seal, which followed his punt, had been killed for sport by a member of a shooting party that he was ferrying across the estuary.

In April 1908, Marriott himself signed into the Arts Club Hugh Walpole (1884-1941, knighted 1937). Walpole had been born in Auckland, New Zealand, but had been educated in England, and was, at the time, working as a lay missioner at the Mersey Mission to Seamen, in Liverpool, as his father, who was shortly to be appointed Bishop of Edinburgh, wanted him to join the clergy as well. However, the single-minded Walpole was keen to be a writer and had brought down, for Marriott's perusal, the manuscript of his first novel, *The Wooden Horse* (published 1909). He later became one of the most successful novelists of his generation. In June that year, Marriott also signed in Ethel Colburn Mayne (d.1941), who had moved to England from her native Ireland in 1905 and who, in addition to writing novels and short stories, was to be the author of one of the standard works on Byron, first published in 1912. Compton Mackenzie (1883-1972) was yet another writer of future significance then in the locality. Marriott recorded, "Compton Mackenzie, then writing his first novel, with his mother, Virginia Bateman, and his sister, Fay Compton, then a solid and sedate little girl with beautiful auburn hair, were living at Riviere, Hayle. Mackenzie and Fay were frequently in St Ives plotting mischief with our two girls, who were about the same age as Fay. The year I happened to be President of the Arts Club and gave the presidential party, Mackenzie wrote for me a brilliant parody of Maeterlink, The Princess Migraine. In the list of characters appeared, "Quarrels, as rehearsed daily by the Sisters Marriott", which was perhaps an exaggeration."[446] Compton also contributed some humorous recitations to a Concert in aid of the St Ives Nursing Association in February 1908 and, during his stay at Riviere House, a three-storey Georgian property with a copper roof, he completed his first two novels - the second one, *Carnival*, setting him on the road to fame that would lead to a knighthood for services to literature. In order to help him concentrate, his new wife, Faith, played Beethoven Sonatas, Schubert and Chopin piano music for three hours at a time! His sister, Fay, followed her father and grandfather on to the stage, starring in many of J.M.Barrie's plays, including *Peter Pan*.

After, and possibly as a consequence of, Marriott's departure, the number of literary members and guests seem to tail off. In 1912, Millie Dow signed in the writer, Austin Phillips, who is featured in Fitz's *Everybody's Doing It* (Fig. 2.273), whilst the Canadian naturalist, Charles G.D.Roberts, is signed in by Nora Hartley in January 1914. A more long-term visitor, however, was the novelist, Frank Barrett. In January 1913, Daisy Whitehouse told her nephew, "This is a theatrical winter. We have already had some good charades last Saturday Eve. A new member of the Club, Frank Barrett, is getting up a little play, *Alfred and the Burnt Cakes*, written by himself and Lionel Brough. I am told Mr Barrett has published 50 novels but I cannot remember the name of one of them."[447] Frank Barrett was the pseudonym of Frank Davis (c.1845-1926), who was born in Tottenham and was the son of a master butcher. He started his career as a journalist, but then became a potter and joined the Savages Club. His obituary recorded, "His small groups of figures, his ability for catching a likeness, his boldly conceived and finely executed specimens of pottery with their rich colouring, give evidence that he might have gone far in that direction, had not his career as a potter been rudely interrupted by the collapse of a kiln containing the entire work of a year." This loss caused him to resume writing and he had instant success with a novel and a play. After that, he maintained a prolific output and his novels proved particularly popular on the Continent, being translated into many languages.[448] Several were made into films.[449] Barrett, and his wife, Joan, who was also an author, lived at 'Rocky Close', St Ives, and he wrote a number of further plays for the benefit of relief funds during the War.[450]

---

444 In 1926, after Hudson's death, Hartley was asked to confirm the identity of the sitter and produced a letter from Hudson dated 31/1/1890, which commented. "I have had the portrait since Wednesday, and now that it is before me here, I like it better than before. I have begun to think, in fact, that you never did a better, and I shall finish by believing that a better was never painted by anyone." See St Ives Times, 24/12/1926. Hartley also contributed illustrations to Hudson's book *Idle Days in Patagonia* (1893).

445 Unfortunately, Tom Whatty died young in 1910 aged 44.

446 Charles Marriott, *Memories of Cornwall's Art Colonies*, Cornish Review, Spring 1949, No 1, at p.69-70.

447 Letter from Daisy Whitehouse to Arnold Whitehouse dated 6/1/1913 - Gloucester Records Office, Whitehouse family archive, Bundle 2/10.

448 *St Ives Times*, 14/2/1919.

449 For instance, *The Woman of the Iron Bracelets* (1920).

450 I am indebted to Steve Holland and the Bear Alley website for information about Frank Barrett.

Fig. 2.213 H.G.Fitzherbert *'The President'* - *Caricature of Jack Titcomb*
(from *Caricatures of the Cornish Riviera* 1910)

2.5.4.11 Presidential parties

The first reference to a Presidential party - some form of entertainment for members put on by the President of the year - is in December 1903, and this was hosted by Allan Deacon. No details of the evening are given, and it was not until 1906 that it became a regular feature. In that year, Fred Milner put on, at the expiry of his year of office, a party, attended by nearly one hundred people, which comprised a concert, some theatricals and dancing. The following year, Albert Lang was President and, in January 1907, he and his wife gave what was called an 'At Home' party, but it was held in the Club-room and featured Bernard Shaw's short comedy *Passion, Poison and Petrification (or the Fatal Gazogene)*, along with several songs, supper and dancing. Shaw's bizarre work, which involved a poisoned soda-water siphon, and which had been performed in public for the first time in 1905, has recently been called "an indigestible tragic romantic comedy of love, jealousy, betrayal and murder", but it obviously was popular, as it was performed in the Arts Club again the following year.

Interestingly, when it was William Fortescue's turn to provide entertainment, shortly after his election as President in November 1907, he engaged his old colleagues from Newlyn to put on a comedietta, *The Bishop's Holiday* and an operetta *The Rose of Auvergne*, suggesting that he still linked up with them for entertainments. The evening was rounded off with songs, refreshments and dancing. As already seen, Charles Marriott, the following year, enlisted the help of Compton Mackenzie.

Thereafter, President's Night became a regular feature of the year, albeit, on occasion, most probably in testing economic times, it was combined with the New Year's Eve Party. It soon became recognised that it was inappropriate to expect the President to pay for the evening's entertainment, and so a sum of £7 10s was customarily voted out of Club funds to cover basic costs. The format of the evening varied, on the whim of the relevant President, but music, dancing and good food were prerequisites. Treve Curnow indicated that his father, C.W.Curnow, who ran Curnow's Commercial Hotel in Tregenna Place, was regularly employed to do the catering. "On President's night, we provided a running buffet. The things we made were out of this world, game pies, fish pies, vols-au-vent, various sandwiches and salads, meringues, iced puddings, French and Genoese pastries, Venetian jellies and creams. They really went to town. The cost was one guinea per head."[451]

---

451 See Marion Whybrow, *St Ives 1883-1993 - Portrait of an Art Colony*, Woodbridge, 1994 at p. 34.

Fig. 2.214 Edmund Fuller as a Greek at the 1893 Carnival Masquerade
(William Trevorrow)

2.5.5 Carnival Masquerades

The additional day in the leap year of 1892 certainly featured something different. In fact, the townsfolk of St Ives had not witnessed anything quite like it before. Those out early in the evening of Monday 29th February will have seen, strolling under cover of darkness, groups of strangely dressed people making their way through the town. A Venetian Noble, a French Chef and a Neapolitan Match Vendor mixed with Turkish and Spanish ladies, a Swedish peasant, a Spanish gypsy and a Dresden shepherdess. Red-shirted Garibaldians were spied alongside the warrior queen, Boadicea, whilst mendicants and sisters of the poor were seen with a White Witch. A discerning eye might also have picked out some figures from mythology, ranging from Terpsichore, the Muse of dance, and Calliope, the Muse of heroic poetry, through to Mephistocles, the Lord of demons. The wife-killing nobleman, Bluebeard, also stalked the streets; indeed, he might have been spotted twice, in rather different garb. Less threatening were two giant twin babies - one in blue and one in pink. All this strange assortment of characters were going to the first St Ives Arts Club Carnival Masquerade Ball (see Appendix B for a list of some of the participants and their costumes). Due to the numbers attending, resulting from the fact that the artists had extended invitations to their close friends from the local community, the event was not held in the Arts Club itself, but in the Public Hall. The lady members of the Arts Club were responsible for its efficient organisation, with Eardley Blomefield acting as their Secretary. A band from Truro, led by Herr Freund, a Professor of Music, was hired for the night, and spirited dancing went on until the early hours.

The success of the event in 1892 led to a repeat in February 1893, along similar lines. The range of costumes was equally wide, featuring well-known historical and mythological figues and a variety of national types, spanning different time periods (see Appendix B). Some of these were captured by William Trevorrow (see Figs 2.214-5), who took photographs for the artists, prior to the arrival in the colony of John Douglas. Trevorrow was probably best known to the artists as the rate collector, but he also ran a music shop in Tregenna Place in addition to his photography business. Sydney Laurence's 'Breton Peasant Girl' and Arnesby Brown's 'Australian Planter - evening dress' were among the outfits that caused some merriment. However, one senses that a number of the locals invited to the second Ball did not enter into the spirit of the occasion, for several turned up in their Royal Artillery Volunteers uniform, two wore the same costume as they had done the previous year and Canon Jones and the Reverend Griffin seem to have felt that their status would have been compromised if they wore anything other than their Church robes.

The list of participants in these two Balls (see Appendix B) is quite informative for a number of reasons.[452] As the events were held in the run up to Show Day in each year, one would expect them to be attended by all the committed resident artists, but the list demonstrates how fluid the colony was. For instance, the Stokeses do not take part in the 1892 Ball, as they had left the colony to go to live in Italy. Finding, however, that nowhere compared to St Ives in the range of subjects that it offered a figure painter, such as Marianne, and a landscape painter, such as Adrian, they had returned by the time of the 1893 Ball. On the other hand, whilst William Titcomb and his fiancée, Jessie Morison, took part in the 1892 Ball, which was held shortly before their marriage in St Ives that April, they were still away on an extended honeymoon at the time of the 1893 event. The Laurences, who had settled in the colony in 1889, were clearly away travelling in 1892, whilst the Robinsons were not around in 1893. Furthermore, some artist wives, such as Annie Eadie and Vesta Simmons in 1892, and Mrs Folliott Stokes in 1893, attend on their own, as their husband was either away or ill. As always, there were a number of artists, whose involvement with the colony was relatively brief or haphazard, whilst the small representation from Newlyn is also noticeable. Whilst Stanhope and Elizabeth Forbes and Ernest Ireland Blackburne attended in 1892, none of the Newlyners were present in 1893.

Fig. 2.215 Louis Grier as a Venetian Gondolier   (William Trevorrow)
This costume appears to have been worn by Julius Olsson
for the 1893 'Carnival Masquerade

452 The 1893 list is particularly useful, as there is no report of Show Day that year.

The note in the local paper of the 1893 Ball merely lists participants and does not pass any other comment on the evening. Therefore, it may not have been as successful as its predecessor. Certainly, the artists did not repeat the format for some years and, when they did, opted for the privacy of the Arts Club. One Fancy Dress Ball in February 1897 seems to have been funded by Adrian Stokes and Millie Dow, and had the artists waxing lyrical about a night's "mirth, music and motion".[453] Another ambitious one was held on New Year's Eve in 1901.[454] On this occasion, whilst the ladies were responsible for the food, a number of the men got involved in the organisation, with that year's committee of Olsson, Fortescue, Robinson, Dow, Dyer and William Titcomb, being supplemented by Bosch Reitz, Deacon, Grier, Lindner and Lang. Herr Freund from Truro was selected again as the pianist, with a violinist to accompany him. In view of numbers, the Club was grateful to be able to use, as well, the next door property, into which James Elgar Russell had recently moved, and applied to the Council for permission to erect a covered walkway, linking the two properties. The Club Minutes record that the evening was a "great success in every way", and another one was organised on the same date the following year. This will have been one of the first New Year's Eve parties that Charles Marriott attended in St Ives, and he could still recall, many years later, the lethal Swedish punch that Olsson was responsible for concocting on such evenings, the process having the aura of "a mystic ceremony".[455] Certainly, New Year's Eve became one of the highlights of the year at the Club. However, the programme on New Year's Eve tended to concentrate on variety entertainment and dancing, with a separate fancy dress evening being held in February, as a release from the tensions building up as Show Day approached.

2.5.6   The Phantom Party

In July 1898, the artists decided on a very different venue for a party - Mrs Ashton's Picnic Gardens at Hawke's Point - and a different theme - white dress only. Labelled as an *al fresco* dance, the evening, which was a huge success, was recalled some twenty-six years later by Greville Matheson, who was on a brief visit to the colony at the time. "It was a perfect summer night, warm but with a pleasant breeze, when, around 8 o'clock, the artists and their guests began to assemble. Everyone was obedient and came dressed in white. Some were in fancy costume - I recollect one tall white Mephistopheles - others came in white jackets and trousers or white skirts. Having only arrived from London on the previous evening, I was content with a pair of flannel trousers, and a painter's linen jacket....We found in Mrs Ashton's garden a place of enchantment, a bit of fairyland. Hundreds of coloured lamps had been hung during the day on trees and bushes, and here and there, and now shone like so many fire-flies. For larger lamps, we had the moon, which was silvering the sands and sea below, and Godrevy light, which flashed on us punctually every few seconds." Lowell Dyer was responsible for one of his famous punch brews, and the stand-up supper was rounded off with fruit salad, mixed in a mighty bowl by Sydney Laurence. "At one end of the tiny lawn by the side of the railway, a small stage had been erected with an immense Japanese umbrella for canopy, and here songs were sung and stories were told from time to time. On the grass, to the music of a small band, we danced. How we danced in those days!...In the semi-darkness, under the starry sky, ghosts danced gaily or went wandering along the path of the mysterious garden, or found their way through the white gate on to the green cliffs. Some, crossing the railway line, explored the leafy labyrinths of the famous nut-grove. Wayfarers making for home may well have been startled as they came along the cliff path. And, as a glorious ending, when the sun was coming up and even the most energetic dancers were wearying, some of the madder ones found their way down to the rocks below Hawke's Point, and, with the wind and rising sun to welcome them, bathed in the chilly sea. We were indeed younger then."[456]

This account, perhaps more than any other record of the colony, captures the Bohemian spirit of the artists. Here was an all night party, with revellers animated by strong drink, frivolous humour and energetic dancing, which gave plenty of opportunity for embraces in hidden places, and was topped by nude or semi-clad bathing at dawn. What excitement for those used to staid Victorian conventions and what scandal for the sober Methodists who learnt of the night's frolics!

2.5.7   Special Dinners

In his satirical take on the colony, Ranger-Gull commented, "It was the Portalone custom to mark every happening by drink and food. If a man sold a picture, they prepared him a little feast of celebration, if he failed to sell a picture, a dinner of sympathy". Ranger-Gull had probably heard of the dinners thrown by the artists for Arnesby Brown, but the first of these was not any old sale of a painting, but a sale

---

453 Extract from *The Cornish Post and Mining News* reproduced in *St Ives Weekly Summary* 6/2/1897.

454 See Arts Club Minutes for 1897.

455 Charles Marriott, *Memories of Cornwall's Art Colonies, The Cornish Review*, Spring 1949, No 1 at p.68.

456 *St Ives Times*, 18/4/1924. Matheson indicates that he was "going back some twenty-six years" and so I have assumed the event happened in 1898.

to the Chantrey Trustees, and the practice had originated in the very early years of the colony, after Adrian Stokes had enjoyed a similar success in 1888. Probably because of Stokes' own movements, the dinner was not held until 31st August. Alfred East took responsibility for designing the Menu (Fig. 1.4), which was headed 'Complimentary Supper to Adrian Stokes Given by his Artist friends of St Ives and Lelant' and included a photograph of the successful work, *Upland and Sky*, and a portrait drawing of the artist. The meal started with Ox-tail soup. There were then a range of 'Joints' - Corned Beef, Roast Chicken, Roast Duck and Tongue - with beans and potatoes, followed by apple tart with Cornish cream, and cheese and cucumber. Twenty artists were in attendance. In addition to Stokes and East, there were a number who had been in the colony some while, such as Harry Robinson, William Eadie, Edward Simmons, the Norwegian, Bernt Gronvold, Wyly and Louis Grier, Ellis Wilkinson and William Titcomb (who was joined by his brother, Jack). Lowell Dyer and Julius Olsson had just arrived, whilst Greville Morris and Allan Deacon were, at that juncture, visiting students from Bushey. Percy Craft and Hugh Norris were Newlyners then in town, but William Borrow, Philip Norman and Thomas Parker were short-term summer visitors.

A number of St Ives artists secured prestigious sales of paintings to both British and foreign Art Galleries during the 1890s, and these probably resulted in enjoyable evenings spent in one or other of the hostelries in the town. However, the first record in the Arts Club Minutes of a special dinner was that arranged in the Club-room by William Titcomb on 13th November 1901 to celebrate the sale by Arnesby Brown of *Morning* to the Chantrey Trustees. In January 1903, Brown was again the beneficiary of a special dinner, to mark his election as an Associate Academician. Being a quiet, reserved man, Brown may not have welcomed being in the limelight on two such occasions in a period of just fifteen months. These special dinners were always male-only affairs, which probably became ever more boisterous and drunken as the evening wore on, and terminated in a sing-song that veered between the bawdy and the downright silly. Ranger-Gull recorded a favourite ditty, relating to a character - the Rajah of Bhong - in the recent, hugely popular musical, *A Country Girl*, which included verses such as,

When on an elephant's back I pass
Somebody beats on a sounding brass-
GONG - the Rajah of BHONG

I can do pretty near every thing,
Only I cannot yet play at Ping-
PONG - the Rajah of BHONG.[457]

The regard held for William Titcomb in the colony is demonstrated by the fact that he was the first artist, whose mere departure from St Ives, warranted a special dinner. This was held on 12th September 1905 and artists present included not only longstanding colleagues, such as Olsson, Talmage, Barlow, Millie Dow, Fuller, Beale Adams, Moulton Foweraker, Elgar Russell, John Douglas, Arthur White and Titcomb's brother, Jack, but also Frank Chadwick, who was back on one of his periodic visits, the writers Charles Marriott and Lewis Hind, the Americans, Elmer Schofield and Henry Keasbey, and visitors Archibald Elphinstone, Harry Browne, Stuart Deacon (presumably brother of Allan) and an artist called Thomas. Titcomb had been a mainstay of the colony for some eighteen years, but the next artist to be honoured with a special dinner on his departure, Elmer Schofield, had merely been based in the town for four years, and had spent nearly half of that time in America. Accordingly, the desire to send him off in style, in October 1907, is a great testament to his engaging personality. The dinner, though, was not, on this occasion, held in the Club-room, but in the Western Hotel, then run by John Henry Tremayne, which was the venue that the artists used for billiards. Olsson presided and Dyer, Allan Deacon, Hayley Lever, Milner, Foweraker, Douglas, Meade and Lanyon were also present. Dyer "gave one of his characteristic humorous speeches and a song", Foweraker sung three songs, whilst Philip Baynes, a comic illustrator on a brief visit with his sister Cecily, gave a clever whistling imitation. Others also sang or played instrumental selections, and the evening finished with *Auld Lang Syne*.[458]

By this juncture, little excuse was needed to put on a dinner and, in April 1909, it was Charles Marriott's turn to be sent off in style, as he left St Ives shortly after the termination of his Presidency of the Club. Again, Olsson presided. Opinions of Marriott were later tempered by his disregard for the work of his former colleagues, when art critic of *The Times*, but, at the time of his departure, he had just written an article for the *Daily Mail*, in which he hailed West Penwith as "England's Art Centre" and St Ives as "the best illustration of the artistic colony".[459] That was surely worth a dinner.

In 1912, two special dinners were laid on by the Club. The first was to celebrate Julius Olsson's sale of *Moonlit Shore*, the previous year, to the Chantrey Trustees. Olsson, by this juncture, was spending less and less time in St Ives, and the Club contacted him to make the offer of a dinner, should he come

457 *Portalone*, ibid at p.78.
458 *St Ives Weekly Summary* 19/10/1907.
459 Reproduced in *St Ives Weekly Summary* 6/2/1909.

Fig.2.216 Signed Address designed by Edmund Fuller
presented to Elmer Schofield at the Queen's Hotel Dinner in 1915
(Archives of American Art, Smithsonian Institution, Washington)

down to St Ives over the winter period. The dinner was held on 12th January 1912 and was attended by twenty-four members and eleven guests - cost 5s 9d a head. Olsson indicated to Moffat Lindner, the President at the time, that the evening would "always remain as one of my happiest memories".[460]

The other dinner, that year, was given to Allan Deacon "for past services to the Club". This is the only occasion that such services were so rewarded. Deacon had been President in 1903 and Secretary from 1904-6, which was commendable, but not necessarily exceptional, and, accordingly, he may also have been constantly involved behind the scenes. However, he had also been very active in the Golf Club and was probably one of the stalwarts of the community. This time there were twenty-three members present and two guests and the cost was 6s 6d per head. Edmund Fuller designed the presentation address.

The final special dinner, that I will cover in this section, really was held for a special reason - the decision by Elmer Schofield, an American, to enlist in the British Army during the First World War. Since his departure from St Ives in 1907, Schofield had kept in touch with his former colleagues, going on sketching trips with Olsson, and returning to visit the town from time to time. Olsson, himself on a return visit, felt that his brave decision should be honoured in some way, and organised a complimentary dinner on 8th September 1915 at the Queen's Hotel, then run by Francis Wheeler, a man of great energy and public spirit, who was a good friend of the artists. Other old colleagues to attend included Moffat Lindner, Louis Grier, Noble Barlow, Edmund Fuller, John Douglas, Herbert Lanyon and Henry Keasbey, whilst Tom Mostyn and Sydney Lee were also in town at the time. Other locals to be invited were the musician, J.C.Montero, George Lord, Lieutenant J.Walters and Wheeler himself. Schofield was presented not only with an illuminated address, prepared by Edmund Fuller, and signed by all attendees, wishing him 'Good Luck' (Fig. 2.216), but also a signed record of "our admiration for his action as an American citizen in enlisting as a Private in the British Army in a time of great national danger". Olsson was deeply concerned that Schofield had enlisted as a Private and arranged with his friend, Thomas Chellew, a local Territorial Army officer, recently promoted to Lieutenant-Colonel, that he should be offered, that October, a Commission as a Second Lieutenant in the Territorial Force. Schofield went on to fight at the Battle of the Somme, but survived the War unscathed.

2.5.8   'At Home' parties

'At Home' parties, in various guises, were a regular feature of the social life of the colony. As in all communities, some were held principally to show off wealth, taste, contacts or a splendid home. Other hosts, though, enjoyed socialising and the cut and thrust of conversation, whether the topic be serious or scurrilous. There also seems to have been a genuine desire to make visitors to the colony, with an interest in the fine arts, feel welcome, and to give them the opportunity of meeting like-minded souls, for there was a general feeling of pride at the reputation that the colony was gaining on both the national and international stages. In some instances, 'Home' was a studio, for these tended to be far larger than any reception room in the standard house.

As mentioned in Chapter 2.1, one of the few things that the artists in St Ives had in common was their interest in Art and, accordingly, current trends in the art world and the state of the art market will have been regular topics of conversation, not only during 'At Home' parties, but whenever a few artists gathered together, whether at the Arts Club, in a studio or in a public house. Lewis Hind recalled a gathering of artists and students at the home of one St Ives artist, probably Folliott Stokes, which was apparently a yearly event. There, for the first time in his life, he "heard ideas and ideals discussed in general conversation. Some steered for a star; they stumbled of course; but their falls did not come from vanity. The motive of the talk for an hour was the absolute necessity in art of individual vision, of permitting nothing to come between the artist and Nature, of working as if there were nothing in the world but the artist and his selection and transfiguration of what he saw."[461] The 1890s, when Hind first studied in St Ives, was a period during which the artists in the colony had high ambitions. Although most had experienced the enthusiasm for *plein air* realism during their sojourns in France, they now saw themselves at the forefront of a new School of landscape and marine painting in Britain, which involved a more lyrical approach, with paintings now primarily directed at evoking a mood. As confirmed by Folliott Stokes in *A Moorland Princess* and *The West Country Arts Review*, the discussions concerned the futilty of the ultra-realist landscape, which was "mere imitation" and the province of "the craftsman" and which, in any event, was now superceded by the camera. Instead, the true artist should seek out those transient moments of ethereal beauty in Nature, store these effects in "the treasure-house of his memory" and then, using his intellectual powers of selection and design, produce on canvas a scene that reflected his own individual vision and bore the impress of his soul - a work that was, indeed, one

---

460   See Marion Whybrow, *St Ives 1883-1993 - Portrait of an Art Colony*, Woodbridge, 1994 at p. 75.

461   C. Lewis Hind, *The Education of an Artist, London,* 1906 at p.33-4.

of true artistic genius.[462] These were intoxicating discussions for artists from humble backgrounds or students starting out on their careers. However, the problem of "steering for a star" was that the harsh reality, for the vast majority of artists, was very different, for few had the vision or talent to come close to achieving such lofty objectives. Accordingly, most of the time, artists had to explain away their failures, not only at securing sales, but also at even getting work hung. Again, Ranger-Gull and Folliott Stokes indicate how this was done.

Despite the emergence of so-called rivals, such as the New English Art Club or the New Gallery, all artists knew, in their heart of hearts, that acceptance of work by the Royal Academy was key to any chance of a successful career, and "being chucked" was a bitter blow.   This led to outbursts about "Philistine R.A.'s, who can't paint, exalted and set for judgment over their less fortunate, but more gifted brethren."[463] Louis Grier, who suffered not only a series of rejections, but also his work being accepted but then not hung, indicated, in 1891, that artists now "consider it to be the sincerest form of flattery to be either 'skied' or refused."[464] In *Portalone*, Lucas, the character based principally on Grier, comments, on getting another rejection slip, "I swore last year that I wouldn't send them anything more. But, like a fool, I thought I'd give them one more chance: this is the result. However, it's the last time of all. I shall send to Paris for the future".[465] Grier, in fact, only had two works hung at the Salon, but one, *The Night Watch* (Fig. 2.201), had earned him a medal in 1891 and he was still able to live on this past glory. Harrison, the character based on Lowell Dyer, who never did have a work accepted by the Academy, overcame the disappointments by labelling Burlington House as "the place the bad pictures go when they die".[466] In these ways, those artists, who had laboured for months on their Academy submissions, were given some comfort, when they heard that all that toil had been in vain. Their painting had not necessarily been rejected because it was poor - it may just have been too advanced!

Fig. 2.217 Herbert Lanyon   *Folliott Stokes*
(courtesy Andrew Lanyon)

---

462 See A.G.Folliott-Stokes, *A Moorland Princess*, London, 1904 at p. 90-1 and *Landscape Painters and their critics* in *The West Country Arts Review*, March 1896.

463 A.G.Folliott-Stokes, *A Moorland Princess*, London, 1904 at p. 90.

464 *Things seen and heard*, *St Ives Weekly Summary*, 5/1891.

465 C. Ranger-Gull, *Portalone*, London, 1904 at p.17.

466 C. Ranger-Gull, *Portalone*, London, 1904 at p.18.

Success at the Academy might assist, but did not guarantee, sales, which, despite protestations to the contrary, were every artist's ultimate goal. On this topic, Folliott Stokes indicated that discussions raged over the extent to which blame for lack of sales could be placed on the public, the critics and/or the dealers. The public were philistines, it was agreed, but this was not their fault, for they had "never been taught what is bad and what is good in art". The dealers, on the other hand, were contemptible because they "often go out of their way to sell popular pictures at high prices, although they know that many of them have little artistic merit".[467] The critics, however, could not all be dismissed out of hand. Whereas a number were competent, only a few "realise the responsibility of their position and have the courage of their opinions"; others did not have "the pluck to risk popularity by telling the truth". Unfortunately, though, the vast majority of critics displayed "drivelling incapacity...blinking owl-like at art from the ivy bush of sloth". "Unable to realise that it is their great privilege to guide the minds of their fellow-countrymen towards larger sympathies and a more catholic intelligence, they year by year drift down the sluggish stream of ignorance, uttering their silly platitudes, unendowed with either the ability or desire to discover beauty or reveal truth."[468] At the end of the discussion, one artist exclaimed, to general amusement, "How long, O Lord, will these monkeys be permitted to jump upon our stomachs?" In a close-knit community of vastly divergent talents, success and failure were both constant companions, and all had to be seen to rejoice in the one and commiserate in the other, whatever black thoughts were forming in their own minds.[469]

One of the most regular holders of social functions was Louis Grier, who was renowned for pontificating on art at length, in flowery language, whilst never missing a chance to name-drop. The visiting American painter, William Wendt, commented that his studio tea parties, often put on for the benefit of his students, were one of the best occasions to meet others in the colony. These were held in 'The Foc'sle', which, as has been seen, was far more tastefully furnished than most studios in the town, and Grier will have ensured, in order to impress new visitors, that his various curios were in prominent positions, so that he could recount their provenance. At such gatherings, Grier would often take centre stage by reading aloud extracts from William Morris Hunt's *Talks on Art*, and Lewis Hind recalled Hunt's comments as "practical, pointed, wise, very helpful, and unencumbered by rhetoric or ornamentation".[470] Another former student, Norman Wilkinson, mentioned how Grier "had a wonderful faculty of being either related to or connected with anyone of eminence whose name cropped up in conversation", and related an incident when Grier's posturing had been shown up. "I remember an evening when he was giving a party in the studio for the students. One or two relative strangers had also been invited; during the course of the conversation, Sir Joshua Reynolds' name was mentioned and when the speaker had finished, Grier said in his airy manner, "It is a curious thing you should mention Sir Joshua - my great uncle was his medical attendant at the time of his death." The statement was received with murmurs of interest. Later in the evening one of the strangers reverted to the subject. "I say, Mr Grier, I have just been looking up the date of Sir Joshua's death and it would appear that your great-uncle must have been at least one hundred and five years of age at the time." Without the least hesitation, Grier looked him straight in the face and said, "Dear me, d'you know I had no idea he was so old." "[471] Grier's pretentiousness, it appears, was known and tolerated, and even found mildly amusing.[472]

Julius and Katherine Olsson were also well-known for their parties, which also were often put on to enable new arrivals, particularly students, to become acquainted with others in the colony. These may also have been quite boozy affairs, as Olsson was renowned for his Swedish punch. Indeed, on hearing that Olsson was unwell in 1908, Elmer Schofield commented, "if he would stop guzzling whisky, it would be better for his health".[473] However, Schofield's wife, Murielle, records more genteel tea parties to which she was invited by Katherine Olsson, some of which were directed specifically at artists' wives, whilst Olsson's students regularly refer to being invited up to dinner in his fine new home, 'St Eia', with its splendid views over the Bay. On occasion, he even laid on entertainment for them.

---

467 A.G.Folliott-Stokes, *A Moorland Princess*, London, 1904 at p. 88-9.

468 Folliott Stokes had already written on such topics in *Landscape Painters and their Critics*, West Country Arts Review, March 1896. In fact, sections of the novel reproduce almost word for word this article. The topic was clearly a much discussed one at the time, as another article in the *West Country Arts Review* deals with it, lambasting critics for always wanting a painting to tell a story.

469 A tailed sonnet in the Italian manner by Harry Robinson entitled *On Some Modern Journalism* in the *West Country Arts Review*, March 1896, suggests that this will have been another topic of conversation. In this poem, Robinson criticizes the modern journalist's overriding interest in title tattle. "He doth his pen anoint / With slang and slander. Impudently pert, / his smartness is another name for dirt". It concludes, "And now the Briton most / Loves back-stairs chat, and takes, with eager eyes, / Libel for truth; for wit and humour, lies."

470 C.Lewis Hind, *Landscape Painting*, Vol 2, London, 1924 at p.146.

471 N Wilkinson, *A Brush with Life*, London, 1969, p.7-8.

472 Ranger-Gull mentions the attitude of the other artists to Lucas, the character in *Portalone*, based on Grier. "No one ever believed the man's tales; but he had become an institution, and the enormous assurance of the telling was in itself a perpetual joy." *Portalone*, ibid at p.65.

473 Letter from Elmer to Murielle Schofield posted 17/11/1908 - Schofield family archive.

Figs. 2.218-9 Hubert Vos   Sketches of Marianne and Adrian Stokes at their New Year's Day party 1890

Another event, which warranted an 'At Home' party, was the presence in the colony of a distinguished visitor. One of the first mentioned was that thrown by Adrian and Marianne Stokes on New Year's Day in 1890. Helene Schjerfbeck told her mother that, "among the guests, there was someone very important from London, Vos, the Dutch painter".[474] Perhaps, Vos, under whom William Titcomb had studied, was bored by the small talk, as he seems to have spent the day doing fine red chalk drawings, not only of his hosts (Figs. 2.218-9), but also of Edward Simmons (Fig. 1.7). These were later published in the *Magazine of Art*. Another such party was thrown in 1904 to celebrate the election of Frank Brangwyn as an Associate Academician, as both he, and his great friend, Alfred East, happened to be in town, when news of his election came through. Brangwyn, being uncomfortable in social gatherings, tended to decline such invitations, but, on this occasion, he and East did agree to attend one reception. "Both of them started with me", Grace Ellison, a friend of East, recalled, "but, unfortunately for the guests, neither of them arrived at their destination. Brangwyn on the way met a cart of slaughtered bullocks on a truck and stayed to make a study. East was very cross with him and did not approve his lack of courtesy. That did not prevent East, however, from getting out at the next station to make a study of a sunset, and I therefore went to the reception alone. Everyone understood. All is forgiven to genius."[475]

East was a regular visitor to St Ives and, being an outgoing person, who was constantly mixing with the rich and famous, tended to hold court at social gatherings. However, during 1908, Napier Hemy, the Falmouth marine painter, spent quite a bit of time in St Ives, due to his interest in the new Catholic Church, and he too liked to hold the floor. Charles Marriott, President of the Arts Club that year, later recalled the amusement of the artists at the rivalry between Hemy and East as raconteurs. "Each of them was full of reminiscences of about the same period, and I can see them now glaring at each other across our sitting room in Porthminster Terrace."[476]

It was the more scurrilous aspects of 'At Home' parties in the colony, to which Ranger-Gull turned his satirical eye in his depiction of the events held by Mr and Mrs Cassilis - based, it would seem, on Harry and Dorothy Robinson.[477] Cassilis was well off and of good family and represented the 'best' social side of the colony. Although nervous and staccato in his talk, he was well-liked, but "long ago the power of

474 Letter dated 5/1/1890.

475 Grace Ellison, *My Tales of A Sailor Artist*, Unidentified newspaper interview from 1930s.

476 Charles Marriott, *Memories of Cornwall's Art Colonies*, Cornish Review, No. 1, Spring 1949, at p.67-8.

477 There are no other detailed descriptions of the characters of Harry and Dorothy Robinson with which to make comparison and this tentative identification is based largely on the fact that the Cassilises lived in a splendid newly built home in Up-long. This suggests either the Robinsons at 'Belliers Croft' or the Olssons at 'St Eia'. Olsson, however, is clearly identified as Badigeon in the novel and his wife was not an artist. Harry Robinson had certainly ceased to paint much at this juncture and was well-liked. A possible alternative is Moffat and Gussie Lindner, but, at this juncture, they were living in rented accomodation, Warren House, and had not yet bought 'Chy-an-Porth'. Lindner was also still enjoying considerable success. The other particularly wealthy artist was Thomas Millie Dow, but his home, 'Talland House', was not newly built.

work had left him". "Because he was afraid to be alone, he kept open house. He was a sort of incarnate sideboard - a place where people found drinks". He had also instituted a sort of *buffet* in the dining-room, which had the advantage of being open when the public houses were closed". He was married to "a bustling woman, a she-artist, who bullied him" and "who pretended that she was well-bred, better than anyone else, because she could afford *paté de foie gras* sandwiches at tea". They lived in a big granite house, with 'artistic' gables and chimneys, and a red-tiled roof, whose rooms had pomegranate-pattern wallpaper and were hung "with rejected masterpieces from the Academy". Almost everyone was welcome at their weekly parties - "a little bit of gossip or scandal was the only entrance fee demanded". Everyone present pretended "that they were, what they were not; and, as Mr Marston, the novelist, (based on Charles Marriott) had remarked, when one considered what they *were*, the effort was surely virtuous and commendable!" "One talked about one's 'poor, dear old father' at these gatherings, in a subtle way, which suggested he was a bishop, but one did not go into details".[478]

"Cassilis himself was in that element of chiffon and cackle which always made him thoroughly happy. His little sniff and giggle were ubiquitous. Every now and then he would catch a male friend by the arm and the two would mysteriously disappear in the direction of the dining-room, from whence after a glass of Benedictine and a coffee bean, they would emerge, rather flushed, and replunge into the wagging sanctuary of scandal". Meanwhile, "Mrs Cassilis flitted about from one lady with the brain of a hen to another with the brain of two hens, and there was a general clink, clatter and hum of talk."[479]

The letters of Murielle Schofield, from her time in the colony during the years 1903-7, provide an unique insight into the social life of an artist's wife. Whilst her husband, Elmer, was much liked, there must have been a degree of perplexity, or even censure, at his decision to leave his wife, for up to six months at a time, to cope with two young children on her own, whilst he pursued his career in America. Shortly after he had left for America in the autumn of 1903, Murielle told him that she, and her mother, who was on a short visit, had been invited around by Mrs Grier, and by Mrs Olsson, where "there were a number of people evidently asked to meet us".[480] She was rather surprised to be asked by Olsson if she wanted a cigarette, but learnt that several of the women in the colony smoked. The Kirkpatrick sisters also invited her round to meet other members of the colony. Before too long, she felt sufficiently comfortable to put on a series of 'At Homes' at her place, but these were much smaller affairs and tended to be restricted to artists' wives. Regular guests included not only Mrs Grier and Mrs Olsson, but also Mrs Dyer, Mrs Barlow, whom she considered "a very bright and charming American woman", Mrs Milner, Mrs Deacon, who was "very pleasant" and invited her to a children's party, Mrs Lang, Miss Pazolt, whom she thought "a nice genuine woman", Mrs Meade, Mrs Fortescue and Mrs Adams, who offered to get her a cat to catch the rats that plagued her home. Fellow American artists, George Gardner Symons and William Wendt, popped up to see her from time to time, including on Christmas Day afternoon, and, after one of her tea parties, she told Elmer, "Both Mr Wendt and Mr Symons flattered me by talking quite seriously on their aims in life".[481] However, the formalities of the period meant that not one person - male or female - is referred to in her correspondence by their forename.

A very different type of 'At Home' party were the musical evenings hosted on Sunday evenings by Herbert Lanyon, after his return from America. An invitation to these was treasured - indeed, Charles Marriott commented that "Sunday evenings at Lanyon's were a regular institution".[482] Given that Marriott left St Ives in 1909, this proves that Lanyon had been organising these evenings long before his marriage in 1916 and his subsequent move to 'The Red House' in The Bellyars. All musicians in the colony will have been asked to contribute, but clearly Lanyon will have been a regular performer himself, as well as being host. In addition to playing popular pieces, he will also have included some of his own compositions, of which he had at least ten published. These included, in 1906, *Mexican Dance*, dedicated to his great friend, Charles Marriott, and another work, *Slumber Song*, dedicated to his baby niece, Olive, which were labelled "Impressions" by the publishers - The Vincent Music Company of London and Thomas J Donlan of Boston. If Whistler could paint Nocturnes, Notes and use other musical terms in his painting titles, why should Lanyon not use a painting term to describe a musical piece?

---

478 The extracts are from C.Ranger-Gull, *Portalone*, London, 1904 at pp.116-7 and 172-4.

479 ibid.

480 Letter from Murielle to Elmer Schofield dated 14/12/1903 - Archives of American Art.

481 Letter from Murielle to Elmer Schofield dated 18/1/1904.

482 Charles Marriott, *Memories of Cornwall's Art Colonies*, Cornish Review, Spring 1949, No 1, at p.70. Marriott, who described Lanyon as one of his greatest friends in St Ives, was asked in 1935 by Lanyon to recommend an art school for his son, Peter. Marriott recommended the Central School of Art and Crafts in London "after his breaking-in by Borlase Smart". Letters from Marriott to Lanyon dated 9/7/1935 and 2/8/1935 (Schofield family archive).

Fig. 2.220 Herbert Lanyon at the piano (Lanyon family archive)

Fig. 2.221 H.G.Fitzherbert *Caricature of Herbert Lanyon*
(from *Caricatures of the Cornish Riviera* 1910)

Figs 2.222-3   H.G.Fitzherbert   *Caricatures of the artist, Sydney Carr, and the dentist, Herbert Fooks*
(from *Caricatures of the Cornish Riviera* 1910). Fooks lived at 1 Porthminster Terrace.

Lanyon's collection of art, much of which was sold at David Lays in February 2004, gives an indication of the artists with whom he most fraternised, as, in the main, the works were minor pieces clearly given as gifts in appreciation of hospitality received.[483] The collection included several works by Noble Barlow, Moulton Foweraker, Alfred Hartley, Fred Milner, John Park and Mabel Douglas, whilst foreign artists represented included the Belgian Louis Reckelbus and the Americans Arthur Beaumont, Will Potter and Frank and Hanna Rion Ver Beck. The ever-smiling Helen Stuart Weir also became a firm friend of the family.

The choice of Sunday evening for these musical nights is a little surprising, given that Lanyon was a Methodist and will have been aware of the attitude of staunch Methodists to the Sabbath. Certainly, Ranger-Gull confirms in *Portalone* that this was yet a further attribute of the artists that was denounced by Methodist ministers. "We can hear the pianos going on Sunday evenings now all over Church-town, and light songs and wantonness."[484]

2.5.9   Billiards and Cards

From the caricatures of H.G.Fitzherbert and Sydney Carr, billiards and cards seem to have been popular ways of passing the extended winter evenings, when most committed members of the colony were in residence. The Western Hotel, run by John Henry Tremayne, was the most popular venue for billiards and Lewis Hind commented, "Here the billiard handicaps take place and eyes learned in the effect of sky and sea are trained to further skill in search of the nice angles between ball and pocket."[485] In November 1898, a set of matches was played against the Camborne Students. These were arranged by Algernon Talmage, who was called "one of the ablest exponents of the game in West Cornwall", and his fellow competitors were Lindner, Olsson, Elgar Russell, Kendrick Wynne and William Badcock, who had just published his Historical Sketch of the district.[486] In the caricatures of Carr and Fitz, a decade or so later, other artists depicted playing billiards include Jack Titcomb, Allan Deacon and Carr himself, whilst members of the local community, with whom the artists socialised around the billiard table, included Herbert Fooks, the dentist (Fig. 2.223), and the Scot, Henry Downing Brown of 'Scot's Craig'.

---

483 At the David Lay sale on 10/2/2004, lots 294-301, 375-382 and 385-6 are believed to have come from the Lanyon family collection. Presumably, the couple of works by Leonard Fuller came into the family collection subsequently, as Fuller only settled in St Ives after Lanyon's death.

484 C.Ranger-Gull, *Portalone*, London, 1904 at p.45.

485 C.Lewis Hind, *In Painters' Land*, *St Ives Weekly Summary* 10/10/1896.

486 *St Ives Weekly Summary* 26/11/1898.

Fig. 2.224 H.G. Fitzherbert
Caricature of Moffat Lindner
(from *Caricatures of the*
Cornish Riviera 1910)

Fig.2.225 Sydney Carr   *Spades! Every Time !!!*
(the late Derek Wintle/Andrew Eggleston)

Cards were also popular and the bridge teas organised at the Arts Club could attract as many as forty people. Bridge was certainly a favourite pastime of Fitzherbert, and he caricatured a number of his acquaintances at cards. Amusingly, both Carr, in his title, and Fitz, in his caption, singled out the same characteristic of Moffat Lindner - that he *always* called spades. Both also show him with an unruly curl.

2.5.10   Cricket

When the art colony was formed in 1885, St Ives did not have a cricket team, and cricket games in the Duchy were quite rare due to the difficulty in finding flat ground for pitches. However, following the close fraternisation between the artists of St Ives and Newlyn during the years 1886-7, Henry Detmold suggested, in late August 1887, that there should be an inter-colony cricket match.[487] Howard Butler recorded the high drama of the encounter, which was played at Tregenna Castle. "September 5th [1887]. We have had a most exciting day. The artists of Newlyn (where there is a colony of young English artists known as the "Square-touch School" hopefully trying to climb into the kingdom of art without going through the straight and narrow path) challenged the artists of St Ives to play them at cricket. Notwithstanding that our team was made up largely of Americans, we beat them 86 to 50. Chadwick made the highest score."[488] However, the day had a sad ending. "It was not during the game but while we were on the field that the ball was tossed into the air and two of the Newlyn men sprang forward to catch it at the same instant neither seeing the other. They came together face to face. It was a most remarkable accident. Scully's nose must have gone into Millard's mouth for it was badly cut by Millard's teeth, several of which were crushed in and the jaw was so strained that he has hardly got the use of it yet. Both fell like dead men. Poor Millard striking on the back of his head and receiving a slight emission of the brain. It was awfully sad. We had been having such a delightful day. Some ran for water, others ran into the town for the Doctor. I held the poor fellow in my arms for fully twenty minutes while others wiped the blood away from his eyes, nose and mouth. None of us knew whether he would die or come to life again."[489] Millard was eventually carried about a mile, with a door being used as a stretcher, to Simmons' house on The Terrace, where he took care of him for three or four days, until friends arrived who hired a house for him to stay in until he recovered. The doctor anticipated this would take at least

---

487 Letter from Stanhope Forbes to Elizabeth Armstrong dated 27/8/1887 - Tate Gallery Archives 9015.2.2.60. Forbes, who was in Wales with his family, regretted not being able to take part.

488 H.R.Butler, Unpublished Autobiography, p.168, Archives of American Art, Smithsonian Institution, Washington DC, Howard Russell Butler papers, Reel 93. This diary note is inserted in Butler's autobiography in 1886 and Jacobs in *The Good and Simple Life* gives this date. However, the *Cornish Telegraph* of 1/9/1887 records the injuries to Millard and Scully.

489 Letter from H.R.Butler to Harriet Butler 5/9/1887 but mistakenly dated 1886. Archives of American Art, Smithsonian Institution, Washington DC, Howard Russell Butler papers, Reel 1189.

a month. Scully, however, recovered more quickly. Butler concluded, "The Englishers are very much cut up over their defeat and we have agreed to play a return match tomorrow. We will probably let them win". Whether or not intentionally, the St Ives artists did indeed lose the rematch and Butler lamented that "there is no prospect of a rubber now that the damp weather has arrived."[490]

Not all games between the sides are so well documented, probably because there was nothing to match the high drama of that first occasion, but it seems clear that, in the formative years of the colony, the two sets of artists played each other a number of times. Indeed, Stanhope Forbes suggested that it was an annual fixture, by calling it "one of the chief sporting events of the year". In 1890, he recorded that the Newlyn side feared defeat as the St Ives artists had acquired two notable batsmen. "But in a fortunate moment, the situation was saved, for Harry Rheam, that notable cricketer, was imported at great expense from Polperro." Writing in 1895, Frank Richards, from Newlyn, summed up the strengths of the teams at that time.

> "Bramley is our captain, and with Forbes, Langley, Tayler, Harris, Rheam, Blackburne, da Costa, myself etc., with Gotch and Mackenzie as umpire and scorer, and Fred Hall, caricaturist, we make up not so bad a team...Adrian Stokes was our opponents' most formidable man at St Ives, backed by Wyley Grier, W.H.Titcomb and Simmons, all of whom were most energetic and good cricketers, and more often than not did all the work for their side.....We Newlyners used always to be looked upon by our opponents at St Ives as a body of men following in the wake of a funeral, yet, when on the cricket field, I think there is little trace of such a melancholy spirit in us."[491]

The Newlyn and St Ives artists did not always compete against each other and, in August 1888, a combined team was selected for a match against Penzance Cricket Club. The artists team, calling themselves the Artists of West Cornwall XI, comprised the St Ives artists Adrian Stokes, William and Jack Titcomb, Allan Deacon, Philip Norman and Herbert Marshall, whilst the Newlyn contingent were Frank Bramley, Chevallier Tayler, Henry Detmold and Frank Bourdillon, with Henry Rheam again being imported from Polperro. Jack Titcomb made the most significant contribution, taking six wickets and a notable catch, but the artists were defeated in humiliating fashion by an innings and twelve runs.

Fig. 2.226 William, eldest son of Edward Simmons,
in cricket gear in St Ives
(William Trevorrow, courtesy Willa Harris)

490 Letter from H.R.Butler to Mary Butler 18/9/1887. Archives of American Art, Smithsonian Institution, Washington DC, Howard Russell Butler papers, Reel 1189.
491 F.Richards, *The Studio*, Vol IV, 1895, p.179-80.

Fig. 2.227 A St Ives artists' cricket team   (Cornish Studies Library)
Adrian Stokes, with blazer, white cap and beard is distinctive as the first seated cricketer from the left, with Frank Chadwick standing behind him, and Henry Rheam to Stokes' left. Very few others can be identified.

Fig.2.228 A Newlyn artists' cricket team   (Cornish Studies Library)
At rear from left: Thomas Gotch, Walter Langley, Unknown, Unknown, Stanhope Forbes, Edwin Harris, Henry Rheam
Seated at front from left: ? Frank Bramley (with scorebook), William Fortescue, Norman Garstin, Chevallier Tayler, Ralph Todd, Fred Millard. At front with bat: Unknown

Fig. 2.229   Spectators watching a game of cricket   (Cornish Studies Library)

The activities of the artists on the cricket field inspired others to consider the formation of a cricket club in St Ives in 1889 and, indeed, Adrian Stokes and William Eadie were two of the principal supporters of this idea. A ground was secured at Higher Tregenna and a game was quickly arranged between the town and the artists on 11th August 1889. Several members of the Newlyn colony were invited to play for the Artists XI, which comprised Adrian Stokes, Allan Deacon, Wyly Grier, Folliott Stokes, Eardley Blomefield, Edward Simmons, William Eadie, Henry Detmold, Frank Bourdillon and Chevallier Tayler. The artists scored 37 to the Town XI's 19 - low scores being typical at this time, due to the poor quality of the pitches.

A number of artists played for the town over the years.[492] In the 1890s, the most regular player was Edmund Fuller, who was Captain in 1898 - "And a right good Captain, too", proclaimed the local paper. William Titcomb was also enthusiastically involved, when he was around, serving on the Committee quite regularly and, in 1901, he provided a board pitch upon which the players could practice. His brother, Jack, also served on the Committee, whilst Sydney Carr donated prizes. However, the artist, who enjoyed the most success, was the Australian art student, Richard Hayley Lever. He was a good batsman and topped the averages in 1900.[493] Fellow Australian art students Will Ashton and Arthur Burgess, who was a useful bowler, also played in 1901, as did another student, Frank Haigh, who topped the bowling and came second in the batting averages that year. Such was the enthusiasm for cricket that summer that the artists challenged the town club again. William Titcomb captained the Artists' Eleven and his side comprised Julius Olsson, Algernon Talmage, Fred Milner, Folliott Stokes, Edmund Fuller, Albert Lang, Thomas Danby, Hayley Lever and Will Ashton. Henry Rheam from Newlyn was due to play but his place was taken by John Uren. On this occasion, the town won by 15 runs.

1902 was a difficult season, with only Lever playing with regularity, and the Club accumulated a deficit during the year. On the proposal of Will Ashton, seconded by William Titcomb, it was decided to put on an Entertainment in April 1903 to raise funds, and a number of the artists contributed to this. Moulton Foweraker, Ranger-Gull and Elgar Russell sang songs, Sydney Carr did some comic impersonations and Ranger-Gull made a humorous speech. However, enthusiasm for the Club wilted and it folded for a few years, leaving Fuller and Lever to play for Lelant. It was reformed, though, in June 1907 and Hayley Lever was made Captain. He even managed to get Elmer Schofield to turn out for the side several times later that year and he impressed sufficiently to move up the batting order from No.10 to No.3. Lever was re-appointed Captain in 1908 but, again, enthusiasm was found wanting and the Club folded once more. When it was reformed in March 1911, the artists were no longer involved.

---

492 Occasional players included John Bromley, Kendrick Wynne, Raffael Farina and the American Richard Levick.

493 At the AGM in 1909, he donated one of his oil paintings to Mr Dyke for the highest batting average of the season.

On several occasions, the male artists were challenged to a game of cricket by the ladies in the colony. In 1894, the game was held on the downs overlooking Hawke's Point and the men were handicapped by having to use broom-handles as bats and having to bowl and field left-handed. The ladies were also allowed fifteen on their side. The Deacons, the Horn sisters and the Langs were to the fore in this encounter, with Albert Lang single-handedly saving the men from embarassment.[494] Another such encounter took place in August 1898, this time on the ground at Higher Tregenna, and similar rules were applied. The report, however, added, "It was suggested that the gentlemen should wear skirts and the ladies use gloves and pads, etc, but as the former had rather hazy notions about fastening the skirts on, and as no gentleman was forthcoming to place the pads on the latter, it was mutually agreed to discard them".[495] Fuller, William Titcomb, John Bromley, Greville Morris, Kendrick Wynne and Raffael Farina played for the gentlemen, who proved too strong, despite their handicaps, for the ladies' team, who included the Horn sisters, Selina Wing and one of the Whitehouse sisters. Nevertheless, the agility of the ladies in running out four of the men was commented upon. Teas for the players and numerous spectators was provided by Mrs Horn.

Burgess indicates that another game was proposed in 1901 but did not come off. However, in 1906, Elgar Russell organised a further match in aid of the St Ives Nursing Fund. The ladies, who included Vera and Irene Carr and Elsie Dow, were allowed 16 players on their side and again an embarrassing upset was on the cards until John Douglas, batting at No.8, scored 23 of the 39 runs required for victory.

2.5.11 Golf

The author and journalist, Harold Begbie (1871-1929), whose parents had retired to Carbis Bay in 1901, commented in *The Morning Post*, "The men of St Ives are all devoted to ocean, plain and rolling down... They are outdoor men, and it is in keeping with their aims that, whenever an hour is snatched from the canvas, it is devoted to the sea-blown golf links."[496] Others suggest, however, that golf mounted a much more serious challenge for the attentions of the artists. In 1902, the New Zealand artist, Frances Hodgkins, commented that the St Ives artists could not wait for Show Day to be over as, having sent off their London exhibits for the year, they could then devote their energies to their first love - golf. Golf certainly seems to have become a passion for a number of both male and female artists in the period prior to the War and, in *Portalone*, the artists were branded as 'golfers and loafers'.

The West Cornwall Golf Club was founded in December 1889 at the instigation of the Reverend R.F.Tyacke, the vicar of Lelant. Adrian Stokes was one of the initial committee of six established to carry out the formation of the Club and the preparation of the links on the Lelant Towans. The fact that it took a mere eleven days to prepare the course gives some indication of its quality at the outset, and an early plea that the farmer, who was allowed to graze his animals on the course, should remove his horned cattle suggests some painful experiences! The first fifty members were invited to enrol without a joining fee, and these included Greville Morris, Wyly Grier, William Eadie, Eardley Blomefield, Louis Grier and Ayerst Ingram. Other artists, who joined during 1890, included Thomas and Caroline Gotch, who were in St Ives that summer, Walter Jevons, Harry and Dorothy Robinson and Harry Browne. Stokes, an inveterate traveller, seems not to have been involved subsequently as an officer of the Club, but played whenever he was around. In 1892, William Dickson was elected as an additional Committee representative "to represent the numerous members" in St Ives and, by this time, Edmund Fuller, Julius Olsson (and his wife) and Albert Lang, all of whom were to play a major role in the Club, had joined. Fuller did several series of caricatures about the rules of the Club and about the exploits of the golfers and the malevolent children who acted as their caddies, showing the members in the distinctive scarlet jackets that became required dress from January 1891 (see Figs 2.233-4). A number of these works were included in his exhibition in a Porthmeor Studio in 1897.

As the decade wore on, interest in golf seemed to increase and Millie and Florence Dow, Beale Adams, Arnesby and Mia Brown, Arthur Meade and his family, Fred and Sophie Milner, William Brooke and his daughter, Moffat and Gussie Lindner, Helen Knapping, Elgar Russell, Allan and Kate Deacon, Algernon and Gertrude Talmage, Jack Titcomb, John Bromley and Daisy Whitehouse all became members. This is likely to be because Albert Lang, a key figure in the St Ives Arts Club, was Golf Captain in each of the years 1896-1900, during which time he transformed the Club's accomodation, standard of play and sociability.[497] A fine player himself, he held the course record for many years. By the turn of the century,

---

494 *St Ives Weekly Summary*, 18/8/1894.

495 *St Ives Weekly Summary* 20/8/1898.

496 Quoted in M.Whybrow, *St Ives 1883-1993 - Portrait of an Art Colony*, Woodbridge, 1994 at p.32. His father, the Reverend Mars Hamilton Begbie (d.1907), and his mother, Anna (d.1915), lived at 'Bemersyde', Carbis Bay.

497 See *Presentation to Mr Lang, St Ives Weekly Summary* 2/3/1901.

Fig. 2.230 The Early Days - Seventh Green
Here, men and women are playing together, whilst the local youngsters earn some pocket money as caddies.

Fig. 2.231 The new clubhouse, built in 1900 by Robert Toy to the design of William Brooke

Fig. 2.232 Outside the Smoking Room - August 1900

(All courtesy West Cornwall Golf Club)

interest was considerable and a Club team of sixteen men against Falmouth in March 1899 included no less than eleven artists - Lang, Meade, Lindner, Brooke, Milner, Olsson, Stokes, Brown, Fuller Maitland, Russell and Adams. Brooke designed the Club's pavilion (Fig. 2.231), which was built by Robert Toy in 1900, was Club Captain in 1902 and later became Secretary of the Club between December 1907 and July 1909. On his resignation, due to ill-health, he was elected a life member in recognition of his indefatigible services. Lindner was a regular Committee member and was Club Captain in 1901 and 1910 and lent the Club £150 in 1901 to enable an extension to the dining room to be completed. Deacon was another regular on the Committee and was Club Captain in 1903. Arnesby Brown and Julius Olsson were also on the Committee several times and Olsson was Club Captain in 1905.

The best golfer amongst the artists, however, was Arthur Meade. Although surprisingly only Club Captain once - in 1919, he won nine Cups in the Club competitions between 1904 and 1926. The only other artist to win a Cup was Jack Titcomb in 1922. Two paintings by Meade hang in the Clubhouse. One is a portrait of the Club's founder, the Reverend Tyacke, which Meade offered to do after his death, by enlarging a small portrait of him that he had done previously. The result, perhaps unsurprisingly, is a little lifeless. The other work, though, is a fine panorama from the sixteenth green looking out towards Godrevy. It was being exhibited at Worcester when Meade offered it to the Club in 1905, as the walls were felt to be a little bare. Another depiction of the links was Moulton Foweraker's *Hayle and the Estuary from the Clubhouse*, which was exhibited at the RBA in 1902.

Another caricaturist among the artist members of the Club was the New Zealander, H.G.Fitzherbert, who was also a good golfer, with a handicap of two. Several members of the Club feature in his book *Caricatures from the Cornish Riviera*, published in 1910, and he also appears to have played at Newquay as well. Lowell Dyer's wit was also likely to have been a feature of golf days, as he was a keen, although eccentric, golfer, for he made all his strokes with the one club, described as "a battered old wooden spoon, with which he did effective work".[498]

Women artists, and wives and female siblings of artists, seem to have been equally interested in golf. The Club was open to women from the outset and a nine-hole ladies course was laid out in 1892. By 1898, this was run almost entirely separately by a Ladies Committee. Kate Deacon (Captain 1906), Beatrice Vivian (Captain 1907) Gussie Lindner (Captain 1910), Helen Knapping, Kate Adams, Mabel Meade, Selina Bromley and Gertrude Rosenberg were some of the keenest members. The finest woman golfer, however, was Katherine Horn, who had briefly studied art alongside her more talented sister, Frances. She was Ladies Captain in 1905, County Champion in 1905 and 1908 and Ladies Secretary in 1908-1910, 1922-1924 and 1936-1949.

In April 1907, the artists of St Ives challenged a party of artists from London to a golf match at Lelant. The idea may have first been mooted when Norman Wilkinson and Oswald Moser, two of Louis Grier's former students, were entertained at the Arts Club on one of their periodic return visits to St Ives in late March, for they were two of the visiting team of ten that played on 11th April. The other London artists were Frank Swinstead, the Principal of Hornsey School of Art, already a regular visitor to the region, the figure painters Henry John Hudson, Collier Smithers and Gerald Moira, the sculptor James Nesfield Forsyth, Harry Browne, another regular visitor to the town, and Messrs Newell and Anderson. They were also accompanied by several female friends. Judging from their hosts at the Arts Club, the St Ives team included Arthur Meade, who captained the side, Albert Lang, Jack Titcomb, Allan Deacon, Lowell Dyer, Julius Olsson, Fred Milner, John Bromley and W.H.Pilcher, Dow's stepson. On the night of the 10th, a dinner for 24 persons was held to welcome the Londoners, but it was thought fit to minute that *Auld Lang Syne* was, at the request of the guests, sung at the early time of 11-30 p.m. in view of the full day's play on the morrow. If that was felt a little whimpish, the guests made up for it the following night by putting on a full evening's entertainment. This involved a lengthy programme of songs, music, speeches and recitations and was ended by an hour or so of dancing finishing at 1 a.m..[499]

The extant members lists at the Golf Club reveal some surprisingly long associations. Edward Fuller Maitland and his wife, who were only involved with the art colony in 1898-9, remained members of the Club until September 1937, despite living in Rye, and the Paris-based American, Frank Chadwick and his Swedish wife, Emma, who are normally only associated with the colony in its early days, only resigned their membership in 1932. However, they are recorded as playing on their frequent return visits and, in 1903, Frank gave a number of prizes for the Club's competitions - one of which was a Japanese cabinet.

---

498 Obituary, *Mr Lowell Dyer*, St Ives Times 7/3/1939.

499 The programme was carried out solely by guests, namely Mrs Carter-Campbell, Miss Olsson, the Misses Baker, Miss Phillips, Miss Wilks and Messrs Swinstead, Wilkinson, Moser, Anderson and Ricardo.

Fig. 2.233 Edmund Fuller *The Bunker*   Fig. 2.234 Edmund Fuller   *Clean Your Clubs, Sir*
(from his series of six scenes, entitled *The Trials of a Tyro*, published by Louis Wolff & Co, which featured a red-jacketed golfer from the West Cornwall Golf Club)

2.5.12 Other activities

Tennis was another favourite activity, the St Ives Tennis Club having been founded in 1884, making it the oldest club in West Cornwall. A number of the early Presidents of the Club, such as Edward Boase, Dr Staff and Robert Sawle Read, were close friends of the artists, as was Lieutenant Alfred Hackman (1844-1904), who was Secretary of the Club for its first twenty years. Alfred Hackman was a retired Naval officer, who lived at 'Carrack-Dhu'. Both he and his wife took part in entertainments put on by the artists (see Fig. 3.50) and he is likely, at social gatherings, to have regaled the artists with stories of his escapades fighting pirates in the eastern seas.[500] The Club's four courts and croquet lawn were situated on the Tregenna Estate and commanded fine views over the Bay, and the highlight of the year was the Annual Tournament in August.   A review of the event in 1902 enthused, "The pavilion gay in its garb of red and white and bright with its rainbow of many coloured flags; the field with its large gathering of moving players and interested spectators; the tender green of the surrounding foliage, with the blue sea as a sparkling background, formed a *tout ensemble* not easily forgotten by the visitor."[501]

Simmons, Blomefield and Dyer were early tennis enthusiasts and, in fact, the 1891 Tennis Club AGM was held in Simmons' studio. Dyer also served on the Committee from time to time, and he and William Titcomb played tennis to a good standard, representing the town in matches on a number of occasions. Titcomb also acted as a tennis referee. His brother, Jack, was a keen player, as well, and he won both the men's singles and doubles in 1896, losing in the finals of the mixed doubles. His opponent in the singles final was another artist, Kendrick Wynne, who also played for the town. Allan Deacon, Sydney Carr, Elgar Russell and Edmund Fuller were other enthusiasts, who served on the Committee, Hugh Blackden played for the team and Sydney Laurence, Thomas Danby, John Bromley, John Douglas and Oswald Moser were some of the male artists who took part in the Annual Tournament.   Daisy Whitehouse, Selina Bromley, Miss Wynne, Katherine Horn and Mrs Sydney Lee were amongst the female artists to participate. On a number of occasions, paintings by artists were offered as prizes, whilst Deacon and Carr gave silver cups.

---

500 In 1868, he was involved in operations against pirates in the River Congo and, in 1873, against Malay pirates.. He also served as naval instructor on a number of voyages with Lord Brassey's cadets to Australia. *St Ives Weekly Summary*, 19/11/1904.
501 *St Ives Weekly Summary*, 10/5/1902.

Fig.2.235   Edmund Fuller
*Tennis Tournament 1910
- Opening Day*

The biggest social event mounted by the Tennis Club was a Ball for sixty people at the new Porthminster Hotel in November 1895. This was organised by Dr Staff and Alfred Hackman, and a committee of ladies, and Herr Freund, from Truro, was again responsible for the dance music. The evening was so mild and balmy that 'sitters out' could enjoy the view of the Bay from the balconies. Another large party recorded was an 'At Home' party at the Tennis Club thrown by Julius Olsson, on the day of the Coronation of George V in June 1911. Despite not appearing to play himself, Olsson was elected President that year, when Robert Read stepped down, and his Committee included H.G.Fitzherbert, Albert Lang and Ernest Morton Nance.

It was rather longer before a hockey club was formed in St Ives and the Bushey student, Hugh Blackden, was one of the early Secretaries, but few other artists appear to have been involved. However, Hugh Walpole, whilst visiting Charles Marriott, "decided, with some reason, that the young people of St Ives needed discipline, and prescribed mixed hockey. I have a vivid memory", wrote Marriott many years later, "of Walpole being pursued over a muddy field on a drizzling day by a small girl who barked his shins and broke his pince-nez. There was no more mixed hockey".[502]

Walking was another popular pastime for artists, particularly on Sundays, when most other activities were frowned upon. Zennor was a favourite destination. Yet, in 1892, John Hobson Matthews commented that the average St Ives local "would as soon think of swimming to Cardiff, as of walking to Zennor" and so, here again, the artists changed attitudes.[503] Indeed, Leslie Stephen had first discovered St Ives on a walking holiday and was renowned for his lengthy Sunday tramps, thinking nothing of walking to Penzance and back, or to Gurnard's Head and back. Whilst those venturing as far as Zennor could rely on Mrs Griggs providing a fine tea, Folliott Stokes mentions parties of artists taking picnics with them, including a kettle and "a small etna for heating it", using fresh water from a stream for their beverages.[504] Lewis Hind recalled his art student days as one of the happiest times of his life, "for St Ives was - and is - a dream place; such seas, such skies, such yellow sands, such walks."[505] Indeed, he enjoyed walking the coast so much that he secured a commission to produce a walking book on the subject - *Days in Cornwall* (1907) - and he recorded that he had been joined in most of the walks by Charles Marriott. At much the same time, Folliott Stokes turned his attention from novel writing and produced walking books on the Cornish coast and moors. For many decades, the books by Hind and Stokes continued to be recommended to walking enthusiasts. Indeed, Stokes' huge fund of knowledge about the Hinterland has ensured that his books are still of great interest today.

These then were the activities, which combined "simplicity of life, refinement and cultivated taste, love of outdoor nature, and freedom from convention" which so appealed to the reporter from the *Westminster Gazette*.

---

502 Charles Marriott, *Memories of Cornwall's Art Colonies, Cornish Review*, No. 1, Spring 1949, at p.69.

503 J.H.Matthews, *A History of the Parishes of Saint Ives, Lelant, Towednack and Zennor in the County of Cornwall*, London, 1892 at p.371

504 A.G.Folliott-Stokes, *A Moorland Princess*, London, 1904 at p. 122.

505 C Lewis Hind, *Napthali*, London, 1926 at p.159.

STUDENT LIFE IN THE COLONY

2.6.1   The St Ives Schools of Painting

In April 1900, an interesting comparison was made between the St Ives and Newlyn colonies. "At Newlyn, the artists - at any rate those who are left - are mostly veterans, men who have won their spurs or have begun to think wistfully of the grey in their beards and the many milestones they have passed. At St Ives, some of the strongest wielders of the brush are broad-shouldered, alert, sanguine, bright-eyed young men who are strenuously working their way to the front. But while at Newlyn, the gaps in the ranks are not being filled by talented newcomers, at St Ives one meets many new names and the younger men are forging ahead and bidding their seniors look to their laurels."[506] This influx of young talent into the colony was entirely due to the Schools of Painting that had been set up in the previous decade.

From the very early days of the colony, St Ives attracted budding art students, particularly those keen to practice landscape and marine painting in the open air. The initial draw was Adrian Stokes, who established himself as one of the leading landscape painters in the country with a succession of highly acclaimed canvases at the Royal Academy and the New Gallery. However, in 1895, clearly in response to a continuing demand, a formal School of Painting was set up by Julius Olsson and Louis Grier. The prospectus for this indicated that it would concentrate exclusively on landscape and marine painting, two genre that did not feature very much, if at all, on the curricula of other art schools, and that, whenever weather conditions permitted, work would be carried out in the open. The School was, therefore, unique and tapped into the then current vogue for *plein air* painting. Accordingly, it attracted not only those keen to learn to paint in attractive surroundings away from a big city, but also students from other major art academies in Britain during their holiday periods, particularly if they had an interest in landscape or marine work.

The School was an immediate success, with ever increasing numbers of students flocking to the colony, and when Olsson and Grier split after a couple of years, with Algernon Talmage stepping in to assist Olsson, Grier set up on his own. In 1898, he was helped by John Noble Barlow, but then, in 1899, Barlow advertised his own classes as well. The Australian, David Davies, also took students in Lelant from 1898 to 1904 and many of the other senior figures in the colony, such as Arnesby Brown, William Titcomb and Fred Milner, had students from time to time. Indeed, St Ives gained such a reputation as a centre for art education that a number of students came from abroad to study in the town. The importance of these Schools in maintaining the health and vibrancy of the colony cannot be over-emphasized. The constant stream of new, young talent ensured that the colony did not stagnate. Indeed, as a number of the visiting students had also experienced the latest trends in Paris, they introduced new approaches, ensuring a constant cross-fertilisation of ideas.

The duration of visits by students varied enormously. There seems to have been no minimum required period of study. Accordingly, some merely enrolled for a few classes in the course of a sketching tour. However, it is clear that a number stayed for several months, with the busiest period being late summer through to March. Quite a few students returned year after year at much the same time, probably fitting in their studies in St Ives with their vacation periods at other art schools. August and September were particularly popular months for such regulars, tying the tutors to the town at a time when other resident artists were keen to avoid the holiday hordes. Several students found that the charms of St Ives beguiled them so much that they ended up by settling in the town. Not all of the long-term students had the talent, the dedication or the inclination to carve out successful careers as professional artists, but many of these lesser lights nevertheless played important roles in the Arts Club or in other aspects of the colony's life.

Periods of training tended to lead to deep friendships, as students worked hard together to help each other and develop their skills, and then socialised with each other in the evenings. Not surprisingly, therefore, quite a number of romances flourished at the Schools. There were also romances between

---

506 *St Ives Weekly Summary* 7/4/1900.

students and established painters in the colony, for students were often taken by their tutors to the Arts Club, took part in entertainments put on by the artists and generally mixed with the artistic community. Despite individual visits often being relatively short, the student presence in the town as a consistent and significant group will have been most marked, boosting the economy yet further and increasing, in particular, the demand for lodgings.

2.6.2   Student life in the 1890s

A number of students, who studied at the the various painting schools in St Ives during the late 1890s, went on to become well-known artists. Perhaps the most successful alumnus was the marine painter and poster artist Norman Wilkinson, who commented, "It was mainly at St Ives that I learned what little I know about painting" and recorded how much he enjoyed his time sketching out of doors under the guidance of Louis Grier.[507] The Liverpudlians, Mary McCrossan and James Hamilton Hay, also flourished at the Schools and Hay recorded that "the careful study of values under Julius Olsson at St Ives" had been one of the most useful parts of his training.[508] However, only Lewis Hind, a journalist turned art student, gives us any real insight into the life of an art student during this period.

Hind recalled his art student days as one of the happiest times of his life. He was, though, an unusual student, as he had never studied art elsewhere and merely wanted to grasp the basics of art, so as to improve his art criticism. Olsson had been recommended to him by Moffat Lindner and, when Hind asked a fellow student Olsson's method, he replied, "Values, always values and then more values".[509] However, as Hind had drawn neither from the cast nor from life before, he did not join in with the other students, who were constantly sketching out of doors on the beaches and around the town, but worked alone in the afternoons in Olsson's Porthmeor studio. He began with still life. Olsson arranged the subject, set up his palette and then left him to it.[510] He was surprised that art students were not actually taught the craft of painting, but muddled along, trying to learn something from the often contemptuous criticisms that they received from the master or his corrections to their efforts. He thought that they learnt most from fellow students. Nevertheless, he became inspired and rented a small studio overlooking the harbour, which at high tide was inaccessible from the quay, and worked really hard not only in his studio, but out of doors, pitching his easel on the beach, on the leeward side of Trencrom and among the blue pools and dunes of Lelant. He was thrilled on one occasion to be invited by Arnesby Brown to sit in his studio for a week of afternoons and copy, from a magnificent Brown pastoral, the leading cow bathed in sunshine.

In Hind's novel, *The Education of an Artist*, the character based on himself is helped extensively by another artist, called Lund, who enjoyed walking and painting the moors - a figure possibly based on Folliott Stokes. Hind records some of the advice that he received, which was consistent with that given in the Schools.

"Once learn to draw, and master values, and the rest will come if it's in you."

"Get your values first. First! First!! - First!!! Then your colour."

"Study the gamut from your highest light to your deepest dark."

"For every second you paint, study your object for sixty."

"You can train yourself to remember colour. The ways of light, direct, reflected, or absorbed, become in time a scientific matter; but form you can't remember..There's not the slightest or humblest form in tree, boat, or beast but must be observed anew from nature."

"You must begin by painting out of doors - on grey days when the changes of light are so gradual that you can paint straight away for two hours or so at a stretch. But you cannot paint out-of-doors on a sunny day. The changes are too rapid."

"Your colour is crude and flat. Break it up more! ....Half close your eyes; then objects out of the line of vision will become blurred. Paint 'em blurred! Lose 'em."[511]

---

507 N. Wilkinson, *A Brush with Life*, London, 1969, p.7-8.

508 Walker Art Gallery, *James Hamilton Hay*, Liverpool, 1973 at p.4.

509 C. Lewis Hind, *In Painters' Land, Black and White*, 12/9/1896.

510 See C. Lewis Hind, *Napthali*, London, 1926 at p.161.

511 C. Lewis Hind, *The Education of an Artist, London,* 1906 at p.26-30.

Fig. 2.236 John Douglas   Photograph inscribed "Grier's Students"   (courtesy Denys Wilcox)
(back from left) William Walke, Guy Kortright and William Lloyd
(front from left) Fred Milner, Folliott Stokes, Will Ashton and Milford Norsworthy

Fig. 2.237 Arthur Burgess
(courtesy Stephen Bartley)

Fig. 2.238 Muriel Coldwell
(courtesy Stephen Bartley)

2.6.3   The classes of 1901-2

Of all the groups of students that passed through the St Ives Schools, we know more about the classes at the School run by Olsson and Talmage during the years 1901-2 than any other. This is because they included four foreign artists, whose accounts of their experiences during what each considered to be a key period in their art education, have survived in one form or another. Three were Australians and, in addition to assorted comments made in interviews later in life by Richard Hayley Lever, who found fame and fortune in America, there are the reflections of Will Ashton - then Sir William Ashton OBE - in his autobiography, and a series of letters written by Arthur Burgess from St Ives to his new-found love, Muriel Coldwell, whom he had met at Olsson's School. The fourth foreign student was the Canadian artist, Emily Carr, who not only wrote about her time in St Ives in her autobiography, but also left sketch books full of work from her time in the town. A number of these sketches feature her fellow students - amusing vignettes, often accompanied by Carr's inimitable doggerel verse. These sources give us a real flavour of what it was like to study under Olsson and Talmage and of how the students lived and socialised in the town. They are particularly invaluable, as they cover what can be considered to be the period when the reputation of Olsson's School was at its zenith.

Two of the Australians, Richard Hayley Lever (1876-1958) and Will Ashton (1881-1963), knew each other from their schooldays in Adelaide, where they had been taught art by Will Ashton's father, James (1859-1935), a painter of seascapes, who had been born in the Isle of Man. Before emigrating to Australia in 1884, James Ashton had been a teacher at York School of Art from 1876 and, accordingly, Will Ashton was born in York. In Australia, James Ashton divided his time between running his own art school in the mornings, and teaching art at Prince Alfred College in the afternoons. Lever and his son attended both, learning the need for careful observation, an understanding of texture and a respect for drawing.[512]   In 1894, James Ashton returned to England for six months, during which he worked privately with Henry Moore, whom his son called "the greatest sea painter in the world at that time", and, during this visit, he saw, and was deeply impressed by, a seascape by Julius Olsson. Accordingly, when he later learned that Olsson had set up a School of Painting, he recommended that Lever, who himself had come over to study in Europe in 1894, should enrol in it.[513] Will Ashton persuaded his parents that he should have the chance to study under Olsson as well and so, although Lever had already studied in London and Paris before arriving in St Ives, Ashton came straight from Australia in late 1900. Ashton recorded, "My arrival at St Ives was the turning point of my life. I travelled all night on the Cornish Express and felt very lonely when I stepped out of the train. Having no idea where to obtain lodgings, I approached the Station Master, who, like most Cornish people, was kind, advising me to see a Mrs Trevorrow, who had a small boarding house just opposite St Andrew's Church. My luggage was put on a hand cart and I followed the porter through what seemed to me such funny little lanes to Mrs Trevorrow. Elizabeth Jane Trevorrow was a small woman, whose tall husband was a fisherman nicknamed 'Tommy Dick'. I lodged with these kindly people during the years that I spent in Cornwall."[514]

Ashton's loneliness was soon dispelled by his reunion with his old friend, Hayley Lever, who had first been signed in to the Arts Club by Louis Grier in November 1900, and they were soon hard at work. Lever, who had found lodgings in Richmond Terrace, recalled that he was constantly painting during his time in St Ives - "when the tide was out and when it was in, at all hours; sunrise, midday, sunset and moonlight".[515] Ashton confirms the concentration on the teaching of values at the School. "Julius Olsson held his classes about the harbour. He had us painting boats, the old buildings on the harbour front, the quaint streets and the fishing fleet with its colourful sails.....Olsson insisted on tonal values and to paint a white boat against the Sloop Inn, which was white-washed, needed careful study. J.O., as he was affectionately known to us, was assisted by Algernon Talmage. They took turns - week and week about. We received criticisms in the Harbour Studio for work done during the days when they were not present, and they would visit us when we were working in the streets and around the harbour. When the weather was wet, we painted still life in the studio and I remember J.O. setting us the problem of painting white chrysanthemums against a subtle background of grey, a real test for the student in the painting of tonal values."[516] Ashton's work is first mentioned in a review of Show Day in 1901, when he exhibited a seascape, and his pictures were stated to be full of movement and were complimented on their good colouring.

512 Will Ashton recorded that the still life subjects set up by his father - pots and pans, glass, fruit, dead rabbits and fish - were aimed to help him understand the texture of what he was painting. He also mentioned that, on entering his father's studio, one was confronted with the motto: "He that attempts to run before he can walk must surely stumble and fall." Will Ashton, *The life and work of artist Sir William Ashton OBE*, Sydney 1961 at p.15.

513 Will Ashton, *The life and work of artist Sir William Ashton OBE*, Sydney 1961 at p.16. There must be a good chance that James Ashton and Lever came over together.

514 Will Ashton, *The life and work of artist Sir William Ashton OBE*, Sydney 1961 at p.16. Ashton mistakenly records the surname as 'Treverrow'.

515 Helen Wright, *A Visit to Hayley Lever's Studio, International Studio*, 70 (May 1920), lxx

516 Will Ashton, *The life and work of artist Sir William Ashton OBE*, Sydney 1961 at p.17-8.

Plates 13 to 15

top -   Robert Langley Hutton
           Pednolva Cottage, St Ives
           (with Pednolva Mine Studio at rear)
           (Millie Dow family collection)

middle -   Richard Hayley Lever
           House Tops and Harbour, St Ives

bottom -   Emily Carr
           Olsson's Studio - Wet Day, St Ives
           (featuring, from left,
           Fearon, Ashton, Simmons (with puppy),
           Burgess (with duck) and Carr)
           (Royal BC Museum, BC Archives PDP-09017)

Plates 16 to 18

top -   Charles Bryant
          The Thames at Westminster
          (ex-Wintle collection
          - wedding present)

middle - Richard Hayley Lever
          Early Morning, St Ives
          (ex-Glanville collection)

bottom - Harry Britton
          Misty Morning, St Ives

242

Plates 19 to 21

top - Marion Frances Horn
The Harbour, St Ives
(David Lay, Penzance Auction House)

middle - Arthur Burgess
Drifting Home, St Ives
(James Makin Gallery;
photo Jessica Williams)

bottom - Hugh Blackden
Boat by The Wharf, St Ives (1897)
(Mallam's, Oxford)

Plates 22 to 25

top left - Beatrice Bright
              Sunset, Porthmeor
              Bright studied periodically in St
              Ives from 1909-1914

top right - Arthur Burgess
              Rowing Boats in a rocky cove
              (Lacy, Scott & Knight)

middle - Alfred Pazolt
              After the Storm
              (Neale's, Nottingham
              - ex-Glanville collection)

bottom - Will Ashton
              Gigs off Pednolver Point, St Ives
              (Private Collection)

The third Australian, Arthur Burgess (1879-1957), from Bombala, New South Wales, arrived in St Ives during the summer of 1901. Burgess' father was a former British Royal Naval officer, who had emigrated to Australia, where he became a land surveyor. A keen and able artist himself, he encouraged his son to draw from an early age. Arthur attended schools in New South Wales and Tasmania, and then trained for three years in an architect's office in Sydney, but he spent all his leisure hours sketching steamships in Sydney harbour. Just after his 21st birthday, he set sail for England, and he spent some time in Staithes before coming down to St Ives to study under Olsson.[517]

As had been the case since 1899, the summer class that year included a group of female students from the Slade School in London, who wanted to study landscape and marine painting during their summer vacation.[518] They always lodged in 'The Cabin' on Westcott's Quay (see Fig. 2.118). In 1901, the Slade girls comprised Ethel Carrick and Hilda Fearon, who had been coming down since 1899 and who went on to win significant reputations, Muriel Coldwell from Shrewsbury, who had enrolled at the Slade in 1897 and had also studied in St Ives the previous year, and Irma Richter (1876-1956), a Paris born girl, who was making the first of several visits. Ethel Carrick (1872-1952), who was born in Ealing, was the second eldest daughter in a family of ten children of a successful draper, and spent much of her youth looking after her younger siblings. She was aged 25 before she was able to persuade her family to allow her to study at the Slade. Hilda Fearon (1878-1917) was, accordingly, some six years younger. She was born in Banstead in Surrey, her father being a wine merchant in the West End of London, and, before enrolling at the Slade, she had studied in Dresden under Robert Sterl from 1897 to 1899.

Other students in the colony that summer were Caroline and Enid Jackson, two of six daughters of a wealthy Cheshire stockbroker. Caroline (b.1862) was the eldest, and, although she had first exhibited in 1888, she clearly had not pursued her art with any vigour previously. This was her second visit, as she had come down the previous year as well, but, for her much younger sister, Enid (b.1875, fl.1900-1908), it was a new experience.[519] Another Liverpool student, who had joined them that summer, and did so in many others, was Ethel Martin (1873-1954), a landscape and figure painter, who won numerous prizes and scholarships whilst at Liverpool.[520] The eldest daughter of a Kent brickmaker, she started exhibiting in 1894, began her training in Liverpool in 1899 and had her first success at the Royal Academy in 1900.

Another budding artist, who fraternised with this group of students from time to time, was John Thurston, who had first joined the School in late 1898 but, as he was then aged 32, he was rather older than the other students. Born in Ipswich, his mother had remarried by the time that he was five years old, and she had four more children with his stepfather, Charles Smith, a wine merchant. He was already specialising in marine painting and had had a work hung at the Royal Academy in 1899.

The summer proved a fertile time for romance, as no doubt through her Australian fellow students, Ethel Carrick met, and fell in love with, the Australian painter, Emanuel Phillips Fox. He had hired the large Porthmeor Studio, originally used by Olsson for the School, to complete his commission depicting Captain Cook landing in Botany Bay, for which Will Ashton modelled as the Captain. Muriel Coldwell also fell in love with fellow student, Arthur Burgess, and his letters to her on her return to Shropshire, give us a fascinating insight into student life in the colony.[521] He confirms, for instance, that the classes will nearly always have contained a number of students, who never enjoyed any success at all. This makes it very difficult to estimate the total number of students that passed through the Schools.[522] He also passes comments on some of the less popular students. In September, he complains to Muriel about the arrival of "a Miss Money covered in jewels, who puts on airs, talks of her aunt's footman and misses her maid. She gets through about 20 cigarettes a day and the sow giggling and shrieking is enough to drive any one mad".[523] This was Elsie Money from Hereford, who stayed overnight with Talmage, Stuart Hobkirk and Hilda Sealey at the Carbis Bay Hotel on the 27th that month - an interesting little party given that Hobkirk had rooms in Carbis Bay anyway! Another student who irritated the others was an elderly spinster, a Miss Read, whom the students christened "the Old Bird". She seems to have shared

517 A poem by Staithes Art Club member H E Conway dated 13/7/1901 mentions Burgess. I am indebted to George Bednar for bringing this to my attention.

518 Established in 1871 through the munificence of Felix Slade, the School was one of the first in Europe to offer the same terms to male and female students and, as a result, attracted a considerable number of female artists. See *The Slade Girls*, *Magazine of Art*, 1883 at p.324.

519 Another sister, Alice Marie Therese (1872-1958), also came down on occasion. Indeed, she joined Caroline in St Ives in the 1920s and played a large role in the activities of the Arts Club.

520 See *Studio-Talk, Liverpool*, *The Studio*, Vol. XXVIII, 1903-4, at p.291.

521 They were engaged in the winter of 1903-4 but it was not until 1911 that Burgess had established himself sufficiently to be allowed to marry her.

522 There are, for instance, many years in which individuals are recorded on the Visitors' List for months on end, making it likely that they were students, albeit that they never exhibited a work and so are not recorded in Dictionaries.

523 Letter from Arthur Burgess to Muriel Coldwell dated 8/9/1901 (Stephen Bartley).

Burgess' lodgings for he complains, "She cannot even be smoked out of the sitting room and brings her box and washes her brushes and cleans her palette on the table while we try to read or write."[524] She also irritated locals by blocking the street with her easel, when painting in The Warren. However, he admits that the Sealy sisters gave her a lively time, causing some jocularity. Nevertheless, she worked hard for, when she eventually left for Scotland, she took a couple of dozen canvases with her, requiring twelve parcels in all. Other students known to Muriel he refers to as 'His Majesty' and 'Pug'.[525]

Ashton and Burgess' accounts reveal other aspects of the relationship between Olsson and his students. There were dinners at what Ashton called J.O.'s "beautiful home high up on the hill overlooking Porthminster Beach" and, on one occasion, when Burgess and Fearon were invited, Arthur reported to Muriel that the Olssons had organised some entertainment. "They had an entertaining kind of a Johnny, who made jokes, sang coolie songs and did card tricks".[526] Emily Carr complained that Olsson only invited his male students to his house, but Burgess' letters reveal that Hilda Fearon and the Jackson sisters were regular guests, and so Carr's exclusion was nothing to do with her sex, but was due to her attitude.

Olsson was a very keen sailor and organised various boat trips for the students. An expedition, which seems to have acquired almost legendary status, was an attempted trip to Seal Caves in 'The Mermaid', Olsson's gig. The party comprised Olsson and his wife, Jo Thurston, Arthur Burgess, Ethel Carrick, Muriel Coldwell, Caroline Jackson, Ethel Martin and Billy Baragwanath, the landlord of the 'Sloop Inn', who used to look after the boat for Olsson. The trip had to be aborted due to rough seas and Olsson was much amused by a sketch done by Caroline Jackson of everyone looking the worse for wear, which he hung in his house. Male students, such as Ashton, Burgess and Thurston, also acted as crew members on Olsson's large yacht, 'The Siren', on longer distance voyages. Olsson himself described the boat as "a floating coffin", and so sailing in her will not always have been enjoyable. However, Ashton mentioned that Olsson "took me with him on many a yachting trip up and down the English Channel as far as Cowes", and recalled, near Falmouth, seeing Napier Hemy at work in his own floating studio. Burgess, for his part, recorded that, on one trip to Padstow, "There was a nasty sea and the old tub rolled. Too much for me. I was very bad and wished I was dead."[527] He was then stuck in Padstow for a week waiting for the weather to improve, with only enough money to buy eggs for every meal. For the Regatta in September, Olsson moored 'The Siren' in Porthminster Bay and hired a gig for his friends, leaving Burgess in charge of 'The Mermaid' to ferry people to and from the pier. Ethel Carrick and Hilda Fearon were amongst those who made the trip.

Fig. 2.239 Arthur Burgess
'The Siren' waiting to be refloated
(Stephen Bartley)

In his letter to Muriel Coldwell dated 11/8/1901, which he illustrated with this sketch, Burgess comments, "Yesterday one of the yacht's legs broke, which made her fall over flat on the beach. The fishermen all said that she would never get up but they, as usual, were doomed to disappointment. Three barrels were tied under her so that when the tide rose, they would gradually lift her up. At about 11p.m. last night, we went down to watch the operations. She rose without any trouble, so we went on board and sat till after midnight."

---

524 Letter from Arthur Burgess to Muriel Coldwell dated 11/8/1901 (Stephen Bartley).

525 Agnes Guyon from Bristol, who exhibited St Ives subjects at BAPFA for several years, will be one of the other students to whom Burgess was referring. Miss Hettie Wilde and her friend from Chagford, Miss Carnsew, will probably be others.

526 Letter from Arthur Burgess to Muriel Coldwell dated 9/10/1901 (Stephen Bartley).

527 Will Ashton, *The life and work of artist Sir William Ashton OBE*, Sydney 1961 at p.18 and Letter from Arthur Burgess to Muriel Coldwell dated 8/9/1901 (Stephen Bartley).

Fig. 2.240 *The Siren*
Cartoon of Olsson, probably drawn by Norman Wilkinson, published in *St Ives Weekly Summary* on 9th April 1904, at a time when there was a great debate about free trade.

Dash it all you will excuse me, but this beastly sea is coming out of the frame.

Look out! dash it all! its wet.

I only began it this morning, must get it back by to-night. Sending-in day, to-morrow. What?

Fig. 2.241 H.G.Fitzherbert *Caricature of Julius Olsson*
(from *Caricatures of the Cornish Riviera* 1910)

'The Cabin', which was often full of eight girls, clearly was quite a focal point of social life and Burgess mentions a photo of him pouring out ale at a supper party "with about five dozen glasses held round me".[528]   One can imagine the frowns that such antics received from the local Methodists, particularly as female students were involved. When 'The Cabin' closed in October 1901, Hilda Fearon was the last resident and, as she was a bit lonely in her new lodgings in The Warren, Thurston and Burgess threw a small party for her in the Temperance Hotel, at which they played euchre.

Also in October, Burgess decided that he wanted his own studio, and, with considerable help from Olsson, he created Norway House Studio from a building in Porthmeor Square. Having his own place to work boosted his output and he was soon telling Muriel that he was doing two panels a day and had a frieze of panels along two sides of his studio. He also ordered seven dozen sheets of cardboard from London for black and white work. In his next letter, he comments, "There is not much fun to be had down here now. The only thing to do is to work."[529]

In early November 1901, Burgess told Muriel about an addition to the class, "We have a new student, a Canadian, and she stays at Hodges. She is neither young, handsome nor thin".[530] This, accordingly, was the first impression made by Emily Carr, later to be considered the leading female Canadian artist of her generation.

Emily Carr was from Victoria, British Columbia. Her father, Richard, an entrepeneur, had been born in Kent, but had made some money gold prospecting in California, whilst her rather stern mother, Emily, was from Oxfordshire. However, her parents had met in California before settling in Victoria in 1863. Daughter Emily was the youngest but one of nine children and her father's favourite, and she found home life difficult after his death in 1888. In 1890, she was eventually allowed to study at the California School of Design in San Francisco, where she stayed for three years, but she found it dull and uninteresting, most of her time being spent in the Antique class. Considered the 'black sheep' of the family by her mother and sisters, life back in Victoria was no easier and she was delighted when her savings from some teaching assignments enabled her to travel to England in August 1899. She enrolled at the Westminster School of Art, but, again, found it an 'uninspiring grind', and she was made to feel unsophisticated. Her decision to come to St Ives was inspired by a desire to work more *en plein air* and she had been told that St Ives was one of the few places in England where one could paint out in the open all the year round.[531] Her knowledge of St Ives was limited to a painting, *St Ives Beach* by Moffat Lindner, which she had seen hanging over the fireplace in the drawing room of the London mansion owned by the parents of her student friend, Mildred Compton. Accordingly, she did not come down to St Ives to train under Olsson specifically. Her choice of tutor was only made on arrival, when she was asked if she wanted "studio tea parties" or whether she really wanted to work. For hard work, Olsson was the man.

According to Carr, the group of students with whom she trained comprised the three Australians - Burgess, Ashton and Lever -, Hilda Fearon, who, for some reason, she refers to as an "Irish girl", an "ultra-Englishman" from London, Noel Simmons, who, in fact, like the Sealy sisters, came from Weybridge, a cockney boy called Albert, an "upper class Englishwoman" whom Carr called Maude Horne (whom I have assumed to be Marion Frances Horn, as opposed to Maud Sealy), a French male student and "the nondescript old women who are found in most studios just killing time." 'The Old Bird' will be an example of this type and may possibly be one of the persons Carr is referring to.[532]

Hilda Fearon was the student who tried to make Carr feel welcome. She pointed out that, as Olsson insisted on the students painting on Porthmeor Beach in all weathers, she would need to get a heavier easel. On seeing Fearon's equipment, Carr exclaimed, "Gracious! That easel is as heavy as a cannon and that enormous brass-bound paintbox! I can't, I won't lug such heaviness" Hilda warned, "J.O. bellows if you cross his will". Unperturbed, the Canadian responded, "Let him roar!" and proceeded to tie a rock in her paint rag and hang it from her easel. Olsson grudgingly accepted this makeshift arrangement, but then insisted that Carr stand to her work and paint with full sun on her subject and full sun on her canvas. Carr objected - firstly, she did not have the strength to stand for lengthy periods and, secondly, the glare of the sun gave her headaches. She also was not too interested in marine scenes and preferred to sketch in the shade on a street corner. Not surprisingly, Olsson found her attitude

528 Letter from Arthur Burgess to Muriel Coldwell dated 11/8/1901 (Stephen Bartley). In his letter of 9/10/1901, he sadly records 'The Cabin' is no more.

529 Letter from Arthur Burgess to Muriel Coldwell dated 15/10/1901 (Stephen Bartley).

530 Letter from Arthur Burgess to Muriel Coldwell dated 3/11/1901 (Stephen Bartley).

531 Emily Carr, *Growing Pains*, Toronto 1946 (Paperback edition 1966 at p.163).

532 Burgess records the departure of 'the Old Bird' in his letter of 8/9/1901 but, in his letter of 3/11/1901, mentions that she is back in the locality.

annoying, albeit possibly admiring her spirit.[533] She found Talmage a more sympathetic tutor, which he put down to his own art training having been a grind, but he was adamant Olsson was the better painter. "J.O. is a genius", he told her.[534]

Carr records that the students met in Harbour Studio at 8 o'clock each morning to receive "crits" on the work done the afternoon before. Both Olsson and Talmage gave the students "crits" three days a week, and Carr complained that "what one taught, the other untaught; it was baffling but broadening".[535] After the "crit", the students went to work out in the open and the tutor on duty came round from time to time to view what they were doing. It was a long day, as they would be expected to work until dusk. Only in severe weather conditions did they work in the studio and, on these occasions, a model might be hired or Olsson would set up a still life.

Whilst Carr may have not enjoyed the concentration on marine work, one of her sketches demonstrates how Fearon eagerly drank in Olsson's teaching. Called *And Where is she at Midnight?*, it features Fearon watching the fishing fleet go out under the light of the moon and studying how the moonlight played on the waters of the Bay. Burgess also reports to Muriel on Fearon's fascination with moonlit scenes. "One night, I was seeing the Jacksons home from J.O.'s - 11p.m.. We came down past 'The Cabin' and met, just outside, Miss Fearon with her paintbox and her cousin with a candle in a cigar box. They had been out looking for the Moon."[536] In November, Burgess himself comments, "We have had some gorgeous moonrises here this [month]. Everyone has been doing moonrises."[537]

With their interest in different subject-matter, Fearon and Carr tended to paint in different areas during the day, but they became firm friends and, in the evenings, they would often hire one of the fisher children to act as a model for them. They would normally work in Carr's digs, under the light of a coal lamp, and, occasionally, some of the other students would join them. If they could not afford a model, then they would sit for each other. Carr's sketch-books are full of these sketches, showing children sitting and standing in a variety of poses (see Figs. 2.244-6 & 2.250).

Fig. 2.242 Emily Carr
And Where is she at Midnight?
featuring Hilda Fearon
(both Royal BC Museum, BC Archives
PDP05 898 & 909)

Fig. 2.243 Emily Carr
Windblown
Hilda Fearon and Noel Simmons
painting on the Harbour Beach.

---

533 Carr did not even manage to learn to spell Olsson's name properly, calling him both on her sketches and in her biography 'Olsen'.

534 Emily Carr, *Growing Pains*, Toronto, 1946 (Paperback edition 1966 p.175).

535 Emily Carr, *Growing Pains*, Toronto, 1946 (Paperback edition 1966 p.168).

536 Letter from Arthur Burgess to Muriel Coldwell dated 8/9/1901 (Stephen Bartley).

537 Letter from Arthur Burgess to Muriel Coldwell dated 3/11/1901 (Stephen Bartley).

Fig. 2.244 Emily Carr   *Sketch of a Girl*
(Royal BC Museum, BC Archives, PDP 05975)

The sketch-books also contain a number of delightful vignettes (see Figs. 3.18-9), demonstrating the high regard that the local fisherfolk, and their children, had for Hilda Fearon. All are titled with Carr's doggerel verse, such as *There's a 'wummun' called Fearon, that the folk of St Ives set great store on.* In these sketches, Fearon is always shown as a diminutive figure, wearing a Tam o' Shanter, with the burly fishermen towering above her. In a further sketch *And for the lovers' quarrel, she has a ready ear,* a young couple, who are having an argument, seek out her opinion, whilst her magnetic personality is further demonstrated in another vignette in which her mere presence on a town bench has attracted the whole local cat population! She clearly was a delightful personality. There are also a few rough sketches of other fellow students (see Fig. 2.251) and, in a lonely moment, when pain and poverty had struck her down, Carr also did a self-portrait - *Toothache and Patches*.

Figs. 2.245-6   Emily Carr   *Woe*   *Girl with doll*
(both Royal BC Museum, BC Archives, PDP05 890 & 884)

At Christmas, the School closed and most of the students went home. Carr decided to do some sightseeing in the locality with Albert, the cockney boy, somewhat to the surprise of Simmons, who dismissed him as "that wretched little cockney". He certainly seems not to have fitted in, for Carr concluded, "He was not quite one of us - no one bothered about him". Olsson and his wife, who had sailed to Sweden, stayed away six weeks longer than anticipated and, upon resumption after the break, Talmage ran the School on his own. Carr found this much more profitable, for Talmage was rather more accomodating than Olsson. "He was a calm, gentle man, one who understood", she wrote.[538] During the holiday, she discovered Tregenna Woods - "haunting, ivy-draped, solemn Tregenna" - and Talmage told her, "Trot up to your woods; that's where you love to be. I will come there and give you a lesson". When Carr expressed surprise that he was prepared to come out of his way for her lesson alone, he responded, "Trot along; one works best where one is happy".[539] Carr, therefore, worked away eagerly in Tregenna Woods and Talmage helped her, advising her, when her colour was going black, "Remember, there is sunshine too in the shadows". She was pleased with the results of her labours, and her fellow students and Talmage also applauded them. She therefore looked forward to showing them to Olsson on his return. Olsson, however, dismissed them immediately as "maudlin rubbish" and shouted at her "Go out *there*" (pointing to the glaring sands) "out to bright sunlight - PAINT"[540]

Extract from *The Olsson Student*

*These are the students
Who laughed at her gear
But now they have left
Doth she wish they were here
To jeer at the cloak..............
With the seams all broke
That covered the coat
Of a date remote
That covered the gown
With a hole burnt brown
That was worn by an
Olsson Student*

Fig. 2.247 Emily Carr   *Students laughing at my gear*
          The students are, from the left, Simmons, Burgess, Fearon, Ashton and Horn.
          (Royal BC Museum, BC Archives, PDP06127)
This was the final image of a series showing Carr walking into Tregenna Woods wearing an increasing assortment of tatty clothing and strange accessories, for which she was renowned, and about which she wrote a poem in her doggerel verse called *The Olsson Student*. Whilst self-mocking, this reveals a lonely, sensitive soul.

---

538 Emily Carr, *Growing Pains*, Toronto, 1946 (Paperback edition 1966 p.173).
539 ibid, p.173.
540 ibid, p.174.

Carr was not the only one to get the lash of Olsson's tongue that morning - the Frenchman and Burgess suffered too. The artistic skills of the unidentified Frenchman are never referred to by Burgess and Carr - what concerned them most was his crush on Burgess.[541] Writing to Muriel, Burgess reported: "The Frenchman made a fool of himself in my studio. He embraced and kissed me - Fancy being hugged and mugged by a Froggy-Frenchy. Ugh! I told him in my best French not to be a fool and that I would not stand it."[542] Nevertheless, on one occasion, he had to summon assistance from Carr, as "the Frenchie" had declared his intention of giving Burgess a "crit" alone in his studio. Carr was pleased to oblige, as she had enlisted Burgess' help in chasing away a fisherman, with religious mania, who had cornered her so as to expound his views on purgatory.

The painting that Burgess had shown Olsson featured steamers. He had a keen interest in craft of all descriptions and was constantly chiding Muriel for her inability to recognise the difference between one type of sailing ship and another. However, he had a particular fascination with steamers and, in one letter, he told Muriel, "I am off over to Hayle this afternoon steamer hunting. A Norwegian one came and anchored here for the tide yesterday so I am off after her with a 20 x 18 canvas."[543] Rather bizarrely, though, he decided that, for his major work for the Royal Academy in 1902, he would attempt a Thames subject featuring steamers. He worked on this during Olsson's absence and had great encouragement from Talmage and the other students. He even ordered a 38" x 20" gold frame for the work, and so was most dismayed by Olsson's cursory dismissal of it on his return. In fact, the dressing down Carr and Burgess received was so severe that, independently, they both decided to give up the idea of becoming an artist altogether and go home. They were only partly mollified when they met Frances Horn, who had had a similar experience before. "Criticism first morning after J.O.'s vacation! Not I. J.O. always returns in a rage. This time it is two rages - his usual and a toothache. You pair of young fools!" she grinned at our grief-wracked faces. "Poor children, I s'pose you knew no better." "[544] Olsson's brusqueness, which reduced at least three of his students to tears, does not reveal the better side of his nature and Carr's departure shortly afterwards is no surprise.

Figs. 2.248-9   Arthur Burgess   Sketches from letters to Muriel Coldwell,
whom he invariably addressed as 'Queen', signing himself 'White Knight'
(Stephen Bartley)

541 The only possible clue to his name is an Arts Club visitor F Murich.
542 Letter from Arthur Burgess to Muriel Coldwell dated 18/2/1902 (Stephen Bartley).
543 Letter from Arthur Burgess to Muriel Coldwell dated 15/10/1901 (Stephen Bartley).
544 Emily Carr, *Growing Pains*, Toronto, 1946, (paperback edition 1966 at p.175).

Figs. 2.250-1   Emily Carr
Girl with hat &
Fellow Student
(Royal BC Museum, BC Archives,
PDP05 906 & 949)

Burgess was sorry when Carr left, commenting, "She was about the only one I had to talk to in the Studio".[545] However, he soon bucked up when one of his works was selected for the Cornish Artists' exhibition at Whitechapel Art Gallery that spring, for this was an unusually prestigious opportunity to exhibit in London.   Lever, Ashton, Guy Kortright, Frances Horn and Gertrude Rosenberg had work selected for this as well However, upon the recommendation of his tutors, Burgess left St Ives around Easter to study at the Slade and, after a brief stint there, spent the summer sketching in the Naval Dockyard at Portsmouth, before returning to St Ives with Muriel that autumn.

Burgess indicates that, by February 1902, Ashton had also acquired his own studio - most probably in St Andrew's Street, close to his lodgings - and had begun to be less regular in his appearances at the Harbour Studio.[546] He was also the only student who did not get a mauling from Olsson on his return from holiday that month, and he seems to have become a particular favourite of the Olssons. He later commented, "Julius and [Katherine] Olsson had no children and treated me as though I was their son" and, for his twenty-first birthday on 20th September 1902, they gave him a letter and a gift and organised a picnic with all the students in attendance.[547] Judging from the Visitors' Lists, his companions that day would have included Hayley Lever, Caroline and Enid Jackson, Ethel Martin and the three Sealy sisters, for Burgess, Coldwell and Irma Richter did not arrive back until October.

Despite Carr confirming that Hayley Lever was a member of her class, he is not mentioned much by either Burgess or herself, which suggests that he was more advanced and worked separately from the other students, for he was already having work hung in Paris. When, after Lever had moved to the States, an American patron spoke to him about his time in St Ives, the artist recalled, "I really worked there. I did not realise then how much my future depended upon those days when I studied diligently from morning until night. Here in America, I work, of course, but one cannot get the solitude for reflection and concentration and therein lies the beauty of those quaint old world villages."[548] The superior quality of the work being produced by Lever and Ashton at this time is demonstrated by the fact that, at the RCPS exhibition in Falmouth in the autumn of 1902, Lever had six and Ashton five works hung, whilst the only other students represented, each with a single work, were Frances Horn, Mary McCrossan, Edith Sealy, Gertrude Rosenberg and Guy Kortright.

545 Letter from Arthur Burgess to Muriel Coldwell dated 18/2/1902 (Stephen Bartley).
546 Letter from Arthur Burgess to Muriel Coldwell dated 18/2/1902 (Stephen Bartley). See 1904 Rate Book re Ashton's studio.
547 Will Ashton, *The life and work of artist Sir William Ashton OBE*, Sydney 1961 at p.18. Ashton calls Olsson's wife Kathleen.
548 Previti Gallery Catalogue, *Richard Hayley Lever*, New York, 1985.

Fig. 2.252 Hayley Lever in St Ives in 1904

That winter, both Lever and Ashton decided to spend time in Paris. Ashton, in any event, confirmed that he studied at Julian's Academy and returned the following winter for further study.[549] Such breaks from St Ives for further training in Paris were encouraged, and Norman Wilkinson recalled his time there in 1900 with fellow St Ives students, Guy Kortright and Percy Heard, albeit not with great fondness, as they had been attacked by a French crowd enraged at Britain's actions during the Boer War. Ashton, though, enjoyed Paris immensely. On his return to St Ives, he painted a large oil *Boulevard Montparnasse, Paris,* from sketches that he had made from his bedroom window in Paris. It was, in due course, to be the first work that he sold to a public gallery.

For most of the students in St Ives, the ultimate accolade was getting a work hung at the Royal Academy. Ashton gives us an inkling of the pride and joy that such success brought, particularly for someone from a country where it was considered an immense achievement. Ashton confirms what Ranger-Gull in *Portalone* suggests - namely that it was the custom of the artists, on the day when news was expected of successes and failures at the Royal Academy, to gather together in the 'Sloop Inn'. Indeed, Ranger-Gull indicates that the landlord recognised that it was the best morning's 'trade' of the year. This was a momentous day, when the artists learned the result of all the hard work, all the emotional turmoil and all the dreams of the past twelve months. For those successful, it was a time of intense satisfaction, but for those rejected, it was a bitter blow. It says much for the community spirit in the colony that the artists had decided that no-one should have to be on their own when the news was imparted. Those disappointed could be consoled by friends, and if this were not enough, then alcohol was there to numb other feelings, whilst all could share in the joy of those unexpectedly successful. In 1904, Ashton records that Olsson brought the news to the pub, having received a telegram from Arnesby Brown, who, as an ARA, had received advance notice. "It named a number of the artists represented, including Hayley Lever with one picture, David Davies with two, and finished up with the magic words, 'Ashton two'. One can imagine my joy at such news! ..... J.O. said to me, "You must come with us to London for Varnishing Day". Ashton continued, "Never will I forget that journey with Julius Olsson, Algernon Talmage, Arthur Meade, E G Fuller, Moffat Lindner and several other artists.[550] When we arrived at Burlington House, I was so excited that I could not find my pictures. But they were there and I was really proud to have my pictures hanging in the same exhibition as my master. I felt that I had not let my parents down. They had sacrificed so much to give me my opportunity which was better than that given to most art students."[551]

---

549 Will Ashton, *The life and work of artist Sir William Ashton OBE*, Sydney 1961 at p.22. Both Ashton and Lever exhibited paintings of the Seine on Show Day in 1903, and Ashton, when signed into the Arts Club by Louis Grier in February 1904, is stated to have come from Paris.

550 Other artists hung that year include Louis Grier, Noble Barlow, John Bromley, Allan Deacon, Harry Robinson, Stuart Hobkirk, Mabel Douglas and Frances Horn.

551 Will Ashton, *The life and work of artist Sir William Ashton OBE*, Sydney 1961 at p.20.

Ashton's pleasure at this success was followed the same year by an acceptance of a work at the Paris Salon and, having won these accolades, he decided that December to return to Australia. Lever went with him, but always intended to return, as he had fallen in love with a girl that he had met in his lodgings (see Chapter 3.5 - Courting the Locals). Ashton indicated that he too had not intended to remain in Australia but, having taken over his father's outdoor sketching class, he fell in love with one of his students, May Millman, whom he married in January 1906.

How then did this group of students fare in their careers? Lever married immediately on his return to St Ives in December 1905 and became one of the most innovative artists working in the colony. However, good reviews did not translate into good sales and, in 1912, he decided to try his luck in America, where he was an immediate success, winning many medals and awards and becoming a member of the National Academy of Design.

Somewhat surprisingly, given that the School does not appear to have been operating in any formal capacity for some years, Ashton indicated in his autobiography that Olsson had given him the chance of taking it over in 1914. Ashton, whose admiration for his tutor can be gauged by the fact that one of his first child's forenames was Olsson, recorded the difficult decision that he had had to take that year. "My old master, Julius Olsson, had written advising us to settle in England, and that I was wasting my time in Australia. Such advice needed much consideration, as several factors were involved. It meant selling up and leaving our parents, and there were two children to consider.... Finally, I decided to take the plunge. Olsson wanted me to take over his painting school, with himself and Talmage for visiting professors. It was a daring move to make and yet we decided to go. But fate was against us. The war with Germany had begun, and it looked as if it would be a long and desperate struggle. Painting outside was, of course, out of the question, so we took a flat in London".[552] They stayed until 1917. On his return home, Ashton became a pillar of the establishment in Australian art, eventually receiving a knighthood, and was responsible for securing a number of sales of work by his tutors and colleagues in St Ives to Australian Galleries and other private collectors. On his frequent return visits to Europe, he kept in close contact, not only with his tutors, but also with a number of his fellow students, staying in France with the Foxes, buying work for his own collection by Hilda Fearon and linking up repeatedly with Arthur Burgess and Charles Bryant, another Australian who studied under Olsson.

Burgess, who had his first success at the Royal Academy in 1904, developed a reputation initially as a naval artist and exhibited large canvases of convoys in heavy seas in mid-ocean, broadly painted, with much impasto. He eventually persuaded Muriel's parents that he was an appropriate son-in-law and they married in 1910. He too paid several return visits to St Ives and kept in close contact with Olsson.[553] By the Second World War, he was recognised as one of the leading marine painters in this country.

Emily Carr went on to study at Bushey for a short period, but then had a nervous breakdown.[554] Noel Simmons and his mother tried to help, but she ended up being committed to a sanitorium in East Anglia for over a year. Burgess linked up with her in London again in the spring of 1904 before her chastened return to Canada. Accordingly, her initial European training period was not a great success, albeit she did admit in her autobiography that sombre Tregenna, "interpreted to me by a good, sound teacher", had given her "so much, so much".[555]

Of the Slade girls, Ethel Carrick married Phillips Fox in 1905 and they settled in Paris, where they both gained significant reputations. They returned to Australia in 1913, but Fox died young in 1915. Ethel spent the rest of her life between Paris and Australia and Ashton was a great help in securing sales of both her work and that of her husband to Australian Galleries. Hilda Fearon continued to come down to study in St Ives until 1907 and it is believed that a blossoming romance between her and Talmage led him to leave his wife and move to London. She became a highly regarded figure painter, having regular success at the Royal Academy, before dying in 1918 from puerperal convulsions whilst pregnant. Talmage was presumably the father. Muriel Coldwell had a couple of successes at the Royal Academy between 1914 and 1917 and later joined the St Ives Society of Artists, along with her husband and Ashton. Irma Richter moved to America, where she taught art and became a leading authority on Leonardo da Vinci.[556]

552 Will Ashton, *The life and work of artist Sir William Ashton OBE*, Sydney 1961 at p.28.

553 He is signed into the Arts Club in both January 1911 and November 1914.

554 Her biographer, Maria Tippett, considers her malady to be hysteria, brought on by stressful situations in a foreign environment, but related to a sexual conflict, possibly resulting from some encounter with her father. Maria Tippett, *Emily Carr - A Biography*, Ontario, 1979 at p.57-61.

555 Emily Carr, *Growing Pains*, Toronto, 1946 (Paperback edition 1966 p.181).

556 Irma A Richter is recorded as exhibiting work between 1909 and 1928 and became a teacher of art at Rosemary Hall, Greenwich, Connecticut. In 1932, she published *Rhythmic Form in Art*, an investigation of the principles of composition in the work of the great masters, and later became an expert on Leonardo da Vinci. Her book *Selections from the Notebooks of Leonardo da Vinci*, first published in 1952, has been reprinted on numerous occasions.

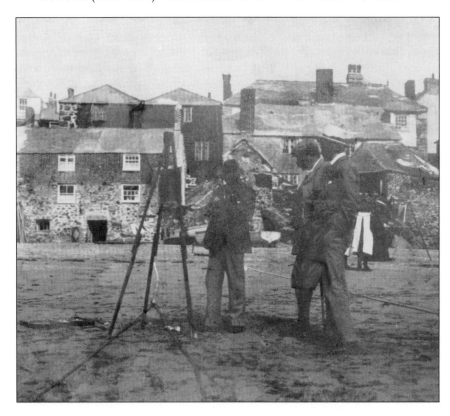

Fig. 2.253 Julius Olsson and Algernon Talmage review the work of Hayley Lever
on the Harbour Beach   (Leonard Clayton Gallery Incorporated and
Clayton-Liberatore Gallery, Bridgehampton, New York)

Of the girls from the Liverpool-Birkenhead Schools, Caroline Jackson continued to visit with regularity, using a St Ives exhibiting address in 1904 and becoming a member of the Arts Club in 1906, but it was probably not until 1909 that she settled in the town, for her first Show Day appearance was in 1910. She came to concentrate on sculpture in plaster and plasticine, her speciality being portrait studies, particularly of local children. Over her career, she had twenty-nine works shown at the Walker Art Gallery in Liverpool. Enid Jackson, who had some success as a figure painter, also used a St Ives exhibiting address in 1903-4, and was in town again in 1905. Ethel Martin, having married a Mr Fridlander in c.1905, still accompanied Caroline Jackson down on visits in 1906 and 1907, and continued to exhibit her work with regularity until 1938.

Of the Surrey crew, Frances Horn exhibited on Show Days most years until 1909, basing herself most of the time with her mother in 9, Pednolver Terrace.[557] However, she had several sketching trips to Brittany and her one success at the Royal Academy was with *The River, Quimperlé* in 1907.[558] She married in 1909 and, although the Art Dictionaries record her married name as Luck, the local paper quite clearly indicates that her husband was William Alfred Elliot Coxon, then resident in Egypt.[559] Marriage (and possible foreign residence) seems to have brought her painting career to an end. Katherine Horn settled in Lelant, living in 'Chygwidden', and became one of the leading female golfers in the locality. Hilda Sealy (d.1936) and her sister, Maud, also settled in Lelant, with Maud later gaining a reputation for her extravagantly decorated raffia hats and chatty parrot.[560] However, Edith Sealy enjoyed some considerable success as an artist, particularly in Paris, and she was hung at the Royal Academy in 1905 and 1906. When she returned to exhibit on Show Days in 1913-1915, her work was labelled post-impressionist and she was regularly hung at the Salon d'Automne in Paris from 1913 to 1924, and probably lived in Paris from 1919. She was also successful at Pittsburgh in 1923. Gertrude Rosenberg was another student to settle in St Ives, living at 18 The Terrace, but she died young, of meningitis, whilst at Oudon in France, in 1912.[561] Her work, however, is represented in the Royal Art Gallery, Canterbury.

557 This was called 9, Talland Road for some years. However, in 1903, she gave her exhibiting address as in Totnes and, in 1904, as in Camberley.

558 In a letter from Murielle Schofield to her husband dated 12/10/1906 (Schofield Archive), she mentions that the Horns are back "- and Miss Horn says she met the Parker Newtons at Concarneau and they were very kind to her."

559 *St Ives Weekly Summary* 26/6/1909. The only possible explanation for this error is that a Mrs Mabel Luck, the wife of Colonel Luck, did exhibit with an address c/o Marion Frances Horn on some occasions.

560 See Dorothy Meade, *Reminiscences of Lelant*, Lelant website.

561 See *St Ives Times* 4/10/1912.

Noel Simmons seems to have made only the one visit to St Ives and, albeit he was later praised as "a draughtsman of exceptional talent" and continued exhibiting until 1938, his output was small.[562] Although on Show Day in 1903, John Thurston was described as "a rapidly advancing marine painter" and he rented one of the Porthmeor Studios in 1903-4, he appears to have had no further success after leaving the colony in 1905. Nevertheless, this all represents quite a considerable achievement by one group of students.

I indicated above that the years 1901-2 probably represented the zenith of the Schools. This was not because of any deterioration in the number or quality of students arriving in the colony, but because Olsson himself played a restricted role after 1902. Adverts thereafter for the 'Cornish School of Landscape and Sea Painting' refer to him as being merely an 'Honourable Visitor', and it appears that the School was effectively run by Algernon Talmage, with some help from his wife, Gertrude. Olsson, therefore, just gave private lessons to a few talented artists, such as John Park, Charles Bryant (see Plate 16), Beatrice Bright (see Plate 22) and Borlase Smart, who showed a particular interest in marine painting. However, whereas Talmage introduced some new initiatives, such as open air figure painting in a private orchard, we have no accounts by any of his students as to what life was like when the School was run solely by him. Talmage, however, was a much-liked character, and a valued teacher, and the regulars, such as Hilda Fearon, the Sealys, the Jacksons and the Horns, continued to return. The James Lanham Ltd sketchbook of one of his most well-known students, the Canadian, Helen McNicoll, is owned by the Art Gallery of Ontario, Toronto, but this does not appear to contain anything of great interest.

2.6.4   Prospective art students - The experiences of Brian Hatton and Milford Norsworthy

In addition to art students coming down to St Ives to study, it appears that the colony had gained such a reputation as an art centre that prospective art students came to seek advice as to how and when they should commence their art training. With the Schools at St Ives being focussed extensively on landscape and marine painting, such students were often told to study elsewhere first, so that they acquired basic skills of drawing the figure before tackling the difficulties of *plein air* sketching. A series of letters, recording the experiences of the sixteen year old budding art student, Brian Hatton (1887-1916), during a visit to the colony in January 1904, are of particular interest.

Hatton's talent had already come to the notice of the elderly George Frederick Watts (1817-1904), who had been sufficiently impressed by the boy's work to suggest that he did not need to go to Art School at all. Hatton was unconvinced by this advice and, therefore, had come down to West Cornwall with some family friends, Dr and Mrs Lancaster, to see how the various art schools operated, and to seek further advice on where he should train. He spent a day in Newlyn with Norman Garstin, a morning with Sherwood Hunter, who taught at the Forbes School, and some time with Forbes himself, who showed him his classes and his studio, where he was working on his Royal Academy submissions. In St Ives, he spent an afternoon in the studio of Russell Dowson, whom he called "a nice old boy", watching him enlarge some watercolours into oils.[563]   However, initially, he found it difficult to gain access to the studios of the principal artists in St Ives, as they were "busy now and don't like people going over their studios unless they buy".[564] It was only when he met at his hotel - Hendra's in Carbis Bay - the retired civil engineer, John Ward Girdlestone, who was a regular student in Olsson's classes, that he managed to gain some useful introductions.[565] In each instance, Hatton made a quick sketch of the artist's head and jotted down a few character traits. He was impressed by the "lovely things" he saw in the studio of Olsson, whom he described as a big man, with a limp, and "considered to be about the best seascaper nowadays". He added, "Girdlestone told me he works at an awful rate. He has before now painted a 6 foot canvas in 12 hours that, with a few finishing touches when dry, was ready to be hung on the line at the Royal Academy."[566] He was also introduced to Algernon Talmage, whom he described as "young and sporting looking - gingery", Stuart Hobkirk and his mother, whom he called "a Red Headed Baroness Ferina-Faron" and Louis Grier, "who had some awfully nice things but seemed rather a queer customer". His sketch of Grier is inscribed - "looks like a wee little monkey - very much mottled about the nose". One of Hatton's strengths at that time was his ability to depict animals and Arthur Meade, whom he called "a very dapper little fellow", made the interesting comment that, if Hatton did decide to settle in St Ives, "a good many artists would be only too glad to have me put animals in their landscapes".

---

562 See review of an exhibition of his watercolour drawings at Chenil Gallery in Chelsea in 1912 - *International Studio* , Vol 48, 1912-3 at p.322-3, where three watercolours, showing fine drawing, are illustrated.

563 This is the only reference that I have found to Russell Dowson in St Ives.

564 Letter to his mother dated 8/1/2004 reproduced in Celia Davis, *Brian Hatton*, Suffolk, 1978 at p.67.

565 Girdlestone and his two sons were first signed in as guests to the Arts Club in November 1891 by Mrs Olsson and he became a regular visitor to the town during the 1890s, staying each time at Hendra's Hotel in Carbis Bay. On these visits, he probably studied under Olsson. He then settled in Carbis Bay and started to exhibit on Show Days between 1899 and 1911. Watercolours of Norwegian subjects seem to have been his speciality. He does not appear to have exhibited elsewhere. He died in 1911 and is buried at Lelant.

566 Reproduced in Celia Davis, *Brian Hatton*, Suffolk, 1978 at p.69.

Hatton had to wait to meet Alfred East and Arnesby Brown, as they were in London for the Royal Academy elections, but East, on his arrival, was very encouraging and showed the boy "some lovely huge landscapes" that he was getting ready for the Academy. Hatton was also impressed with the two pastoral subjects that Brown was working on.and described them to his mother. "One of them [was] a drove of cows coming over a bridge...in late afternoon light more or less behind them; they looked very fine and hot and dusty. The other was a Hay wagon and men and a boy haymaking in evening light full on them, but with chequered lights from trees"[567]. These were *The Bridge* (Walker Art Gallery, Liverpool) and *Full Summer, Ludham* (Nottingham Castle Museum).

Most artists Hatton consulted in St Ives disagreed with Watts' opinion that he should forego art school, feeling that nowadays teachers did not attempt to interfere with, or unduly influence, a pupil's work, but they nevertheless thought that Hatton should continue with his education before concentrating on art. Not surprisingly, given that Talmage, Brown and Meade (and many others in the colony) had studied there, the Herkomer School at Bushey was highly recommended as an alternative to Paris, but some time at art school was felt to be imperative, as "he would learn in three months what it would take him years to learn by himself". Reporting to Brian's mother on the meetings in St Ives, Mrs Lancaster commented, "The artists that Brian met on Monday were the men that will be his judges in the future, the present ARAs and RAs and one felt down there that there was calm dispassionate judgement. They were kindness itself to him and said he was full of promise, but it was the old story, only education and work will give him his future success."[568] Sadly, Brian's artistic career was cut short in the First World War.

The other artist featured in this section, Harold Milford Norsworthy (1886-1917), was also killed in the First World War and, as he is one of only two artist members whose death is commemorated on the copper plaque in the St Ives Arts Club, it seems appropriate to record the additional information that I have uncovered about him, particularly as he seems to be that rare phenomenon - a locally based boy, who was inspired by seeing artists at work to become an art student. Born in Wandsworth, Norsworthy is first mentioned locally as a member of the town cricket team in September 1898 and it appears that, at this time, he was living with his mother, Mildred, in Lelant, his father William Milford Norsworthy having died in Penzance in June 1894.

There seems little doubt that Norsworthy is the boy from St Ives called 'Milford', who had been told by the art students in St Ives to be sure to look up Emily Carr, when he went to study under John Whiteley at Bushey in 1902, and Carr writes amusingly about him in her autobiography. She tells us that Milford had a doting mother but "a stepfather who considered both stepsons and art unnecessary expense".[569] It appears that Mildred Norsworthy, having enquired in St Ives as to what was best for her artistically inclined son, had been told that he should study the figure at Bushey, before training in St Ives.

Fig. 2.254 -260   Brian Hatton   Quick sketches, in his letters, of artists met in St Ives.
Clockwise, from top left, Olsson, Meade, East, Girdlestone, Grier, Dowson and Talmage

---

567 ibid.
568 ibid at p.70.
569 Emily Carr, *Growing Pains*, Toronto, 1966 at p.178.

Fig. 2.261 Emily Carr   *A Study in Evolution - Bushey*   (featuring Carr and Milford Norsworthy)
(Royal BC Museum, BC Archives, PDP06156)

She pleaded with Carr to keep an eye on him, to look after his pocket money, for otherwise he would spend it all on the first day, and to ensure that he chewed his food, as he had poor digestion! Carr duly took him under her wing and, in her inimitable way, shouted, whenever she saw him eating, "Chew, Milford, Chew!". Indeed, she scandalised the other students by going off sketching with him on her own, and he features in her work *A Study in Evolution - Bushey* - a three-part piece showing their *plein air* sketching trip being brought to an abrupt and painful end by a swarm of insects. However, in January 1903, Norsworthy was back in St Ives and, as he was signed into the Arts Club that month by Algernon Talmage, he is likely to have enrolled in his class. During 1903 and 1904, he took part in various classes in St Ives, featuring in the photograph of Grier's students taken by John Douglas (Fig. 2.236), and often staying at 3 Warren View. He exhibited on Show Day in 1904 and also at the RCPS exhibition in 1906. He then moved to study at the London School of Art, where, in 1908, he won a prize for still life in a class taken by Frank Brangwyn.[570] There is very little evidence to suggest a continuing connection with St Ives, but clearly his former colleagues felt sufficiently highly of him to commemorate his death in 1917, shortly after his first successes at the Royal Academy, albeit, as he was no longer a local resident, he does not feature on the town War Memorial.[571]

2.6.5   Sketching tours for students

In addition to the classes run in West Cornwall, some of the artist teachers organised for their students sketching tours to other parts of the country or even abroad. Such concentrated trips will have helped students to get to know their tutor and each other much better.

In 1903, the advert for the Cornish School of Landscape and Sea Painting indicated that watercolour tuition was now an additional option under Albert Moulton Foweraker, who had settled in Carbis Bay in 1901. He became a member of the RBA in 1902 and, although his major works were in oils, he is now best known for his watercolours, particularly his exquisite depictions of twilight subjects. As watercolours were popular, particularly with female students, this addition to the School's curriculum will have been welcome, as neither Olsson nor Talmage (nor, incidentally, Grier nor Barlow) tended to paint in this medium.

In January 1904, Foweraker, then called a Director of the School, organised what was hailed in the local paper as a ground-breaking "Spanish Expedition". "The ancient and romantic country of Spain, as a theatre of landscape for painters and students, is almost unexplored", it trumpeted, as if quoting from Foweraker's prospectus. "It has great natural beauties, and *plein air* work is full of new schemes and arrangements of colour, and, especially, opportunities for the study of form and drawing abound on every side in the Ancient Moorish cities. Yet, hitherto, these artistic opportunities have been almost untouched."[572] This was put down to difficulties of language and the need to travel "under unusual conditions", problems which Foweraker from his previous experience could circumvent. The party included "several well-known painters" along with the novelist, Cyril Ranger-Gull, and Folliott Stokes, who were both to lecture on Spanish art and history.

---

570 See *The Studio* Vol 45, October 1908, at p.75,
571 After 1906, the only mention of him I have found locally is when he took a book out of the Arts Club library in 1910.
572 *St Ives Weekly Summary*, 23/1/1904.

Fig. 2.262 Cyrus Cuneo   *An outdoor sketching class at St Ives*   (*Black and White*, April 1903)
The tutor depicted appears to be John Noble Barlow

In such company, the first Spanish expedition will not have been a dull affair.[573] It was supposed to end with an exhibition of work in a London Gallery, whilst Ranger-Gull was said to have made arrangements with a firm of publishers, presumably Greening & Co, for the best work to be reproduced in a book.[574] I can find no evidence of either of these grand plans coming to fruition, but the trip seems to have been sufficiently successful to have persuaded Foweraker to run such ventures thereafter on his own account. In 1905, he advertised winter art classes in Andalucia, giving his address as 'Villa Camara' in Malaga. Classes were held in Malaga in January and February, in Cordoba in March and in Granada in April. He ran such painting trips for a number of years and Spanish subjects predominate in his output of this period.

Although Foweraker did not retain a connection with the Cornish School of Landscape and Sea Painting for very long, one of the new initiatives introduced by Algernon Talmage, when he assumed control of that School, was an annual trip to Picardy concentrating on landscape painting. Fred Milner, the American Henry Keasbey and Lizzie Whitehouse are some of the artists that exhibited Picardy subjects in the years 1906-8. No doubt for reasons of expense, Noble Barlow restricted his sketching tours for his students to this country. Shaugh Bridge in South Devon, Studland in Dorset and Shere in Surrey were popular destinations and Garstin Cox and Herbert Fitzherbert were some of the students that accompanied him.

2.6.6   New Schools

Talmage's departure in 1907, and Grier's increasing lack of application, did not stop the continual flow of students into the town. Barlow continued to run classes until the War, the visiting American, Frank Hutton Shill, ran a School between 1907 and 1910 and painting lessons continued to be advertised by a whole range of artists, such as Beale Adams, Lynn Pitt, Mary McCrossan, Arthur White and Richard Hayley Lever - many themselves former students. By 1912, Alfred Hartley had also set up a School principally devoted to etching. Whilst there are no extant accounts of these Schools, it is clear that the student body in the colony was still thriving and played an important role in the town.

---

573 Foweraker, Ranger-Gull and Stokes were great friends and were part of a group interested in a wide range of cultural activities, involving art, drama, literature, natural history and music. Foweraker's arrival in St Ives signified an increase in the number of dramatic productions put on by the artists, and these were often stage-managed by Stokes. Foweraker was also a talented musician and, in August 1903, he was choirmaster for an evening of sacred music held at Lelant Parish Church, during which a hymn, with music by himself and words by Ranger-Gull, was played by Herbert Lanyon.

574 *St Ives Weekly Summary*, 23/1/1904.

COMICS IN THE COLONY

Art in St Ives was not always a serious business and, in addition to the renowned wit of painters, such as Lowell Dyer and Louis Grier, there were several artists who produced comic work not only for the amusement of their colleagues, but for publication in a range of different media.

2.7.1   The humorous work of Edmund Fuller

Despite his considerable success as a marine artist, Edmund Fuller became best known nationally for his comic postcards. One of the first artists to spot that humour would be an attractive additional ingredient to boost, yet further, the new craze for sending postcards, he produced an astonishing number of comic images. His own notebook, recording publishers, lists of titles and prices achieved, shows that this was a profitable, albeit relatively brief, venture.[575]

Fuller used watercolour for his comic pieces and, from examples of original art work seen, sketched them generally on 10" x 7" paper. The humour was unsophisticated, often being based purely on lame puns. However, Fuller was good at caricature, used the limited colours available for printed work cleverly and included a considerable amount of carefully observed detail. Accordingly, irrespective of their humorous content, which has not always stood the test of time, many of these images contain attractive features, demonstrating a talented watercolourist at work.

The first reference to comic work by Fuller is in the reviews of his exhibition in Olsson's Porthmeor Studio in 1897, which make mention of the presence of a few unpublished humorous sketches and caricatures, particularly relating to golf. The *Western Morning News* commented, "He has evidently obtained some of his studies from links which are not far from St Ives. They are all exceedingly clever and most amusing."[576] As an early member of the West Cornwall Golf Club, Fuller will have experienced the tribulations of playing on this newly-formed course and, as golf was a sport that suddenly burgeoned in popularity at this juncture, he found a ready market for his comic pieces. He records selling an initial set of twelve golf sketches to W.M.Power, with copyright, for £36, but it is not known whether these were ever published. He soon followed this up with a further set of twelve, with titles such as *A Scratch Player* or *An Uneven Match*. On this occasion, he merely sold the copyright to the publishers, Hildesheimers, for £10. However, his best known golf set, entitled *The Trials of a Tyro*, featuring six depictions of a hapless red-jacketed golfer, with a malevolent child caddy, is clearly set on the links of the West Cornwall Golf Club (see Figs. 2.233-4).

Fuller was a good all-round sportsman, playing cricket and tennis as well, and, boosted by the success of his golf sketches, he turned his attention next to other sporting mishaps or misnomers. Hildesheimers, for instance, in addition to taking the twelve golf scenes, took, most probably in 1899, fourteen on cricket (e.g. *A Maiden Over, Long-Leg and Short-Leg*), twelve on football (e.g *Dark-Blue forwards, Light-Blue backs*) and twelve on cycling (e.g *A Gear Case, Bone-shaken*). Cycling was again a pastime with a burgeoning popularity, and Henry Graves & Co Ltd also bought, for £24, a series of eight cycling sketches (e.g.*Riding with a bell(e))*), dating from 1898, whilst Woolstone Bros published another set of eight, which was most novel, as the cards told an unfolding story. A girl with a puncture is helped by a chivalrous male, but the pair, having decided to cycle on together, manage to collide with each other coming down a hill, knocking them both unconscious.[577] Love, however, triumphs. As each card was not particularly illuminating on its own, the whole series needed either to be bought but not used, or sent in stages to the same recipient, and the idea does not appear to have caught on. Fuller also produced several works on shooting (e.g. *Small Bore*), hunting (e.g. *Full Cry*) and fishing (e.g. *Fly Fishing*) and Raphael Tuck & Sons Ltd, one of the best known postcard publishers, and Jonas Wolf & Co also took a selection of golf, cricket, cycling, hunting and fishing scenes at this time. All these, however, are now rare, but there are three series of postcards that seem to have been especially popular.

---

575 Fuller may well have enjoyed considerable success with his comic work even before the postcard boom of the early 1900s, as his notebook seems to record total income, in 1897, of £174-6-0 and, in 1898, of £141-2-0. However, there is no indication of how these totals are arrived at.

576 Reproduced in *St Ives Weekly Summary* 12/6/1897.

577 This is the only series that I can find no mention of in Fuller's notebook of his comic works.

Fuller makes reference in his notebook in January 1900 to some sketches, which he called "misreadings from Shakespeare". This was a concept that he was to develop into a large series, which proved attractive to several publishers. Fuller's idea was to use couplets from Shakespeare plays as titles for his comic depictions of modern day life. Accordingly, a scene in which the occupants of a flash new car have been hurled clear, after it struck a narrow bridge, is entitled, *"Are we undone? Cast off? Nothing remaining?" - Timon of Athens, Act IV, Sc 1* (Fig. 2.265). Motoring proved a fertile new source of inspiration for Fuller's comic eye, as did the activities of trippers on Porthminster Beach. The series, though, gave rise to endless possible scenarios and, as well as reverting to tried and tested subjects, such as golf, he also included scenes outside his own personal experience, such as big game hunting.

Fuller got particularly immersed in this series in the autumn of 1901 and his notebook reveals the incredible speed at which he was able to produce these works, for during October he completed eleven titles, during November twenty-four and, in the first few days of December, a further eighteen more. Tucks paid £28-7-0 for two parts of the series, which they published under the title *Shakespeare Up-To-Date*, Hills & Co bought twelve for £36, Davidson Bros acquired and published six, Landeker & Brown bought four with motoring themes, which they published under the title *The Poetry of Motoring*, whilst others were acquired by Jonas, Wolf & Co and Stewart & Woolf. It seems somewhat surprising that publishers were happy to allow an artist to sell works with a similar theme to rival publishing companies, but clearly this was acceptable then. Whilst the concept was a good one and clearly appealed, Fuller's "misreadings" rarely seem very amusing today.

Another series that was popular was what Fuller called his 'Post Office' sketches. This comprised twelve scenes and was based around commonly seen post service signs. However, there is nothing on the postcards to indicate that they are part of this series, and so the humour can now easily be missed. Fuller did these in September 1903 and they were published by Stewart & Woolf. Several works, in typical Fuller fashion, rely on 'Mail' being interpreted as 'Male'. *The Last Mail* (Fig. 2.264), therefore, sees an unfortunate man being chased along a beach by a variety of ugly or elderly spinsters. It is Fuller's characterisation of these females that is more amusing than the insipid pun. Rather subtler is *No Collection on a Sunday*, depicting a vicar preaching to a sparse congregation in church, or *Gone Away, Left No Address*, showing two burglars leaving the grounds of a nice house carrying their swag.

Perhaps the most popular series that Fuller produced comprised lampoons of the Dutch, based almost entirely on the comic potential of the voluminous balloon-like breeches worn by Dutchmen, which were invariably heavily patched and seemed to stretch up to their armpits. Fuller records nearly forty titles in this series, done during October and November 1903, and, again, he seems to have sold them to a variety of publishers. Wunderlich & Co took twenty-six, Hildesheimers six, Max Ettlinger & Co Ltd six, whilst Tucks also produced a *Quaint Holland* series. However, the cards now appearing on the market were printed by Woolstone Bros. *Grateful Shade*, showing two children utilising the shade thrown by a Dutchman's breeches, or *Dutch Ware*, showing copiously patched breeches, are typical of the humour. However, in two scenes, *Art Critics* and *Sauce Hollandaise* (Fig.2.263), Fuller does depict artists working *en plein air*. The latter is one of the best of the series, from both comic and artistic viewpoints, for it shows a young child onlooker painting a funny face on the rear of the trousers of an artist, as, obliviously, he works away at his easel on the beach.

Fuller's notebook, which records this frenzied activity on his comic works during the years 1899 to 1903, ends in 1903 and there is nothing to suggest from postcards now coming on to the market that he did any further work in this vein.[578] As his cards had no particular Cornish connection, they could be sold all over the country, and some were adapted later into birthday, Christmas and other greetings cards. They were still popular in the 1920s but, having sold the copyright in most cases, Fuller enjoyed no further benefit from the success of any particular series. Having taken advantage of the extraordinary boom in the postcard market in the early years of the century, he happily reverted to his marine paintings and other interests. Fuller, however, was unique amongst St Ives artists in entering the comic postcard market and the number of publishers, who were taken with his work, demonstrates how his humour matched that of the age. His motoring sketches, featuring early cars, are now the ones that fetch the highest sums.

---

578 Fuller records selling for £21 to Raphael Tuck & Sons Ltd a Don Quixote series. I know of no cards or books reproducing these but the rather disappointing original art work came up at auction at Plymouth Auction Rooms on 18/6/2008 Lot 73. On 6th March 2008, at Clevedon Salerooms, amongst a host of items from Fuller's estate, including his notebook re his comic works, were the original art work for *My Old Dutch* and two Shakespearean misreadings, featuring motoring scenes *Fly further off, my Lord, fly further off'* and *How now my noble Lord? What all afoot?*.

Fig. 2.263 Edmund Fuller *Sauce Hollandaise*   (postcard)

Fig. 2.264 Edmund Fuller *The Last Mail*
(Stewart & Woolf postcard - series No 206)

Fig. 2.265 Edmund Fuller *"Are we undone? Cast off? Nothing remaining?"*
Timon of Athens, Act IV, Sc.1.
(Davidson Bros postcard - series 6081)

Fig. 2.266 Herbert Lanyon   *H.G. Fitzherbert*
(courtesy Andrew Lanyon)

2.7.2   The caricatures of 'Fitz'

Herbert George Fitzherbert (1875-1943), who was always referred to as 'Fitz' or H.G. Fitzherbert, had limited success with his paintings, but has secured for himself a significant place in the history of the colony, due to the two books of caricatures of his fellow residents that he produced in 1910 and 1913. Albeit these are of mixed quality and were only distributed locally, they provide a very different and fascinating slant on the artists, their leisure activities and the characters in the town with whom they socialised. Indeed, Fitzherbert demonstrates how he himself - like many of his fellow artists - was now actively involved with many different segments of the local community.

Fitzherbert has, in previous books, been referred to as an American, but, in fact, he was a New Zealander and was born at Marsden, Lower Hutt, Wellington. He was the eldest son of the engineer-artist, Sir William Fitzherbert (1843-1906), and was educated in Lower Hutt and then in Wanganui.[579] In the early years of the century, he came over to England to study at the Slade and contributed two cartoons to *Punch* in 1904. On 22nd January 1906, shortly before his father's death, he was married at St Paul's, South Kensington to Elsie Clement Smith, aged 21.[580] Their first child was born in November that year in 'The Count House', Carbis Bay, indicating that they had rented this property after the departure of the Ellises, pending the resumption of mining operations. However, in 1908, they moved to the five-bedroomed property, 'Seagulls', in Headland Road in Carbis Bay, which was their base for the rest of their stay in the area.[581] In September 1907, Fitzherbert and Herbert Lanyon put on a joint exhibition of "character sketches and artistic photos" in Lanyon's Attic Studio in St Andrew's Street, and it appears that the pair remained close friends. Fitzherbert was a member of the West Cornwall Golf Club by November 1907 and he joined the Arts Club in January 1908.

---

579 His father built him a studio in the garden at Marsden and he also painted with Nairn's group at Pumpkin Cottage, Silverstream, a summer house rented for members of the Wellington Art Club. A watercolour of the cottage by Fitzherbert is in the Fletcher-Trust Collection.

580 She was then living at 1 Glendower Place and her father, Clement Madeley Smith, was described simply as 'Gentleman'.

581 The property is advertised for sale in *St Ives Weekly Summary*, 18/4/1908. See Kelly's Directories for 1910 and 1914. This has been renamed, but still exists, next to 'Puffin Cottage'. I am grateful to Wendy Smaridge for this information.

Initially, on Show Days, he merely exhibited his comic sketches, done under the name 'Fitz', and, in 1910, he produced his first book of caricatures - *Caricatures from the Cornish Riviera*, which was published locally by Martin Cock, who had just set up the *St Ives Times*. It contained some fifty drawings, most of which are dated 1910, but the earliest examples, which are often significantly inferior in quality, date from 1908. The range of local personalities that he lampooned reveals the circles in which he mixed but, although I have seen several attempts at identifying the subjects, there is little consensus. Accordingly, for those who own a copy of this delightful book, I include in brackets the page number where any caricature mentioned can be located therein.

The book has a bizarre preface, which, even at the time, was considered unfunny. Fitz was keen on country sports and the largest group of caricatures feature his fox hunting colleagues. The best is *The Great Western Hounds in full cry* (p.39 - Fig. 2.267), but he also captures leading figures, such as William Craze from St Erth (p.51), who had been Mayor in 1877, 1887-8 and 1901, and Sir Thomas Robins Bolitho (p.55), the former High Sherriff of Cornwall, who was then Master of Foxhounds. This latter depiction of bedraggled horse and rider is a far cry from the impressive portrait of his Lordship on Barum in the region of Zennor done by fellow hunting enthusiast, Alfred Munnings, just a couple of years later.

Other caricatures capture friends from the then popular shooting parties, such as John Henry Tremayne (p.17), the proprietor of the Western Hotel, the venue where the artists played billiards. The caption reads, "I know this gentleman very well. Good shot? Oh, fair; He is pretty hot at rabbits, - if they keep still". Unperturbed, Tremayne even took out an advertisement in the book. Other hotel proprietors, such as Francis Wheeler of the Queen's Hotel (p.65), also feature, suggesting that Fitz was a regular in their bars, whilst other personalities around the town that are captured are the former Mayor Capt Thomas Row Harry (p.73 - Fig. 3.5), the Town Clerk and Coroner, Edward Boase (p.91 - Fig. 3.21), the auctioneer, William Benney (p.7 - Fig. 4.8), the Borough Surveyor, Francis Edward Wintle, who married Sydney Carr's daughter, Irene, (p.99 - Fig. 3.67), the Dentist Herbert Fooks (p.33 - Fig. 2.23), the surgeon, Dr William Smyth, the Barclay's Bank cashier, Edwin Anthony (p.53), local solicitor, Aubrey Bawden (p.19 top) and Edward Newton, the Secretary of RCPS (p.11 - Fig. 3.43). Fitzherbert may also have been involved with the Territorial Army, even before the War, as Major Thomas Chellew (p.35 - Fig. 3.7), the drill instructor, and Sergeant-Major Chaytor (p.23) are also featured, whilst, in 1913, a sketch by Fitzherbert graced the cover of a newly published song, entitled *Cornwall*, dedicated to No. 7 Company Cornwall Royal Garrison Artillery, with words by Folliott Stokes and music by W.R.Reeves. Fitzherbert was also a keen golfer, not only playing at Lelant, but also at Newquay, which he refers to, on the map incorporated into the frontispiece, as the 'longest in the world'. A rather good caricature features the secretary there - Willis (p.95).

Fig. 2.267 H.G.Fitzherbert *The Great Western Foxhounds in full cry*
(from *Caricatures of the Cornish Riviera* 1910)

Figs. 2.268-9   H.G. Fitzherbert
Caricatures of Edmund Fuller (left) and *Louis Grier*
(from *Caricatures of the Cornish Riviera* 1910)

There is greater consensus in relation to his depictions of artists The only artist shown at work is Julius Olsson (p.13 - Fig. 2.241). This is by far the best of the caricatures in the book, as it shows Olsson, renowned for his last minute productions of large canvases for the Royal Academy, holding a lifebelt, as he struggles to stop his moonlit sea flowing out of the frame. Fitz's depiction of the distinctive features of Noble Barlow, with bushy eyebrows and pointed beard, is also a fine caricature (p.31). Unsurprisingly, Herbert Lanyon is depicted at the piano (p.75 - Fig. 2.221). The caption to a rather sombre Edmund Fuller (p.27 - Fig. 2.268) is 'In Maiden Meditation. Fancy Free', for reasons unknown, whilst Louis Grier, with bushy moustache, is depicted in his customary cape, with the rather lame caption 'Cape Cornwall is 'not' the only Cape in England' (p.21 - Fig. 2.269). Jack Titcomb is portrayed as *The President* (p.87 - Fig. 2.213), as he was President of the Arts Club that year, whilst Folliott Stokes is labelled *A Moorland Prince*, after his novel *A Moorland Princess*, set around Zennor (p.89 - Fig. 2.93).

The caricatures confirm that, on winter evenings, the social life of the artists, and their friends from the town, seemed to revolve significantly around the billiard and card tables. Sydney Carr (p.15 - Fig. 2.222) and a rather puzzled looking Allan Deacon, in a fancy waistcoat (p.63 - Fig. 2.196), are depicted playing billiards, whilst Moffat Lindner, in a check jacket, is shown at cards (p.79 - Fig. 2.224). Other artists featured are considered to include Alfred Bailey (p.83 - Fig. 2.158) and Arthur Meade (p.81), who will not have been amused by his depiction as a fat, gruff bruiser, with large moustache and beret.[582] Fitzherbert exhibited fourteen of these caricatures at the RCPS show that autumn, priced at just 2 guineas each.

Fitzherbert's second series of caricatures, which was published, again by Martin Cock, in December 1913, was called *Everyone's Doing It*. This was a lengthy, pull-out, frieze-like depiction of characters running, ostensibly following the beagles. This clearly seems to have been inspired by Henry Rankin Poore's *The Fox Chase*, painted between 1901-5 on a narrow eight-foot canvas for the mantle of the fireplace in the dining room of Florence Griswold's House - the epicentre of the art colony at Old Lyme, Massachusetts.[583]   Quite how Fitzherbert knew of this work, which portrayed, in a humorous light,

---

582 It has been contended in the past that the caricature on p.77 of the book - 'The Heart Convention' features Arthur Meade. However, the most reliable source - the copy of the book owned originally by John Blowey - indicates that this character is called Robertson and that Arthur Meade is the rather fearsome figure shown on p.81.

583 Poore's work is illustrated in M Jacobs, *The Good and Simple Life*, Oxford, 1985 on pp.168-171.

Fig. 2.270 Edward Hain (junior), Reginald Boase (solicitor), Henry Keasbey and Herbert Fitzherbert

Fig. 2.271 Edward Anthony (bank cashier), Unknown, Herbert Fooks (dentist), Jack Titcomb,
Moffat Lindner, William Lloyd and Noble Barlow

Fig. 2.272 Anthony Bawden (solicitor), Louis Grier, Herbert Lanyon, Thomas Uren (Mayor)
and Henry Brown (of 'Scot's Craig')

Figs. 2.270-2   Sections from Fitz's *Everyone's Doing It*
(David Wilkinson, Book Gallery, St Ives - photography - David Romeo)

Fig. 2.273 Pearce 'Jackers' (Town Crier), William Trewhella and Colonel Henry Williams
(former Mayors), Davy Martin (ostler), Austin Philips (writer), and Martin Cock

Fig. 2.274 William Veal (fishmonger), Louis Sargent, unknown, Folliott Stokes and Count Larisch

Fig. 2.275 James Stevens ('Jimmy Limpots'), Billy [Schelke?], Walter Sterling,
W Prophet, Osborne ('Shanghai') and Jackie Farrell

Figs. 2.273-5   Sections from Fitz's *Everyone's Doing It*
(David Wilkinson, Book Gallery, St Ives - photography - David Romeo)

several Lyme artists running after a fox, past others at work and play, is unclear, for there is no suggestion that he had visited Old Lyme himself. Accordingly, one must presume that he had heard about it from an American artist visitor, with Old Lyme connections, who had passed through St Ives.[584] The beagle theme resulted from the relatively recent formation by Edward Hain (junior) of the Porthia Beagles, which attracted considerable interest locally.

The work is far more adventurous than its predecessor, for all the figures have to be shown in profile and in motion, and are generally depicted overlapping each other, requiring a degree of perspective. It is a considerable success, particularly as the actual caricatures are of a far more consistent quality than in the initial book. Quite a number of the personalities, who featured previously, are lampooned again, but, whereas the first book included only Fitz's acquaintances from the middle classes, this work includes a number of the fishermen, such as Jimmy Limpots, and other local characters, such as 'Shanghai', 'Jackers', the Town Crier, and Davy Martin, the ostler at the Queen's Hotel. Even some sporting celebrities, such as the County rugby player, Barrie Bennetts, and the Redruth referee, Dennis Lawry, are featured.

The leading seven figures are shown in hunting gear and so, presumably, they were the principal lights of the Porthia Beagles. At the front, appropriately, is Edward Hain, who was then living in Pednolver Terrace, next to Lowell Dyer. Behind him are Reginald Boase, the son of Edward Boase, who was also a solicitor and deputy Town Clerk, the American artist, Henry Keasbey, who is portrayed as a tall, clumsy man with big feet, and Fitzherbert himself (Fig. 2.270). The other hunting men are the local solicitor Mascie Taylor, Robert Read's son, Richard, and Francis Wheeler, the proprietor of the Queen's Hotel, who is shown on his backside, whilst a beagle surreptitiously lifts a leg over his upturned riding hat (Fig. 3.46). Artists in the chase include Lindner and Barlow, shown holding palettes, Jack Titcomb, with a set of golf clubs, Folliott Stokes, portrayed as a wild man of the moors with a club, a stylish Louis Grier, with check plus-fours, Herbert Lanyon with bugle, a rather effete Will Lloyd and a dandified Louis Sargent. Others who moved in artistic circles at that time included the publisher, Martin Cock, the writer, Austin Phillips, and Count Larisch, then much feted by members of the colony due to his connections to the Bavarian Royal Family. The extent of the print run is not known, but, as it featured so many of the local community, it soon sold out, but surviving copies of what is a considerable accomplishment, which is of such social historical value, are rare.

Fig. 2.276 H.G.Fitzherbert *Kits and Fitz*
(courtesy Ellen Shepherd)

---

584 Frederick Waugh knew Poore, having worked with him in Barbizon in 1884.

On Show Day in 1912, Fitzherbert exhibited some work in oils for the first time - landscapes with good atmospheric effects - and he appears to have taken lessons from Noble Barlow. Between 1912 and 1922, he had just four works hung at the ROI, but *The Times* was taken with his 1913 exhibit there, *Frosty Morning*, which was hailed as "a sketch in which the swift beauty of handling has the same effect as the beauty of words in a lyric".[585]

Fitzherbert appears in images as a dapper fellow, well dressed and invariably wearing a cravat. In self portraits, he shows himself wearing a top hat and smoking a cigar. Evidence has emerged, however, of an affair that he carried on for some years, with Catherine Power, known as Kit, from County Waterford, who used to pay regular visits down to St Ives each summer with her sister, Mary Reddie, who later was a friend of Frances Hodgkins. The romance could have blossomed due to a joint love of country pursuits, and, each year, they managed to spend time together at Juan-les-Pins in the South of France. Kit, being a Catholic, refused to contemplate marrying Fitz, in view of his marital status, but, in 1912, he gave her a copy of *The Rubaiyat of Omar Khayam*, inscribed 'Kits from Fitz' and containing on its frontispiece not only a self-portrait but a depiction of them picnicking together under a tree (Fig. 2.276).

After serving with distinction in the War, Fitzherbert appears to have settled in Exmouth, but clearly retained some links with St Ives, for he contributed two works to Mary Lanyon's Doll's House and did not resign his membership of the Golf Club until 1925.[586] In 1927, he started to contribute, with some regularity, to *Punch* and continued to do so for the rest of his life, despite moving to South Africa in 1933, in an effort to obtain respite from asthma. He died in Johannesburg in 1943.

Fig. 2.277 Sydney Carr   *Venus and Adonis*
(the late Derek Wintle/Andrew Eggleston)

---

585 *St Ives Times* 10/10/1913.
586 The Doll's House works were *Bruges* and *Clodgy*, with the former being dated 1925.

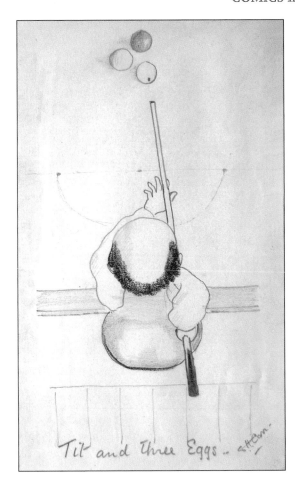

Figs. 2.278-9 Sydney Carr *Tit and three eggs*
Spheroids
Caricatures of Jack Titcomb
(the late Derek Wintle/Andrew Eggleston)

2.7.3   The caricatures of Sydney Carr

It was with great excitement that I discovered, amongst the papers of the descendants of Sydney Carr, a series of caricatures, in pencil, for these were never published and so are completely unknown. Thirteen have survived and, although none are dated, they probably were produced at much the same time as those by Fitz. Unfortunately, the identity of the majority of the characters portrayed has not been recorded and has remained elusive, despite making comparisons with Fitz.[587] Unmistakeable, though, is his depiction of Moffat Lindner, shown, as by Fitz, in check jacket, with an unruly curl in his hair, and playing cards - *Spades! Every Time!!!* (Fig. 2.225). Like Fitz, Carr confirms that a lot of time was spent during winter evenings not only playing cards but around the billiards table, and there are also two delightful caricatures of Jack Titcomb, with cue in hand (Figs. 2.278-9). Clearly renowned for his large posterior, *Spheroids* pokes fun at his figure, whilst *Tit and three eggs* is an overhead view of him lining up a shot, in which his balding pate is likened to a bird's nest, with billiard balls as the eggs! He himself, of course, was the Tit.

Perhaps the most interesting of the Carr caricatures, however, are the pair concerning Havelock and Edith Ellis. One can imagine that, even among relatively enlightened members of the community, the writings of Ellis on sexual inversion raised a few eyebrows, and the unusual nature of their marriage, which saw Edith on her own for lengthy periods of time and each indulge in relatively open affairs with other women, must have caused, in different segments of the town, a mixture of outrage, incomprehension and, possibly, mirth. Carr's title for one of his caricatures, *Naughty!* (Fig. 2.77), perhaps sums up neatly, in one word, the general feeling. In the scene, a nude Edith appears to be telling off a beaming Havelock for touching her bottom, a reference perhaps to Edith's known preference for lesbian relationships. His other caricature, which he called *Venus and Adonis*, is rather subtler. In the mythological story, Venus, who is "sick-thoughted with love", tries to seduce Adonis, but cannot rouse him to sexual desire. On discovering, the following day, that Adonis had been killed in a hunting accident, she pronounces a curse on love. In Carr's depiction, Havelock, as Adonis, is indeed shown unmoved, but Edith, whilst again naked, is not trying to tempt him, but is instead covering herself up and has a look of disgust on her face. One can imagine that this pair of sketches caused peels of laughter when shown to Carr's close friends.

---

587 One called *There goes another 6d* seems to be of the rather lugubrious Hitchens, who features in *Caricatures of the Cornish Riviera* at p. 25. The only other ones with titles are *A Club Meeting* and *Rex!*

Fig. 2.280 Ruth Simpson
Portrait of Frank Ver Beck (detail)

2.7.4   The comic world of Frank Ver Beck

With Fuller having given up his comic work, Carr having left for Teignmouth and Fitzherbert having enlisted, the horrors of the War years would not have been able to have been alleviated by a dash of humour, had it not been for the arrival in the colony in 1913 of the American comic illustrator, William Francis Ver Beck (1858-1933).[588]

Frank Ver Beck was best known as an illustrator of children's books, usually with a humorous bent. He had produced illustrations from the 1890s for a number of other authors, but the turning point in his career was the publication in 1906 of *Ver Beck's Book of Bears*, and he became very well-known for his comic depictions of animated teddy bears. In fact, he was described by the local paper as "the originator of the Teddy Bear".[589] He followed this up in 1910 with *Ver Beck's Bears in Mother Gooseland*. This was a work to which his second wife, Hanna Rion, contributed as well, as the subtitle records "The New Lines by Hanna Rion, The Old Lines by Mother Goose herself". She was also a well-known writer, having published a novel and several books on gardening.[590]

The arrival of the Ver Becks was particularly welcomed by Herbert Lanyon, as Hanna Rion had initially been a professional musician and composer, performing, on the piano, joint concerts with her first husband W.V.Abell, whom she had married in 1894.[591] Accordingly, the Sunday evening soirées at Lanyon's house now included a further star turn. In July 1914, Frank gave Lanyon a copy of *Ver Beck's Book of Bears* and inscribed it with a little drawing and, the following year, when he published *The Little Bear Lost - A Short Little Tale from Bruintown* (Fig. 2.283), he gave a copy to Lanyon, inscribing it, "Dear Mr Lanyon, If you should go to Bruintown, please be as kind to this little bear as you have been to Frank Ver Beck".[592] Later, when presumably Lanyon was unwell, he sent him a drawing of one of his bears playing the bagpipes, with the message "Cheer up, Old Man!!" (Fig. 2.281).

---

588 Their presence is first noted by Bleistift, *Art and Artists*, *St Ives Times*, 7/11/1913, when he mentions that they had been working in the town "since last midsummer".

589 *St Ives Times*, 21/6/1918, in the account of his stepdaughter's wedding.

590 Her published work included *The Garden in the Wilderness* (1909 - under the pseudonym, A Hermit), a novel, *The Smiling Road* (1910), and *Let's Make A Flower Garden* (1912), all of which had been illustrated by Ver Beck.

591 She studied musical composition under Heinrich Barth in Berlin

592 In 1923, after he had left St Ives, when he returned to the theme with *The Little Bear who ran away from Bruintown*, he again sent an inscribed copy to Lanyon. My thanks are due to James Church for alerting me to the Ver Beck/Lanyon friendship and for providing me with images evidencing this.

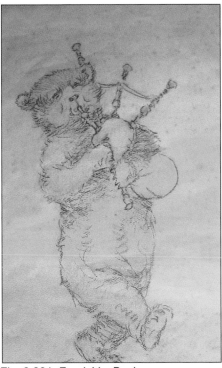

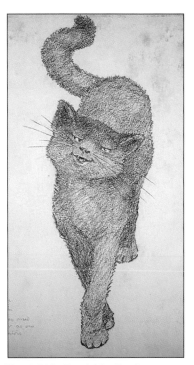

Fig. 2.281 Frank Ver Beck
Cheer Up, Old Man!!
(Lanyon family archive)

Fig. 2.282 Frank Ver Beck
Tanky Tunk
(Lanyon family archive)

Ver Beck's talents, however, were not restricted to bears and, on Show Day in 1916, he also exhibited some comic illustrations of turtles, for a book to be called *The Amazing Adventures of Timothy Turtle*. The book was published that year under the title *Timothy Turtle's Great Day* but is extremely rare. However, John Douglas recorded some of the illustrations in a series of photographs (see Fig. 2.284). The Show Day reviewer commented, "It is difficult to say at what age children would cease to admire these quaint studies - methinks they would last as long as a person's sense of humour".[593] Other stories that he published during his time in England included *Piggywiggen - A Little Pig Who Went to Market*, *The Elephant Child* and *The Donkey Child*. The latter two seem to be from a series of Little Black Sambo titles that he did about the adventures of African-American boys, which may now be considered of dubious political correctness.

Fig. 2.283 Frank Ver Beck Cover illustration from
The Little Bear Lost - A Short Little Tale from Bruintown
(Lanyon family archive)

Fig. 2.284 Frank Ver Beck
Timothy Turtle meets his froggy friends
(John Douglas - courtesy David Wilkinson)

593 *St Ives Times*, 16/3/1916.

Fig. 2.285 Frank Ver Beck *St Ives, Where Numerous Cats Abide, and Where Tanky Tunk Found a Happy Home*
(Skinner, Inc. Boston and Bolton MA)

Another project that he worked upon in St Ives, which may not have come to fruition, was a book called *The Little Cat Who Journeyed to St Ives*, about the adventures in St Ives of the tom-cat, Tanky Tunk (Fig. 2.282).[594] In 2003, ten illustrations for this book were sold at Skinner Inc, Boston.[595] The frontispiece was based on a photo of St Ives taken from Porthminster Point, with a border of cats drawn round it and the title decoration superimposed (Fig. 2.285). Other illustrations featured Tanky being attacked by geese and at the helm of a boat with an owl in the bows.

With many of the artists having children of their own, Ver Beck's publications were appreciated in the colony, but it is likely to have been his dry humour at social gatherings that made him friends. He certainly seems to have mixed well with other artists, whilst in St Ives. He sat for two portraits by Frances Hodgkins and Ruth Simpson, the latter, now in the Royal Cornwall Museum, revealing a distinguished countenance, with round glasses and grey hair, and showing him in a blue painting smock, clutching a cigarette (Fig. 2.280). One might imagine that an artist of his ilk would have indulged in caricature from time to time and two pen and ink sketches of Noble Barlow and Folliott Stokes have been located. The latter, so beloved of caricaturists, is again portrayed as a big man, with centre parting, large moustache and check trousers.

---

594 A postcard to Herbert Lanyon in August 1919 in which he comments, "I feast tonight on green peas - Tanky too shall have some" suggests that he was working on it still at that juncture. My thanks again to James Church.
595 Auction dated 21/11/2003 Lots 93-102.

PART THREE

THE BEACH ST. IVES.

THE ARTISTS AND THE TOWNSFOLK

IN THE PRE-WAR ERA

THE ARTISTS AND LOCAL BUSINESSMEN

3.1.1   Introduction

One of the most intriguing aspects of the social history of the colony is how the artists got on with the locals, particularly as the Cornish were quite insular and considered anyone from outside the County to be a 'foreigner'.   Whilst standard summer tourists were an irritation that had to be put up with for a few months a year, given their importance to the health of the local economy, the decision by ever greater numbers of artists to settle in the town made them a conspicuous presence at all times, which could not be ignored. St Ives, like most towns in Cornwall, had, for many generations, been dominated by Methodists, but it had gained a reputation, even in the Duchy, as being notoriously strict in its observance not only of the Sabbath, but also of teetotalism. Accordingly, the ways of the artists were very different to the sober mode of life encouraged by Methodist ministers. It is not surprising, therefore, that, in some quarters, the artists' lifestyle was often frowned upon.[596] Even the Editor of *The Cornishman* lamented the coming of "lady artists, gentlemen artists, their sisters, their cousins and their aunts", and commented, "They romp, they sing at the most ridiculous times of the night, they flirt, they spoon, they sketch - in fact their 'Bohemian' ways...astonish us."[597] The sin of 'sketching' particularly amused Stanhope Forbes. However, more open-minded members of the community, who could often match the artists in terms of wealth and education, if not in cultural experience, soon appreciated other attributes of the artists, for they had an immediate impact on business, as a result of the requirements not only of themselves, but also of the additional tourists that they attracted to the town. Furthermore, members of the colony demonstrated a determination, from the outset, to become actively involved in the cultural and sporting life of the town. Accordingly, they were soon fraternising happily with local dignitaries, professionals and tradesmen.

3.1.2   Local dignitaries

One of the first local Societies that the artists joined was the St Ives Choral Society. This immediately enabled them to mix with some of the local hierarchy, for the President of the Society was Edward Hain, the pre-eminent figure in the town, the Treasurer was James Read, a senior Bank Manager, the Secretary was Edward Boase, the Town Clerk, who had married James Read's daughter, and the librarian was James Read's son, Robert Sawle Read, a ship broker and close associate of Hain, whilst the Committee also included William Trewhella, a member of a long-established St Ives family. All of these important dignitaries were to become long-term friends of the artists.

Edward Hain (1851-1917) was the fourth person with that name in the Hain dynasty, and his great-grandfather had established a small fleet of sailing vessels that operated from St Ives. Showing no interest in going to sea, Edward was sent to the local branch of Bolitho's Bank to train in accountancy and book-keeping, and then moved to London to work in a tea merchant's office. In 1878, he presented his father with an ultimatum - either the family business purchase steamships or he would resign. In addition to significant investment from the Bolitho and Hain families, a large number of locals were persuaded of the merits of the venture and the first steamship was commissioned from Readhead's yard at South Shields. By 1901, when the various ship ventures were amalgamated into one company, there were twenty-two steamers and, by 1913, there were thirty-six, with five more on order. All had been funded by revenue, without any call on capital.

Despite this thriving business, which enabled him to build, in 1892-3, a huge new home, 'Treloyhan Manor', designed by Silvanus Trevail, on the cliff edge between St Ives and Carbis Bay, Hain still had time for both local and national politics. He was first elected on to the St Ives Town Council in 1883 and served as a councillor and alderman for twenty years, being Mayor in 1884-6, 1889, 1895 and 1899. He also served on Cornwall County Council for fifteen years and, between 1900 and 1906, he was the local Member of Parliament. In 1912, he was appointed High Sheriff for Cornwall and was knighted for his services to British shipping. He was also the first person to have conferred upon him the freedom of the Borough of St Ives. Whilst he himself was often away from the town, his children, Edward and

---

596 At the time of the 1851 Census, 32% of the population of the County were Methodists, whereas only 13.2% were Church of England - T. Shaw, *A History of Cornish Methodism*, Truro, 1967 at p.3.

597 *The Cornishman*, 6/10/1887.

Fig. 3.1 Edward Hain, his father and his three children.
Grace, who died young, Kate and Edward.
(St Ives Trust Archive Study Centre)

Fig. 3.2 Lady Hain, her daughter, Kate,
and Ruth Williams on The Wharf
(St Ives Museum)

Kate, fraternised repeatedly with the artists and their families. Edward (junior), as already seen, set up the Porthia Beagles, which 'Fitz' depicted, and 'Kitty' was well-liked by the artists. For instance, in 1913, she went to Rome with Mabel Douglas, where they were shown the sights by Louie Whitehouse, who was then living there.[598] Sir Edward died in 1917, having never truly recovered from his son's death in 1915 at Gallipoli. Kate inherited the Porthia Estate, comprising over 2500 acres, on her brother's death, but sold this in 1930, when she moved to live in Hampshire with her second husband, Eric Bullivant. 'Treloyhan Manor', had previously been sold, following Lady Hain's death, to a hotel company, and is now a Methodist Conference Centre.

Fig. 3.3 'Treloyhan Manor'   (St Ives Trust Archive Study Centre)

598   Letter from Jeannie to Arnold Whitehouse dated 6/4/1913 - Gloucester Records Office, Whitehouse archive (Bundle 2/10).

Robert Sawle Read (1863-1932), the eldest son of the banker, James Read, was born when his father was working in Penzance. He too trained as a banker, but became a ship broker, working closely with Edward Hain. They were partners in the firm, Foster, Hain and Read, and he was appointed the local managing director of the Hain Steamship Company. They also both had stakes in the Porthminster Hotel. Read lived initially in Albany Terrace in St Ives, before moving in the mid-1890s to 'Beaumont', Talland Road, and then, by 1910, to the even more substantial 'Lansdowne' in The Bellyars, long since converted into numerous flats. Following the demise of the Choral Society, he joined Louis Grier's acting company in 1890 and socialised regularly with the artists, taking part in the Carnival Masquerades in 1892-3. He was also a keen sportsman, being, for many years, President of the local tennis and rugby clubs. Described on his death as "open-minded, open-hearted and open-handed", he too was a great servant of the town.[599] He was first elected to the Town Council in 1891 and served as Mayor in 1897-8, 1904-6 and 1912-3. He was also a Justice of the Peace and County Magistrate. He appears to have had a keen interest in art, as he rented one of the Malakoff Studios for a number of years, and, after the death of his first wife, Jane, in 1917, he married, in June 1920, Lizzie Blackburn Hutton (d.1963), then aged forty, one of the sisters of the artist, Robert Langley Hutton.

William Trewhella (1844-1938), a member of an ancient St Ives family, will also have first fraternised with the artists, due to his position on the Committee of the Choral Society, and he again was invited to take part in the Carnival Masquerade in 1893. He referred to himself in Kelly's Directory as a seine owner, for, in 1876, he had acquired from his father, Matthew, shares in the Friendship Pilchard Fishery Co. However, with the decline in the fisheries, he probably made more money as a property developer. Although diminutive in stature (see Fig. 2.273), he was a highly regarded figure. He was first elected to the Town Council in 1892, made a Justice of the Peace in 1893 and became Mayor in 1894, the year that St Ives suffered a terrible flood. Having initially lived in The Terrace, he acquired, in 1891, from Dr Nicholls 'Brunswick House', which he re-named 'Trewyn', meaning 'the fair place'. This had originally been built by a local entrepreneur, James Halse, but, over the years, he altered and extended it significantly, even erecting a new front in 1905. He also bought and demolished properties to enlarge his garden. His billiard room, erected in 1908, subsequently became Barbara Hepworth's studio. As noted below, two of his sons, Bernard and Cecil, married members of the artistic community, whilst his eldest son, William, became, for some years in the 1920s, Vicar of Zennor - a district with which the family had long associations, as it was one Matthew Trewhella, who was reputedly enticed away by the Zennor mermaid!

Fig. 3.4 'Trewyn' in the 1950s   (St Ives Trust Archive Study Centre)

---

599 *St Ives Times*, 18/11/1932.

Fig. 3.5 H.G.Fitzherbert *Father Neptune*
Caricature of Capt Thomas Row Harry
(from *Caricatures of the Cornish Riviera*)

Another Mayor, who became a good friend of the artists, was Captain Thomas Row Harry. Born in St Ives in 1835, Harry had had an adventurous career at sea, which had taken him to far-flung corners of the globe.[600] In particular, he had been Captain of the Australian grain clipper, *Hesperus*, for many years. On his retirement in 1889, he had immediately been elected on to the Town Council and served as Mayor in 1896, 1900 and 1903. During his first period of office, he was presented to Queen Victoria, and he briefly gained notoriety in the London press in the mid-1890s, after his irate tirade at Sir Hudson Kearley, of the Board of Trade, who had dismissed the need for a Harbour of Refuge at St Ives.[601] With his impressive long, white beard shaking as he spoke, he had been dubbed 'Father Neptune', a title used by 'Fitz' for his caricature of Harry (Fig. 3.5). William Titcomb was another artist, who admired Captain Harry, as he painted his portrait (Plate 38), not under commission, but as "a direct expression of respect by a clever artist for a fellow townsman who has endeavoured to conscientiously discharge a public and important duty".[602] Harry too employed Silvanus Trevail, in 1895, to design a fine new house for himself on Porthminster Hill, which he called 'Morwenstow'. This was later known as 'Chy-an-Dour' and, despite this pedigree, has recently been demolished. Harry's daughter, Charlotte, was also well-known in the artistic community, as she married the Reverend Griffin, who was a good friend to the artists.

Another key figure in the town in the new century, who owned work by the local artists, was Colonel Henry Willey Williams. Born in St Ives in 1838, he had started as a booking clerk at Waterloo Station in 1856 and worked his way up to become City Superintendent for the London and South Western Railway, a position that he held for seventeen years, before moving to the London and St Katherine Dock Company. He ended an illustrious career as sole manager of Royal Victoria and Albert Docks, before returning to his native town in 1901 to take an active role in local affairs, becoming an influential member of the Cornwall Sea Fisheries Committee and Mayor in 1910-11.[603] He also was offered the freedom of the Borough.

Fig. 3.6   Colonel Henry Willey Williams

---

600 See David Tovey, *W H Y Titcomb, A Newlyner from St Ives*, Tewkesbury, 2003 at p.118.

601 See W.J.Jacobs, *Memories of Eighty Years 1880-1960*, at pp.41-2. Copy held at St Ives Archive Centre.

602 *St Ives Weekly Summary* 21/12/1901.

603 *Fair Play*, reproduced in *St Ives Weekly Summary*, 24/11/1900.

3.1.3 Professionals

Once the artists started to stay in the town for extended periods, they needed the services of local professionals, such as bankers, solicitors, doctors and dentists, and friendships soon developed.

James Read, who had been born in 1823 in Penryn, had moved to St Ives from Penzance in the early 1870s to become Manager of St Ives Bank. In the early 1890s, this became part of the Consolidated Bank of Cornwall. He was one of the first locals to invite the American artist, Howard Russell Butler, around to his house in 1886 and Butler, who had no doubt initially consulted him over the transfer of funds from America, recorded enjoyable musical evenings spent in his company.

James Read, who, after the death of his first wife, Emma, married a woman thirty-four years his junior, had four children - Jessie, Robert, Mary and Orlando.[604] His daughter, Mary, married the solicitor, Edward Boase, who had been born in Marylebone in 1858. They lived initially in Islington and Lincoln, where he was practising, but decided to base themselves in Cornwall in the mid-1880s, presumably when Edward was offered the post of Town Clerk at St Ives.[605] However, they never lived in St Ives, but were based initially in Madron, before moving to 'The Hollies', Alverton Terrace, Penzance, probably in 1892. Boase rapidly established himself in St Ives, becoming also Clerk to the Harbour Authority and Clerk to the Hayle local board and sanitary authority and Coroner for West Cornwall, retaining all these posts until the early 1920s.[606] Like his brother-in-law, Robert Read, Boase soon mixed with the artists and, after the collapse of the Choral Society, he took part, with his brother, Richard, in Louis Grier's acting company in 1890. His sister, Kate, born in Hampstead in 1862, was also a regular performer at the artists' entertainments, and they both joined in the Carnival Masquerades, as did James Read's youngest son, Orlando, then training to be an accountant.

Edward Boase also practised as a solicitor in St Ives, Hayle and Penzance and his son, Reginald, joined him for a time, becoming Deputy Town Clerk and Deputy Coroner (see Fig. 2.270). In most instances, the artists will not have provided the local professionals with any unusual work, but Edward Boase received a considerable amount of national publicity when he was instructed, in 1890, by Edward Simmons to sue the Royal Academy, as it had incorrectly marked his painting *John Anderson, My Jo* as sold, and had failed to remedy the position despite repeated requests. Boase argued that this had prevented Simmons from making a sale of the painting. Such an action caused a huge stir in the art world and Simmons was accused of indulging in "cheap American advertising", but eventually Boase did obtain a formal apology from the Academy. The publicity will have done neither Simmons nor himself any harm.

Thomas John Chellew (1869-1940) was another local solicitor, who fraternised with the artists. Born in St Ives, he did his articles in London and returned to the town in c.1892. He is first recorded in Kelly's Directory in 1893, when he was living in Draycot Terrace and practising in Skidden Hill, and he acted for many of the local mining concerns and seine companies. He took part in the Carnival Masquerade in 1893 and featured in a number of the artists' entertainments. Having married Maud, the eldest daughter of Colonel Henry Williams, he had, by 1910 - Williams' year as Mayor - , become Clerk to the Magistrates. He and his wife lived at 'St Merryn', Trelyon, and, by 1922, he had taken over as Town Clerk from Edward Boase. He was also President of the Rugby Club and a leading freemason, but H.G.Fitzherbert caricatures him in his role as Drill Instructor for the Territorial Army (Fig.3.7), in which he rose to the rank of Lieutenant-Colonel. It was due to his contacts that Olsson managed to secure a commission for Elmer Schofield in the War.

Fig. 3.7 H.G. Fitzherbert
Caricature of Thomas Chellew
(from *Caricatures of the Cornish Riviera*)

---

604 At the time of the 1891 Census, he is recorded as a widower, but, by 1901, when he was 78, he is liiving with his second wife, Gertrude, then aged 44, and his unmarried elder daughter, Jessie, then aged 39!

605 His eldest child, Reginald, was born in Islington in 1882 and his second child, Kate, was born in Lincoln in 1884.

606 It is interesting, however, that, in Colonel Williams' reminiscences, he indicated that he had to point out, when he became Mayor, that various practices of the Council relating to disclosure of private interests in contracts and such like, upon which Boase should have advised, were wrong - see Col.H.W.Williams, *Some Reminiscences (1838-1918)*, Penzance 1918.

Fig. 3.8 H.G.Fitzherbert
Caricatures of Barrie Bennetts and Dennis Lawry
(from *Everyone's Doing it*) (David Wilkinson)

Fitzherbert features four other solicitors in his caricatures - Anthony Bawden and Mascie Taylor, who were based in St Ives, the latter being a particularly regular guest at the Arts Club, and Dennis Lawry and Barrie Bennetts, who were based primarily in Penzance. However, the latter two are both depicted in sporting garb. Lawry (c.1870-1924) was a stalwart of rugby in the County, serving as Secretary of Cornwall Rugby Union for over twenty-five years, and is depicted as a pot-bellied referee, whilst Bennetts, who played rugby for England and who later went into partnership with Edward Boase, is shown as a flying winger. In the 1920s, Bennetts was a regular performer at the Arts Club on violin and viola.

Dr George Thomas Albert Staff LKQCP Irel. and Dr John Michael Nicholls (1858-1937) LRCP Lond.were the two local G.P.'s. George Staff, who also acted as Admiralty surgeon, had come from Queensland in 1880 and lived in 'Chy-an-Porth' on The Terrace. He was the Medical Officer of Health for the District, when the artists first settled in the town. However, Michael Nicholls, who was born in Redruth and who moved to St Ives in the mid-1880s, direct from his hospital training, had taken over that role by 1893 and was to be the principal doctor in the town until 1936. As already indicated, it was Nicholls, whom William Jacobs described as "the most handsome young man I ever saw....and the envy of all the eligible young ladies in the neighbourhood", who forced the local Council to improve the local drainage facilities, shortly after his arrival.[607] He also was elected Mayor in 1892 and served as the St Ives representative on the County Council from 1901, when Hain resigned, for over twenty-five years. For a long time unmarried, he lived until 1891 at 'Brunswick House' (later 'Trewyn'), enjoying the extensive gardens there, and then for over twenty-five years at 'Penwyn', a semi-detached property with marvellous views, situated on The Terrace, close to the entrance to the railway station (now the Regent Hotel).[608] Nicholls, who was an amateur painter himself, appears to have converted one of the large rooms in the property into a studio, with a northern light, and examples of his work are held by St Ives Museum.[609] The property, however, was one of those sold by the Cowley Estate in 1919 and Nicholls moved into 27 The Terrace until his death in 1937.[610] Both doctors are featured in *Portalone*. Nicholls (in the novel, Dr Peters) was described as a handsome, vigorous, large-hearted Cornishman, with white teeth and grey moustache, who rode like the summer wind over the moors to attend his patients at Zennor, with his giant greyhound beside him.[611] However, according to Ranger-Gull, the artists considered Nicholls a "reckless devil" and preferred the more refined Dr Staff (in the novel, Mr St John), "who sang chansonettes in their houses".[612] There might also have been concerns about Nicholls' reputation with the ladies!

607 See W.J.Jacobs, *Memories of Eighty Years 1880-1960*, privately published, 1960 at p.13 (copy at St Ives Archive Centre).

608 The Trewhella family called an apple tree in the grounds 'Dr Nicholls' apple tree'.

609 See description of property when for sale in 1927 - *St Ives Times*, 25/11/1927.

610 His wife, formerly Miss Grace Brooking, of Halsetown, committed suicide, whilst depressed, in 1933. She was only aged 48, but had fallen off a ladder the previous year and had subsequently suffered severe head pains, causing insomnia. *St Ives Times* 5/5/1933.

611 Nicholls' obituary confirms that, in his youth, he was "a spruce, sporting doctor, well-known for the magnificent horses he rode and for his delight at residing in such a lovely country district" - *St Ives Times*, 16/1/1937. Jacobs also records, "It was a picture to see him riding on his rounds to the country districts on a beautiful black horse followed by two St Bernard dogs" - W.J.Jacobs, *Memories of Eighty Years 1880-1960*, privately published, 1960 at p.13 (copy at St Ives Archive Centre).

612 C.Ranger-Gull, *Portalone*, London, 1904 at p.86-7.

Fig. 3.9 Edmund Fuller   Letterhead design for James White

3.1.4   Tradesmen

The artists had particular requirements that entrepreneurial shopkeepers soon learnt. For instance, the tailor needed to increase his supply of plus-fours and check jackets, the dress shop needed more fashionable clothes, with additional frills, and a greater selection of hats, whilst the off-licence needed many more bottles of whisky and a good supply of tobacco!

One of the local businessman, who recognised at an early juncture, the importance of the artists was James Uren White, who had been born at Madron and who had worked at the offices of *The Cornish Telegraph* in Penzance, before setting up in St Ives as a stationer and printer in 1882. After producing a short-lived monthly pictorial in 1885-6, he founded, in May 1889, St Ives' first newspaper, the *St Ives Weekly Summary and Visitors' List*. Indeed, his opening lines, written in doggerel verse, explaining his reasons for the launch of the paper, indicate that the impact of the artists had played an important part in his decision, for they ran,

> *"This year the pictures in th' Academy*
> *By artists who last Summer made St Ives*
> *Their happy hunting-ground and rendezvous,*
> *Must help materially to swell the ranks*
> *Of cultured folk who come down year by year*
> *To visit our health-giving neighbourhood....."*

White appreciated that the artists were an integral part of the community and, accordingly, always made certain that their achievements were recorded. Therefore, in addition to full reviews of nearly every painting exhibited on Show Days, the paper included notes of works hung at London and major provincial exhibitions, awards won and sales effected, so that local people could take pride in the achievements of "their artists". Visitors too, whilst checking out who else was staying in town, were made aware of the artists' accomplishments, in the hope of tempting further sales. Furthermore, the entertainments put on by members of the colony for local causes were also fully reported, so that their presence and impact locally could not be missed. Sometimes the mere fact that an artist had returned from his travels made news. William Jacobs, who served a five year apprenticeship under White, described him as a hard taskmaster, but he was generally considered a very pleasant, genial man. Edmund Fuller seems to have been a particular friend, for he was asked to design White's headed notepaper (Fig. 3.9), and White used a woodcut by him for the cover of his short Handbook for Visitors, which was the first Guide to the town.[613] Although White sold his paper to *The Cornishman* in 1910, he sold his press and type to Martin Osborne Cock (c.1879-1940), who started the *St Ives Times* a few months later.

---

613   See W.J.Jacobs, *Memories of Eighty Years 1880-1960*, privately published, 1960 at p.81 (copy at St Ives Archive Centre).

Fig. 3.10 James White's shop at No 1, Fore Street
(St Ives Trust Archive Study Centre/St Ives Museum)

Born in Pelynt, Cornwall, Martin Cock initially came to St Ives in his teens to reside with his uncle, James Wearne, who ran a Stationery and Printing Business. Having gained some experience as a manager of a London printers, he came back to St Ives in 1905 and took over his uncle's business. Cock's decision to launch a new paper in 1910 was a brave one, for William Jacobs had established the *Western Echo* in 1899, but this, being directed principally at the 'Down-along' section of the town, had noticeably less coverage of the artists' activities. For a decade, St Ives supported all three papers, but, shortly after the War, the *St Ives Weekly Summary* became subsumed into *The Cornishman*. In the early years of the War, when Cock needed help at the *St Ives Times*, James Uren White, who had continued as a correspondent for a number of Cornish papers, assisted with editing duties, until he became ill in 1916. Although continuing with some reporting until 1924, he was in poor health until his death aged 72 in 1927.[614]

The local tradesman, who made it his business to satisfy as many of the needs of the artists as possible, was James Kempthorne Lanham (1848-1931).[615] Born in London, Lanham opened a general merchants store in the High Street in St Ives in 1869, when he was just twenty. His business was listed in Cornwall directories as 'Fancy Repository & tobacconist' in 1873, and 'Ale & Porter Merchant' and 'Wine & Spirit Merchant' in 1883. He is reputed to have started to sell artists' materials in the early 1880s, on the suggestion of Whistler, who had had to send all the way to Cambridge for his paints.[616] However, it was not until 1887 that the term 'artists' colourman' was used by Lanham in the description of his business for the Cornwall Directories. He also added that year 'with associated gallery', and the exhibition gallery that he established at that time became the principal outlet for the sale of work by the St Ives artists in Cornwall (see Chapter 3.4.2.2). The entry in Kelly's Directory in 1889 reveals the extensive range of the business, for Lanham now described himself as 'Artists' colourman, china, glass and earthen ware dealer, general ironmonger & cutler, general draper & furniture dealer, & ale & porter bottler, wine & spirit merchants'. As a result, Lewis Hind, in listing St Ives' attractions, was moved to comment, "There is a shop - a wonderful shop - where everything that an artist can possibly require as painter, householder or as batchelor may be purchased."[617]

---

614 See *St Ives Times*, 13/6/1924 and 8/7/1927.

615 Lanham's date of birth, about which there has been some uncertainty, due to the 1881 and 1891 Censuses implying that it was in 1843-4, is recorded on his gravestone in Barnoon Cemetery as 29/10/1848.

616 Marion Whybrow records in *St Ives 1883-1993 - Portrait of an Art Colony*, Woodbridge, 1994 at p.39 that Lanham had told this story to the artist Arthur White.

617 *In Painters' Land*, *St Ives Weekly Summary* 10/10/1896.

Fig. 3.11 Lanham's shop in the High Sttreet   (St Ives Trust Archive Study Centre)

Lanham took the greatest pains to ensure that he supplied the very best materials, visiting every prominent art gallery on the Continent and sourcing his paints from a wide range of countries.[618] It is unlikely that Lanham made such journeys purely on his own initiative; in all probability, they reflect numerous discussions with artists in the colony as to their recommendations, following their painting experiences on the Continent. Growing confident of his expertise, Lanham advertised nationally, for example in *The Year's Art*, and listed as his suppliers James Newman, G.Edouard, Schoenfeld and Winsor & Newton for oil and watercolours, and G.Edouard for soft pastels. He also promoted 'Cow-Hair Landseer Brushes, with polished Cedar handles; first introduced into England by me. These are largely in use by Foreign Artists. Very beautifully made, and suitable for oil and water painting'. He also sourced the best canvas, sometimes from Belgium, and discussed with the artists the manner in which they preferred this primed.

Realising that the artists at Newlyn required a similar service, Lanham visited that village each week, going round the artists' studios and calling, in particular, at the Forbes School, where students were soon won over by the quality of what he had to offer.[619] Among those to rate his canvases was Alfred Munnings, who had been recommended them by Laura Knight. In his autobiography, he wrote, "I see myself with a thirty-by-twenty-five inch canvas - beautiful canvas from Lanham's with a surface upon which any artist would have loved to paint." He then recalled a painting of a black and white cow - "painted on another of Lanham's canvases, this time with an absorbent, china-clay priming", which was bought by a Canadian. When many years later, he visited Canada and saw it in his house, it looked as bright and fresh as the day it was painted - "a tribute to the china-clay canvases prepared in those days at St Ives."[620]

In addition to supplying all painting materials, Lanham also made frames for the finished works. In the early 1890s, he offered to supply 'Japanese Art Frames - Design Simple and Effective', responding early to the enthusiasm of the period for Japanese art. In 1895, he advertised 'Studio or Trial Frames, Finished in Deep or Pale Gilt, with Bead and Bevel, 4 1/2 to 7 ins wide', as well as Japanese Frames and Newlyn Art Frames, 'supplied in Natural Colour, intended for the Artists' own decoration, or can be Bronzed Pale or Deep Gold'. Subsequently, he advertised Japanese frames made of 'Japanese Gold Canvas' (1897), and in 'rich, dull gold canvas' (1904). This concentration on Japanese style frames suggests that Japanese art was more influential in the colony than might be evident from the paintings themselves. One of the most commented upon features of the exhibition, *Lyrical Light : St Ives 1889-1914*, at Penlee House Gallery & Museum, Penzance in 2008, was the extraordinary quality of many of the frames for the works, and these are likely to have been produced in St Ives by Lanham's.

---

618 See his Obituary, *St Ives Times*, 5/6/1931.

619 See Gladys Beattie Crozier, *Mr and Mrs Stanhope Forbes as Teachers at the Newlyn School of Painting*, *Girl's Realm*, November 1904.

620 Alfred Munnings, *An Artist's Life*, London, 1950 at p.280-1.

The fact that James Lanham also set up an Art Gallery in his premises, where the artists could exhibit their work, led Norman Garstin to comment that Lanham's was "at once the source of all, and the goal of most, of the pictures that are painted in St Ives; for from it a stream of colours that are ground in London, Paris, Dusseldorf and Brussels, are for ever trickling in slow rivulets, or flowing in rich streams, as the energy and style of the painters require, into the various studios of the town, and floating back again in the form of pictured waves, or sands, or sunsets, to decorate the walls" of the Gallery.[621] As well as organising these exhibitions, Lanham's also arranged transport of major works, which were often up to nine feet wide, to both national and international exhibitions, constructing packing cases, where required. There are few records of damage in transit, but it was felt that Julius Olsson's hopes of being elected an Associate of the Royal Academy were hampered, in 1907, when his painting, *Moonlit Bay*, was severely damaged, when oil from a barrel of fish, which had been placed on its case, leaked over the painting. The fact that the damage was caused by the leaking oil, and not the weight of the barrel, is testament to the sturdiness of Lanham's crates.

Lanham not only did business with the artists, but became friends with them and entertained them at his home, 'The Retreat', in Street-an-Pol, on the site of which now stands the Guildhall. Saturday afternoon tea at Lanham's home became a regular feature. Quite what the artists made of his first wife, Lucy Stephens, is not known, for Virginia Woolf records that she wore false curls all round her face and that Lanham's servants whispered that their master had married her "from an advertisement".[622]

Fig. 3.12 H.G.Fitzherbert
Caricature of James Lanham
(from *Everyone's Doing It*)

However, several leading artists attended her funeral, when she died, aged only 56, in 1899. Amongst these, were the visiting American artists, William Wendt and George Gardner Symons, who had enjoyed Lanham's hospitality. Wendt, in fact, gave Lanham one of his paintings, and Lanham's own collection must, at one time, have been most interesting.

This family tragedy was followed shortly by another, when Lanham's only son, Arthur, died in 1903. In 1908, however, Lanham remarried, his new wife being Helen Whitfield from Wootton-under-Edge, in Gloucestershire, and the pair soon proved of great comfort to Louis Sargent, an artist of nervous disposition, who first arrived in St Ives that year in a fragile state and immediately suffered a relapse. However, the Lanhams took him into their own house, nursed him and set his recovery on course by selling some of his paintings.

Fig. 3.13 Packing for the Royal Academy at Lanham's
(St Ives Trust Archive Study Centre)

621 Norman Garstin, *Studio Talk, The Studio*, Vol. VIII, 1896, p.242-3.
622 Virginia Woolf, *Moments of Being*, London, 1976.

James Lanham retired in 1911 and the above account demonstrates his immensely significant contribution to the success of the art colony. His story is not only the most telling example of a local entrepreneur spotting and exploiting the business potential of the artists, but also demonstrates how a true partnership was forged for the mutual benefit of both parties.[623]

On his retirement, Lanham sold his business to Benjamin Bramham. However, I have not found one reference to Bramham, and, so far as I am aware, he does not feature in Fitz's caricatures, which suggests that he did not engage with the artists to the extent that Lanham had done. The timing of his acquisition could hardly have been worse and the War years will have been a difficult time. However, in 1919, the business was taken over by Martin Cock. Cock now had an extraordinary range of businesses and was able to advertise them, for free, in his newspaper. A correspondent for a Glasgwegian paper described him as a most enterprising man. "His main lines of business are printing, selling wines and spirit and artists' colours and acting as a local house agent. He is also a stationer, a newsagent and a tobacconist in his spare time."[624] Cock also prided himself on being able to acquire speedily anything that any resident or visitor desired. One impressed local penned a poem in tribute, which contained the verse:-

If perchance you want the Moon,
At Lanham's you can buy it,
Let them know you want it soon,
Promptly they'll supply it
(Delivered that same afternoon).[625]

The Skipper :   *"Tell you what! I'll lend her to you for a week. All you've got to do is to keep the sails*
                       filled and she'll run herself."
Temporary Skipper :   *"Oh, I wasn't bothering about the* Sales. *I was wondering how to fill the blessed sheets!"*

Fig. 3.14   Francis Roskruge   Cartoon for *St Ives Times*, on Matheson taking over as temporary editor

---

623 Lanham died in 1931 and his widow was joined at 'The Retreat' by her sister, Mrs L.B.Foxwell, and niece (Miss Maud Whitfield) (see *St Ives Times*, 31/12/1937). On her death, the property was acquired by the Council and demolished, to enable the erection of the present Guildhall.

624 Article by B.C., reproduced in *St Ives Times*, 31/8/1923.

625 From poem by Anon, *What is Lanham's?*, *St Ives Times*, 17/7/1925.

The artists' materials section was just in "one little nook", but "only give an address, and it will furnish and stock a studio", utilising "the fruit of sixty years' experience and selection".[626] Tonkin Prynne, the foreman, had been working there since 1890 and had perfected his systems. His canvases remained highly prized, and Lanham's remained the principal supplier of all the artists' painting needs. In the late 1920s, Cock's adverts proudly included a comment from a London businessman, "I have never seen such a varied and unique selection of mouldings anywhere in England and, candidly, there are few towns on the Continent that can offer such facilities".[627]

Cock also made a concerted effort to gain further business from Newlyn. He was instrumental in 1920 in getting the first exhibition mounted at the Passmore Edwards Gallery after the War, following a six year gap, and, rather than making weekly visits, he established, in 1924, a new depot for artists' materials at the works of the Newlyn Art Metal Industries. Cock also sought to capitalise on the increasing interest in the decorative arts by becoming one of the sole outlets for Newlyn Copper and by stocking, in addition, Poole pottery, Royal Devonshire ware and serpentine and Goss china. It was also Cock, who persuaded Alec Walker, when he had outgrown his premises in Newlyn, to move his Crystéde works to St Ives, rather than to Dorset, as originally planned.

Although he never sought Municipal honours, Cock took a keen interest in public affairs, and was, inter alia, for some time, Secretary of the St Ives Swimming Association, working with Herbert Lanyon, who was President. He was also Chairman of the St Ives Conservative Association, where he worked closely with George Bradshaw. His later years - he died in 1940 - were beset by illness, and he was grateful for the extensive role played by Greville Matheson, in the editorship of the *St Ives Times*, following his retirement to the town in 1920, whilst two of his sons, Gerald and John, ran all the varied business interests of Lanhams. Again, the art colony owed a huge debt to the Cock family.

3.1.5   Property developers and agents

As already indicated in Part Two, the artists' requirements for accomodation and studios led them to deal on a regular basis with a number of locals. As much of St Ives was owned by the Cowley Estate, Reginald Glanville, Lord Cowley's property agent, based in Truro, frequently needed consulting, and he came across to St Ives on a regular basis, becoming good friends with a number of artists. He appreciated art, for he developed a collection, which included works by Émile-Louis Vernier, Adrian Stokes, Arnesby Brown, Richard Hayley Lever, Sigisbert Bosch Reitz and Alfred Pazolt. In his absence, however, they had to deal with Glanville's local agent, George Toman, with whom, as seen, they did not get on. Mention has also been made of the artists' relationship with the developer, Robert Toy, who built many of the homes in which the artists lived, and of the extraordianry entrepreneurial enterprise shown by former Mayor, George Williams, who was responsible for the Porthmeor Studios complex, and William Paynter, who erected the Piazza Studios. A number of other leading figures in the town owned property that was rented out to artists, but it was again James Lanham, who tended to deal with the letting aspects. With visiting artists bound to visit his shop for their painting materials, it made sense for any studio and accomodation vacancies to be made known to him.

3.1.6   Joining the establishment

A number of artists felt motivated to become more involved in the affairs of the community by standing for places on the local Council or by becoming Borough Magistrates or by taking part in local politics. Harry Robinson, who was described as "a man of remarkable culture and refinement....with literary and scholarly attainments of a high order", was the first artist to take an active role in the town in a formal capacity, when he was appointed a magistrate in 1897.[628] Having trained as a barrister, before turning to art, he clearly had some legal knowledge and took his duties seriously. On his early demise in 1904, fellow magistrate, Captain Harry, commented, "The late Mr Robinson was a good man, who, while administering the law, was anxious to do justice, and at the same time temper justice with mercy." His obituarist added, "He not only had the courage of his own opinion, but he fearlessly expressed the same whenever he felt it his duty to do so. This characteristic was exemplified in every phase of his life, his innate love of fair play and outspokenness earning for him the respect, esteem and admiration of everyone."[629]

Shortly after Robinson's appointment, Louis Grier decided, in 1898, to stand for the Town Council and was duly elected. He indicated at the time that he felt that it was important for artists to become

---

626 J.C.Carbis, *The Gateway to St Ives, St Ives Times*, 5/7/1929.

627 See, for instance, *St Ives Times*, 11/4/1929.

628 *St Ives Weekly Summary*, 8/10/1904.

629 *St Ives Weekly Summary*, 8/10/1904.

Fig. 3.15 William Titcomb *Basket Making*   (exhibited Show Day 1891)
This is a unique record of this St Ives industry. Thomas C. Warren of
124 Teetotal Street was one of the leading basket makers of the day.

involved in order to stop the town becoming absolutely hideous. "The spirit of Mr Gradgrind is too much with us in municipal affairs, and a little aesthetic leaven is very desirable".[630] In 1901, Grier was re-elected on to the Town Council, and Arthur Burgess passed comment to his girlfriend, "St Ives was rather lively on Friday night - the Municipal Elections. Grier managed to wriggle in. I don't know whether his students lost their heads or not but next morning the beach was simply white with old sketches, monotypes etc."[631] Grier did not need much excuse for a party. He devoted his next three year stint principally to the Free Library (see Chapter 3.4.3 below).

Political persuasion was an individual matter, but two artists, William Titcomb and Julius Olsson, got themselves involved in local politics. They joked to a reporter, however, that they had only done so as a result of a wager as to "who could longest survive the ventilation of the local hall in which meetings are usually held".[632] Titcomb became President of the local Liberal Association and actively promoted Clifford Cory as a candidate to oppose the Conservative, Edward Hain. At a meeting in July 1903, the comment was passed that, for twenty years, the people of St Ives had been disenfranchised "and the constituency had been regarded as private property". This was because, first, Thomas Bedford Bolitho (1887-1900) and, then, Edward Hain (1900) had been elected unopposed. Titcomb proposed a resolution condemning the "reactionary legislation" of the Government, the enormous increase in expenditure, the "retrograde proposals for the abolition of Free Trade and the suggested imposition of taxes on the food of the people".[633] The Liberal campaign was successful and Cory, later Sir Clifford Cory, was elected for the first time in 1906.

Olsson was then a Liberal supporter as well and, by 1907, had followed the lead of Harry Robinson by agreeing to become a Borough Magistrate. Despite leaving St Ives in 1912, he is surprisingly still listed as a J.P. in all the Kelly's Directories up to 1935. Despite reasonably regular return visits - and one recorded appearance on the bench in 1928 - , he is unlikely to have been able to perform many of his duties, and one wonders whether he liked the kudos of having the initials after his name. However, the seeming lack of any attempt to remove him from the position demonstrates the respect with which he was held in St Ives.

Georgina Bainsmith had strong views on the role that women could play in municipal affairs and first stood for a place on the Town Council in 1912. Captain Harry was her proposer, but she proved unable to break down the prejudice against women at that time and, despite several further attempts, was not successful.

---

630 *St Ives Weekly Summary*, 10/12/1898.

631 Letter from Arthur Burgess to Muriel Coldwell dated 3/11/1901 (Stephen Bartley).

632 J.M.Gibbon, *St Ives and its Artists, Black and White*, 30/12/1905.

633 *St Ives Weekly Summary*, 4/7/1903.

THE ARTISTS AND THE FISHERFOLK

3.2.1   Introduction

As already indicated, the initial attitude of the Down-along section of the town towards visitors was very different to that of the businessmen of the community, for the fisherfolk did not want change. They did not care to admit that their own livelihoods were under threat and that they needed to adapt time-honoured ways. Enormous differences in class, wealth, education, mode of life, dress and religious belief also made it difficult, at first, for the artists to establish easy relationships with the fishing community. They were classed not only as 'foreigners', but also as 'Uplongs' - members of the wealthier section of the community, who lived in the upper reaches of the town and who, historically, were distrusted. However, whereas, in many towns, the wealthy members of society mixed with each other, and paid little attention to the plight of the poor, it was the lives of the fisherfolk that the early artists wished to portray. Therefore, they needed to get to know them and understand their values, so as to entice them to sit as their models, and the location of their studios in Down-along ensured that the artists rubbed shoulders with them every day. In the colony's infancy, there were, according to Folliott Stokes, "occasional loggerheads; surface misunderstandings between two impetuous races, whose idiosyncrasies neither understood", but, before too long, "they mutually respected and comprehended each other, and the hatchet of ignorant animosity was buried."[634] This was very important, for not only did the increase in size of the colony result in an ever-increasing demand for models, but the fisherfolk's input on the accuracy of the representations made by the artists was most welcome. Respectful friendships developed between artists and models, and long-term settlers appreciated how to adapt their lives, so as not to upset the religious beliefs, moral values or quaint superstitions of the fisherfolk. However, it is clear that some of the most fervent Methodists in the community disliked all that the artists stood for and harboured a simmering resentment against them, as they became an ever greater feature in the town, for their very way of life was seen to encourage "backslidin'". There was also an extremely active Temperance Society, who disapproved of the artists' fondness for alcohol. Normally, such tensions bubbled below the surface, but visiting preachers, unfamiliar with the compromise reached between artist and Methodist, or visiting artists, unaware of the sensibilities of the locals, could spark outbursts quite easily.

3.2.2   Pre-colony visitors - the differing reactions to Hook and Whistler

A comparison between the visit of James Clarke Hook in 1860 and that of James McNeill Whistler in 1884 provides a stark demonstration of the manner in which different approaches to the fisherfolk resulted in vastly differing responses. Hook was not only a devout Methodist, like most of the fishermen, but also a champion of the working man. Accordingly, during his lengthy visit to the town in the late summer of 1860, he took time to talk to the fisherfolk about their lives, and was impressed that "there was everywhere among the fishermen that unmistakable air of being in earnest about work".[635] He also admired their enterprise in leaving home, during the summer months, to fish in the North Sea, as there was no fish to be had then in the locality. Hook, therefore, did not view them as coarse, ignorant and superstitious, but as honest, sober, brave and industrious - the very qualities of the working classes that he sought to champion. The fishermen naturally responded to his lack of condescension and were honoured to model for him. They may not have seen a figure painter at work before, as most of the early artist visitors to the town had been landscape and marine watercolourists. Imagine the fascination of both the models, and their friends from the fishing community, as the artist's sketches of their faces took shape. Portraiture was the province of the very rich, and the camera was still in its infancy, and so to see the likenesses of themselves captured on canvas must have been a great thrill. And then to be told that the paintings would be displayed in the Royal Academy in London, for all the leading figures in Society to view! No wonder the early colonists were regaled with stories of 'Squire Hook' and one old salt, to whom Hook had given a telescope, considered it his most prized possession.[636]

---

634 A.G.Folliott Stokes, *A Moorland Princess*, London, 1904 at p.86. Stokes, of course, wrote these words in his novel about the colony of St Ars, but he was clearly referring to his own experiences in St Ives.

635 Allan Hook, *Life of James Clarke Hook RA*, privately published.

636 See *St Ives as an Art Colony* in *Babcock's Historical Sketch of St Ives and District*, 1896 & W H Bartlett, *Summer Time at St Ives, Cornwall, Art Journal*, 25/9/1897.

Later artist visitors to St Ives were lucky that Hook was the first artist to stay any appreciable length of time in the town, for they could not have asked for a better role model. He had clearly dispelled, to a significant degree, the notion held elsewhere that artists were merely lazy good-for nothings. There are, however, few sources to tell us how the increasing numbers of artist visitors during the 1860s and 1870s inter-reacted with the fisherfolk. W.H.Hudson, however, indicates that the outspoken atheism and brusque manners of John Brett, who spent a month in the town in September 1872, greatly offended the Cornish fisherfolk, who were finally convinced that he was a little queer in the head when they saw him apply paint, not with a brush, but with a palette knife.[637]

Whistler's visit in January 1884 was prompted by his pupil, Walter Sickert, who had much enjoyed painting in the town on a family holiday in the summer of 1883. His fellow pupil, Mortimer Menpes, recorded how Sickert had assumed a "jersey and top boots and had completely won over the fishermen, fascinating them with his kindly bonhomie".[638] With the gifts of fish that Sickert received from the fishermen, almost on a daily basis, he had then managed to ingratiate himself with the elderly landlady with whom they stayed at 14 Barnoon Terrace. This annoyed Whistler intently, as he considered these arrangements undermined his position as the Master. He asked Menpes, "Why don't they give me fish? It is the Master who should receive these gifts."[639] Accordingly, he set out to win over the fishermen himself. "Often he, too, would talk to the fishermen, and it was interesting to see Whistler copying the tactics of the follower [Sickert], talking of sea and boats, and gracefully playing round the subject of fish; but somehow or other the St Ives fisher folk never gave him fish, and Whistler was far too proud to ask. "It must be given," he would say, "of their own free will." What marvellous finesse, and tact, and cunning, and humour, I have heard wasted on those coarse fishermen! What veiled entreaties and flatteries! Yet never a mackerel did his fluency bring forth, never a sprat."[640] The monocled Whistler, however, was dressed, not in jersey and top boots like Sickert, but in what Menpes called "almost a tomtit scheme" - a very short jaunty jacket, a straw hat cocked completely over the right eye and square-ended patent-leather dancing pumps with bows on them.[641] The fishermen were never going to feel at ease with someone like him.

Still determined to oust Sickert as the landlady's favourite, Whistler, one day, on seeing fishermen carrying a huge ray, the size of a dining room table, through the town, bought it, on impulse, for half-a-crown, feeling that "it would outdo in size, if not in quality, anything that Walter had yet procured".[642] However, the fishermen, having pocketed the money, merely left it on the pavement and, without means of transporting it, Whistler, after a cursory inspection, left it to rot. The fishermen will not have been impressed by such waste - or the need to clear it away.

Fig. 3.16 James Clarke Hook   *Leaving Cornwall for the Whitby Fishing* (RA 1861)
(Juliet McMaster)

---

637 W.H.Hudson, *The Land's End*, London, 1908, at p.170.

638 Mortimer Menpes, *Whistler as I Knew Him*, London, 1904, p.139.

639 ibid, p.140.

640 ibid, p.140.

641 ibid, p.136.

642 *Reminiscences of Whistler, The Studio*, 1903, Vol 29 at p.254.

Fig. 3.17 Mortimer Menpes
Double portrait etching of Whistler

Whistler's attempts to curry favour with his landlady were probably doomed to failure in any event, as Menpes records how Whistler had already gone out of his way to humiliate her. "It had suddenly occurred to him that the landlady somehow was in a way neglecting us. She had not realised our position, or rather the position of the Master; she had not yet, as he himself picturesquely put it, "placed us"." Accordingly, one breakfast time, Whistler rang the bell to summon her from the kitchen and gave her a lecture on how gentlemen, such as themselves, required coffee after dinner and that it should be served in a small dainty cup of porcelain, rather than in a large breakfast cup. Having had the landlady "quaking and nervously shaking her head", Whistler announced, "Now I think she realises better our position, and that we have certain habits of what is fit and proper."[643]

The fishermen will not need to have heard accounts of such appalling behaviour to have picked up on the overbearing arrogance of the man and his condescending attitude. Funnily enough, Menpes, in recording yet another story of a fisherman putting Whistler in his place, also confirms the great respect that the fisherfolk still had for Hook - as it is surely him to whom the fisherman refers.

> "Whistler did not quite give up his idea of winning over the fishermen of St Ives. Many a time, as we strolled along the beach, he stopped and talked with the men. One day he was out painting on the sands, and, seeing a fisherman mending his nets, the Master, still with the fish scheme on his mind, took the opportunity of explaining to him the beauties of the scene upon which he was working. "Ah, yes," said the fisherman, as he paused in his work: "I know all about that sort of thing. There was a great painter down here once; he did a sketch of me, and after it was finished, he gave it to me." - "Well, and do you value it much?, asked Whistler, looking up. "O, yes," said the man. "You see, sir, he was a great artist in London, a member of the Academy." This piece of information had not the astounding effect upon his hearer that the fisherman had intended; and Whistler, feeling considerably damaged in his ardour, went on to put questions about the life this painter led at St Ives. The natural enthusiasm of the fisherman's answers depressed him still more. He said to me afterwards, as we were walking home, "Just think: this fisherman talks to me, the Master, enthusiastically about a man whose work can never live!" "[644]

3.2.3   The reactions of the early foreign colonists

One of the extraordinary aspects of the art colony in St Ives was the number of foreign artists that were drawn to the town. Indeed, in the very early years of the colony, there appear to have been more foreign artists in the town than English ones. As there are few records of the reactions of the early British colonists to the fisherfolk, we are left with the records of the experiences of some of the foreign artists.

---

643 Mortimer Menpes, *Whistler as I Knew Him*, London, 1904, p.137-8.
644 ibid, p.142-3.

To the great credit of the fisherfolk, there are no accounts of xenophobia. However, the Finn, Helene Schjerfbeck, did complain, "The English haven't bothered to do anything in order to make us foreigners feel comfortable - unlike the French everywhere in France - but once you get used to this way of life, it is all right."[645] As Schjerfbeck did not speak English and the locals were unlikely to be conversant in French, an inability to communicate with each other may have been part of the problem.

One of the first foreign artists known to have visited St Ives was the American, William Trost Richards, and he appears to have got on well with the fisherfolk, for they went out of their way to explain to him all aspects of the seine fishery. He was amused, however, that one fisherman, who approached him when he was painting some houses in the town one day, did not understand that the value of a picture was not in anyway related to the value of its subject, for the man commented, "one fellow made a thousand pounds by a picture of those houses, but for my part, I can't see anything much in them."[646] This was not an unusual experience, for Arnesby Brown recorded how Cornish farmers could not understand why a picture of a cow should fetch more than the cow itself. "One of them asked me once to 'take' his horse and cart, expecting to pay 5s. When I named a figure, he thought I had gone dotty."[647]

Once artists started to take studio space in Down-along, they came into more direct, and more frequent, contact with the fisherfolk. The American, Howard Butler, who created the first Porthmeor Studio, told his family in 1886, "I am thrown a great deal with the poor people here. There are carpenters and fishermen and ship chandlers all around me working in similar shops to mine. I often talk with them and if I don't know them all, I am known to all....I like the men and the boys - they are a rough lot, but there are some fine rustic characters among them. But the women all seem to be fiends. They will beat a child of three years old - and the little girls are most insolent. All are slovenly, given to overdressing, lazy and filthily dirty."[648] Helene Schjerfbeck was also none too impressed with the girls, once they had passed the age of 17. "Nowhere have I seen young girls' faces and expressions as dull and impassive as here."[649] Anders Zorn's wife, Emma, on the other hand, was shocked at the low morals amongst the fisherfolk, which she believed stemmed from the cramped and dirty surroundings in which they lived. She commented that boys of eighteen and nineteen were made to marry fourteen-year-old girls simply to keep the latter from being corrupted.[650]

3.2.4 Areas of tension

However considerate the artists were towards the sensitivities of the locals, there was bound to be some resentment to their intrusion. Edith Ellis tried her best to get to know the locals, taking an interest in their welfare, inviting them up to London to stay with her and employing them whenever she could but, on her departure, one of her neighbours confided, "You've been one here against all, in a manner of speaking, for it do take years with we to treat a stranger like one of our own. We've been reared to look on all uplongs as natural foes, and though we all likes you, my dear, still it 'ave been a matter of principle wi'some, and wishing you no harm neither, just to show they could frustrate you in any undertaking."[651]

Not only were artists natural foes as 'Uplongs', but there was also clearly some concern amongst the devout that their new-fangled ways would lead to a degeneration in moral standards. The following conversation between two of Ellis' neighbours sums up the locals' dilemna.

"It's a pity as ever any foreigners or uplongs took to come hereabouts to live. Decent folks had better mind themselves, for example is very catching, as our minister only told us on Sunday, if you can mind it."

"Iss, sure enough" the other said solemnly "but, after all, strangers do bring we both money and work, for I gets double for my eggs now to what I used to from the neighbours years ago."

"Tut!", the first responded, "What's that at all, alongside o' 'avin' their whimey ways and upstart fal-lals to put up wi' all over the place? Their very frills spells backslidin', seems to me."[652]

645 Letter to Maria Wiik, undated, 1887, translated by Erkki Toivanen.
646 Letter from W.T.Richards to G.Whitney dated 1/8/1879 - Archives of American Art, W.T.Richards Papers, Reel 2296.
647 J.M.Gibbon, *Painters of the Light - An Interview with Arnesby Brown ARA, Black and White*, 29/7/1905.
648 Letter from H.R.Butler to his mother dated 20/8/1887, Archives of American Art, Smithsonian Institution, Washington DC, Howard Russell Butler papers, Reel 1189.
649 Letter to Maria Wiik, undated, 1887, translated by Erkki Toivanen.
650 Letter to Hugo Greber dated 3/1/1887, Zorn Museum Archives.
651 Edith Ellis, *My Cornish Neighbours*, London, 1906 at p.194
652 ibid at p.32-3

As acknowledged by Ellis' neighbours, the artists, and the tourist masses that followed them, did have a significant impact on prices. One artist in *Portalone* commented, "I cannot understand why people hate us so. It must be sheer unreasoning stupidity, for we bring trade and custom to the town". However, a local responded, "You say as the artists bring traade to Portalone. Not to the largest number of Portalone folk they don't. The tradesfolk up to Church-town do well and prosper as never before. What's the end o' that? Why, prices go up and stick up, and the fishermen have to pay 'un! It's harder for a fisherman to live here than it was before you artists came." Ranger-Gull continued, "The painters were silent. This was a new aspect of the question altogether. The fact chilled them. It chipped their pedestal, so to speak, and they had long found pleasure in the vague and splendid imagination that they were the Lords Bountiful of Portalone."[653]

Resentment at the artists' impact on the cost of living was exacerbated by a feeling, in certain quarters, that the fisherfolk were being exploited by the artists without any recompense. "Damm'ee", one exasperated old salt in *Portalone* cries, "You comes down here and you paints our boats and our houses and then you sells them. And what do we get out of them? They're our boats, not yours"![654]

A number of the locals, particularly those involved in manual labour, also had difficulty accepting that what the artists did was work. Accordingly, the adjective 'lazy' was probably that used most often to describe them. Indeed, in a story told by Algernon Talmage to Charles Marriott, the word 'artist' had become a term of abuse. "A fish cart was being driven up Skidden Hill, when the horse jibbed. After exhausting an extensive vocabulary of abuse, the driver, walking in the road, exclaimed, as if with his last breath, "You - you Pygmalion *artist*!"[655]

It needs to be recognised, therefore, that the artists impacted on the various sections of the local community in different ways. Indeed, *Portalone* suggests that divisions arose within local families, between those who profited from the artists' presence, and those who did not, and changes in thought, speech and mode of life could be detected in those who did deal with the artists.

Fig. 3.18 Emily Carr
The old men tell her how the fish
<u>will</u> not be caught as they would wish

Fig. 3.19 Emily Carr
There is a "wummun" named Fearon,
who the folk of St Ives set great cheer on

These vignettes from the sketchbook of the Canadian, Emily Carr, demonstrate the high regard that the local fisherfolk had for fellow art student, Hilda Fearon. Another one is titled *The women tell her of such woes, as how the wind won't dry their clothes.*   (Royal BC Museum, BC Archives, PDP 05 896 & 893)

653 C.Ranger-Gull, *Portalone*, London, 1904 at p.125-6.
654 ibid, at p.29.
655 Charles Marriott, *Memories of Cornwall's Art Colonies*, Cornish Review, Spring 1949 No 1 at p.67.

3.2.5   The trials of *plein air* sketching

Artists sketching in their midst might have been something that the fisherfolk had witnessed, with some regularity, from the 1860s, but natural curiosity still meant that an artist working out of doors was likely to find himself surrounded by onlookers. This can be seen, for example, in Sydney Carr's photograph of a woman artist painting a horse and cart against the backdrop of the harbour beach (Fig. 3.21) or in the sketches of Hilda Fearon at work done by Emily Carr (Fig. 3.19). It took extreme confidence, therefore, to paint on without being disturbed by all sorts of comments being made behind one's back, few of which are likely to have been complimentary. Even if onlookers were silent, the encroachment on an artist's space could be most off-putting and established names, such as James Clarke Hook, were still forced to be rude to Cornish onlookers, who could not take a hint.[656] Albert Ludovici Jnr was astonished to hear that one artist, who had had a crowded St Ives beach scene hung at the Royal Academy in 1883, had not been able to summon up the courage to paint it on the spot, with inquisitive eyes looking on, but had instead retreated to the terrace of the Tregenna Castle Hotel, viewing the subject through opera glasses![657]

Small boys are frequently mentioned in this connection as the scourge of *plein air* artists and the Australian, David Davies, indicated that it was considered good sport to hurl fish as missiles at the artists.   Lewis Hind recalled an incident demonstrating how deflating comments could be. "One day, having caught the *plein air* infection, I set up my easel in a remote corner of St Ives beach and tried to convey the wonderful look of yellow sand, blue sea, and pools of water, any lovely colour you like, left by the receding waves. I was enjoying the job immensely. The sun was dipping. I was flushed with ecstasy, when three little local children in pinafores approached and carefully examined my handiwork. Soon the eldest child said aloud, in an emphatic voice, "I don't like that picture". When I narrated this adventure at the St Ives Arts Club that evening, one of the men said, "You should write that. Your account is much more amusing than your painting." "[658]   However, it is easy to understand how children, being naturally inquisitive, found the activities of the sketchers fascinating, and clearly some artists went out of their way to explain what they were doing. Elmer Schofield, for instance, depicts himself in Fig. 3.20 surrounded by attentive children, whilst a further vignette by Emily Carr of Hilda Fearon, entitled *As sticketh close the blight to rose, Close flock the kids we're* [sic] *she goes*, shows her with a gaggle of young children hanging off each arm.

Despite the sight of sketchers becoming common-place, the problem of intrusive spectators was still being experienced in the 1920s. Whilst working at Phillack, the American, Wilson Henry Irvine, had a man of about 25 standing very close to him for over an hour, staring without saying a word. As he ignored all hints that he was being a nuisance, Irvine was forced to stop work and stare at him for a full minute before he went off, again without saying a word.

Fig. 3.20 Illustration from letter from Elmer Schofield to John Sloan (undated, summer 1904)
(Sloan papers, Delaware Art Museum, Wilmington)

---

656 W.H.Hudson, *The Land's End*, London, 1908 at p.192-3.
657 A Ludovici Jnr, *An Artist's Life in London and Paris*, London, 1926 at p.74.
658 C Lewis Hind, *Napthali*, London, 1926 at p.172-3.

Fig. 3.21   Sydney Carr   Spectators watching a female artist at work
(the late Derek Wintle/Andrew Eggleston)

3.2.6   'No sketchin' on a Sunday'

The Cornish were very devout and a majority of the locals in St Ives were Methodists of one denomination or another - Wesleyans, Bible Christians, Primitives and such like. Many of the fisherfolk tended to be attracted by the fiery oratory and fervent prayers of the Primitive Methodists. The American, Edward Simmons, observed that, in St Ives, "The butcher, grocer and carpenter were all preachers on Sunday" and, without doubt, the issue that caused the most discord between the artists and the locals was the strictness with which the local Methodists observed the Sabbath.[659] No work of any kind was permitted on a Sunday, and a number of other activities, such as playing the piano or the singing of popular songs, were frowned upon as well.[660] Wilson Henry Irvine, for instance, indicated that he was scowled upon merely for trying to take a photograph, this being deemed to be 'work'. The fishing fleet, therefore, did not go out either on a Saturday or Sunday night, and some fishermen even removed the bait from their pots on Saturday evening so that nothing should be caught on the Sabbath. As the East Coast fishermen, who also fished in the nearby waters, did not hold such strong views, there were frequent clashes when they attempted to land fish on a Monday morning, culminating in the Newlyn riots in 1896, when the Mount's Bay fishermen boarded the Lowestoft boats and threw their catch into the harbour. In the enquiry that followed, the fishermen referred to their faith as "the brightest and best part of our lives" and stated that they would rather die than break the Sabbath.[661] Most of the fishermen were also strict teetotallers, and Stanhope Forbes complained to his father that "the effect of this abstinence from strong drink and indulgence in strong prayers, is to make them a most disagreeable set of people, full of hypocrisy and cant".[662] Folliott Stokes was also unimpressed by "a dour and narrow-minded methodism", which he felt had "spread a fungus-like growth over the minds of the people and endeavoured, with Pharasaical perversity, to stamp out of their hearts the God-given joy of life". As a result, Sundays in Cornwall became, in his view, "as sterile and negative a day of rest and recreation as the world can show".[663]

However strongly the artists might have objected to the views of the Methodist community, they were in the minority and soon learnt that sketching on a Sunday out of doors would not be tolerated. In October 1890, the local paper reported, "A Japanese artist, who visited St Ives on a recent Sunday and commenced painting...had a lively half hour with a large number of children. They threw missiles at him and threatened to tell the policeman if he didn't clear out!".[664] He was probably quite lucky not to have experienced more direct action. One female artist, on being warned to desist from sketching on

---

659 E.E.Simmons, *From Seven to Seventy : Memories of a Painter and a Yankee*, New York and London, 1922, at p.163.

660 See C Ranger-Gull, *Portalone*, London, 1904 at p.45.

661 Extract from the Submission of the Mount's bay Fishermen's Committee to the Home Secretary at the time of the 1896 Newlyn Riots.

662 Letter from Forbes to his father dated Sunday, February 1884.

663 Letter re *A Cornish Theatre*, St Ives Weekly Summary, 5/12/1903.

664 *St Ives Weekly Summary*, 11/10/1890.

the Sabbath, was informed, "And you're lucky to have me telling you so politely. If you were further up the alley, they'd say it with a bucket of water."[665] Furthermore, the incident related in *Portalone* of an artist and his easel being thrown into the harbour, with little concern for whether or not he could swim, seems, like many of the stories contained in that novel, to be based on fact. Certainly, over twenty years later, the same is said to have happened to Arthur Hayward, whose dog was thrown in as well, for good measure.[666] Writing about the town in 1920, Frank Emanuel, an irregular visitor over a period of thirty years, became very heated about the situation.

> "Should one unaccustomed to the practices of these ignoramuses venture out with a notebook, if only to sketch some little detail in a quiet spot, busybodies will soon be heard shouting out "No sketchin' allowed on Sundays", and, if he persist, they will molest him. The bigots have even been known to enter private studios in which artists have been reported at work on Sundays and to have destroyed or damaged works intended for exhibition... I have known of inoffensive lady artists' work destroyed by native women on week-days on some idiotic charge, and destroyed, moreover, with impunity. This lawlessness should be put down with a strong hand by the local authorities if St Ives fishermen are not to remain a laughing-stock and worse."

Emanuel's account suggests that the situation had got worse, as not only were the fisherfolk invading private property, irrespective of whether activity was taking place on a Sunday, but were also acting as censors. Such actions might have been isolated incidents, but the preservation of the Sabbath was an issue on which the locals would not budge and, well beyond the period covered by this book, activities in St Ives on a Sunday were strictly curtailed to the annoyance of decades of visitors. Indeed, in 1929, the issue caused a nasty disturbance that resulted in St Ives attracting adverse headlines around the world. Interestingly, a few weeks before the disturbance, Greville Matheson clearly picked up on a degree of heightened tension on the subject, resulting from strong preaching from the Reverend W.A.Bryant, the Primitive Methodist minister, for he covered it in one of his poems.[667]

1. On Sunday, 'tis a curious place
crammed full of charity and grace.
You may go to church, to chapel too,
but other things you may not do,
in St Ives upon a Sunday.

2. At home you mustn't stand or sit,
and watch the folk go by, or knit.
You mustn't walk upon the grass,
or smile to see a lady pass.
You mustn't yawn, you mustn't laugh;
you mustn't take a photograph.
You mustn't wear a Homburg hat,
you mustn't stroke the household cat,
in St Ives upon a Sunday.

3. By 'bus or train you must not go,
or motor idly to and fro.
You mustn't park upon the quay,
look through your glasses at the sea,
or saunter slowly through the town
with coloured parasol or gown,
or trousers with conspicuous check,
or College scarf around your neck,
in St Ives upon a Sunday.

4. *The Sunday Times* you mustn't buy,
polluting both your mind and eye;
and crossword puzzles, sinks of sin,
you must not wallow vainly in.

You mustn't turn your wireless on
to hear the news and which has won;
you mustn't use your gramophone,
you mustn't give your dog a bone,
in St Ives upon a Sunday.

5. All fiction is, of course, taboo
from Edgar Wallace to le Queux;
'tis only sermons you may read;
and you mustn't drink, you mustn't feed;
you mustn't snuff; you mustn't smoke;
you mustn't try to tell a joke;
you mustn't sneeze; you mustn't cough;
you mustn't take your jacket off
in St Ives upon a Sunday.

6. You mustn't sketch or even seek
a subject for the coming week.
Of course, you mustn't bathe, or be
upon the sands and ask for tea.
You mustn't glance into a shop;
if somebody falls, you mustn't stop;
if someone tumbles off the quay,
you must walk away and let them be,
in St Ives upon a Sunday.

7. It is a very curious place,
crammed full of charity and grace.
You may go to church, to chapel too,
but other things you may not do,
in St Ives upon a Sunday.

---

665 See *St Ives and the Arts*, *Daily Mirror*, 11/10/1928.
666 Certainly, Wilson Henry Irvine was told in 1923 that an artist had been thrown into the harbour for working on the waterfront on a Sunday - Journal of Wilson Henry Irvine, 20/2/1923, Archives of American Art, Smithsonian Institution, Wilson Henry Irvine papers, Reel 3564.
667 *St Ives Times*, 16/8/1929.

The local paper, that year, also records the increasing annoyance of the residents at the activities of the newly introduced speedboats. A young girl, who lived on The Terrace, was run down and badly gashed, whilst swimming, fishermen complained of the boats damaging their nets and lines, and scaring the fish away, whilst poems published decried the incessant noise.[668] This tension all boiled over on a Sunday in late August, when the owner of the speedboat company and his sister decided to go for a spin in one of their boats. Accordingly, as commentators around the world pointed out, the speedboat was not even plying for hire, but was merely being used by its owner - no different from some one driving their own car. Having been roughly jostled as they embarked, the mood amongst the fishermen darkened so appreciably that a visitor felt compelled to swim out to the boat on its return to warn the occupants that their lives would be in danger if they attempted to land. Thus thwarted, the fishermen then stormed into the two cafés that were legally providing refreshment for visitors and forced them to close, causing several ladies to faint in fear. The incident was roundly condemned both locally and internationally, but it did lead to a total ban on speedboats at St Ives.

3.2.7   The simmering mistrust of fervent Methodists

Just as the artists had to adapt their lifestyle so as not to upset local sensibilities, the town's Methodists had to accept that the artists had become a prominent feature of the community, however much they disapproved of their lifestyle. Such acceptance was given grudgingly, as some of the most fervent Methodists had difficulty with *all* art. One of the artists in *Portalone* exclaims about the fisherfolk, "Brutes, swine they are! We come down here, we settle, we make trade brisk, we practically keep them in a bad winter, and they hate us. All art is vile to them. In their dour Calvinism, they hate it and are afraid of it."[669] As already discussed in Chapter 2.4.1.3, one person, whom the artists had to deal with on a regular basis, who displayed a deep-seated hatred for all that they stood for, was George Toman, the local representative of Lord Cowley's property agents. He simply considered artists as "paint-wasters".

Such lack of understanding was not confined to the uneducated amongst the congregation, and a number of Methodist ministers found the artists an easy target for criticism. Particular problems were caused when "red-hot revivals" were initiated. Fearing that the new Bishopric of Truro was making inroads into their congregation, the Methodists would organise, from time to time, speakers of particular vigour to visit the town. These men, unused to the ways of the artists, would rail against what they saw, stirring up the fishermen. In a sermon in *Portalone*, Godlessness, Sabbath-breaking, and drink were labelled by the minister as the artists' most heinous crimes. "What place of worship do they attend? Who fills the drink shop a stone's throw away from here?...We can hear the pianos going on Sunday evenings now all over Church-town, and light songs and wantonness." However, this was not all, for he criticised their frills and their fal-lals and commented, "A young maid's head is easy turned when carnal comeliness is all that's thought of or spoke of".[670] The nude in art was, naturally, an anaethma to Methodists and, in the novel, an inoffensive female student, just down from the Slade, is viciously assaulted by a group of fishwives, merely because she is walking down the street carrying a nude study. On another occasion, an artist quietly at work on his own in his studio is disturbed by two fishermen breaking through his roof, as they falsely believed that one of their young female relations was posing in the nude for the artist. *Portalone* is, of course, merely a novel, but so many of its incidents have a ring of authenticity, as is demonstrated by the events leading up to an attack on the artists by the fishermen in 1897.

3.2.8   The trouble at the 1897 municipal elections

The one time that a dispute between the fishermen and the artists made headlines in the press was in 1897. The incident, which involved a number of *plein air* sketchers being attacked on the harbour beach by a group of fishermen, occurred on the morning after the municipal elections. It can be explained away as the result of a misunderstanding, following some unwise remarks made by the defeated candidate, but closer analysis suggests that it illustrates the simmering tensions that were ever present between the Methodists and the artists, which could be ignited by an unfortunate comment or action. Accordingly, the story is worth reviewing in some detail.[671] It was even featured in the *Daily Mail*, under the heading *Pilchards v. Palettes - The Newlyn School attacked by fishermen*. The use of the term 'Newlyn School' might seem odd, given that the incident involved local artists working in St Ives, but the reporter was keen to make reference to the Newlyn riots of the previous year. Accordingly, albeit in a semi-jocular manner, the thrust of the piece was, if the Cornish fishermen have picked fights with their East Coast brethren and now with inoffensive artists, who are they going to pitch into next?!

---

668 See poem *Speed - St Ives Times*, 16/8/1929. After the disturbance, Filson Young, the BBC producer, and his party were also "kept prisoners in the boat out in the Harbour for three-quarters of an hour" after a dispute about the fare and were landed without their shoes and socks and so had to walk barefoot back to Carbis Bay. *St Ives Times*, 13/9/1929.
669 C Ranger-Gull, *Portalone*, London, 1904 at p.28.
670 ibid at p.45.
671 The *Daily Mail* article is reproduced in *The Cornishman* 11/11/1897.

However, the article does record that, in the view of several artists, the root of the problem was a completely separate matter - the application for a liquor licence by the Porthminster Hotel, which had been heard a couple of weeks previously.

The Porthminster Hotel had opened in 1894. Its Directors included Edward Hain, Robert Sawle Read, Joshua Daniel, a J.P. and former Mayor, and Dr Nicholls, many of whom had significant financial stakes in the venture. When the development was first proposed, it was stated that the hotel did not intend to have a licence but, finding that this had put it at a severe competitive disadvantage to the Tregenna Castle Hotel, it applied for one initially in September 1895, but was turned down. The local paper commented, "We wish that some of our earnest temperance workers would cultivate a sense of proportion. The Hotel is unlikely to become a centre of demoralisation and morbid alcoholism".[672] With the business still struggling, it re-applied for a licence in the busy tourist summer of 1897, but was again faced with fierce opposition from fervent supporters of the Temperance Movement.[673] Several attempts were made to get the licence application heard, but it proved difficult to get a quorum of licensing justices. Opposers to the licence accused the Town Clerk, Edward Boase, who, as Secretary of the Hotel company, had a vested interest in the result, of deliberately arranging adjournments until he could get together the necessary number of justices to pass the application.[674] This persuaded the magistrates to refuse to adjourn for a third time, leading Boase to have to apply to the High Court to force them to hear the application.

By the date of the eventual hearing in mid-October, the artist, Harry Robinson, had become a J.P., raising the distinct possibility that he was appointed with this particular hearing in mind.[675] The Primitive Methodist minister, the Reverend J.Crompton, was one of the objectors to speak, urging refusal on the grounds of "good order and morality", but other objectors felt that they were not given appropriate opportunities to air their views.[676] When the vote was taken, the six licensing justices were split equally. Accordingly, Robinson's vote proved crucial, as it ensured that the Mayor, Captain Harry, had to give the casting vote. This he did in favour of the grant of the licence, largely on the basis of what appears rather spurious, and certainly not impartial, advice from Edward Boase.[677]

Fig. 3.22 H.G. Fitzherbert
         Caricatures of Edward Boase
         (top - from *Caricatures of the Cornish Riviera*
         bottom - from *Everyone's Doing It*)

---

672 *St Ives Weekly Summary*, 14/9/1895.

673 For instance, a reader had just reported to the local paper that a member of the Movement had been publicly denounced as "a moral coward and not worthy of the Temperance cause", merely for failing to attend a meeting, despite being out of town both when the meeting was publicised and when it was held! - *St Ives Weekly Summary*, 10/7/1897.

674 *St Ives Weekly Summary*, 18/9/1897.

675 Certainly, when Robinson rose to speak at the subsequent Mayoral Banquet, he was applauded as if he was a key figure.

676 *St Ives Weekly Summary* 16/10/1897. The Rev. Crompton pointed out that "throughout the country the increase in drunkenness and crime was in proportion to the number of licensed premises". Other objectors said that the Hotel was intended to attract families and that it was inappropriate for women and children to be staying in a place with a licence.

677 Captain Harry indicated that he did not think that the number of full licences granted in the town - 12 - was excessive with a population of 6000 and felt that the magistrates were being asked to lay down a law that there should never be another licence granted. However, he relied most on Boase's argument that, if a licence was granted, the police had more powers to combat drunkenness at the Hotel. However, it was not made clear how there were likely to be 'drunken carousels' at the Hotel without a licence. *St Ives Weekly Summary*, 16/10/1897.

Fig. 3.23 Artist-designed letterhead for the Porthminster Hotel (1903)
(Schofield family archive)

The decision, and the manner in which the hearing was held, still rankled with the objectors at the time of the municipal elections a few weeks later. Captain Harry was one of four Councillors seeking re-election, and their only opponent was Robert James Lees, who had been a public figure in Peckham Rye, where he had conducted a Christian mission. Lees, during his time in St Ives, had preached often at the Primitive Methodist chapel and had become very popular with the fisherfolk. Indeed, he had completely overshadowed the local minister, causing some friction.[678] However, now with the support of the Reverend J.Crompton, he put himself forward as the "fishermen's candidate". Lees thought that he had uncovered financial irregularities by the outgoing Councillors, and made wild, unsubstantiated accusations of bribery, jobbery and evil doing against them.[679] These enraged many people in the town, and several parents made it known to the headmistress of the school at which Lees' daughters were temporarily being educated that, unless she barred them, they would withdraw their own children from the school. Not unnaturally, this unwise move only served to increase Lees' antipathy to the local 'establishment', and he suspected that the artist, Folliott Stokes, had been one of the parents involved.[680] Accordingly, tensions were high on polling day and, when after a false rumour had spread that Lees had been elected, it transpired that he had, in fact, lost badly, a considerable disturbance resulted, with a crowd of some one thousand people preventing a number of Councillors from leaving the Town Hall. Those that attempted to break out were physically molested and were compelled to take shelter in the nearby houses of friends, and it will be no coincidence that Edward Boase, a key figure in the Porthminster Hotel licence saga, was the most roughly handled, being "thrown down and violently assaulted".[681] Eventually, the police, armed with batons, had to clear a way through the mob and provide a safe passage for the beleaguered Councillors.

Lees, who immediately returned to London, subsequently complained to the *Daily Mercury* that their reporter's account of the incident was biased, "as he was blind to any defects which may appear in the Bohemian artists, with whom he fraternised" and indicated that, in truth, the whole of the disturbance "originated with the artists".[682] He then recounted how, at 4 p.m. on polling day, a member of a group of 'art students' had come up to one of the Methodist ministers and said, "I say, old chappie, will you come and take a drink?". This had been perceived as a gross insult by the fishermen, and nearly resulted in an exchange of blows there and then. The comment, however inappropriate, again highlights the significance of the drink question at the time. Lees also contended that, as soon as the result was eventually declared, "several artists, brandishing their sticks, rushed into the crowd, saying they would

678 See W.J.Jacobs, *Memories of Eighty Years 1880-1960*, privately published, 1960 at p.83 (copy at St Ives Archive Centre).

679 The outgoing Councillors, in a published note dated 28/10/1897 denounced Lees' "reckless accusations of bribery and jobbery and evil doing against honourable men who have lived their lives openly amongst you, as did their fathers before them; men whose records are clean, and who have devoted many years of service without fee or reward." *St Ives Weekly Summary*, 30/10/1897.

680 *The Cornishman*, 4/11/1897.

681 Others to be attacked were the successful candidates, Joshua Daniel and William Blight, and former Mayor Edward Hain.

682 Reproduced in *The Cornishman*, 4/11/1897.

299

clear a way" and that these artists included the group of 'art students', who had caused the trouble earlier on. This latter claim by Lees is dubious, but one of the group of 'art students', called Wynne, did become embroiled in the affray, as he had been spotted, with his elderly father, a doctor, crossing the square. Both were beaten insensible, albeit the young man, coat off and with his back to the Town Hall, had landed several solid blows in self-defence before going down.[683]

The following morning, a group of fishermen, still smarting from the events of the previous day and aware of Lees' indictment of the artists, confronted a group of sketchers on the harbour beach, initially pelting them with fish, before making it clear by actions and words that they should pack up and leave. Some physical force seems to have been used, as the *Daily Mail* reported that "one knight of the mahl stick had his raiment rent to pieces at the scaly hands of his antagonist", and the police were called. Perhaps the choice of target resulted from resentment at the sight of ever-increasing numbers of sketching umbrellas on what the fishermen considered to be their terrain.

The artists were outraged by Lees' claims that they were to blame for the disturbance, and Harry Robinson, having made exhaustive enquiries of his artist colleagues, wrote to the local paper to report that there had been "no rushing of artists, no brandishing of sticks by artists and no clearing of the way by artists", simply because there had, in fact, been no artists at all in the vicinity for some two hours before the result was announced.[684] However, Robinson does not make mention of Wynne and his group, who clearly were involved, either because they were not art students at all, or because he did not consider that students of that ilk should be associated with the term 'artists'. Without knowing the names of those involved, it is difficult to determine whether Lees' comments merely reflected his hang-up about artists in general or whether some art students were indeed involved. All that can be gleaned from the reports about Wynne is that he and his father were visitors to the town and that he had just arrived from Matabeleland, where he had been recovering from a serious illness. However, it is clear that they were visiting the artist, Kendrick Wynne, who had been involved with the art colony for over a year, and a Miss Wynne, presumably his sister, who had taken part in various entertainments.[685] Accordingly, it is easy to see why Lees linked the Wynne involved in the affray with the artists. Indeed, Lees may well have been correct that he was an art student, albeit at the time a fledgling one, as a Reginald Wynne - presumably the young man concerned - takes part in various entertainments put on by the artists over the next nine months, cutting quite a dash with the ladies.[686]

Robinson attacked the efforts of Lees and others to create a "class antagonism where none ought to exist. Most of us have received kindness and assistance from the fishermen in the pursuit of our calling. We can have no other desire than to live in unity with them; and there can be no reason why they should regard us with other than good feeling. On our part, we have striven, and shall strive, that no conduct of ours shall interfere with the good relations which have subsisted between us and the fishermen of St Ives; and if agitators will only let us and them alone, we shall succeed."[687]

At the Mayoral Banquet held a week or so later at the newly-licensed Porthminster Hotel, the disturbance was naturally referred to by several speakers. Louis Grier played down the seriousness of the incident on the beach, saying it was of the most trivial character, and thought that, in general, the artists "owed a serious debt to the fisher people". However, Adrian Stokes considered that the artists had been "attacked in a somewhat rude manner by a small section of the inhabitants", but needed to "make allowance for a little primeval ignorance still existing in the neighbourhood of the Island, which was not an island" - a comment clearly intended to raise a laugh at the Banquet, but which did not help when reproduced in black and white in the next week's paper.[688] However, normal relations appear to have resumed fairly speedily and the day after the incident on the beach, the artists were back there sketching, unmolested.[689] Nevertheless, William Jacobs indicated in his memoirs that it was this incident which persuaded him to found the *Western Echo* to reflect the views and interests of the Downalong section of the town.

---

683 See *The Cornishman*, 4/11/1897 and *St Ives Weekly Summary* 6/11/1897.

684 *St Ives Weekly Summary*, 6/11/1897.

685 Kendrick Wynne had been signed into the Arts Club by Robinson himself in March 1896, when he was stated to have come from Paris, and had become a member of the Arts Club in October that year. He had also taken part in Show Day in March 1897, performed, along with Miss Wynne, at the Library entertainment in April 1897 and rented a Piazza studio.

686 Both Kendrick Wynne and Dr Wynne were present at the Arts Club on the same evening later in the year (11/12/1897) and a Reginald F.Wynne took part in entertainments in December 1897 and July 1898. The marriage at Radstock of a John Kendrick Wynne MD of St Ives was noted in *St Ives Weekly Summary* 3/3/1903.

687 *St Ives Weekly Summary*, 6/11/1897.

688 *The Cornishman*, 11/11/1897.

689 William Jacobs records that, just before leaving the town, Lees "wrote a most entertaining book entitled *A Corner Wall Mystery*, in which he held up to ridicule several leading residents of St Ives" - W.J.Jacobs, *Memories of Eighty Years 1880-1960*, privately published, 1960 at p. 83 (copy at St Ives Archive Centre). Unfortunately, a copy of this has not yet surfaced.

Fig. 3.24 William Titcomb   *Ego Sum Nolite Timere*   (Titcomb family archive)

3.2.9 Models from the fisherfolk

Whereas it is important to highlight the tensions that existed, from time to time, within certain sections of the community, it would be quite wrong to suggest that the relationship between the artists and the fisherfolk was always strained. As has been seen, when disputes did arise, it tended to be the result of the actions of newcomers - be they artists, politicians or preachers. On the whole, relations between the fishermen and the long-term resident artists were most amicable and, as admitted by Robinson and Grier, the artists owed a considerable debt to the fisherfolk, for they satisfied one of the artists' major requirements - the need for models. With their weather-beaten features, and extravagant beards, their distinctive clothes and the dignified air that seemed to come from years at sea scanning the horizon, aged fishermen made an irresistible subject for artists and the additional cash for sitting doing nothing was very welcome.   William Bartlett, writing in the *Art Journal* in 1897, commented,

> "Artists, always pretty numerous [at St Ives], are, I think, very welcome to the fisher folk, and the superannuated old salts who sit and sun themselves on the benches lament exceedingly if the usual number of 'sketchers' shows any signs of falling off. The painters, indeed, provide them with food for conversation as well as for the eye. I remember one very advanced impressionist creating an idea among these local art critics that, as his productions were quite unintelligible, he must be a little queer in his head; also sundry details connected with his get-up and his methods generally were all considered strong evidence of his want of sanity."[690]

One need only have regard to a few of the most significant paintings of the activities of the fisherfolk, such as, for example, Frederick Sargent's *Catch of Pilchards* (Back Cover), Edward King's *Sale of Herrings* (Front Cover) or William Titcomb's *A Pilot* (Fig. 3.31), all of which feature more than twenty fishermen, to appreciate the extraordinary number of locals that will have modelled for the artists. Even more are featured in Dorothy Robinson's masterwork, *A Volunteer for a Lifeboat* (Plate 30), demonstrating that the coastguards and the lifeboat crew had no difficulty modelling for a woman. Given that few of the artists were experienced sailors, they were also very dependent on the fisherfolk to advise them if they had made errors in the depiction of such matters as sails or rigging, and the artists soon learnt to check that their depictions of the fishermen's boats and equipment passed the test of these keen-eyed experienced mariners. When so many members of the local community were involved in such a project, the sense of anticipation as the painting developed and the sense of pride, as likenesses were captured on canvas, must have been immense. Accordingly, the unveiling of the finished work on Show Day will have generated enormous interest amongst the fisherfolk.

Whilst most paintings by the St Ives artists featured the fisherfolk in realistic settings, appropriate to their calling, a work such as William Titcomb's *Ego Sum Nolite Timere* (Fig. 3.24), in which local fishermen modelled as the disciples in a depiction of the miracle of Christ walking on the water, must have created an enormous stir in such a religious community. To be depicted as oneself was one thing, but to be shown as one of the Lord's closest followers was an enormous honour, and photographs of Titcomb's painting were prized possessions of the models.

690 W.H.Bartlett, *Summertime at St Ives*, Art Journal, October 1897.

Fig. 3.25 John Douglas *Ephraim Perkin* (c.1900)

The ability to persuade large numbers of local fishermen to pose for a single picture was limited, as most of the younger fishermen needed to attend to their primary calling. Helene Schjerfbeck, when describing the early art classes run by Adrian Stokes, commented, "We draw fishermen in sou'westers and oilskins. Unfortunately, they spend most days at sea fishing and only seldom find time to pose for us. In the summer, it is easy to find models, but now that there's fish to be caught the locals have become uninterested."[691] Accordingly, it was the retired fishermen, who had the time to pose repeatedly for the artists and who enjoyed the company, and the additional cash. The following is just a selection of some of the characters that sat for the artists.

In his account of the fishermen models at St Ives, William Bartlett mentioned that "One fine old type of fisherman had been painted by so many of the annual visitors that he was firmly convinced that, in the event of his coming to London, he was certain to be recognised."[692] Bartlett goes on to comment that, "He used to show, with a considerable amount of pride, a telescope that he had received from Mr Hook", which suggests that he was a member of the Perkin family, who featured in a number of Hook's paintings of 1860. Certainly, Ephraim Perkin was a popular model in the 1890s, featuring, inter alia, in Sigisbert Bosch Reitz's *Portrait of a Fisherman* (Paris Salon 1891) and William Titcomb's *Old Sea Dogs* (RA 1891) and *Jubilee Day, St Ives* (1897), and his photographic portrait by John Douglas (Fig. 3.25) ranks as one of the latter's finest achievements.

Capt Dick Harry, who was in his eighties when the artists first settled in the town, was a master mariner by profession and had been a Primitive Methodist Class-leader for more than forty years. "He was not educated in the modern sense of the word, but he knew his Bible by heart, and his life was full of its spirit."[693] Not surprisingly, therefore, he agreed to act as model for the principal figure for William Titcomb's *Primitive Methodists at Prayer, St Ives*. He also modelled for William Eadie's *"As you are now so once were we, Therefore prepare to follow me"*, a painting depicting a young girl welcoming her grandfather into his daughter's home, the title of which was taken from a gravestone near Lelant church-tower.[694] He was, in fact, sitting for another painting by Titcomb, when he died in 1890.

---

691 Letter to Maria Wiik, undated, 1888 - reproduced in translation in Marjatta Levanto, *Helene Schjerfbeck - Convalescents*, Helsinki, 1988 at p.46.
692 W.H.Bartlett, *Summertime at St Ives*, Art Journal, October 1897.
693 Undated extract from *The Artist* in the Titcomb family papers.
694 The painting depicted the interior of a cottage near Trenwith Mill (behind what is now the Royal cinema).

Another well-known character, who modelled for Titcomb, the principal figure painter in the colony, was Wilhelm Schmidt, who was known as 'Prussian Bill' or 'Old Worm's Fool'. He came to St. Ives originally as the cabin boy on a German sailing ship carrying smuggled goods and stayed on in St. Ives, after Worm, the Captain of the ship, largely due to Prussian Bill's testimony, was acquitted of smuggling. He was brought up by one of the Primitive Methodist families and was a regular in the congregation. He, therefore, featured, along with Tom Bassett, in Titcomb's painting *A Mariner's Sunday School*, which featured the interior of the Fore Street chapel, and also in his work *The End of the Day* (Fig. 2.24), with John Roach, known as 'Old Bull', and 'One-Eyed' Barber. With his shiny, bald pate, which Titcomb utilised for effects of reflected light, and his bushy, triangular-shaped beard, the broad-shouldered 'Old Bull' made an ideal model and Titcomb used him in *A Pilot* (Fig. 3.31) and other works as well. The Roach family lived close to Titcomb's studio and a relative recorded that Titcomb had helped them out financially on occasion. Titcomb will not have been the only artist to have quietly provided assistance to his models in difficult times.

'One-Eyed' Barber, whose proper name was William, was one of the true characters amongst the fisherfolk. Folliott Stokes described him as "a man of fine physique, with the face and brow of an old prophet", who possessed "a remarkable store of interesting facts, and not less interesting fancies".[695] He was loved by the children of St. Ives, not only because of the wooden dolls, called Joannies, that he would carve out of old oars in no time at all (see Fig. 3.26), but also because of his rhymes. His talent for making up rhymes in his head at a moment's notice was well-known throughout St. Ives and was a talent shared by his daughter. Stokes commented, "I have heard him addressing his wife in sonnet after sonnet of amusing conceits".[696] He would use his time modelling to think up new rhymes, which he would then proclaim to the artist at the end of the session.

Fig. 3.26 John Douglas   *'One-Eyed' Barber carving a Joannie*

---

695 A G Folliott Stokes, *From St Ives to Land's End*, London, 1908, at p.37.
696 ibid.

George Quick, who featured in several of Titcomb's paintings (see Fig. 3.35), was a celebrated preacher, better known as Georgie Crutch, as he was lame. He was a fascinating character, who had had no religious inclinations whatsoever until a powerful experience, when he believed he had been visited by God during the night, led to his conversion.[697] Thereafter, he devoted himself to evangelical work, his preaching activities taking him as far as Bath. He was described as "rugged, grizzled and weather beaten, with a voice like the roaring of the sea: quaint and original: uneducated, but learned in the things of God - a preacher of unusual power, and a welcome visitor to the sickbed. His religion was intense, real and irresistible."[698] His epitaph in Barnoon cemetery reads, "fisherman, saint, hero, 40 y a local preacher". After Titcomb had sent him a photograph of two paintings in which he had featured, he wrote, in thanks,

> "You have given me a very precious present, and I thank you for it. I mean, by God's help, to make these two pictures a blessing to many. I am sure it must have been a pleasure to paint it for God, as you have done. I wish I could write for Him or speak to Him, or paint for Him. It would be sending a voice out into the darkness, which must reach many, and guide them to light. I can do very little, but He condescends to use very poor creatures sometimes, does He not?"[699]

3.2.10 Recording a way of life

Whilst figure painters became less prominent in St Ives in the new century, as the colony developed a reputation as a centre for marine and landscape painting, the activities of the fisherfolk still continued to attract countless artists. For instance, the watercolourist, Charles Mottram, appears to have gone out with the fleet on numerous occasions, capturing the boats at work in the Bay. The magical sight of the fishing fleet leaving the harbour in late evening, with rust-coloured sails lit up by the warm glow of the setting sun, attracted William Fortescue, Claude Barry and many more, whilst Noble Barlow (Fig. 3.45) and the American, George Herbert McCord, attempted the more difficult task of depicting the boats returning under moonlight in the middle of the night, with golden shafts of light, emanating from the lanterns in their bows, dancing over the waters of the Bay. Many details of the three principal fishing seasons were captured. The Austrian, Rudolf Hellwag, depicted the bustle on the harbour beach, as the mackerel boats were made ready for the new season. Numerous artists were fascinated by the drama of the seine fishery, played out just offshore, as shoals of pilchards, gleaming like silver jewels, were caught, tucked and brought ashore. Charles Simpson, in 1923, depicted all aspects of the herring fishery, as witnessed from his studio on the harbour beach - the boats returning in the early morning, the catch being unloaded into carts backed by ponies into the lapping waters, then sorted, packed and sold by auction on the beach, before being taken away in carts over the cobbles. Other artists captured these scenes as well, with fish sales on the beach being a particularly popular subject. These paintings have recorded for posterity a way of life, with which the artists were very familiar, but which was soon to disappear. Unlike photographs of these scenes, their paintings are in colour and provide an unique historical record, which, due to the collaboration between the artists and the fisherfolk, tends also to be correct in detail.

3.2.11 Helping in troubled times

With their studios situated in the fishing quarter and with their close connections to their models, the artists could not fail to witness the economic travails of the fisherfolk in hard times, when fish were scarce or prices for catches were low, or to share the grief of the community, when, as happened all too frequently, boats were wrecked and lives were lost at sea. Therefore, in the subscription lists to relief funds, artists feature prominently, but, in an age where dependants of a deceased breadwinner could often face the workhouse, such acts of charity were expected. However, there were clearly occasions when artists went further, such as when Herbert Lanyon paid for Humphrey Hart, after he had suffered a serious accident whilst working on the railways, to have an operation in London.[700] Other recorded acts of kindness include Edmund Fuller arranging for his maid to look after Sarah Escott's deranged mother once a week, so that the young girl, forced to leave school at twelve to become her mother's carer, could get out of the house once in a while.[701] Perhaps there is no greater evidence of sincere friendships growing up between artists and fisherfolk than the use of names of artists for the fisherfolk's children; thus a member of the Stevens family was called Louis Monro Grier Stevens and a member of the Care family John Douglas Care.

---

697 The account of this experience, in his own words, is recorded in Ed.C.Noall, *History of the Fore Street Methodist Church*, 1962, p.26.

698 Ed.C.Noall, *History of the Fore Street Methodist Church*, 1962, p.26.

699 ibid.

700 See Marion Whybrow, *St Ives 1883-1993 - Portrait of an Art Colony*, Woodbridge, 1994 at p.68.

701 ibid at p.51.

Plate 26 Anders Zorn   *Fish Sale, St Ives*

Plate 27 Anders Zorn   *Fisherman, St Ives* (1888)

The purchase of this painting by the French Government and its display in the Luxembourg Museum, Paris resulted in many artist visitors to St Ives.

Plate 28 Alberto Ludovici Junior   *Fish Sale, St Ives* (1883)   (Sotheby's)

It was while Ludovici was painting this work on the harbour beach that another artist confided in him that a horror of onlookers had forced him to paint a similar scene from the grounds of the Tregenna Castle Hotel, using field glasses to view the subject!

Plate 29   Richard Hayley Lever   *Storm*   (Spanierman Gallery, LLC, New York)

Plate 30 Dorothy Robinson *Second Crew for the Lifeboat - A Volunteer*   (Salford Art Gallery)

Plate 32 William Llewellyn *St Ives* (pre-1888)
(Hy Duke & Son, Dorchester)

Plate 31 Henry Harewood Robinson
Two Nibbles (pre-1888)
(David Messum Fine Art Ltd)

Plate 33 Frank Emanuel   *Waiting for Pilchards*
(reproduced as an undivided back postcard)

Plate 34 William Banks Fortescue   *Loading Fish at Low Tide, St Ives*
(Private collection/ Photo Christie's Images/ The Bridgemen Art Library CH352999)

Plate 36 Mabel Douglas
Theresa Abell at the Arts Club
(Priscilla Fursdon)

Plate 35 Monica MacIvor
The Lost Chord
- a portrait of her sister
(William Pelly Gallery)

Plate 37 Eardley Blomefield
Charlotte Harry
(exh. Show Day 1891)
(Edward Griffin collection)

Plate 38 William Titcomb
Capt Thomas Row Harry
(Harry family collection)

THE ARTISTS AND LOCAL CLERGY

Whereas the artists might have been irritated by the attitudes of some of the most fervent Methodists, they were not irreligious themselves. Indeed, many had a strong faith, enjoyed close friendships with their clergy and executed commissions on their behalf. A number even donated work to local churches.

During his visits in 1886 and 1887, the American, Howard Butler, attended the services at the Parish Church, "because there is no other place to go to". The Vicar was the Reverend John Balmer Jones (1837-1901), who had been educated at King's College, London and Trinity College, Cambridge, before taking holy orders. He had been a curate at both St Ives (1863-4) and Hayle (1867-9) before becoming Vicar of St Ives in 1869. Butler, who was a Unitarian himself, commented, "The service seems to me to be particularly high and I cannot feel much in sympathy with it, but after the performing is all over, the Vicar generally says something good and to the point. He is a most earnest man. I have become quite attached to him and I like the curate too, who is a pleasant fellow and a capital hand at tennis.[702] They are examples to clergymen of other denominations in their attention to their flock. They seem always to be making visits. I often meet them in the vicinity of my loft notwithstanding the fact that most of my neighbors are dissenters or they are non-church goers or belong to the Salvation Army."[703] On Sunday afternoons, Butler would visit the home of fellow artist and parishioner, William Eadie, who had five small children. Eadie too became friendly with the Vicar, whose portrait he exhibited at the 1887 WCAU exhibition. Indeed, one of the first major works that Eadie executed in St Ives was *Sunday Morning in St Ives Church, Cornwall*, showing Canon Jones preaching, which was exhibited at the Royal Academy in 1889.[704]

The Reverend Jones was universally liked and worked tirelessly for the improvement of the town and his parishioners, never taking a holiday. He was made a Canon in 1894. One of his great ambitions was that a new church should be built for the fishermen. He had first suggested this in 1892, and the artists had got involved in several fund-raising activities. However, it was only after his death, in 1901, that serious progress was made towards realising this aim. The site in Norway Lane was donated (see Fig. 2.192) and, in 1903, contracts were exchanged for the erection of the building, which was called the Mariners' Church, by Robert Toy, to the design of Edmund Sedding of Plymouth. It was eventually dedicated in 1905, but always proved a bit of a white elephant, as most of the fishermen remained Methodists. Since 1945, it has been the home of the St Ives Society of Artists.

In the spring of 1887, a new curate arrived in St Ives, who was to enjoy a long association with the town and the friendship of many artists. The Reverend Richard Edward Griffin (1861-1918) was born in Weymouth and had studied at St John's College and then St Stephen's House in Oxford.[705] He was ordained priest in 1888 and was curate to the Reverend Jones for five years. A portrait of him by William Eadie (Fig. 3.27) was included in the Art Union show in November 1887 and further portraits by Eardley Blomefield and Harry Bishop were exhibited on Show Day in 1891. Blomefield also exhibited on that occasion a portrait (Plate 37) of Miss Charlotte Harry, daughter of Captain Thomas Row Harry, who was to become Griffin's wife the following year.[706]

In 1892, Edward Griffin was appointed Vicar of St Johns-in-the-Fields, Halsetown, and the American, Sydney Laurence, who seems to have been a particularly close friend, painted for him a depiction of the church and the adjoining vicarage in its isolated position (Fig. 3.30). In 1896, Griffin made an appeal for the restoration of the organ in the church and, to assist this cause, paintings were donated by the Australian Will Osborn, William and Jessie Titcomb, Sydney Carr, Walter Jevons, Percy Northcote, John Douglas, Mrs Latham Greenfield, her sister, Rose Cooper, Alexandrina Laurence, Gertrude Rowe, future wife of Algernon Talmage, and Emily Cogill.

---

702 This curate was the Reverend C.F.Jones, who subsequently moved to Fowey.

703 Letter from H.R.Butler to his mother dated 20/8/1887, Archives of American Art, Smithsonian Institution, Washington DC, Howard Russell Butler papers, Reel 1189.

704 This was sold quickly to a Mr Porter, described as "a merchant of London", but is now in the St Ives Town Collection. *St Ives Weekly Summary*, 22/6/1889.

705 Griffin could trace a connection to Thomas Hardy of Nelson fame. His great-grandmother was Hardy's sister.

706 The Griffins had four children but their only son, known as Tommy, died aged only 37 in 1940 - see *St Ives Times* 30/8/1940.

Fig. 3.27 William Eadie
Reverend Griffin (1887)
(ex- Edward Griffin collection)

In 1901, Griffin commissioned William Eadie, then a sidesman at St John's, to paint portraits of the twelve Apostles on a screen to be erected under the Chancel Arch.[707] Various well-known local figures paid contributions to sit as models for the Apostles and a contemporary account comments that the features of the originals could be clearly recognised. From the artists' community, Sydney Carr sat for St James-the-Great, the American Percy Simpson, a sidesman at the church, for St Philip, Eadie himself as St Matthias and his son, John, as St John. Other models were the Vicar himself (St James-the-Less), the long-term churchwardens, Capt Harry (St Matthew), and Lieutenant Alfred Hackman (St Thomas), Mr C.L.Williams, sidesman and local station-master, (St Simon Zelotes), and three fishermen as St Peter, St Andrew and St Bartholemew. Local legend has it that the model for the Apostle depicted as bald - Lieutenant Hackman - failed to pay his contribution (Fig. 3.29). However, Hackman was balding and the version of the story incorporated in *Portalone* - namely that it was the moustache of the miscreant that was omitted - is correct.[708] This still makes Hackman the guilty party. Whilst the series gives us the only known resemblances of Percy Simpson and Eadie himself (Fig. 3.28), the paintings are poor. In 1979, the screen was removed from its original position and now stands in the Memorial Corner.

Figs. 3.28-9 William Eadie   Details from his portraits of himself as St Mathias and Alfred Hackman as St

---

707 Eadie was a sidesman at the church, having presumably transferred his allegiance from the Parish Church.
708 C Ranger-Gull's *Portalone*, London, 1904, at p.74-5. When Hackman died in 1904, thirteen artists attended his funeral. *St Ives Weekly Summary*, 19/11/1904.

Fig. 3.30 Sydney Laurence   *St Johns-in -the-Fields and the Rectory, Halsetown*   (detail)
(ex- Edward Griffin collection)

In 1902, the artists again got together to help with a bazaar for the Church's Heating Fund. Many of the wives ran stalls, Arthur Meade was in charge of a series of pictures illustrative of life in different fluids - some 100,000 times magnified - and Talmage and Frances Horn appeared in a farce, *The Happy Pair*. Other artists who made contributions to St John's include William Fortescue, who designed, in conjunction with the ornamental artist, Miss W.K.M.Coode, a new oak altar and reredos, and Thomas Millie Dow, who designed a stained glass window above the central altar, which was dedicated in 1903 by his wife, Florence, in memory of her father, William Cox.

Griffin, who was described, in his obituary, as having "every instinct of one of England's gentlemen", was a popular clergyman and "a friend to all in need", and the extent of his involvement with the artistic community can be judged by the collection of work that he acquired.[709] This included paintings by Arnesby Brown, Julius Olsson (2), Adrian Stokes, William Titcomb (2), Sydney Laurence (7), Helene Schjerfbeck, Dorothy Robinson (2), Eardley Blomefield (3), William Eadie, Gwilt Jolley, Edmund Fuller and the Australians, Will Ashton and Will Osborn.   He remained Vicar at Halsetown for twenty-three years before becoming Vicar of St Veryan in 1915.

Fig. 3.31 William Titcomb *A Pilot*
This depicts Bernard Walke preaching to the fishermen on the quayside,
a place where they felt more comfortable than in church.

---

709 *St Ives Times*, 18/3/1918.

Other curates at the Parish church, who became well-liked by the artists, were Bernard Walke and Joe Hellier. Walke, who was to cause such controversy due to his Catholic sympathies, whilst Vicar of St Hilary, near Marazion, became a curate in St Ives in 1902 and lived at Ayr Cottage with his mother and his brother, William, who seems to have enrolled as an art student (see Fig. 2.236).[710] Bernard Walke immediately made a significant impression on both artists and fishermen and he is featured in William Titcomb's paintings *A Pilot* (Fig. 3.31) and *The Church in Cornwall : A Rogation Day Procession* (Cheltenham Art Gallery). Realising that the fishermen were put off coming to the Parish Church because of middle class snobbery about matters such as dress and cleanliness, and that the typical Anglican service was considered boring and uninspiring, Walke sought to introduce more ritual and passion into proceedings, and even preached to the fishermen in their own environment - the quayside (Fig. 3.31). When he was removed from his curacy in December 1904 by the Bishop of Truro on the grounds that he and the Vicar, the Reverend Marsh, could not work together, Charles Marriott and Sydney Carr were some of those who wrote strong letters in his support. Indeed, Marriott described Walke as one of his greatest friends in St Ives and later recalled how he was "universally beloved".[711] Hellier arrived as a curate in 1903 and was considered zealous and hard-working and an earnest preacher. After leaving St Ives in 1905, he holidayed with the Titcombs in Germany and, after a spell as a missionary, eventually married Sydney Carr's daughter, Vera.

The Reverend Sidney Frank Marsh, who served as Vicar at the Parish Church from the death of Canon Jones in 1901 until 1936, does not appear to have been as well liked. He had been a teacher at Liskeard, before taking holy orders, and was an accomplished musician. However, he soon suffered the tragic loss of his wife, Louisa, aged only 34 in June 1903, and her funeral was attended by the Lindners, the Carrs, the Mottrams, the Douglases, Millie Dow, William Brooke, Louis Grier and Elgar Russell. However, in a letter dated 1st February 1904, Murielle Schofield told Elmer that Marsh had got engaged again to Gwendoline Mary Snow-Clifton. "People think too soon after his wife's death. She is heavy looking but has a beautiful neck and arms and large hips - many a man has married for the same attractions". They got married that September, but the Reverend Marsh seems to have been stalked by tragedy, for his second child died aged 20 months in 1909. Furthermore, whilst Herbert Lanyon's two children, Peter and Mary, acted as train-bearers at the wedding, in 1923, of his eldest son, Francis, to a Californian, Muriel Snook (see Fig. 3.32), Francis, then an officer in the RAF, was killed in a car accident in India in 1929.

Fig. 3.32 Herbert Lanyon Peter and Mary Lanyon, as train-bearers at the wedding of Francis Marsh (Lanyon family archive)

Fig. 3.33 Alfred Pazolt The Catholic Chapel in St Ives 1902-9

---

710 William went on to Salisbury Theological College, but was killed in a car accident in 1911. The driver was a fellow student, who had been driving too fast. *St Ives Weekly Summary*, 18/2/1911.

711 Charles Marriott, *Memories of Cornwall's Art Colonies*, *The Cornish Review*, Spring 1949, No.1, at p.70.

Fig. 3.34 H.G.Fitzherbert
Caricature believed to be of Alfred Pazolt
(from *Caricatures of the Cornish Riviera*)

In the early years of the art colony, there was no Catholic Church in St Ives and so Roman Catholics, such as Marianne Stokes and Dorothy Robinson, had to worship in Penzance. Martin Gwilt Jolley, who was also a Roman Catholic, painted a Madonna for his Church there, but as the local Catholic churches have had no compunction in selling off artists' donated work over the years, the current whereabouts of this are not known. However, in 1902, a site was acquired in central St Ives and a small upper room, above some old shops, was used as a chapel (Fig. 3.33). The American-born marine painter, Alfred Pazolt, lent £1500 to the Church Building Fund and enlisted his old friend, John Pius Boland, now an M.P., to publicize the new initiative.[712] Pazolt's own photographs of the first church and general views of St Ives were used in the article. After seven years, this room proved woefully inadequate and the present Catholic Church at the top of Skidden Hill was erected.

When Pazolt married, on 29th August 1906, Mary Teresa Freeman, the eldest daughter of John Freeman of Penryn, whose wealth came from granite quarries, he became related to Charles Napier Hemy, as Hemy's second wife, Amy, was Mary's sister. Hemy was a staunch Roman Catholic himself - he had once contemplated becoming a Dominican priest - and his decision to base himself in St Ives during 1908 was, without doubt, due to his desire to see the completion and dedication of the new Catholic Church in the town. The result was that three of his exhibits at the Royal Academy in 1909 were St Ives scenes - *The Harbour Lights, St Ives*, *Godrevy Light* and *A Sleeping Sea*. All were night scenes and, unusually, were executed in watercolour. Another work, again a watercolour, *St Ives on Christmas Day 1908*, is now owned by Penlee House Gallery & Museum, Penzance. The Pazolt family's donations to the new Church included a new set of the Stations of the Cross in coloured plaster, and stained glass, showing The Immaculate Conception, for the Rose Window over the High Altar.

In 1909, however, Alfred Pazolt decided to move to Ryde on the Isle of Wight, for reasons most probably connected with his enthusiasm for sailing, and the log of the Catholic Church for 1909 reads, "The close of this year saw the departure from St Ives for the Isle of Wight of Mr and Mrs Alfred Pazolt, with their two maid servants and their man, Stevens; this removal, involving also the departure of Mrs Stevens and five children, means a loss of eleven to the St Ives congregation." However, Alfred's father, Henry, and his sister, Caroline, remained in St Ives and continued to be great benefactors of the Church. Another artist, who was a great servant of the Catholic Church, was Arthur White, who, despite being a member of the Wesley Chapel, was the organist there for some twenty-five years.

712 See J P Boland MP, *An Irish Saint in Cornwall*, *The Catholic Home Journal*, 1902 - copy at St Ives Archive Centre. Pazolt had travelled with the Irishman John Pius Boland in 1896 from Bonn, where they had met at a Catholic Students' Convention, to Athens, where Boland competed in the first Olympic lawn tennis event, winning both the singles and the doubles. Boland's diary for this trip is the reason for Dr Heiner Gillmeister's interest in Pazolt and I am very indebted to him for his research on Pazolt.

Fig. 3.35 William Titcomb *Piloting Her Home*   (charcoal drawing)
featuring 'Georgie Crutch' (hands on bed), John B.Stevens (standing)
Peggy Rouncefield and her daughter, Miriam Hart

One might imagine, given the difficulties that Methodists tended to have with artists, that friendships would not have developed between Methodist ministers and anyone from the colony, but the Reverend Francis Robinson, who was a Methodist minister in the town in the late 1880s, had an eye for beauty and wrote several fine articles in 1889 describing the attractive scenery around St Ives, even highlighting the merits of Louis Grier's painting *A Golden Autumn Evening, St Ives*. On a return visit to the town in 1902, he stayed at 'Windy Parc' with the Titcombs. Albeit an Anglican himself, Titcomb was fascinated by the fervour of the local Primitive Methodists and his trio of paintings depicting the congregation of the Fore Street Chapel have made that simple place of worship famous around the world. As a result, he donated to the Chapel the original large charcoal drawings for such works, and these have recently been restored. That of *Piloting Her Home* (Fig. 3.35) has also been exhibited at Penlee House Gallery & Museum, Penzance, for it is an extraordinary work of art in its own right. It was a scene witnessed by Titcomb, as he came to pay his last respects to one of his models, Peggy Rouncefield, who was seriously ill, before departing on his extended honeymoon. The fervour of the prayers, led by 'Georgie Crutch', had caused the old woman to sit up in bed, raising her hands as she talked familiarly to Jesus and welcoming her impending fate. In fact, she recovered and so Titcomb was able to get the participants to re-enact the scene on his return.

ENLARGING 'THE MENTAL VISION OF THE TOWNSPEOPLE'

3.4.1   Introduction

As early as 1891, a local correspondent paid tribute to the artists for "the marked influence they have brought to bear on the artistic education of the residents.....Working in the open, as a large majority of our artists do, ample opportunities have been afforded to watch day by day the evolutionary principle of the pictures, as they were developed from one stage to another. It has often been interesting to observe the earnestness with which an artist is watched whilst at work, and to listen to the common-sense criticism of uneducated, but intelligent, members of the working class."[713] This confirms that the artists were not merely dismissed as interlopers or as objects of idle curiosity, but generated a genuine interest in their methods and objectives. Such interest might be off-putting, on occasion, but was also quite welcome, for the correspondent continued, "This inartistic and common-sense criticism, strange to say, is what is most valued by the artists, for....the inartistic critic has no pre-conceived notion of what the colouring, grouping or construction of a picture should be, and consequently gives the expresssion of an unbiased and unprejudiced judgment."[714] Artists, therefore, by painting out of doors, ensured a greater inter-reaction with the townsfolk and were able, much quicker, to educate them on some of the mysteries of art.

The influence of the artists, however, was much wider than this. At the Mayoral Banquet in 1900, Edward Boase proposed a toast to the St Ives Art Colony as it had exercised "a beneficial moral influence on the town by helping in the enlargement of the mental vision of the townspeople".[715] This was not an isolated view, as Sampson Taylor Rowe, two years previously, in an article entitled *Old St Ives - Its Artists and its Fishermen*, had stated that the presence of the artists had led to the development in the local community of "more liberal opinions....and broader views of the modern condition of social life."[716] These comments indicate that the impact of the artists was much broader than is normally credited, and this chapter looks not only at the manner in which their art was exposed to the locals, but also at the influence that they had on other cultural activities, such as music, drama and sport, their support for worthy local causes, particularly the Free Library, and their involvement in campaigns on such matters as women's rights and animal cruelty.

3.4.2   Art

Before the formation of the art colonies, exhibitions of fine art were rare events in Cornwall, with paintings merely forming a minor section of the exhibitions mounted, under the auspices of the South Kensington Museum, by the Royal Cornwall Polytechnic Society in Falmouth and the West Cornwall Art Union in Penzance. In any event, such paintings often tended to be by amateurs or students. Once artists had settled in the Duchy, such exhibitions began to include more work by professional artists, but they rarely contained major works, for these were produced principally for the exhibitions in London, Paris and Pittsburgh. There was, however, one occasion each year, when such major paintings could be viewed by locals - Show Day - and this became the highlight of the artistic calendar in St Ives.

3.4.2.1 Show Day

The phenomenon that Show Day in St Ives became in the 1930s and 1940s, when special trains were laid on from London and crowds of visitors every March thronged through the artists' studios to view the paintings that they were sending off to the Royal Academy, was a world apart from the small, exclusive 'At Homes' that took place in the early years of the colony. Aware that in London, a number of artists held Private Views in March/April prior to submitting their work to the Royal Academy, this practice was introduced at Newlyn in 1887, when Stanhope Forbes and Percy Craft opened their studio to a number of invited guests at the end of March.[717] There is no mention of a similar event in St Ives that year, and it is most unlikely that it occurred, as very few of the St Ives residents seem to have submitted work to

---

713 *Cornish Telegraph*, 9/4/1891.
714   ibid.
715 *St Ives Weekly Summary* 10/11/1900.
716 Sampson Taylor Rowe, *Old St Ives - Its Artists and Fishermen*, *St Ives Weekly Summary*, 9/4/1898. Rowe was Gertrude Talmage's father.
717 The works on display included Forbes' *Their Ever Shifting Home*, a subject that had been painted partly in St Ives.

the Royal Academy. The following year, however, the idea was taken up by the artists in St Ives and, over a period of a fortnight, there were a series of Private Views.[718] Unfortunately, the artists concerned are not named and their works were not reviewed in the local press.

In 1889, the event's significance had become appreciated, and the local paper contained a full description of the paintings on display during 'At Homes' by Louis and Wyly Grier, Harry and Dorothy Robinson, Adrian and Marianne Stokes, William Eadie, William Titcomb, Julius Olsson and Charles Davis, although, in fact, a number of artists exhibited their work, not in their studios, but in the Public Hall. In addition, the reviewer apologised for missing the work of Edward Simmons, adding, helpfully, that this could be seen in the American section of the forthcoming exhibition in Paris! Already, however, such functions had become social events. "Who ever came to *see pictures* at a 'Private View'? Certainly, the 'Cimabue Brown' girls, the handsome young gentleman in the bold stockings and knickerbockers and Randolph-Churchillian moustache, the patriarchal lawyer, who loves his cups of tea ('but no sugar, thank you'), the burly retired naval lieutenant and the whole family of the Bohemiam brotherhood who have come to assist in the social functions, give no earnest heed to the pictures, at least not those in frames. The girls are here for fashion's sake, to see and be seen. The 'mashers' are here to help them and the elders to enjoy the fun."[719]

The practice whereby the artists held independent Private Views over a period of weeks seems to have continued for some years, with reviews of their work being spread over several issues of the local paper. Unfortunately in 1893, there are no reviews at all and, in 1894, only the works of Sydney Laurence, Edmund Fuller, Noble Barlow, Walter Jevons and Emily Latham Greenfield are mentioned, although clearly many other artists were showing that year. It is not clear when a specific day - normally, a Monday - was selected for all artists' studios to be open at the same time, but this was certainly the case by 1896, when Lewis Hind describes the scene:-

"The village is in holiday attire. Since early morning, vehicles laden with ladies in their best bonnets, and men in new serge suits, have come galloping gaily down the hill that leads from the outside world. The steep streets are bright with laughing groups. Women lift their silken skirts and plunge bravely into the tortuous bye-ways, round angular corners, through ancient doorways, and up rickety stairs. All these little journeys have the same issue. The top stair abuts on a passage, and the passage opens into a studio, and in the studio stands a young man, who bows, grasps your hand, and then retires to greet another guest, while you examine the display of pictures, and presently, when your host draws within earshot, you murmur "Excellent!" or "Delightful!" or "Very Good!" or "Superb!" or, perhaps, if he is a very old friend, and has painted more than common well, you grasp his hand and say, "My dear fellow, you have done it this time."

It takes the best part of a day to get round these studios. Their number is endless. Some are new, some have been converted from sail lofts, or pilchard packing dens, or any large apartment whose architecture would admit of a window with a north light. They perch upon the brow of the cliff, glass windows flashing in the sun; they hide themselves in the innermost recesses of the congeries of crooked courts; they stand like sentinels above the harbour, and they line the Porthmeor Beach, upon which the broad waves of the Atlantic rear and tumble. St Ives is not always in this holiday mood. This is the day that corresponds to the London Show Sunday. Soon the visitors will have all departed, the finery will be laid away, and, by the time the night comes up with her garniture of stars, St Ives will be as sleepy and sedate as she has been any time during the past centuries. Tomorrow, the pictures will be packed, a special train will run them up to London, and towards the end of the week that precedes 'Varnishing Day', the painters themselves will be following their pictures to London."[720]

The change to a single open day heralded a significant development. Private Views were occasions for a select group of friends - fellow artists, known collectors, models, landladies and acquaintances from the Arts Club and from around the town. Setting aside a whole day (sometimes two) for members of the general public to wander in and out of their studios at will made more commercial sense and certainly encouraged greater numbers of visitors to make the trip to St Ives for the event. It became an occasion that could not be ignored by the locals, and Lilian Faull records how the excitement swelled as the day approached. However, it was not the art that interested girls like her, but the fashions. "This was a great day in the town for we saw ladies of grace and position walking from the station - no buses and few cars - over our cobbled streets to the Studios which were mostly in the lower part of the town. I used to go to Grandma Faull's Parlour and look out of the window to see the lovely dresses as the Visitors passed below."[721]

---

718 *The Cornishman*, 29/3/1888.
719 *The Cornishman*, 11/4/1889.
720 C.Lewis Hind, *In Painters' Land, The Ludgate*, October 1896.
721 Lilian Faull, *The Faulls of St Ives*, Penzance, 1972 at p.74-5.

Fig. 3.36 Show Day at the Piazza Studios in the 1930s

Writing in 1907, Hind commented on the crush that was now a feature of the occasion. "All day the population swarmed and gazed. In the huddle of studios that are packed away in the Brobdingnagian beehive on the Porthmeor shore, against whose granite foundation walls the Atlantic breakers dash, one could move neither backwards nor forwards. Fishermen and painters stood like sculptured figures on Mahomet's coffin on the open staircases that shoot this way, that way, and upwards from the ground. In every studio, you were jostled by a wide-eyed crowd of gazers."[722]

The fact that the fisherfolk were not only welcomed to partake in the spectacle by the artists, but were sufficiently intrigued by the crowds to do the rounds of studios themselves, says much for the mutual respect that eventually developed, after early misunderstandings. The result was, in the words of Charles Vulliamy, a student at Newlyn, "a most curious, a unique crowd of picture-gazers. Pallid high-brows, with their black stocks and floppy hats, stand by the side of chubby old fishwives; and ladies who would cut a seemly figure in the tea room at the Trocadero are elbowed by tough sailormen from the quay. Thus, in a strong smell made up of fish, tar, creosote, oil-paint, and things which are better imagined than described, a truly democratic set of sight-seers moves from studio to studio."[723]

The fisherfolk did not join in merely out of curiosity or from a desire to mingle with the upper classes, but to view the finished paintings, which they had often seen in progress as the artists sketched around the town and in some of which, as likely as not, one or more of their colleagues were portrayed. They were not afraid to pass comment on what they saw, either, for Hind records the opinion of one old Cornish dame, on looking at a broadly painted seascape, "It looks likelier, my dear, the further you go away from it." As he observed, "That old dame had the root of the matter in her."[724] It also appears that, during these sorties into the painters' lairs, the locals began to pick up artistic terminology, for Charles Marriott was most amused to overhear one layman saying to another, "Your brown boots are a bit high in tone, old chap"![725]

---

722 C Lewis Hind, *Days in Cornwall*, London, 1907 at p. 147.

723 Charles Vulliamy, *Unknown Cornwall*, London, 1925 at p.75.

724 C Lewis Hind, *Days in Cornwall*, London, 1907 at p. 147-8.

725 Charles Marriott, *Memories of Cornwall's Art Colonies*, *Cornish Review*, Spring 1949, No.1 at p.68.

Fig. 3.37 Arnesby Brown *Labourers*   (RA 1898)

Children from the fisher-community were also tolerated, if not always welcome, and the reviewer of Show Day in 1898 recorded a couple of amusing incidents. Arnesby Brown that year exhibited *Labourers*, a painting of several tired horses turned out after a hard day's work on to a bleak common (Fig. 3.37), and the critic commented, "Perhaps the most sincere flattery to the skill of this Painter was paid by a troublesome small boy, who was so much impressed by the shininess of the old brown horse's coat, glowing in the evening sunlight, that he stealthily approached the canvas, and, having rubbed his not too clean hand on the side of the poor tired creature, proceeded to examine his thumb to see how wet the sweat of the painted horse had made it! Another of these unconscious flatterers was, in another studio, trying to bathe his hand in the pictured glow of the setting sun, and was much disappointed that his little grubby paw did not get dyed in the ruby light of the sunset!"[726]

Visitors enjoyed these adventurous sorties into the private lairs of the artists and a local reporter commented in 1899, "There undoubtedly is, to most of us, a special charm in seeing the works of our Artists in their birth-place, and this charm is heightened by the artistic litter of the studios, with the sketches - some mere suggestive outlines in charcoal; some only experiments in colour such as we may see in the Turner Collection; and some so far finished that to the generalising eye of the British Philistine, half an hour or so is all that is necessary for the production of a perfect picture from a nearly finished sketch. Apart from the romance of the Bohemianism of Art, there is in the breakneck approach to many of the studios an element of danger, which has, in this prosaic end of the century,...a charm and romance of its own."[727]

One might have anticipated that the artists would have welcomed such added exposure for their efforts but, on a further occasion, Hind commented, "These show times are not the happiest days in the lives of painters. What they want - what we all want - is rich, steaming, abundant but discriminating praise. All Monday, and nearly all Sunday, St Ives painters cowered in the corners of their studios, watching the world muddy their floors, misunderstand their dreams, admire their frames, and the view from the window. To the sensitive, the ordeal is agony."[728]

During the War, Show Day was suspended in the years 1917 and 1918, but it regained its popularity in the early 1920s. A programme was produced listing the studios that were open and the artists who were exhibiting and, later in the decade, a map of the studios, drawn by Francis Roskruge, was issued as well. Safety concerns, as a result of the vast crowds attending, meant that police had to be employed to regulate numbers in certain studios and the combined weight of visitors in the wooden Piazza studios resulted in structural movement that caused great anxiety. Tea was invariably served in the Arts Club and this was one of the few occasions when the artists from Newlyn and other Cornish colonies were entertained. Show Day, accordingly, remained the principal event of the year amongst the artistic community in the town and artists worked feverishly away as the date approached, putting the finishing touches to their best works of the season.

726 *St Ives Weekly Summary*, 26/3/1898.

727 *St Ives Weekly Summary*, 1/4/1899.

728 C.Lewis Hind, *Picture Monday at St Ives, Pall Mall Gazette*, April 1905.

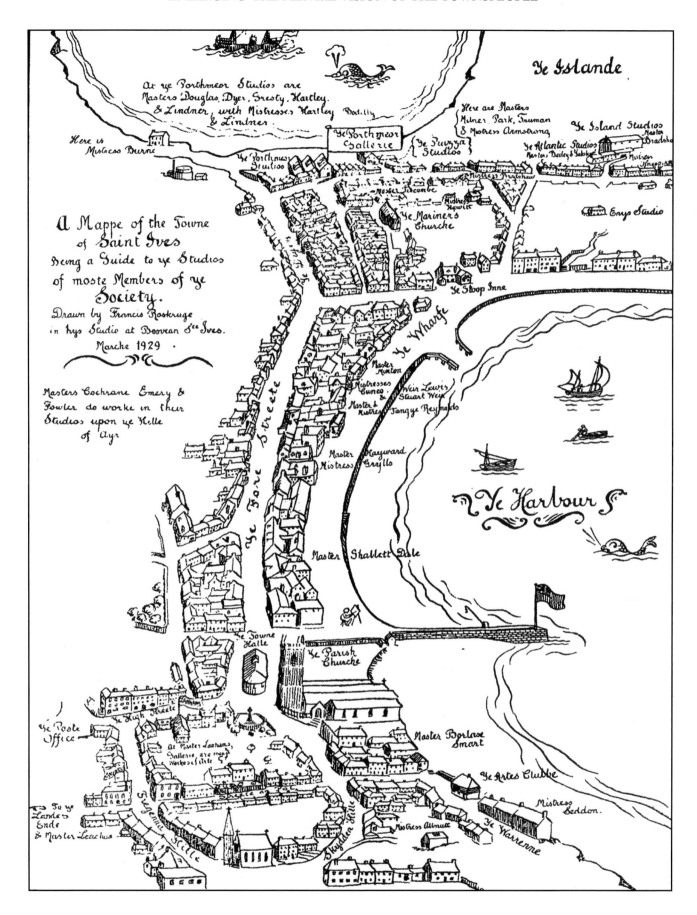

Fig. 3.38 Francis Roskruge's Map of the Studios (1929 version). This confirms, inter alia, the location of 'Poncyn Studio', one of the Malakoff Studios, (Allnutt), 'Morvah Studio' (Seddon), 'Ocean Wave Studio (Smart), 'Market Strand Studio' (Shallett Dale), 'Blue Studio' (Grylls), 'Harbour Studio' (Hayward), 'Downalong Studio' (Cuneo), 'Rose Lodge Studio' (Weir) and 'Shore Studio' (Minton).

Fig. 3.39 Lanham's shop, with posters advertising an exhibition of pictures.
Storeman, Alex James, is in the doorway.
(St Ives Trust Archive Study Centre)

3.4.2.2 Lanham's Galleries

Show Day was the only occasion during the year that all the studios were open at the same time and, in general, artists did not welcome casual visitors to their workplaces. Accordingly, for most tourists, the only place at which paintings by the artists could be viewed was at Lanham's Galleries. Although this became the principal outlet for the sale of work in Cornwall by St Ives artists, there is a frustrating lack of information about the paintings that were hung and sold there. No catalogues were printed, as the works hung were changed every month, and very few reviews exist of the exhibitions mounted.

Harry Robinson, in Badcock's guide, published in 1896, recorded, "In the year 1887, a small gallery for the exhibition of works by members of the community was, at the insistence of the artists, opened by Mr Lanham. It has since been enlarged and improved. Pictures are selected and hung by a Committee of Artists chosen by the Exhibitors from amongst themselves."[729] This account makes it clear that, yet again, the venture was the result of discussions between the artists and a local businessman. The enlargement appears to have happened in 1889, as an article in *The Cornishman* that August commented, "A new art exhibition for the West of England has sprung into existence, and the quaintly attractive town of St Ives bids fair to become a centre, where the celebrated artists at St Ives, Newlyn and other parts of West Cornwall will group together their work for the benefit of the public and themselves until the nucleus will expand and obtain a widespread and favourable reputation. The credit of originating this idea is due to James Lanham, the well-known importer of artistic materials, and he has borne the entire expense of tastefully decorating a room over his extensive warehouse, where the paintings are set off by a background similar to that in vogue in all great exhibitions."[730]   The artists, therefore, will have had an input concerning the decorative scheme. A new name may have been adopted as well at this time, as adverts in 1892 refer to the premises as the West Cornwall Gallery of Fine Arts.[731]

---

729 In the Cornish Directory for 1887, Lanham calls himself "artists' colourman with associated gallery".

730 *The Cornishman*, 8/1889.

731 See, for instance, *St Ives Weekly Summary* 6/8/1892.

The show in 1889, that launched the refurbished Gallery, is the only one that gets any significant coverage in the local papers prior to the First World War. The hanging committee comprised Adrian Stokes, Edward Simmons, Harry Robinson and Louis Grier and amateur artists and mediocre professional artists were discouraged from applying. Artists from Newlyn, however, were invited to exhibit, and work was contributed by Stanhope and Elizabeth Forbes, Frank Bramley, Henry Tuke, Chevalier Tayler, Henry Detmold, Percy Craft and J.D.MacKenzie. Frank Brangwyn, who had been working in Cornwall that year, was also represented, along with the permanent St Ives residents Edward and Vesta Simmons, Harry and Dorothy Robinson, Louis and Wyly Grier, Sydney and Alexandrina Laurence, Julius Olsson, Marianne Stokes, Greville Morris, William Eadie and Eardley Blomefield.[732]

The Gallery was a room, "hung with dark red", over Lanham's extensive warehouse in the High Street and the steep stairs leading to the Gallery were decorated with prints of Botticellis and other Florentine masters.[733] Norman Garstin, when he visited the Gallery in 1896, commented in an article in *The Studio*,

"Here, under an awning, that softens the strong glare of the sky-light, you find a charming little show, always fresh and interesting. Every month it is re-arranged, new blood infused; the fearful gaps made by that ruthless devastator of exhibitions, the buyer, are filled up; and so from year's end to year's end, this gallery flourishes like a tropical forest, dropping now and then a leaf though knowing no season but one.

People might hastily assume that a picture gallery in a small town like St Ives would be of a monotonous character; but this is not so because, though the town is small, the artistic colony is large and of most varied constituents; furthermore the St Ives painters are nomadic in their instincts; they sally forth like the Barbary pirates from the little port and ravage distant lands of their beauties."[734]

By this juncture, Lanham had made available other rooms, for individual shows, and Garstin viewed a selection of works by William and Jessie Titcomb of Venice, by Gwilt Jolley of Capri and by the Canadian, Mary Bell.

Fig. 3.40 This photograph from Louis Grier's papers is believed to show Lanham's Galleries
(Denys Wilcox)

732 Brangwyn, who also worked in Mevagissey, recalled that he sold a work there to Charles Grier, a brother of Louis and Wyly, who was a doctor - see Marion Whybrow, *St Ives 1883-1993 - Portrait of an Art Colony*, Woodbridge, 1994 at p. 35.
733 Extract from *Westminster Gazette*, reproduced in *St Ives Weekly Summary*, 19/9/1896.
734 Norman Garstin, *Studio Talk, The Studio*, Vol. VIII, 1896, p.242-3.

Lanham had to get used to the sensibilities of the artists. Having tried, helpfully, in 1893, to give them some additional publicity by putting a few of their paintings in his shop window, he got a severe rebuke for his pains. Following an Arts Club resolution (see Fig. 3.41) , which read, "We, the undersigned, think it most unbecoming in members of this Club to allow their pictures to be exhibited in shop windows", a letter was despatched to Lanham accordingly.

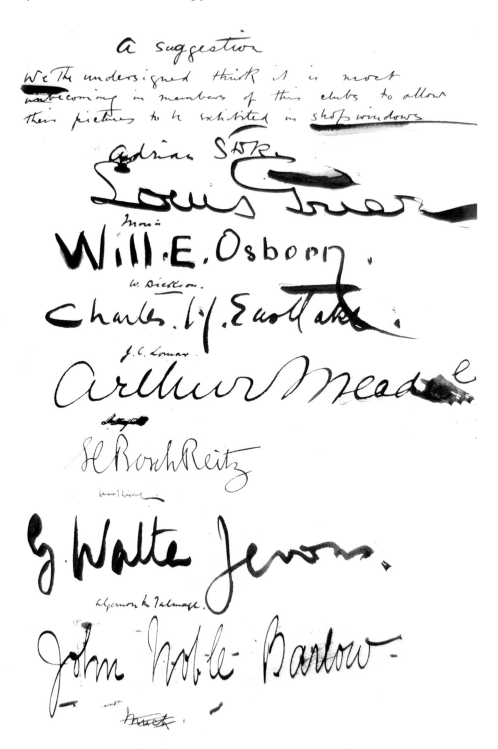

Fig. 3.41 Extract from Arts Club Suggestions Book, where, prompted by Grier's renowned flamboyant signature, the artists have amused themselves by signing alternatively as large or as small as possible. Signatories are Adrian Stokes, Louis Grier, Greville Morris, Will Osborn, William Dickson, Charles Eastlake, John Lomax, Arthur Meade, Sigisbert Bosch Reitz, Edward Lingwood, Walter Jevons, Algernon Talmage and Noble Barlow.

TABLE F   HANGING COMMITTEES FOR LANHAM'S GALLERIES

The records of elected hanging committees are incomplete. The following are some examples.

1889	Adrian Stokes, Edward Simmons, Harry Robinson, Louis Grier.
April 1897	Noble Barlow, Louis Grier, Lowell Dyer, Harry Robinson, William Titcomb.
October 1897	Noble Barlow, Millie Dow, Harry Robinson, Adrian Stokes, William Titcomb.
November 1898	Julius Olsson, Harry Robinson, Arnesby Brown, Millie Dow, Moffat Lindner.
February 1900	Julius Olsson, Harry Robinson, Algernon Talmage, Folliott Stokes, Millie Dow.
October 1900	Arnesby Brown, Millie Dow, David Davies, Harry Robinson, William Titcomb.
November 1904	Arnesby Brown, Arthur Meade, Fred Milner, Julius Olsson, William Titcomb.
November 1905	Arnesby Brown, Allan Deacon, Millie Dow, Moffat Lindner, Algernon Talmage.
November 1906	Arnesby Brown, Moffat Lindner, Arthur Meade, Julius Olsson, Elmer Schofield.
March 1907	William Fortescue, Louis Grier, Julius Olsson, Elmer Schofield, Algernon Talmage.
November 1907	Arnesby Brown, Alfred Hartley, Fred Milner, Arthur Meade, Julius Olsson.
November 1911	Louis Grier, Alfred Hartley, Moffat Lindner, Fred Milner, Louis Sargent.
November 1912	Moffat Lindner, Alfred Hartley, Arthur Meade, Fred Milner, Louis Grier.
November 1913	Moffat Lindner, Alfred Hartley, Arthur Meade, Louis Grier, Lowell Dyer.
November 1916	Moffat Lindner, Alfred Hartley, Arthur Meade, Louis Grier, Langley Hutton.
November 1917	Lindner, A Hartley, Meade, Langley Hutton, Emile Fabry, Frederick Beaumont
November 1919	Lindner, Meade, Milner, Frederick Beaumont, Claude Francis Barry, Langley Hutton.
1922	Lowell Dyer, Alfred Hartley, John Park, Borlase Smart, Frank Moore, William Fortescue.
1924	Moffat Lindner, John Park, Borlase Smart, Alfred Hartley, Arthur Hayward, Nell Cuneo.
1925	Moffat Lindner, John Park, Alfred Hartley, Fred Milner, Nell Cuneo, Pauline Hewitt.
1926	Moffat Lindner, Fred Milner, George Bradshaw, Francis Raymond Spenlove, John Park, Nora Hartley and Pauline Hewitt.

The hanging committee was elected principally from the artist members of the Arts Club, and every attempt was made to ensure that the best artists available were elected on to the committee. Works were selected on the basis of their artistic merit, rather than their commercial appeal. Nevertheless, it was reported in 1894 that sales were very good, although Lanham was dismayed that the volume of pictures submitted meant that many had to be rejected each month. In 1897, some rule changes were introduced. There was clearly some concern that sub-standard work by some of the art students was being included in the Gallery, and so, in future, members of the hanging committee were not allowed to vote on the works of their pupils. Furthermore, in an effort to ensure that the gallery remained the premier showcase for the artists, exhibitors were also not allowed to have works on sale in any other Public Gallery or shop in St Ives.

In 1905, a Special Meeting of the Arts Club was called, as it was felt that the arrangements concerning Lanham's had become unsatisfactory. At this juncture, it appears as if outsiders had the right to vote and act on the hanging committee, with the result that "nobody knew how they were to use their rights in a Club to which they did not belong". The Club, therefore, agreed to re-assume sole responsibility for the management of the exhibitions and published a set of rules governing the election and operation of the hanging committee. The committee was to consist of five persons and only Club members could be appointed. As non-attendance at the monthly hangs was clearly a problem, detailed rules were set out for a quorum and for the substitution of recalcitrant members. The idea of having a supplementary committee, from which gaps in the original committee could be made up, soon failed to work, and, for a while, committees were appointed twice a year - at the time of the AGM in November and around Show Day. This reflected the fact that some artists, such as Arnesby Brown, for instance, were principally winter visitors. August and September often proved difficult months for the hanging committee to operate, as so many artists were away and, in such circumstances, James Lanham had to hang the exhibitions himself. However, in doing so, he nearly always upset someone. The rules relating to the composition of the hanging committee did not mean that exhibitors had to be Club members, and works from Newlyn and elsewhere continued to be hung.

One of the few occasions, in the pre-War period, when a full listing of artist exhibitors is given was in connection with a Five Guinea show "for a special purpose" in April 1908, albeit that purpose is not revealed. In addition to the artists that one would expect to contribute at that time, there were works by the Americans George Gardner Symons and Henry Keasbey, the New Zealander Herbert Babbage, regular visitor Alfred East, the recently departed Algernon Talmage, soon to depart Max Ludby, new arrivals William Parkyn and Arthur White, and recent students Norman Wilkinson, Hayley Lever, John Park, Gertrude Rosenberg, Frances Horn, William Evans Linton, Gwendoline Hopton and Elizabeth Wilde.

Fig. 3.42   Artist showing his work outside Lanham's

After Lanham's business was taken over, in 1911, by Benjamin Bramham, the Galleries seem to have been run much as before. The War years will have been difficult and, in October 1916, the Arts Club Committee issued an edict that artists should only exhibit their pictures at Lanham's Gallery.   Such a direction was clearly not adhered to, as, the following year, it was stipulated that artists, who did exhibit their works elsewhere, would not be hung at Lanham's. Alfred Hartley and Louis Grier were amongst those keen to ensure that such a rule was rigidly enforced. By this juncture, though, some artists were desperate for sales.

In 1917, Bramham redecorated the premises and decided to change the name to the St Ives Art Gallery. However, when Martin Cock took control in 1919, the Lanham's name was re-introduced. He, too, was soon reprimanded by the artists. "The Committee are of the opinion that the way paintings and drawings are now shown crowded together and overlapping is undignified and against the interests of the artists and yourself".[735] Cock soon learnt how the artists liked things done, and one major new benefit was that reviews of the exhibitions at Lanham's became more regular, as he was also running the *St Ives Times* at that juncture. Edgar Skinner and Borlase Smart were occasional contributors. However, one Scottish visitor, in 1923, described the Gallery as full of "pictures of St Ives which nobody buys".[736] Possibly as a result of this, Martin Cock decided to improve and renovate them in 1924. There were now three separate Galleries - Gallery No 1 was hung by the Arts Club, Gallery No 2 was available for one man shows, whilst, with the increased interest in the decorative arts in the 1920s, Gallery No 3 became increasingly devoted to craftwork shows. Accordingly, it staged several exhibitions of art needlework, by such artists as Doris Barry, Ruth Davenport and Lucy and Vera Bodilly, as well as two exhibitions featuring Marcella Smith's raffia hats. With the advancing years of the colony's members, memorial exhibitions also started to become a regular feature. Some of these, like those for William Fortescue and William Cave Day in 1924, went on to Plymouth Art Gallery.

The exclusive monopoly on the display of paintings in the town that, with the support of the artists, Lanham's Galleries had had for over forty years, ended in 1928, when the newly-formed St Ives Society of Artists decided to rent No 5 Porthmeor Studios, as an exhibiting venue. There had clearly been some disaffectment with the exhibitions at Lanham's in the preceding years, but this had partly been due to artists not sending their best work there. In any event, in the hope of boosting sales, the artists now wanted to have complete artistic control over the decoration and presentation of the exhibition space. There is also likely to have been a feeling that, at Lanham's, there were too many other lower cost articles competing for the attractions of prospective purchasers, and it is telling that handicraft was excluded from the Society's exhibitions.

The new Gallery created by the Society did not mean the end of the exhibitions at Lanham's. Indeed, the Society's decision prompted Martin Cock to have a further refurbishment of the Galleries, which vastly improved the lighting and general appearance. Accordingly, there were now two major venues for the display of paintings in the town, and it was noted, after the first exhibition was opened at the Porthmeor Galleries, that there were over 300 paintings for sale - 204 at Lanham's and 109 at Porthmeor. As the Society increased its membership, the additional hanging space offered by Lanham's was welcomed and exhibitions continued there for many decades, albeit the quality (and, accordingly, price) of work on offer tended to be lower. Sadly, the records of the company, which would have provided such an invaluable source, have been destroyed.

---

735 See Arts Club Minutes 11/6/1919.
736 Article by B.C., reproduced in *St Ives Times*, 31/8/1923.

3.4.2.3 The Passmore Edwards Gallery Exhibitions, Newlyn

Wherever exhibitions of art were held in West Cornwall, contributions were always encouraged from all the Cornish art colonies. Accordingly, St Ives artists were well represented at the West Cornwall Art Union exhibitions that were held in 1887, 1889 and 1891 at the short-lived Penzance Art Museum, which had been built next to the School of Art in Morrab Road.[737] They also contributed to the Country Fisheries Exhibition, organised by Thomas Gotch, in Truro in 1893. In 1895, a new venue became available, when the philanthropist, Passmore Edwards, built a Gallery in Newlyn. However, the Gallery was donated to the artists just as many of the original Newlyn settlers began to move away, and so the Newlyn artists needed contributions from other Cornish artists to make a decent and varied show. Even at the opening exhibition, there were only twenty-six Newlyn artists helped by some seventy outside members. St Ives artists, who contributed to that first exhibition, were Harry Robinson (*In Captivity*), Dorothy Robinson (*Little Angler*), Algernon Talmage, whose *Moonrise in January* was considered the finest landscape in the show, Walter Jevons, Folliott Stokes, Arthur Meade, Arnesby Brown (*Wherries running down to Yarmouth*), Alfred Warne-Browne, Lowell Dyer, Sydney Carr and Selina Wing.

After this, there are very few records of the works hung at the Gallery and the extent of the contributions from St Ives. In 1901, Arthur Burgess, in one of his letters to his girlfriend, Muriel Coldwell, mentioned that their mutual friend and fellow student, Hilda Fearon, had had her work rejected by Lanham's, but will have "a better chance of getting them accepted at Newlyn", implying that the competition was not as severe in Newlyn.[738] A catalogue for the Winter Exhibition of 1911 has survived and this shows St Ives contributions from Olsson, Barlow, Fuller, Fortescue, Milner, Alfred and Nora Hartley, Arthur White, Hayley Lever, Mary McCrossan, Claude Barry and Charles Stiffe, who lived in Lelant, as well as from the visiting American, J.S.Bristol, and the former Barlow student, Herbert George, but the prices quoted indicate that these were all minor works. The extant, but incomplete, sale records of the Gallery (see Table G) do not suggest that the St Ives artists, with the exception of Olsson, found many purchasers for their work on that side of the peninsula. In the main, however, just as with the shows at Lanham's, one is left frustrated that these exhibitions have passed largely unrecorded.

TABLE G   KNOWN SALES OF PAINTINGS BY ST IVES RESIDENT ARTISTS AT PASSMORE EDWARDS GALLERY, NEWLYN[739]

1896 - Sydney Carr, Edmund Fuller	1905 - William Fortescue, Hayley Lever
1897 - Julius Olsson, Harry Robinson, Bertha King	1906 - Herbert George, Arthur White
1898 - William Fortescue, Bertha King	1908 - Alfred Hartley, Nora Hartley
1901 - Harry Robinson, Dorothy Robinson, Lizzie Whitehouse	1910 - Julius Olsson, Alice Nicholson
1902 - Julius Olsson, Sydney Lee	1912 - Julius Olsson, Lizzie Whitehouse
1903 - Harry Robinson, Elinor Postlethwaite	1913 - Julius Olsson
1904 - Julius Olsson, Charles Mottram, Elinor Postlethwaite	1914 - Arthur Beaumont, R.L.Hutton

3.4.2.4 The Royal Cornwall Polytechnic Society Exhibitions, Falmouth

Like the WCAU exhibitions, the RCPS exhibitions in Falmouth were part of the initiatives encouraged by the South Kensington Museum and comprised a similar strange mixture of inventions, mechanical devices and art and craftwork. They were considered to be important events and excursion trains were run from all round the county bringing interested people, including students at the mining schools, to the exhibition.[740] However, few of the local professional artists sent work to the RCPS exhibitions of the late 1870s and early 1880s. Henry Tuke was the most regular contributor, whilst Napier Hemy, Henry Martin, J.C.Uren, William Casley, Maria Tuke, Richard Harry Carter and J.B.Babb sent work to the occasional show. 1888 saw the first contributions from St Ives artists. This may have been at the instigation of Ayerst Ingram, who had been working in St Ives that year. Louis Grier, Ellis Wilkinson and Percy Northcote sent work to that show, with Grier's *Moonrise* and Wilkinson's *Vegetables for the Schooner, Hayle River* being two of the most highly priced pieces, but it was not until 1890 that a significant number of St Ives artists began to exhibit there. The shows were irregular, but tended to be bi-annual. Unlike any of the other local exhibitions, full catalogues of all work exhibited were printed and have been retained by the Society. These have proved an invaluable source.

---

737 This was the dreamchild of Henry Malcolm Geoffroi, the initial headmaster of the Penzance School of Art, but it folded after just four years. The building is now the Penzance Library, but the original Gallery space is still visible.
738 Letter from Arthur Burgess to Muriel Coldwell dated 3/11/1901 (Stephen Bartley).
739 Compiled from Ed. Melissa Hardie, *Artists in Newlyn and West Cornwall 1880-1940*, Bristol, 2009 at pp.54-61.
740 See *Cornish Telegraph* 15/9/1887.

For the most part, the works contributed were moderately priced but, just occasionally, one of the top artists would send a major work, and these will clearly have made a big impression in the show. For instance, Frederick Sargent, the only time he exhibited here, which was in 1894, sent the huge and magnificent *A Catch of Pilchards off St Ives* (Back Cover), priced at £420. This work now hangs in The Guildhall in St Ives, as does Edward King's major work from his brief visit to the colony, *Sale of Herrings* (Front Cover), which was exhibited in 1895 priced at £150. The following year, William Titcomb stole the show, with his two depictions of the steel works at Rotherham, which now hang in the Kelham Island Industrial Museum in Sheffield. Both were priced at £200 and were not in fact hung at the Royal Academy until the following year. The 1904 exhibition contained a number of fine works, headed by Alfred East's sole exhibit, *Japanese Girls Returning from an Evening Party*, priced at £400. It also included some Royal Academy exhibits - Allan Deacon's *A Fisherman's Fireside* (£150), Harry Robinson's *Between the Wood and the Sea* (£80) and his wife's *The Ancient Mariner* (£80). Deacon was again to the fore at the 1906 show with another of his Royal Academy exhibits, *The Peacemakers* (£150) (Fig. 2.197), whilst Edmund Fuller's *Drifting Cloud Shadows* was also priced over £100. Julius Olsson's most important exhibit was *Moonrise and Afterglow*, which was priced at £250 in 1910, and Noble Barlow's was *Lamorna Valley* in the 1913 show.

Figs. 3.43-4 H.G.Fitzherbert
Caricatures of Eddy Newton,
Secretary of RCPS
(top - from *Everyone's Doing It,*
bottom - from *Caricatures of the Cornish Riviera*)

In general, though, the top artists in St Ives only exhibited occasionally or sent minor work. Nevertheless, the shows provided an invaluable outlet for lesser artists, for students and, interestingly, for foreign visiting artists. In fact, in the mid- to late-1890s and 1900s, St Ives artists tended to dominate the shows. For example, the 1898 exhibition contained work by Julius Olsson (2), William and Jessie Titcomb (2 and 1 respectively), Algernon and Gertrude Talmage (2 each), William Fortescue (7), Arthur Meade, Fred Milner, Edmund Fuller, Moulton Foweraker (4), J Elgar Russell (4), Sydney Carr (5), the Americans Sydney Laurence and Richard Levick, Stuart Hobkirk (5), John Bromley and his future wife, Selina Wing, Guy Kortright, Mary McCrossan (2), Edith Hayes, Lizzie Whitehouse (2), Emily Latham Greenfield (6), Helen Knapping (2), Walter Riddall, Frederick Bertram, H M Maynard, A R Phillips (5), Bertha King (2), Georgina and Kate Bainsmith, Catherine Walton (2), Elinor Postlethwaite and Beatrice Vivian. Of the works priced at over £30 in the show, all bar two were provided by the St Ives artists. Edmund Fuller's *Clear Shining After Rain* at £100 was the most expensive work, followed by Emily Greenfield's *The Enchanted Cove* at £85.

Of the foreign artists, Sydney Laurence was the most regular exhibitor. Others who sent work were the Americans Arthur Hoeber, Richard Levick, Percy Simpson, Alfred Pazolt, Henry Keasbey, Arthur Beaumont, Will Potter, Anna Hills and Alexandrina Laurence, the Australians Hayley Lever, Will Ashton and Sidney Long, the New Zealander Herbert Babbage, the Canadian Harry Britton and the Dutchman Sigisbert Bosch Reitz. [741]

Given the extent of the St Ives contributions to the RCPS exhibitions, the Secretary there, Eddy Newton, was well-known in St Ives, and he was featured in both of Fitz's books of caricatures. Fitzherbert labels him "A Fellow of infinite jest". Albeit Newton's somewhat lugubrious expression might indicate that such comment was ironical, a struggling artist, like Fitz, is unlikely to have wanted to make an enemy of an exhibition selector!

3.4.2.5 Local patrons and collectors

The extent of local patronage of the artists is hard to gauge, as most collections have long since been dispersed, and the St Ives Museum, to which a number of works have been donated, refuse to reveal the identity of the donors.

Somewhat surprisingly, few of the St Ives figure painters sought to supplement their income by doing portraiture. This was a lucrative sideline for artists such as Stanhope Forbes, Henry Tuke and Thomas Gotch, but it was not one that interested the major St Ives figure painters. Apart from his impressive portrait in pastel of Captain Harry (Plate 38), which was not a commission, and a sketch of the fisherman, Nat Oliver, no other portraits are known to have been completed by William Titcomb during his time in St Ives. Likewise, William Fortescue also seems largely to have avoided portraiture, although he did present the town with a portrait of Mayor Thomas Uren. Wyly Grier became a noted portrait painter in Canada, but the only local known to have sat for him was Captain J. Hollow, whilst Gwilt Jolley, who did some figure work, is only recorded as having done a portrait of Dr Michael Nicholls.[742] Therefore, it was the moderately talented William Eadie, who was the principal option for locals wanting portraits of their families, and he appears to have enjoyed some success in this regard, from the outset, as his exhibits at the 1887 shows, in Penzance and St Ives, included not only portraits of Canon Jones and his curate the Reverend Griffin, but also Lieutenant Alfred Hackman, Dr Staff, and Edward Boase's predecessor as Town Clerk, William Tolmie Tresidder.[743] Later portraits include one of the leading figures in the town's musical societies, Joseph White, and W.Lang, the Mayor of Liskeard. Eadie found a particularly keen supporter in William Faull (1861-1927), the local ironmonger, who was born in the town, became Mayor in 1903 and was a long-serving magistrate.[744] His daughter, Lilian, recalled the sittings:-

> "It was decided that we were all to have our portraits painted by William Eadie, an artist who was living in Halsetown. Frank was too young but Willie was painted wearing a white sailor suit and I wore a pink frock and pinafore, while Henry was dressed in a plaid frock and pinafore and shown eating grapes from a bunch that he held. Those grapes drew us time after time to our sittings and I have been told that the final reward was grapes for all of us. Mr Eadie had a flair for painting Antiques and always incorporated a piece of antique furniture in whatever interior he produced. Each of us is shown seated on a Chippendale chair and, to my mind, it mitigates against the fact that I am shown wearing black button boots, which I never wore. I think the Artist must have used his daughter's feet for his model in this case."[745]

William Faull acquired other paintings by Eadie as well, including the large painting, featuring Captain Dick Harry, 'As you are now, so once was I, As I am now, so you may be', which Eadie had exhibited at the Dowdeswells Exhibition in 1890 priced at £80. However, the only other artist that Lilian mentions as represented in her father's collection was Edmund Fuller. Her father owned two watercolours by him - "one showed the seine net surrounded and obviously full of fish, the other showed fat Italians taking pilchards from the wood casks and eating them on the spot." Lilian adds in relation to the latter, "Colourful, doubtless true to fact, but nauseating".[746]

---

741 Of passing interest, the 1891 exhibition contained some oil paintings by Herbert Lanyon, normally only known for his photography, whilst the 1897 show featured, in the amateur section, a young Borlase Smart, aged 16, exhibiting a watercolour and a study in charcoal from the cast.

742 *St Ives Weekly Summary*, 18/10/1890.

743 See obituary notice re Hackman in *St Ives Weekly Summary*, 19/11/1904 and re Staff in *St Ives Weekly Summary*, 22/8/1908.

744 See *St Ives Times*, 25/11/1927 - *The Late Mr Wm Faull J.P. - An Appreciation.*

745 Lilian Faull, *The Faulls of St Ives*, Penzance, 1972 at p.53.

746 ibid at p.89.

What is particularly surprising is that the Cornish Museums, notably the Royal Cornwall Museum, Truro, failed to supply any patronage whatsoever. As a result, there are very few prime examples of the paintings of St Ives artists in Cornwall. The St Ives Town Council did own some major works by Millie Dow, William Titcomb, Julius Olsson, Arthur Meade, Fred Milner, Louis Grier, Algernon Talmage, Harry Robinson, William Eadie, Moffat Lindner, Greville Morris and others, most probably donated to it by local collectors or the artists themselves, but maintained them in such poor condition that, in 1968, it was considered to be uneconomic to restore them and fourteen works were sold off.[747] Both the lack of care and the decision to sell were scandalous. Lilian Faull was so outraged that she bought back the Eadie painting that she had donated to the Council. This was a work called *Contented with Little* and showed a typical Halsetown interior, with a large old fashioned dresser with jugs and basins on it and a round table, where a Mother was cutting bread for a boy and girl, modelled by two of Eadie's own children.[748] What interest such a painting would arouse now.

There are, however, three particularly fine paintings remaining in the St Ives Town collection. William Jacobs indicates that Frederick Sargent's *Catch of Pilchards off St Ives* (Back Cover) was donated to the town by Edward Hain's daughter, Kate, and it would not be a surprise, if the other large painting hanging on the stairs at the Guildhall, Edward King's *Sale of Herrings, St Ives* (Front Cover), came from the same source. I have also established that the third major work, Middleton Jameson's *Toilers of the Sea*, exhibited at the Paris Salon in 1890, was donated by Colonel Henry Williams.[749] In addition, Borlase Smart's appreciation of the work of Louis Grier, written shortly after his death in 1920, confirms that, at that time, his acknowledged masterpiece, *The Night Watch* (Fig. 2.201), was owned by the Holman family, who ran a successful engineering business in Camborne.[750] However, it is unlikely that work of this quality was a regular feature of local collections, and it is revealing that, with the exception of William Titcomb's portrait of Captain Harry (Plate 38), then (but not now) owned by the Town Council, none of the St Ives paintings lent to the important exhibitions of Cornish art, at Nottingham in 1894 and Whitechapel in 1902, came from local collections. The prices commanded by major works put them beyond the reach of even moderately successful locals, who are more likely, if interested in the artists' productions, to have made their purchases from Lanham's or the other Cornish exhibitions, where cheaper, less significant works were on offer. There is a fairly constant stream of such works appearing in the Penzance auction houses, having been owned by local families for several generations, and, whilst some of these will be gifts from the artists for services rendered, many will have been acquired originally from these exhibitions or from the artists directly.

One of the most interesting collections, that has recently come on the market, is that of Reginald Glanville, the property agent for Lord Cowley. This was only sold by his descendants in November 2004 at Neale's of Nottingham. Glanville, who lived in Truro, is likely to have made friends with the artists during his dealings with their homes and studios, and his collection included several studies by Arnesby Brown, done in the Zennor area, a painting of Marazion Marshes by Adrian Stokes, as well as a sketch for his famous painting, *The Setting Sun*, a seascape by the American-born Alfred Pazolt (Plate 24), a sketch by the Dutchman, Sigisbert Bosch Reitz, a painting of Italy by Gwilt Jolley, and, most interestingly, a watercolour of St Ives Bay by the Frenchman, Émile-Louis Vernier, such a key figure in the establishment of the colony. The stand out work, however, was Hayley Lever's *Early Morning, St Ives* (Plate 17), which set a record price for this artist in this country. This, we know from a letter that Lever wrote to Glanville, was one of two works purchased off the artist in 1911, and the quality of most of the collection would suggest that the works were bought by Glanville, rather than received as gifts.[751] Glanville lent his painting by Jolley to the exhibition that the artist held in Plymouth in 1892, and other local lenders were Robert Read, John Vivian and the Reverend Griffin, who clearly had all acquired examples of his work by that juncture.[752]

Mention has already been made of the Reverend Edward Griffin's collection, the bulk of which was sold by Bonhams, Par in September 2008, without any mention of the provenance. Indeed, they were not even aware that the portrait of a priest by William Eadie included in the sale was of Griffin himself (Fig. 3.27) or that the portrait of a girl by Eardley Blomefield was of his wife, Charlotte. The best works included in this sale were a painting by Adrian Stokes of a ship in trouble off Porthmeor (Plate 7) and a

---

747 The works sold were Julius Olsson's *Sunset on a breaking sea*, Millie Dow's *The Enchanted Wood*, William Titcomb's *Blue Maids - Mending Day*, Louis Grier's *Moorland Scene*, Fred Milner's *Corfe Castle*, Arthur Meade's *Autumn Ploughing*, Algernon Talmage's *Cows by a Moonlit Stream*, Greville Morris' *Evening*, Harry Robinson's *The Cellist*, William Eadie's *Halsetown Interior*, Moffat Lindner's *Dutch Boats*, John Bromley's *Man's Head* and *Water Mill in Sussex* and, finally, *Nuns Preparing Dressings* by one of the Whitehouse sisters, probably Lizzie - see *St Ives Times and Echo* 29/11/1968.
748 Lilian Faull, *The Faulls of St Ives*, Penzance, 1972 at p.53.
749 It was owned by Colonel Williams when shown at the 1903 Free Library Exhibition.
750 *St Ives Times*, 19/11/1920.
751 See letter from R.H.Lever to R.Glanville dated 23/4/1912 - Mornington Estate papers, County Records Office, Truro GHW/12/3/6/1/161/20.
752 *St Ives Weekly Summary*, 30/7/1892.

double-sided work by Arnesby Brown. However, a still life by Helene Schjerfbeck had previously fetched a significant sum, whilst the seven paintings in the collection by Sydney Laurence evidenced a close friendship with that maverick artist. Two further foreign artists, the Australians, Will Osborn and Will Ashton, were represented in the collection, and the presence of significant numbers of works by foreign artists in these local collections indicates that they had little difficulty integrating into the community. Indeed, many of the works are likely to have been gifts, in response to acts of kindness.

By far the most impressive work originally in the Reverend Griffin's collection was a large painting by Noble Barlow, *Early Morning*, which depicted Barlow's favourite tree-skirted pool in the Lamorna Valley. Given its far superior size and quality to anything else in the collection and its date of 1914, there must be a good chance that it was presented to him by his parishioners when he left St Johns-in-the-Fields in 1915. After his death in 1918, it was given by his widow to his brother, Frederick, a Southampton based doctor, who had himself developed a great interest in St Ives art during his visits to the town. Indeed, an inventory of his house contents in 1928 reveals a large and fascinating collection, and this document is particularly interesting as it records how he acquired the paintings and, if purchased, the price paid. The collection included oils by Adrian Stokes (paid £4), Julius Olsson (inherited, presumably from his brother), Algernon Talmage (paid £2), David Davies (paid £1), William Eadie (paid £1), Kendrick Wynne (present), Folliott Stokes (paid 10s 6d), Hugo Tabor (present), John Thurston (paid £2), Frank Moore (paid 10s 6d) and two by Lizzie Whitehouse (paid £1 & 10s 6d), as well as a further work by Noble Barlow, his 1899 New Gallery exhibit *Midnight Toilers* (Fig. 3.45), which depicted the return of the fishing fleet in the middle of the night. This, like a number of others, is noted as a 'present' and so perhaps Frederick gave some medical advice during his visits. There were also several watercolours by Edmund Fuller (paid no more than £1 each). However, the collection was most notable for the large number of works by Sydney Laurence that it contained - fifteen oils and eighteen watercolours - the prize piece being no less than Laurence's greatest Cornish work, *Setting Sun on the Cornish Coast*. Griffin family folklore indicates that, in 1904, Laurence was desperate to raise funds for his Alaskan gold prospecting adventure and that Frederick, whom he clearly knew well, for he had given him a painting as a wedding present in February 1896, obliged by buying his 1894 Paris Salon success for just £100. Nevertheless, as Frederick did not pay more than £5 for any of his other purchases, this was still a big investment.[753] Accordingly, it is perhaps understandable why Laurence, in later years, told his Alaskan admirers that he had sold the painting to the French Government. This sounded rather better than having to admit that, after failing to find a buyer for a decade, he had ended up flogging it, for a song, to his Vicar's brother, to finance a madcap venture, which resulted in him not only deserting his wife and children, but also losing everything. The sale to Frederick Griffin also explains why the painting has ended up in Southampton Art Gallery, for it was donated by Frederick or his heirs to their local Gallery in the early 1930s.

Fig. 3.45   John Noble Barlow   *Midnight Toilers*
(Frederick Griffin collection)

753 The descendants of Thomas Albert Lang also have a collection of Laurence paintings, perhaps acquired in similar circumstances.

By comparison, the rest of the Laurence paintings bought by Frederick Griffin were moderate pieces. Most of the watercolours were bought for £1, as were some oils of waves breaking on rocks at Porthmeor, but he did pay £5 for a large watercolour, *Storm Clouds*, measuring 36" x 23", depicting boats and gulls on Porth Kidney Sands by the entrance to the Hayle estuary, and the same sum for an oil of a 'Tramp', anchored out in the Bay with sails half furled to dry, measuring 42" x 33". Accordingly, apart from the one major purchase, made in special circumstances, Frederick Griffin's collection demonstrates how cheaply artists were prepared to sell their work to a friend.

In 1927, the newly formed St Ives Society of Artists organised a Retrospective Exhibition, the purpose of which was to encourage contemporary artists by highlighting the rich history of the colony. Whilst recording that the response from local collectors was so great that the hanging committee could have filled three times the space allotted, few indications are given of the identity of the collectors. Two, however, are specifically mentioned.[754] Arthur Curnow, of Carrick, who provided catering services for the artists, was said to have a fine collection, and his contributions to the exhibition were two works by each of Julius Olsson and Louis Sargent. Mrs Wheeler of the Chy-an-Drea Hotel also lent works by Moffat Lindner and Arthur Meade. Borlase Smart later confirmed that the collection put together by Francis Wheeler at the hotel, which also included works by Olsson, Noble Barlow, Louis Sargent, Louis Grier, John Park, Hayley Lever, and the Americans Frederick Mulhaupt and J.S.Bristol, had all been purchased off the artists.[755] Wheeler, who was the son of Ferdinand Wheeler of Lostwithiel, had, until the end of the First World War, run the Queen's Hotel, a favourite venue for the artists, but he then took over 'Chy-an-Drea'. He was a man of great energy and public spirit and had made an impression as a 'Progressive' Councillor before his untimely death in March 1923, aged only fifty.

Not all local collections of paintings will have been amassed willingly, for hard-up artists, on numerous occasions, will have offered paintings in return for goods or services supplied. Treve Curnow indicated that a number of his father's paintings had been acquired in this way, and Noble Barlow is even reputed to have exchanged a painting with his dentist for a set of dentures![756] Lena Bray records that her grandfather, the builder, Robert Toy, was one person, who was unimpressed by such payments in kind, for he "was wont to complain, as he nailed yet another painting or photograph to the wall, that he couldn't feed his thirteen children on pictures".[757]

Locals, who had to be particularly long-suffering in this regard, were owners of public houses, for one regular bill that artists liked to settle by the offer of a painting was their tab at the bar. They could then view their work, while they drank, and hope that it might generate the interest of a visitor in their output. As already mentioned in Chapter 1.4, Ranger-Gull indicates that such an arrangement was resisted initially by the landlord of The Sloop, but he had been forced into accepting this re-creation by the artists of the ambience that they had experienced in the Breton hostelries. Ranger-Gull also recounts how Lucas, the figure based on Grier, was most indignant that the landlord, after a spring-clean, had

Fig. 3.46 H.G.Fitzherbert   *Caricature of Francis Wheeler*
(from *Everyone's Doing It*)

754 See *St Ives Times*, 20/5/1927.

755 See *St Ives Times*, 9/6/1933.

756 See Marion Whybrow, *St Ives 1883-1993 - Portrait of an Art Colony*, Woodbridge, 1994 at p. 26.

757 Lena and Donald Bray, *St Ives Heritage*, Truro, 1992 edition at p.31.

re-hung his Whistlerian piece, *Symphony*, upside-down, although no-one else had noticed![758] Having corrected the position, the landlord, in an effort to console the artist, commented, "It's a braave, fine picture, whichever way up you do look at it"! There is no record of what this early collection of work comprised, but Wilson Henry Irvine, during his visit in 1923, spied work on the walls of the pub by Hayley Lever and fellow American, George Bruestle.

Those artists living in Up-long tended to frequent the Porthminster Hotel and its walls, until recently, displayed paintings by Moffat Lindner, Arthur Meade, Fred Milner, Alfred Warne-Browne, Herbert Truman, Marjorie Mostyn and one of the best examples of the work of Borlase Smart, but, sadly, this collection has now been disbanded. It was interesting that the collection of the Queen's Hotel in Penzance, sold off in 1984, also contained some works by St Ives artists.[759] Indeed, the cover illustration for the auction catalogue was of Edmund Fuller's large painting of the harbour from the Malakoff, whilst the sale included no less than nine works by Hayley Lever and a painting of St Ives by Christopher Nevinson. The Hotel still retains work by Noble Barlow, the German Franz Muller-Gossen and a collection of work by William Parkyn. It also has a version of Harry Robinson's 1887 painting, *On the Foresand, St Ives*, showing a fishwife and her basket on the harbour beach. The finest painting owned by a local Hotel, however, is Claude Francis Barry's *St Ives at Sunset*, a massive canvas owned by the Carbis Bay Hotel, which clearly will have been purchased, rather than gifted. This depicts the view from the top of Skidden Hill across the town as the fishing fleet set out. Another huge canvas of the same scene, but at twilight, which is still impressive, if not so successful, is owned by the Treloyhan Manor Hotel, and may, therefore, have been part of Edward Hain's collection originally.

3.4.3   The Free Library and the Loan Exhibition of 1903

The need to make more easily available to the public instructive reading material was a significant issue at the end of the century, and this was a campaign that the artists supported with considerable vigour. Initially, the objective was to provide a place of recreation and instruction for the young men of the town - "a public house without the drink, where you may sit, talk, read and think". Accordingly, in March 1891, largely upon the initiative of the Mayor that year, Joshua Daniel, the St Ives Institute and Reading Room, located in Fore Street, was opened, with both Wyly Grier and William Titcomb on the committee.[760] Grier hoped that they could gradually acquire a good library, "for they must cultivate their youths in order to develop genius", whilst Titcomb got involved, as he already had some experience of this type of Institute, having, shortly beforehand, inherited the Wickersley Institute in Yorkshire, a similar philanthropic enterprise.[761] Writing just a year later, Matthews suggests that it was not just young men that utilised the Reading Room, for dropping in after lunch "to study Lloyd's List and the Western Mercury" had already become part of the daily routine for a number of St Ives inhabitants.[762] In order to help the funding of the Institute, the Boxing Night concert organised by the artists in December 1892 was for its benefit.

In 1896, however, more ambitious plans came to fruition when the great philanthropist, Passmore Edwards, agreed to fund the erection in St Ives of a Free Library, as he had in many other towns both in Cornwall and elsewhere. These had often been designed by Silvanus Trevail, but, despite trying to enlist the support of Edward Hain and Captain Harry, for whom he had designed properties in St Ives, the commission was given to Symons and Sons of Blackwater. The site, on the corner of Tregenna Place and The Stennack, was donated by local M.P., Thomas Bedford Bolitho, but was criticised by Trevail for having only eleven feet of frontage.[763] After the Library opened in 1897, it still needed to be furnished, and the artists helped to raise over £266 by putting on a series of entertainments over a three day period in April of that year. This was one of the fullest programmes that the artists put on, combining a series of musical pieces each day, with a number of *tableaux vivants*, designed by Marianne Stokes, Millie Dow and Harry Robinson. Nearly every single artist in the colony was involved in some aspect - see Appendix C.[764] Generous gifts of books were also made by Leslie Stephen, Thomas Millie Dow, William Brooke, Sydney Carr, Lowell Dyer, Louis Grier and the Whitehouse sisters. Interest in the Library was considerable and, in 1899, the librarian reported that over 16,000 books had been borrowed during the year.

---

758 C.Ranger-Gull, Portalone, London, 1904 at p.18-9.

759 Phillips, New Bond Street, Auction dated 13/11/1984.

760 The premises were said to have been previously occupied by W.C.Richards - presumably William Cornish Richards recorded in Kelly's Directory as a grocer in Fore Street in 1889 but not in 1893.

761 See *St Ives Weekly Summary*, 28/2/1891 & 7/3/1891.

762 J.H.Matthews, *A History of the Parishes of Saint Ives, Lelant, Towednack and Zennor in the County of Cornwall*, London, 1892 at p.370.

763 See R. Perry and H. Harradence, *Silvanus Trevail : Cornish architect and entrepeneur*, London, 2008 at p.127-8.

764 See *St Ives Weekly Summary* 24/4/1897.

Fig. 3.47 Sydney Carr   Celebrations by the Library, Tregenna Hill
(courtesy Derek Wintle/copy photo Andrew Eggleston)

By 1903, however, when Louis Grier, as Town Councillor, was President of the Free Library Committee, the position had become most unsatisfactory, with many of the books requiring rebinding or replacement. Grier suggested that the Library Committee should be complemented by the addition of Millie Dow and Harry Robinson, both literature buffs, as well as representatives from five of the religious denominations in the town, and this enlarged Committee made a series of recommendations, including the establishment of a Reference Section. In order to help fund these improvements, it was decided, on the suggestion of the artist members, to mount a Loan Exhibition of Paintings and Curios in order to generate, amongst the general public, new enthusiasm for the Library, and for learning in general.

Lilian Faull, whose father, William, was Mayor that year, recalled her father's "keen interest, as one of *the* events of his Year of Office" and that the exhibition was "well patronised from all walks of life".[765] It certainly proved a major logistical challenge, as over 400 exhibits were contributed. Most of the artists lent works to the show, but the stand-out paintings were most probably William Titcomb's *The Wealth of England : The Bessemer Process of Making Steel* (RA 1897 - Kelham Island Industrial Museum), Edmund Fuller's *Doomed* (RA 1896), Dorothy Robinson's *The Ancient Mariner* (RA 1898), Harry Robinson's perennial exhibit *Between the Wood and the Sea* (RA 1894) and Middleton Jameson's *Toilers of the Sea* (Paris 1890), which had already been acquired by Colonel Williams. Olsson, Grier, Talmage, Foweraker, Hobkirk, Fortescue, Russell, Jack Titcomb, Pitt, Thurston, Park and Phil-Morris were also represented, as were the female artists Sarah and Daisy Whitehouse, Mabel Douglas, Mrs Latham Greenfield and Edith Sealey. Foreign artists involved were Alfred Pazolt, Will Ashton and Richard Hayley Lever, whilst James Lanham lent a work by Rudolf Hellwag. Herbert Lanyon, John Douglas and Georgina Bainsmith contributed photographs.

765 Lilian Faull, *The Faulls of St Ives*, Penzance, 1972 at p.80.

Of greater interest almost, as they shed light on previously unknown interests of the artists, are some of the curios that they lent. Louis Grier sent a linen chest and chairs used by John Wesley and a number of ancient stringed instruments, including his prized guitar lyre used in the band of Charles II (see Fig. 2.169). Millie Dow's several contributions included a jewelled sword from the palace of King Theban, Mandalay and a model of a knight and horse in armour. Allan Deacon lent Chinese embroidery from the Imperial Palace and a case of French duelling pistols, whilst the Whitehouse sisters lent some valuable old lace, including a lace cap dating from around 1750. They also lent their coin collection, but this was probably eclipsed by that of Sydney Carr, who was considered to have an exceptionally fine selection of gold and silver coins.

It was felt that no other comparably sized town in Britain could have mounted such an important collection of work but, although from an educational viewpoint, it was considered an outstanding success, it only raised £16 after expenses. Greater funds were raised by the series of concerts and entertainments that were put on each evening during the week that the Exhibition ran. The artists' contribution was an evening of music and *tableaux vivants* (see Appendix C).

3.4.4 Music and drama for local causes

Prior to the arrival of the artists, public entertainments in St Ives will have been sober affairs - some classical music played by worthy amateurs, some choral singing and the odd patriotic song. Howard Russell Butler found the one that he was invited to attend excruciating - so bad, in fact, that it was almost amusing. These entertainments were transformed by the artists, as not only did they introduce much more variety, but they were also prepared to have fun. This did not result in a drop in the standard of performances, as a number of artists were talented musicians, composers and actors, some even with professional experience, and their artistic capabilities transformed set designs. Accordingly, farces, comic recitations, glee singing and *tableaux vivants* were amongst the items that they introduced into the programmes. Most of the entertainments were designed to raise funds for worthy local causes, and these were not confined merely to those in the artists' sphere. Accordingly, the beneficiaries included such diverse organisations as the Fire Brigade, the Reading Institute, the St Ives Choral Society, the new Library, the St Johns-in-the-Field Organ Fund, the Rugby and Cricket Clubs, the National School Extension Fund, the St Ives Nursing Association, the Parish Church Club's Piano Fund, the St Ives Orchestral Society, the Methodist New Connexion's New Chapel and Schoolrooms Fund, the local Territorial Army unit and the Mayor's Boer War Fund.

One of the first public entertainments put on by the artists was in aid of the St Ives Choral Society. Both Harry and Dorothy Robinson, and the Grier brothers, had joined shortly after their arrival in the town, and Harry Robinson, having discovered, after his election on to the Committee in October 1886, that the Society's finances were in a poor shape, suggested, following the success of the 1887 WCAU exhibition in Penzance, that there should be an Art Union exhibition in St Ives, with artists donating works in aid of the Society. The event was held during November 1887 and most of the artists in St Ives at the time donated a work. There were also contributions from some of the Newlyn artists. However, the Finn, Helene Schjerfbeck, at that time renting Robinson's garden studio, probably felt morally obliged to contribute, as she later confided to her brother, "When the English sing, it sounds as if they are about to throw up"![766] The exhibition was supplemented by some works from the collection of Doctor Rosewall, which included paintings by Hogarth, Canaletto, Wovverman, Albano, Vernet, Cresswell, Dingle and Browning.[767] Accordingly, Rosewall, whose daughters took part in the Carnival Masquerades in 1892-3, must have been one of the few art connoisseurs in town prior to the arrival of the artists.

Musical entertainment was provided in the evening of each of the four days that the exhibition was open, with Moffat Lindner and James Clarkson Uren being additional participants, and some £44 was raised for the Society.[768] The other members of the Committee of the Society, who included Edward Hain, James and Robert Read, Edward Boase and William Trewhella, must surely have been impressed that the artists, so soon after their arrival, not only had all been prepared to donate work, but also had worked hard to put on an exhibition and entertainment for the benefit of all. They had certainly put the fun into fundraising, whilst *The Cornishman* considered that the Society had "done such good work in promoting the cause of musical culture in the locality".[769]

At one of the Society's concerts in April 1888, Robinson premiered two of his own compositions, *They have taken away my Lord* and *Lullaby*, the latter being particularly well received, whilst songs were also sung by Wyly and Louis Grier. However, despite these efforts, the Society had run back into debt by 1889 and folded for a while.

---

766 Letter to Magnus Schjerfbeck dated 1889, the 26th, Saturday evening.
767 *Cornish Telegraph*, 10/11/1887.
768 Both Robert Toy and his wife won prizes in the draw, perhaps fuelling their interest in art!
769 *Cornish Telegraph*, 10/11/1887.

The Choral Society was not the only body in town that gained from the musical talents of Harry Robinson and the Griers, and they took part in a number of other musical entertainments in the early years of the colony. Before his departure to America in the mid-1890s, they were often joined by Herbert Lanyon, who was also in demand on the piano, and he contributed a number of his own compositions to a variety of public concerts.[770] Alfred Warne-Browne and his wife and Katherine Olsson are also recorded as taking part in various entertainments at this time.

After the collapse of the Choral Society, Louis Grier and some of his friends from the local community decided to link up with several Newlyn artists to put on Gilbert and Sullivan's operetta, *Trial by Jury*, in Penzance in December 1890. The group was referred to as 'Louis Grier's Company' and he directed the production and acted as stage manager.[771] Edward Boase, appropriately, acted as the judge, whilst his brother, Richard, was the defendant. The Grier brothers were the two ushers, whilst Robert Read, William Craze, who had been Mayor of St Ives in 1887-8, and Newlyn artists Thomas Gotch, Frank Richards, Trythall Rowe and Ernest Ireland Blackburne were amongst the jury. Joseph Uren White, the newspaper proprietor, was the foreman. The performance, which was considered to have been carefully rehearsed, was highly praised for the quality of both the acting and the singing, and the audience was convulsed with laughter throughout. This proved the last time that the St Ives artists needed to draft in Newlyners for their entertainments, as henceforth there were more than enough artists with musical and acting talents in St Ives.

Unlike in Newlyn, where Percy Craft was very much the driving force behind all productions, no one artist in St Ives regularly took on the position of stage manager, and a variety of artists assumed leading roles at different times. In the early 1890s, Boxing Night became the traditional evening for the artists to contribute to public entertainments. 1892 saw the first appearance of the 'St Ives Nigger Minstrels', whose performance consisted of "songs and choruses, a whistling solo, a stump speech, a dance, conjuring tricks, solo on tin whistle and numerous jokes and conundrums etc".[772] This was a group of artists, who, under Robinson's direction, sang glees and negro spirituals together and put on similar variety entertainment, under different names, such as the 'St Ives Artists' Glee Club' and the 'Magpie Minstrels', during the course of the 1890s. William Titcomb, Arthur Meade, Fred Milner, Millie Dow and William Brooke were regular participants. Such good natured fun will have amused most of the audience, but, for fervent Methodists, this was wanton entertainment.

One of the most regular beneficiaries in the 1890s was the Fire Brigade and the artists were eternally grateful for their services, when, in December 1895, a serious fire broke out in Arthur Meade's Porthmeor Studio. Accordingly, that month, the artists put on the hit comedy *Our Boys*, in Olsson's new large studio for the benefit of the firemen. The play was a comedy in three acts, that had been written by Henry James Byron. It had been first performed in January 1875 and its initial run until April 1879 made it still, in the 1890s, the world's longest-running play. Lead parts were taken by Harry Robinson, Max Ludby, John Noble Barlow, Algernon Talmage, Alexandrina Laurence, Dorothy Robinson, Emily Cogill and one of the Kirkpatrick sisters, probably Lily, whilst the programme was designed by Edmund Fuller (Fig. 3.49). For several years thereafter, the artists took part in further entertainments designed to raise money for the Fire Brigade.

There was a marked increase in activity in the years 1896-8 when a series of talented performers joined the colony, particularly as this coincided with an increase in numbers due to the opening of the new Schools of Painting. Gordon Killmister (1856-1899), a Cheshire-born architect, who had turned to art in mid-career, was a fine pianist, often performing his own compositions, and he helped to produce and direct a number of entertainments. He arrived in the town at much the same time as fellow Bushey student, Hugh Blackden (1871-1900), who made more of a mark in both colonies as a musician, rather than as an artist (see, however, Plate 21).[773] Described as "genial, kind and unworldly", Blackden, who had been born in Bournemouth and was a graduate of Emmanuel College, Cambridge, was a skilled composer who "delighted many a public and private audience with his charming solos on the mandolin".[774] With Moffat Lindner's future wife, Gussie Baird-Smith and her sister, Isabel, also accomplished on guitar and mandolin, there were several concerts, such as that for the St John's Organ Fund, featuring mandolin and guitar bands.

770 In June 1890, Karl Braden, a student from Bushey, was meant to give a banjo solo at a Fire Brigade concert, but failed to turn up!

771 *St Ives Weekly Summary*, 20/12/1890.

772 *St Ives Weekly Summary*, 31/12/1892.

773 He enrolled at the Herkomer School in Bushey in 1894 and stayed there for four years, playing the mandolin at village entertainments. In St Ives, he also became Secretary of the Hockey Club and was involved in arranging the tennis tournament in August 1899 when he donated one of his pictures as a prize for the Ladies' Singles Champion. However, he only exhibited a handful of works in the years 1898-1900.

774 He served in South Africa as a Private in the Imperial Yeomanry (50th Company), but died from an attack of fever and sunstroke on 14th June 1900 - *St Ives Weekly Summary*, 23/6/1900.

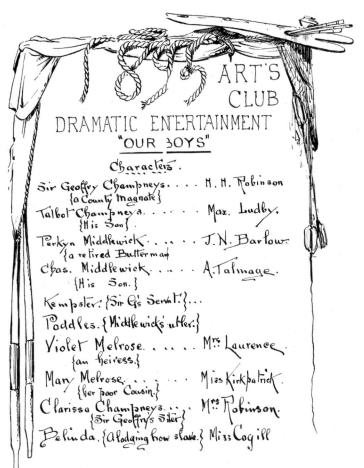

Fig. 3.48-9 *Our Boys* programme (1895),
designed by Edmund Fuller

Beale Adams' wife, Kate, was also a fine piano soloist and performed in duets and trios with William Fortescue, newly arrived from Newlyn with his 'cello. Other members of the trio in this period included the marine painter Hely Smith, an old friend of Olsson, then based in Looe, on flute, Edith Lee (née Elgar), the wife of the painter and printmaker, Sydney Lee, on violin, and Sarah Trevorrow, daughter of the music shop owner, William Trevorrow, also on violin.[775] Sarah, who, in 1899, married the American artist, George Gardner Symons, taught violin and was also much in demand as a soloist on that instrument. At the same time, Max Ludby, then living in Carbis Bay, produced, wrote and acted in a series of comedy sketches, with Sydney Laurence, John Bromley and another former Bushey student, Thomas Danby, often taking leading parts.[776] Indeed, the humorous songs of Danby, who enthusiastically involved himself in all the artists' extra-curricula activities, were always a hit. Algernon Talmage also acted a number of comic roles, whilst humorous recitations were the speciality of John Douglas.

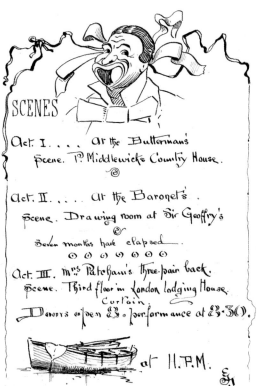

For the variety entertainment in January 1897, which featured Ludby's new farcical comedietta, *In the Springtime of Youth*, he and Fuller designed a new 'drop scene', which was let down during intervals between acts. In the centre of the scene was a medallion, cable framed, representing the approach to Venice, backed by pictured hangings of rich red drapery. On the right, were portrayed a wealth of summer flowers of dazzling colours, whilst on the left "were the graceful folds of a curtain whose brilliant white satin was looped up and edged with a flashing fringe of deep gold".[777]

---

775 It has been suggested that Edith Lee was related to Edward Elgar but, although her maiden name was Elgar, her father was Frederick Elgar, an oil cake merchant from Rochester. She was also born in 1867, just ten years after the musician.

776 Thomas Hardridge Danby studied at Bushey in 1895 and was involved with the St Ives colony for several years from 1899, exhibiting on Show Day in 1901 and 1902 and playing golf and cricket with the artists. In 1902, his sister, Helen, was also involved in various entertainments.

777 *St Ives Weekly Summary* 23/1/1897.

During this period, there was clearly a tight-knit spirit amongst the artists in the colony, and it was with a sense of dismay that they heard, first, that Gordon Killmister had succumbed to pneumonia, on a visit back to his native Macclesfield, in November 1899, and, then, that Hugh Blackden had died in June 1900 whilst serving his country in the Boer War.[778] Ironically, his last performance in St Ives had been in an entertainment in November 1899 to raise funds for the widows and orphans of soldiers killed in that conflict.

Tableaux vivants played a significant role in a number of the productions, and it was noted with regard to the entertainment put on in January 1891 that it was the first time that such *tableaux* had been presented in St Ives. There were six, on this occasion, with a range of historical, Shakespearian, comic and realistic subjects. The one that caused the most amusement, demonstrating that the artists could laugh at themselves, was called *The Fore-Sand, St Ives* and featured an artist trying to pitch his easel in the midst of the bustle of a fish sale on the Fore-Sand, before being summarily ejected by two fishermen. Louis and Wyly Grier (and their sister), Folliott Stokes, Sydney Laurence, Eardley Blomefield and Harry Browne were joined in the *tableaux* by Alfred Hackman and his wife and the children of Thomas Row Harry and of Robert Read, whilst Dr Nicholls, with whom Gertrude Rosenberg was staying at the time, provided many of the costumes and allowed everyone to practise in his house.

For the Easter Monday Entertainment in 1892, the *tableau* subject chosen was Dorothy Robinson's painting *Too Late*, featuring the five foolish virgins, a work that was highly regarded in the town. However, the most extensive set of *tableaux* that were performed was in connection with the entertainment to raise funds for the furbishment of the new Library in 1897. The entertainment ran over a period of four days, with at least ten comic *tableaux* being produced for each day. These were arranged by Marianne Stokes, Thomas Millie Dow and Harry Robinson and were normally accompanied by music. This was one of the first occasions that the children of the artists became involved, with parts in the *tableaux* being taken by Sydney Carr's daughters, Irene and Vera, and the daughters of visiting American artist, John Carleton Wiggins. It is interesting that, later in the decade, many of these *tableaux* had Japanese themes, reflecting the great interest among British artists at the time in Japanese art. One was described as a "happy combination of tea-cups, waving fans, paper sunshades, almond eyes, brushed-back hair and symetric profiles".[779]

In 1898, the St Ives Choral Society was revived, with Robinson as Joint President, Elgar Russell as Joint Secretary and William Titcomb and Kate Adams on the Committee. Russell seems to have been the principal organiser of events hereafter, as Robinson devoted himself to the newly formed St Ives Orchestral Society, where he was intimately involved in training, conducting and organising the fledgling Orchestra. This was a huge commitment, which clearly impacted upon his art and, possibly, his health. These Societies seemed perpetually short of funds and, in one performance in 1900, designed to pay off debts, comedy sketches were contributed by the Newlyn artists Lionel Birch and Norman Garstin and their respective wives. Both societies struggled on for a while, but eventually folded. This did not prevent an attempt to launch a St Ives Philharmonic Society in 1902, which again the artists supported.[780]

The relatively barren year of 1901 probably reflected the changed mood, resulting from the ongoing War, but the arrival that year of Albert Moulton Foweraker produced a resurgence of interest in dramatic activities, and a body calling itself the 'St Ives Artists' Dramatic Society' put on shows, not only in the town, but also in Redruth.[781] The quality of acting in these was felt "to equal if not surpass many professional touring companies", with the interest of the audience being rivetted in particular by the magnetism given off by the acting and elocution of Foweraker himself.[782] Foweraker, however, who knew of the terrible fire, in 1887, at the Theatre in his home town of Exeter, that had killed nearly two hundred people, vowed in 1902 never to put a foot in the Public Hall at St Ives again, as he considered its fire safety precautions woefully inadequate.[783]

The art students of the time, such as the Australian Will Ashton, Frances Horn, Frank Haigh and Percy Heard, were again to the fore, whilst a further bonus was the involvement of Gertrude Talmage's sister, Mrs Archer Julian (née Lily Rowe), who had enjoyed a musical career as a contralto in London and whose acting had "breeziness and dash".[784] Yet another boost was the return from America in 1902 of Herbert Lanyon, who, despite his injured hand, played a hugely significant role in musical circles

778 *St Ives Weekly Summary*, 16/11/1899.

779 Parish Church Club - New Year's Entertainemnt. *St Ives Weekly Summary* 7/1/1899.

780 It is interesting that Harry Robinson does not feature in a concert given by the St Ives Orchestral Society in May 1901.

781 *St Ives Weekly Summary*, 15/2/1902.

782 *St Ives Weekly Summary*, 11/1/1902.

783 *St Ives Weekly Summary*, 10/5/1902.

784 *St Ives Weekly Summary*, 18/1/1902.

Fig. 3.50 John Douglas   Entertainment featuring from the left Mrs Hackman, Harry Robinson, Miss Harry, Edmund Fuller, Rose Cooper, Georgina Bainsmith and Lieut Alfred Hackman.

The reverse of the photo lists those who have requested copies and, in addition to the participants, these include Miss Little, the Rev J.B.Jones, Folliott Stokes, Sydney Carr, Mrs Morris (mother of Greville Morris) and Mrs Whitehouse. As the latter died in 1900, the entertainment will date from the late 1890s.

in St Ives for the rest of his life. Folliott Stokes began to turn his writing skills to wordings for songs and, in 1903, published an article in the *Playgoer*, entitled *A Plea for a Cornish Theatre*.[785] In this, he decried the lack of a single theatre in the Duchy, for "England contains no more romantic, emotional, and pleasure-loving people than the Cornish", as demonstrated by their folklore and their earlier fondness for medieval miracle plays. At present, though, he considered that they were overrun by a dour and narrow-minded Methodism.

After 1903, the number of entertainments put on by the artists were less regular. There are probably several reasons for this. Harry Robinson's organisational skills, as well as his musical enthusiasms, will have been sorely missed, following his death in 1904, whilst Foweraker spent increasingly extended periods in Spain. His safety concerns about the Public Hall may have been an issue as well. 1906, however, saw an increase in activity, with Horace Taylor (1881-1934) and his family playing significant roles. Taylor, who had studied at the Royal Academy Schools and in Munich, was best known for his novel caricatures, done in oils, as opposed to black and white. He was a friend of Charles Marriott, whose portrait he exhibited on Show Day in 1906.

In August 1907, there was another performance of *Trial by Jury*, directed by Foweraker, which *The Cornishman* felt was "so beautifully staged and cleverly performed" and "in a hall, which must have been bad enough as a chapel but would be regarded by most people as an impossible home for concert parties, the opera or drama".[786] After that, artists' entertainments in the public domain were rare indeed. Perhaps, the financial climate was not as buoyant, or the leading figures in the past had just got older and less enthusiastic. The increase in the size of the town and a change in taste may also have been contributory factors. A final flourish, however, was the performance of the comedy, *Little Mrs Cummin*, in November 1910. This had only been performed in London at the Playhouse Theatre that January. John Bromley acted as stage manager, as he had done a number of times previously, and Edmund Fuller,

785 Reproduced in *St Ives Weekly Summary*, 5/12/1903.
786 Reproduced in *St Ives Weekly Summary* 31/8/1907.

Fig. 3.51 H.G.Fitzherbert Selected caricatures from the programme for *Little Mrs Cummins*

his frequent accomplice in the production of stage sets, caused some amusement with his poster, which read *Don't miss comin' to see Mrs Cummin*. H.G.Fitzherbert, who took a part in the play, also produced an illustrated sheet, with caricatures of the characters (Fig. 3.51), the lead roles being taken by visitors, Mr and Mrs Charles Kent.

The regularity with which these entertainments were put on by the artists suggests that they were appreciated by the locals, not only for raising money for a variety of different causes in the town, but also for providing some novel entertainment of a good standard and considerable variety. In all probability, it was the middle-class sections of the town that derived the most pleasure from these performances. However, Christine Morton Raymont records how the artists were also keen to reach out to the fisherfolk as, for one concert, they arranged to invite the cleaner of the hall in which the performance was held. At the interval, "one of the artists came and asked her how she liked it. "Aw, 'tes beautiful", she said, "but I wish to Gawd 'twas awver [over]"!"[787]

3.4.5 Women's rights

One of the aspects of the life of the artists in the town that would have been most shocking to traditionalists amongst the local population was the role that women members of the artist colony played. Instead of being "angel of the house and protector of the sacred hearth", female artists pursued their own careers and were prepared to be seen "working" in public. They also fraternised openly with their male colleagues, without chaperones, and were members of their dissipate Club. Their more ostentatious manner of dress, with its "frills and fal-lals", also "spelt backslidin'". Accordingly, by their mere presence in the town, the female members of the colony forced attitudes to change to the role of women in society. However, some were keen feminists and took part in public campaigns to improve the lot of women, particularly the women's suffrage movement.

The extent of the struggle that they faced is amply demonstrated by the reaction of a discussion group, in April 1892, promoted by the Reverend Griffin and William Hebblethwaite, of the Blue Bell studio, who was the Secretary of the Parish Church Club. The proposition discussed was "That the principle which regulates the legal subordination of women to men is wrong in itself". Both Griffin and Hebblethwaite spoke in favour, but this was clearly too advanced a concept for the locals, as everyone else present, without exception, voted against it.

---

787 C. Morton Raymont, *Memories of Old St Ives*, St Ives, 1958 at p.23.

Gussie Lindner was one of the first women in St Ives to champion the right of women to vote and she became a leading figure in the local branch of the National Union of Women's Suffrage. From 1910, she organised regular public meetings on the issue and also chaired meetings at her home, 'Chy-an-Porth'. However, there was no call in Cornwall for violence, as change by constitutional methods was advocated. Gussie's Lindner's friend, Edith Ellis, was a strong supporter of the movement, having been for many years a leading feminist. She came up with a novel idea - a "love strike". She told one American lecture audience: "In Cornwall, my home, I asked an old farmer what he thought of this plan. He replied, "Good gracious, women would get the vote within a fortnight".

Georgina Bainsmith was also a strong campaigner for equality for women and became the Head Organiser for Devon and Cornwall of the Political Information Offices for Women. She was also on the International Council of the Union of Women. However, locally, although she stood a number of times in both Municipal and County elections, she did not have the personality to overcome the prejudice against women.

The outbreak of War rendered such issues of secondary importance, but, when peace came, women were at last given the right to vote - a major step forward. The St Ives women artists played very little part in this, but by ensuring that the topics were raised and discussed, they slowly began to chip away at ingrained local prejudices and to persuade other local women to expect more than they had in the past. Indeed, in 1928, not only did Katherine Arnold-Forster, of Eagle's Nest, Gussie Lindner's socialist friend, become the town's first female magistrate, but St Ives elected its first female M.P., Hilda Runciman, only the twelfth woman to be returned to Parliament.[788] Cannot the artists claim some credit for this?

Fig. 3.52 Hanna Rion Ver Beck in 4 Norway Lane, St Ives
(Priscilla Fursdon)

---

788 A few years later, Robert Langley Hutton's sister, Lizzie, (then the widow of Robert Sawle Read) also became a magistrate.

Hanna Rion Ver Beck (1874-1924) was the second wife of the American illustrator, Frank Ver Beck and was a multi-talented lady, passionately interested in music, literature, art and gardening. In addition to writing her own books and helping with those produced by her husband, and doing some painting, she became fascinated, during her time in St Ives in the War years, with the new theory developed by Dr Carl J Gauss and Dr Kronig for painless childbirth through "twilight sleep". This term applied to the combination of analgesia (pain relief) and amnesia (loss of memory), resulting from an injection of morphine and scopolamine, which led to a state in which the woman did not remember the pain of childbirth. Rion wrote a number of articles on the subject for Lord Northcliffe's *Weekly Despatch* before publishing in 1915, a book, *The Truth About Twilight Sleep*, which proclaimed, "Through Twilight Sleep, a new era has dawned for woman and through her for the whole human race." So enthused was she with this concept that she trained as a maternity nurse and, in collaboration with Lord Northcliffe, established eleven maternity hospitals around the country. She also claimed herself to have brought forty six 'twilight sleep' babies into the world. Unfortunately, it did not prove a new dawn for women, and the procedure fell out of favour.[789]

3.4.6 Animal welfare

One member of the artistic community, William Hebblethwaite, the occupier of the Blue Bell studio in St Andrew's Street, took it upon himself to to try to bring to an end the wanton cruelty that was often inflicted upon birds and animals by the locals, especially by the children of the fisherfolk. From his letters to his landlord and from his comments in the Arts Club suggestions book, he may well have been a serial complainer, and he clearly upset a number of people with his attitude. However, he had an aversion to animal cruelty and the naturalist, W.H.Hudson, tells how Hebblethwaite, by his own efforts, amidst considerable hostility, had secured strict protection for gulls in the town. However, as he heard the story from grateful locals a decade or so after Hebblethwaite's death, he calls him Mr Ebblethwaite!

"The fishermen always had a friendly feeling for the birds, as is the case in all the fishing places on the coast, but they did not protect them from persecution, although the chief persecutors were their own children. People, natives and visitors amused themselves by shooting gulls along the cliff and harbour. Harrying the gulls was the most popular amusement of the boys; they were throwing stones at them all day long and caught them with baited hooks and set gins bated with fish on the sands and no person forbade them. Then Mr Ebblethwaite appeared on the scene. He came from a town in the north of England, in broken health, and here he stayed a number of years, living alone in a small house by the waterside. He was very fond of the gulls and fed them every day, but his example had no effect on others, nor did his words when he went about day after day on the beach trying to persuade people to desist from these senseless brutalities. Finally, he succeeded in getting a certain number of boys summoned for cruelty before the magistrates, and though no convictions followed nor could be obtained, since there was no law or by-law to help him in such a case, he yet in this indirect way accomplished his object. He made himself unpopular, and was jeered and looked black at and denounced as an interfering person, especially by the women, but some of the fishermen now began to pluck up spirit and second his efforts, and in a little while it came to be understood that, law or no law, the gulls must not be persecuted." [790]

In 1905, Robert Blatchford (1851-1943), the editor of the socialist paper, *The Clarion*, wrote an article on St Ives, which he called "the loveliest town in England", and, in this, he repeatedly mentioned the attractions of the vast colony of gulls. "I have never seen anything like them. They are so beautiful, so numerous and so tame." He made enquiries of a fisherman, who looked at them "with softened eyes" and said, "They are tame. They belong here. We don't allow anyone to harm them.... Men used to shoot them and throw stones at them. A cruel, foolish thing, I call it... But we have stopped all that. We don't allow it; and you'll never see a boy throw a stone at a gull. Yes, they are worth seeing, and they are useful too. They snap up all leavings of the fish off the shore, and keep us a nice clean beach; and they do no harm to anybody."[791] Such a complete change in attitude was solely down to Hebblethwaite, and the gulls became one of the attractive features of St Ives that was most commented upon by visitors.[792]

Despite Hebblethwaite's success in curbing cruelty to gulls, Hudson found in 1907 that the locals still turned a blind eye to the setting of baited hooks and gins to capture other birds, whether winter migrants or local species, despite the fact that this resulted in numerous birds being maimed.

---

789 'Twilight sleep' fell out of favour as it completely removed the mother from the birth experience and gravely depressed the baby's central nervous system, leading to babies often being drowsy, depressed and with poor breathing capacity. (Information from MedicineNet.com).

790 W H Hudson, *The Land's End*, London, 1908 at p.219-20.

791 Reproduced in *St Ives Weekly Summary* 10/6/1905.

792 See also *St Ives Cornwall - As Others See Us*, *St Ives Weekly Summary*, 29/2/1908.

Fig. 3.53 John Douglas   *Gulls*   (courtesy Andrew Lanyon)
Douglas was fascinated with the play of light through flocks of gulls and took numerous photographs of the subject, one of which won a silver medal in a competition run by *The Tatler* in 1923.

In fact, Hudson was appalled at the huge number of maimed birds that could be seen around the town painfully hopping on one foot or crawling with the help of their wings over the ground in search of food. When confronted, those involved seemed to think it all a great sport and were impervious to the suffering experienced by the birds.[793]   A successful action brought by the R.S.P.C.A. in 1917 against Charles Paynter, who had been found with thirty hooks baited with worms to catch birds, probably marked the end of this practice.[794]

Hebblethwaite did not restrict his efforts to gulls and also arranged for boys to be summoned for cruelty to donkeys, as these seem to have been systematically mistreated as well. Here again, his actions were applauded in a number of quarters, but attitudes were so ingrained that it would take some years before such cruelty was universally condemned.[795] Accordingly, a visitor writing to the local paper, in 1920, complained about the cruelty displayed by youths driving ponies, and said that he had made exactly the same complaint seven years previously.[796]

Hebblethwaite was very much ahead of his time on this issue, and Hudson indicated that he found at least twenty people to tell him Hebblethwaite's story and to praise the beneficial impact that he had eventually had.

---

793 W H Hudson, *The Land's End*, London, 1908 at p.214-7.

794 *St Ives Times*, 16/2/1917.

795 *St Ives Weekly Summary*, 9/8/1890.

796 *St Ives Times*, 13/2/1920.

COURTING THE LOCALS

3.5.1 Introduction

It is perhaps not surprising that the art colony at St Ives should have proved to be a fertile seed-bed for romance. Most of the artists who settled in the colony in its early years were relatively young, arriving shortly after completing their art education, whether in France and/or Britain, and the formation of a series of painting schools in the town in the late 1890s resulted in a mass of much younger students, of both sexes, working in the town, often for extended periods. Whilst life in St Ives was still hide-bound, in many respects, by Victorian values, there were much greater opportunities for the sexes to mix regularly, in informal surroundings, than in most other towns, particularly as the Arts Club was open to women. It would have been odd, therefore, if a number of relationships had not developed between students, or between established artists and students. A number of these have been referred to already, such as the Australian, Arthur Burgess, falling in 1901 for fellow student, Muriel Coldwell, and his Australian colleague, Emanuel Phillips Fox, being struck by another visiting Slade student that year - Ethel Carrick. Students who caught the eye of more established artists, included Augusta Baird-Smith, who married Moffat Lindner, and Selina Wing, who married John Bromley. Romance, however, was not confined to nubile young students. The visiting Canadian, Mary Bell, met her English husband, Charles Eastlake, in St Ives in 1893, whilst Harry Britton became engaged to a fellow Canadian visiting artist, Henrietta Hancock, during his stay in the town in 1910-12. The American Guy Wiggins, who had first visited St Ives as a boy in the company of his father, fell in love on his return in 1914 with an English tourist, Dorothy Johnson, who was staying in the same hotel - 'Chy-an-Drea'. However, what I want to look at in more detail in this section are those romances that flourished between local girls and visiting artists, particularly as, in a number of instances, these were with foreign artists, which resulted in the girls being whisked away to live in a totally different world. How did these romances come about, how were they viewed and did they endure?

3.5.2 The John sisters

The most extraordinary story relates to two St Ives sisters - Mary and Edith John - who married two American artists - Frederic Winthrop Ramsdell and Herbert Waldron Faulkner.[797] Mary (b.1866) and Edith (b.1871) were the daughters of Thomas Trewhella John, a commercial traveller, and his wife, Eliza Wearne, the daughter of Roger Wearne, who had been Mayor of St Ives in 1834 and 1839. They, and their three brothers, Edwin, Trewhella and Ernest, lived in Tregenna Terrace and, although their father was exceedingly proud of his daughters and took them to Plymouth to be fitted with stylish suits so as to make them better dressed than any other girls in town, he was renowned as a difficult and domineering man, prone to depression. Christine Morton Raymont remembers him as a "very gloomy man. Few people came to the house when he was there and all the blinds had to be kept drawn".[798] However, he was clearly successful, for he described himself as a "seine owner" in Kelly's Directory in 1883. After their mother's death in 1887, the situation at home cannot have been easy for the girls, although they got on with Mary Pearce, the housekeeper employed by their father, who was now working as a commission agent from 'Albert House', in Albert Place - just around the corner from his home.[799] Raymont, who became close friends with both sisters, recalled Mary as "so clever and amusing", "very delightful in her way of treating children" and with thick, dark hair hanging in a long plait reaching below her waist.[800] Edith was "quite a beauty" and utterly charming.

In 1894, having broken off her engagement to a suitor from a wealthy St Ives family approved by her father - the "boring" Jim Chellew, Edith, then aged 22, fell in love with Frederic Winthrop Ramsdell, an American artist who had been lodging nearby in Tregenna Terrace. He was then principally a portrait painter, and he had already enjoyed some success at the Paris Salon and at the Chicago World

---

797 I am greatly indebted to Celia Faulkner Crawford, the granddaughter of Herbert Faulkner, for this story, told in her privately published book *Four Grandparents*. She also supplied me with Christine Morton Raymont's *The John Family in St Ives*, an unpublished manuscript, and many family photos and papers. She also put me in contact with Edith Scott, the granddaughter of Winnogene Ramsdell, Winthrop's sister, who has been most helpful on the Ramsdell side of the story.

798 Christine Morton Raymont, *The John Family in St Ives*, at p.7.

799 See Kelly's Directory 1893.

800 Christine Morton Raymont, *The John Family in St Ives*, at p.1.

Fig. 3.54   Mary, Edith and Ernest John
(Celia Faulkner Crawford)

Fig. 3.55   Frederic Ramsdell
(Manistee County Historical Museum)

Fig. 3.56   Herbert Faulkner
(Celia Faulkner Crawford)

Columbian Exhibition of 1893. He had come to St Ives to visit an old friend from his student days in Paris - the Liverpudlian Walter Jevons. Indeed, Jevons, Ramsdell and their friend, Herbert Faulkner, had all been imprisoned overnight on a sketching trip to the Loire Valley on suspicion of being spies![801] During their courtship, Winthrop persuaded Edith to sit for him, and he depicted her side-on as she sat in a long green dress, playing a musical instrument.[802] However, Edith's choice of man could not have been further from her father's wishes - he was a foreigner, he was an artist and he was deformed by curvature of the spine. Despite being charming and amusing and the son of a wealthy American attorney, these other attributes made Edith aware that her father's consent would never be forthcoming, particularly as such a marriage would mean that she was bound to go to live in America. Accordingly, with Mary's help, the couple got married, without her father's consent, and eloped.[803]

Thomas Trewhella John's reaction to this subterfuge was worse than anyone could have imagined. He dismissed the servants and closed the house, leaving his daughter, Mary, homeless. Mary's grand-daughter, Celia Faulkner Crawford, recalls how Mary, telling this story, some fifty years afterwards, turned scarlet, as she said, "He turned me out of the house!", her eyes flashing with rage. Mary, accordingly, was forced to live with her maternal grandmother, Mrs Smedley, in St Ives, a staunch Methodist, who had remarried after Roger Wearne's death, but fallen on hard times.[804]

Before leaving on his honeymoon, Ramsdell had begged Mary, who was an excellent letter writer with an attractive hand, to write, with news of the wedding, to his old friend, Herbert Waldron Faulkner, with whom he had studied at the Art Students League in New York and who had been a frequent companion during his European trip. Herbert replied with appreciation, enclosing a sketch of Florence, where he was staying. Mary naturally wrote back to thank him, and so began a regular correspondence. An exchange of photographs prompted Herbert to write to say that he was coming to St Ives to ask her to marry him. Mary agreed to meet him at St Erth and, on the way over by rail from St Ives, bribed the guard to allow them to have a compartment to themselves on the return trip. She spotted him first - a tall, thin, gawky figure, wearing striped trousers, a tail-coat and a top-hat. "There's Uncle Sam!", she said to herself. By the time that they reached St Ives, they were engaged, and were married two weeks later on 12th September 1895 in the Parish Church, her strict Methodist upbringing immediately forgotten. Faulkner himself had endured an unhappy childhood, spent mostly with his mother at an uncle's house, as his father had been a failure at everything that he tried. Herbert had also been weak and sickly and was the only one of his parents' six children to survive. However, he impressed everyone with his unfailing courtesy and manners. Writing much later about the Church at St Ives, Faulkner commented, "To me, it seems as if my life began there. My Mary's companionship so completely rounded out an existence which, up to that time, had been thwarted, starved and discouraged. We both came out of the portal of that little church with larger lives, to face bigger responsibilities but with complete confidence in the future and in one another."[805]

How did these two extraordinary marriages fare? Despite only having met a fortnight beforehand, that of Mary and Herbert was very happy. Nevertheless, the first couple of years, spent in America, brought its trials, for they were both distraught when their first child died shortly after birth and then Herbert managed to burn down the apartment block in which his studio was located.[806] On returning to Europe, they then had to cope with the death, probably through suicide, of Mary's eldest brother, Edwin.[807] After spending some time in St Ives in 1897, they settled in Paris, where they stayed until 1908.[808] They enjoyed a good social life with other American artists living there and had two children, Waldron and Louis, that Mary doted upon. Indeed, she produced two 'baby books' for her children recording their early lives, to which Herbert added some charming watercolours. Meanwhile, Herbert played a leading role in the American Arts Association in Paris and enjoyed considerable success as a painter of Venetian scenes. Accordingly, there would have been numerous trips to that idyllic town. Their return to America in 1908 was to ensure that their children obtained an American education. They settled in Washington, Connecticut and built their own home, which they named 'Tregenna'. With painting sales not so easy,

801 Waldron Faulkner, *A Portrait of the Artist, Herbert Waldron Faulkner*, Washington, 1966 at pp.16-18.

802 The Ramsdell family also have some marine studies done during Frederic's time in St Ives.

803 The witnesses were Edith's siblings Trewhella and Mary.

804 There was a custom in St Ives for long leases to be granted for the life of the survivor of three nominated persons. Mrs Smedley had nominated her three children, only for them all to predecease her, leaving her in straightened circumstamces in her old age.

805 Celia Faulkner Crawford, *Four Grandparents*, Washington D C, 1995 at p.23.

806 Faulkner, whilst tending his fire, had been called away to eject a tramp. *St Ives Weekly Summary* 26/12/1896.

807 Edwin, who was much loved by his sisters, had wanted to be a doctor, but had been forced by his father to take an office job in Manchester, which he hated. Raymont records that "he became ill and wandering out he fell into the canal and was drowned" - Christine Morton Raymont, *The John Family in St Ives*, at p.3. Edwin's state of mind may not have been helped, firstly, by the departure abroad of his two sisters following their marriages but also by the departure to America in 1897 of his youngest brother, Ernest, where he was looked after initially by Winthrop Ramsdell's parents in Manistee. He later settled in Philadelphia.

808 Letters from Eliza Smedley to Edith Ramsdell dated 5/4/1897 and during July 1897 refer to Herbert and Mary being in St Ives, albeit they spent much of the interim period in Paris.

Herbert devoted himself to a range of other activities - woodcarving, giving lectures on European art and history and writing books on flowers. In November 1916, the St Ives paper recorded how the Faulkners, dressed in the colours of England and wearing English flags, had been in charge of the English booth, decorated by Herbert with the English coat of arms, at an Allied Market held in Washington Green to raise funds for the War effort.[809]   The pair remained devoted to each other - the only problems being Mary's occasional bouts of severe depression, which sometimes required her to be hospitalised. Given the problems experienced by her father and elder brother, this may have been a congenital complaint. When Herbert died in 1940, he was still declaring his love for his "devoted and wondrous sympathetic" Mary. Looked after by children and grandchildren, Mary outlived him by twenty-one years.[810]

Edith's marriage was also happy, but fate, in the end, was not so kind to her. Naturally, after their marriage, Edith had to be introduced to Winthrop's parents, who lived in Manistee, Michigan and, in 1895, they had their first child, Winnogene, named after one of Winthrop's sisters. An interview with Winthrop in the local Manistee paper in December 1895 records that he was planning a one-man show in Chicago before returning to Europe in the spring of 1896.[811] Back in France, they lived in Fontenay-aux-Roses near Paris. Raymont, who visited them in 1897, commented, "The little family was delightful; Edith was perfect as wife and mother, Winthrop most amusing and Gene...'une grande fille'".[812] Their circle of friends included Anders Zorn, who had worked in St Ives in 1887-8, the writers Émile Zola and Israel Zangwill, and the composer, Ethelbert Nevin.[813] For a short period after Mary and Herbert's move to Paris in 1897, the two sisters no doubt met up with regularity. The difference between humble St Ives, with its dour Methodism, and fashionable Paris, in the company of leading artists and writers, must have been immense, but the two girls each seem to have made the transition easily.

In 1898, Winthrop and Edith spent some time back in St Ives to say farewell to her aged grandmother, Mrs Smedley, as they had decided to return to America. There, they lived with Winthrop's parents in the huge Victorian mansion, known as 'The Lindens', which had been built by his father, Thomas Jefferson Ramsdell, in 1876. T.J., as he was known to the family, was not only the leading attorney in Manistee, but a serial entrepeneur, with large property interests. Manistee had been a wild, outback town on his first arrival in 1860 and he became involved in any enterprise that advanced the town. For instance, he started the first hardware store in Manistee, was instrumental in the establishment of the first newspaper and was President of the First National Bank.

Fig. 3.57   Frederic Ramsdell   *The Breakfast Table*   (Anne Ramsdell von Helf)
This features Edith and her daughter, Gene, in 'The Lindens'.

---

809 *St Ives Times*, 3/11/1916.

810 Ernest Morton Nance, an admirer of Mary from her youth, asked her to marry him after she had become a widow, but she would not leave her family in America. Christine Morton Raymont, *The John Family in St Ives*, at p.6/7.

811 *Manistee Daily News*, 7/12/1895.

812 Christine Morton Raymont, *The John Family in St Ives*, at p.12.

813 Letter from Roger Ramsdell to Edith Scott dated 22/10/1969 lists his father's friends as including Émile Zola, Anders Zorn, Joseph Pennell, Ethelbert Nevin, Albert Chevalier and Israel Zangwill and mentions that he knew Whistler. Waldron Faulkner records Zangwill as a friend of his father in Paris as well.

'The Lindens' was a massive three storey building, with a tower, and Winthrop and Edith had a separate section to themselves, and Gene and her new brother, Roger (b.1900), were able to use the forty foot square ballroom on the third floor as their playroom. Edith was given a warm welcome, as the Ramsdells were delighted with her gentle ways and her English speech.[814] Her brother, Ernest, also socialised with the family and was intimately involved with the Ramsdells in the establishment of a local sailing club.[815] When Mary's children later came to visit their aunt, they were very much in awe of the house and remembered magical times. Life in the Ramsdell household was apparently uninhibited and fun.

Winthrop Ramsdell was in demand in Manistee for his portrait work and completed a fine painting of Edith and their daughter, Gene, entitled *The Breakfast Table* (Fig. 3.57). However, he is perhaps best known as an artist for his art nouveau poster design for American Crescent Cycles in 1899, which has become a classic. He was also given prestigious commissions by his father. When T.J. organised the construction of a new building for the First National Bank, Winthrop decorated the vestibule with a history of Manistee. When the local theatre burnt down in 1900, T.J. came to the rescue and built a new opera house at vast cost (Fig. 3.58).[816] Winthrop was again entrusted with the decor and depicted, in the vault of the dome, Edith, topless, as Venus, riding her chariot through the heavens, surrounded by cherubs (Fig. 3.61). In order to pose, Edith had to mount high scaffolding and spent many chilly hours, scantily clad in a couple of yards of sheer silk mull.[817] When Winthrop heard that the clubby wives of the lumber barons were calling the new building 'Ramsdell's Folly', he incorporated their faces on to the voluptuous nudes with which he decorated the lobby! After the performances, members of the touring troupe and the leading figures in the town retired to 'The Lindens', where they danced in the ballroom to music from an orchestra imported for the occasion from New York or Chicago.[818] The commercial traveller's daughter from St Ives must occasionally have had to pinch herself. Was this real?

In addition to his portrait work in Manistee, Winthrop began to branch out into landscape painting, becoming involved with the fledgling art colony at Old Lyme, Connecticut. In 1907, he acquired an old farmstead, dating from 1778, near Long Island Sound as a summer home and, after 1909, he spent increasing amounts of time during the summer and autumn at Old Lyme. He was actively involved with the formation of the Lyme Art Association in 1914 and was its first President.[819] Indeed, his son, Roger, recorded that he was so often away that they had little time together, but that he always looked upon his father "as a God and an angel".[820]

For Edith, however, such happiness was not to last, for Winthrop died in 1915, at just fifty years of age. T.J.'s subsequent death in 1917 was probably not so much of a surprise, given that he was aged eighty-four. What was a shock, though, was that he died practically penniless, having made a series of speculative investments. Left with no income and faced with a number of severely disappointed siblings-in-law, Edith had little option but to find employment.[821] Raymont gives us glimpses of her life as a widow. In the early 1920s, she was working at the Cosmopolitan Club in New York. She did, however, manage to accompany Herbert and Mary on several trips, including a brief return visit to Carbis Bay to see old friends and cousins in June 1924.[822] In 1926, when Raymont visited the sisters in America, Edith was renting an old school building close to Mary in Washington, Connecticut.[823] However, the impact of the Depression, following the Wall Street Crash in 1929, seems to have persuaded both Edith and Roger, who had taken an art degree at Yale, to move back to England, with Edith settling back in Carbis Bay, where she lived for the last twenty-five years of her life. Gene, having married the artist, Robert Jackson, stayed on in America. Tragically, during the War, Gene died young from cancer and Edith was unable to get across to be by her side. Roger (d.1975), a talented artist, but a profoundly unconventional and carefree spirit, worked as a set director for Laurence Olivier and others at the Old Vic.[824] However, as he was occasionally reduced to scrubbing pub floors for a crust himself, it is unlikely that he will have been much support financially to his mother. Edith's final years may have been impoverished and lonely, but she enjoyed twenty-one years of a life and life-style that was far beyond her wildest dreams as a young girl in St Ives.

---

814 Christine Morton Raymont, *The John Family in St Ives*, at p.13.

815 *The Onekama Sailing Club, Manistee News Advocate*, 23/2/2003.

816 The estimated cost of the building was $25,000 but the final figure was over four times that. It opened on 4/9/1903 but has had a chequered history, suffering long periods of neglect. However, it has now become the focal point of community pride and is seen as the paradigm of the town's resurgence.

817 See *'Star' of Opulent Era Stages Comeback, Detroit News*, 8/7/1951.

818 It was probably through the Manistee theatre that Winthrop Ramsdell became friends with the entertainer, Albert Chevalier.

819 The 1915 Retrospective of his work contained 89 canvases of Lyme subjects. A further retrospective was held by the Lyme Art Association in 1921. Two of his works are owned by the Florence Griswold Museum, Old Lyme.

820 Letter from Roger Ramsdell to Edith Scott dated 22/10/1969.

821 The Wall Street crash seems to have finally put paid to the Ramsdells' fortunes and it was widely believed that the fire which burnt down 'The Lindens' in the 1930s was an insurance scam.

822 During the visit, Herbert Faulkner was a guest at the Arts Club of E Morton Nance.

823 Christine Morton Raymont, *The John Family in St Ives*, at p.11.

824 The address at his funeral service was given by the actress, Constance Cummings.

Fig. 3.58   The Ramsdell Theatre, Manistee

Fig. 3.59 Thomas Jefferson Ramsdell
            (Manistee County Historical Museum)

Fig. 3.60   'The Lindens', Manistee
             (Manistee County Historical Museum)

Fig. 3.61   Frederic Ramsdell
             Edith Ramsdell as Venus
             in the dome of the Ramsdell Theatre
             (Manistee County Historical Museum)

Fig. 3.62 Frederic Ramsdell
            Edith Ramsdell as a sea maiden
            (Anne Ramsdell von Helf)

3.5.3   Aida Gale and Sarah Trevorrow

The two other romances that led to local girls being transported to America are less well documented. That which flourished between the visiting Australian student, Richard Hayley Lever, and Aida Gale clearly came about, as they shared the same lodgings in Richmond Terrace. Born in St Austell, Aida was four years older than him and, in the 1901 Census, was described as a Governess, but she had secured first place in all England in her music exams, with her contralto voice being highly regarded by leading musicians of the day.[825] Accordingly, she had had the opportunity for a career as a professional singer, but she appears to have decided against such a life, even before her marriage, and there are few references to her performing in St Ives. In December 1904, Lever returned to Australia, with his great chum, Will Ashton. It is not known whether Aida accompanied him so as to be introduced to his family and to Australia, or whether she spent an anxious year, hoping that he would fulfil his promise to return. In any event, almost immediately after he arrived back in St Ives in December 1905, they got married. The wedding was stated to be a quiet affair, as there had been a recent bereavement in Lever's family. However, despite his marriage, it seems that he never intended to settle in St Ives permanently, as the local paper recorded, "Hayley Lever has just returned from an Australian voyage and will be in England for a few years to complete his studies."[826] Aida, however, probably did not envisage ending up living in America.

This choice resulted from Lever's great friendship with the American artist, Elmer Schofield, who was based in St Ives between 1903 and 1907. Indeed, the couple's first son, born in August 1907, was called Elmer Domenico Hayley Lever. "Poor little chap!", commented Schofield to his wife.[827] In any event, when Lever became restless in St Ives in 1912, the family tried their luck in America. Almost immediately, Schofield told his wife that Lever thought New York "the most wonderful and delightful city in the world".[828] What Aida felt at being transported from her native Cornwall to this bustling metropolis, with a young child in tow, is not known. As her husband's paintings were immediately acclaimed on all sides, she was no doubt pleased that he was happy and successful, and they mixed with some of the leading figures in the American art scene, as Lever's paintings were in demand at all the top galleries. Lever became a painting instructor at the Art Students League in New York (1919-1931) and was made an associate of the National Academy of Design in 1925 and a full member in 1933. He even won a prestigious commission to paint President Coolidge's yacht. Lever was not as successful as a portrait painter, but Aida sat for him on a number of occasions, often nude, and these naive studies have their own following, albeit they tell us little about Aida herself. Other paintings by Lever indicate she was a keen gardener. However, the difficult economic circumstances in the 1930s took their toll and, in 1938, their home in Caldwell, New Jersey, to which they had moved in about 1930, was re-possessed. They subsequently moved to Mount Vernon, New York, but the last decade of Aida's life - she died in 1949 - cannot have been easy, as the onset of arthritis hampered her husband's painting and the increasing eclecticism of his work, which was felt to be the product of "an agitated spirit", found few followers.

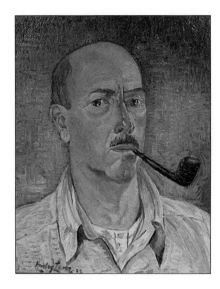

Figs. 3.63-4
Richard Hayley Lever
Self-Portrait (1932) &
Portrait of Aida (1916)

---

825 *St Ives Weekly Summary*, 30/12/1905.

826 *St Ives Weekly Summary*, 30/12/1905.

827 Letter dated 11/8/1907 - Schofield Family Archive.

828 Letter from Elmer to Murielle Schofield dated 17/12/1912 - Smithsonian Institution, Archives of American Art, Schofield Papers (Reel 5043).

Fig. 3.65   George Gardner Symons in 1916
(Archives of American Art,
Smithsonian Institution)

When Sarah Trevorrow, the daughter of a seller of musical instruments in Tregenna Place in St Ives, was asked by her father, William, to pop down to the Post Office for him in 1898, she could never have foreseen the dramatic consequences that this errand would have upon her life. On the way, she bumped into two American artists from Chicago - George Gardner Symons and William Wendt - and, for Symons, it was love at first sight. As the Trevorrow family were well-known in artistic circles - William not only for his shop but also for his sideline as a photographer, and Sarah for her exceptional talent as a violinist - Symons was able to pursue his courtship with alacrity and the pair were married, for some reason in Islington, on 17th May 1899, with Wendt as best man. He reported to his friend, Samuel McCrea, a couple of days later, "The happy couple now reside in blissful ecstasy in Paris while I am uncaught and unfettered in England."[829] Unlike the John sisters, Sarah was able to make a number of return visits to St Ives to see her family - for instance, in 1901-2 and 1903-4, and, on her father's death in 1908, they stayed for an extended time. There were also a number of return visits prior to 1914.

After the War, Symons obtained what Elmer Schofield called "a very fine studio apartment" in New York and built a studio at Laguna Beach in California. He also painted a lot in the Berkshire Mountains in New England. Schofield remained a close friend and would have stayed quite often, as they painted together in California in the 1920s, culminating in two well-received joint shows in the Stendahl Galleries in Los Angeles in 1928-9. Sarah and her husband made some further return visits during the 1920s, her mother now living at Angarrack, and, in the summer of 1929, were regularly seen in the town.[830] They were intending a further visit in 1930, but, unfortunately Symons died that January, aged 67. Instead of returning to Cornwall at this juncture, Sarah, now known as Zar, re-married the American impressionist figure painter, Louis Betts (1873-1961), and enjoyed a splendid lifestyle with homes in New York, Sherborne Falls, Massachusetts and Laguna Beach, until her death in New York aged 92.[831]

3.5.4   The Carr sisters

The four romances featuring Ramsdell, Faulkner, Lever and Symons all involve foreign male artists falling for local girls. However, other than Talmage's union with art student Gertrude Rowe, from Redruth, I am not aware of any British male artist marrying a girl from the local community in the Pre-War period. Was this due to prejudices involving class or status or was the upbringing of girls in St Ives so far removed from that of the artists that compatibility was difficult? Clearly, the John sisters and Sarah Trevorrow had no problems in adapting, but the position may not have been so easy if they had remained in St Ives within the bosom of their own families. Any prejudice would not have been solely on the part of the artists, and many well-to-do members of the local community would not have considered, initially, that an artist was an appropriate match for a favoured daughter, as demonstrated by the reaction of Thomas Trewhella John.

829 Letter to S H McCrea dated 19/5/1899 (courtesy Edenhurst Gallery, San Francisco).

830 Wilson Henry Irvine notes "Symons is coming over this summer" in his Journal (24/3/1923). See also *St Ives Times*, 17/1/1930.

831 St Ives Archive Centre - 'Memories- The History of Beatrice Estelle Trevorrow'.

The position was very different, though, for children of the artists, as they grew up in the town, went to school with the locals and socialised with the children of the artists' friends from the community. By 1910, weddings between children from the artistic community and local families began to take place, and, in a number of cases, these clearly were considered "events of the year".

Sydney Carr's two daughters, Irene and Vera, who had begun to play significant roles in artists' entertainments from 1903, were clearly well-liked. Irene, in fact, showed some artistic talent as well, exhibiting some dainty miniature portraits on Show Day in 1908. Her marriage, in June 1912, to Francis Edward Wintle, who had been Borough Surveyor in the town for three and a half years, before being made Deputy Governor of Liverpool Prison (later Governor of Isle of Wight Prison), was a major social event of the year, with a reception for 120 people at the Porthminster Hotel.[832] Irene, who designed her own dress, clearly appreciated art, for most of the artists in attendance at the wedding gave her paintings. These included oil paintings from Noble Barlow, Alfred Hartley, Gertrude Talmage, the Australian Charles Bryant (Plate 16) and the Americans Henry Keasbey and William Potter, a watercolour portrait by Mabel Douglas (Fig. 3.68) and other watercolours from Moulton Foweraker, Lizzie and Daisy Whitehouse and Mrs F.M.Evans, etchings from Claude Barry and Fred Milner and a personalised bookplate by Edmund Fuller (Fig. 3.66). The latter shows that, in addition to art and dressmaking, Irene was also interested in tennis and in literature and music, playing the violin. Other artists in attendance included Julius Olsson, William Fortescue, Beale Adams, Folliott Stokes, Elgar Russell, Herbert Fitzherbert, Nora Hartley, Marcella Smith, Georgina Bainsmith, Katherine Horn and Caroline Jackson. Local notables, who were also present, included Sir Edward and Lady Hain, Commander Chellew and Major Chellew, Albert Lang and Edward and Reginald Boase, amongst many others, demonstrating that the artists had now become part of the central fabric of the town.[833]

Fig. 3.66 Edmund Fuller
Bookplate for Irene Wintle

Fig. 3.67 H.G. Fitzherbert
Caricature of F.E. Wintle
(from *Caricatures of the Cornish Riviera*)

---

832 Wintle, whose father was the Reverend F.T.W.Wintle of Bere Ferrers, Devon, had been educated at Plymouth College. Despite having served whilst at St Ives with the Duke of Cornwall's Light Infantry, his application to volunteer for service in the War had been turned down, as the Home Office refused to release him. Sadly, he died in 1927 from a cerebral haemorrhage, aged only 50. See *St Ives Times*, 2/9/1927.

833 See full page review in *St Ives Times* 21/6/1912.

Fig. 3.68 Mabel Douglas *Irene Carr*
          (portrait miniature
          given as a wedding present)
          (Carr family archive)

Fig. 3.69 Theresa Abell   (Priscilla Fursdon)

Also in attendance at Irene's wedding were Bernard and Annie Walke - in fact, Bernard took the service, rather than the Reverend Marsh. Sydney Carr had been a strong supporter of Walke, when he was a curate in St Ives, and was incensed when he was removed from his position in 1904, writing several letters to the local press and to the Bishop protesting at the decision. Walke's fellow curate in St Ives, Joe Hellier, was also at the wedding, and, as noted above, after a period as a missionary, he returned to marry Irene's sister, Vera.

3.5.5   The Trewhella brothers

Whilst Francis Wintle was a town dignitary, he was not born in St Ives and the first member of the artist community to marry into an established St Ives family was Theresa Rion Abell (1896-1927), the daughter of Frank Ver Beck's wife, Hanna Rion, from her first marriage to the musician W.V.Abell. Theresa arrived in St Ives with her mother and step-father in the summer of 1913 and had an interest in both art and drama. As her beauty matched that of her mother, she was in much demand as a model, and Mabel Douglas produced a fine portrait of her (Plate 36), whilst sitting at one of the Arts Club sketching sessions. She also took part in Arts Club productions, and a quick pencil sketch by her stepfather captures her performing as a clown there on 21st March 1917. Indeed, she enjoyed a brief career as a vaudeville artist, performing during the complete runs at the Empire Theatre, London, of *Razzle-Dazzle* in 1916 and *Hankey-Panky* in 1917. Accordingly, despite his friendship with the artistic community, she was probably not what former Mayor, William Trewhella, of 'Trewyn', whose family counted themselves one of the oldest in Cornwall, had in mind for a daughter-in-law.[834] However, his second son, Captain Bernard Trewhella, who had lost an arm in the War, was smitten, and the wedding, in June 1918, was the social event of the year.[835] The Read, Chellew and Nicholls families, and many others known to William Trewhella through public office, were well represented, and numerous artists, who would have known well both bride and groom, attended. A notable absentee, however, was Theresa's stepfather, Frank Ver Beck, with whom she did not get on. Pictures were again a popular present.

---

834 William Trewhella's wife was the sister of Edith Wearne, later Smedley, the grandmother of the John sisters.

835 It is reviewed at length in *St Ives Times* 21/6/1918. Bernie Trewhella, who lived into his nineties, is also buried in Zennor churchyard.

Fig. 3.70 H.G.Fitzherbert *Caricature of Richard Read* (from *Everyone's Doing It*)
Richard Read, who was the second son of Robert Sawle Read, was best
man at the wedding of Bernard Trewhella, for they shared a sense of
comradeship having both lost limbs in the War

A certain degree of tension developed between the newly-weds respective mothers, as Mrs Trewhella did not take kindly to Hanna Rion thumping the keys of her grand piano at 'Trewyn', as if she was in a Concert Hall, or to her insisting that her daughter give birth under the influence of 'twilight sleep'. However, she will have been mortified not only at Hanna Rion's death in 1924, aged just 49, but also at the death of Theresa, shortly after giving birth to her second child in 1927. Theresa was buried in Zennor churchyard, as William Trewhella's eldest son was Vicar there in the 1920s. Despite the number of artists at the wedding, only Caroline Jackson attended the funeral.

The Trewhella family clearly had artistic sensibilities, as William's third son, Ernest Cecil, married another member of the artistic community, Lilas Barrett, in 1925. Lilas was the daughter of the writer, Frank Barrett, and had been exhibiting at Lanham's since 1917. Their romance blossomed after Lilas was laid up at Cecil's home, Restronguet Farm, after a serious riding accident. It was again a huge wedding, with numerous artists in attendance, and many of the wedding presents were pictures or etchings personally executed by the donor.[836] Also popular as gifts, by this juncture, were examples of Leach pottery. Lilas (d.1962) continued with her art, after her marriage, for some while, exhibiting with the St Ives Society of Artists, before the demands of being a farmer's wife and the mother of two children took their toll. These unions, however, display the further merging of 'art and town'.

---

836 A long list of wedding presents is given in *St Ives Times*, 23/1/1925. Artists who gave their own work included Moffat Lindner, George Goosey, Marjorie Ballance, Alfred Hartley, Edgar Skinner, Frances Tysoe Smith, Pauline Hewitt, Francis Roskruge and Charles Hobhouse.

PART FOUR

SKIDDEN HILL ST. IVES.   Edmund G. Fuller

WAR AND AFTERMATH

THE WAR YEARS

4.1.1 'The land of the dead'

In 1912, Richard Hayley Lever wrote to Elmer Schofield in America describing St Ives as 'the land of the dead' and pleading with him to help him "get out of this mud here".[837] The colony had certainly changed. The leading figures, such as Brown, Olsson and Talmage, had left to pursue their career aspirations in London, and the reviewer of Show Day in 1912 dwelt as much on who was *not* exhibiting, as he did on the works on show. The schools of painting that had drawn down fresh blood to the colony had ceased to operate on any formal basis, and the enthusiasm for landscape and marine painting in the open air, which had led so many artists to select St Ives as a base, had dwindled, as young artists became increasingly interested in more modern, intellectual movements, such as Cubism and Futurism, which were often inspired by the city rather than the countryside. Furthermore, those artists, who had settled in the early years of the colony, were now well into their fifties, with growing families and less energy. There were those too, who had "discovered that the fame dreams of youth would never be realised, and were content to admire, where they formerly worshipped."[838]

The reduced number of artist visitors was conspicuous, with the local paper commenting in 1913, "The artists in St Ives at the present time are less than they have been for many years - and they are still decreasing".[839] A reader felt that one cause of this was that there was less to paint, as "the incursion of visitors has been the cause of the destruction of many quaint and picturesque dwellings, especially in the lower part of town, to make room for a cheaper class of lodging house".[840]

Financial conditions were clearly difficult as well. Lever had not only had eight consecutive years of success at the New Salon in Paris, but had also won awards at Pittsburgh, been selected to represent Britain at the Venice Biennale and received critical acclaim in London circles. Yet, he was forced that year to resign as a member of the RBA and ROI, as he could not afford the subscription. If Lever, who deserved success more than any other artist in St Ives at the time, could not make ends meet, what hope was there for any other artist in the colony? 'Bleistift', the local art scribe at the time, recorded that artists were constantly complaining about lack of sales. He offered his own explanation. "Hitherto the patron of the easel-picture has been the cultured upper-middle class - a class which has now largely given itself over to a constant round of golf, bridge and motoring, with the result that its mental power has decreased, as its selfishness has increased."[841] The New Zealander, George Sherriff, after his initial sojourn in the colony between 1905-8, condemned the indulgences of the wealthy in very similar terms on his return to Wanganui, when deploring the inability of an artist to make a living in Britain, adding, for good measure, their expenditure on yachts, horse-racing and other forms of gambling. Indeed, he may well be 'Bleistift', as he was back in the colony at the time of Bleistift's reviews. Sherriff, though, also blamed picture dealers for palming off 'old master' rubbish on the ignorant, collectors for demonstrating a lack of patriotism by giving large sums for foreign works, simply because they were foreign, and, more controversially, the increase in women artists. "These painters have, as a rule, parents to support them, and so can afford to sell at starvation prices. The owner of many studios told a friend of mine that half his studios were rented by ladies. They are starving out the professional artist, who, as a rule, has a wife and children to support." Furthermore, in Sherriff's view, lack of sales for "great works" led to a slump in quality, as artists were forced "to degenerate into pot-boilers".[842]

There were serious problems in other sections of the community as well. The pilchard fishery had collapsed completely. Even in 1904, when there had been a good catch on one occasion, it was described as "a rare and beautiful sight", and, most years, the men involved barely earned enough to feed their families. Being a capital intensive venture, seine companies went bust, or stopped trading, and the storage area at the back of Porthminster Beach became a seine boat graveyard. The herring fishing was not much better. There were occasional good catches, but no consistency. At the Mayoral Banquet in 1907, the Mayor bemoaned, "The fishing industry is practically gone and I sympathise with the fishermen in their misfortune". By 1912, the fishing fleet at St Ives comprised just forty luggers.

---

837 Letter dated 12/1/1912 - Schofield family archive.

838 Adapted from A.G.Folliott-Stokes, *A Moorland Princess*, London, 1904 at p.131.

839 *St Ives Times*, 21/2/1913.

840 *St Ives Times*, 7/3/1913.

841 Bleistift, *Art and Artists*, St Ives Times, 3/10/1913.

842 *A Wanganui Artist in England*, *Wanganui Chronicle*, 16/1/1908.

The St Ives fishermen were also at a great disadvantage, as they could not afford motor powered boats. In December 1909, it was recorded that only one motorised fishing boat operated from St Ives, whereas there were two hundred from Yarmouth fishing in the area, and efforts thereafter to get more motorised boats working from St Ives were hampered by the lack of available instruction on their operation. 1912 proved a dreadful fishing season, with catches less than half what they had been in 1906 and a fifth of what they had been in 1902.[843] As a result, one hundred fishermen appeared before magistrates for non-payment of rates. The situation was now desperate, and the local paper next notes sorrowful family groups congregating, with regularity, on the pier, as they waved off parties of young fishermen, sometimes twenty at a time, who had decided to sail for America to start afresh. The old way of life in St Ives had gone for ever.

One glint of hope was a wide-held belief that the mining industry in the area could be revived on a profitable basis, and significant steps, at great cost, were taken towards this end. In 1907, St Ives Consols, at the top of the Stennack, was re-opened, as was Wheal Trenwith, the following year, where radium had been discovered. As has already been mentioned, the Ellises were paid good money to leave the 'Count House' in Carbis Bay, and options were even taken over the old North Providence mine on Pednolver Point, where the engine house had been converted into a studio. One proposal, with revenues of twenty million pounds being bandied about, was to dredge the Bay for tin, but Colonel Henry Williams, the local fisheries officer, soon put paid to this, as the proposed operations were exactly in the area where herring were caught. The limited chances of revitalising the mining industry were snuffed out by the outbreak of the War, and investors lost all their money.[844] Therefore, the economic situation in St Ives was bleak, even before hostilities commenced.

4.1.2   The impact of War

The impact of War was immediate. On 28th July 1914, Fred Milner, who was desperate to get away from the tourist masses to go sketching in the Cotswolds, commented, "The place is absolutely crowded. I believe 'Chy-an-Drea' are refusing dozens every day. I shall be <u>so</u> pleased to get out of it and be absolutely quiet at work."[845] Sixteen days later, his summer sketching plans scotched by the declaration of war, he reports, "Here the harbour seems very deserted as nearly all the men were in the naval reserves and have gone to their ships. I find it very difficult to do any work, as one's mind is full of the serious outlook."[846] Milner realised that the outbreak of War had, at a stroke, destroyed the art market

Fig. 4.1 Herbert Lanyon   *Fred Milner*
(courtesy Andrew Lanyon)

843 See *St Ives Times* 11/10/1912 and 29/12/1912.
844 In the case of Wheal Trenwith, where there was real potential, the position was complicated by significant German ownership.
845 Letter to Mrs Brumfit dated 28/7/1914 - Tate Gallery Archives 9511.16.
846 Letter to Mrs Brumfit dated 13/8/1914 - Tate Gallery Archives 9511.17.

Fig. 4.2 Sydney Carr *Count Georg Larisch*
(June 1910)   (Carr family archive)

Fig. 4.3 H.G.Fitzherbert
Caricature of Count Larisch
(from *Everyone's Doing It*)

and that those artists, who relied on sales to meet their expenses, would soon struggle desperately financially. However much he appreciated that his plight was nothing compared with that of the refugees that soon started flooding into the country from Belgium, or the men who were forced to fight at the front, he could not stave off the deep depression that made him query whether it was worthwhile to paint at all. His letters are full of comments, such as "Everything seems depressing", "There seems nothing to work for", "What is the use?".[847]

If artists had become concerned at their prospects when War was first declared, they became profoundly depressed when outdoor sketching restrictions were imposed in 1915. Initially, the artists had assumed that Cornwall's situation would make the War seem rather distant - and, indeed, some of the newly arrived artists, such as the New Zealander, Frances Hodgkins, who had been displaced from Paris, had chosen St Ives for this very reason. Accordingly, reports of German submarines sinking local ships was a big shock. Worse was to follow, as Hodgkins told her mother in February 1915. "Spies have been very active in Cornwall & the St Ives people are feeling very sick because they were so nice to a young German Count who took a Studio here last year. After war was declared Studio was raided - charts of every cove, road, track, rock, tides and currents were found and copious diaries. The Count himself escaped - we heard there was a German submarine in Newquay Harbour 2 days ago."[848] This is clearly a reference to Count Georg Larisch, who had been welcomed at the Arts Club from time to time since 1910 and featured in Fitz's *Everyone's Doing It* (see Fig. 4.3). Larisch, who had been born in 1855, was son of Count Leo Larisch von Moennich and Princess Helene Stirbey. In 1877, he married Marie Louise, the illegitimate daughter of Ludwig Wilhelm, Duke of Bavaria, and the actress Henrietta Mendel. Marie was both the confidante of her aunt, Empress Elisabeth of Austria, and the go-between in the affair between Elisabeth's husband, Crown Prince Rupert, and his mistress. The Larisch marriage ended in divorce in 1896, not least because only two of the five children of the marriage were indisputably Georg's! His wife, who had plenty of stories to tell of the Royal Family, was apparently given a large sum of 'hush money' in return for agreeing to exile in the United States, where she published her notoriously unreliable memoirs anyway in 1913. One can imagine the dinner tables in St Ives buzzing with accounts of the revelations.

I have not found any other account of the incident recounted by Hodgkins to determine whether there is any truth in the allegation. Larisch, it seems, was a professional cartographer and oceanographer, and so he would quite naturally be interested in the local coastline and have many charts. A photograph of

847 Letters to Mrs Brumfit dated 1914-5 - Tate Gallery Archives 9511.20, 21, 24.
848 Letter dated 4/2/1915 - Ed. L Gill, ibid, at p.303.

him by Sydney Carr, whose family he befriended, shows him in June 1910 in oilskins, with telescope in hand (Fig. 4.2). The family also retain a *fifty* page letter, written to Irene Carr, from a ship off South America, where he was working.[849] The Lloyd family, with whom he was also friendly, were told by him that he left in a hurry, as he was concerned that he would be interned, and they retained for many years a trunk, with all his maps and drawings, and so these do not appear to have been impounded. Therefore, the incident could be a further example of the paranoia that was later to lead to the expulsion of D.H. Lawrence and his German wife from the County. Nevertheless, following this raid, artists suddenly became suspicious personages, particularly to those locals who had never really welcomed the arrival of the Bohemian brotherhood. A few days later, sketching restrictions were imposed. These prevented sketching anywhere without a permit and no sketching at all was permitted on the coast or within sight of the coast, albeit it was still possible around the harbour itself. Even in such out of the way places as Zennor, where enemy landings were nigh on impracticable, the coastwatchers were much in evidence.

In September 1915, the position became even worse, after an alleged abuse of a sketching permit, and all sketching in Cornwall was banned.[850] Quite clearly, the position was now impossible, and a strong letter was published in the local paper from Moffat Lindner, Millie Dow and Julius Olsson, who happened to be staying with Lindner at the time. This made the point that the vast majority of winter visitors to the town were artists and these would now go elsewhere, causing loss all round. "The artists will suffer, both through the restriction and the loss of pupils, the lodging-house keepers through the lack of their winter lodgers, and the tradesman and the town generally through the loss of customers."[851] The letter suggested that the Mayor should assume responsibility for the issue of permits, as most artists, whether residents or regular visitors, would be known to him. It also confirms that, even at this late date, the artists were still seen as crucial to the prosperity of the town during the winter months. Eventually, a limited number of permits, for three months at a time, could be obtained from the Penzance Divisional Coast Watching Officer, but it was difficult for the artists to feel at ease, particularly when the news from the front was so poor and people were so much on edge.[852]

4.1.3   War work

By mid-1915, any hopes of a quick end to the conflict had vanished and every able-bodied man was required to assist in some way in the War effort. Guy Kortright became a Captain in the 21st Monmouthshire Regiment and Will Lloyd, having volunteered, served in France, fighting at Passendale, winning the Military Cross and rising to the rank of Major. Commendably, a number of artists of foreign nationality volunteered anyway. The New Zealander, H.G.Fitzherbert, was one of the first to join up and he became a Lieutenant in the 1st Devon Yeomanry, winning the Military Cross for conspicuous bravery in the field. He will have seen service in the Dardenelles campaign at the Battle of Gallipoli and then in Egypt in 1915-6 and later in Palestine and France. Fitzherbert was soon followed by his fellow countryman, Herbert Babbage, who joined the 4th Duke of Cornwall Light Infantry for home defence duties and was posted to Wales to guard railway facilities used for the distribution of coal. As already mentioned, the American, Elmer Schofield, also decided to enlist in 1915. Explaining his decision to his friend, Robert Henri, Schofield said, "At my time, one does not, as a rule, take up the soldier's profession but it was not love that forced me on - but the strong desire to do what I could to prevent Germany goose-stepping over the world and help force her out of France."[853]

Most of the artists were too old to be forced to fight, and others, like Robert Langley Hutton, whose health had broken down in Burma, and Charles Simpson, who had damaged his hearing as a child when kicked by a pony, were able to demonstrate that they were unfit. Garstin Cox also proved himself unfit and ended up doing munitions work with his father in Camborne. Edmund Fuller was another to undertake some munitions work from October 1915, although not in the locality, but he was none too impressed with the attitude of the Trade Unions.[854] Georgina Bainsmith, keen to demonstrate that women could play an important role, became principal overseer, for two years, of the fuses department of the Woolwich arsenal munition factories, manned only by females. Twice the arsenal was bombed and she recorded that, on one occasion, the enthusiasm of the women was such that work continued despite notice of an approaching raid. In one week, the factory, working twenty-four hours a day, managed to produce 45,000 fuses.[855] She was also awarded a medal by the Aerial League, a pressure group keen to develop aeroplanes for defence purposes.[856]

849 The Lloyd family have a photograph taken by Larisch of a forty foot wave off Cape Horn.
850 See *St Ives Times* 1/10/1915 - *The Restriction on Sketching*.
851 *St Ives Times,* 1/10/1915.
852 See *St Ives Times*, 14/7/1916, which reproduces the relevant regulation.
853 Quoted in T Folk, *The Pennsylvania Impressionists*, Madison and Teaneck, 1997 at p.58.
854 *St Ives Weekly Summary*, 7/10/1915.
855 See *Mrs Bainsmith*, *St Ives Times*, 3/1/1919.
856 She is credited, in fact, with getting Gustav Hamel to bring his aeroplane to Cornwall in 1913. See *St Ives Times*, 3/1/1919.

Fig. 4.4 Herbert Lanyon
         Elmer Schofield in Army uniform
         (Schofield family archive)

Fig. 4.5 Herbert Babbage
         in his Home Guard uniform in 1914
         (courtesy Margaret Edgar)

Eighteen members of the Arts Club joined the St Ives Volunteer Training Corps, when it was formed in March 1915, and Fred Milner that June records the time that this took up. "Our drill is the ordinary infantry drill, rifle drill and shooting. We drill Monday, Tuesday, Wednesday and Friday and shoot Thursday and Saturday afternoon and evenings."[857] There were no doubt periods of tedium, but the banter passing back and forth probably fostered a new type of camaraderie.

As the horrors of the War started to unfold, it was not long before close friends of the artists received the dreaded telegram informing them of the deaths of loved ones. Edward Hain's only son was killed in November 1915 at Gallipoli, news from which his father never recovered, Moffat Lindner's nephew, Leonard, died during the Battle of Jutland, Edward Boase's son was lost at sea in April 1917 and Thomas Chellew's son, John, died, aged only 19, in June 1917. From the artist fraternity, Herbert Babbage died in 1916 during an operation at Cardiff, whilst former student, Milford Norsworthy, a Second Lieutenant in the East Kent Regiment, was killed in France in March 1917. The local paper also reported the deaths of the only sons of Stanhope Forbes and William Titcomb. Amongst those badly injured were William Trewhella's son, Bernard, who had an arm amputated, and Robert Read's son, Richard, who lost a leg in a flying accident.   Georgina Bainsmith's son, Bruce, who was serving in the Canadian Light Infantry, was also badly wounded, losing three fingers of his left hand and having a piece of shrapnel pierce his lung.[858] It was a period when perceived shirkers were given short shrift and the etcher, Frank Moore, then living at 'Pednolva House', Draycott Terrace, was denounced in public by Councillor Edward Daniel. However, he had the grace to apologise, when Moore pointed out that he was not only over age, but also unfit.[859]

4.1.4 Belgian refugees and other charitable causes

The women artists in the colony, led by Gussie Lindner and Lizzie Whitehouse, soon realised that they could play a major role in promoting and organising charitable relief. The result was that the War years saw the artists not only taking leading roles in adopting various relief causes, but also working in closer conjunction with members of the local community than they had ever done before.

---

857 Letter to Mrs Brumfit dated 16/6/1915 - Tate Gallery Archives 9511.30.

858 See *St Ives Times*, 30/4/1915.

859 *St Ives Times*, 18/6/1915.

The first major issue was the plight of thousands of Belgians forced to flee following the German invasion of their country, and Gussie Lindner's proactive approach ensured that St Ives was the first town in Cornwall to welcome a group of refugees from that country. The first Belgian Refugees Committee included Millie Dow, Herbert Lanyon, Moffat Lindner, Edgar Skinner, Lizzie Whitehouse, Mary Cameron, Caroline Pazolt and, most appropriately, one of the Belgian artists, who had been forced to seek refuge in the town, Louis Reckelbus, a watercolourist of some renown. From the ninety-nine refugees initially received, sixty-two remained at the end of 1915. Many artists were weekly subscribers to the Belgian Relief Fund and regular collectors of goods and money for them included Mesdames Lindner, Dow, Grier, Robinson, Farina, Hewitt and Cameron, and Caroline Pazolt. Frances Hodgkins also helped by using a number of the mothers and their children as models.

Whilst the plight of the Belgians in the town was a constant source of concern as the war dragged on, their presence also ensured that many concerts and other fund-raising activities were organised to assist their countrymen, particularly as several of the refugees were talented musicians. The violinist, Harriet Solly, and the singer, Irene Blox, were particularly involved at such events, both in the town and at the Arts Club, and they organised some leading artists of various Belgian operas to perform in St Ives, in June 1916, for the benefit of the British Society for the Relief of Belgian Wounded Soldiers. On several occasions, Harriet Solly linked up with Marian McKenzie, who had been the principal contralto at a number of opera festivals around the world. McKenzie clearly liked St Ives, as she returned on several occasions for some months, giving singing lessons, whilst staying at the Chy-an-Drea Hotel. The result was that the quality of the musical performances in the town during the War years exceeded anything that had been heard before. The Belgian Red Cross and a fund for destitute Belgian children were also supported regularly, with Irene Blox organising some *tableaux vivants* in February 1917 for the benefit of the latter. One of these was entitled *English Children Welcoming Belgian Children*. In addition to Reckelbus, Solly and Blox, Miss Blondieu, who painted in watercolour, and Mrs Symays, who wrote short stories, were made honourable members of the Arts Club, and many of the Belgians integrated well into the local community. The final cost of supporting the Belgian Refugees, until their departure in 1919, was put at £5,300, of which £3,500 had been raised in St Ives. Joshua Daniel, who co-ordinated the relief, was awarded the Médaille du Roi Albert in 1920 by the King of the Belgians for his considerable efforts.

In October 1915, the St Ives War Hospital and Field Supply Depot was established and a number of the female artists played leading roles in collecting and distributing parcels of clothing, equipment, reading material and other aid for troops at the Front and for the Territorials. The Whitehouse sisters, as they had been during the Boer War, were at the forefront of the efforts of Arts Club members on behalf of the Depot, and a Sewing Party was organised and met regularly. Parcels were sent off to a variety of organisations, including the English, Belgian and French Red Cross, and, in the first year alone, an astonishing 59,201 articles were made at the Depot by some seventy-two regular workers.[860]

Fig. 4.6 Sarah Elizabeth Whitehouse   *War Hospital Supply Depot, St Ives, 1916*   (postcard)

---

860 *St Ives Times*, 27/10/1916.

Fig. 4.7 Charles Simpson   *The Serbian Retreat into Albania*   (RA 1916)

One fund-raising event for the War Supply Depot, arranged by the artists in January 1916, was an exhibition of *tableaux vivants* at the Central Hall, during which works by Fra Angelico, Titian, Holbein, Romney, Reynolds and Millais were re-created. The *tableaux* were directed by William Spittle, a Birmingham artist, who had moved to the town in 1913 and taken one of the Piazza Studios, and he was hailed by a visitor as "a genius in this art".[861] John and Selina Bromley also organised a Garden Open Day in September 1916, during which various events were put on in five gardens around the town, including 'Talland House' and Robert Read's house, 'Lansdowne'. These included musical performances by singers from London and a concert organised by Elgar Russell and Mrs Chellew, which included not only Harriet Solly, Kitty Hain and Cecil Trewhella, but also Richard Jack ARA, on a visit from London. There were also two plays produced by Selina Bromley, and a treasure hunt organised by Edgar Skinner at 'Talland House'. Frank Ver Beck also offered for sale some of his Teddy Bears and, for the first time, his 'War Babies', an original idea that had been taken up by Selfridges and Harrods.

Another cause, that was keenly espoused by the Lindners, was the Serbian War Relief Fund. In advocating the endeavour, Gussie Lindner wrote, "The 1915 retreat of the Serbians across the snows of Albania, accompanied by various hospital missions, will remain for all time one of the greatest tragedies in history, a tragedy that was shared by many gallant Englishwomen and which has resulted in an everlasting affection between them and the Serbians".[862] It was also a subject selected by Charles Simpson for his Royal Academy exhibit of 1916, for he had been asked to produce illustrations for a book on the experiences of a Lieutenant Beavor in the Balkans, although this never came to fruition.[863] By the end of the War, Serbia had lost over 365,000 soldiers, some 26% of all mobilized personnel, with some 114,000 soldiers disabled and 500,000 children orphaned, and the Lindners continued with their fund-raising activities for this cause for some years.[864]

Bereaved children became an increasing concern, as the death toll mounted, and Gussie Lindner held drawing room sales at her home, 'Chy-an-Porth', for Dr Barnado's. Frank Barrett's 'pastorel operette', *Prince Pan*, was premiered at a garden fete, held at 'Treloyhan Manor', in July 1917, for the benefit of the French Red Cross and the Y.M.C.A.. The cast of actors and musicians was drawn from the Arts Club, the Belgians and the local townsfolk, and included a number of children, demonstrating how the War efforts had brought all sections of the community closer together, and the performance was considered "the most original and beautiful work of its kind that has ever been seen in St Ives."[865] Elgar Russell and the Whitehouse sisters also helped with entertainments for the benefit of the First

861 *St Ives Times*, 7/1/1916.
862 *St Ives Times*, 14/9/1917.
863 See John Branfield, *Charles Simpson*, Bristol, 2005 at p.50.
864 See Wikipedia - The Serbian Campaign.
865 *St Ives Times*, 27/7/1917.

Aid Yeomanry Nursing Corps at Calais. The number of causes that warranted support in such horrific times was never-ending and, for instance, Ida Praetorius organised a Blue Flag Day for wounded and disabled military horses. A more personal touch was taken by Herbert Lanyon and his father-in-law, John Vivian, who entertained twenty-one wounded soldiers from the Camborne Convalescent Home at their respective homes for a day in July 1917.

A couple, with whom the Lindners worked closely during the War years on fund-raising ventures, was Sir Herbert Thirkell White and Lady White, who had moved into 'The Cottage' on Talland Road, the property owned by the Dow family, which had been known as 'Closeburn' during the occupancy of the Kirkpatrick sisters. Sir Herbert was known to Florence Dow, from her time with her first husband in Burma, for he had served there for thirty-two years, becoming Lieutenant-Governor from 1905 to 1910. One of Sir Herbert's passions was bridge - he wrote a book on the game in the 1920s under the pseudonym, Buccaneer - and, accordingly, bridge tournaments made a regular appearance in the list of activities that were put on to raise funds for the various relief causes. The Whites loved their retirement in St Ives. They socialised regularly with the artists and attended their dramatic performances, becoming particularly good friends with George Bradshaw, who was one of only four mourners invited to attend his burial at sea off Falmouth in 1931.[866] Two photographic portraits of Sir Herbert taken by Walter Stoneman in 1918, as part of his ambitious plan for a National Photographic Record, are owned by the National Portrait Gallery.

The constant round of fund-raising events put a strain on the limited finances of some artists, who responded by offering paintings for sale or as raffle prizes. Lizzie Whitehouse, Elgar Russell, Louis Reckelbus, Arthur Meade, Edmund Fuller and Charles Simpson were amongst those who adopted this course, whilst, after a serious fire destroyed the Salvation Army Citadel in Market Strand and a number of homes and stores on 22nd March 1915, Edmund Fuller, William Parkyn and Arthur Lyons, who had arrived in the town from Paris, offered to paint 24" x 22" canvases to be sold to the highest bidder, with all proceeds going to the St Ives Fire Relief Fund. Parkyn also painted and donated to the town a depiction of H.M.S.Albion, on which a large number of St Ives men were serving. These men were given a rousing welcome, with crowds lining the street and the whole town *en fete*, when they returned for their first leave in May 1916, having been in the Dardenelles since the inception of the War.[867]

4.1.5 The Arts Club

Unsurprisingly, the activities of the Arts Club during the War years were strictly curtailed. President's Night and Fancy Dress parties were inappropriate, and any entertainments put on were generally for the benefit of a charitable cause. Nevertheless, Fred Milner, who was Secretary between 1915-17 and an ardent music lover, passed comment that the Club had been able to host some of the best concerts that he had ever heard. This was due to the presence, in 1914, of "a lady violinist of quite front rank as an amateur, a favourite pupil of Joachim's", probably a reference to Harriet Solly, and, in 1916, of the refugee Belgian Artistes of renown, who had come down for the concert that June.[868] It was also felt that wartime should not be all doom and gloom for the children and so the Lindners put on, in January 1915, a children's entertainment for the benefit of the local Dr Barnado's home, to which friends from the Town were invited, and, in 1917, a children's play by Frank Barrett, *Little Red Riding Hood*, was performed for the benefit of the St Dunstan's Institute for Blind Soldiers. The scenery for this was painted by Robert Langley Hutton and it was stage managed by one of his sisters. Iris Cooke, Hope Lindner and Lilas Barrett were amongst those acting and it was felt to have been "an unqualified success in every way", raising over £22.[869]

!917 saw severe food shortages and Joan Barrett published a poem, *The Women Who Save the Bread*, highlighting the vital role that women could play in eking out provisions.[870] A copy of this was obtained by Queen Alexandra.[871] In these circumstances, Moffat Lindner, who was President in each of the years 1914-7, suggested that members of the Club should find some land upon which to cultivate crops, and two plots were allocated by the Borough Surveyor at Nanjivey. Eight members of the Club - Lindner, Meade, Milner, Douglas, Dyer, Nora Hartley, Hanna Rion Ver Beck and Miss Walton Evans - worked the land under the supervision of Edgar Skinner (1862-1925), who had first become a member of the Club in December 1907, but who settled in the town in 1910.[872] A retired Bank Manager, Skinner had spent some time in Italy before

---

866 See David Tovey, *George Fagan Bradshaw and the St Ives Society of Artists*, Tewkesbury, 2000 at p.108-9.

867 *St Ives Times*, 19/5/1916.

868 Letters to Mrs Brumfit dated 30/12/1914 & 23/8/1916, Tate Gallery Archives 9511.23 & 36.

869 See *St Ives Times*, 19/1/1917.

870 This is reproduced in *St Ives Times*, 26/10/1917.

871 See *St Ives Times*, 9/11/1917.

872 In a letter in *St Ives Times*, 6/11/1925, he says that he had been resident in the Borough fifteen years.

Fig. 4.8 H.G.Fitzherbert *William Benney*
(from *Caricatures of the Cornish Riviera* 1910)

coming to St Ives.[873] Although elected as a painter, he exhibited his watercolours rarely, but he did write a number of art reviews during the War years.[874] He was a particular fan of the paintings of Frances Hodgkins, and he and his wife, Edith, who was a regular contributor of poetry to the local paper, are featured in their home, 'Salubrious House', in her work, *The Edwardians* (Auckland Art Gallery - Plate 1). Skinner, who was a good linguist and was keenly interested in music and literature, was well-liked amongst the artistic community for his kindly disposition, but, having taken over the role of Borough Accountant in 1916, he had various battles with the Local Council over the level of his pay, waged inappropriately in the letters section of the local paper, to which he was a regular contributor.

The War years were clearly difficult financially for a number of artists and local auctioneer, William Benney (Fig. 4.8), began to hold auction sales of paintings. Moulton Foweraker and Elgar Russell were two artists, who decided to raise funds in this way.[875] The Arts Club Committee was appalled and, in October 1916, issued a notice stating, "The Committee are of the opinion that the holding of auction sales of pictures is not only undignified but detrimental to the best interests of art and artists and trust that members of the Arts Club and other artists will signify their disapproval of such methods by signing this notice". Foweraker ignored the edict, as he held a further auction of thirty watercolours and pastels in January 1917, whilst, the following month, Benney held an auction of seventy works by Cornish artists at Camborne, suggesting that financial constraints were biting hard and that cash was required, however "undignified" the process.[876]

Russell's use of an auction may have antagonised some of his old colleagues, but his involvement in the organisation of events in the town and in the affairs of the Club came to a sad end, after he pleaded guilty, in 1918, to assaulting Wilmot Couch and was fined £5. Due to his plea, details of the incident are not recorded, and it is not known whether Russell was drunk at the time, but Edward Boase pleaded,

---

873 See Bernard Leach, *Beyond East and West*, London, 1978 at p.151.

874 He did participate on Show Day in 1914 and 1919.

875 The auction of work by Foweraker and Russell was held on 25/1/1916.

876 Foweraker may have already decided to leave the district as, in March 1918, the contents of his boarding house at Carbis Bay, 'The Headlands', were for sale as well. See *St Ives Times*, 8/3/1918.

in mitigation, that he suffered from his heart and nerves.[877] Rather than help an old friend at a difficult time, the Committee of the Arts Club demanded his resignation and, although he retained his property, 'St John's' (GER £42), in Primrose Valley, to which he had moved in 1917, it appears as if he spent much of the last few years of his life, prior to his death in 1927, living, in indifferent health, with his sisters at Sutton-at-Hone.[878]

Just a month after Russell's conviction for assault, another member of the Arts Club made a poor impression in Court. Louis Grier was the key witness in a case involving the illegal use of petrol by Doctor Watkinson, a medical attendant to Sir Ratan Tata, then terminally ill at the Porthminster Hotel. Watkinson, who himself suffered from a weak heart, had claimed that he had used his car to visit Grier at his studio for a consultation. Grier confirmed that he was seriously ill, for he had already consulted seven doctors! However, he could not explain why Watkinson, to whom he had been accustomed to give painting lessons, had stayed for five hours! By responding to all difficult questions, "I don't recall", he made himself look not only very foolish but also deceitful, and his testimony was dismissed as worthless.[879] Accordingly, Watkinson was convicted.

4.1.6   A silver lining

Despite the gloomy news from the War, there were several pieces of encouraging news on the financial front, particularly in 1917. Through the efforts of Colonel Henry Williams, the Government made loans, totalling £4000, in 1914, to the Cornish fishermen, in order to enable them to install motors in their boats. Of this sum, £1308 was allocated to the men working from St Ives, and the installation of motors led to an immediate improvement, "with more sorts of fishing and more regularity".[880] Within just sixteen months, particularly due to good herring catches, the St Ives men had been able to repay £675 of their loan. There were further enormous catches of herring in 1917, leading Edgar Skinner to comment, "Many men who never in their lives have had enough to support the wants of themselves and their family, for longer than a fortnight ahead, are now the happy possessors of £100 or more."[881] Many of the middle classes also suddenly felt far more prosperous in late 1917, due to the sale of the Hain Steamship Company to P & O. Original subscribers, having paid £10 for their shares, were very pleased with the quoted price of £34, prior to the offer, but were amazed to receive eventually £80 per share, as the destruction of ships during the War, led to P & O being prepared to pay a hefty premium. To what extent artists benefitted from wallets being fatter in the town is not known, but some good news was most welcome.

4.1.7   Peace at last

After the War finally ended, the Arts Club appointed a Peace Celebrations Committee, comprising Dyer, Lanyon, Yabsley, Robert Morton Nance, Lilas Barrett and Dossie Cooke. Designs were invited in June 1919 for a card to be presented to those who had served in the War and, of the designs submitted by Fuller, Smart, Lilas Barrett, Dossie Cooke and Marjorie Ballance, that by Smart was selected and presented to the Mayor. In 1920, it was also Borlase Smart's design for the memorial tablet for the four members of the Club killed in the War, rather than those put forward by Hartley and Fuller, that was accepted, and Fuller was asked to execute the design in copper.

---

877 *St Ives Times*, 7/6/1918.

878 See letter from the Club dated 17/7/1918 in the Arts Club Minutes and Russell's Obituary in *St Ives Times*, 8/4/1927.

879 *St Ives Times*,12/7/1918.

880 *St Ives Times*, 2/6/1916.

881 *St Ives Times*, 14/12/1917.

ST IVES IN THE 1920s

4.2.1   The Times

A number of factors led to the reduced popularity and relevance of the rural art colony after the War. The harsh realities of the conflict had impacted on everyone, in town and country alike. Industrial progress could no longer be ignored, and the nostalgic vision of an idyllic rural community divorced from the modern world had been shattered for ever. St Ives, in any event, like many other art colonies, was no longer particularly remote or unspoiled, and the local inhabitants had moved into the modern age. Amongst artists, financial realities also struck home, as the excesses of the Edwardian era came to an abrupt halt. Sales at inflated prices were no longer so easy, and living expenses became more testing. The carefree era had passed. Budding artists were more interested in modern artistic trends, in which representational painting played an ever decreasing role. Society itself had also become less interested in rural retreats and more concerned with utopian urban ideals. The heyday of the rural art colony was over.

4.2.2   The Town

The town still had the ability to inspire visitors. One, writing in 1921, exclaimed, "St Ives is a painter's paradise. It is so unfailingly picturesque that there is scarcely a foot of the older part of the town that does not provide a 'subject'. Artists are as plentiful as blackberries, and there are few hours of the day during the summer months in which one does not stumble across half-a-dozen or so men and women at their easels capturing effects of light and shade in ancient archways or quaint streets."[882] Long-term residents, however, saw many changes that impacted upon the town's quaint charm.

After the War, house prices soared, and, consequently, there was much new development. The death of Lord Cowley in 1919 led to over one hundred of his properties in the town being disposed of, resulting in much more piecemeal development. The Council itself embarked on a huge housing scheme of over one hundred properties in the Ayr district, and land owned by the Hain family in Carbis Bay was sold off in 1930, beginning the complete despoilation of that district. On a visit in 1933, the editor of *The Artist*, Harold Sawkins, expressed the hope that St Ives might still preserve its heritage, "Even now I see signs of what is obvious change - the studios turned into cafés, the beautiful old cottages pulled down for more modern buildings." Perceptively, he concluded, "Is this the beginning of the end of *old* St Ives?" Indeed it was.

With the motorisation of the fishing fleet, one of the most magical sights of the pre-War period - the brown-red sails of the local boats caught in the light of the setting sun as they departed for the fishing grounds - was witnessed no more. Whilst the fleet was now more adaptable, the fishing remained desperately inconsistent. Pilchards were not seen at all and, even when there was a huge herring catch, the fishermen still lost money, as the price for the fish dropped dramatically and the size of the catch caused extensive damage to their nets and gear. The American artist, Wilson Henry Irvine, records, in 1923, being asked for money by one fishermen, whose wife was due to give birth imminently, as neither of them had eaten for days, whilst the younger men constantly asked him about life in America, as they were contemplating emigration. A Canadian in town reported similar enquiries.

The town, more than ever, was dependent on tourism, and visitors now often arrived in motor cars or char-a-bancs, neither of which were suited to the town's narrow streets and steep hills. Whilst initially tourists found it quaint to park on West Pier, this soon proved woefully inadequate, leading ultimately to the demolition, in its entirety, of Pudding Bag Lane, one of the picturesque streets most beloved by artists, so that the site could become a car park. The Malakoff, which boasted one of the finest vistas of the town, also had to be turned into a coach park. Furthermore, these new-fangled machines brought fresh perils to the streets of the town, and the local paper is full of reports of accidents. For instance, former Mayor, William Trewhella and his wife, were both knocked down by a car and seriously hurt, as they walked back, one Sunday, from Church to their home, 'Trewyn'; the artist, Kathleen Bradshaw, was lucky to escape merely with a badly gashed leg, when her companion reversed her car off Wharf Road into the harbour waters at high tide, whilst the whole community was left in deep mourning, in 1923, when Robert Hodgeson Read, the son of leading citizen, Robert Sawle Read, who had already served

---

882 *St Ives Times*, 20/5/1921.

as a Councillor, was killed, aged 31, in a motor-cycle accident on his way home from the Golf Club. The worst accident, however, involved Moffat Lindner's daughter, Hope, who, whilst ferrying people to vote at an election, collided with another car at a crossroads, killing all three occupants of the other vehicle. It was a bad junction and she had sounded her horn, but there was a suspicion that she had been travelling too fast.

4.2.3   The Colony

Whereas St Ives may not have lost its ability to attract artists, there was a clear reduction in the quality of the residents, students and visitors in the colony, and it struggled to maintain its reputation both nationally and internationally. The end of the War, perhaps unsurprisingly, resulted in a mass exodus, as a number of artists had stayed on in the town purely because of the hostilities. Unfortunately, this included most of the young artists of promise, such as Frances Hodgkins, Claude Barry and Louis Sargent. The colony also suffered a number of losses through death - Noble Barlow (1917), Millie Dow and Robert Langley Hutton (1919) and Louis Grier (1920). This left the colony dominated for the first time by a group of elderly painters, such as Moffat Lindner, Arthur Meade, Fred Milner, William Fortescue and Alfred Hartley, whose career highs were far behind them. For a young student in the early 1920s, such as Averil Mackenzie-Grieve, the colony was disappointing. "The coterie of painters in St Ives had reached a low ebb. The young Bohemians who had settled years before in the fascinating little port, using the net lofts above the quays and shores as studios, had grown old and academic, content to turn out competent paintings year after year, each in his own genre. A bare half-dozen could rely on what one might call sure seats in the Royal Academy and other established galleries in London. There were a number of middle-aged spinsters who, living uncomfortably in their studios, cheaply achieved a sort of domestic Bohemianism."[883]

There was also a change of emphasis in the colony. Whereas in the pre-War years, artists worked almost exclusively in oils, sending canvases of vast dimensions to international exhibitions, there was now a much wider range of media employed and a growing interest in the decorative arts. Oil paintings became smaller, so as to become more acceptable and more affordable for middle class homes, whilst the cheaper and more delicate medium of water colour attracted the increasing numbers of female artists. The astonishing boom in etchings and aquatints during the decade led to the formation of a St Ives Print Society, whilst great interest was shown, for the first time in St Ives, in the decorative arts. Accordingly, at Lanham's Galleries and elsewhere, there were regular exhibitions devoted not only to work from the much applauded Leach Pottery, which had been established in 1920, but also to art needlework, painted models, jewellery, craftwork and even Marcella Smith's hat creations.

Fig. 4.10 Frances Ewan   *St Ives Fisherman*
(St Ives Trust Archive Study Centre)

---

883 Averil Mackenzie-Grieve, *Time and Chance*, London, 1970 at p.37.

4.2.4   The Journal of Wilson Henry Irvine

The Journal of the American artist, Wilson Henry Irvine, recording his stay in St Ives in the spring of 1923, is unique, for it is the only known day by day record of an artist's inter-reaction with the community. It is also most revealing, for it not only gives an insight into how the relationship between the fisherfolk and the artists had progressed by this juncture, but also paints a picture of an artist community that was much changed - one that was distinctly unfriendly and unwelcoming towards a foreign artist. Indeed, Irvine found that the fisherfolk were much more civil to him than the local artists.

Just a couple of days after his arrival, Irvine commented, "Am gradually getting able to pick out men among the fishing people whom I have met or passed the time of day. They are all civil and kind, as all people seem to be who follow the sea. They are extremely poor here and many are being helped. There are four families below our attic studio - all very poor." A neighbour soon warned him not to sketch on a Sunday, and he repeatedly cursed his luck that, during the period of particularly bad weather that he experienced at St Ives, he could always rely on Sunday, when he could not work, being a fine day. However, having entered the words "damn weather" in his diary, he noted that, since his arrival in St Ives, "Have not heard an oath or near it or an obscene word or remark or seen a drunken man".[884] He also later mentioned that his wife had received a severe ticking off from their cleaner and washerwoman, Mrs Caulkins, whom he described as "a Salvation Army lass and a good mother and neighbor", for complaining about the "bloody weather". This was the same woman, he noted, who happily admitted that "it was the custom among the fisherfolk for the daughters to get in a family way, then marry."[885]

In general, he found the fisherfolk helpful and scrupulously honest. Several times, his unfamiliarity with the English currency could have been exploited, but they always pointed out his mistake, and refused to accept money for gifts of fish made to him. One warned him that the tide came in very quickly, where he had set up his easel, and that it might be best, if he moved.[886] Another got a board for him to stand on when the position he favoured was wet, and also kept an eye on the tide for him. Another warned, "Don't dare put in the old green goods lady. If you do, she will do what she did once - smash up your canvas."[887] The fisherfolk were also not afraid to pass comment on his work. He had got the sail all wrong. They also regaled him with stories of the other artists. Alfred Bailey was colour-blind, they thought, whilst John Park "can paint anything - make a picture of anything".[888] They also put him off hackneyed motifs. On finding a "stunning old court" - probably Hick's Court, with its unusual stone arch -, he was assured by an old lady, that they had all painted it, "four deep sometimes, my dear man".[889]

On Irvine's very first day, a schooner got into difficulties in the Bay and he watched the exciting spectacle of the lifeboat at work, as it took the men off the schooner and made light of bringing in the great boat by torch light. When he heard that the men in the lifeboat were on 15s each, he commented, "It makes me feel cheap in kicking about a smoky stove or any of our hardships" [890] A month later, one of the local boats, *Mitzpah*, ran on to the rocks at the back of The Island at night in thick fog and was completely destroyed. Irvine suggested to the Mayor that a relief fund should be set up and was the first to donate. He commented, "I gave £5, and for all the kindnesses of these men to me, it seemed too little."[891]

The manner in which Irvine was immediately accepted by the fisherfolk contrasted greatly with the lack of courtesy, indeed rudeness, shown by the local artists towards him. Irvine arrived in St Ives on 20th February and yet it was not until 2nd April, some six weeks later, that he recorded, "Douglas, painter here, talked to me while at work!! The first here."[892] On another occasion, he was painting in The Warren, when someone suggested that he should join the Arts Club but, on hearing that he was American, suddenly went lukewarm on the idea, prompting Irvine to comment, "I should hate America if I thought our own fellows were not kinder to a visiting painter."[893] He also mentioned an encounter with an artist, whom he called "Spark" and described as "as good a painter as there is here, save Simpson" - clearly a reference to John Park - , who disconcerted him by silently watching his palette like a hawk all the time.[894] Even as late as April 19th, Irvine recorded, "Usual bunch of painters going by, rubbering, staring but never a word." Indeed, the only two artists, who did eventually make an effort to be friendly

---

884 Journal of Wilson Henry Irvine, 1/3/1923, Archives of American Art, Smithsonian Institution, Irvine papers, Reel 3564.
885 ibid 12/3/1923.
886 ibid 15/3/1923.
887 ibid 14/3/1923.
888 ibid 5/3/1923.
889 ibid 7/3/1923.
890 ibid 22/2/1923.
891 ibid 23/3/1923.
892 On 13th March, he mentions an artist, who looks at his canvas and says "Oh, hum!", and then moves off.
893 Journal of Wilson Henry Irvine, 24/3/1923, Archives of American Art, Smithsonian Institution, Irvine papers, Reel 3564.
894 ibid 14/4/1923.

Fig. 4.11 John Douglas   *The Harbour, St Ives*   (courtesy Austin Wormleighton)
This photograph comes from the Olsson family archive, but Irvine and Douglas shared a passion for
photography and Irvine bought many examples of Douglas' work for use with his paintings.

towards him, were John Douglas and Lowell Dyer. Irvine's experience suggests not only the onset of
xenophobia, something quite unheard of before, given the number of foreign artists that had been
warmly welcomed previously, but also a complete loss of self-confidence. Irvine seems to have been
perceived not as a fine painter, who could spread the word about the enchantments of St Ives to his
fellow countrymen, but as a serious threat to a potential sale in a depressed market.

4.2.5   The Arts Club

One of the novel features of the colony in the 1920s was the dramatic increase in the number of residents
with considerable knowledge of, and skill in, the fields of literature and drama. Whilst the landscape of
Cornwall could inspire such persons as much as it did artists, it seems clear that it was the existence of
the art colony, which contained many kindred spirits, and of a well-established Arts Club, that persuaded
so many to retire to or settle in the town. Accordingly, after the War, there was an influx into the Arts Club
of new, enthusiastic members, many of whom had talents in fields other than art. This clearly altered the
atmosphere of the Club and, whereas in the pre-War period, it was unusual for a resident artist not to be
closely involved, there is, in the 1920s, a surprising lack of reference, in the records of the Club, to some
of the leading artists, such as Charles and Ruth Simpson, John Park and Borlase Smart. However, it
does appear that, in the late 1920s, the Arts Club thrived to an extent greater than ever before, with non-
artist professional members producing a regular programme of quality entertainments, during the winter
season, that drew large audiences. This fostered a considerable community spirit.

Whilst old stagers, such as Moffat Lindner, Lowell Dyer, John Bromley, Arthur Meade, Jack Titcomb,
Herbert Lanyon and Fred Milner were regularly elected on to the Committee, with several serving further
terms as President, it was the newer members who tended to be appointed as the key organisational
officers (see Appendix A). The Secretary in 1918-9 was Edgar Skinner, who became very involved with
the Leach Pottery in its early years. It had been his wife, Edith, who had first recommended Bernard
Leach to Frances Horne, when she was looking for a potter for her newly established St Ives Handicraft
Guild, and Leach found Edgar's business acumen helpful during his initial struggles. Upon his death in
1925, his grave was adorned with Leach tiles - 'He went through life with outstretched hand of help".[895]
The Treasurer of the Club in 1918-9 was a retired Doctor, Adam MacVie, who lived in Park Avenue and
exhibited on Show Day on several occasions and with the Cornish artists at Plymouth in 1922.

---

895 For obituary notices, see *St Ives Times* 11/12/1925 and 18/12/1925.

Fig. 4.12 Frank Moore sketching in Norway Lane
(St Ives Trust Archive Study Centre)

In December 1920, drawing classes were started again on Monday and Thursday evenings, under the supervision of Marcella Smith, who had made rapid progress during the War years. The following year, the then President, Frank Moore, suggested that the Club should form a sketch club, as at Langhams, where members had two hours to produce a sketch on a given subject. An exhibition of some forty works by members of the sketch club was held in April 1922. Moore, who was President in both 1921 and 1922, was hailed in 1925 by the French magazine, *La Revue Moderne*, as one of the best contemporary printmakers in England, and it was also at his suggestion, at an Arts Club meeting in October 1922, that the St Ives Print Society was set up.

Frank Barrett, whose entry in *Who's Who*, listed chess and mechanical invention amongst his hobbies, and his wife, Joan, continued to be stalwarts of the Club, until Frank's death in 1926, whilst their daughter, Lilas, took part in a number of dramatic performances.[896] Rolf Bennett and his wife, Katherine Harrington, were two other acclaimed writers in the colony. Bennett, whilst living at Penbeagle, St Ives had made his name with various novels published during the War about the adventures of a Naval Officer, Frank Lawless, one of which was made into a film, whilst his wife was also a novelist - one of her short stories, *O'Hara's Log*, being hailed as one of the leading works of 1922. On returning to St Ives, having served as a gunner in the Royal Garrison Artillery, Bennett was elected Secretary of the Club in 1922.

There are few records of particular entertainments staged in the early 1920s, but one Club member, Patrick McMahon, who occasionally exhibited with the artists and contributed poems to the local paper, was very moved by an Oriental piece that was put on in January 1923, which was set in a street in Morocco, with a potter at work on a vase, a snake-charmer with magic flute and street vendors of various commodities, all dressed in beautiful costumes. He felt that the piece, which no doubt reflected Bernard Leach's input, was so good that the general public should be given a chance to view it, and he wrote to the local paper with this suggestion.[897]

The Minutes of the Arts Club for the 1924-5 winter season reveal not only the appointment of a keen Secretary, but also a dramatic increase in activity. The new Secretary, Engineer-Captain Francis Roskruge D.S.O., O.B.E., who held that office in the years 1924-6 and who was then elected President in 1927-8, was a highly decorated retired naval officer, who had fought in both the Boer and First World Wars. On his retirement to St Ives, he took up printmaking, with some success, but he became recognised as one of the finest actors in the town and he clearly played a significant role in the resurgence of interest in entertainments at the Club. The 1924-5 season saw the appointment, once again, of an Entertainments Sub-Committee, which comprised Herbert and Lilian Lanyon, for musical evenings, Cecil Bromley Magnus and his wife, Alice, for theatrical performances and Greville Ewing Matheson for literary events.

---

896 In 1925, Joan Barrett published a children's book *The Story of a Cat and Two Naughty Magpies.*
897 *St Ives Times*, 2/2/1923.

Cecil Magnus, who had only joined the Club in March 1924, was a nephew of John Bromley and had acted in New York in the 1890s in plays written by his father, Julian Magnus. He was joined in St Ives by his mother, Kate (d.1926), Bromley's sibling, and his own sister, Rosa, who also took an active role in the Arts Club, prior to her early death in 1930.[898] Matheson, who was the son of the Reverend David Matheson and who was named after his grandfather, Greville Ewing, the architect of Scottish Congregationalism, was a highly intelligent literary connoisseur, who had been passenger manager of the Union Castle Line and had started its publicity department, the first of its kind in the shipping world. He retired to St Ives in 1920, but had visited the town on a number of previous occasions, and was clearly responsible for Edmund Fuller winning several commissions for designs for the shipping company (see Figs. 2.179-181). Matheson also asked Fuller to design the extension to his home 'Boskerris', Trencrom Lane, Carbis Bay, which was to form a library to hold his collection of some 10,000 books. These included many complete sets, as well as others that he had arranged to have bound in designs of his own choice. After consulting Cornish expert, Henry Jenner, on appropriate Cornish names, he called it 'Boskerris Vean'. Fuller also produced a bookplate for him (Fig. 4.19), showing him puffing away at a cigarette, as he sat in his library surrounded by piles of books, with golf clubs and cricket gear at hand. Photographs of the library (Figs. 4.13-4) show that it also housed a snooker table and that the few gaps between the shelves were crammed with pictures. Unfortunately, his wife, Emily, a talented musician, died, aged 66, in 1924, but, in 1928, he remarried Isobel Littlejohn, the eldest daughter of Sir Henry Duncan Littlejohn of Edinburgh.[899]

Figs. 4.13-4   Greville Matheson's Library at 'Boskerris Vean',
designed by Edmund Fuller
(courtesy David Chadwick)

898 Kate, Rosa and Alice (d.1933) are all buried in Barnoon Cemetery.

899 For a full review of Matheson's career, see Tom Richards, *Greville Ewing Matheson - His Books and the Boskerris Vean Connection*, St Ives Times and Echo, 25/4/1997.

The 1924-5 season saw the start of a trend, that continued throughout the rest of the 1920s, where an entertainment was staged, during the winter season, lasting from late October to early April, on almost every Saturday night, whilst nearly every Tuesday afternoon featured a tea talk. At the end of that season, which proved a record year for profits, Roskruge noted that the average attendance had been, for Plays eighty-eight, for Charades seventy-three, for Concerts sixty-eight and for Tea Talks forty-one, with some fifty to sixty members regularly involved. The Ladies Committee, responsible for refreshments at each event, was kept exceptionally busy. As, on several occasions, the Club had been packed out with over a hundred persons present, new smaller chairs were acquired and a hinged bench installed on the east side of the Club-room. The increase in interest in theatrical activities led to membership being extended to persons from the operatic and theatrical professions, something that had been resisted before, and membership numbers now approached one hundred and fifty.

Artist members, who took regular acting roles, in addition to Roskruge, included Pauline Hewitt, George and Kathleen Bradshaw, Nell Cuneo and her sons, Desmond and Terence, former Olsson student, Therese Jackson, Jack Titcomb, George Turland Goosey and Helen Seddon. Quite often, the plays performed were written by Arts Club members. Greville Matheson was quite prolific and his contributions included the comedies *Heva*, *Selfish Mr Samuel* and *Forty Thousand*. Stewart Darmady, who joined the Club in November 1924 and took over from Roskruge as Secretary in 1927, proved a real stalwart for over twenty years, joining the Entertainment Sub-Committee in 1926 and being a regular member of it until his departure from the town in 1948. He had previously contributed to *Punch*, the *New Statesman* and the *Windsor Magazine*, and he wrote a number of plays in different styles. These included the 'serious play' *The Visitor*, the romantic play *A Happy Ending* and several other short pieces, such as *A Trunk Call*, *A Tragedy* and *A Valuable Rival*. Later, he also wrote a piece about John Knill, and his play, *The Adam Tragedy*, was considered so meritorious that it was forwarded to the B.B.C. as worthy of production. He and his wife, Jessica, (see Fig. 4.17) were joined by their children, Michael and Elizabeth, and the family not only were key members of the Club, but also were intimately involved with all drama productions in the town.

One-off contributions included a farce by Cecil Magnus, which introduced various local celebrities, and Percy Ballance's *A Bridegroom's Nightmare* in November 1926, which, as he had recently married, may have contained some true to life scenes. One evening, in 1928, featured *The Beating Heart and the Story of an 'Orrid Cruise*, described as "thrown together' by the young Terence Cuneo, whilst a later drama written by him, *Blood and Sawdust*, was so popular when it was premiered on 28th December 1929 that it was repeated the following week. A joint effort was the farcical sketch *The Escape of the Last Artist from St Ives*, performed in December 1926, which featured Roskruge and his wife, Richard and Mabel Shone, Jack Titcomb, John Bromley, Pauline Hewitt and Stewart Darmady amongst others.[900] Unfortunately, no scripts have been retained in the Arts Club records in relation to any of these entertainments, but, as a result of numerous requests, that for a show called *The Rivals* - Not *by Sheridan*, which was staged in March 1928, was published in the local paper.[901] The piece featured personifications of St Ives and Carbis Bay, vying to outdo each other by listing their respective attributes, until the unwelcome siren voices of Penzance and West Penwith offstage brought them together to make common cause. However, unfortunately, Matheson, its author, attempted to incorporate into the script the names of the vast majority of members of the Club, and many of the local tradesmen, by way of increasingly painful puns. One trusts other scripts were more accomplished.

Few of these plays written by members were ever performed professionally, but the Arts Club did premiere one play that was to enjoy a long run in London - *The Constant Nymph* by Margaret Kennedy, who was related to the Millie Dow family. Kennedy, who was a budding novelist, had joined the Arts Club at the end of 1920, and her first book, *The Ladies of Lyndon*, published in 1923, was universally admired. However, her second novel, *The Constant Nymph*, caused outrage in certain circles, due to her descriptions of the romantic and sexual thoughts of an adolescent girl, just fourteen years old at the commencement of the story. She received furious letters from women around the world, saying that the character desecrated modern girlhood, and there was much gossip in the town, as to how she could know about such things! The book, however, proved a runaway success. It was adapted into a play in 1926, and was first performed at the Arts Club, before enjoying a run at the New Theatre in London, with Noel Coward taking a leading role. It has since been the subject of at least four films, the first of which was made in 1928 and featured Ivor Novello, who was in the audience at the Arts Club.[902]

---

900 A sketch, *Greek as she is taught*, put on by Richard Shone and Jack Titcomb in January 1929, was clearly influenced by an article written the previous year by Greville Matheson on an old phrase book, *English as she is spoke*, compiled by a Portugese, Pedro Carolino, who, unperturbed by his own inability to speak English, used a Portugese-French dictionary and a French-English dictionary, with most amusing results.

901 *St Ives Times*, 3/1928.

902 Kathleen Frazier, *My Story*, St Ives, at p.16. The first film, in 1928, was directed by Adrian Brunel and Basil Dean, and featured Ivor Novello, Mabel Poulton, and Elsa Lancaster. In 1933, Dean directed another version, with Victoria Hopper and Brian Aherne. Best known is that made in 1943, which was directed by Edmund Goulding, and featured Charles Boyer and Joan Fontaine (who was nominated for a Best Actress Academy Award).

Another play written by an Arts Club member and performed at the Arts Club, which resulted in considerable national interest, was *Duffy and the Devil*, the first Cornish dialect play written by Robert Morton Nance. At the turn of the century, Nance, whose grandparents lived in St Ives, had shown considerable promise as a marine painter. Having studied at Bushey and then worked in St Ives in 1898, his works were hung at the Royal Academy and at the New Gallery. However, following the death of his first wife in 1902, he concentrated his attentions on the history of sailing ships and sailing ship models, ultimately producing the definitive book on the subject, *Sailing Ship Models*, in 1924.

Fig. 4.15 The cast of Robert Morton Nance's first Cornish dialect play, *Duffy and the Devil* - from the left, Kathleen Frazier as Duffy, "the giddy giglet", Kenneth Hamilton Jenkin as Terry Top the Demon, Morton Nance as Squire Lovell of Trove, and May James (wife of Stanley James) as the housekeeper.

Shortly after his second marriage to fellow Bushey student and accomplished weaver, Annie Maud Cawker, in 1906, the couple settled at Nancledra, between St Ives and Penzance, which he called "a real old village, with nothing modern about it, with a village school and real village children, whose politeness was a delight". He decided to interest the children in acting, for they were clever, and they performed a play, "which was a shoddy little thing sent down from London". Considering that the children would "do much better with something written in their own language", he put together *Duffy and the Devil*, his first literary effort.[903] This aimed at carrying on the West Penwith tradition of guise-dance drolls - local folk-tales turned into plays for Christmas acting, which incorporated the local speech and broke, from time to time, into rhyme or song.[904]

Fig. 4.16 Andrew Glover   Cast of the Old Cornwall Society's performance of *George and the Dragon*, c.1924 featuring A. K. Hamilton Jenkin, Phoebe Nance, R. J. Noall, Bernard Leach, Michael Cardew and Robert Morton Nance.
(Royal Institution of Cornwall, Royal Cornwall Museum, Truro)

903 *St Ives Times*, 17/1/1930.
904 R.Morton Nance, Preface to *The Cledry Plays - Drolls of Old Cornwall for Village Acting and Home Reading*, Penzance, 1956.

Having moved to Carbis Bay in 1914, Nance generated considerable interest in the Cornish language and in Cornish folk-lore after the War, and was instrumental in the formation of the St Ives Old Cornwall Society in 1920. The play was performed in the Arts Club in March 1925 and Nance gave several talks to members on Cornish miracle plays, whilst Henry Jenner, the first President of the Old Cornwall Society, and Kenneth Hamilton Jenkin, who was to become the expert on Cornish Mining history, also spoke to members. The play was performed locally a number of times and attracted the attention of Filson Young, the B.B.C. producer, who arranged for it to be first broadcast on the radio in 1928, with several Arts Club members taking parts. The huge interest aroused locally in Cornish history and the Cornish language led to the establishment of the Cornish Gorsedd in 1928 and, after Jenner's death, Nance was appointed Grand Bard of Cornwall in 1934, a position he retained until his death in 1959.

Charades also played a regular and popular role in the entertainments arranged for Saturday nights, often followed by dancing. A combined sketch and charade, entitled *The Making of a Charade*, was repeated by request, and other titles included *Crossword Puzzle*, *Balkans*, *Counterfeit* and *Brooke's Monkey-Brand Soap*. The musical evenings, arranged by the Lanyons, also drew large audiences, even though Herbert Lanyon himself did not perform much. In great contrast to the pre-War years, few of the other artists, or their relations, were talented musicians, and performances tended to be put on by members elected purely for their musical abilities. One of the true stalwarts was Kathleen Frazier, a young local girl, who lived at 22 The Terrace, whose talent had been spotted and promoted by Herbert Lanyon. He told her mother, "Kathleen has got her foot on the ladder and she's going to the top".[905] This proved correct, as she went on to become the official accompanist for the B.B.C.. She was made a member of the Arts Club in 1918 and recalled, in her autobiography, that, as a young girl, "it was a great thrill to go there and meet famous Painters and Writers, and Sculptors and, of course, Potters, such as Bernard Leach".[906] She also took an active role in the Club's theatricals and, when she moved to Bristol in 1945 to take up her position with the B.B.C., she was presented by the Club with an Illuminated Address "beautifully executed by Shearer Armstrong", bearing the words of the old Scottish song, "Will ye no come back again? Better lo'ed ye canna be", which she described as "one of my most treasured possessions."[907]

Barrie Bennetts, the former England rugby player, caricatured by Fitz (Fig. 3.8), was now a partner in Edward Boase's solicitors' practice and serenaded members on his viola, whilst Hurst Balmford, who moved to the town in the mid-1920s, was also accomplished on violin and viola. A significant impact was made by the arrival in the colony in 1925 of the musical composer and arranger, J.C.Holliday, who had toured with the famous music-hall entertainer, Albert Chevalier. He introduced 'Revue' Evenings into the Club's programme, which were considered "a novelty and revelation", and the events that he organised were always packed out. One piece that he wrote in 1925 was called *Zennor (A Morris Dance)*. It was most unusual for an evening to be devoted to a single performer, but, in January 1925, John Douglas commanded the floor on his own, singing songs and giving a number of his humorous recitations. Another different evening, in 1926, was a Scottish night, organised by two new members, who were to be stalwarts - Colonel James Marshall Findlay (d.1945), who had been appointed property agent for the Porthia Estate of the Hain family, and his wife, Cecile, who involved herself in numerous local causes, acting as a quasi-Lady of the Manor after the death of Lady Hain and the departure from the area of her daughter, Kate. Findlay had become Commander of the 8th Scottish Rifles during the Great War and was awarded the D.S.O and bar and mentioned in dispatches on five occasions.[908] He became President of the British Legion, Chairman of the Conservative Association and a County Councillor, whilst his wife became a magistrate.[909] One of their daughters, Anna, was a woodcut artist, who exhibited with the St Ives Society of Artists, whilst another was a talented musician, who took part in a number of entertainments.

The tea talks, held on Tuesday afternoons, covered a wide range of subjects. They were normally given by members, but, in February 1921, the Secretary of the newly-established National Trust was asked to speak, and invitations were extended to old friends from the local community, such as Lady Hain, Robert Read, William Trewhella and Dr Nicholls. With the War still a vivid memory, a number of talks were of members' experiences during the conflict. General Sir Herbert Blumberg, who was married to the marine artist, Eliza Tudor Lane (d.1931) and who had joined the Club in 1925, spoke on his time as Commander-in-Chief and Governor of certain Greek Islands and on a number of other military subjects.

---

905 Kathleen Frazier, *My Story*, St Ives, at p.16.

906 ibid.

907 ibid at p.44.

908 He was converted to a professional member following the publication of *With the 8th Scottish Rifles (1914-1919)* in 1926. This was reviewed in *St Ives Times* 19/3/1926 and re-published in 2004.

909 See his Obituary in *St Ives Times*, 23/2/1945.

Fig. 4.17   Cast of the St. Ives Players' performance of Ibsen's *A Doll's House* at The
Assembly Rooms, Camborne, featuring, from the left, Alexander Marsh, Margaret
Jacobs, Jessie Darmady, Monica Lidgey, David Leach and Stewart Darmady
(Royal Institution of Cornwall, Royal Cornwall Museum, Truro)

He was soon elected Treasurer, a post he retained until 1931. George Bradshaw, who had won a D.S.O and risen to the rank of Lieutenant-Commander in the Submarine Service, gave a talk on Submarines, whilst fellow retired naval officer, Francis Roskruge, and Captain Richard Shone, husband of the artist, Mabel Shone, spoke of their time at sea. Jack Titcomb recounted his war-time experiences as a Special Constable, whilst Norman Cooke, who was Treasurer of the Club between 1923-6 and again from 1932-1940, reminisced about his time as a Coast-Watcher. Little is known about the artistic or literary accomplishments of Cooke, but he is recorded as the ratepayer for a studio in the Barnoon area of town as early as 1911 and, in 1920, he acquired 'Dunvegan', Carbis Bay, the house that Edmund Fuller had designed for himself. However, his two daughters, Dorothy, always known as 'Dossie', and Iris, were considered to be art students of considerable promise in the early 1920s and entertained the members, from time to time, on piano and violincello respectively.

A number of tea talks featured reminiscences of some of the senior members of the colony, such as Moffat Lindner, Lowell Dyer and Fred Milner. Indeed, Lindner's talk was so popular that he repeated it on at least three occasions. Art related talks included one by Bernard Leach on *Old Japanese, Korean and Chinese Art*, and another on pots, whilst Alfred Hartley spoke on etching. Roskruge spoke on a variety of topics, whilst, unsurprisingly, Matheson and Darmady were also regular speakers. One of the most popular speakers, however, was the novelist, Crosbie Garstin, son of Norman Garstin, who talked about his adventures in Africa and Cambodia. One novelty tea-time event was a soap carving contest!

Extra special nights during the year, when a large attendance was guaranteed, were the New Year's Eve party and President's Night. Roskruge's minutes for the celebration of the arrival of 1925 give a flavour of such parties. Members gathered at 9 p.m. and a variety entertainment was put on for an hour, for which names of volunteers were put into a hat, and each performer, after the conclusion of his or her "stunt", drew out a name for the next piece. It also included some "music recitations". At 10.15 p.m., there was a break, during which Lowell Dyer's annual brew of punch was passed around and a moderate supper of sandwiches and biscuits was consumed, and, then, the band, hired for the night, kicked off the dancing, which continued until 1.00 a.m.. There was a further break at 11.15 p.m. for lemonade and claret cup to be served and, at midnight, there was an interval, during which *Auld Lang Syne* was sung by all, "hand in hand and standing in three concentric circles". There was no particular formula for President's Night, although it normally also included a band, dancing and refreshments. Sometimes, one or more short plays were put on or a member gave a talk. The one held by John Douglas in April 1926 required members to wear a token representing some well-known painting. The ladies' prize was won by Mrs Beddard, who brought a bill from the Gas company, representing *The Charge of the Light Brigade*! Fancy Dress parties also continued to be popular, the one in January 1926 being slightly different as it specialised in fancy head-dresses. A children's fancy dress party over the Christmas period also became a regular feature.

In September 1924, it was decided to write to past Presidents of the Club to ask if they would donate a small example of their work to hang in the Club-room. Whereas some obliged, there were a number, such as Adrian Stokes, Arnesby Brown and Julius Olsson, who did not agree with the concept, a viewpoint which was in keeping with the early decision taken by the Club to have just photographs of work on display for aesthetic reasons.

Fig. 4.18   Daphne Pearson *Greville Matheson*
(Spring 1933)   (courtesy Margaret Reed)

Fig. 4.19 Edmund Fuller
Bookplate for Greville Matheson

In 1924, the Club learnt that the rent of the Club-room was to be doubled to £16. Given that the rental had not altered from the outset back in 1890, this rise was long overdue, but the Club, aware of their landlord's advancing years, were keen to learn of his future plans for the property. Eventually, in September 1928, the Club bought the freehold of the property for £600, Jenkyn having paid for the release of the rights of way of the adjoining fish cellar owner. George Turland Goosey, who had been a practising architect in America, before joining the colony, supervised the alterations required, which involved the insertion of an internal staircase and the creation on the ground floor of a room as a library, two dressing rooms, a storeroom and toilets. A little later a stage was built in the upper room, after joists had been strengthened to "permit dancing". 5% Debentures were issued to members willing to lend money to cover the costs of the purchase and the subsequent alterations.

4.2.6   Literary friends

The influx of writers into the colony led to an increased interest in literature and, in 1919, a St Ives Literary Society was formed, with Edgar Skinner, as first President. Artists to present papers at the Society included Alfred Bailey (*Walt Whitman* & *The Need for Art in the Present Age*) and Bernard Leach (*The Influence of European Literature in Japan*) and, in 1923, there was a discussion evening on the subject *Is a leisured class indispensable to Art?* This prompted one artist to write to the paper. "I fail to see that the question calls for any discussion as it has been proved beyond doubt that the 'leisured class' is essential to itself only and is as helpful to the movement in art about as much as the smell is to the movement of a motor car".[910] However, it was the arrival in the town in 1920 of Greville Matheson that led to increased interest in the Society and to literature receiving as much publicity as art.

Matheson, who was described as a man with an exceptionally brilliant brain, took an increasingly active role in the editorship of the *St Ives Times* during the 1920s, as Martin Cock began to suffer health problems, and, almost every week, the paper included several contributions by him, under the pen name M.A.Honest, an anagram of Matheson. These included articles on drama, literary or artistic subjects, and reviews of books and plays of interest to locals, either because they were written by local residents or because they related to local subjects. Rolf Bennett, Katherine Harrington, Margaret Kennedy, Joan Barrett and Stewart and Jessica Darmady were just some of the locals to produce new novels, whilst Will Lloyd and Irene Wintle, Sydney Carr's daughter, produced volumes of poetry.[911] Books recording their

910 *St Ives Times*, 16/3/1923.

911 Irene Wintle produced a slim volume of poems called *Harvest* in 1929. Lloyd's poems were reviewed in *St Ives Times* 4/1/1929.

military experiences were also written by General Blumberg, Colonel Findlay and Sir Herbert Thirkell White.   In addition to *The Constant Nymph*, Frank Bennett's *The Woman of the Iron Bracelets* (1920) and Charles Procter's *The Notorious Mrs Carrick* (1924) were made into films and aroused considerable interest when shown locally. Matheson also dug back into Cornish history to find early accounts of St Ives, asked well-known artists or writers, who had been residents in the past, to reminisce about their sojourns in the town and interviewed aged locals to obtain their memories of times past. In addition, he often wrote comic verse in response to news items, many of which were published by James Lanham Limited, in 1936, in *Painters, Poets and Others in St Ives*. Verses inspired by the art colony tended to relate to Show Day or the (lack of) judgement displayed by the Royal Academy hanging committee. For instance, *A Ballade of Optimism* commences,

> *From studio to studio*
> *The mournful message went its way*
> *The news that travelled to and fro*
> *Filled many a household with dismay,*
> *The sun went out, the world was grey,*
> *And there was wrath in all the place,*
> *For Fate is stern and nought can stay*
> *Those simple words "For want of space".*[912]

Matheson encouraged the other writers resident in the locality to contribute articles and poems to the newspaper, and there were occasional contributions from artists, such as Ruth Davenport. His brother-in-law, Charles John Pugh, who lived with him, was another regular correspondent, using the pen-name, J.C.Carbis. One piece that caused rather a stir, resulting in the local paper selling out, was a review of Show Day in 1924 by the Cockney 'Marcus', one of the pen-names of the novelist, Charles Procter, as he lampooned both the fishermen and the artists.

"It says in the guide book that the chief industry of St Ives is fishin', but I reckon that's only a rumour. They've got a fleet of fishin' boats, but I think they only keeps 'em so's ter give the artists somethink ter paint, and the visitors somethink ter to take photos of...'cos it's always the wrong kinder weather for the local fleet ter go out in. I never knew till I got to St Ives 'ow particlor fish is about the weather they gets caught in. If there's a' East wind blowin', the fishing boats don't go out, 'cos the fish won't come up ter get caught; if it's rainin', it ain't no use the fishermen goin' out, 'cos the fish objects, I suppose, ter gettin' wet; if it's stormy, the fish goes round and gets themselves caught at Newlyn, and if the weather's fine, the fishermen can't go out 'cos they ain't got no bait. And if they've got bait and the weather's orlright, and the fish is there waitin' ter be caught, it's very likely Sunday and the boats can't go out 'cos the men 'as ter go to chapel."

In the light of this, Marcus considered that the reason that pilchards had stopped coming to the Bay was because "the last shoal waited so long ter get caught that orl the fish died of old age". He continued by poking fun at the habit of retired mariners of walking up and down by their fishing lodges, as if they were still on deck. "I ain't sayin' as 'ow the fishermen ain't energetic. I never was in a place where the men does so much walkin' without gettin' anywhere. Y'see, they only walks four paces each way, but they keeps it up for 'ours and 'ours, and some of 'em 'olds the short-distance walkin' championship."

Turning to the artists, Marcus continued, "No, yer can't kid me that the chief industry of St Ives is fishin'. The chief industry is art, or, any'ow, paintin' pictures, which ain't quite the same thing, for I've seen a lot of pictures wot ain't art. St Ives is full of artists wot lives by paintin' pictures wot nobody don't buy, and 'ow some of 'em looks so prosperous is a mystery ter me. I reckon artists and fishermen must 'ave found out some way of livin' without earnin'." The purpose of Show Day, therefore, in Marcus' view, was "to prove to the fishermen, and their missuses and kids, that the artists does do some work, even if they don't earn no money". It meant that "for one day everybody in the town, and a lot from outside the town, is a' art critic. Some of 'em as lives in the town, and mixes with the artists reg'lar knows just wot ter say. They goes about sayin' ' 'Ow perfectly charmin', if the artist is listenin', and waits till they gets outside before they bursts out larfin', but others wot ain't bin brought up genteel asks the artist wot 'is picture is supposed to represent...or remarks that 'is pictures don't make 'em feel so sick this year as they did larst or words ter that effeck....One bloke told me 'e was paintin' for posterity and I couldn't help wonderin' wot posterity 'ad done to 'im that 'e should 'ave a grudge against 'em." Given that most of the paintings were to be submitted to the Royal Academy, Marcus considered that "there must be more optimists in St Ives than any other place I've ever struck. Most of the pictures I saw stands as much chance of gettin' 'ung at the Royal Academy as a celluloid cat does of coming whole out of a furnace....There was 'still lifes' so blomin' still that yer might be forgiven for thinkin' they was dead, and seascapes wot looked like

---

912 Greville Matheson, *Painters, Poets and Others*, St Ives, 1936 at p.6.

a jam factory in eruption or confetti floating in pea soup, and some as looked like the effecks of a bilious attack". However, Marcus' favourite studio, where he stayed the longest, was the one "where the artist asked me ter step inter the back office where the chief exhibits was a decanter of Scotch and small bottles of soda".[913]

Predictably, a few people failed to see the funny side of the article and wrote letters of complaint, resulting in Greville Matheson publishing *A Ballade of Marcus*, which contained the refrain,

> *He did not know - perchance not care -*
> *That in St Ives and Carbis Bay*
> *A lack of humour is not rare*

Marcus himself, in his response, commented, "I'm told they was larfin' over Marcus in the cottages down-a-long and while they was doing their short-distance walkin' championships and a gent at the 'Red 'Ouse' [Lanyon] larfed till 'e cried, and people was even 'eard to laugh in the 'Sloop' and in the Arts Club about wot I said about pictures."[914] The following year, Marcus was at it again, commenting that, in the intervening months, he had been giving lessons on 'The Gentle Art of Leg-Pulling'.[915] Procter, who had first joined the Arts Club in 1922, was, at this juncture, a regular visitor to the town, but later settled at 'Caerthillion', with his daughter, Sheila, who became Curator of the Gallery of the St Ives Society of Artists, and he contributed rather kinder reviews of numerous shows over the years.

Matheson's involvement with the *St Ives Times* led to the paper having an extraordinarily high intellectual content for a local rag, and this was clearly popular with the distinct group of artists, writers, musicians and dramatists that now formed a sizeable segment in the town. Quite what the fisherfolk thought of it all is not recorded. They presumably just bought *The Western Echo*.

Visiting Artist : *Dangerous job that of yours - fishing?*
Fisherman : *Not 'arf as dangerous as itud belong to be*
if us 'ad to go to sea in they boats you artises paints

Fig. 4.20 George Turland Goosey Cartoon for *St Ives Times* 18/12/1925

---

913 *St Ives Times*, 28/3/1924.
914 *St Ives Times*, 11/4/1924.
915 *St Ives Times*, 20/3/1925.

4.2.7 Art-related employment

Whilst artists had always had some beneficial effect on local employment prospects, due to their requirements for domestic servants and general helpers, the increased interest in the decorative arts in the 1920s briefly gave rise to optimism that more employment opportunities would be available in art-related concerns. Certainly, Frances Horne, when she formed, in 1920, the St Ives Handicraft Guild, which specialised in weaving and basket making, hoped that this would provide alternative employment for women, who had formerly been involved in the fishing industry, and for men disabled by the War. Unfortunately, however, it attracted only middle class women, and the only disadvantaged person to work for the Guild was a man, who had been badly gassed in the War. The most notable of the enterprises that Frances Horne helped to establish was the Leach Pottery, which soon acquired an international reputation, but, here again, initial hopes that it would prove a significant employer of local people were dashed, as the pottery merely relied on the services of one handyman. However, the transfer of the production of Cryséde's hand-painted silks to a new factory built on the site of old fish cellars on the Island in the mid-1920s did provide significant new employment opportunities, which were much sought after.[916] Emily Woolcock, great-grand-daughter of Alfred Wallis, commented, "If you got in at Cryséde, you were "it" ". Tom Heron, father of Patrick, who ran the works, was rated a marvellous boss, albeit discipline was strict. "We were allowed to sing but not to speak. So you can just imagine what hundreds and hundreds of machines were going like, and we singing....They were wonderful people to work for. It was really a happy place, very very happy and I remember the day I left, I broke my heart. We were never laid off. Never, never laid off. They always found something for us to do."[917] Unfortunately, Alec Walker, jealous of Heron's success, sacked him in 1929 and his own mental difficulties resulted in his own dismissal shortly afterwards. Bereft of both its inspiring manager and its creative genius, the business struggled thereafter.

4.2.8 Entertaining the locals

Whereas, in the pre-War period, the artists had regularly put on entertainments in the town for the benefit of the locals, this did not happen very often in the 1920s.[918] The influx of non-artist members into the Arts Club had, in any event, meant that artists were often in the minority in the cast of the Club's entertainments, but the Arts Club, in general, largely ceased to put on public performances. This might be partly due to the new era, which witnessed the introduction of the cinema, the wireless and the gramophone, resulting in higher expectations of more sophisticated entertainments, than the slapstick variety shows that the artists had tended to put on in the past. However, the quality of the Arts Club productions in the 1920s was considered very good and, when it did arrange an entertainment in 1929 at the Palais de Danse, the local paper commented, "Although members of the Arts Club present plays frequently in the Club privately, there are few occasions on which the general public have opportunities of seeing them, but when they do occur, large audiences are attracted."[919] Accordingly, although the Arts Club had been opened up to a wider section of the community, there was a greater risk of the Club itself being seen as exclusive.

Another reason for the lack of public performances by the Arts Club was the formation, in 1922, of the St Ives Dramatic Society, as a result of interest arising from some *Scenes of Shakespeare* performed in the Public Hall in December 1921. The Society's first production, in May 1922, was *Diana of Dobson's*, which received high praise from Rolf Bennett, who described himself as a former drama critic. He considered that it inaugurated "a new era in the social life of St Ives", for it was the first time that a performance had been put on by "a properly constituted local society, with a long and ambitious programme before it and, what is more to the purpose, a society composed of people not just 'roped in' for a single performance, but pledged to carry on the work begun so ably". He felt that the Society would "bring together in greater sympathy and understanding...'art and town' ".[920] Whilst a number of members of the Arts Club, such as the Darmadys and Therese Jackson, were stalwarts of the new Society, the level of commitment required appears to have put off a number of artists with dramatic talent. Francis Roskruge, who not only took leading roles, but was also responsible for scene-painting, was the only artist to be regularly involved, although parts were taken, on occasion, by George Bradshaw and Pauline Hewitt. The newly arrived Fred Bottomley was also appointed 'Business Manager' at the 1929 AGM. However, instead

---

916 By June 1926, there were about one hundred employees, although skilled workers employed previously from Newlyn were brought over by charabanc each day.

917 Extracts from an interview with Roger Slack, quoted in John Pearl-Binns and Giles Heron, *Rebel and Sage : A Biography of Tom Heron 1890-1983*, Bishop Auckland, 2001 at p.42.

918 One of the few instances was a *Fantasy Play*, written by Francis Roskruge, which was put on at the Palais de Danse on 5/2/1926 in aid of the St Ives Ambulance. This featured Roskruge, Bromley and his sister, Mrs Magnus, Robert Morton Nance and his wife, Greville Matheson, Marjorie Ballance and Vera Bodilly.

919 *St Ives Times*, 12/4/1929. However, the only artists involved were the Bradshaws, Francis Roskruge, Anna Findlay and Elizabeth Cork. It did feature, however, the young Peter Lanyon.

920 *St Ives Times*, 12/5/1922.

of promoting a "spirit of comradeship", as hoped by Bennett, the St Ives Dramatic Society seems to have led to cliques developing.[921] Accordingly, one group of artists, comprising George and Kathleen Bradshaw, Pauline Hewitt and Nell Cuneo and her son, Terence, preferred to put on plays themselves, often written by Nell Cuneo, for events such as Conservative Association parties, whilst Jack Titcomb and Arthur Hayward appeared in a play to raise funds for the British Legion in 1927.[922] The burgeoning size of Carbis Bay led another group of dramatically inclined artists and writers, who were resident in the locality, to put on plays at the Carbis Bay Institute, which had been erected in 1923.[923] Again, these were often written by locals, such as Greville Matheson, Robert Morton Nance and Charles Pugh, and, in contrast to the Arts Club, were open to the public.[924]

Musical performances provide the starkest contrast with the pre-War period. Both the St Ives Choral Society and the St Ives Orchestral Society flourished in the 1920s under the leadership of conductor and singer, Ernest White, but no artists were involved at all. Even Herbert Lanyon does not appear to have given any public performances, whilst Will Lloyd seems to have become more involved with Walter Barnes in Penzance.

4.2.9   Sport

The artists also largely disappeared off the sports scene in the 1920s. Arthur Meade and Jack Titcomb won a couple of the competitions at the Golf Club, but artists rarely featured in the teams and there is little mention of groups of either sex playing with regularity. No artists played cricket for the town and cricket matches featuring the artists against the town, the Newlyners or even the ladies of the colony appear to have ceased. Similarly, artists rarely took part in the annual tennis tournament. Even billiards seems to have ceased to be popular.

4.2.10   Local Children

The arrival in the colony of Borlase Smart after the War brought much needed energy, enthusiasm and organisational skills. One of his initiatives was to get the local schoolchildren interested in art. Accordingly, in 1924, the senior children at the local school were invited to visit the studios on Show Day and the local headmaster, Charles Bray, expressed his appreciation in a letter to the *St Ives Times*, complimenting the artists on the courtesy that they had shown the children and commenting that such visits had "a very high educational value".[925] Following on from this, in July 1925, some two hundred works by local schoolchildren were exhibited in Balcony Studio, before being shown at the RCPS. After this, a tour of the studios and Lanham's Gallery by a group of children from the local school became a regular feature and the interest shown by the children in the works on display was often commented upon. On one occasion, when a visitor complained about the bad behaviour of children at exhibitions, Smart responded, "I had scores of young children in my studio. They showed an intelligent interest in what they saw, especially if any work on view contained 'local interest'. I always make it a practice to endeavour to interest the children in the various pictures, and anything I feel may appeal to them, I give them a little talk on it. I have invariably found them very attentive listeners, and that they appreciate such consideration is shown by their general behaviour."[926] Sarah Escott, remembering her Show Day experiences as a child, commented, "We traipsed up and down steps, in lofts over fish cellars. It was amazing that they could live and paint such beautiful pictures in such primitive conditions."[927]

A number of artists got involved in local scout and girl guide groups. Marjorie Ballance was the District Commissioner for the Girl Guides, whilst Herbert Lanyon became President of the local Boys Scouts Association and Francis Roskruge became Scoutmaster of the St Ives Rover Troop, the first in the County. In 1923, Lanyon and Roskruge, who lived close to each other in The Bellyars, persuaded their neighbour, John Cork at 'Chy Morvah', to allow the gardens of their three properties to be the venue for what they termed the annual Scouts' 'Jolliday'.[928] In addition to a series of activities laid on outside, which included portraits done by Kathleen Bradshaw and Francis Roskruge for just 1s 6d, these days included concerts put on in Lanyon's studio, and they proved a highly popular annual event.

---

921 Stewart and Jessica Darmady also set up the St Ives Old Scholars Dramatic Society, encouraging leavers from the St Ives schools to take up drama and put on performances locally.

922 See *Jane, St Ives Times,* 4/3/1927.

923 The site was initially leased from the Lawry estate and the building's erection was made possible by a generous gift of timber by David Macfarlane Horne. The freehold was acquired in 1930. See *St Ives Times,* 30/6/1930.

924 For instance, in March 1923, an entertainment at the Institute featured *Dick Whittington* by Pugh, *The Humours of Jan and Doll* by Nance and *Selfish Mr Samuel* by Matheson - *St Ives Times,* 9/3/1923.

925 *St Ives Times,* 4/4/1924.

926 Letter to *St Ives Times* 1919.

927 See Marion Whybrow, *St Ives 1883-1993 - Portrait of an Art Colony,* Woodbridge, 1994, at p.36.

928 See *St Ives Times,* 7/9/1923.

Fig. 4.21 Edmund Fuller   Design for Certificate for
St Ives Elementary Schools Swimming Association

4.2.11 Serving the Community

During the 1920s, several male members of the artistic community devoted considerable time to local matters, whilst a number of female artists and artists' wives continued their work on women's issues and for local charitable causes.

Most probably inspired by his father-in-law, John Vivian (c.1853-1919), who had been a member of the County Council, since its inception, Herbert Lanyon began to take an active interest in local matters after the War. He stood, and came a creditable second to Dr Nicholls, in the County Council election in 1919, arguing, inter alia, the need for a Secondary School in St Ives. Georgina Bainsmith also stood, but was humiliated, capturing a mere forty-two votes. The passage of the Representation of the People Act the previous year did not change ingrained prejudices overnight. When Lanyon stood for the local council later in the year, he described himself, interestingly, as an artist, as opposed to a photographer or musician, and, backed by the highly respected Colonel Williams, he secured the highest number of votes. In 1920, he was joined on the Council by Borlase Smart. Lanyon seems to have soon wearied of the grind of the role and did not seek re-election when his three year term expired. Smart was much more actively engaged, but, as he planned to be away from St Ives for a large part of 1925, he did not seek re-election in 1924. However, he found that the experience had proved most educational and "had quickened him in his business faculties".[929] In 1928, Francis Roskruge, who was well regarded by a wide section of the community, was made a Justice of the Peace and, on his first appearance on the bench, was joined by Julius Olsson, making one of his rare visits.

Fig. 4.22 Herbert Lanyon
Self-Portrait in later life
(Lanyon family archive)

929 *St Ives Times*, 17/10/1924.

Fig. 4.23 Regatta Day in St Ives   (postcard)

Whilst Smart, after his return to the colony in 1928, devoted himself principally to the fortunes of the St Ives Society of Artists, Lanyon took on a number of figure-head roles. In addition to his role as President of the local Boy Scouts Association, he was also, for many years, chairman of the St Ives Swimming Association, which had an important annual swimming match and regatta attracting professional swimmers from around the country. This was one of the events of the year, which Virginia Woolf recalled with fondness from her youth - "the crowd of little boats, the floating flags along the course, & the Committee boat, dressed with lines of bunting, from which naked figures plunged, & guns were fired. A certain distant roll of drums & blare of trumpets ... The band playing on the Malakoff ....Two or three little booths for the sale of sweets & cakes lined the Terrace, & the whole population of St Ives paraded up & down in their reds & greens.... Reduce it all to a French impressionist picture & the St Ives Regatta is not a sight to be despised."[930]

Lanyon's other long-term roles included the Presidency of the local section of the St John's Ambulance Brigade and of the St Ives Town Band, for whom he obtained new premises, and the Vice-Presidency of the Fire Brigade. He was also President, in its Jubilee Year in 1919, of the National Children's Home and Orphanage. In the meantime, his wife, Lilian, and Florence Dow, were on the Committee of the St Ives Nursing Association. On a more political note, Lanyon, in 1920, became President of the local branch of what started out as the unfortunately named Middle Classes Union, but which became known as the National Citizens Union. This was intended to be a non-party, non-sectarian movement, which had the motto "fair play and equitable treatment for all", but its principal aim was to draw attention to the dangers of communism and bolshevism. Georgina Bainsmith was also on the local Committee.

The developments in Russia clearly worried many people and Olsson, visiting the town at the time of the 1928 election, wrote to the local paper, "I was a pre-War Liberal, but find now that the only party that can and will fight the insidious canker of communism is the Conservative party, which I now back for all I am worth."[931] Despite this, a Liberal, and what is more, a female, Hilda Runciman, was elected, albeit she later stood down in favour of her husband, Walter.

Of a very different political persuasion were Will and Katherine Arnold-Forster, who lived at 'Eagle's Nest', near Zennor. Will, who exhibited on occasion with the St Ives artists, had been closely involved in the League of Nations and they were active supporters of the League of Nations Union, of which Gussie Lindner was local President and Chairman. Katherine became the first female to be made a Justice of the Peace in St Ives in 1928, whilst Will became the first local Labour candidate. The famous garden that they developed at 'Eagle's Nest' was the scene of many garden parties for these causes and the Women's Peace Pilgrimage.

Georgina Bainsmith also continued to devote herself to a number of local causes. She was a member of the Penzance Board of Guardians and, along with Florence Dow and Elizabeth Cork, was on the Committee of the St Ives Infant Welfare Centre. She was also a member of the Penzance branch of the Brabazon Society, which aimed to bring comfort to those in hospitals and prisons.

---

930 Diary of Virginia Stephen, 14/8/1905.

931 *St Ives Times*, 2/3/1928.

PART FIVE

OLD HOUSES, SKIDDEN HILL
(NOW DEMOLISHED)   ST. IVES.

Edmund G. Fuller

THE IMPACT OF THE ARTISTS

UPON THE TOWN

"A LOCALITY CAN HAVE NO BETTER FRIEND THAN AN ART COLONY"

5.1.1   Introduction

Although John Hobson Matthews indicated that, prior to the construction of the branch line to St Ives in 1877, tourists were exceedingly rare, his assessment of the town's position in 1892 made him remark, "St Ives relies on visitors, the majority of whom belong to a wealthy class, for the support of its inhabitants."[932] This comment not only confirms that the traditional industries of St Ives had continued their headlong decline, but also that there had been an astonishing transformation in tourist numbers. From being a town that did not welcome visitors, St Ives had become, over the short period of fifteen years, *dependent* on them. The role that the artists played in this transformation was considerable and their impact was ongoing. Whereas the 1891 Census for St Ives had shown yet a further drop in the population, the 1901 and 1911 Censuses both revealed an increase, making St Ives one of the very few former industrial towns of Cornwall to prosper in these two decades.[933] By the turn of the century, Mayors were constantly paying tribute to the contribution that the art colony had made to the success of St Ives as a tourist centre. In a speech at the Mayoral Banquet in 1901, William Faull commented that the "artists' pictures had made St Ives a resort for visitors", whilst, at the Banquet in 1904, the retiring Mayor, Captain Thomas Row Harry, told his audience, "We owe a great deal more to the gentlemen of the art colony than we suppose, but I fear that we seldom give them the credit that they deserve. Never a year passes without the walls of the Royal Academy being adorned with pictures, portraying every variety of the beautiful scenery of our county, from that of storm-swept coast to sylvan scene, by rock and glen of the interior. What is the consequence? Nothing less than this, that, aided by the sanitary progress of the town, there is year by year an ever increasing list of visitors who bring occupation and emolument to many of our people.....I can assure you, gentleman, that a locality can have no better friend than an art colony."[934]

These words, of course, were delivered to an audience that included artists, who were close friends. To what extent do they ring true? With so many attractive natural features, tourists would have discovered St Ives in any event, but the artists certainly helped to accelerate the process and, what is more important, they appear to have played an important role in the way in which the tourist industry developed in the town. The artists not only transformed the tourist season and increased the number of visitors to the town, but they also influenced the type of tourist, who came. This higher class of visitor did not want the vulgar trappings of most seaside resorts, and so St Ives was able to pride itself on being different. The Town Council, in the pre-War period, in any event, appreciated this, so that, although the town had to expand to cater for the vast increase in tourists, inappropriate development was kept to the minimum, and the features which attracted artists and visitors alike were retained. The artists were not slow to decry lapses, and the friendships that had developed between artists and local dignitaries ensured that the artists' standpoint was always appreciated.

5.1.2   The transformation of the tourist season

There is no doubt that the first major impact that the artists had on the town was on the fortunes of the local landladies. In Kelly's Directory for 1873, there is merely a single 'lodging house' listed, confirming the paucity of tourists before the rail link. Accordingly, prior to 1877, artists would have constituted a significant percentage of the visitors to the town. By the time of the next Kelly's Directory in 1883, the number of 'lodging houses' had increased to fourteen, the majority of which were situated on The Terrace, Tregenna Terrace or Barnoon Terrace. This demonstrates the immediate impact of the railway, but these establishments are only likely to have been busy in the short summer season of August and September. Whereas in the 1860s and 1870s, artists had tended to favour the autumn period for their sketching tours, by the 1880s, the attractions of West Cornwall as an all year round sketching destination were becoming more widely known. Accordingly, artists not only increased the number of visitors significantly, but dramatically extended the season.

---

932 J.H.Matthews, *A History of the Parishes of Saint Ives, Lelant, Towednack and Zennor in the County of Cornwall*, London, 1892 at p.368.

933 The population figures for the St Ives parish were 6094 in 1891, 6699 in 1901 and 7170 in 1911.

934 *St Ives Weekly Summary*, 9/11/1901 & *St Ives Weekly Summary*, 12/11/1904.

Fig. 5.1 Cynicus (Martin Anderson)   *The Last Train to St Ives*   (postcard)

The first Visitors' List was published in the local paper in late May 1889 and, accordingly, that year is the first year when one can truly gauge the effect of the artists (see Table B - p.34). Only three properties were shown as having guests in May but, by the end of June, this had increased to sixteen, and a number of artists had arrived for an extended visit. However, by mid-August, the number of lodging houses listed was over sixty. St Ives, therefore, was already attracting considerable numbers of summer tourists and the sprinkling of artists recorded during that period was of no great consequence. The key statistic, though, is that, at the time of the last published Visitors' List - on 26th October - , there were still eighteen lodging houses listing visitors, of whom ninety-five per cent were artists. This was how the artists completely transformed the lodgings market, for they required accomodation all year round and so provided a steady income stream for landladies during the winter periods that, in the past, would have been dead.

This beneficial aspect of the artists' presence continued for decades. Accordingly, as already mentioned, one artist character in *Portalone* felt that the artists practically kept the fisherfolk in a bad winter, whilst, as late as 1915, in a letter to the local paper, Moffat Lindner contended that the sketching ban would have a serious impact on winter trade in the town, for most winter visitors were still artists.[935]

5.1.3   The impact of the artists on tourist numbers

Prompted by Terrick Williams' recollections in 1930 of his early visits to St Ives, the first of which was in 1890, Charles Procter provided his analysis of how artists were ultimately responsible for spoiling the havens that they had unearthed. "An artist discovers a beauty spot, paints it, exhibits his pictures of it, and talks about his discovery to fellow artists, with the result that more, and still more, artists visit the place and portray its charms; more, and still more, pictures of the place appear on the walls of the Academy and other Exhibitions, and, as a result, the tourists, first in single spies and then in battalions, begin to arrive. And within a few years, the place has changed from an old world town into a popular holiday resort, tumble-down sail-lofts have become studios, garages and cafés, and the price of everything has gone up, and up, and up."[936]

This process is very easily discernible in the growth of tourism in St Ives. When discovering a new location full of paintable motifs, artists were often in two minds as to the extent to which they should publicize their find. On the one hand, they wanted time to capture on canvas as many of the motifs as possible, before other artists tackled similar subjects, but, on the other, the presence of fellow artists

---

935 See C Ranger-Gull, *Portalone*, London, 1904 at p.28 and *St Ives Times,* 1/10/1915.
936 Charles Procter, *Art, Talk and St Ives*, *St Ives Times*, 18/4/1930.

made the whole painting experience, and, in particular, the evenings in such out of the way places, much more convivial. In 1887, Anders Zorn's wife, Emma, having told her cousin of all St Ives' multifold attractions, commented that it had "one disadvantage - St Ives is a place for artists". Nevertheless, she was soon writing to inform her of good friendships made amongst the artist community, which had made their time in the town so enjoyable. However secretive artists were about their finds - and artists such as the American, Howard Russell Butler, found it terribly difficult not to boast to friends of new discoveries - , the word got out as soon as their paintings were exhibited. In the absence of tourist literature, artists were influenced in their choice of sketching destinations by paintings by other artists seen at exhibitions. As Butler himself put it, "It is under the inspiration of one Salon that subjects for the next are chosen".[937] Therefore, the not insignificant artist segment of the tourist crowds to St Ives was clearly inspired to visit by the works and reputation of their painting colleagues, and the extraordinary international element within the artist enclave in the town was due to the early and continuing successes of the colony in Paris. In this regard, Harry Robinson records how influential Anders Zorn's painting, *Fisherman, St Ives* (Plate 27), had been, as, having been bought by the French Government in 1888, it was hung in the Luxembourg Museum in Paris, where it had been viewed, with admiration, by successive intakes of students from around the world.[938] Indeed, it was probably this painting that had first attracted Terrick Williams and his friends from the Julian School in Paris, who included the Australian, Emanuel Phillips Fox, and the Dutchman, Sigisbert Bosch Reitz, to come to St Ives in the first place in 1890.

Capt Harry made reference, in his speech at the 1904 Mayoral Banquet, to the influence upon tourist numbers of the paintings of the St Ives artists hung on the walls of the Royal Academy. These certainly will have been very influential on members of London society and on the most enthusiastic art lovers from around the country, who made a special trip up to London to see the Academy show. Indeed, as early as 1889, it was noted in the local paper that the paintings by St Ives artists at the Academy the previous year had helped swell "the ranks of cultured folk" who came down year by year.[939] However, this was not the only location that paintings by St Ives artists could be seen, as it was traditional for Royal Academy exhibits to do the rounds of leading provincial Art Galleries, such as Manchester, Birmingham and Liverpool, in subsequent years. Furthermore, there were, at that time, a number of relatively newly-endowed Galleries, such as Nottingham and Rochdale, actively encouraging Cornish artists to exhibit with them. The exhibitions at Bristol were also a popular destination for Cornish paintings. Accordingly, these annual exhibitions introduced the attractions of St Ives to art lovers all around the country.

The St Ives artists also soon effected sales to leading public galleries as well, so that their work was on show not just for a few weeks, but for most of the year. For instance, by the date that Captain Harry was speaking, not only had the Chantrey Trustees bought work off Adrian Stokes and Arnesby Brown, but the Harris Museum at Preston had acquired Cornish works by Arnesby Brown, Arthur Meade and Fred Milner, Dudley Art Gallery had works by Alfred East and William Titcomb, Leeds Art Gallery had St Ives work by Adrian Stokes and Henry Detmold, the Walker Art Gallery, Liverpool had works by Marianne Stokes, Arnesby Brown and Moffat Lindner, Nottingham Castle Museum had works by William Titcomb and Marianne Stokes, Manchester Art Gallery had works by Arnesby Brown, Thomas Millie Dow and Greville Morris and Birmingham had acquired Alfred East's major Cornish work, *Hayle from Lelant*. Accordingly, the achievements of the St Ives artists, and their depictions of the locality's scenic attractions, were soon known nationally amongst educated members of society. Indeed, in describing the town in 1925, a reporter for the *Daily Mail* considered that his readers would best be able to visualise its attractions by reference to paintings seen. "Its picturesqueness is, indeed, actually incredible. It is as though all the pictures of quaint harbour scenes, of brown-faced fishermen in brown jumpers, and white boats in green water and stone piers, which have adorned the walls of the Royal Academy and the windows of picture shops in London in the last fifty years, had all become real in one moment before your eyes."[940]

Subsequent to Capt Harry's speech, largely through the efforts of Elmer Schofield, the St Ives colony also gained a significant reputation in America, not only through the Cornish paintings of a whole succession of talented American artists, who came to the town, but also because St Ives artists were hung with regularity at the prestigious Carnegie International Exhibition in Pittsburgh. This resulted, for instance, not only in increased tourist traffic from the States, but in fifty American artists working in St Ives in the summer of 1914. Accordingly, the artists played an exceptionally important role in making the beauties of St Ives internationally known and, in an age where photography was still often presented in black and white, they captured these scenes in glorious colour.

---

937 Letter from H.R.Butler dated 3/7/1885, Archives of American Art, Smithsonian Institution, Washington DC, Howard Russell Butler papers, Reel 1189.

938 See *St Ives as an Art Colony* in *Babcock's Historical Sketch of St Ives and District*, 1896.

939 *St Ives Weekly Summary*, 25/5/1889

940 Reproduced in *St Ives Times*, 7/8/1925.

5.1.4 The impact of the artists on the tourist type

Matthews commented, in 1892, that the average St Ives local did not really appreciate the aspects of the town that were so attractive to the educated London visitor. "He has never been onto Porthminster beach in his life, and would as soon think of swimming to Cardiff, as of walking to Zennor". Instead, "He (the native) thinks things would be tolerable if a nice new marine parade were built around the shore of the harbour, and the Island turned into public gardens, like they have at Penzance."[941] Not all locals were of such opinion, and the Town Council, when they decided to re-brand St Ives as a tourist centre in the late 1870s, had a vision of the town as a "health resort". However, given the poor reputation that St Ives had at such time for cleanliness, and the ever-present odours of the fishing industry, it is uncertain to what extent the Council would have been successful, without the artists, for it was their paintings and their presence that attracted visitors from "the ranks of cultured folk". The listings of types of guest that stayed at Hendra's Hotel, or even at Edith Ellis' holiday cottages, quoted in Chapter 2.3.2, reveal Cabinet ministers, Colonial governors, soldiers and sailors, engineers, diplomats, North Country manufacturers, newspaper editors, schoolmasters, ministers of religion of all denominations, University professors and such like. These were just the type of tourist that the Town Council had hoped to attract, rather than the mass tripper, and the special ambience that resulted from the presence of the art colony was of great appeal to such visitors.

James Uren White's unusual concept of including a Visitors' List in his newspaper clearly reflected the type of visitor that was being attracted to the town by the artists, for its purpose was to alert residents and other tourists of the presence of distinguished persons in the town, so that visiting cards could be dropped off at their lodgings. The concept would not have been appropriate in a mass tourist destination and the fact that it endured for over twenty-five years again signifies the distinctive type of resort that St Ives was in the period prior to the First World War.

As, due to the art colony, St Ives was successful at attracting the more refined tourist, the occasional demand for inappropriate "improvements" could be resisted, and it was the absence of the excesses of a typical seaside resort that made St Ives so attractive to the educated visitor. The Socialist campaigner,

Fig. 5.2 Sydney Carr   *St Ives Harbour at low tide*
(the late Derek Wintle/Andrew Eggleston)

---

941 J.H.Matthews, *A History of the Parishes of Saint Ives, Lelant, Towednack and Zennor in the County of Cornwall*, London, 1892 at p.371

Robert Blatchford, commented, "There is no vulgar Grand Hotel; no hideous iron pier; there are no advertisement hoardings; only one sign visible in all the view."[942] Harold Begbie, writing in *The Daily Mail*, made similar observations, "Tempest and tourist sweep over St Ives, but fail to shake it out of its immemorial calm. It invites the visitor to no sea-front, and provides the tripper with no spindly jetty. The town band is the sea, whose music rolls through the steep and narrow streets by day and night; and the only wandering minstrels are the white-breasted, blue-winged gulls, which wheel and circle over the huddled grey roofs from glistening dawn to majestic sunset."[943]

St Ives, with its plethora of sandy beaches, still had many attributes that would have appealed to what the Council perceived as "the vulgar type of tripper", but the presence of the artists, and of the tourists that they encouraged, raised the tone - and the prices - so that St Ives did not need to pander to them. Instead, Begbie felt that the tourists did not impinge on the atmosphere of the resort too much. "The visitors who overflow the place for certain months catch the tone of the village and become a part of its daily life. They, in their turn, strike no jarring note. You meet the men coming over the downs with their hands full of wild flowers, or sitting in cottage doors conversing with sea-wise fishermen. You see the woman wandering over the white sands, or sitting under the shade of the cliffs busy with needlework, while bare-legged children peer into translucent pools, half-hidden by weed-hung rocks."[944]

5.1.5   Artists as tourist attraction

In addition to alerting tourists to the beauty of the area, the artists became an attraction in themselves. Not only were they admired for their talents, but their free and easy lifestyle, away from many of the strictures of Victorian Society, was peculiarly fascinating, if not a little envied.

Given the vogue for *plein air* sketching, the artists were always visible around the town, and an article in the *Westminster Gazette* in 1896 confirms that Victorian tourists were also quite keen to indulge in a spot of celebrity-gazing, for it listed other locations where artists might be spotted.

> "The artists are chiefly in evidence in the morning. You may meet them in the narrow ancient streets, where one has constantly to plunge into doorways to avoid being crushed by the carts of the 'Jowders' (fish merchants). You may see the men of the painter colony, stalwart figures in tweed suits and knickerbockers, and the women (amongst them a Rossetti face crowned by a Tam o'Shanter cap) - you may see them diving into dark archways and up rough wooden steps to their studios, great wooden sheds hung with brown sails or fishing nets instead of tapestry...You may lunch with the artists at a simple restaurant which bears as its sign a palette and brushes; or, if you are lucky enough to get an introduction, you may spend an evening at their Club, which meets in a room above a carpenter's workshop, in a queer, Dutch-looking building, black with tar."[945]

The success of Show Day is another example of this trend. What all commentators on the event agreed was that Show Day in St Ives was far more interesting than Show Day in Newlyn, where, after 1895, the artists' paintings were all hung in the Passmore Edwards Gallery. What visitors to St Ives enjoyed, as much as, if not more than, the paintings on display, was the ability to enter the artists' private lairs. These were perceived, by some, as sacred spaces, where the artist worked for long hours with his model or his sketches, seeking the inspiration of his muse. The paint-stained beams and the general artistic clutter bore the imprint of individual personalities. The possible presence of preparatory sketches gave an insight into how the finished work had developed. The whole experience brought the visitors far closer to the artists than the sight of a well-framed canvas hung on a gallery wall, and the event became increasingly popular.

Unsurprisingly, once artists had come to be perceived as an attraction in themselves, there were people, who wanted to fraternise with them on a more regular basis, either by becoming annual visitors or by settling in the town. Accordingly, there grew up around the professional artists, a group comprising amateur artists and students, who had little prospect of making art a career, but who liked to role play. There were also writers, musicians and actors, who enjoyed the company of artists and sought to participate in their Club. As the correspondent to the *Westminster Gazette* noted in 1896, the combination of "simplicity of life, refinement and cultivated taste, love of outdoor nature, and freedom from convention" produced a most attractive lifestyle.[946]

---

942 Reproduced in *St Ives Weekly Summary*, 10/6/1905.
943 Reproduced in *St Ives Weekly Summary*, 22/7/1905.
944 ibid.
945 Reproduced in *St Ives Weekly Summary* 19/9/1896.
946 Reproduced in *St Ives Weekly Summary*, 19/9/1896.

Fig. 5.3 L.E.Comley   *William Titcomb sketching on Barnoon Hill*
(Titcomb family archive)

The presence of writers within the colony led to further promotion of the town's attributes, for, even in their works of fiction, the attractions of the locality were highlighted. Correspondents for newspapers and magazines were also effusive in their praise of the town's ambience. Robert Blatchford, the editor of *The Clarion* and leader of what became known as the Clarion movement, advocated convivial groups, such as cycling clubs, choirs, Socialist scouts and glee clubs. Accordingly, his article on St Ives in *The Clarion* in June 1905, in which he called it "the loveliest town in England", will have had an important influence on his readership. However, he did not detail things to see and do, but talked almost exclusively of colour, as if he was viewing the town simply from an artistic standpoint. "Conceive, then, a perfect day in spring, with a gentle breeze from the South-West. Conceive a wonderful English sky, glorious with noble ranges of sailing clouds; a wonder of snowy, downy whites, of delicate opal greys, of glistening luminous opal blues. Conceive a dimpled, rippled sea, splendid with all the glories of marine colour, from beryl green to regal purple. Conceive the clean crescents of white sand, and the bold grey cliffs strewn with flowers and crowned with olive-green verdure and graceful trees. Conceive the gray rocks, pencilled with lines of sage-green weed, and starred with crimson and orange coloured lichen. Conceive the ragged amber reefs, and the creamy, lacey foam, and the spouting, flashing spray. Conceive the broad blue bays and the bronze and silver and pearl and copper sails of the boats and trawlers. Conceive the gleam and glint of the soaring, sailing, hovering gulls - thousands of gulls. Conceive the misty distance where, in the purple deeps, you can see the breakers round the Herah Rocks swirling like blown snow. Conceive the harbour, with water of peacock blue, and a huddle of brown and yellow fishing craft...The place is perfect. The air is elastic, nimble: it smells of salt spray and sunshine, and woodsmoke and wild flowers. To breathe such air, to feel such sunshine, to look upon such beauty, to listen to the shrilling of the gulls, the growling bass of the surf, the swish and hiss of the green sea on the sand and shingles, thrills one with a feeling of gaiety, of happiness, of life."[947]

947 Reproduced in *St Ives Weekly Summary*, 10/6/1905.

Fig. 5.4 The Island, St Ives   (postcard, courtesy St Ives Trust Archive Study Centre)
This shows women carrying their washing down on to Porthmeor Beach to dry it on the rocks.
Washing can be seen already on the beach and on The Island in the background.
The studios fronting the beach can be seen on the right.

Just a month or so later, it was the turn of author Harold Begbie to extol the beauties of St Ives - this time in the *Daily Mail*. "In Cornish phrase, the little grey village in the midst of the bright blue waters 'belongs' to the sea. It strikes no jarring note. It suggests neither period nor style. It is one with ocean, an eternal place on eternal shores, very child of the great true mother at whose breast it lives tenderly, bravely, and so quietly". Like Blatchford, Begbie noted the range of colour seen in its surroundings, but his eye also fell on the fisherfolk. "Then, too, the people themselves make for colour and gladness. The men in russet-coloured jumpers, and the women in pink linen dresses, fill the streets with freshness. The lack of gardens means that the washing must be hung in the streets, and as the housewife of St Ives is apparently never weary of the washtub, it comes to pass that all the narrow courts and alleys are hung with gaily coloured garments, like bunting hung for the welcome of a hero."[948] Such word pictures of St Ives, reproduced in the national press, again reinforced the reputation of the town, as a holiday destination for the more refined tourist.

The fascination with the artists themselves did not diminish, and a visitor in the 1920s, for whom the town was "a veritable gem of beauty, and inexhaustible in its attractions to artists", felt that what was particularly special was "the art atmosphere of St Ives". "The presence of other artists, who have made a success of their work, sustains and encourages the young aspirant. Many a morning as you wander through the narrow alleys of Down-along, you may meet a figure, dressed almost as casually as the fisherfolk, hastening along, a canvas tucked under her arm. You turn to your companion and whisper, 'that is the brilliant M. whose pictures hang in the Academy' - or that plainly-dressed elderly woman, who goes in to make her purchases at the butchers, with a crowd of less-gifted housewives, you recognise as one of the foremost water-colour artists of the day."[949] This ability to mingle easily with well-known names and to enjoy a healthy, cultured existence in an outstanding beauty spot had led St Ives, by this juncture, to become a favoured retirement venue, not only for practitioners of one of the Fine Arts, but for military personnel and all "ranks of cultured folk". It was the presence of the artists that initiated this trend, and they are seldom given credit for the impact that they had on the type of tourist destination that St Ives became.

5.1.6 The impact of the artist postcard and poster

The early 1900s saw the birth and flowering of the postcard industry. In 1899, what became the standard size of 5.5" x 3.5" was set, but, at this juncture, the whole of one side had to be devoted to the address, leaving the image and the message to be squeezed onto the other. In 1902, however, the 'divided back'

948 Reproduced in *St Ives Weekly Summary*, 22/7/1905.
949 D P Sedding, *St Ives Times*, 14/1/1921.

design was approved by the Post Office, so that the message and the address could be put on one side, whilst the whole of the other side could be devoted to the image. As a result, the postcard craze took off and, in 1908-9, for example, 860 million cards passed through the post in Britain.[950]

The postcard meant that, for the first time, colour images of St Ives became widely available and this was soon recognised as a marvellous way to promote the town's tourist industry. Many painters, aware of the stigma of 'trade', were uneasy about getting involved in such commercial activities, but two St Ives artists saw it as a wonderful opportunity to raise their profile in an unprecedented way. I have already considered the comic postcards of Edmund Fuller (see Chapter 2.7.1), but these had no obvious St Ives connections to encourage tourists. However, the postcards of Frank Lewis Emanuel (1865-1948) were colour reproductions of his own paintings of the town, and so brought St Ives art into many new homes.

Born in Kensington, Emanuel was the eldest son of Lewis Emanuel, a London solicitor, and his wife, Julia. He studied at University College London, the Slade School and Julian's in Paris and he first visited St Ives with his parents in 1892-3, exhibiting at the Royal Academy in 1893 *An Old Cornishman*.[951] He returned to St Ives in the early 1900s, for he contibuted *A City of the Sea - St Ives Bay* to the 1902 Whitechapel Exhibition. It was clearly during this visit that Emanuel completed the sketches of the town that were published by Raphael Tuck & Sons in an early series of postcards called *Quaint Corners*. In another series, *Picturesque Cornwall*, he depicted the activities of the fishermen, both in the harbour and out in the Bay, particularly during the seine fishing season. Indeed, a number of his paintings, such as *Waiting for Pilchards* (Plate 33), were reproduced on 'undivided back' postcards and thus pre-date 1902, showing that he spotted the commercial potential of the new medium at the very outset. Emanuel went on to become one of the most prolific of the early postcard artists, producing similar series featuring other seaside art colonies in this country and France, but nowhere else did he find as many subjects as the dozen or so that he reproduced from St Ives.

Fig. 5.5 Frank Emanuel
Ebb-Tide, St Ives Harbour
(postcard)

Fig. 5.6 Frank Emanuel
Getting Ready for Pilchards
(postcard)

---

950 See A.W.Coysh, *The Dictionary of Picture Postcards in Britain 1894-1939*, Woodbridge, 1984 at p.9.

951 In 1892, he stayed at Albany House, St Ives with his parents, joined the Arts Club and exhibited *Sand and Surf* at the RBA. He was also present at the Arts Club in February 1893, took part in the Carnival Masquerade that month, and contributed a large work to the Country Fisheries Exhibition in Truro that July.

Fig. 5.7 Frank Emanuel
Outside Staircase, St Ives
(postcard)

Fig. 5.8 Frank Emanuel
In the Fishermen's Quarter, St Ives
(undivided back postcard)

Whereas prolific postcard producers, such as Alfred Robert Quinton, Harold Lawes, G.F.Nicholls, Charles Hannaford, Walter Hayward Young ("Jotter") and Martin Anderson ("Cynicus"), produced a number of cards featuring depictions of St Ives scenes, the only other resident of the colony in this period to have his work reproduced in postcard form was the little known artist, Yarker Richardson. Richardson only exhibited on Show Day in 1908, but dated works place him in St Ives from 1902 to 1913 and he produced a series of St Ives scenes for Frith's. Another artist, who had several of his major paintings of the St Ives fisherfolk reproduced as postcards, was Edward King, but, as he only worked in St Ives in the mid-1890s, it is not clear when these were produced. One card features his magnificent large work, *Sale of Herrings* (Front Cover), now in the Town collection. In the 1930s, the potential of the postcard as an advertisement for both the town, and the artist, was recognised by John Park, Leonard Richmond and, in particular, Herbert Truman, who produced over sixty cards of Cornish and Devon scenes.[952]

The railway continued to be the principal means of visiting the town and, in 1922, the Great Western Railway Company opened a competition for the most attractive poster advertising the Cornish Riviera. This was before 'commercial art' of this nature had been made acceptable by several Royal Academicians producing designs, at the instigation of former Olsson student, Norman Wilkinson, for London Midland & Scottish Railway Company in 1924. Nevertheless, Borlase Smart, seeing the potential of such posters, suggested that artists in St Ives should submit designs and, in April that year, an exhibition was held in his studio, featuring the artwork submitted by himself, John Park, Edmund Fuller, George Bradshaw, Francis Roskruge, Percy and Marjorie Ballance, Pauline Hewitt, Dossie Cooke and a Miss Webb. Smart was, at that juncture, a Town Councillor and, when his colleagues on the Council viewed the exhibition, Edward Daniel remarked that "this was yet another instance of the Art Colony helping the town of St Ives, which they had done for so many years".[953] It is not known whether any of the artists were successful on this occasion, but Smart did have one of his designs accepted by GWR for a poster advertising St Ives, Carbis Bay and Lelant, and, in the 1930s, the heyday of the railway poster, classic designs, featuring St Ives, were created by Leonard Richmond and Herbert Truman, which are still reproduced now.

Whereas the artists' paintings would only have been seen by a limited number of educated members of society, their postcards and posters were seen by a much wider public, leading to the further development of St Ives as a tourist destination.

---

952 It is interesting that artist photographers, such as Lanyon, Douglas and Carr, did not exploit the postcard market.

953 *St Ives Times*,26/4/1922.

COMBATTING 'THE SPIRIT OF MR GRADGRIND'

5.2.1   Introduction

The artists were always keenly aware of what it was about the town that made it so attractive to them and, occasionally, they were moved to take action, if there were development proposals that they realised would not only impact severely on their own enjoyment of the town's ambience, but also prove very off-putting for the more refined type of tourist that the town hoped to attract. Indeed, when explaining his decision to stand as a Councillor in 1898, Louis Grier commented, "The spirit of Mr Gradgrind is too much with us in municipal affairs, and a little aesthetic leaven is very desirable".[954] The following are examples of occasions, when the artists felt compelled to protest as a body.

5.2.2   The Glanville letter

Grier's comment came at a time when the artists started to become alarmed at some of the developments that were taking place in the town. A whole succession of new terraces were being built in Up-along, whilst Lord Cowley was planning an estate of some seventy bungalows on land adjoining 'Treloyhan Manor'. As many of the artists were well acquainted with Lord Cowley's property agent, Reginald Glanville, as they themselves rented studios or homes off his Lordship, they decided to write him a letter, expressing their concerns. It was sent with a covering letter from William Brooke, who, as a former architect, may have been one of the initiators of the protest. Interestingly, the Mayor and a number of Councillors appended their signatures to the letter, fully endorsing its contents. With such leading figures clearly feeling unable to write themselves to Glanville in such terms, the letter, written on Arts Club paper, and dated 26th November 1898, is, accordingly, a remarkable example of the artists taking the lead in municipal affairs.

"Sir, we, the undersigned, Artists now residing in St Ives, watch its growth with interest and considerable apprehension. Artists and visitors are drawn to St Ives, not by its beautiful sea alone; but by its unlikeness to other watering places. This distinction, we cannot but feel, is in danger of being lost through hastily conceived building schemes, and thoughtless removal of characteristic features. We would urge upon you as the representative of large landowners here, that there is a future before St Ives as a place of all-the-year-round resort by well to do people in search of health and change, if only those things be preserved which now attract them, and which they can get nowhere else. We would suggest that it is for these people, who turn from other watering places in search of something quite different, that provision should be made by building; and that the erection of long terraces and rows of lodging houses will not attract, but assuredly repel them; and make of St Ives a poor rival, (and that for a month or two in the year only) of Newquay, Ilfracombe and other watering places in the West of England. Our love for the place, to the growth of which we have contributed, must be our excuse for addressing the landowners in St Ives and those who represent them. We would also beg you to use your power and influence to prevent the destruction of objects of natural beauty and interest, - trees, and granite boulders - and especially those gnarled and wind twisted thorn trees which help to give this country its distinctive character, we are Sir, your obedient servants - Thos Millie Dow, F W Brooke, Lowell Dyer, Julius Olsson, H Harewood Robinson, Adrian Stokes, C G Beale Adams, Fred Milner, Marianne Stokes, Mary Lovett Cameron, Edward Fuller Maitland, M D Harewood Robinson, L Kirkpatrick, J Noble Barlow, Moffat Lindner, Emma Chadwick, Francis B Chadwick, Bertha King, E E Mainwaring, Percy Mason, A K Baird-Smith, M E Meade, Louis Grier, John M Bromley, Arthur Meade, S C Bosch Reitz, W H Y Titcomb, Stuart **Hobkirk,** J H Titcomb, W B Fortescue, Arnesby Brown, Mia Brown, J R Weguelin, G Walter Jevons, John C Douglas, S E Whitehouse, H M Maynard

We the undersigned residents desire to associate ourselves with the Artists of St Ives in the above letter - R S Read, Mayor, Edward Hain jr, George J A Staff, Geo B Rosewall, William Trewhella, J M Nicholls, W Tolmie Tresidder, Thos Row Harry"

---

954 *St Ives Weekly Summary*, 10/12/1898. Mr Gradgrind was the philistine teacher in Charles Dickens' *Hard Times*.

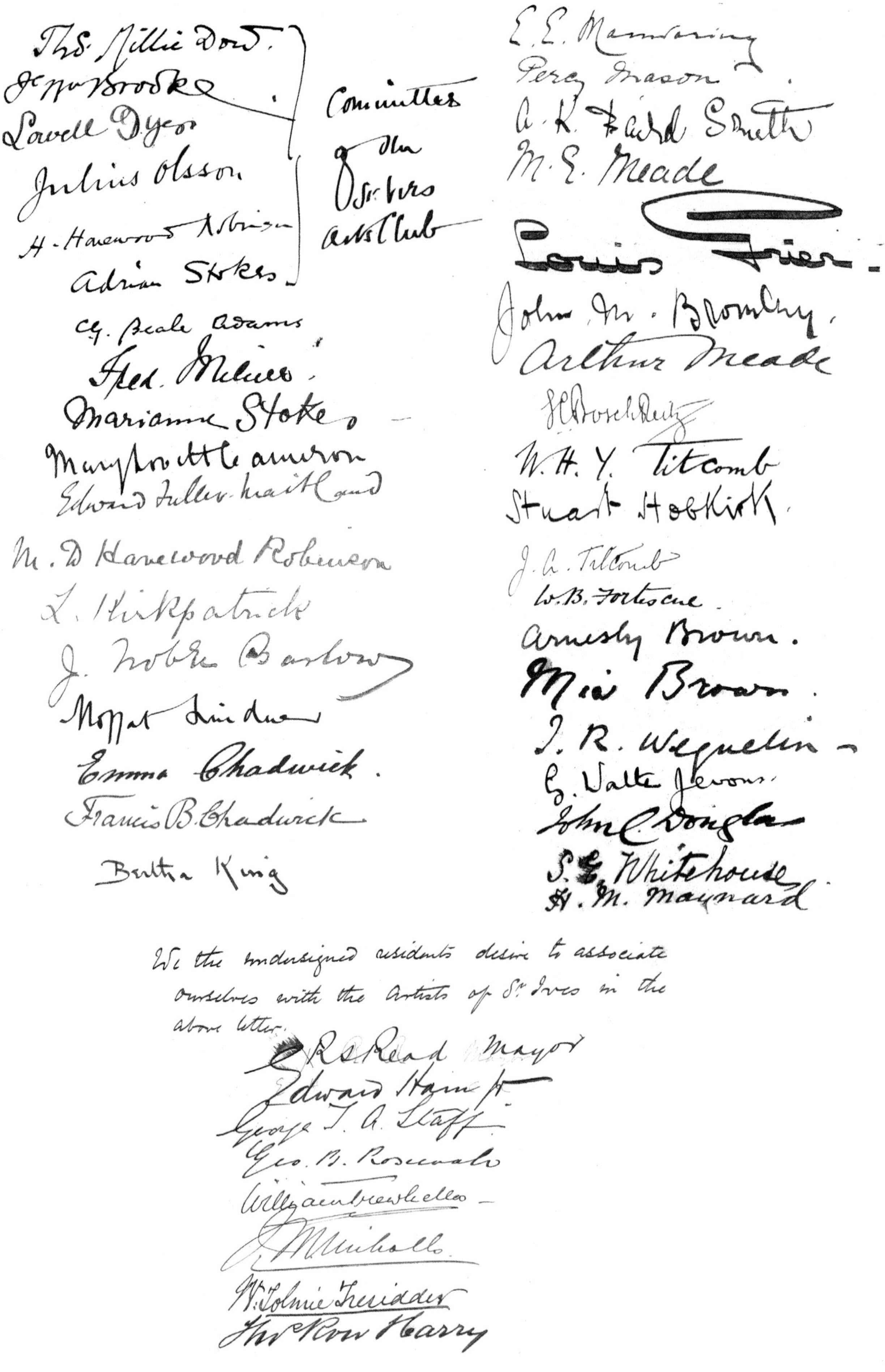

Fig. 5.9 Signatories to the 1898 letter to Reginald Glanville (St Ives Arts Club)

The artists admitted that their sole justification for writing in such terms was their "love of the place, to the growth of which we have contributed". The letter emphasized the uniqueness of St Ives, leading to its status as an "all-the-year-round resort", and the considerable commercial risks of jeopardising this by making it only appealing to summer trippers. Whilst largely wholly general in scope, the removal of native thorn trees and granite boulders during developments had clearly irked at least one artistic eye. Whilst Lord Cowley did not proceed with his development, this was more to do with the receipt of £10,000 from Edward Hain for the land, rather than the artists' letter!

5.2.3   The threat to convert St Ives into a china clay port

After the War, as the pressure for progress increased, there were other occasions when the artists felt compelled to make a public proclamation of their views. As the former Borough Accountant, Edgar Skinner, commented, there was little point in "improvements" that "improved away the unique quality that warrants the advertising of St Ives on the walls of the Royal Academy and other picture exhibitions all the world over".[955] However, the proposal that alarmed the artists the most was one to allow china clay to be loaded in the harbour. This was put forward by the Porthia China Clay Company, then run by Dennis Shipwright, a war hero and Member of Parliament, who was the first husband of Sir Edward Hain's daughter, Kate. Given the poverty in the town, this appealed to some sections of the Council as a way of increasing prosperity, seemingly totally oblivious of the detrimental impact that it would have, not merely on the fishing industry, but more importantly on the tourist trade. A group of artists wrote a strong letter to the local paper, arguing that "the whole character of the town will be changed and, instead of being a place beloved by the visitors who come here over and over again, it will become a place to be avoided."[956] Greville Mattheson also wrote a piece in the paper, predicting that St Ives would become a white-dust entombed ghost town. Despite the significant contacts of the Hain family, the proposal was eventually dropped.

5.2.4   Slum housing - refurbishment versus demoliton

By far the bitterest dispute between the artists and the Council concerned the latter's Five Year Slum Clearance Scheme, which was encouraged and approved by the Ministry of Health in the early 1930s. As the number of houses potentially affected by this plan was nearly one hundred and fifty, the artists were very concerned that the quaint characteristics of the old town would be destroyed completely, to the severe detriment of the tourist industry, and wanted to ensure that, where-ever possible, houses should be re-conditioned, rather than demolished. Somewhat arrogantly, and certainly tactlessly, Borlase Smart suggested, in a letter to the Council, that two members of the St Ives Society of Artists should be available to advise on new building plans, so that the character of the old town be retained as far as possible.[957] The involvement in this debate of the artists, amateurs in such matters, intensely annoyed Councillor Sullivan, a local teacher with strong socialist views, who was closely involved with the plan, and he included an extraordinary tirade against them in a letter to the local paper.

"These Don Quixotes who tilt at windmills, these Oswald Moseleys in miniature, are not concerned with facts. They are not concerned as to how a large number of their fellow citizens live. In their prejudiced class-conscious minds, anything is good enough for the working man. Let them keep their hovels, they say, so that we can come down now and then from our £1,000 mansions and paint the outsides of these dwellings. We do not desire to paint the interiors, they say. We do not wish to paint the leaky roofs, the crumbling walls, the uneven walls, the non-ventilated bedrooms, in which five or six or seven fellow human beings toss every night in uneasy slumber. We shall not paint a picture of that woman creeping out stealthily in the dead of night to throw an accumulation of filth on the nearest beach, because she has not even a closet in which she can dispose of it. And so in order to please these so-called artists, this Council must refuse to carry out the behests of the Ministry of Health. It must refuse to re-house these people in decent homes, at a cost of something less than half a crown a week, and it must condemn fellow creatures to live under conditions which they themselves would not consider fit for a dog or cat to live in."[958]

Not unnaturally, the letter, which went on to label the artists "non-entities", caused a furore, and Councillor Sullivan was eventually forced to apologise. However, the debate concerning re-conditioning or demolition rumbled on throughout the decade, and the artists even arranged for the Royal Institute

---

955 *St Ives Times*, 6/11/1925.

956 *St Ives Times*, 28/3/1924. Artists appending their name to the letter included Herbert Lanyon, Frank Moore, Arthur Meade, Louis Sargent, John Bromley, Arthur Hayward and Mary Williams. Other names were R Edwards, Cecil Magnus, M.M.Goosey and C.S.T.Fowler.

957 Extract from Minutes of Society in 1933.

958 *St Ives Times*, 29/9/1934.

Fig. 5.10 Herbert Truman   *Pudding Bag Lane*   (postcard)
Truman has depicted the street as being far wider than it was.

of British Architects to give free advice on the question. In the end, many houses were demolished, but the artists had ensured that the debate was held and that, where-ever possible, old houses were saved. One of the greatest losses was the complete destruction of Pudding Bag Lane, beloved by artists and visitors alike, to make way for a car park. A visitor in March 1936, having spotted, at the Porthmeor Gallery of the St Ives Society of Artists, a painting by Herbert Truman of the street, showing "bright sunshine gleaming on ancient white walls, and red-faced fishwives gossiping", went in search of the place, but was stunned to find that "the hammers of the housebreakers have done their work. The white-walled cottage, which inspired Herbert Truman's picture, is now a mass of broken stones.....An old woman was gazing upon the ruins. 'Shameful', she muttered".[959] The story not only demonstrates the sense of outrage at the decision shared by artist, visitor and local alike, but also neatly gives an example of the manner in which paintings could inspire visitors.

The saga concerning slum housing demonstrated that 'art and town' were not as close as they had been in the pre-War period, when the artists numbered leading dignitaries amongst their closest friends. Whereas, previously, local Councillors were fully appreciative of what the artists had contributed to the development of the town and its tourist industry, those in the 1930s wanted to modernise St Ives, so that it could compete with other flourishing holiday resorts. As the artists saw that this would impact on its original appeal, they became considered to be reactionary and their past contributions forgotten. Accordingly, in one bust-up with the Town Clerk in 1934, Borlase Smart felt compelled to write, "The art colony has advertised this town for the last fifty years throughout the world and by comparision with which the propaganda of the Publicity Committee of the Council and the Chamber of Commerce is a mere pin-prick, and such a half-century of endeavour has not cost the town one penny."[960] At a time, when the contribution of the early artists has again been forgotten, it is a point worth re-affirming.

---

959 *Passing of Pudding Bag Lane, St Ives Times*, 13/3/1936.
960 *St Ives Times*, 7/9/1934.

SUMMARY OF IMPACT

In summary, let me draw together, in brief outline, the various ways in which I have demonstrated that the artists and the local community impacted on each other.

5.3.1   Commercial aspects

The artists helped significantly to convert St Ives from a failing industrial town into a prime tourist destination, dealing principally with a wealthy, cultured class of visitor. They transformed the tourist season into a year-round industry, benefitting, in particular, the local landladies. They provided locals with a variety of different employment opportunities, ranging from full-time domestic servants and cooks, through to casual helpers and errand-boys and, of course, models. They also improved, beyond measure, the business of many local shopkeepers, and, although this raised prices, which did lead to resentment from those unable to benefit from the artists' presence, there would have been considerably greater hardship, particularly during the winter months, without them. Whilst Ranger-Gull lampooned the artists, who "found pleasure in the vague and splendid imagination that they were the Lords Bountiful" of St Ives, such an attitude was perhaps understandable, on occasion.[961] The artists also had their own particular requirements, as regards housing, studios, painting materials and exhibition space, which a number of local entrepreneurs were able to exploit most profitably.

5.3.2   Physical aspects

The artists ensured that quaint aspects of St Ives were retained for far longer than would have been the case, if St Ives had become a standard tourist resort, for their own artistic appreciation of these dovetailed with that of the more refined tourist that they, and the town in general, sought to attract. They also did their best to ensure that these features were not adversely effected by the developments necessary to cater for the increased tourist traffic for which they were partly responsible. Their own requirements for homes had some impact on the type of new housing that was erected, and several of them built or developed properties of novel design that became significant features in the townscape. This aspect of the artists' presence has not been appreciated at all in the past and there has been no attempt to list any of the artists' former homes. Whilst it is now too late to save 'Bellier's Croft' (see Fig. 5.11), does not the current state of 'Chy-an-Porth' (Fig. 5.12) raise concerns? In addition, the artists' requirement for studios in the fishing quarter led to many industrial buildings receiving a new lease of life, preventing their demolition, and the Porthmeor area in particular, was transformed from an industrial section of the town into an art enclave, featuring several purpose built blocks of studios. Accordingly, the surviving Porthmeor Studios block can now be seen to be of immense historical importance.

Fig. 5.11 'Bellier's Croft' after the fire in 2007 that resulted in its demolition
(St Ives Trust Archive Study Centre)

---

961   C.Ranger-Gull, *Portalone*, London, 1904 at p.125-6.

Fig. 5.12 A very overgrown 'Chy-an-Porth' in 2009

5.3.3 Cultural aspects

The artists were not just a small segment of the population that lived in their own exclusive world. Particularly due to the vogue for *plein air* sketching, art became a subject that could not be ignored and the locals, even if not actively involved as models, took an interest in what the artists produced and how they produced it. Discussions between artists and locals as to their objectives fostered novel patterns of thought. However, the artists had a much wider influence on cultural activities, by stimulating greater interest in music, drama and literature and by promoting greater variety in entertainments. Whilst having talent as serious musicians and actors, their most marked initiative was the introduction of humour and fun into performances. They put on farces, blacked themselves up as minstrels, sang glees, told humorous stories and put on the first Carnival Masquerades and *tableaux vivants* that St Ives had witnessed. All these performances were for worthy local causes and so the artists not only entertained the townsfolk, but won thanks and respect from the beneficiaries. They also played significant roles in the golf, cricket and tennis clubs, encouraging the development of those sports, and they were always generous in the provision of prizes. Their lifestyles may have been frowned upon by some, but, generally, their presence was considered to have encouraged greater broadness of vision on the part of the townsfolk. I have mentioned, in particular, the decided impact that I feel that they had on local attitudes to the place of women in society and animal welfare.

5.3.4 Local input

It would be wrong to suggest that the benefits of the inter-relationship between the artists and the locals flowed only in one direction. The artists owed a huge debt to entrepreneurs, such as James Lanham (and later Martin Cock), who satisfied all their painting (and many other) needs and organised an exhibition venue for them. Robert Toy built them some fine houses, and George Williams and William Paynter were prepared to speculate by erecting purpose-built studios. James Uren White and Martin Cock gave them exposure in the local press, and dignitaries such as Edward Hain, Captain Harry, Edward Boase and Robert Sawle Read were endlessly supportive of their efforts. In many instances, locals were forced to accept paintings as payments in kind from hard-up artists, but the benefits that the colony brought to the town were generally recognised. Accordingly, true partnerships developed between artist and entrepreneur, and between the artists as a body and the community at large, for the common good. Unheralded before, it is a fascinating story that reflects great credit on both sides, and deserves to be more widely appreciated. In fact, the achievements of the art colony in the art world cannot be properly assessed without an awareness and appreciation of the inter-relationship between the colony and the community.

THE ST IVES ARTS CLUB - LIST OF OFFICERS (1890-1930)

YEAR	PRESIDENT	SECRETARY	TREASURER
1890	Adrian Stokes	Harewood Robinson	E W Blomefield
1891	L.Stephen/A. Stokes	Harewood Robinson	E W Blomefield
1892	Harewood Robinson	Louis Grier	E W Blomefield
1893	Lowell Dyer	Harewood Robinson	E W Blomefield
1894	Lowell Dyer	Harewood Robinson	E W Blomefield/William Titcomb
1895	Julius Olsson	Harewood Robinson	Arthur Meade
1896	Adrian Stokes	Harewood Robinson	William Titcomb
1897	Harewood Robinson	J Elgar Russell/Julius Olsson	William Titcomb
1898	Millie Dow	William Brooke	Lowell Dyer
1899	Moffat Lindner	William Brooke	Lowell Dyer
1900	William Titcomb	W B Fortescue	Lowell Dyer
1901	Julius Olsson	Harewood Robinson	W B Fortescue
1902	Arthur Meade	Harewood Robinson	W B Fortescue
1903	Allan Deacon	Harewood Robinson	T A Lang
1904	Arnesby Brown	Allan Deacon	T A Lang
1905	Fred Milner	Allan Deacon	T A Lang
1906	T A Lang	Allan Deacon	J M Bromley
1907	W B Fortescue	Charles Marriott	J M Bromley
1908	Charles Marriott	J H Titcomb	J M Bromley
1909	Julius Olsson	J H Titcomb	J M Bromley
1910	J H Titcomb	Beale Adams	J M Bromley
1911	Moffat Lindner	William Lloyd	J M Bromley/Sargent/C F Barry
1912	Moffat Lindner	William Lloyd	T A Lang
1913	Arthur Meade	R L Hutton	T A Lang
1914	Moffat Lindner	Frank Moore	T A Lang
1915	Moffat Lindner	Fred Milner	Lowell Dyer
1916	Moffat Lindner	Fred Milner	Lowell Dyer
1917	Moffat Lindner	Fred Milner	Lowell Dyer
1918	Lowell Dyer	Edgar Skinner	Dr Adam MacVie
1919	William Lloyd	Edgar Skinner	Dr Adam MacVie
1920	Arthur Meade	Borlase Smart	Herbert Lanyon
1921	Frank Moore	Borlase Smart	Herbert Lanyon
1922	Frank Moore	Rolf Bennett	Herbert Lanyon
1923	Herbert Lanyon	Frank Moore/George Bradshaw	Norman Cooke
1924	Herbert Lanyon	Francis Roskruge	Norman Cooke
1925	John Douglas	Francis Roskruge	Norman Cooke
1926	Moffat Lindner	Francis Roskruge	Norman Cooke
1927	Francis Roskruge	Stewart Darmady	General Blumberg
1928	Francis Roskruge	Stewart Darmady	General Blumberg
1929	J H Titcomb	Stewart Darmady	General Blumberg
1930	George Bradshaw	Stewart Darmady	General Blumberg

LADIES COMMITTEE

1904	Deacon, Dyer, Grier, Meade, Lindner, Olsson
1905	Milner, Dow, Lang, Rosenberg, Deacon
1906	Deacon, Milner, Douglas, S E Whitehouse
1907	Douglas, Fortescue, Deacon, Lang, Milner, Bromley
1908	Douglas, Marriott, Hichens, Fortescue, Dyer, Horn
1909	Olsson, Dow, Robinson, Meade, Hartley, Douglas
1910	Hartley, Milner, Meade, Dyer, Douglas, Lindner
1911	Douglas, Dyer, Barry, Lang, S E Whitehouse
1912	Douglas, Lang, Lloyd, Milner, S E Whitehouse
1913	Meade, Lloyd, Douglas, D Whitehouse, Praetorius, Hutton
1914	Lloyd, Douglas, Lang, Milner, S E Whitehouse, Hutton
1915-6	Milner, Fortescue, Cameron, Hutton, D Whitehouse, Douglas, Parkyn
1917	Cameron, Milner, Douglas, Hutton, D Whitehouse

APPENDIX B

SELECTION OF ARTISTS TAKING PART IN 1892-3 CARNIVAL MASQUERADES

Member	1892 Dance	1893 Dance
Eardley Blomefield	St Ives - 60 years ago	Pierrot
Sigisbert Bosch Reitz	Venetian Noble - 16th century	Artillery Captain
Arnesby Brown	Twin Baby - Blue	Australian Planter - evening dress
Rose Cooper	'Black and White'	Bulgarian
William Croxford		Chinaman
Miss Jessie Davidson[962]	Turkish Lady	Evening Dress
William Dickson	Twin Baby - Pink	Clown
Mrs Dickson	Ivy	Narcissus
Lowell Dyer	Blue Beard	Astrologer
Mrs Dyer	Fatema	Snake Charmer
William Eadie		Highland Chief
Mrs Eadie	Little Sister of the Poor	Scotia
Miss Mia Edwards (later Brown)		Dancing Girl
Frank Emanuel		French Cook
Stanhope Forbes	Blue Beard	
Mrs Elizabeth Forbes	'Green Tea'	
Edmund G Fuller	Cow Boy	Greek
Mrs Fuller	Winter	Snowdrop
Miss Fuller	Calliope	Beatrice
General Fuller (father of EGF)		Spirit of 1993
Mr H.T.Geoghegan[963]	French Chef	
Mrs Emily Latham Greenfield	Terpsichore	Sorceress
Louis Grier	'Black and White'	Turk
Miss Blanche Douglas Hamilton	Haidee	
William Hebblethwaite	Garibaldian	Croatian Peasant
Walter Jevons	Officer of the Guard - Louis XV	Crown and Punch
Martin Gwilt Jolley	Mendicant Monk	
Mrs Gwilt Jolley	Red Cross Nurse	The Missing Word
Albert Lang		Uniform Royal Engineers
Sydney Laurence		Breton Peasant Girl
Mrs Alexandrina Laurence		The Sunrise
Edward Lingwood		16th century Court Dress
Miss Emily Little[964]	Dame Primrose	Study in Grey
Mrs Amy Lluellyn	Directoire	Poudree
John Chadwick Lomax	Neapolitan Match Vendor	Yeoman of the Guard and Judy
Arthur Meade		Ancient Greek
Mrs Meade		18th century
Miss Jessie Morison (later Titcomb)	Pompadour	Puritan Lady
Charles Muirhead	The Bogie Man	
Percy Northcote		Mendicant
Julius Olsson	Fire Brigade Man	Venetian Gondolier
Mrs Katherine Olsson	Swedish Peasant	
Will Osborn	Franciscan Monk	
Mrs Pansy Rainey (née Grier)	Miranda	Fate Thalia
Harry Robinson	Mephistocles	
Mrs Dorothy Robinson	English Lady - 14th century	
Miss Gertrude Rosenberg	My Great Aunt	St Eia
Adrian Stokes		Barrister
Mrs Marianne Stokes		Roman
Mr A G Folliott Stokes	Le Grand Seigneur	
Mrs Folliott Stokes	Red Cross Nurse	Marie Antoinette
Mrs Vesta Simmons	Judith	
William Titcomb	Spahi	
Miss Tully		Euterpe - Goddess of Music[965]
Miss West[966]	Poudree	
Miss West	Kate Greenaway	
Mrs W Whitehouse		Balchristie
Miss Whitehouse		Moonlight
Miss Whitehouse		Marigold

---

962 Liverpool artist, who exhibited on Show Day and at the RA in 1892 and with the Cornish Artists at Nottingham in 1894.

963 Visitor in 9/1891, joined Golf Club 12.1891 and exhibited Show Day 1892. Living in West Kensington when made donation to Flood Relief Fund in 1894. A Miss Geoghegan also took part.

964 Former Bushey student. Exhibited Show Day 1895 and noted as ratepayer for a small studio on Harbour Beach until 1898.

965 Possibly the well-known Canadian artist, Miss Sydney Strickland Tully (1860-1911).

966 The three Misses West - Alice Lizzie West (b.1852, fl.1889-1915), Maud Astley West (b.1858, fl.1880-1916) and Marian May West (b.1871) - daughters of the publican, James West, from Poplar, London, were visitors with him from 9/1891. Alice was a figure and domestic painter, whilst Maud was a watercolour flower painter, who had taught at St Bees in Cumberland. Both exh. at RA & SWA. Marian was an art student. They were visitors again in 10/1892, 9/1895 & 9/1896.

APPENDIX C

SELECTION OF PUBLIC ENTERTAINMENTS TO WHICH THE ARTISTS CONTRIBUTED

Year	Month	Event	Participants
1890	December	*Trial by Jury* performed at St John's Hall, Penzance	"Mr Louis Grier's Company". Featured Wyly and Louis Grier and Edwin Harris, E Ireland Blackburne and Thomas Gotch. L Grier director and stage manager.
1891	December	Boxing Night Concert	'Merchant of Venice' - Bosch Reitz (stage manager). Incl. F Stokes, Robinson, W Titcomb, Meade, Jessie Morison & sister, Also Lanyon (piano).
1892	April (Easter Monday)	Parish Church Club (for piano fund)	Stage design - Jolley, Stage manager F. Stokes. Tableaux (featuring Jevons and Mrs Greenfield) incl. Dorothy Robinson's *Too Late*. Also sketch *Lodgings to Let* incl.Fuller, A Richardson.
	December	Boxing Night Concert (for Library)	"Freezing A Mother in law" incl. F Stokes, E G Fuller, A Talmage. Variety from 'St Ives Nigger Minstrels' - nearly all artists.
1893	December	Boxing Night Concert	Meade (songs), Robinson (recitation)
1894	February	Entertainment (for Fire Brigade)	Robinson (piano solo & recitation), Meade & Lang (vocal duet), Richardson (comic lecture) Ramsdell (mandolin solo)
1895	December	Entertainment (for Fire Brigade)	Comedy *Our Boys* performed by artists in Porthmeor Studios following Meade's studio fire
1896	November	Parish Church Club	Misses Baird-Smith (mandoline/guitar duets), Douglas (recitations), Russell, Manning, Miss Wiggins (songs).
	December	Boxing Night Concert (for Fire Brigade)	Killmister (piano - own composition *Quick March*), Artists' Glee Singers (Meade, W & J Titcomb, Milner, Lang & Dow), with Robinson (conductor) and L Kirkpatrick (accompanist). Fortescue (cello solo). Mrs Adams (piano solos). Douglas (recitation).
1897	January	Variety Entertainment	Arranged by Killmister, Scenery by Ludby & Fuller; Mrs Sydney Lee (violin solos), Killmister (piano - own compositions), Drama - *The Art of Never Forgetting* - Ludby Comedy written by Ludby - *In the Springtime of Youth* - Ludby, Laurence, Dobbs, Bromley
	April	Entertainment (for Library)	Killmister (piano solo), Sarah Trevorrow (violin solo); Blackden (mandolin solo); Mrs Lee (violin); Mrs Adams (piano); Russell, Meade, KIllmister (songs); Douglas (recitation) Tableaux - all the above plus Wynne, Titcomb, Dobbs,Carleton Wiggins' daughters, Mrs Greenfield & Misses Whitehouse, Rosenberg, Richardson, Horn, Wynne & Carr.
	December	Entertainment (for St Ives Nursing Association)	Music: Killmister (piano solo), Sarah Trevorrow (violin solo), Hely Smith (flute solo), Douglas (recitation), Blackden and Mrs Adams (mandolin/guitar duet). Comediatta: *The Journey's End* - Hely Smith, Russell, Alexandrina Laurence. Tableaux: Misses Wing, D Whitehouse, Mrs G Talmage, Bromley, Laurence.
	December	Boxing Night Concert (for Fire Brigade)	St Ives Orchestral Society (conducted by Robinson), Sarah Trevorrow (violin solo); Meade (song), Mrs Adams & Fortescue (duet - piano/cello), Meade, Milner, W Titcomb, Brooke & Lang (song, conducted by Robinson).

Year	Month	Event	Participants
1898	February	Lelant Feast Entertainment (for Church Heating Fund)	'St Ives Glee Club' (incl. Meade, Lang, Dow, Lindner, Brooke, & Mesdames Adams, Dow & Levick); Fortescue (cello solo); Douglas (recitation).
	July	Entertainment (for St Ives Church Schools)	Comediatta - *The Duchess of Bayswater & Co* - Russell, Talmage, Bromley, Alexandrina Laurence. Scenery - Barlow, Bromley & Talmage.
	December	Boxing Night Concert	St Ives Orchestral Society (conducted and trained by Robinson); Douglas (recitations), Robinson (song); Trevorrow (violin solos)
1899	February	Entertainment (for St Ives Orchestral Society)	St Ives Orchestral Society (conducted by Robinson); 'The Artists' Glee Party' (Meade, Milner, Brooke, W Titcomb, Dow & Lang, conducted by Robinson and accompanied by Miss L Kirkpatrick); Meade (song); Mr and Mrs Lionel Birch (comic sketches); Mrs Adams and Bertha King (piano solos)
	November	Mayor's Fund (Boer War)	Danby, Talmage, Blackden, Miss A Baird-Smith, Mrs Adams, Mrs Lindner (mother of Moffat). 'Artists' Glee Club' feat. Meade, Lindner, Dow, Brooke and Lang. Conductor - Robinson.
	December	Cricket Club Concert	Farce - *The Burglar and the Judge* - Talmage, Bromley & Danby.
1900	February	Magpie Minstrels Concert (for war widows and orphans)	Incl. Adams, Brooke, Cameron, Douglas, Hobkirk, Lang, Lindner, Milner, F Stokes & Talmage & Mesdames Bromley, Laurence & Talmage.
	April	Concert (for St Ives Orchestral Society)	St Ives Orchestral Society (conductor - Robinson); Mrs Adams (piano); Comic Pieces incl. *A Case for Eviction* - Mr and Mrs Lionel Birch & Mr and Mrs Norman Garstin.
	November	Entertainment (for Choral Society)	Sketch - *My Friend, Jarlet* - Talmage, Romilly Feddon, Leonard Lewis, Mrs Carr. Stage Manager - F Stokes. Mrs Adams (piano), Fortescue (cello).
1903	August	Entertainment (for Free Library)	Tableaux Vivants - William & Jessie Titcomb, Stuart Hobkirk, Harry Browne, Oswald Moser, Elgar Russell & Misses Whitehouse, Bodilly, Dickinson & others. J Titcomb (song); Irene and Vera Carr (dance). Also later in week Foweraker, Russell & Lanyon.
1906	December	Entertainment (for St Ives Nursing Association)	Fortescue (cello), J Titcomb (nightingale), Kortright (triangle), Dow (quail) *Aladdin in Japan* - Carr, Marriott, Dow, Meade children
1907	August	No.1 Company (DCA)	*Which* and *Trial by Jury* - directed by Foweraker, who acted as the Judge. Also H Taylor, H Fitzherbert, C Marriott & Carr, Marriott and Taylor daughters, Scenery by P Heard and Barlow
1909	January	Parish Church Restoration	H Taylor, C Marriott & Meade, Deacon, Marriott and Carr children. J Bromley (stage manager), W Fortescue (cello)

ACKNOWLEDGEMENTS

As this book draws on the research that I have done over the past fifteen years, I am still indebted to many of the people whose assistance has been gratefully acknowledged in my previous books. However, I should like to thank a number of people, whose contributions to this book have been especially important.

Janet Axten, the supervisor at the St Ives Trust Archive Study Centre, has been a magnificent help, for not only has she supported the project whole-heartedly from its outset, alerting me to relevant files and suitable photographs in the Centre's impressive collection, but she also kindly read through the draft manuscript of the book and made many helpful suggestions. It was Brian Stevens of the St Ives Museum, who first alerted me to the Rate Books and the Mornington Estate papers, which have proved crucial sources. He and his wife, Margaret, have also been of much assistance on many other aspects. Marion Whybrow, whose ground-breaking book on the colony in 1994 set the ball rolling, has been immensely helpful and supplied a number of images. Over the years, a number of officers at the St Ives Arts Club have allowed me generous access to their incomparable records and I am particularly grateful to Irene Allen, John Berriman and Marie Keeling.

Chris Hibbert, the Manager of the Borlase Smart John Wells Trust, has been immensely helpful and generous in sharing information on the findings of the Trust during the current Porthmeor Studios fund-raising project, as also have the Trust's Historic Buildings Consultants, Nick Cahill and Eric Berry.

I am most obliged to Brian Mitchell and his wife for allowing me to peruse the Visitors' Book of Hendra's Hotel and for supplying me with a number of images relating to the Hotel, and to Alison Symons, for allowing me access to Mrs Grigg's Visitors' Book.

I am also indebted to a number of volunteer helpers at the St Ives Trust Archive Study Centre for sharing their knowledge, particularly Pam Badman, who is undertaking an exhaustive study of the Mornington Estate papers, Wendy Smaridge, Rita Lait, John McWilliams and John Sell, whilst John Allan has supplied me with many photographs from the Centre's impressive collection. Considerable thanks are also due to the staff at the Cornish Studies Library in Redruth, who have been unfailingly helpful and have copied for me copious pages from those indispensable records, the *St Ives Weekly Summary* and the *St Ives Times*.

Descendants of artists have been very generous in their provision of information and photographs and I would particularly like to thank the following:- James Church (Lanyon/Schofield), Andrew Lanyon (Lanyon), Priscilla Fursdon (Ver Beck/Rion/Abell), Celia Faulkner Crawford (Faulkner), Edith Scott, Anne Ramsdell von Helf and William Eick (Ramsdell), Nicholas Halliday (Lindner), Bill Lloyd (Lloyd), Stephen Bartley (Burgess), Norma Neal (Knapping), Lynda Holland (Smith), Jane Cooper and Roger, Michael and Anne Whitehouse (Whitehouse), the late Derek Wintle, Margaret Hellier and Jeremy and Nina Wintle (Carr), Jean Cooper (Olsson), Willa Harris (Simmons), Brain Smart (Smart), Diane Osborne (Sherriff) and Gay Jarman (Brown). Pamela Robinson has also been most helpful with regard to her ancestor, Robert Toy; likewise, Margaret Reed as regards Greville Matheson. Dr Heiner Gilmeister generously shared his quite exceptional research into Alfred Pazolt, whilst others who kindly shared their research were Sebastian Halliday ('The Count House', Carbis Bay) and Jill Block and Lady Carol Holland ('Tremorna').

Given that the book contains over 450 images, I am indebted to very many people and organisations for the supply of photographs - duly acknowledged, I hope, in the captions. For those who have supplied them without charge or at discounted rates, I am most grateful. James Church, who has photographed or copied many images from the Lanyon/Schofield archive, and Andrew Eggleston, who photographed the Carr archive, deserve especial mention.

This book marks a first in that I designed it myself, but I am deeply indebted to Joe Frost of Joe Frost Design for explaining to me some of the intricacies of Adobe Indesign and for helping me along the way. He also has done a magnificent job on the numerous illustrations in the book, many of which were in a sorry state before he applied his considerable technical know-how and dexterous touch. His help with the cover design was also much appreciated.

Once again, my wife, Sherry, has been most understanding and supportive.

SELECTED BIBLIOGRAPHY

Will Ashton, *The life and work of artist Sir William Ashton OBE*, Sydney 1961

Georgina Bainsmith, *Francis Newman in Private Life*, in Giberne Sieveking, *Memoir and Letters of Francis W. Newman*, London, 1909.

W.H.Bartlett, *Summer Time in St Ives*, Cornwall, *Art Journal*, 25/9/1897

Lena and Donald Bray, *St Ives Heritage*, Truro, 1992

Arthur Burgess, family papers

Howard Russell Butler papers, Archives of American Art, Smithsonian Institution, Washington DC

Emily Carr, *Growing Pains*, Toronto 1946

Emily Carr papers, Royal BC Museum, BC Archives

Celia Davis, *Brian Hatton*, Suffolk, 1978

Havelock Ellis, *My Life*, Heinemann, 1940

Mrs Havelock Ellis, *A Cornish Experiment in Cottages*, *The World's Work and Play*, September 1906

Mrs Havelock Ellis, *My Cornish Neighbours*, London, 1906

Mrs Havelock Ellis, *The Mine of Dreams*, London, 1925

F.L.Emanuel, *The Charm of the Country Town - St Ives, Cornwall*, *Architectural Review*, July 1920

Herbert Faulkner, family papers

Lilian Faull, *The Faulls of St Ives*, Penzance, 1972

H.G.Fitzherbert, *Caricatures of the Cornish Riviera*, St Ives, 1910

H.G.Fitzherbert, *Everyone's Doing It*, St Ives, 1913

A.G.Folliott-Stokes, *A Moorland Princess*, London, 1904

Stanhope Forbes papers, Tate Gallery Archives

J.M.Gibbon, *St Ives and its Artists*, *Black and White*, 30/12/1905

Ed L Gill, *The Letters of Frances Hodgkins*, Auckland, 1993

Louis Grier, *A Painters' Club*, *The Studio*, Vol 5, 1895

Vera Hemmens, *A Cornish Chelsea*, *The Daily Graphic*, reproduced in *St Ives Times* 8/1923

C.Lewis Hind, *Newlyn v. St Ives*, *The Studio*, 1895

C.Lewis Hind, *In Painters' Land*, *The Ludgate*, October 1896.

C.Lewis Hind, *Picture Monday at St Ives*, *Pall Mall Gazette*, April 1905.

C.Lewis Hind, *The Education of an Artist, London,* 1906

C.Lewis Hind, *Days in Cornwall*, London, 1907

C.Lewis Hind, *Napthali*, London, 1926

W.H.Hudson, *The Land's End*, London, 1908

Wilson Henry Irvine papers, Archives of American Art, Smithsonian Institution

W.J.Jacobs, *Memories of Eighty Years 1880-1960*, privately published, 1960

Herbert Lanyon, family papers

Will Lloyd, family papers

Emma Loam, *Carbis Bay - Past and Present*, St Ives Archive Centre

A.Ludovici Jnr, *An Artist's Life in London and Paris*, London, 1926

Charles Marriott, *Memories of Cornwall's Art Colonies*, *The Cornish Review*, Spring 1949, No 1

J.H.Matthews, *A History of the Parishes of Saint Ives, Lelant, Towednack and Zennor*, London, 1892

Mortimer Menpes, *Whistler as I Knew Him*, London, 1904

Mornington Estate papers, County Records Office, Truro

Ed.C.Noall, *History of the Fore Street Methodist Church*, 1962

Frederic Winthrop Ramsdell, family papers and photographic collection of Manistee Civic Museum

Cyril Ranger-Gull, *Portalone*, London, 1904

Christine Morton Raymont, *Memories of Old St Ives*, St Ives, 1958

Christine Morton Raymont, *The John Family in St Ives*, unpublished manuscript

Harry Robinson, *St Ives as an Art Colony*, in *Babcock's Historical Sketch of St Ives and District*, 1896

Sampson Taylor Rowe, *Old St Ives - Its Artists and Fishermen*, *St Ives Weekly Summary*, 9/4/1898

Elmer Schofield papers, Archives of American Art, Smithsonian Institution, Washington DC and family papers

Ed. Jeanne Schulkind, *Virginia Woolf - Moments of Being*, New York, 1985

D.I.Sedding, *St Ives and its Studios*, *St Ives Times*, 1/1921

E E Simmons, *From Seven to Seventy*, New York and London, 1922

Leonard Spray, *A Novelists' Hunting Ground*, in *The Star*, reproduced in *St Ives Weekly Summary* 6/1/1912

St Ives Trust Archive Study Centre - photographic collection and other archives

St Ives Arts Club records

St Ives Museum - Rate Books

St Ives Times - passim

St Ives Weekly Summary - passim

West Country Arts Review 1896

William Titcomb, family papers

Whitehouse family archive, Gloucester Records Office, Churchdown District - D6035

Marion Whybrow, *St Ives - Portrait of an Art Colony 1883-1993*, Woodbridge, 1994

Norman Wilkinson, *A Brush with Life*, London, 1969

Col.H.W.Williams, *Some Reminiscences (1838-1918)*, Penzance 1918.

Names of artists in italics